Christianity
and Social Work

*Readings on the Integration of
Christian Faith and
Social Work Practice*

THIRD EDITION

Beryl Hugen and T. Laine Scales

Editors

The editors and publisher gratefully acknowledge permission to reprint or adapt material from the following works:

Ethical integration of faith and social work practice: Evangelism, by David A. Sherwood, *Social Work and Christianity*, vol. 29 (1), pp 1-12, © 2001, Reprinted with permission of North American Association of Christians in Social Work.

Table 1 from *Changing for Good,* by James Prochaska, John Norcross and Carlo C. Diclemente, © 1998, Reprinted with permission of Harper Collins Publishers, Inc.

Excerpts from *Sacred Stories of Ordinary Families: Living the Faith Everyday,* by Diana R. Garland, © 2003, Excerpts used with permission of Jossey Bass Publishers.

CONTENTS

Exploring Foundational Christian Beliefs and Values for Social Work

Spiritual and Religious Dimensions in Social Work Practice

PREFACE

The first edition of this book developed from the experience of teaching social work on the undergraduate level at Christian colleges and finding that almost all social work textbooks were produced for the secular market. Most texts were at best neutral, with others often antagonistic to Christian concerns. There was clearly a need for a text that would not only offer a Christian perspective on the social work profession as a whole, but also on specific topics within the profession. In discussions with colleagues, they also saw a similar need.

After some research and discussion it seemed that the best approach was to produce a collection of articles dealing with a variety of topics and issues related to the practice of social work. Effort was given to recruit Christian social workers from a wide variety of colleges and universities and practice settings who could address topics in which they were most competent.

The development of the third edition has followed a somewhat similar pattern. We began by surveying NACSW members and Christian college teachers inquiring which chapters in the second edition they felt were most informative and useful and should be included in a third edition. In addition, we asked what new topics or issues would be important to address in this edition. From this feedback, we again sought to recruit contributors.

The contributors represent a variety of academic and social work practice settings, along with a broad range of theological and social work perspectives. All the contributors in this edition are social workers, but clearly offer unique perspectives to the contemporary debate regarding the role of Christian faith in human service delivery. The contributors were not given a strict outline to follow, but rather were supplied with the basic purposes of the book and general stylistic guidelines. As editors, we have attempted to allow the authors' ideas to stand with as few editorial changes as possible. This collection is intended for a variety of audiences, including social work practitioners, educators, and students at the undergraduate and graduate levels. The book is organized so that it can be used as training or reference materials for practitioners, or as a textbook or supplemental text in a social work class.

The reader may agree with some of the contributors' ideas and disagree with others. It is our hope that the reader, whether agreeing or disagreeing, will be stimulated to integrate his or her Christian worldview with the professional social work perspective on helping. We sincerely hope that readers will catch a glimpse of the potential contributions that being a Christian in social work can make to the competent and holistic practice of professional social work and, not incidentally, to the furtherance of the gospel of Jesus Christ and the growth of His Kingdom.

Acknowledgements

Special thanks are due the contributors. We have had the entirely enjoyable task of working with a group that without exception not only produced substantive manuscripts, but shared a clear commitment to the integration of Christian faith and social work practice.

We thank our respective institutions, Calvin College and Baylor University for their support. Special thanks go to Rick Chamiec-Case, Executive Director of NACSW, for his support and encouragement, and to Bob Alderink from Calvin College Communications and Marketing for his work on the layout.

We also are indebted to the Calvin College Social Work Department's Summer Seminar Programs held at Calvin College in 2004 and 2006. Several new chapters in the book were written for these seminars and refined through the thoughtful and challenging feedback offered in these seminar groups. A thank you is also owed to the Calvin College Social Work Department for underwriting most of the costs of these seminars through a generous gift donated to the Department by the late Dr. Theodore R. and Jeanne Deur.

We also wish to acknowledge the influence of Alan Keith-Lucas on the initial thinking and development of this project. Both his life and writings continue to provide encouragement and motivation for many social workers in the continuing effort to integrate their Christian faith and social work practice.

CHAPTER 1

INTRODUCTION

Beryl Hugen and T. Laine Scales

One of the developments in social work in the second half of the 20th century has been a marked decline in the recognition of the Christian religion in the teaching and practice of professional social work. The secularization of the social work profession, the notion of religion in both an ideological and institutional sense having little or no part in forming or informing the world of social work, has been very extensive (Hugen, 1994). For many in the social work profession, this question of the relationship of Christian faith and social work is inconsequential, irrelevant, and for some, an inappropriate topic for professional investigation. Even presently, when spirituality is being recognized by the profession as a legitimate area of inquiry, Christianity, as one spiritual voice, is recognized only hesitantly.

This is unfortunate for a number of reasons. First, social work once used the language of Christianity as a basis for its existence. Historically, such language was widely and eloquently used by both social work educators and practitioners. Second, spirituality, and to a large degree Christian spirituality, is very much part of our society and continues to play a significant role in providing moral rationale and reasoning to our political, social, and charitable institutions. As a result, many social workers want to know what role Christian faith plays in a helping profession—specifically, the professional existence and activities of social work. The purpose of this book is to help respond to this question.

A Christian Worldview and Social Work

Looking at history, and particularly the history of social welfare, it would be hard for anyone to deny that the Christian church is one of the true originators of charity. Out of ancient Israel's concern for justice and mercy toward the sick, the poor, the orphaned, the widowed—from Micah and Hosea, Jeremiah and Isaiah—grew the compassion of Jesus and the devotion of Paul. Both the justice and love of God set forth and exemplified in the Judeo-Christian tradition have given motivation and direction to much of western culture's charities. Historically, the whole shape and operation of organized welfare is inexplicable apart from this religious conviction and commitment. Jewish, Catholic, and Protestant thought have continuously shaped the ideological basis of social work practice. One writer has suggested that these religious traditions, along with the secular philosophy of humanism, are the four foundational roots out of which has emerged the value base of the social work profession (Kohs, 1966). Many social workers find the assumptions, beliefs, and values of the Christian faith helpful in providing a frame of reference for understanding and responding to both individual and societal problems.

For the Christian, the standard or "plumbline" (Amos 7:8) used to make judgments has always been the principles set forth in the Bible. Hence it is important and necessary for Christian social workers to relate or test the values of the profession with the principles of a Christian worldview. To be explicit about such moral principles provides an opportunity to reconnect with the profession's religious bearings and roots. To do so may also help recover dimensions of social work teaching and practice that have been alienated from their theological roots.

Many social workers who are Christians do not hold to the idea that there is such a thing as Christian social work—only Christians in social work (we belong to this group). They believe that one's Christian perspective comes into play in social work practice when one is deciding *what* to do, *when* to do it, *how* to do it, and *why* one should do it. They clearly identify with those who seek to follow Christ in a servant role focusing upon the alleviation of pain and suffering and the establishment of justice and peace in the world. The beginning chapters of the book, chapters 2 through 6, offer Christians in social work - from students, whose calling and motivation to enter the profession are informed by their Christian faith, to seasoned professionals, whose desire is to further develop Christian approaches to helping - a variety of frameworks to help link their Christian faith, personal identity and professional social work practice.

In chapter 2, David Sherwood lays out a framework for a Christian worldview for social work practice. Beryl Hugen, in chapter 3, addresses how one's Christian faith and one's professional work are related through the Christian concept of calling. In chapter 4, T. Laine Scales, Helen Wilson Harris, Dennis Myers, and Jon Singletary, social work faculty members at a Christian university, share several student views of the journey toward integration of faith and social work practice. Students tell their stories of seeking God's plan, dealing with obstacles, and seeking companionship for the journey. Cheryl Brandsen and Paul Vliem, in chapter 5, contribute to a deeper understanding of the historical religious roots of social welfare by recovering the story of a system of social reforms begun by Basil and his contemporaries in the 4th century. Their understanding of justice motivated leaders to expand human rights and social welfare beyond kinship and religious affiliations. Lastly, Sarah Kreutziger, in chapter 6, offers a historical look at how Christian principles gave shape to a framework for programmatic policy and practice of an early twentieth century Christian settlement house program.

Exploring Foundational Christian Beliefs and Values for Social Work

It is increasingly being recognized that social work, despite its preoccupation in the last half century with science and with developing objective and empirically validated practice techniques, is also a normative profession (Siporin,

1982, 1983). Normative means that the social work profession is also concerned with how persons and societies ought to behave "on principle," and that the purposes and goals of the social work profession are anchored in particular foundational beliefs and values. A normative principle is an objective rule that when properly applied distinguishes between what is right and wrong. Such rules may be applied to the behavior of individuals, whether client or professional, to social institutions, as well as social and political change processes. So when the social work profession advocates for a more just redistribution of resources that are deemed valuable to society, a value basis, belief, or normative principle for such a redistribution proposal is needed. For example, to advocate for a national health care plan because one believes that for persons in the United States adequate health care is a basic human right, requires a value or normative principle as to what is the basis for such a right. Human behavior, both individual and collective, is also socially defined as good or bad, normal or deviant. Whether one chooses as a social worker to enforce such normative standards or advocate for their change, the essential "morality" of these norms or standards requires justification.

Social work has always been guided by such normative principles, although the basis of these principles rarely has been clearly explicated. For Christians, the normative principles used to make moral decisions have always been based upon the values and beliefs set forth in the Bible. An important professional task for Christian social workers, therefore, is to relate or test the values of the profession with values and beliefs derived from a biblical perspective. Articulating these Christian beliefs and values—helping the reader develop the specific content of a Christian worldview related to social work—is one of the focuses of this book, and is addressed in section two, chapters 7 through 12.

In chapter 7, Rick Chamiec-Case offers a model, the Filtering Role Model of Integration, for how social workers can draw upon the beliefs and values of their Christian faith to meaningfully inform their work. Mary Anne Poe, in chapter 8, identifies central biblical principles and theologies (at times in tension) related to the understandings of human nature, social welfare, and the problem of poverty. In chapter 9, Jim R. Vanderwoerd provides underlying Christian principles for the place of macro practice as an essential element of social work practice. Mary Ann Brenden addresses in chapter 10 how Catholic social teaching, by virtue of its harmony with social work values and ethics, is a valuable resource for strengthening the social justice focus of social work education and professional practice. In chapter 11, Mary Anne Poe offers a conception of justice that goes beyond justice as fairness to describe justice as an ideal that reflects the human longing for wholeness and harmony in social relationships. Christian principles provide criterion for measuring this state of justice in relationships. Finally, Jim R. Vanderwoerd, in chapter 12, identifies several key biblical beliefs and values that provide a foundation from which to understand a Christian vision for 21st century social welfare, drawing on understandings of social structures rooted in neo-Calvinist understandings within Reformed Protestantism and Catholic social teaching.

Spiritual and Religious Dimensions in Social Work Practice

Today there is a growing movement within the social work profession to affirm that spiritual and religious beliefs are integral to the nature of the person and have a vital influence on human behavior. These spiritual and religious dimensions are being increasingly recognized as important features of social work practice at all phases of the social work helping process and in all areas of practice. This perspective embraces a holistic conception of the person and has more recently been elaborated as the bio-psycho-social-spiritual perspective. This view reintroduces spiritual issues as a legitimate focus for social work practice and provides for a more complete understanding of client strengths, challenges, and resources. As a result, there is now a need for the development of theoretical frameworks and practice models, including assessment tools and intervention strategies that flow from this perspective.

Social work research also has shown that although many social workers see religious and spiritual issues as important parameters in practice and important in their own lives as well as in the lives of their clients, many are hesitant to initiate discussion of spiritual issues with clients (Canda & Furman, 1999; Derezotes & Evans, 1995; Joseph, 1988). Much of this hesitation is due to the lack of knowledge and skill in this area. Greater sensitivity to the concerns of the religious client has also been shown to be related to the social worker's own spiritual awareness—the ability to integrate the personal, spiritual, and religious self with the professional self. Again, there has been a reluctance to incorporate such knowledge into social work education, considering such discussions an intrusion into a private sphere.

This movement within the profession to embrace a bio-psycho-social-spiritual focus in practice, along with the promotion of a professional learning environment that is more supportive of personal religious and spiritual experiences, has resulted in the development of models for incorporating spirituality in a wide variety of practice areas. Christians in social work now have the opportunity to truly minister to the whole person. Several chapters in section three address these spiritual dimensions focusing on a broad range of practice areas.

In chapter 13, Hope Haslam Straughan reviews and critiques several theoretical perspectives on individual spiritual development. David R. Hodge and Crystal R. Holtrop present a variety of spiritual assessment tools useful in different social work practice settings in chapter 14. In chapter 15, Jason Pittman and S.Wade Taylor offer a comprehensive model for incorporating Christian spirituality in substance abuse practice. Chapters 16, 17, and 18 each address the role of spirituality and religion in practice with a specific vulnerable population. Beryl Hugen outlines in chapter 16 the role of a religious orientation in practice with persons experiencing severe mental illness. Cheryl K. Brandsen proposes a model for addressing spirituality in end of life care with the elderly in chapter 17. The role of spirituality and religion in child welfare, specifically foster care, is presented in chapter 18 by Jill Mikula and Gary Anderson. In chapter 19, Helen Wilson Harris leads us on a journey into understanding the nature and approach to professional helping according to Alan Keith Lucas, and in particular "one of his core ideas—that all good helping involves the skillful use of reality, empathy, and support—dimensions of the helping process that reflect the very nature of God." In the concluding chapter (20) in this section, David A. Sherwood offers a Christian perspective on ethical decision making in social work practice.

The Changing Environment for Social Work Practice

Social work as a profession has undergone a variety of changes in the twentieth century. Many of these reflect both significant material and technological changes in our society, along with a shift in our ideas about relationships between people and their social environments, particularly government. The early twentieth century was fertile ground for the development and expansion of broad governmental responsibility for social welfare. The idea of the welfare state and of the centrality of government and public service seemed both inevitable and probably necessary.

But the latter part of the twentieth century was much less hospitable to the concept of the welfare state. A perceived lack of results from publicly funded and delivered human services along with a focus on renewing civil society propels today's government leaders to call for community and faith-based organizations to take increasing responsibility for the social and economic needs of communities and persons in poverty. A central question is whether government can better meet the country's critical social needs by working in partnership with the faith community, focusing particularly on congregations and faith-based community development organizations.

Several legislative and legal changes have helped facilitate this increased involvement of faith-based organizations in the delivery of social services. The Section 104 "Charitable Choice" provision of the 1996 welfare reform legislation enabled religious organizations to receive government funding for the delivery of social services, without requiring changes in governance, employment practices, or religious characteristics (Center for Public Justice, 1999). President Bush's development of the Office of Community and Faith-Based Initiatives along with several recent legislation initiatives has given further support to this movement. Social workers who are able to understand and relate to both the public (governmental) and faith-based service communities are today in an important and advantageous position to influence the development of policies and programs that help meet important social needs in their communities (Aker & Scales, 2003). The increased involvement of faith-based organizations in human service delivery also brings new challenges, as the purposes and missions of some of these faith-based organizations include an evangelistic outreach. Previously, such faith-based organizations have been seen as "pervasively sectarian"—too religious to receive public financial support. How do social workers in these congregations and faith-based organizations balance the mandate for professional service delivery with an evangelistic mission? Chapters 21-24 focus on this larger changing environment of social work practice.

In chapter 21, Diana Garland provides insights related to faith in family life for congregational ministries with families seeking to strengthen this aspect of family life. Timothy Johnson, in chapter 22, identifies the Black church's practice of Christian charity and how "its current orientation to living out the Christian discipline of "holistic grace and hospitality" serves as a microcosmic case example of social welfare and systematic helping that undergirds the profession of social work." In chapter 23, John Cosgrove focuses on the contemporary and growing phenomenon of formal relationships between individual congregations in the developed and developing worlds. Christian social workers who wish to have direct "hands on" involvement in the developing world may need look no further than their local congregation for an opportunity to serve that is both professionally and spiritually rewarding. Lastly, in chapter 24, David Sherwood posits a limited and cautious perspective for the role of evangelism in social work practice.

Humility and Competence

One of the primary goals of this book is to apply a Christian perspective to the realities of contemporary social work practice. It is important to remember that in offering a Christian understanding and response to social problems it does not mean that Christians in social work have all the answers. The Bible may provide guidance, but it does not always provide clear and specific direction for the sometimes confusing moral and ethical situations social workers encounter in practice. As Christian social workers, we know that we live and practice in a broken world, and that our only real comfort is that we are not our own, but we belong, body and soul, in life and in death, to our faithful Savior Jesus Christ.

It is easy to assert the evident Christian goodness of helping people. And it can be easier still to assume that a Christian perspective on the profession and practice of social work furthers that good. But goodness of motivation may be and frequently is unrelated to outcome. There is always the possibility that our Christian perspectives are no more than self-serving rationales (promoting judgmentalism, discrimination and selective helping motives) rather than the product of a thoughtful analysis. With this book, therefore, we have attempted to offer a Christian perspective for social work practice that is within the parameters of contemporary models of professional social work research and scholarship. We believe that all knowledge is God's knowledge, and clearly social work practice and scholarship can also inform the Christian community.

References

Aker, R., & Scales, T.L. (2004). Charitable choice, social workers and rural congregations: Partnering to build community assets, In T.L. Scales, & C. Streeter (Eds.), *Rural social work: Building and sustaining community assets*. Pacific Grove, CA, Brooks/Cole, 226-239.

Canda, E.R., & Furman, L.D. (1997). *Spiritual diversity in social work practice: The heart of helping*. New York: The Free Press.

Center for Public Justice. (1999). A guide to charitable choice: An overview of section 104.

Derezotes, D.S., & Evans, K.E. (1995). Spirituality and religiosity in practice: In-depth interviews of social work practitioners. *Social Thought, 18* (1), 39-54.

Hugen, B. (1994). The secularization of social work. *Social Work and Christianity*, 21(4), 83-101.

Joseph, M.V. (1988). Religion and social work practice. *Social Casework, 60* (7), 443-452.

Kohs, S.C. (1966). *The roots of social work*. Association Press.

Siporin, M. (1982). Moral philosophy in social work today. *Social Service Review, 56*, 516-38.

Siporin, M. (1983). Morality and immorality in working with clients. *Social Thought, 15* (3/4), 42-52.

CHAPTER 2

THE RELATIONSHIP BETWEEN BELIEFS AND VALUES IN SOCIAL WORK PRACTICE: WORLDVIEWS MAKE A DIFFERENCE

David A. Sherwood

In some circles (including some Christian ones) it is fashionable to say that what we believe is not all that important. What we do is what really counts. I strongly disagree. The relationship between what we think and what we do is complex and it is certainly not a simple straight line, but it is profound. Social work values, practice theories, assessments, intervention decisions, and action strategies are all shaped by our worldview assumptions and our beliefs.

I believe that a Christian worldview will provide an interpretive framework which will solidly support and inform commonly held social work values such as the inherent value of every person regardless of personal characteristics, self-determination and personally responsible freedom of choice, and responsibility for the common good, including help for the poor and oppressed. And it will challenge other values and theories such as might makes right, exploitation of the weak by the strong, and extreme moral relativism. At the same time, other worldviews, including materialism, empiricism, and postmodern subjectivism will lead to quite contrasting conclusions regarding these values.

Worldviews Help Us Interpret Reality

What is a "Worldview?"

Worldviews give faith-based answers to a set of ultimate and grounding questions. Everyone operates on the basis of some worldview or faith-based understanding of the universe and persons— examined or unexamined, implicit or explicit, simplistic or sophisticated. One way or another, we develop functional assumptions that help us to sort through and make some sort of sense out of our experience. And every person's worldview will always have a faith-based component (even belief in an exclusively material universe takes faith). This does not mean worldviews are necessarily irrational, unconcerned with "facts," or impervious to critique and change (though they unfortunately might be). It matters greatly how conscious, reflective, considered, or informed our worldviews are. The most objectivity we can achieve is to be critically aware of our worldview and how it affects our interpretations of "the facts." It is far better to be aware, intentional, and informed regarding our worldview than to naively think we are (or anyone else is) objective or neutral or to be self-righteously led by our biases which we may think are simply self-evident truth.

These worldviews affect our approach to social work practice, how we understand and help people. What is the nature of persons—biochemical machines, evolutionary products, immortal souls, all of the above? What constitutes valid knowledge—scientific empiricism only, "intuitive" discernment, spiritual guidance (if so, what kind)? What kinds of social work theories and practice methods are legitimate? What are appropriate values and goals—what is healthy, functional, optimal, the good?

Worldviews and the Hermeneutical Spiral: A Beginning Place

I like to use the concept of the *"hermeneutical spiral"* (the term is not original with me, cf. Osborne, 1991, Wood, 1998). We always come to the world, including social work practice, with our faith(worldview assumptions)—wherever we got it, however good or bad it is, and however embryonic it may be. This worldview faith strongly affects what we perceive (or even look for). But the world (God's creation, in the Christian worldview) is not a totally passive or subjective thing. So, we run the risk of coming away from any encounter with the world having our faith and our categories somewhat altered, perhaps even corrected a bit. Then we use that altered faith in our next encounter with the world.

So, for me, the starting place for integration of my beliefs and social work practice is always at the level of basic faith, worldview assumptions. What are the implications of my core beliefs? And what are the implications of the idea, theory, interpretation, or practice that I am examining? To use a currently fashionable phrase, how do they "interrogate" each other? What kind of assumptions about the nature of the world lie behind Freudian theory? Behavioral theory? The scientific method? The strengths perspective? The social work belief that all persons have intrinsic value (a radical notion not particularly supported by either modernism or postmodernism in their materialist, subjectivist versions)?

To put it another way, we all form stories that answer life's biggest questions. As I become a Christian, I connect my personal story to a much bigger story that frames my answers to these big questions. For Christians, the biblical story of God's nature and action in human history, culminating in Jesus Christ, is the "meta-narrative" that frames our personal stories and within which the meaning of our stories is rooted. Middleton and Walsh (1995, p. 11) summarize the basic worldview questions this way (with my illustrative additions):

1. **Where are we? *What is the nature of the reality in which we find ourselves?*** Is the nature of the universe meaningful or absurd? Created or accidental? Materialistic only, or also spiritual?

2. **Who are we? *What is the nature and task of human beings?*** What does it mean to be a person? What is human life? What is its source and value? Is there such a thing as freedom or responsibility?

3. **What's wrong? *How do we understand and account for evil and brokenness?*** And how do we account for our sense of morality, love, and justice? Is evil only stuff I happen not to prefer? Or are some things really good

and other things really wrong? Is love only lust or well-disguised self-centeredness? Does justice have a claim on us and what we call "ours"?

4. **What's the remedy?** *How do we find a path through our brokenness to wholeness?* What kinds of things will help? Do we need a Savior or just a positive (or cynical) attitude? Will chemicals or incarceration do the trick?

Interpreting the Facts

"Facts" have no meaning apart from an interpretive framework. "Facts" are harder to come by than we often think, but even when we have some "facts" in our possession, they have no power to tell us what they mean or what we should do.

That human beings die is a fact. That I am going to die would seem to be a reliable prediction based on what I can see. In fact, the capacity to put those observations and projections together is one of the ways we have come to describe or define human consciousness. But what do these "facts" mean and what effect should they have on my life?

One worldview might tell me that life emerged randomly in a meaningless universe and is of no particular value beyond the subjective feelings I may experience from moment to moment. Another worldview might tell me that somehow biological survival of life forms is of value and that I only have value to the extent that I contribute to that biological parade (with the corollary that survival proves fitness). Another worldview might tell me that life is a gift from a loving and just Creator and that it transcends biological existence, that death is not the end of the story. Different worldviews lend different meanings to the same "facts."

The major initial contribution of a Christian worldview to an understanding of social work values and ethical practice is not one of unique, contrasting, or conflicting values. Rather, a Christian worldview gives a coherent, solid foundation for the basic values that social workers claim and often take for granted (Holmes, 1984; Sherwood, 1993, 2000, 2007). Subsequently, a Christian worldview will shape how those basic values are understood and how they interact with one another. For example, justice will be understood in the light of God's manifest concern for the poor and oppressed, so justice can never be defined only as a procedurally "fair" protection of individual liberty and the right to acquire, hold, and transfer property (Lebacqz, 1986; Mott, 1982; Wolterstorff, 1983, 2006).

The Interaction of Feeling, Thinking, and Behavior

Persons are complex living ecological systems—to use a helpful conceptual model common in social work—systems of systems, if you will. Systems within our bodies and outside us as well interact in dynamic relationships with each other. For example, it is impossible to meaningfully separate our thinking, feeling, and behavior from each other and from the systems we experience outside ourselves, yet we quite properly think of ourselves as separate individuals.

The lines of influence run in all directions. What we believe affects what we experience, including how we define our feelings. For example, does an experience

I might have of being alone, in and of itself, *make* me feel lonely, or rejected, or exhilarated by freedom, for that matter? Someone trips me, but was it accidental or intentional? I have had sex with only one woman (my wife Carol) in over sixty years of life. How does this "make" me feel? Are my feelings not also a result of what I tell myself about the meaning of my experience? But it works the other way too.

All this makes us persons harder to predict. And it certainly makes it harder to assign neat, direct, and one-way lines of causality. The biblical worldview picture is that God has granted us (at great cost) the dignity and terror of contributing to causality ourselves through our own purposes, choices, and actions. We have often used this freedom to hurt others and ourselves, but this also means that we are not mechanistically determined and that significant change is always possible.

And change can come from many directions—thinking, emotions, behavior, experience. We are especially (compared to other creatures) both gifted and cursed by our ability to think about ourselves and the world. We can form purposes and act in the direction of those purposes. Our beliefs about the nature of the world, other persons, and ourselves interact in a fundamental way with how we perceive reality, how we define our own identity, and how we act.

If this is true in our personal lives, it is equally true as we try to understand and help our clients in social work practice. And it is no less true for clients themselves. What we believe about the nature of the world, the nature of persons, and the nature of the human situation is at least as important as the sheer facts of the circumstances we experience.

Worldviews Help Construct Our Understanding of Values

Cut Flowers: Can Values Be Sustained Without Faith?

One significant manifestation of the notion that beliefs aren't all that important is the fallacy of our age which assumes that fundamental moral values can be justified and sustained apart from their ideological (ultimately theological) foundation. Take, for example, the fundamental Christian and social work belief that all human beings have intrinsic dignity and value.

Elton Trueblood, the Quaker philosopher, once described ours as a "cut-flower" generation. He was suggesting that, as it is possible to cut a rose from the bush, put it in a vase, and admire its fresh loveliness and fragrance for a short while, it is possible to maintain the dignity and value of every human life while denying the existence or significance of God as the source of that value. But the cut rose is already dead, regardless of the deceptive beauty which lingers for a while. Even uncut, "The grass withers, and the flower falls, but the Word of the Lord endures forever" (I Peter 1:24-25).

Many in our generation, including many social workers, are trying to hold onto values—such as the irreducible dignity and worth of the individual—while denying the only basis on which such a value can ultimately stand. We should be glad they try to hold onto the value, but we should understand how shaky such a foundation is. A secular generation can live off its moral capital only so long before the impertinent questions (Why should we?) can no longer be ignored (Sherwood, 2007).

Doesn't Everybody "Just Know" That Persons Have Dignity and Value?

But doesn't everybody "just know" that human beings have intrinsic value? You don't have to believe in God, do you? In fact, according to some, so-called believers in God have been among the worst offenders against the value and dignity of all persons (sadly true, in some cases). After all, a lot of folks, from secular humanists to rocket scientists to New Age witches to rock stars, have declared themselves as defenders of the value of the individual. Isn't the worth of the person just natural, or at least rational and logically required? The plain answer is, "No, it's *not* just natural or rational or something everyone just knows."

I received a striking wake-up call in regard to this particular truth many years ago when I was a freshman at Indiana University. I think the story is worth telling here. I can't help dating myself—it was in the spring of 1960, the time the Civil Rights movement was clearly emerging. We were hearing of lunch room sit-ins and Freedom Riders on buses. Through an older friend of mine from my home town I wound up spending the evening at the Student Commons talking with my friend and someone he had met, a graduate student from Iran named Ali. I was quite impressed. My friend Maurice told me Ali's father was some sort of advisor to the Shah (the ruling despot at that point in Iran's history).

The conversation turned to the events happening in the South, to the ideas of racial integration, brotherhood, and social justice. Ali was frankly puzzled and amused that Maurice and I, and at least some other Americans, seemed to think civil rights were worth pursuing. But given that, he found it particularly hard to understand what he thought was the wishy-washy way the thing was being handled. "I don't know why you want to do it," he said. "But if it's so important, why don't you just do it? If I were President of the United States and I wanted integration, I would do it in a week!" "How?" we asked. "Simple. I would just put a soldier with a machine gun on every street corner and say 'Integrate.' If they didn't, I would shoot them." (Believable enough, as the history of Iran has shown)

Naive freshman that I was, I just couldn't believe he was really saying that. Surely he was putting us on. You couldn't just do that to people. At least not if you were moral! The conversation-debate- argument went on to explore what he really did believe about the innate dignity and value of the individual human life and social responsibility. You don't just kill inconvenient people, do you?

I would say things like, "Surely you believe that society has a moral responsibility to care for the widows and orphans, the elderly, the disabled, the emotionally disturbed." Incredibly (to me at the time), Ali's basic response was not to give an inch but to question *my* beliefs and values instead.

"Society has no such moral responsibility," he said. "On the contrary. You keep talking about reason and morality. I'll tell you what is immoral. The rational person would say that the truly *immoral* thing is to take resources away from the strong and productive to give to the weak and useless. Useless members of society such as the disabled and mentally retarded should be eliminated, not maintained." He would prefer that the methods be "humane," but he really did mean eliminated.

It finally sunk into my freshman mind that what we were disagreeing about was not facts or logic, but the belief systems we were using to interpret or assign meaning to the facts. Ali was a thoroughly secular man; he had left Islam behind. If I were to accept his assumptions about the nature of the universe (e.g. that there is no God, that the material universe is the extent of reality, that self-preservation is the only given motive and goal), then his logic was flawless and honest. As far as he was concerned, the only thing of importance left to discuss would be the most effective means to gain and keep power and the most expedient way to use it.

In this encounter I was shaken loose from my naive assumption that "everybody knows" the individual person has innate dignity and value. I understood more clearly that unless you believed in the Creator, the notion that all persons are equal is, indeed, *not* self-evident. The Nazi policies of eugenics and the "final solution" to the "Jewish problem" make a kind of grimly honest (almost inevitable) sense if you believe in the materialist worldview.

The "Is-Ought" Dilemma

Not long afterward I was to encounter this truth much more cogently expressed in the writings of C. S. Lewis. In *The Abolition of Man* (1947) he points out that both the religious and the secular walk by faith if they try to move from descriptive observations of fact to any sort of value statement or ethical imperative. He says "From propositions about fact alone no *practical* conclusion can ever be drawn. 'This will preserve society' [let's assume this is a factually true statement] cannot lead to 'Do this' [a moral and practical injunction] except by the mediation of 'Society ought to be preserved' [a value statement]" (p. 43). "Society ought to be preserved" is a moral imperative that no amount of facts alone can prove or disprove. Even the idea of "knowing facts" involves basic assumptions (or faith) about the nature of the universe and human beings.

The secular person (social worker?) tries to cloak faith by substituting words like natural, necessary, progressive, scientific, rational, or functional for "good," but the question always remains— For what end? And Why? The answer to this question always smuggles in values from somewhere else besides the facts.

Even the resort to instincts such as self-preservation can tell us nothing about what we (or others) *ought* to do. Lewis (1947, p. 49) says:

> We grasp at useless words: we call it the "basic," or "fundamental,"
> or "primal," or "deepest" instinct. It is of no avail. Either these words
> conceal a value judgment passed *upon* the instinct and therefore not
> derivable *from* it, or else they merely record its felt intensity, the
> frequency of its operation, and its wide distribution. If the former,
> the whole attempt to base value upon instinct has been abandoned:
> if the latter, these observations about the quantitative aspects of a

psychological event lead to no practical conclusion. It is the old dilemma. Either the premise is already concealed an imperative or the conclusion remains merely in the indicative.

This is called the "Is-Ought" dilemma. Facts, even when attainable, never have any practical or moral implications until they are interpreted through the grid of some sort of value assumptions. "Is" does not lead to "Ought" in any way that has moral bindingness, obligation, or authority until its relationship to relevant values is understood. And you can't get the values directly from the "Is." We always come down to the question—what is the source and authority of the "Ought" that is claimed or implied?

The social work Code of Ethics refers to values such as the inherent value of every person, the importance of social justice, and the obligation to fight against oppression. It is a fair question to ask where those values come from and what gives them moral authority and obligation.

A Shaky Consensus: "Sexual Abuse" or "Intergenerational Sexual Experience?"

For an example of the "Is-Ought Dilemma," is child sexual abuse a fact or a myth? Or what is the nature of the abuse? Child sexual abuse is an example of an area where there may seem to be more of a consensus in values than there actually is. In any event, it illustrates how it is impossible to get values from facts alone. Some intervening concept of "the good" always has to come into play.

Fact: Some adults have sexual relations with children. But so what? What is the practical or moral significance of this fact? Is this something we should be happy or angry about? Is this good or bad? Sometimes good and sometimes bad? Should we be encouraging or discouraging the practice? Even if we could uncover facts about the consequences of the experience on children, we would still need a value framework to help us discern the meaning or practical implications of those facts. And to have moral obligation beyond our own subjective preferences or biases, this value framework must have some grounding outside ourselves. What constitutes negative consequences? And even if we could agree certain consequences were indeed negative, the question would remain as to what exactly was the cause.

In the last few years there has been a tremendous outpouring of attention to issues of child sexual abuse and its effects on adult survivors. I must say that this is long overdue and much needed. And even among completely secular social workers, psychologists, and other therapists there currently appears to be a high degree of consensus about the moral wrong of adult sexual activity with children and the enormity of its negative consequences on the child at the time and in later life. As a Christian I am encouraged, especially when I recall the self-described "radical Freudian" professor I had in my master's in social work program who described in glowingly approving terms high levels of sexual intimacy between children and each other and children and adults as "freeing and liberating" (that was the early 1970s).

However, if I look more closely at the worldview faith underlying much of the discussion of sexual abuse and its effects, the result is not quite so comforting to me as a Christian. The moral problem tends not to be defined in terms of a well-rounded biblical view of sexuality and God's creative design and purpose or an understanding of the problem of sin. Rather, it tends to be based on a more rationalistic and individualistic model of power and a model of justice that pins its faith on reason. Sexual abuse grows out of an inequity in power which a person rationally "ought not" exploit. Why not, one might ask.

But what if we take away the coercive element and get rid of the repressive "body-negative" ideas about sexual feelings? What if much or all of the negative effects of non-coercive sexual activity between adults and children is the result of the misguided and distorted social attitudes which are passed on to children and adults? Defenders of "non-exploitive" sexual activity between adults and children can (and do) argue that any negative consequences are purely a result of sex-negative social learning and attitudes. Representatives of a hypothetical group such as P.A.L. (Pedophiles Are Lovers!) would argue that what needs to be changed is not the "intergenerational sexual behavior," but the sexually repressive social values and behavior which teach children the negative responses. These values are seen as the oppressive culprits. Then, the argument might go, should we not bend our efforts to eradicating these repressive sexual values and attitudes rather than condemning potentially innocent acts of sexual pleasure? Indeed, why not, if the only problem is exploitation of power?

You should also note that this argument in favor of intergenerational sexual behavior is not exclusively scientific, objective, or based only on "facts." It has to make faith assumptions about the nature of persons, the nature of sexuality, the nature of health, and the nature of values. By the same token, my condemnation of adult sexual activity with children is based on faith assumptions about the nature of persons, sexuality, health, and values informed by my Christian worldview. It is never just "facts" alone that determine our perceptions, conclusions, and behavior.

Right now, it happens to be a "fact" that a fairly large consensus exists, even among secular social scientists and mental health professionals, that adult sexual activity with children is "bad" and that it leads quite regularly to negative consequences. Right now you could almost say this is something "everyone knows." But it would be a serious mistake to become complacent about this or to conclude that worldview beliefs and faith are not so important after all.

First, not everyone agrees. Although I invented the hypothetical group P.A.L. (Pedophiles Are Lovers), it represents real people and groups that do exist. The tip of this iceberg may be appearing in the professional literature where it is becoming more acceptable and common to see the "facts" reinterpreted. In preparing bibliography for a course on sexual issues in helping some time ago, I ran across a very interesting little shift in terminology in some of the professional literature. One article was entitled "Counterpoints: Intergenerational sexual experience or child sexual abuse" (Malz, 1989). A companion article was titled "Intergenerational sexual contact: A continuum model of participants and experiences" (Nelson, 1989). Words do make a difference.

Second, we shouldn't take too much comfort from the apparent agreement. It is sometimes built on a fragile foundation that could easily come apart. The fact that Christians find themselves in wholehearted agreement with many secular helping professionals, for example, that sexual activity between adults (usually male) and children (usually female) is exploitive and wrong may represent a temporary congruence on issues and strategy, much more so than fundamental agreement on the nature of persons and sexuality.

But back to the "Is-Ought" dilemma. The fact that some adults have sexual contact with children, by itself, tells us *nothing* about what, if anything, should be done about it. The facts can never answer those questions. The only way those questions can ever be answered is if we interpret the facts in terms of our faith, whatever that faith is. What is the nature of the world? What is the nature of persons? What is the meaning of sex? What constitutes health? What is the nature of justice? And most important—why should I care anyway?

Worldviews Help Define the Nature and Value of Persons

So—Worldviews Have Consequences

Your basic faith about the nature of the universe has consequences (and everyone, as we have seen, has some sort of faith). Faith is consequential to you personally, and the content of the faith is consequential. If it isn't *true* that Christ has been raised, my faith is worthless (I Corinthians 15:14). And if it's *true* that Christ has been raised, but I put my faith in Baal or the free market or the earth goddess (big in New England these days) or Karl Marx (not so big these days) or human reason, then *that* has consequences, to me and to others. What are we going to *trust*, bottom-line?

In I Corinthians 15, the apostle Paul said something about the importance of what we believe about the nature of the world, the *content* of our faith. He said, "Now if Christ is proclaimed as raised from the dead, how can some of you say there is no resurrection of the dead? If there is no resurrection of the dead, then Christ has not been raised; and if Christ has not been raised, then our proclamation has been in vain and your faith is also in vain . . . If Christ has not been raised, your faith is futile and you are still in your sins . . . If for this life only we have hoped in Christ, we are of all people most to be pitied" (12-14, 17, 19).

I've been a student, a professional social worker, and a teacher of social work long enough to see some major changes in "what everyone knows," in what is assumed or taken for granted. "What everyone knows" is in fact part of the underlying operational *faith* of a culture or subculture—whether it's Americans or teenagers or those who go to college or social workers — or Southern Baptists, for that matter.

When I went to college, logical positivism was king, a version of what C. S. Lewis called "naturalism," a kind of philosophical materialism. It said that the physical world is all there is. Everything is fully explainable by materialistic determinism. Only what can be physically measured or "operationalized" is real (or at least relevantly meaningful). In psychology it was epitomized in B. F. Skinner's behaviorism.

I remember as a somewhat bewildered freshman at Indiana University attending a lecture by a famous visiting philosophy professor (a logical positivist) from Cambridge University (whose name I have forgotten) entitled "The *Impossibility* of any Future Metaphysic" (his take-off on Kant's title "Prolegomena to any Future Metaphysic"). I can't say I understood it all at the time, but his main point was that modern people must permanently put away such meaningless and potentially dangerous ideas as spirituality, the supernatural, and any notion of values beyond subjective preferences. We now know, he said, that such language is meaningless (since not empirical) except, perhaps, to express our own subjective feelings.

In a graduate school course in counseling, I had an earnest young behaviorist professor who had, as a good behaviorist, trained (conditioned) himself to avoid all value statements that implied good or bad or anything beyond personal preference. When faced with a situation where someone else might be tempted to make a value statement, whether regarding spaghetti, rock and roll, or adultery, he had an ideologically correct response. He would, with a straight face, say, "I find that positively reinforcing" or, "I find that negatively reinforcing." (I don't know what his wife thought about this kind of response). Notice, he was saying "I" (who knows about you or anyone else) "find" (observe a response in myself at this moment; who knows about five minutes from now) "that" (a particular measurable stimulus) is "positively reinforcing" (it elicits this particular behavior now and might be predicted to do it again).

Above all, the idea was to be totally scientific, objective, and *value-free*. After all, values were perceived to be purely relative, personal preferences, or (worse) prejudices induced by social learning. And "everyone knew" that the only thing real was physical, measurable, and scientific. If we could only get the "facts" we would know what to do.

But this was, and is, a fundamental fallacy, the "Is-Ought" fallacy we discussed earlier. Even if facts are obtainable, they have no moral power or direction in themselves. If we say they mean something it is because we are interpreting them in the context of some values that are a part of our basic faith about the nature of the world.

Shifting Worldviews: The Emperor Has No Clothes

In the meantime we have seen some rather amazing shifts in "what everyone knows." I am old enough to have vivid memories of the 1960s and the "greening of America" when "everybody knew" that people under 30 were better than people over 30 and that human beings are so innately good all we had to do was to scrape off the social conventions and rules and then peace, love, and total sharing would rule the world. An astounding number of people truly believed that—for a short time.

In the '70s and early '80s "everybody knew" that personal autonomy and affluence are what it is all about. Power and looking out for Number One became the articles of faith, even for helping professionals like social workers. Maximum autonomy was the obvious highest good. Maturity and health were defined in terms of not needing anyone else (and not having any obligation to anyone else either). Fritz Perls "Gestalt Prayer" even got placed on romantic greeting cards:

> I do my thing, and you do your thing.
> I am not in this world to live up to your expectations.
> And you are not in this world to live up to mine.
> You are you and I am I,
> And if by chance we find each other, it's beautiful.
> If not, it can't be helped.

If you cared too much, you were labelled enmeshed, undifferentiated, or at the very least co-dependent.

And here we are in the 21st century and, at least for awhile, it looks as though values are in. Time magazine has had cover stories on ethics. We have had occasion to feel betrayed and outraged at the exposure of unethical behavior on the part of corporate executives, accountants, stock brokers, and especially government officials. Even more amazing, philosophy professors and social workers are not embarrassed to talk about values and even character again. "Family Values" are avowed by the Republicans and Democrats. The books and articles are rolling off the presses.

But we should not be lulled into a false sense of security with this recovery of values and ethics, even if much of it sounds quite Christian to us. The philosophical paradigm has shifted to the opposite extreme, from the modern faith in the rational and empirical to the postmodern faith in the radically subjective and relative, the impossibility of getting beyond our ideological and cultural horizons. Our culture now despairs of any knowledge beyond the personal narratives we make up for ourselves out of the flotsam of our experience and fragments of disintegrating culture (Middleton & Walsh, 1995). Postmodernism says each person pieces together a personal story through which we make sense out of our lives, but there is no larger story (meta-narrative) which is really true in any meaningful sense and which can bind our personal stories together.

It is remarkable, as we have seen, how rapidly some of these assumptions can shift. The seeming consensus may be only skin-deep. More importantly, unless these values are grounded on something deeper than the currently fashionable paradigm (such as a Christian worldview), we can count on the fact that they will shift, or at least give way when they are seriously challenged. It's amazing how easy it is to see that the emperor has no clothes when a different way of looking is introduced to the scene. Remember, both enlightenment empiricism and postmodern subjectivity agree that values have no transcendent source.

What Is a "Person?"

Controversies regarding abortion and euthanasia illustrate the profound consequences of our worldview faith, especially for worldviews that deny that values have any ultimate source. Even more fundamental than the question of when life begins and ends is the question: What is a person? What constitutes being a person? What value, if any, is there in being a person? Are persons owed any particular rights, respect, or care? If so, why?

If your worldview says that persons are simply the result of matter plus time plus chance, it would seem that persons have no intrinsic value at all, no matter how they are defined.

From a purely materialist point of view, it may be interesting (to us) that the phenomena of human consciousness and agency have emerged which allow us in some measure to transcend simple biological, physical, and social determinism. These qualities might include the ability to be self-aware, to remember and to anticipate, to experience pleasure and pain, to develop caring relationships with others, to have purposes, to develop plans and take deliberate actions with consequences, and to have (at least the illusion of) choice. We may choose to define personhood as incorporating some of these characteristics. And we may even find it positively reinforcing (or not) to be persons. But then what? In this materialist worldview there are no inherent guidelines or limits regarding what we do to persons.

Do such persons have a right to life? Only to the extent it pleases us (who-ever has the power) to say so. And what in the world could "right" mean in this context? But what if we do choose to say that persons have a right to life? What degree or quality of our defining characteristics do they have to have before they qualify? How self-conscious and reflective? How capable of choice and action?

It is common for people to argue today that babies aren't persons before they are born (or at least most of the time before they are born) and thus that there is no moral reason for not eliminating defective ones, or even just unwanted or inconvenient ones. And there are already those who argue that babies should not even be declared potential persons until they have lived long enough after birth to be tested and observed to determine their potential for normal growth and development, thus diminishing moral qualms about eliminating "wrongful births" (Singer, 1996). After all, what is magic about the birth process? Why not wait for a few hours, days, or weeks after birth to see if this "fetal material" is going to measure up to our standards of personhood? And at any point in life if our personhood fails to develop adequately or gets lost or seriously diminished through accident, illness, mental illness, or age, what then? Was my college acquaintance Ali right? Is it immoral to take resources from the productive and use them to support the unproductive? Do these "fetal products" or no-longer-persons need to be terminated?

A Solid Foundation

If I balk at these suggestions, it is because I have a worldview that gives a different perspective to the idea of what constitutes a person. I may agree, for example, that agency—the capacity to be self-aware, reflective, remember and anticipate, plan, choose, and responsibly act—is a central part of what it means to be a person. But I also believe that this is a gift from our creator God which in some way images God. I believe that our reflection, choice, and action have a divinely given purpose. This purpose is summarized in the ideas of finding and choosing God through grace and faith, of growing up into the image of Jesus Christ, of knowing and enjoying God forever. All of this says that persons have a special value beyond their utility to me (or anyone else) and that they are to be treated with the care and respect befitting their status as gifts from God. Even when something goes wrong.

Having a Christian worldview and knowing what the Bible says about God, the world, and the nature of persons doesn't always give us easy answers to all of our questions, however. And having faith in the resurrection of Jesus Christ doesn't guarantee that we will always be loving or just. But it does give us a foundation of stone to build our house on, a context to try to understand what we encounter that will not shift with every ideological or cultural season. I can assert the dignity and worth of every person based on a solid foundation, not just an irrational preference of my own or a culturally-induced bias that I might happen to have. What "everybody knows" is shifting sand. Even if it happens to be currently stated in the NASW Code of Ethics for social workers.

Some Basic Components of a Christian Worldview

Space does not permit me to develop a detailed discussion of the components of a Christian worldview here, but I would at least like to try to summarize in the most basic and simple terms what I perceive to be quite middle-of-the-road, historically orthodox, and biblical answers to the fundamental worldview questions I posed at the beginning (cf. Middleton & Walsh, 1995). This suggests the Christian worldview that has informed me and has been (I would hope) quite evident in what has been said. This little summary is not the end of reflection and application, but only the beginning.

1.   **Where are we?** We are in a universe which was created by an eternal, omnipotent, just, loving, and gracious God. Consequently the universe has built-in meaning, purpose, direction, and values. The fundamental values of love and justice have an ultimate source in the nature of God which gives them meaning, authority, and content. The universe is both natural and supernatural.

2.   **Who are we?** We are persons created "in the image God" and therefore have intrinsic meaning and value, regardless of our personal characteristics or achievements. Persons are both physical and spiritual. Persons have been given the gift of "agency"—in a meaningful sense we have been given both freedom

and responsibility. Persons created in the image of God are not just autonomous individuals but are relational-created to be in loving and just community with one another. Persons are objects of God's grace.

3.   **What's wrong?** Oppression and injustice are evil, wrong, an affront to the nature and desire of God. Persons are finite and fallen—we are both limited in our capacities and distorted from our ideal purpose because of our selfishness and choice of evil. Our choice of selfishness and evil alienates us from God and from one another and sets up distortion in our perceptions, beliefs, and behavior, but we are not completely blind morally. Our self-centeredness makes us prone to seek solutions to our problems based on ourselves and our own abilities and accomplishments. We can't solve our problems by ourselves, either by denial or our own accomplishments.

4.   **What's the remedy?** Stop trying to do it our way and accept the loving grace and provisions for healing that God has provided for us. God calls us to a high moral standard but knows that it is not in our reach to fulfill this standard completely. God's creative purpose is to bring good even out of evil, to redeem, heal, and grow us up—not by law but by grace. "For by grace you have been saved through faith, and this is not your own doing; it is the gift of God—not the result of works, so that no one may boast. For we are what he has made us, created in Christ Jesus for good works, which God prepared beforehand to be our way of life." (Ephesians 2:8-10).

Why Should I Care? Choosing a Christian Worldview

Moral Obligation and Faith: Materialism Undermines Moral Obligation

To abandon a theological basis of values, built into the universe by God, is ultimately to abandon the basis for any "oughts" in the sense of being morally bound other than for purely subjective or cultural reasons. Normative morality that is just descriptive and cultural ("This is what most people in our society tend to do"), subjective ("This is what I happen to prefer and do," or "It would be convenient for me if you would do this"), or utilitarian ("This is what works to achieve certain consequences") has no power of moral *obligation*.

Why should I care? On materialist or subjective grounds I "should" do this or that if I happen to feel like it or if I think it will help me get what I want. But this is using the word "should" in a far different and far more amoral sense than we ordinarily mean by it. It is a far different thing than saying I am *morally obligated or bound* to do it.

Many will argue that reason alone is enough to support moral obligation. This is the argument used by Frederic Reamer in his excellent book on social work ethics, *Ethical dilemmas in social services* (1990), based on Gewirth (*Reason and morality*, 1978). If, for example, I understand that freedom is logically required for human personal action, then this theory says I am logically obligated to support freedom for other persons as I desire it for myself. But I have never been able to buy the argument that reason alone creates any meaningful moral obligation for altruistic behavior. Why *should* I be logical, especially if being logical doesn't appear to work for my personal advantage? Any idea of moral obligation beyond the subjective and personally utilitarian seems to lead inevitably and necessarily to God in some form or to nowhere (Sherwood, 2007; Evans, 2004, 2006; Smith, 2003).

The "Method of Comparative Difficulties"

Although it is logically possible (and quite necessary if you believe in a materialist or postmodernist universe) to believe that values are only subjective preferences or cultural inventions, I have never been able to completely believe that is all our sense of values such as love and justice amounts to. There are, in all honesty, many obstacles in the way of belief in God as the transcendent source of values. But can we believe, when push comes to shove, that all values are either meaningless or totally subjective? Elton Trueblood calls this the "Method of Comparative Difficulties" (1963, p. 73; 1957, p. 13).

It may often be hard to believe in God, but I find it even harder to believe in the alternatives, especially when it comes to values. It's easy enough to say that this or that value is only subjective or culturally relative, but when we get pushed into a corner, most of us find ourselves saying (or at least *feeling*), "No, *that* (say, the Holocaust) is really wrong and it's not just my opinion." (Cf. C. S. Lewis, "Right and Wrong As a Clue to the Meaning of the Universe," *Mere Christianity*, 1948)

Dostoevski expressed the idea that if there is no God, all things are permissible. C. S. Lewis (1947, pp 77-78) said that "When all that says 'it is good' has been debunked, what says 'I want' remains. It cannot be exploded or 'seen through' because it never had any pretensions." Lust remains after values have been explained away. Values that withstand the explaining away process are the only ones that will do us any good. Lewis concludes *The abolition of man* (1947, p. 91):

> You cannot go on "explaining away" forever: you will find that you have explained explanation itself away. You cannot go on "seeing through" things forever. The whole point of seeing through something is to see something through it. It is good that the window should be transparent, because the street or garden beyond it is opaque. How if you saw through the garden too? It is no use trying to "see through" first principles. If you see through everything, then everything is transparent. But a wholly transparent world is an invisible world. To "see through" all things is the same as not to see.

Looking for Christian Implications

A Christian worldview is not going to give us simple answers to all of our questions. It is not as though there is a simple translation of Christian values and principles into practice implications, or that there is a unitary "Christian" version of every human activity from French cooking to volleyball to politics.

Even though we may agree on fundamental values and principles, such as love and justice, as fallen and finite human beings, the more specific we get in terms of translating love and justice into particular attempts to solve concrete problems the more we are likely to honestly and conscientiously disagree with one another in our interpretation of what the problem is or what, in fact, might actually do more good than harm in attempting to deal with it (Sherwood, 1999).

I assume, for example, that if we are Christians and we have read the Bible, we have been impressed with our obligation to work for social justice and to help the poor. But what are the causes of poverty and what can we do to help the poor that will do more good than harm? Not simple and not obvious.

May I be so bold as to say that there is **no** simple, single "Christian" answer to those questions? We are going to be working to deal with poverty (and conscientiously disagreeing about how to do it) until Jesus returns. And I will submit that there is *no* policy or program to help the poor, individually or collectively, privately or publicly that will not *advance some* of the legitimate values that we have at the *risk or cost of some* of our other legitimate values.

So, everything we do will be a compromise of sorts and will need to be adapted as much as possible to the unique situation. But what we do needs to be an imperfect solution shaped both by our Christian faith and by our professional social work values, knowledge, and skills.

A Christian perspective is not always totally unique or different in every respect from what another perspective might offer, but it always informs and critiques these perspectives. An example from social work is the NASW Code of Ethics. Even some Christian social workers may be laboring under the impression that it somehow contradicts Christian values. Far from it. Anyone who has this impression should take a closer look at the Code of Ethics. There is no principle in the Code that a Christian cannot strongly affirm. In fact, I would argue that a Christian worldview is quite compatible with the social work Code of Ethics, and in fact is the soil out of which much of the Code has sprung (Sherwood, 2000, 2002, 2007).

As we have discussed before, one of the core social work values in the Code is the inherent dignity and value of every person. Now, what in modernism or postmodernism gives such a value ground to stand on and to claim obligation over us? Not much. When push comes to shove, the inherent dignity and value of every person is pretty hard to sustain under assumptions of relativism, subjectivism, material determinism, and survival of the fittest.

At the same time that a Christian worldview upholds this core social work value, it also informs and critiques it. For example, a Christian perspective might say that individual freedom is not the only or necessarily always the highest value when legitimate values come into tension with each other in a given situation. The good of others and the community (deriving from both love and justice) has a powerful moral claim in every situation. Yet individual freedom tends to be granted privileged status in most social work ethical thinking.

So, not all social workers, Christian or otherwise, will necessarily agree on how to prioritize legitimate values when they come into conflict with one another, which they inevitably do in complex cases. One of the admirable virtues of the current Code of Ethics is its clear recognition in the preamble and throughout that legitimate values *do* come into tension with one another in actual practice situations, that professional judgment will *always* be required to prioritize them, and that conscientious and competent professionals will *not always* be in agreement.

Furthermore (given the hermeneutical spiral), it must be remembered that other perspectives may inform and critique our Christian perspectives. Many contemporary Christians seem to need to be reminded, for example, that individual peace and prosperity do not necessarily rank high in the list of biblical virtues compared to sacrifice for the common good (Sherwood, 1999).

Seeing Through a Mirror Dimly: Real Values But Only a Limited, Distorted View

So, I believe in God as the ultimate source and authenticator of values. I believe that real values exist beyond myself. And I believe these values put us under real moral obligation. To believe otherwise, it seems to me, ultimately makes values and moral obligation empty shells, subjective and utilitarian, with no real life or content. It may be true that this is all values are, but I find it very hard to believe. Belief in a value-less world, or one with only "human" (that is to say, purely subjective) values, takes more faith for me than belief in God.

But (and this is very important) this understanding of values as having ultimate truth and deriving from God is a very far cry from believing that I fully comprehend these values and the specific moral obligations they put me under in the face of a particular moral dilemma when these values come into tension with one another and priorities have to be made. Much humility is required here, an appropriate balance. At any given moment, my (or your) understanding of these values and what our obligations are is very limited and distorted. In fact our understandings are in many ways subjective, culturally relative, and bounded by the interpretive "language" available to us. And any particular place where I can stand to view a complex reality at best only yields a partial view of the whole. Remember the story of the blind men and the elephant ("It's like a snake," "It's like a wall," "It's like a tree").

We can see, but only dimly. God has given us light but we will only be able to see completely when we meet God face to face (I Corinthians 13:8-13). In the meantime we are on a journey. We are pilgrims, but we are not wandering alone and without guidance. We see through a mirror dimly, but there is something to see. There is a garden beyond the window.

> Love never ends. But as for prophecies, they will come to an end;
> as for tongues, they will cease; as for knowledge, it will come to an
> end. For we know only in part, and we prophesy only in part; but
> when the complete comes, the partial will come to an end. When I
> was a child, I spoke like a child, I thought like a child, I reasoned

like a child; when I became an adult, I put an end to childish ways. For now we see in a mirror, dimly, but then we will see face to face. Now I know only in part; then I will know fully, even as I have been fully known. And now faith, hope, love abide, these three; and the greatest of these is love. (I Corinthians 13:8-13)

Now we have received not the spirit of the world, but the Spirit that is from God, so that we may understand the gifts bestowed on us by God. And we speak of these things in words not taught by human wisdom but taught by the Spirit, interpreting spiritual things to those who are spiritual. Those who are unspiritual do not receive the gifts of God's Spirit, for they are foolishness to them, and they are not able to understand them because they are spiritually discerned. Those who are spiritual discern all things, but they are themselves subject to no one else's scrutiny. "For who has known the mind of the Lord so as to instruct him?" But we have the mind of Christ. (I Corinthians 2:12-16)

Now the Lord is the Spirit, and where the Spirit of the Lord is, there is freedom. And all of us, with unveiled faces, seeing the glory of the Lord as though reflected in a mirror, are being transformed into the same image from one degree of glory to another; for this comes from the Lord, the Spirit. (II Corinthians 3:17-18)

References

Evans, C. S. (2004). *Kierkegaard's ethic of love: Divine commands and moral obligations*. New York: Oxford University Press.

Evans, C. S. (2006). Is there a basis for loving all people? *Journal of Psychology and Theology, 34*(1), 78-90.

Gewirth, A. (1978). *Reason and morality*. Chicago: University of Chicago Press.

Homes, A. (1984). *Ethics: Approaching moral decisions*. Downers Grove, IL: InterVarsity Press.

Lebacqz, K. (1986). *Six theories of justice: Perspectives from philosophical and theological ethics*. Minneapolis, MN: Augsburg Publishing House.

Lewis, C. S. (1947). *The abolition of man*. New York: Macmillan Publishing Company.

Lewis, C. S. (1948). *Mere Christianity*. New York: Macmillan Publishing Company.

Malz, Wendy. (1989). Counterpoints: Intergenerational sexual experience or child sexual abuse. *Journal of Sex Education and Therapy, 15*, 13-15.

Middleton, J. R., & Walsh, B. J. (1995). *Truth is stranger than it used to be: Biblical faith in a post-modern age*. Downers Grove, IL: InterVarsity Press.

Mott, S. (1982). *Biblical ethics and social change*. New York: Oxford University Press.

Nelson, J. A. (1989). Intergenerational sexual contact: A continuum model of participants and experiences. *Journal of Sex Education and Therapy, 15*, 3-12.

Osborne, G. R. (1991). *The hermeneutical spiral: A comprehensive introduction to biblical interpretation*. Downers Grove, IL: InterVarsity Press.

Reamer, F. G. (1990). *Ethical dilemmas in social service* (2nd Ed). New York: Columbia University Press.

Sherwood, D. A. (1993). Doing the right thing: Ethical practice in contemporary society. *Social Work & Christianity, 20*(2), 140-159.

Sherwood, D. A. (1999). Integrating Christian faith and social work: Reflections of a social work educator. *Social Work & Christianity, 26*(1), 1-8.

Sherwood, D. A. (2000). Pluralism, tolerance, and respect for diversity: Engaging our deepest differences within the bond of civility. *Social Work & Christianity, 27*(1), 1-7.

Sherwood, D. A. (2002). Ethical integration of faith and social work practice: Evangelism. *Social Work & Christianity, 29*(1), 1-12.

Sherwood, D. A. (2007). Moral, believing social workers: Philosophical and theological foundations of moral obligation in social work ethics. *Social Work & Christianity, 34*(2), 121-145.

Singer, P. (1996). *Rethinking life and death: The collapse of our traditional ethics.* New York: St. Martin's Press.

Smith, C. (2003). Moral, believing animals: Human personhood and culture. New York: Oxford University Press.

Trueblood, D. E. (1963). *General philosophy.* New York: Harper and Row.

Trueblood, D. E. (1957). *Philosophy of religion* New York: Harper and Row.

Wolterstorff, N. (1983). *When justice and peace embrace.* Grand Rapids, MI: Eerdmans Publishing Company.

Wolterstorff, N. (2006). Justice, not charity: Social work through the eyes of faith. *Social Work & Christianity, 33*(2), 123-140.

Wood, W. J. (1998). *Epistemology: Becoming intellectually virtuous.* Downers Grove, IL: InterVarsity Press.

CHAPTER 3

CALLING: A SPIRITUALITY MODEL FOR SOCIAL WORK PRACTICE

Beryl Hugen

In making a career choice, many Christian students find the social work profession a good fit with their religious faith. Or at least at first glance it appears so. For example, as part of the application process for the social work program I teach in, students are asked to explain why they have chosen social work as a major. What motivates them to enter this field of study? Some answer the question by relating past experiences with social work services or role models who were social workers, but almost all describe a moderate or fairly strong religious impulse to serve people and society.

Many specifically relate their faith to their choice of social work—stating something like this: In being loved by God, they in turn wish to share some of this love with those who are poor or hurting or are in need of help of some kind. Some of these students believe that to be a Christian in social work they must work in an agency under religious auspices, whereas others plan to work in programs that do not have a specific religious base or affiliation, but are part of the larger community of governmental social welfare responses to those in need. Despite these differences, almost all are interested in finding ways to integrate their faith and their newly chosen field of study.

But it doesn't take long in their social work studies for these students to begin to recognize the complex tensions between their religious faith, agency auspices, and the secular values of the social work profession. This discovery is not surprising; social work is, after all, a secular profession. At times, students find the profession very critical of religion, even suspicious of anyone who claims to have religious motives for helping others.

This feeling is understandable, for in the last forty to fifty years, the social work profession has simply ignored religious insights and accepted the principle of separating the sacred and secular. Religion came to be seen as having no particular insight to offer or relevance for everyday professional practice. Because of this attitude, the recent professional literature does not offer much help to students in thinking through the relationship of religious faith and professional practice. It is ironic that social work, which claims as its unique focus the "whole person" in the whole environment, has for so long neglected the religious dimension of life.

Not only do students continue to come to the profession with religious motivations, but the roots of social work are largely grounded in religious faith (Devine, 1939). Social work originated and came of age under the inspiration of the Judeo-Christian traditions and the philanthropic and service motivation

29

of religious people. As Leiby (1985) indicates, the Christian biblical command to love God and to love one's neighbor as oneself was directly translated into a sense of moral responsibility for social service. As the social work profession secularized in the 20th century, these earlier religious rationales and models for service were replaced by doctrines of natural rights, utilitarianism, and humanistic ideology.

Dealing with human need apart from religious motives and methods is actually a very recent development in the history of charity and philanthropy. The notion of a secular profession focused on responding to human suffering would have struck many of our professional ancestors as quite inconsistent and confusing. Many of them were religiously motivated and expressed their faith by means of social work as a vocation, a calling from God to serve their brothers and sisters who were in need. With their perception of social work as a calling, a vocation, they formalized a link between their religious faith and social work practice.

What is meant by viewing social work as a calling? Several recent articles have addressed this "old fashioned" concept of calling or vocation, sensing its power and value for current social work practice (Gustafson,1982; Reamer, 1992). However, these writers essentially have attempted to take the religious concept of calling and use it in a secular fashion. They have done so in order to provide a moral purpose for the profession—to counteract what they perceive to be the focus on self-interest inherent in the social work profession which has become increasingly professionalized, specialized and bureaucratic.

My intent in this chapter is to explain, or more accurately to reintroduce, the religious model of calling as used by Christian social workers, past and present, in linking Christian faith and professional social work practice. Both its attractiveness and shortcomings as a model will be addressed. My purpose is not only to help social workers and the profession understand or correct misunderstandings related to this model, but also help social workers better understand the broader issues related to the spirituality of social work practice, in that other religious models and spiritual traditions address many of the same integration of faith and practice questions. Also, reintroducing the model of calling will lead us to see the significance of how the perspectives and writings of our religiously motivated social work ancestors—of which there are many— can contribute to the profession's current discussions regarding spirituality and social work practice.

Religion, Faith, and Spirituality

Before discussing the model of calling, it is helpful to define what is meant by the terms spirituality, religion, belief and faith. The profession has long struggled with this definitional dilemma. The dilemma has focused on how to reintroduce religious or spiritual concerns into a profession which has expanded beyond specific sectarian settings and ideologies to now include diverse sources of knowledge, values and skills, and how to respond to the needs of a much more spiritually diverse clientele. Addressing this dilemma, Siporin (1985) and Brower (1984) advocated for an understanding of spirituality that includes a wide diversity of religious and non-religious expressions, with such an inclusive understanding of spirituality encouraging social workers to reflect upon their clients both within and outside of particular institutional religious settings and ideologies.

From this beginning, Canda (1988a, 1988b) further developed a concept of spirituality for social work that incorporates insights from diverse religious and philosophical perspectives. He identifies three content components to spirituality—values, beliefs and practice issues—"all serving the central dynamic of a person's search for a sense of meaning and purpose, developed in the context of interdependent relationships between self, other people, the nonhuman world, and the ground of being itself" (Canda, 1988a, p. 43).

In the same vein, the work of James Fowler, known more for his model of faith development, is particularly instructive. Fowler (1981) states that to understand the "human quest for relation to transcendence," the key phenomenon to examine is not religion or belief but faith (p. 14). According to Fowler, who draws upon the ideas of religionist Wilfred Smith, *religions* are "cumulative traditions," which represent the expressions of faith of people in the past (p. 9). Included in a cumulative tradition are such elements as "texts of scripture, oral traditions, music, creeds, theologies," and so forth. *Belief* refers to "the holding of certain ideas" or "assent to a set of propositions" (p. 13). *Faith* differs from both religion and belief. Fowler describes faith as a commitment, "an alignment of the will...in accordance with a vision of transcendent value and power, one's ultimate concern" (p. 14). One commits oneself to that which is known or acknowledged and lives loyally, with life and character being shaped by that commitment. Defined in this way, faith is believed to be a universal feature of human living, recognizably similar everywhere, and in all major religious traditions.

What does faith consist of then? Fowler describes three components of what he calls the contents of faith. The first he terms *centers of value*, the "causes, concerns, or persons that consciously or unconsciously have the greatest worth to us." These are what we worship, things that "give our lives meaning" (p. 277). The second component of faith is described as our *images of power*, "the power with which we align ourselves to sustain us in the midst of life's contingencies" (p. 277): these powers need not necessarily be supernatural or transcendent. Finally, faith is comprised of "the *master stories* that we tell ourselves and by which we interpret and respond to the events that impinge upon our lives." Essentially, our master stories reveal what we believe to be the fundamental truths, "the central premises of [our] sense of life's meaning" (p. 277).

In discussing spirituality and faith, Fowler and Canda both emphasize its pervasive, all encompassing nature in an individual's life. Faith or spirituality is not a separate dimension of life or compartmentalized specialty, but rather an orientation of the total person. Accordingly, the three components of faith— centers of value, images of power, and master stories (Fowler, 1981)—and spirituality—values, beliefs, and practices (Canda, 1988)—exert "structuring power" in our lives, shaping our characters and actions in the world, including our work. Faith and spirituality are defined here as the essence of religion. Faith and spirituality take on a Christian religious meaning when the centers of value, images of power, and master stories of one's faith, the central dynamic of one's search for a sense of meaning and purpose, are grounded in the creeds, texts of scripture, and theology of the Christian tradition. I will attempt to present the Christian religious concept of calling within these more inclusive frameworks of spirituality and faith.

Calling in Action

Perhaps the best way to develop an understanding of the religious concept of calling is to start with an illustration. Robert Coles, in his book *The Call to Service* (1993), tells of a six year old black girl who initiated school desegregation in the South in the early 1960s. Tessie, a first grader, each day facing an angry and threatening mob, was escorted by federal marshals to school. The mob almost always greeted her with a litany of obscenities. Tessie's maternal grandmother, Martha, was the family member who usually got Tessie up and off to school each morning.

Coles reports that one day Tessie was reluctant to go to school— claiming to feeling tired, having slipped and fallen while playing in a nearby back yard, and having a difficult time with a current substitute teacher. Tessie suggested to her grandmother that she might stay home that day. Her grandmother replied that that would be fine if Tessie truly wasn't well, but if she was more discouraged than sick, that was quite another matter. She goes on to say:

> It's no picnic, child—I know that, Tessie—going to that school. Lord Almighty, if I could just go with you, and stop there in front of that building, and call all those people to my side, and read to them from the Bible, and tell them, remind them that He's up there, Jesus, watching over all of us—it don't matter who you are and what your skin color is. But I stay here, and you go—and your momma and your daddy, they have to leave the house so early in the morning that it's only Saturdays and Sundays that they see you before the sun hits the middle of its traveling for the day. So I'm not the one to tell you that you should go, because here I am, and I'll be watching television and eating or cleaning things up while you're walking by those folks. But I'll tell you, you're doing them a great favor; you're doing them a service, a big service.
>
> You see, my child, you have to help the good Lord with His world! He puts us here—and He calls us to help Him out. You belong in that McDonogh School, and there will be a day when everyone knows that, even those poor folks—Lord, I pray for them!—those poor, poor folks who are out there shouting their

heads off at you. You're one of the Lord's people; He's put His Hand on you. He's given a call to you, a call to service—in His name! There's all those people out there on the street (p. 3-4).

Later Coles questions Tessie whether she understood what her grandmother meant by "how you should be of service to those people out there on the street." She replied:

If you just keep your eyes on what you're supposed to be doing, then you'll get there—to where you want to go. The marshals say, 'Don't look at them; just walk with your head up high, and you're looking straight ahead.' My granny says that there's God, He's looking too, and I should remember that it's a help to Him to do this, what I'm doing; and if you serve Him, then that's important. So I keep trying (p. 4-5).

The heart of what Tessie had learned was that for her, service meant serving, and not only on behalf of those she knew and liked or wanted to like. Service meant an alliance with the Lord Himself for the benefit of people who were obviously unfriendly. Service was not an avocation or something done to fulfill a psychological need, not even an action that would earn her any great reward. She had connected a moment in her life with a larger ideal, and in so doing had learned to regard herself as a servant, as a person called to serve. It was a rationale for a life, a pronouncement with enormous moral and emotional significance for Tessie and her grandmother. This call was nurtured by the larger black community, her pastor, family, and the biblical values of love and justice—the stories of exile and return, of suffering and redemption—the view of the powerful as suspect and the lowly as destined to sit close to God, in His Kingdom.

Coles himself recounts how ill-prepared professionally he was to understand this family and their sense of calling:

I don't believe I could have understood Tessie and her family's capacity to live as they did, do as they did for so long, against such great odds, had I not begun to hear what *they* were saying and meaning, what *they* intended others to know about their reasons and values— as opposed to the motivations and reactions and "mechanisms of defense" I attributed to them. Not that there wasn't much to be learned by a psychoanalytic approach. Tessie and her companions, like human beings everywhere (including those who study or treat other human beings), most certainly did demonstrate fearfulness and anxiety; she also tried to subdue those developments by not acknowledging them, for instance, or by belittling their significance. Mostly, though, she clung hard to a way of thinking in which she was *not* a victim, *not* in need of "help" but someone picked by fate to live out the Christian tradition in her life. "I'm trying to think of the way Jesus would want me to think," she told me one evening. When I asked how she thought Jesus wanted her to think, she replied, "I guess of others, and not myself, I'm here to help the others" (p. 26).

Calling: The Meaning of Work

For some Christians, like Tessie and her grandmother, connecting one's work to the divine intentions for human life gives another dimension to the meaning and purpose of one's work and life. Certainly adequate pay, financial stability, social status and a sense of personal fulfillment remain significant criteria in choosing a career, but they are not the central motivation. The central motivation is the means by which one's Christian religious tradition has tied one's work and faith together, this concept of vocation, or calling.

Martin Luther originally formulated the notion of vocation or calling largely in reaction to the prevailing attitude toward work in medieval society. Medieval thinkers devalued work. They believed that in and of itself, work had little or no spiritual significance. They held, like the Greeks earlier, to the idea that the highest form of life, the form in which humans can realize their noblest potential, is the contemplative life of the mind. By thinking, we liken ourselves to God. Work was thus a hindrance to an individual's relation to God, which could be cultivated only in the leisure of contemplation. Because peasant serfs did most of the work in medieval society, and because the earthly character of their occupations prevented them from participating directly in the religious life, they received grace through the church by means of the sacraments.

Not only the life of productive work, but also the practical or active life, consisting of doing good to one's neighbor, was viewed by many medievals as an impediment to the true goals of the religious life. The activity given precedence was always the contemplative life. An early church father, St. Augustine (1950) wrote: "the obligations of charity make us undertake virtuous activity, but if no one lays this burden upon us, we should give ourselves over in leisure to study and contemplation" (p. 19). The need for the active or charitable life was temporary, whereas contemplation of God was eternal.

Luther's concept of vocation or calling fits neatly within the compass of this thought since he draws a basic theological distinction between the kingdom of heaven and the kingdom of earth. To the kingdom of heaven belongs our relationship to God, which is to be based on faith; to the kingdom of earth belongs our relationship to our neighbor, which is to be based on love. A vocation, properly speaking, is the call to love my neighbor that comes to me through the duties attached to my social place or *station* within the earthly kingdom. A station in this life may be a matter of paid employment, but it need not be. Luther's idea of station is wide enough to include being a wife or a husband, a mother or a father, a judge or politician, as well as a baker, truck driver, farmer or social worker. Thus, the call to love one's neighbor goes out to all in general. All of these callings represent specific and concrete ways of serving my neighbor, as I am commanded to do by God Himself.

What do we accomplish when we discharge the duties of our stations in life, when we heed the call of God to serve our neighbor in our daily tasks? Luther believed the order of stations in the kingdom of earth has been instituted by God Himself as His way of seeing to it that the needs of humanity are met on a day-by-day basis. Through the human pursuit of vocations across the array of earthly stations, the hungry are fed, the naked are clothed, the sick are healed, the ignorant are enlightened, and the weak are protected. That is, by working we actually participate in God's providence for the human race. Through our work, people are brought under His providential care. Far from being of little or no account, work is charged with religious significance. As we pray each morning for our daily bread, people are already busy at work in the bakeries.

Luther conceived of work as a way of serving others. He never recommended it as either the road to self-fulfillment or a tool for self-aggrandizement. We, of course, find it natural to assess the attractiveness of a particular job on the basis of what it can do for us. But Luther saw quite clearly that work will always involve a degree of self-sacrifice for the sake of others, just as Christ sacrificed himself for the sake of others.

During the time of Luther, and for many centuries preceding him, people thought of human society as stable, static, and as incapable of change, as the order of nature itself. Shortly after Luther's time, however, European civilization underwent a dramatic transformation under the combined influence of a rapidly expanding market economy, accelerated urbanization, technological innovation, and vast political reorganization. In the face of these astounding changes on all fronts of social life, people soon saw that the structure of human society is itself in part a product of human activity, changeable and affected by sin. Once people recognized this fact, it became clear, in turn, that to the degree human activity is motivated by sinful desires and worldly ambitions, the society thus produced is also likely to be structurally unsound and in need of reform. For example, an economy based upon greed and a government based on the arbitrary use of power stand in just as much need of repentance as the individuals who are a part of them. For this reason, other reformers insisted that not only the human heart, but also human society must be reformed in accordance with the Word of God. The emergent vision of the Christian life at the dawn of modern social work practice, then, required not only that people obey God in their callings, but that the callings themselves be aligned with the will of God.

Calling Within Social Work

Although historically there have been many models of spirituality in social work, the calling model perhaps has been the most prominent, or at least the most extensively referred to in the social work literature. In fact, in the very early years, it was the dominant model. This dominance is certainly related to the fact that Protestantism was the dominant religious form at the time. Many early social workers in their writings refer to the relationship of their spirituality and social work within this calling model. Their response is not surprising, since many of them grew up in devoted religious families, many had theological training, and still others were very active as lay people in their churches. All found in their spiritual experiences something which gave impetus, meaning, and value to their work of service.

The following examples illustrate the prominence of the calling model and how it has been articulated and practiced by a variety of different leaders within the profession.

Edward Devine, a leader in the Charity Organization Society and the first director of one of the first schools of social work, records in his book *When Social Work Was Young* (1939) the early experiences in social work education and summarizes these experiences as follows:

> The real start towards the professional education of social workers as such was made in 1898, when the Society launched its summer school of philanthropy with thirty students enrolled.
>
> For several years this summer school gathered from all parts of the country a substantial number of promising candidates, and a brilliant corps of instructors, who for one day, or sometimes for an entire week, expounded and discussed the fundamentals of the slowly emerging profession. Jane Addams, Mary Richmond, Zilpha Smith, Mrs. Glendower Evans, Graham Taylor, Jeffrey Brackett, John M. Glenn, Mary Willcox Brown, before and also after she became Mrs. John M. Glenn, James B. Reynolds, Mary Simkhovitch—a full roster of the lecturers in the school would be like a list of the notables in the National Conference of Social Work. Certainly no religious gathering could have a deeper consecration to that ideal of learning how to do justly, and to love mercy, and to walk humbly, which Micah described as being all that is required of us (p. 125-6).

He ends the book by stating that in his opinion the spirit of social work finds its power, value, and purpose from the biblical Sermon on the Mount.

Richard Cabot (1927) addressed the model of calling more specifically in an article entitled "The Inter-Relation of Social Work and the Spiritual Life." He writes:

> religion is the consciousness of a world purpose to which we are allied...when I speak of the purpose being a personality, I speak of the person of God of whom we are children... I think it makes absolutely all the difference in social work to know this fact of our alliance with forces greater than ourselves. If a person wants to find himself and be somebody he has got to find his particular place in the universal plan. In social work, we are trying to help people find themselves, find their places and enjoy them. The chief end of man is to glorify God and to enjoy Him forever (p. 212).

Cabot also articulated several spiritual powers applicable to social work practice that come to those who hold this faith: courage, humility and the ability to stand by people. He goes on to explain that the goal of social work is to:

...maintain and to improve the channels of understanding both within each person and between persons, and through these channels to favor the entrance of God's powers for the benefit of the individuals....Unblocking channels is what social workers do. The sort of unblocking that I have in mind is that between capital and labor, between races, or between the members of a family who think they hate each other....Spiritual diagnosis, I suppose, means nothing more than the glimpse of the central purpose of the person, unique and related to the total parts of the world. Spiritual treatment, I suppose, is the attempt to open channels, the channels I have been speaking of, so as to favor the working of the world purpose. In this way social workers participate in the providence of God (p. 215-16).

Perhaps the most prominent example of the power and dominance of the calling model is illustrated in Owen R. Lovejoy's presidential address to the National Conference of Social Work in 1920, entitled "The Faith of a Social Worker." In the speech he attempts to draw upon the foundations of faith of the members in order to aid in their approach to discussions during the Conference and to help create a real basis for unity. He begins by first disclaiming any intention of committing the Conference to any specific creed of social service. His desire, rather, is to discover "some of the those underlying principles which bind people together."

He states that all social workers have a philosophy of life, a faith, a "basic enthusiasm," and those who act on this faith can choose to:

regard this as a sacred ministry and claim their commission as the ancient prophet claimed his when he said: "The Lord hath anointed me to preach good tidings to the meek, to bind up the broken hearted, to proclaim liberty to the captives, the opening of prison to them that are bound, to give a garland for ashes, the oil of joy for mourning, the garment of praise for the spirit of heaviness." Certainly this is not a slight task to which we are called, but the expression of a joyful faith carried with cheerfulness to those in the world most in need of it...a field of service based on the conviction that men are warranted in working for something corresponding to a divine order "on earth as it is in heaven (p. 209).

He warns those "who look upon the visible institutions connected with their religion as the essential embodiment of faith," recognizing such a sectarian position frequently leads to imposing one's own values on others and proselytizing—similar issues we face today. He ends the address stating that the secret of their usefulness as social workers is found in the following litany.

> God is a Father,
> Man is a brother,
> Life is a mission and not a career;
> Dominion is service,

> Its scepter is gladness,
> The least is the greatest,
> Saving is dying,
> Giving is living,
> Life is eternal and love is its crown (p. 211).

It is difficult to imagine an address on such a topic being given today. Such was the significance of spirituality and the calling model in the social work profession at that time.

The calling model's chief apologist, however, was Ernest Johnson, a prolific writer and interpreter of Protestant religion and the social work profession. His writings detail the principles which he hoped would govern efforts to bring Protestantism to bear through the social work profession in meeting human needs. Recognizing that Protestantism had a majority position and influence in the culture, he strongly advocated, with some exceptions, for a pattern of social work based on the calling model. The result was to minimize the operation and control of agencies and social welfare enterprises by churches or religious groups and maximize Protestant participation in non-sectarian agencies.

Later in life he recognized that Protestantism, particularly when its pre-eminent position was beginning to wane, would never obtain complete cultural dominance or create an approximation to the ideal of a Christian society—the Corpus Christianum. The result, he lamented, would be only a partial trans-formation of the culture—and regrettably, a partial accommodation on the part of Protestantism to the culture. But despite this limitation, he still believed the Protestant pattern or model of influencing social work enterprises and social movements "indirectly" (through the means of one's calling or vocation) was essentially sound. Johnson (1946) states:

> It [the calling model] affords the most effective channel through which our churches, in the midst of a religiously heterogeneous population, can bring to bear their testimony through community endeavor and make their impact on a secular culture. This means, however, a recovery of the sense of lay Christian vocation, which has been so largely lost. The major Protestant contribution to social work can be made, I believe, through the consciously Christian activities of persons engaged in non-sectarian enterprises and movements. In the existing situation in America a revival of a sectarian, possessive attitude toward social work would be definitely reactionary....
> In a word, then, we need to devise our social strategy in the light of our Protestant history, with its emphasis on freedom, and in the light of our cultural situation, which puts a premium on vocational work as Christian testimony. We can make our best contribution without seeking to enhance Protestant prestige, seeking rather to influence contemporary life and to meet human need through the activities of those whose lives have been kindled at our altars and nourished in our fellowship (p. 2-4).

As Johnson relates, the calling model has not always functioned as intended. Already in 1893, one leader of the new social work profession, responding to the widening gap between religion and the emerging influence of scientific models in social work, characterized social work as "a revolutionary turning of thought in our society from a religious service to God to a secular service to humanity" (Huntington, 1893). Along this line of thought, Protestant theologian Reinhold Niebuhr (1932) grappled with the practical consequences of the calling model for social work. With three-fourths of social workers then functioning under secular auspices, many had become "inclined to disregard religion." This development he regarded as a significant loss for social work—"destroying or remaining oblivious to powerful resources and losing the insights religion provided in keeping wholesome attitudes toward individuals" and "preserving the sanity and health in the social worker's own outlook upon life" (p. 9). He believed social workers needed, therefore, a renewed sense of vocation or calling. In addition, this loss of calling partially contributes to what church historian Martin Marty (1980) later referred to as "godless social service," or the migration (privatization) of faith or spirituality from social work.

Conclusion

Because of our distance from the thoughts and assumptions of our predecessors in social work and perhaps from the language of spirituality itself, efforts regarding such historical reflections as these may seem awkward and archaic. The goal is not, however, to recreate the past, but rather to identify the models of spirituality that guided our social work ancestors and then to find ways to translate and apply the spirit of these models to our present situation.

This model of calling offers significant insight into current discussions relating spirituality and professional social work practice. Within this calling model, religious faith is not the private possession of an individual, but is grounded in tradition and divine revelation, permeating the whole of life, connecting public and private spheres, and linking the individual with the community. The model also places professional techniques and methods in the context of larger goals and values that give life meaning and purpose for both clients and practitioners.

Historically, religiously motivated persons and groups found their faith propelling them into actions of concern for others, especially the poor and the vulnerable in society. These social workers have affirmed in a variety of ways their shared belief that the faith dimension of life leads to a transcendence of individualism, and to a commitment to others—to social work practice motivated by a calling to a life of service.

The model presented is helpful to social workers from the Christian faith tradition, but also to others who seek to acquire a better understanding of the meaning and effects of spirituality in their own and their clients' lives. A social worker's own cultivation of spirituality is a crucial preparation for the competent application of knowledge and skills in practice. The model is particularly helpful in taking into account the distinctive values, sources of power and master stories of one particular religious and cultural tradition, Christianity—represented by many persons like Tessie and her grandmother whom social workers daily encounter in practice, as well as by many social workers themselves.

Although the model does not resolve the tensions and conflicts which exist between the Christian spiritual tradition and the current largely secular profession, it does provide a beginning framework for integrating Christian spirituality and social work at both the personal and professional levels. The profession's roots are significantly tied to this particular model of spiritual/professional integration, and many social workers as well as clients continue to define their lives, personally and professionally, in the context of this Christian-based spiritual call to service. The Christian values of love, justice, and kindness; its stories related to the poor, the vulnerable, and those of liberation from oppression; and its emphasis on self-sacrifice, are the "passion of the old time social workers" that many find attractive and wish to bring back—albeit in a form more adaptable to a more diverse clientele and changed environment (Constable, 1983; Gustafson, 1982; Reamer, 1992; Siporin, 1982, 1985; Specht & Courtney, 1994).

References

Augustine, St. (1950). *City of God*. XIX, 19, New York: Modern Library.

Brower, I. (1984). *The 4th ear of the spiritual-sensitive social worker*. Ph.D. diss., Union for Experimenting Colleges and Universities.

Cabot, R. C. (1927). The inter-relation of social work and the spiritual life. *The Family*, 8(7), 211-217.

Canda, E. R. (1988a). Conceptualizing spirituality for social work: Insights from diverse perspectives. *Social Thought*, 14(1), 30-46.

Canda, E. R. (1988b). Spirituality, religious diversity and social work practice. *Social Casework*, 69(4), 238-247.

Coles, R. (1993). *The call of service*. New York: Houghton Mifflin Company.

Constable, R. (1983). Religion, values and social work practice. *Social Thought*, 9, 29-41.

Devine, E. T. (1939). *When social work was young*. New York: Macmillan Company.

Fowler, J. W. (1981). *Stages of faith*. San Francisco: Harper and Row.

Gustafson, J. M. (1982). Professions as "callings." *Social Service Review*, 56(4), 105-515.

Huntington, J. (1893). Philanthropy and morality. In Addams, J. (Ed.), *Philanthropy and social progress*, New York: Crowell.

Johnson, E. F. (1946). The pattern and philosophy of protestant social work. *Church Conference of Social Work*, Buffalo, New York.

Leiby, J. (1985). Moral foundations of social welfare and social work: A historical view. *Social Work*, 30(4), 323-330.

Lovejoy, O. R. (1920). The faith of a social worker. *The Survey*, 44, 208-211.

Marty, M. E. (1980). Social service: Godly and godless. *Social Service Review*, 54, 463-481.

Niebuhr, R. (1932). *The contribution of religion to social work*. New York: Columbia University Press.

Reamer, F. G. (1992). Social work and the public good: Calling or career? In Reid, N. P. & P. R. Popple (Eds.), *The moral purposes of social work*, (11-33), Chicago: Nelson-Hall.

Specht, H. & Courtney, M. (1994). *Unfaithful angels*. New York: The Free Press.

Siporin, M. (1982). Moral philosophy in social work today. *Social Service Review*, 56(4), 516-538.

Siporin, M. (1985). Current social work perspectives on clinical practice. *Clinical Social Work Journal*, 13, 198-217.

CHAPTER 4

INTEGRATING CHRISTIAN FAITH AND SOCIAL WORK PRACTICE: STUDENTS' VIEWS OF THE JOURNEY

T. Laine Scales, Helen Wilson Harris, Dennis Myers, and Jon Singletary

Perhaps you remember family vacations that included road trips across the country; trips that started with the unfolding of a map on the dining room table or an internet search for driving directions. You found your current location on the map, then found your destination on the map and only then began the exploration of various routes to get there. The journey really started before the map was secured or the computer was booted up. It very likely started as you considered your destination and the purpose of your trip. Once you knew where you were going, your focus could move to the "how to" of getting there.

In this chapter we will share several student views of one of the most challenging journeys for Christians in social work: the journey toward integration of faith and social work practice. We are a group of four social work faculty members at a Christian university, Baylor University in Waco, Texas. We spend a lot of time pondering this journey toward integration. We think about Christianity and social work very personally, in relation to ourselves and our callings. We talk about this often with other faculty members on retreats or in meetings. Most important, we explore this topic with students in advising, in classrooms, and most recently, in conducting a research project with our students. We have been intentional in our exploration of this topic because we have been deeply affected by our own responses to the question "Where am I on the journey toward integrating Christian faith and social work practice?"

Our purpose in writing this chapter is three-fold. First, we want to share with you the stories from Christian students at our university who have been on this journey toward becoming a social worker. We collected interviews from students and alumni during the year 2004-05. All participants were seeking or had completed one of three programs: Bachelor of Social Work (BSW), Master of Social Work (MSW), or in some cases, our dual-degree program, in which they sought the MSW from the School of Social Work and the Master of Divinity (M.Div.) from Baylor's George W. Truett Theological Seminary. Our second purpose in writing is to comment on the various themes emerging from the students' reflections as they shared stories of seeking God's plan, dealing with obstacles, and seeking companionship for the journey. Finally, we will invite you to join with other Christian travelers as we figure out together various ways to integrate Christian faith and social work practice.

We are addressing our comments primarily to student readers, though we realize that faculty members, social work practitioners, and others may read this chapter. Our hope is that students and others who are introduced to the stories of our Baylor students will be prompted to reflect on their own journeys. We expect that for our readers, these conversations about calling have been and will continue to be a central part of the dialogue concerning Christians in social work: a dialogue involving other students, advisors, supervisors, teachers, families, and friends. One last caution: this chapter is not based on our data analysis and is not presented as research findings. We are beginning to report those findings in other publications (Singletary, Harris, Myers, & Scales, 2006). Instead, this is a more personal sharing of selected quotes from students and faculty that we hope will serve as information and inspiration as you consider your calling and your pilgrimage. We invite you to travel with us.

The Road Trip of a Lifetime

For the Christian student, the most compelling question of "Where am I going?" has been answered ultimately: "I am going to God, to eternity with my creator, to Heaven." But if life is truly a journey leading us to our Home, it seems very important "how we get there." It is frequently easier for Christian students to talk freely about their eternal destination while struggling significantly with determining the course of their life journeys. Which of the many career paths available shall we take? What is it we are to "do" with this life we have been given? We look at the "life map" of possibilities and consider our options while many voices, from parents to mentors to detractors, offer opinions. Shall we travel major highways with large loops that let us travel quickly and efficiently but that help us or make us skirt around the inner cities where the bustle of life and pain of others is almost palpable? Shall we travel the back roads of life where the pace is slower and the interactions more measured and deliberate? Will our travels take us through many small adventures or will this journey center on one or two defining highways?

For the Christian social worker, there is a real sense that we serve a Navigator who has charted our path, who created us with particular gifts and talents to accomplish the purposes of God's creation. But getting the message and instructions of the Navigator that are specific to our journey is often the challenge. Has God called me to a specific work? And if so, how will I "hear" the call and know the path? We find ourselves asking, "What are the roads or pathways that will get me to the work and then through the work to which God is calling me?"

Students who understand that they have been "called" to social work describe that time of hearing the Navigator's voice in a variety of ways. Becoming a social worker is a process, a journey that may begin from any place at any time. Some social workers can trace the beginning of their travels to childhood: parents who modeled for them the giving of self in service of others and encouraged the journey of helping. For some, the journey toward social work may have begun later in life, after several apparently false starts down roads that were blocked or just seemed to be the wrong direction. Eventually they realized that the Navigator provided directional signs and clarity and that those initial forays were strength building that led to clarity and focus.

While all social work students may be on a journey, for Christian social workers, the paths toward life as a Christian and toward professional social work are often traveled simultaneously. Even a student who has been a Christian for many years may be walking a path of deepening faith. Therefore, Christian social work students explore questions such as these: "How does my journey as a Christian intersect with, compliment, replicate, or diverge from travel along my journey toward professional social work? Will I be confronted with the choice between two roads, one representing my faith journey and the other representing my professional journey? Or is there truth in the statement that social work and Christianity really are quite compatible with one another? Is it possible that we have been called by the Navigator to forge a new road that brings our path across the most vulnerable, the most wounded, those lost needing a guide to get back to the road?"

Why Social Work Education?

Our students' stories remind us that all journeys must begin somewhere, even though the map has not been secured or the destination is not in view. Some students are very comfortable with wandering. Some are taking a leisurely journey that may be spontaneous and filled with last- minute decisions about destinations and activities, a bit like buying a month-long rail pass and traveling around Europe. In some instances, students may enter social work to check it out, wander around, and decide along the way what is interesting. In contrast, other students are on a carefully defined path to a very specific destination. They have a particular vocational goal in mind and their social work education is a point on their map. One student described where she hopes to be in ten years:

> I want to have started a non-profit [agency] for doing job training
> for women. For impoverished women—that's what I would like to
> be doing in ten years. To get there, I think in two years I am going
> to be working at an agency doing very micro work.... I really need
> to have that perspective. [1]

One can imagine this student viewing social work classes as particular points on a map that will lead to the ten-year goal.

In some cases, students found their way to social work after developing a commitment to a particular population. For example, one young woman found that she was gifted in working with children, so she planned to pursue teaching in a school setting. In conversation with her own teachers she began to broaden her view of careers in which she might work with kids. Soon she was imagining social work as an option. In her own words:

> I just easily attached to kids; they easily attached to me. And I was
> just a real good people person. People said it all the time,... [With

social work] I would have more job options… and if I'm a school teacher, then that's what I do with kids, I just teach them, but with social work I could do a whole bunch of different things and I liked that.

Another student began social work in order to work with children and adolescents, but, through experience in internships and classes, opened her mind to consider work with additional populations:

I always thought… I was going to work with children. And it's switched a lot. … our society's changing as well, so Alzheimer's and caregivers are going to be big needs our population is going to have…I definitely could see myself in that kind of field…I have lots of options….

Another student's ultimate goal is ministry, but this student intentionally sought a social work education to gain particular skills and information. Encountering two other travelers with social work competencies motivated this student to walk with them.

I want to connect to people and really help them work through these issues that they've got. I thought that I could do that in seminary, and I think that you can, but when I got in there—that's where the catch was—when I started asking questions about wife beatings and children getting hit—those things. And when the only two people in the room that knew were social work students, that was what really did it for me. This is some information that I have always wanted to know. How do I get this information? And social work has that information with it.

While the student quoted above wanted to join the social workers (through Baylor's M.Div-MSW dual-degree program) to gain particular knowledge or skills, another student wanted to journey alongside social workers because she appreciated the value base of the profession.

The first draw that was in my mind was that I thought that social workers worked with the poor, that was the initial lead in. But also, helping the oppressed and the poor in justice issues from a biblical basis and seeing that as a value of the social work profession… So social work values are definitely places that attracted me as a means of vocation or a job where I live out the values.

Where am I Going?

In contrast to students who had a clear picture about why they chose social work education, other students were wandering, with or without a compass. One student was simply lost in the journey and stated bluntly "I have no direction on my future at this point." Another traveler expressed outwardly a feeling of confidence that she would find the way as she goes, but at the same time, admits an "uneasy feeling" as well.

> To me, at this point, there's still just—it's all very unclear. I'm pushing around things right now, but I'm learning that there are so many options out there and that I have to just kind of give it time to know things will develop, and I'll find it as I go. So I'm doing my education to help give me some more options and some more places, but I can't see down the line right now. And it's kind of an uneasy feeling, not knowing which direction or any of the options that are available—in either direction.

This inability to see around the corner is both the joy and the challenge of traveling free and easy, wherever the wind may take us. We may know that good things can happen along the way and that the path will be there when we need it. But, the uneasiness described above leads to a natural question for students: will we really like what we find along the way? And, perhaps a more troubling question: when we arrive at our destination, will the satisfaction we find be worth the time and effort we have invested?

Sometimes it is easier to see where we are on the path by looking behind us, at where we have been. This student reflects on the calling to social work as a process; looking back, she can see that there were signposts of confirmation points on her journey.

> I don't think it was one instance, like one minute, all of a sudden, I was like," I'm called to social work." I think it was a process the constant affirmation. I believe when people are walking with God, and in His word every day, and are really seeking Him, then He'll lead you in a certain direction, and so as I've been seeking Him throughout college, my college experience and life, I've felt confirmed over and over again to continue in the path of social work. And more so every day, even today, more so than yesterday.

Am I on the Right Road?

One of the lessons we learned from the students we interviewed was that entering and staying on the path to a vocation in social work can be an uncertain and complicated task. Their experiences made us more aware of the unexpected turns, intersections, and detours that accompany most who travel this way. These honest, onsite reports of the terrain will alert you to the possibility that you may encounter obstacles in the pathway—you or others in your life may question the direction you are going, the accuracy of your map, and the worth of your destination. You will discover that others have traveled the path that you are now on or that you are thinking of entering. They have much to say about the challenges you face and about how God keeps them on the path and helps them make sense of the journey.

Some students told us that, in the beginning, they didn't want to be on the path toward a career in social work. It seems that God's plan for their life's journey was very different from the life map envisioned by the student. This reflection illustrates how God's plans may not be our plans:

> I remember a point where I sat there and I said, "I don't want to go this direction." I remember praying and saying, "God, you got something confused here. You got the wrong plan for the wrong girl." There was a point where I really remember just about screaming my head off going, "God; you're just off, here! I don't understand why you're doing this!"

Another student described the experience of misinterpreting God's plan:

> "I think, for me, I misinterpret God, definitely because I am a self-ish person and have my own agenda and my own plans that aren't necessarily in conjunction with His, so I do get a little confused and can't see the line—but I definitely know that from my experience, He's used other people and you know, initially by just planting a seed in my heart, or maybe a desire or maybe just a little interest.

It seems that once these students reluctantly entered the path of God's plan for their Christian vocation, confirmation that they were in the right place reassured the travelers. Students reported confirmation from a number of sources.

> I really think, looking back, especially because of that factor, that it was nothing other than God saying, "We're going to have to take major steps to intervene on this girl's life, because she is not listening to anything I'm saying to her! I've put this desire in her heart, I've put this, like, internal factor in her that is driving her towards social work, and she is just abandoning it!" So, that's what I think that God definitely had a huge…part in that, for sure.

One student described the sense of peace that confirmed the chosen path:

> I think it's completely natural for me to be in social work. And if I try to pursue other things, it really doesn't give me that sense of peace, it gives me more of a sense of like I don't belong there. That's really the role that social work plays and that's how I feel as far as my calling, when I know that when I'm doing something that God doesn't want me to do, I don't have that peace. And when God wants me to do something and that's where I should be, and that's where I am, I have that sense of peace and I'm fine with it even if it makes me uncomfortable, but I feel just natural to be there."

Encountering Obstacles

After overcoming their resistance, and then heading out on to the social work path, some students reported that they encountered unanticipated obstacles along the way. Some of these challenges, such as the family members who questioned their choices and the public perception of social work, affected their decisions to begin the journey while others, such as a loss of professional destination created a temporary disorientation.

Family concerns

Confusion or concern may be the response of parents and family members to students who choose social work as a career. Family members may want to understand the motivation and reasoning that underlie this sometimes controversial decision. These two quotes from students reflect the concerns that some family members may have about the choice of social work as a career:

> No matter what I do, there is [from my parents] this, "ok what is your reasoning behind this?" I think that is a real big key thing, is to see where my motivation is coming from, and seeing, what makes me do this, to make sure I am doing it for the right reasons. Also, I think, part of it is for bragging rights, so that when people ask them, [parents] can say, "well, she's doing it because she wants to dah, dah, dah." I get a kick out of that - that that's one of the things that they do.

Another student described a negative reaction to the career path from family:

> Oh, well, they definitely have not influenced me to be called to— I mean, they are—my grandparents still are in denial that I am a social work major. I mean, no one in my family wanted me to be a social work major. So, they really have not done anything to encourage me to do that. But I think they just really wanted me to do business. But, I don't know.

Public perception of social work

Professional prestige and societal recognition may affect career choice. This was not an often mentioned concern in these interviews but there were at least several references to this potential obstacle. One student described a narrow perception of social work when initially considering the profession, asking "Aren't they just CPS [Child Protective Services] workers? That was my whole idea of social work." Another student suggested that "social work, I guess widely speaking, isn't that glamorous of a profession." He described the questions others ask:

> "...is social work a real profession?"... people look down on social workers. They don't think that that's a real thing. In court, they don't listen to their testimony, they don't think its real, but that's just how it was with Jesus."

Obstacles as a path to new directions

Obstacles can detour the traveler in a direction that actually leads to God's intention for the social work student. Consider this observation:

I wish I could say I was that trusting and that easy to influence on it, but one of the characteristics I have, and it usually has a negative connotation to it, but for me it's a good thing, is being stubborn. I am someone who's not very easy to move and be manipulated and I just don't, I tend to want to stay in the same spot because it's kind of, I don't like to move into the unknown very easily and so for me, it seems like it's one instance after another and I keep getting hit from different directions until I'm finally going, ok maybe this, maybe I'm being told something here. That includes some of the people that I know. I'm wanting to go on this path and I keep getting stumbling blocks that are really actually people who are kind of going, "you might want to consider doing this, you're fitted for this."

All of these social work students were seeking a path that would lead them to a place where they could ethically live into their vocation and their faith. The stories provide maps for travelers that aspire to the same destination. The pathway can be clearly marked with signs of confirmation and direction. We also have seen that, along the way, social work students who embrace Christian faith may encounter unanticipated obstacles that may disorient and even cause them to lose their way. Amazingly, the God who called them to the journey is also able to set their feet on the life-long path of service and Christian vocation. And, fortunately, Christian social workers do not ever have to walk alone.

Fellow Travelers

Social workers know perhaps better than most that no one successfully journeys alone in this life. As you learn how to walk alongside the people you serve, you also may begin to wonder "Who will travel with me? Family, faculty, supervisors, student colleagues, God?" You may experience the presence of God calling in many ways; some direct and some indirect, but a part of God's calling is found in the voices of those who go with you on the journey.

Students in our program discussed their understanding of God's call through the influence of other people. We heard about direct and indirect influence of family members, co-workers, social workers, faculty, or others who helped students understand social work as an option for responding to God's call. Interpersonal relationships helped students discern God's call to the profession of social work and to know that there was someone on the journey with them. Here we highlight some of these relationships on the journey.

Who will guide my journey? God.

In trusting God's presence in our midst, we heard students describe the meaning of this for their journeys. One student said that God's "hand was there and just kept guiding me through." Another student offers, "the calling for me is just following what God wants me to do and where God is leading me to." And also, "With me, I feel like God really, strongly directed me towards this."

Who will go with me? Family and friends

The most common travelers alongside students were their family and friends. Sometimes these loved ones question the turns we make on the journey. Sometimes, they aren't sure how to support us along the way. Looking back on years of family strife, a student reflected on her family's role in her journey saying, "I don't know if my family necessarily, in a positive way, influenced my decision for social work." Yet, other students had different experiences as families ventured forth with them: "I knew that by choosing a profession where I would be helping people," said one student, "I would be understood by my family and they would support that decision because that's what I wanted to do." Another student also voiced the encouragement of family traveling with them, "I think that there is an experience where your family, they are helping me through a lot of this. That's one thing I feel very blessed with, is that they have been very supportive."

Who will go with me? Social workers such as faculty, classmates,
and field supervisors

Significant relationships are influential in helping you make your way down the road into professional social work practice. There are many others who travel alongside you in the adventure of becoming a professional, and social work education offers students unique and practical experiences in developing strength for the journey. Students spend a great deal of time with classmates, faculty, and field supervisors, who are a part of their journeys of discernment. They often recognize right away the importance of these relationships.

One new student described one of her attractions to the program: "I knew the faculty was very friendly and very interested in their students succeeding." Students commented on the relationships faculty intentionally developed with students on this journey. "I think it's pretty much invaluable," said one student, "At least if it's set up properly, because you can draw on the experience of your professors, who have years of experience in the field, as well as the experience of the people who are even writing the textbooks." Professors are described as mentors in students' lives as they walk alongside them, "they really push to a high standard, but they're also there to, not hold your hand, but support you, encourage you, and I just got a really strong sense of community, and support."

Faculty understood the importance of engaging with students. After a weekend of discussions about our own vocational journeys, faculty in our program wrote about the role they envisioned for themselves in walking alongside students: "My assessment is that sharing about our journeys and aspirations enabled us to see and appreciate the complexity and richness of the fabric of our collective relationship," offered one professor. Another added her reflections, "My renewed awareness of my own calling and what has contributed to living it out has made me more aware of the potential significance of every interaction I have with students. I find myself asking my advisees and other students more open-ended questions about their purpose and urging them to see their inner promptings and long-held dreams."

As students, you also have supervisors guiding you while you learn, preparing you for the road ahead: "I talk to my supervisor constantly about what is going on with this client," said one person we interviewed. "She lets me do the work, but she is there for advice and consultation. This is uncharted territory for me, but I am learning so much." Students express appreciation for the learning that comes in supervision. One offers, "It was tremendously helpful to me that my supervisor went out on an assessment with me. I was able to discuss advanced practice with her and it was really good to have her feedback from the assessment." And another echoes the support on the journey of learning: "In the middle of the crises of moving the clients I was on the phone with my supervisor. I wasn't sure what to do, and she talked me through it. But she also let me do it on my own, for which I am now thankful. It was a great experience."

Who will go with me? Clients

In social work education, you will have opportunities to reflect upon and then practice traveling with your clients, whether you are in generalist practice, direct practice, or practice with larger systems, you will be asking how to accompany your clients and how they will accompany you on this journey.

Our students may be aware of where they have stumbled along the way, but they are not sure that the people they serve understand the challenges of their journeys. "Sometimes, it's harder to meet people's needs because sometimes you have to convince them they have needs, or they don't realize they have needs," said one interviewee. What this suggests is that students are learning the reciprocal nature of walking alongside others. They walk with clients in hopes of making a difference in their journeys. One student said, "If you can intervene and somehow help them realize that they are worth something and they have true potential, I feel like it changes so many things." After a similar experience with a client, another student said, "That made me feel good because I didn't force anything on him, I just lived right and tried to treat him like I treat anybody else."

As students on the journey into the profession walk with clients, they want to help them, but we know they also learn to "have the clients be the expert of their experience," as one student put it. In this, the clients also walk with students. They help students move further along the journey.

Integration of Christian Faith and Social Work Practice.

Now we have come to the heart of what we learned from our interviews. If you are reading this book you probably have some interest in exploring the integration of Christian faith and social work. Maybe you are faculty members, like us, who have thought about this for years. Maybe you are a student, who is exploring various aspects of what it means to travel this road. Social work students who embrace Christian faith seek a path leading to places where they can integrate professional values and ethics with their religious beliefs. The journey down this path usually creates a unique set of opportunities, challenges and blessings..

Opportunities

For some students, Christian faith adds an extra measure of compassion to their work. This student articulated how faith integration may allow the worker to understand the client more completely.

> My faith shapes who I am—kind of like my thought processes....
> as I'm in social work, I'm learning to evaluate situations and just
> know who I am and what my beliefs are, but then to see that person
> for who they are and to work with them in where they're at. So.....I
> think how I approach situations may be different. I may be a little
> more compassionate than somebody else would be.

Another student explored a similar theme, acknowledging that her own Christian values are a lens through which she sees the world, but this lens does not prevent her from valuing the different perspectives of her clients.

> I'm at peace, I guess, as far as, I'm able to discuss with clients about
> their own views and their own wants and desires for whom—for
> who they are. Without imposing my own values. Because I realize
> that my values are, maybe, different from theirs. But that doesn't
> mean that I cannot help that person.

Perhaps most significantly, a number of students reported the important interplay between their faith and their professional identity and practice. This student described this as "accountability":

> Another great blessing I have had is that it [social work] has made
> me,—it has held me accountable to my faith. But it has made me
> more genuine in my faith. It has really made me examine what it
> means to be a Christian—what it means to minister. The word min-
> istry to me just means doing good social work......The profession
> has held me more accountable to my faith, and my faith has held
> me more accountable to my profession.

Challenges and Dilemmas

For some of the students we interviewed, the potential dissonance between faith and practice created significant, but not overwhelming concerns along the way. For one student this blend was a "dangerous" idea:

> "I think that calling and social work sometimes can be dangerous
> words to associate together for the social work profession because
> you don't want to minimize the professionalism of social work. And
> by classifying social work as a ministry, is very dangerous. I think
> that it does take out the element of professionalism that's there. But
> at the same time—and I am still, I am definitely in the learning pro-
> cess of this—you need to know how to effectively balance faith and
> practice, because you are never going to be just a social worker....I
> am going to be going somewhere as a Christian, with the title social

worker. And I think that's a wonderful and such an amazing blessing to have that opportunity, but it can be very dangerous because you are representing two amazing things. … And I think that's why so many people are so afraid of having faith in practice, and those two words together are like an oxymoron to so many people. I think it's sad, but I think there is a delicate balance there.

Other interviewees, preparing for ministry roles, echoed the potential dissonance between the role of social worker and the role of minister.

"I like the fact that in social work, you know—there are certain things you can do that you can't seem to do in ministry. And there's the other catch where there are certain things you can't do in social work that you can in ministry. For example, with a pastor, they can openly go in and say, this is what I believe and all of this. In social work, it's not really—that's kind of frowned upon."

Students admitted that learning to do this integration was a process; one that sometimes involved some "hard knocks." One student, who described the process of integration as "a little confusing," told us about a learning experience.

For the most part, it's just a hard issue. You take it case by case. I had a hard experience this past semester in my agency where I did an intake and I asked my client if she ever prayed and it helped our conversation and I didn't regret doing it but my supervisor and I had to talk a long time about why that would have been a bad idea and it was hard. In the end I really saw where he was coming from. I just want to know what is best for the client. I just want to be led by the Holy Spirit and not necessarily by the [NASW] Code of Ethics. It's just really hard for me, but I am learning a lot and I am open to learning a lot more."

Some students reported that trying to reconcile the values of the social work profession with Christian values presented a major obstacle for them. One felt frustrated stating "I don't know that I have been able to integrate it [faith and social work] to the point that I feel that it works; I feel really torn." Another student described in more detail:

"I think that there are major conflicts with how I was raised and the element of faith in my life. And that was something I struggled with a lot in undergrad is kind of taking on my parents' values and the things that I learned in the church, you know things that I was supposed to do and how I was supposed to act, and my expectations on life, and what I needed to do I felt like conflict greatly with social work, and that troubled me."

These are the dilemmas that students mention as they embark on a journey that fully embraces the authentic integration of social work and Christian faith.

While the struggles are significant and formative, there are also encounters with blessings and opportunities that mark the journey.

Blessings

In spite of encountering challenges, the students we interviewed reported a wide array of blessings and opportunities associated with the blending of Christian faith and professional identity. At a deeply personal level, students indicated that their intentional efforts at integration resulted in "the feeling of inner harmony", "freedom and flexibility", and helping "me realize more of who I am and making me understand... what I want to do." Sometimes the reward is a feeling of comfort and joy as reflected in this statement: "I prayed about it, and I feel great about it."

One frequently mentioned outcome of the intentional integration of faith and practice was that faith was strengthened in the process. For example, "my social work education has shaped my faith and has made me— its kind of really helped me be a better Christian." These words echoed this same conclusion—"it [social work] has made me more genuine in my faith." This kind of integration may also have the power to change important assumptions. One student described herself as "a Christian wearing the hat of a social worker," with training that " is going to be shaping how I speak to people, even though it [professional education] may not have changed everything how I feel, but it has changed how I think."

The process of blending faith and practice seemed to have beneficial consequences for interactions with clients. Consider this observation—"I think that's my biggest thing that I've enjoyed ...it's what pulled me into it is being able to identify a need and to be aware of needs more than probably the average person is. One student counted among her blessings: "I have gotten to work with people who I never would have ever talked to or met..." While there may be dilemmas and challenges related to an intentional quest to integrate Christian faith and social work practice, you may also find blessings and opportunities to discover and claim along the way. Whatever you encounter, please know that you do not have to travel alone. Christians have expressed this idea in the worship hymn "The Servant Song"

> *We are trav'lers on a journey,*
> *Fellow Pilgrims on the road*
> *We are here to help each other*
> *Walk the mile and bear the load*

Don't Travel Alone

Engaging the dilemmas and claiming the blessings becomes more possible if you will allow others to travel alongside of you. Perhaps you may find mentors who are willing to walk with you and share the benefit of their own experiences on this journey. Find a Christian social worker or faculty member who cares about you and the integration of faith and practice. Form meaningful and trusting relationships with other social work students who are motivated by their Christian faith. Consider joining the North American Association of Christians in Social Work (NACSW) and take advantage of the opportunity to collaborate with a community of Christians in social work and to discover resources that are available to help you as you celebrate and struggle with the integration of faith and practice.

It Really Is All About the Journey

The scripture is replete with journey metaphors that help us understand that our relationship with God and our response to God's call is about the day to day living out of our faith rather than rushing headlong toward a destination. Moses, called to deliver the people, died after a life of leadership with the discovery that his ministry was about the journey, not about the destination. Saul was out looking for donkeys when Samuel found him and communicated God's call for leadership. David was tending sheep when God called him to lead an army and eventually a nation. Jesus' ministry occurred from village to village as he traveled, preached, healed, and loved. He called to his disciples (who were not sure where he would take them), "Come follow me." He invited them to participate with him in ministry rather than to arrive at a particular destination.

We know from the life and ministry of Jesus that the journey is not always easy or without challenges. The words of our students confirmed that in spite of challenges, they found strength to continue, by faith, as followers of Jesus, to travel with him as he equips us and leads us to the hungry, the poor, the broken in body and spirit, the dying, the rejected and lonely, the least of these. Let us journey on together, bound by the call to be fellow travelers with the one who taught us best about the ministry of presence.

We end our chapter with a prayer offered up for social workers by our dean Dr. Diana Garland, long-time NACSW member and former president. It is our intercession on behalf of you who are joining us on the journey.

We are grateful, Lord God, that when you call us on this journey,
You don't call us to walk it alone.
We thank you for one another to share the journey,
To comfort and en-courage one another.
Hold us together, Lord; hold our hands and steady us on the way.
Show us just the next steps to take—
We don't need to see all the way, for we trust the destination to you.
Give us courage to go, step by step, with one another and with you.

Note

[1] This and all other quotes are from interviews conducted in 2004-2005 with Baylor University students and alumni. To protect their anonymity, names will not be cited.

Reference

Singletary, J., Harris, H. W., Myers, D., & Scales, T. L (Spring, 2006). Student narratives on social work as a calling. *Aretê, 30*(1), 188-199.

CHAPTER 5

JUSTICE AND HUMAN RIGHTS IN FOURTH CENTURY CAPPADOCIA

Cheryl K. Brandsen and Paul Vliem

In his Alan Keith-Lucas lecture at the 2005 NACSW conference, Nicholas Wolterstorff concluded his remarks on justice with an insight that drew spontaneous applause from the listeners. He briefly summarized the long and venerable Christian tradition of aiding the poor, dating back to antiquity. He noted that most social work textbooks overlook this, beginning their narrative instead with secular activists in the early 1800s. Wolterstorff found this "secular bowdlerizing of the history of social work academically irresponsible and morally reprehensible" (2006, p. 139). Wolterstorff challenged listeners to recover an accurate and complete story of the beginnings of social welfare, a story that would remind social workers that they stand in a "long and rich tradition" of doing justice, a tradition that "could not fail to inform, inspire and encourage all of us" as we carry out our professional responsibilities through the lens of Christian faith (p. 140).

A broad goal of this chapter, then, is to contribute to a deeper understanding of the historical religious roots of social welfare and in doing so remind social workers of the potential richness and shortcomings of religious attempts to help in earlier times that are often obscured from memory and consciousness. Although we focus on Judeo-Christian motivations integrated into Greek culture, other religious traditions also have valuable insights to offer students and practitioners and are worthy of critical investigation. Such investigations are beyond our scope here.

More specifically, we consider the social thought of three 4th century Cappadocian Fathers: Basil of Caesarea (330-379 C.E.), Gregory of Nazianzus (330-390 C. E.), and Gregory of Nyssa (335-394 C. E.), Basil's younger brother.[1] These men made substantive contributions to the theological debates of their time, but they also had much to say about social and economic concerns of their time. As we argue here, the Cappadocian Fathers worked within a particular conception of justice that took seriously what we in social work call "human rights." Neither this conception of justice nor the notion of human rights is something the Cappadocian Fathers articulated into a comprehensive thought system. An analysis of their sermons, however, reveals that in fact they were motivated by the Hebrew and Christian scriptures' understanding of justice, filtered through the lens of Greek culture, which resulted in practices supportive of human rights. Our focus is primarily upon Basil since he is credited with being the first bishop in the Christian East or West who organized philanthropic institutions and extended the Church's influence into health and social welfare (Constantelos, 1981). Given how closely the three interacted, the Gregories are also included in this analysis.[2]

Social Welfare Provisions in Fourth-Century Cappadocia

We focus on the fourth century because it is during this time that the delivery of social services becomes institutionalized in Cappadocia; in fact, little evidence exists that poverty assistance was practiced in a structured way prior to the fourth century (Holman, 2001). This institutionalization of services occurs through the Church. Why the Church rose to this challenge during this era cannot be substantively addressed here. The Christianization of the Graeco-Roman empire beginning with Constantine's rule (306-337), unprecedented human need, and the bishops' desires to carve out for the Church and themselves a legitimate role in society constitute at least part of the story for the Church's role in institutionalizing social welfare services (Brown, 1995; Stark, 1996).

Prior to the Church's attempts at institutionalizing social welfare services, the two main mechanisms of assistance were public provisions and private gifts, or the gift economy. To understand the sermons of the Cappadocian Fathers in context, it is important to have some sense of how these provisions were granted and to whom. Public provisions were directed only to citizens who were homeowners. The main public provisions provided were food gifts (*annona*), usually in the form of grain or bread doles, granted to certain cities at the emperor's discretion. These doles appeared to keep most people from destitution, even though the primary motivation for such was to strengthen the city and maintain public social equilibrium, not help the weak or destitute poor. *Alimenta* was also provided, at times, to families with children. This provision of food and sometimes cash, provided immediate provisions to destitute parents who appeared to be in such dire situations that they were at risk for committing infanticide or selling their children into slavery (Holman, 2001; Ierley, 1984).

The private gift economy functioned within a patronage system as the primary mechanism for social and political organization. Because tax revenues provided no more than bare essentials, the gift-economy system was integral to a smoothly running society. In this system, wealthy patrons were obliged to perform certain liturgies (i.e., public service projects performed by private citizens with their own economic resources), and citizens were expected to respond with public honor, respect, and praise. Examples of liturgies include additional food in times of scarcity, public entertainment such as theatres and circuses, and public works such as baths and monuments. The wealthy were motivated to engage in liturgies by their desire for honor and public recognition in their current lives, but also by their desire to be remembered into immortality (Countryman, 1980; Holman, 2001; Veyne, 1976).

In return for gifts, citizens were expected to reciprocate with honor, praise, and political allegiance toward their wealthy patrons. Citizen praise was to be public, and in honoring the patron's generosity the recipients often conferred honors upon the donor that were greater than the gift itself. This practice of public honor reinforced that the obligation was repaid and also told the donor publicly that more was now expected. This exchange went far beyond a reciprocal, economic exchange. It operated as a political tool whereby the generosity of wealthy leaders established bonds of obedience with followers, functioning then as a basis for social and political organization and power relationships. In this system, "social inequality was not only understood, but essential for the system to work" (Holman, 2001, p. 32). As with public provisions, the gift economy was not intended to address social inequality. It operated outside of any concern for the poor, although the poor sometimes benefited (Veyne, 1976).

Famine and Food Shortages in Fourth-Century Cappadocia

Basil and the Gregories worked within this kind of welfare system. During Basil's tenure as priest and then bishop, usury, high taxation of the poor, and unfair land policies were common practices, magnifying distinctions between rich and poor. To make matters worse, the poor suffered even further as a result of food shortages between 368 and 375 that resulted from summer droughts and severe winters and, more specifically, a famine in 368-369. Of this period, Nazianzus recalls, "there was a famine, the most severe within the memory of man. The city was in distress, but there was no help forthcoming from any quarter, nor any remedy for the calamity" (McCauley, Sullivan, McGuire, and Defarri, 1953, p 57).[3] Nyssa describes the plight of the poor in this way:

> We have seen in these days a great number of the naked and homeless. For the most part they are victims of war who knock at our doors. But there is also no lack of strangers and exiles, and their hands, stretched out imploring, can be seen everywhere. Their roof is the sky. For shelter they use porticos, alleys, and the deserted corners of the town. They hide in the cracks of walls like owls. Their clothing consists of wretched rags. Their harvest depends on human pity. For meals they have only the alms tossed at them by those who pass by. For drink they use the springs, as do the animals. Their cup is the hollow of their hand, their storeroom their pocket or rather whatever part of it has not been torn and cannot hold whatever has been put into it. For a dining table they use their joined knees, and their lamp is the sun. Instead of public baths, they wash in the river or pond that God gives to all (Holman, 2001, p. 194).

As the fear and eventual reality of famine set in, the situation grew more extreme when those who had resources hoarded them and sold them to desperate neighbors at an exorbitant price. Schools closed, workers began to starve, and many faced the dilemma of selling children into slavery to avoid death by starvation. Basil vividly describes the fierce agony of parents faced with such choices. After taking inventory of his meager possessions, a father asks:

What will he do? His eyes then come to rest upon his own little ones, as if here he may, by taking them to the market and exposing them for sale, hold back that death that now hangs over all of them... What thoughts now rise in the mind of the father? Whom will he first sell? ... Must it be my eldest? But I must not put to shame his rights as the eldest? Shall I sacrifice my youngest? His tender age torments me; unable yet to understand this tragedy? He has the face of both his mother and his father; he is fit for study, for learning. O dread misery! On which of them must I inflict this terrible wrong? On which of them shall I impose the life of a beast? How can I forget my own nature? If I keep them all with me, one by one I shall see them die of hunger. If I sell one, how shall I face the eyes of those left; I who am now guilty in their eyes of treachery and betrayal? How shall I remain in my house, deprived by my own act of my own children? How shall I come to the table, furnished with their price? (Toal, 1959, p. 328-329).

And to illustrate the character of the rich in response to such suffering, Basil says:

At length with tears the father goes, to sell the dearest loved among his children. But you do not bend before the face of such agony; no thought of nature enters your mind. Hunger drives this suffering creature, but you hold out, and play him, and prolong his agony. He offers as the price of food his heart's blood. Your hands that drag riches from the deeps of his pain not alone do not tremble in fear, but with them you haggle over the price. To gain more you offer less; by every trick you look to add to the unhappy man's affliction. Tears do not move you to pity; nor his groans of anguish soften your heart. You are immovable and implacable (Toal, 1959, p. 329).

It is to these kinds of abuses that Basil and the Gregories preach a series of sermons about poverty and wealth.

The Poverty and Wealth Sermons

An examination of key sermons preached by Basil and the Gregories in response to the famine and food shortages provides a window into their particular conception of justice.[4] Basil delivered three influential (but unconnected) sermons on wealth and property use: Homily VI, VII, and VIII. Nyssa delivered a two-part sermon thought to be dated in this same time period entitled *On the Love of the Poor*, and Nazianzus delivered, Oration 14, *On Love for the Poor*. As a result, Basil and the Gregories successfully secured money, property, and other goods from the rich to distribute to the poor— not only the *penes* or citizen paupers but also, and more interestingly, the *ptochos* or destitute non-citizen poor—earning them the title of "lovers of the poor" (Brown, 1995; Sterk, 2004).[5]

Homily VI: Basil's Homily VI, *I Will Pull Down my Barns*, is based on Luke's parable of the rich fool who continually builds larger barns to store his surplus grain (Luke 12: 16-18). Basil's hope is that the rich will open their granaries to meet the food shortage. Here he presents the image described earlier of the father being forced to choose between dying of hunger and selling his children into slavery. The theme of Basil's address is that the earth's surplus is given for stewardship, not possession. Here Basil pleads with the rich:

> You, if you will hear me, opening wide all the doors of your store-houses, give full outlet to your riches. And just as a wide stream is distributed through the fruitful earth by many channels, so let your riches flow, that by many ways they may reach the homes of the poor. Wells, when they are drawn from, flow forth in a purer and more abundant stream. Where they are in disuse they grow foul. And so do riches grow useless, left idle and unused in any place; but moved about, passing from one person to another, they serve the common advantage and bear fruit (Toal, 1963, p. 329).

To those who believed they have a right to keep what they perceive is theirs, Basil has strong words. He warns:

> ... Who is the robber: He who seizes what belongs to another. Are you not a grasper of everything; are you not a robber? You who treat as absolutely yours what you received that you might dispense to others. He who strips another man of his clothing, is he not called a robber; and he who does not clothe the naked when he could, should he not be called the same? That bread you hold in your clutches, that belongs to the starving. That cloak you keep locked away in your wardrobe, that belongs to the naked. Those shoes that are going to waste with you, they belong to the barefooted. The silver you buried away, that belongs to the needy. Whomsoever you could have helped and did not, to so many have you been unjust (Toal, 1963, p. 332).

The reward for generous sharing will not be fully realized in this life but the next. Good works, says Basil, will "carry you back to the Lord, where, standing before our common Judge all the people shall call you their nourisher and their benefactor, and give you those other names that signify kindness and humanity" (Toal, 1963, p. 327). God himself, the angels, and "all who are gathered from the whole world shall call you blessed. Eternal glory, a crown of justice, the kingdom of heaven, these shall he receive who was a just dispenser of the things which perish" (p. 328). With such a reward promised, Basil asks:

> What keeps you from giving now... Are your barns not full...Is the law of God not plain to you? The hungry are dying before your face. The naked are stiff with cold. The man in debt is held by the throat. And you, you put off your alms, till another day? (p. 331).

Homily VII: Basil's Homily VII, *Against the Wealthy*, addresses the rich, law-abiding young man of Matthew 19 who queried Jesus about what he needed to do to receive eternal life. Jesus' response—to give away all possessions and join Jesus' disciples—left the young man sad. But how can it be, Basil wondered, that if this man truly loved his neighbors as he says, he has an accumulation of wealth:

> If your claims were true, namely that you observed from your youth the commandment of love … from where do you derive this abundance? The care of the needy is an expensive undertaking. Even if each receives only the little his need requires, nevertheless, all distribute these goods even as they provide for themselves. Consequently, the one who loves his neighbor as himself possesses nothing in excess of his neighbor's. However, you obviously have many possessions. … Clearly your wealth and superabundance indicates a lack of charity (Holman, 2001, p. 105).

In short, to love one's neighbor implies generous and immediate giving to those in need. Storing up one's wealth to pass on to heirs or the poor after death is insufficient to demonstrate such love.

Homily VIII: Homily VIII, *In Time of Famine and Drought*, like Homily VI, pleads with those who have food supplies to share with those in need. Basil delivered this homily in a public worship service likely dedicated to a call for public repentance. Basil begins by urging his listeners to remember the Old Testament prophet, Amos, who attempted to lead his people through similar difficult times of drought. God sent the Israelites such calamities in an effort to turn their indifference toward God into diligence. So too, says Basil, God sends the drought and famine faced by the Cappodocians because of their indifference to the needs of the poor:

> … our uncontrolled and culpable behavior is manifestly obvious: seizing on behalf of others, we do not share; we commend good works yet withhold them from those who are without. We are freed slaves, yet we do not have pity on our fellow slaves. We are nourished when hungry, yet we rush by the one in need. In want of nothing, having God as our treasurer and the one who defrays the costs, we become skinflints and asocial in relation to the poor. Our sheep multiply, yet the naked outnumber them. The storehouses are crowded with narrow corridors with abundant reserves, yet we have no mercy on those who mourn. For this cause the righteous tribunal threatens us. For this cause also, God will not open his hand, because we ourselves shut out brotherly love. For this cause, the farmlands are dry: because love has fled (Holman, 2001, p. 185).

Seeking true repentance and doing justice is the needed response to open God's hand, says Basil. He pleads for his listeners to pray with lament, wash the feet of guests, nourish fatherless children, provide for widows, destroy unjust accounting books, and wipe out oppressive usury contracts.

To put an even finer point on human need, Basil describes in vivid detail the experience of someone dying from starvation, calling it "a more miserable end than all other deaths." Deaths by fire, by the sword, or even by wild animals "assure that the distress will not be prolonged." Famine, by contrast, is "a slow evil":

> The heat of the body cools. The form shrivels. Little by little strength diminishes. Flesh stretches across the bones like a spider web. The skin loses its bloom, as the rosy appearance fades and blood melts away. Nor is the skin white, but rather it withers into black while the livid body, suffering pitifully, manifests a dark and pale mottling. The knees no longer support the body but drag themselves by force, the voice is powerless, the eyes are sunken as if in a casket, like dried-up nuts in their shells; the empty belly collapses, conforming itself to the shape of the backbone without any natural elasticity of the bowels (Holman, 2001, p. 190).

Basil concludes this description by asking rhetorically how someone capable of ignoring a starving person should be treated: "Whoever has it in his power to alleviate this evil but deliberately opts instead for profit should be condemned as a murderer" (Holman, 2001, p. 190). On the other hand, those who feed the hungry will, at judgment time, "hold the first rank...stand first in honor, the supplier of bread will be called before everyone else; the kind and bountiful will be escorted to life before all the other righteous (p. 191). Furthermore, the giving of food as an individual act does more than cover the sin of the benefactor on judgment day; in fact, it restores the created order. Basil urges his listeners to "destroy the original sin by freely distributing food. For as sin came through Adam's evil act of eating, so we ourselves blot out his treacherous consumption if we remedy the need and hunger of a brother" (p.191). [6]

On the Love of the Poor—On Good Works:[7] After Nyssa exhorts his audience to develop ascetical practices that purify the soul and to reject the evils of stealing from and cheating the poor, he proceeds by depicting several scenes of hordes of destitute people crowding city streets; these include victims of war, strangers from other places, and the sick, especially the lepers. Later Nyssa presents a pointed contrast between rich and poor: between "a myriad of Lazaruses" who are poor, maimed, and covered with sores, driven away by dogs and beatings for their begging and the rich who, in contrast, are gorging themselves on food and wine. Nyssa implores his listeners to not pass over these people but to share their resources generously: "Nourish those in need, immediately and without hesitating. The gift will not result in loss: don't be afraid. The fruits of merciful acts are abundant. Sow your benefactions and your house will be filled with a plentiful harvest" (Holman, 2001, p. 195). Reminding his listeners that "It is God himself, who in the first instance manifests Himself to us as the author of good and philanthropic deeds..." (p. 196), Nyssa calls for his people to imitate God—who loves mercy and good deeds—in their own beneficence.

In modeling the beneficence of God, Nyssa reminds his listeners that the poor and sick further merit respect and have worth because they "bear the countenance of our Savior..." (Holman, 2001, p. 195). And if this truth that the poor have put on the figure of God is not sufficient motivation to share with them, Nyssa reminds his listeners that "the poor are the stewards of our hope, doorkeepers of the kingdom, who open the door to the righteous and close it again to the unloving and misanthropists...for the deed done to them cries out to the one who fathoms the heart in a voice clearer than the herald's trumpet" (p. 195).

On the Love of the Poor—On the Saying, 'Whoever Has Done It to One of These Has Done It to Me:' The second part of Nyssa's homily begins with a picture of Judgment Day, a king seated on magnificent throne, bestowing rewards on those who acted justly toward those in need, and condemning those who ignored human need. The tone of Nyssa's homily is one of fear; he himself says that this threat of judgment "continues to terrify me" (Holman, 2001, p. 200). The way to avoid this threat is to obey God's commandments as set forth in Matthew 25:40: feed the hungry, give drink to the thirsty, clothe the naked, take in the stranger, care for the sick, and visit the prisoner.

The particular population whom Nyssa has in mind here are the homeless and uncared for lepers begging in the streets. He describes their physical condition in detail as well as the exclusionary social practices of the healthy toward those with leprosy: lepers are forbidden from public fountains even though dogs with bloody tongues are allowed; they are cast out of their homes while pigs and dogs are given cover; they are left without human touch even though donkeys have their hoofs washed and backs brushed by owners.

Nyssa pleads with his listeners to remember who these lepers are: they are "a human person like yourself, whose basic nature is no different from your own" (Holman, 2001, p. 201). Even more, they are "Man born in the image of God, entrusted with the governance of the earth and the rule over all creatures, here so alienated by sickness that one hesitates to recognize him" (p. 201). The compassion generated by remembering the lepers must be visible in concrete practices of care.

Nyssa chides his listeners for considering the kind of help that sends lepers far away with food: such a plan only intends to banish the lepers from everyday life. Rather, just as angels are not put off by human flesh and blood, and just as Jesus became human and "put on this stinking and unclean flesh," the care of lepers should similarly be characterized by taking the sick in and caring for them with human hands (p. 201). For those who use the fear of contagion as an excuse, Nyssa challenges them: "Is there anyone indeed among the strong whose health deteriorates by association with the sick, even if they are in extremely close contact while providing medical care? No; this does not happen.... So why do you still hold back from applying the commandment of love?" (p. 205). More pastorally, Nyssa allows that it is difficult work to care for the wounds of the lepers, yet worthy projects require effort.

Oration 14: Nazianzus' Oration 14, *On Love for the Poor*, one of his longest and most grand orations, provides a full account on the importance of loving the poor.[8] Nazianzus does not center his oration on a single biblical text but rather integrates a variety of biblical characters and examples into the narrative. He begins with an extended discussion of virtues and concludes that of all these, love—*philanthropia*—is the first and greatest of these virtues, and that love of the poor—*philoptochia*—is where love is perfected. And while it is important to be mindful of all those who have needs, Nazianzus, like Nyssa, turns to a lengthy and detailed description of the physical and social effects of leprosy.

He describes those with leprosy as "men dead yet living; mutilated in many parts of their bodies, so afflicted they scarcely know who they are or who they were or where they came from" (Toal, 1963, p. 47). They do not know whether to grieve for the part of their bodies already lost or those parts yet wasting, for those who have died or for those waiting to die without anyone to bury them. Relationships often thought inseparable—those between parents and children—are driven apart by the disease. Upon banishment, the lepers "wander through the days and the nights, impoverished, naked, shelterless, their wounds uncovered, recalling past times, calling upon their Creator, making use of one another's limbs in place of those they have lost..." (p. 48).

Like Nyssa, Nazianzus reminds his listeners that the lepers were "born with the same nature, formed of that same clay from which we in the beginning were formed;" indeed, the afflicted are "our brothers in God.... [They] have received the same divine image as we have...they have put on the same Christ...and to them the same pledge of the Spirit has been given.... (Toal, 1963, p. 49). They are, in fact, people for whom Christ has died, "heirs with us of eternal life" (p. 50). Because of this, "we should fix in our minds the thought that the salvation of our own bodies and souls depend on this: That we should love and show humanity to these" (p. 46). Later, after contrasting boldly the lifestyle of the wealthy and healthy with those who have leprosy, Nazianzus again reminds his listeners to share generously:

> ...let us through almsgiving become owners of our own souls; let
> us give of what is ours to the poor, that we may be rich in heaven.
> Do not give to the body only; give the soul its share. Do not give to
> the world only; give a portion also to God....Give even all to Him,
> Who has given all to you. You will never outdo God's generosity,
> even should you give your all, even should you add yourself to what
> you give....(Toal, 1963, p. 54).

Echoing Basil and Nyssa, Nazianzus also takes up the notion of steward-ship, reminding his listeners that those who own property often receive such through aggression and greed, made permissible by law. He does not, however, condemn wealth per se but rather the misuse of it that turns created freedom into slavery. Nazianzus asks his listeners to do the following:

> But I would have you look back to our primary equality of right,
> not to the later division;[9] not to the law of the strongest, but to the

law of the Creator. Help nature with all our might. Reverence the ancient freedom. Reverence yourself. Cover the shame of your own kindred. Help the afflicted. Comfort those in sorrow. You who are strong, help the weak. You who are rich, help the poor. You who stand upright, help the fallen and the crushed. You who are joyful, comfort those in sadness. You who enjoy all good fortune, help those who have met with disaster. Give something to God in thanksgiving that you are of those who can give help, not of those who stand and wait for it; that you have no need to look to another's hands, but that others must look to yours…. Be as God to the unfortunate, by imitating the mercy of God (Toal, 1963, p. 56).

Nazianzus concludes his oration by reviewing a host of Hebrew and Christian scripture passages that make clear God's commands to care for the poor are normative obligations. He urges, in conclusion:

…let us, while there is yet time, visit Christ in His sickness, let us have a care for Christ in His sickness, let us give to Christ to eat, let us clothe Christ in His nakedness, let us do honour to Christ, and not only at table, as some did, not only with precious ointments, as Mary did, not only in His tomb, as Joseph of Arimathea did…, not only doing him honour with gold, frankincense and myrrh, as the Magi did … ; but let us honour Him because the Lord of all will have mercy and not sacrifice, and goodness of heart above thousands of fat lambs. Let us give Him this honour in His poor…. (Toal, 1963, pp. 63-64).

Philanthropia

These sermons, responses to the famine crisis, were intended to move Christian audiences to share in alleviating suffering and end the profiteering that some engaged in because of the famine. The sermons were intended to be practical—to move people to right action on behalf of their neighbors—and not intended as a systematic and comprehensive treatment of how the Cappadocians should understand justice.[10] Nevertheless, the sermons, taken collectively, do accomplish certain purposes that work toward justice. Before making this case, however, it is important to address the notion of *philanthropia*, a concept which, in contrast to justice, often appears as the defining hallmark of the Graeco-Roman Christians. For the Greek Christians, "the God of the Byzantines was the personification and manifestation of love" (Constantelos, 1991, p. 30). Out of this self-giving love of God flowed human philanthropic practices directed to anyone in need, regardless of whether such was a relative or citizen. So important was the human demonstration of *philanthropia* that lack of attention or concern to those in need, following I John 4:7, was a sure sign that one did not know God, because God is love.

The Cappadocian Fathers often appear to ground their work in the notion of *philanthropia*—an "…active, practical love for one's fellow human beings, expressed in kindness—and benevolent action" (Daley, 1999, p. 434).[11] Nazianzus begins his praise for Basil's magnificent *ptochotropheion* (discussed later) by saying "A noble thing is philanthropy and the support of the poor and the assistance of human weakness" (McCauley et al., 1953, p. 80). In Oration 14, Nazianzus argues that *philanthropia* is the greatest among virtues, and that love of the poor (*philoptochia*) is supreme. All three Cappadocian Fathers understand *philanthropia* to be one of God's supreme attributes in relationship to human beings (Constantelos, 1991). All three call on their audiences to imitate God, the author of philanthropic deeds, in their beneficence toward others.

To outsiders as well, *philanthropia* was one of the distinguishing marks of Christians. Emperor Julian, a contemporary of the Cappadocian Fathers and antagonistic toward Christians, remarked regretfully that the impious Galileans (i.e., Christians) had practiced their benevolence so generously that they had attracted new members to their community. Furthermore, "No Jew ever has to beg, and the impious Galileans support not only their own poor but ours as well" (Ep. 896).

Justice in the Poverty and Wealth Sermons

While it is the case that *philanthropia* is one of the premier markers of Christian practices in fourth century Cappadocia, it is not the case that justice goes missing. Next we consider how the idea of justice is manifested in the sermons summarized above.

First, each of these sermons draws heavily from Hebrew and Christian Scripture passages that emphasize justice or *misphat*.[12] Whether it is the legal code of the Torah, the prophets' accusations against those who break the legal code, or the psalmists' lamentations about violations of the legal code, the downtrodden—widows, orphans, strangers, and the poor—are singled out as test cases for whether justice prevails. Here is where the greatest vulnerabilities existed in Israel; to *do* justice, the Hebrew writers insisted on attention to those at the bottom. The downtrodden and excluded were to be lifted up and incorporated into the community.

Moving to the Christian Scriptures, Jesus' separation of the sheep from the goats as recorded in Matthew 25 is similarly infused into the sermons. Interestingly, the poor, the stranger, the sick, and the imprisoned are singled out as those who give witness to the doing of justice.[13] The list is different from that of the Hebrew scripture, but once again, the most vulnerable are noted. The prisoners, often denied their rights unjustly, and the sick, most pointedly the lepers, are at the bottom of the social class ladder in Graeco-Roman society, along with the poor and the strangers. By having their needs met, they too are lifted up and incorporated into the community. Clearly this is a variation of the Hebrew writers' understanding of justice for widows, orphans, strangers, and the poor.

Second, the Cappadocian Fathers make the hungry, the economically impoverished, and the sick more visible. On the one hand, ironically, these groups are very visible. Recall Nazianzus' earlier depictions of dismembered lepers, Nyssa's "Lazaruses," and Basil's vivid descriptions of starving bodies and anguished parents selling their children for food. The Cappadocians did not need to go looking for suffering; rather, it appeared in front of them daily and persistently as they traveled the roads, bargained in the marketplace, and attended worship services. Yet because such persons had no moral standing apart from civic affiliations and kinship ties, no one was required to offer assistance. The patronage system simply did not recognize these needy as person's bearing rights for assistance. In fact, the poor as a special group deserving economic assistance was not recognized at this time; they had "no conceptual place" in urban society (Horden, 2005, p. 362). The poverty and wealth sermons, says Holman (2001), "force a visual awareness, using vivid images and contrasts...to get people to *notice* the poor" (97). The Cappadocian Fathers, in calling detailed attention to particular people in need, served as "agents of change" (Brown, 2002, p. 8).

Third, the Cappadocian Fathers did not stop, however, with simply bringing those in need into sharper focus and depending on whatever native sense of sympathy existed in the rich to be evoked. They went beyond this, advocating that rights previously reserved only for citizens be extended to the needy, regardless of citizenship or kin ties. Those cut off from the community because of an "unclean" disease such as leprosy, those who had lost their land (and thus their citizenship) because of debt, and those who had always been outside the community, were now to be the objects of public giving because of their need; this is in fact what justice requires, argue the Cappadocian Fathers, drawing heavily from the Hebrew Scriptures. Both rich and poor share an "original basic equality," according to Nazianzus (Oration 14), suggesting that all are equal with respect to the basic necessities given by God. Honor this ancient freedom, pleads Nazianzus.

The Cappadocian Fathers remind their audiences that sharing resources with the downtrodden is owed to them because they are human beings. They share a common human nature with the rich, given they have all been born with the same "nature" and formed of the same clay. Putting a finer point on this, the Cappadocian Fathers call the poor "brothers," highlighting the extension of kin networks to groups usually marginalized. Highlighting rights owed to family is something understood in the patronage system. Constructing the poor as fictive kin translates the Cappadocian Fathers' message into a cultural system with which the audiences are familiar.

This strategy of invoking Hebrew injunctions and integrating them with Graeco-Roman society effectively re-shapes who counts as citizen. Even if one is poor, sick, without land, or a stranger—or whatever state of disenfranchisement exists—the common humanity of such "kin" commends them to the rich as having rights to assistance. Because the needy share a common nature with other human beings, "...the poor are here constructed as having 'equal rights' to justice, compassion, and all aspects of the heavenly inheritance" (Holman, 2000, p. 484).

Finally, in addition to being understood as kin, and thus entitled to the benefits of Graeco-Roman citizenship, the needy are also constructed by these sermons as citizens of God's kingdom. The downtrodden bear God's image, remind the Cappadocian Fathers; they are covered with the countenance of God and they are people for whom Christ has died. Because they bear God's image, caring for them is caring for Christ: Visit Christ, care for Christ, clothe Christ, and honor Christ, urges Nazianzus. Because they bear God's image, they have rights. Nazianzus urges listeners to "imitate the justice of God" so that no one will be poor (Toal, 1963, p. 55). Those who desire to imitate God's justice, says Nyssa, will recall the Matthew 25 account, an account that carefully and precisely sets forth "our court of justice" to "teach us the grace and the value of beneficence" (Holman, 2001, p. 196). Basil reminds that failure to help those whom one could have helped is an injustice (Homily 6.9).

The oppressed also have a role in this new Christianized system of patronage. They can participate in the gift exchange—an integral part of the patronage system—in their new civic identity. They are agents for the rich in heavenly gift exchanges. The rich who help the poor will earn honors that surpass the honors attached to earlier generous gifts to the polis. In fact, those who give to the poor will earn not only the coveted titles of 'benefactor' and 'nourisher,' they will receive eternal honor from God and the angels singing their praises (Basil, 6.3).

The oppressed, however, are not only agents; they also serve as legal witnesses for God as Judge (Holman, 2000). The extent to which the downtrodden have been lifted up becomes a visible witness to God of the extent to which the rich have cared for the poor. The poor have power over the gates of heaven, assisting God in determining who gets admitted. And the rich found to be lacking in doing justice would not be able to use their wealth to buy off the judge, or rely on trained orators and friends to act as their advocates and character references, as they were accustomed to doing (Van Dam, 2002).[14] As citizens of a heavenly kingdom, the poor now hold even greater power than did the poor in the gift economy system.

Primary Justice and Human Rights

What kind of justice might we call this? What conception of justice, not named by the Cappadocian Fathers yet affirmed in their sermons, motivates their deep passion for lifting up and bringing into the community as legitimate citizens those who had no visible or moral standing in society? Borrowing from Wolterstorff (2006), the particular conception of justice that the Cappadocian Fathers embrace is primary—or basic—justice.[15] As such, primary justice works toward ensuring that people receive that to which they are entitled; primary justice has to do with rights. Justice is present in social relationships when people are enjoying those things to which they have a right. Injustice is present when people are deprived of that to which they have a right. These rights are rights with regard to someone else, argues Wolterstorff; they are normative social bonds between people. Others come into our presence bearing legitimate claims on how they should be treated. Failing to do the things we should to further their well-being and doing things we should not do violates this normative social bond and wrongs the other.[16]

In their sermons, then, the Cappadocian Fathers argue that the downtrodden have basic human rights. Basil and the Gregories bring to the forefront the misery of the marginalized and assert that they have a right to means of sustenance. The rich are in possession of what belongs to the poor; the poor are wronged because they are denied that which belongs to them as a natural right. The rich have failed in sharing the resources that further well-being, and they have gained what they have unjustly. Arguing that the poor have a right to means of sustenance is recognizable language to social workers familiar with the 1948 United Nations *Declaration of Human Rights.* Article 25.1, for instance, affirms that:

> Everyone has the right to a standard of living adequate for the health and well-being of himself and of his family, including food, clothing, housing and medical care, and necessary social services, and the right to security in the event of unemployment, sickness, disability, widowhood, old age, or other lack of livelihood in circumstances beyond his control (cited in Reichert, 2003, p. 255).

Persons who come into our presence bearing legitimate claims on how they are to be treated are entitled to such rights because of their worth, argues Wolterstorff (2006). To treat others in belittling ways, to not afford them the respect they are due, is to wrong them. Respect for human worth requires that persons be treated in respectful ways; they have a right to such treatment.

Similarly, the Cappadocian Fathers ground the honoring of rights in human worth. Not only are the downtrodden entitled to receive that due to them because they are now citizens, and thus worthy recipients in the patronage system, but also because they bear God's image and are of indescribable worth to God. At one level, as citizens, their worth springs from their newly constructed identity as fictive kin and their incorporation into the life of the community. At a deeper level, their worth is intrinsic to them because of their relationship to the divine—as image-bearers of God.[17] And although the 1948 United Nations *Declaration of Human Rights* cannot ground human worth in a relationship to the divine, like the Cappadocian Fathers, the Declaration connects human rights to the "inherent dignity and worth" of "all members of the human family" (cited in Reichert, 2003, p. 251).

Duty and obligation, distinct from rights, constitute another dimension of the moral order, according to Wolterstorff. Rights have to do with "moral recipients" while duties attach to "moral agents" (2006). If a parent abuses a child, the parent as a moral agent has shirked her duties as a parent and is guilty. Her child, deprived of his right to care that enhances his well-being, is wronged. He has been treated as if he were of little worth. If the focus in doing justice is only directed to duties, as it often is, the focus remains on the guilty moral agent, but the fact that another person is wronged remains invisible.

The Cappadocian Fathers simultaneously address moral recipients and moral agents. Clearly they bring the wrongs experienced by the downtrodden— the moral recipients—into full view, creating for them a legitimate place in the emerging Christian culture and an identity that includes them as image-bearers of God. The Cappadocian Fathers also address the duties and obligations of the rich as moral agents. The rich who fail to share their resources and the rich who gain their wealth through unjust practices are guilty.[18] While in the gift economy, stinginess would meet with public dishonor, in the heavenly economy, failing to do justice puts one at risk for not being admitted to the Kingdom. Failing to engage in the practice of almsgiving, either directly to the poor or through the Church, constitutes a rupture in doing justice.[19] While the Declaration of Human Rights focuses mostly on rights and moral recipients, the recognition "of barbarous acts which have outraged the conscience of mankind" surely speaks to unjust practices of moral agents.

From Rhetoric to Action

The rhetorical moves of the Cappadocian Fathers to construct the poor as part of the kin network and entitled to patronage assistance are accompanied by concrete relief. Nyssa, for instance, wisely reminds his listeners "But dialectic will hardly enrich those [the poor] in such straits" (Holman, 2001, p. 195). Nazianzus, in his Oration 43, *On St. Basil the Great*, provides a first-hand account of Basil's efforts in securing concrete assistance, two of which we mention briefly.[20]

First, Basil set up feeding programs to deal with the immediate crisis of the famine. Nazianzus recalls that Basil, using the power of his priestly office, with "his words and exhortation he opened up the stores of the rich…" (McCauley et al., 1953, p. 58). His considerable rhetorical skills were accompanied by administrative skills unusual for the day, says Nazianzus. Taking contributions in through the Church, Basil gathered surplus food supplies into one place and distributed these to those in need. Nazianzus tells us that Basil provided the poor with bread, meats, and pea soup, and his efforts in doing so were not from a distance. In spite of his privileged position that would have allowed him to transfer the responsibilities of hands-on care to a servant or slave, Basil himself, "imitating the ministry of Christ…ministered to the bodies and the souls of the needy, combining marks of respect with the necessary refreshments, thus affording them relief in two ways (McCauley et al., 1953, p. 58).

Even more impressive in caring for the poor and sick was Basil's *ptochotropheion*, a place to feed, care for, and patronize (*trepho*) the destitute poor (*ptochos*) (Holman, 2001).[21] It was built within walking distance from the city of Caesarea. Nazianzus describes the *Basileias*, as it came to be called, "a new city:"

> Go forth a little from this city and behold the new city, the storehouse of piety, the common treasury of the wealthy, where superfluous riches, sometimes even necessities, thanks to the exhortations of Basil, are laid up, unexposed to the moths and no source of joy to the thief, escaping the assaults of envy and the corruption of time (McCauley et al., 1953, p. 80).

The *Basileias*—a "magnificently constructed house of prayer," according to Basil—provided places of care for six populations: the poor, strangers and homeless persons, orphans, lepers, the elderly, and the sick (Way, 1951, p. 210;

Crislip, 2005). These "social services," as Crislip names them, went far beyond providing custodial care to educating orphans, teaching skills useful in a trade, rehabilitating the injured, and giving comfort care to the dying. The *Basileias* also included a church at the center of the complex, a "stately residence" for bishops and their guests, "inferior quarters" for caregivers, and workshop buildings in which to train people for various occupations. Caregivers included professionally-trained physicians and nurses (some of whom were monks), and escorts (often clerics) who provided hands-on care, prepared meals, and cared for the grounds (Way, 1951, p. 210-211).[22] Housing and services were free to all.

The *Basileias* became a community where the language of caring for the sick and needy was accompanied by action. Basil himself set the standard for such action, caring for the sick and dressing their wounds with his own hands: "Others had their cooks and rich tables and enchanting refinements of cuisine, and elegant carriages, and soft flowing garments. Basil had his sick, and the dressing of their wounds, and the imitation of Christ, cleansing leprosy not by word but in deed" (McCauley et al., 1953, p. 81).

The attitudes and practices of Basil and his urban monk caregivers at the *Basileias* had a significant impact on other bishops. Basil served as a model of leadership that all those in power who care for the sick and poor be part of concerted attention in governing (Sterk, 2004). The *Basileias* itself was hailed as a marvel in its time and stood as an inspiration for and standard by which to judge subsequent facilities and practices (Crislip, 2005). And, just as the Cappadocian Fathers' sermons spoke in parallel tracks of classical Greek societies and a heavenly kingdom, the *Basileias* also reflected these two levels. The *Basileias* stood as an upside-down city, says Van Dam (2002). It was a city that took in, cared for, and protected previously marginalized groups; here the poor were visible and valued, and bishops stood in as patrons and lovers of the poor (Daley, 1999; Van Dam, 2002).[23]

Conclusion

Although present day practices in social welfare have their roots in earlier times, we do not mean to suggest by this discussion that we return unthinkingly to fourth-century social welfare practices. In fact, the church as a delivery system for social welfare services is highly contested in current policy-making circles. So what might 21st century social workers gain from gleaning the writings of the Cappadocian Fathers? What might Wolterstorff have had in mind when he suggested that recovering the long tradition of Christians concerned for justice could inform and encourage social workers? We conclude by offering three suggestions.

In comparison to the Elizabethan Poor Laws, the Cappadocian Fathers provide a different—and in many ways, a more positive—entry into understanding how we care for the poor. Rather than further disenfranchisement of the poor through institutions, almshouses, and prisons, the Cappadocian Fathers worked toward fully franchising the destitute poor as citizens of worth who have been treated unjustly. While modern social workers might disagree (among themselves and with the Cappadocians) on the mechanics for implementing justice, they can nevertheless unabashedly join the Cappadocians in their commitment to and pleas for justice.

Relatedly, the Cappadocians provide us with a window into how social welfare was conceptualized and implemented in a cultural context different from the U.S. While we can learn such things by geographical travel (working or studying, for instance, in a different country), we can also come to an appreciation of alternate social welfare models in diverse cultural contexts by historical analysis. With the Cappadocians, we witness a time when the Church was doing many things effectively with regard to social welfare. We witness a time when the Church was passionate about caring for the marginalized and committed to putting their passions into action. We witness a time when the Church tried hard to operationalize what it means to treat people as worthy of dignity and respect.

We also see in the Cappadocians a model of delivering social welfare that seamlessly integrates charity (or *philanthropia*) with justice. The Cappadocians saw overwhelming human need and responded personally with concrete actions to alleviate suffering. They also worked, especially Basil, to set in place administrative and government policies that would lessen opportunities for exploiting the poor. Modern dilemmas and discussions about whether particular practices extend charity or work toward justice do not seem to enter into the Cappadocians' efforts. They did what needed to be done with efficiency, compassion, and directness.

Enlarging the boundaries, then, of who is to be brought into community and ensuring that all receive that to which they have rights grounds the efforts of the Cappadocian Fathers. Philanthropic practices are certainly visible, of course; for that time and place in human history, doing justice is carried out primarily by personal sharing and generous almsgiving to the church. But motivated by a deep appreciation for inherent human rights and a profound respect for honoring human dignity, the Cappadocian Fathers aim in their sermons for nothing less than fully-orbed citizens whose practices are shaped, within a familiar and particular cultural system, by the commitments of the Hebrew and New Testament writers to do justice. From this comes Nazianzus' appeal to his 4th century listeners about lepers, a plea no less compelling for 21st century social workers committed to the pursuit of justice and human rights:

Give help. Help others to live. Give food, clothing, medicines, apply remedies to the afflicted, bind up their wounds, ask them about their misfortunes, speak with them of patience and forbearance, come close to them, you will not be harmed…. (Toal, 1963, p. 57).

Notes

[1] All three were born into wealthy families of privilege; Basil and Gregory of Nyssa were born into a Christian family while Gregory of Nazianzus' father converted to Christianity when he realized how Constantine patronized Christians at the Council of Nicea in 325. Basil and Nazianzus were close friends for many years beginning with their classical education. Of the three, Basil is known as "Basil the Great" (Phan, 1984). Following the completion of his classical education in 356, he traveled extensively throughout Egypt and Syria, becoming interested in and later involved with the monastic movement and an ascetic lifestyle. He was baptized in 357, ordained as a priest in 365, and appointed bishop of Caesarea in 370 (Rousseau, 1994; Van Dam, 2003; von Campenhausen, 1998). Nyssa and Nazianzus were both bishops in Cappadocia during Basil's appointment as bishop.

[2] For ease of communication, we follow what appears to be acceptable practice in secondary sources, that is, referring to Gregory of Nazianzus as 'Nazianzus' and Gregory of Nyssa as 'Nyssa.' When referring to both, we use "Gregories.'

[3] Severe weather that affected food supplies persisted beyond the famine of 368-369. For first-hand descriptions of these, see Basil's letters in Ep. 48 and 86 (Way, 1951) and Ep. 321 (Way, 1955).

[4] Basil also interacted with emperors and governors to secure resources for the poor, although we do not address these interactions here. Interested readers might consult Basil's letters to these rulers; see, for instance, Ep. 85, 88, 94, 104, 110, 142, 143, 237, 247, 303, 308, 310, 312, 237, 247 in Way, 1951, 1955.

[5] The *penes* were paupers who did hands-on work and lived by their own labors, in a trade or business (in contrast to the wealthy who lived on their own investments and by the work of others). They functioned within the context of a community, had a home, and civic relationships and responsibilities. Because they were citizens, they were legally entitled to participate in the gift economy system, thus benefiting from any gifts bestowed to the community at large. Participation was grounded in citizenship, not economic need (Countryman, 1980; Horden, 2005). The *ptochos* consisted of the destitute, the indigents, the persons at the fringes of society in need of immediate help if they were to survive (Holman, 2001). They were not citizens of a community but rather strangers, refugees, or victims of ship-wrecks or war. They might also be former citizens, but now were cast out, likely because of leprosy or some large loss of wealth. Because they had no civic or familial ties to the community, they were not legally able to participate in the gift economy; wealthy patrons had no intrinsic obligation to help such persons. Although these poor were highly visible in the community, begging by the roadside or in the church courts, they were "excluded . . . from the self-image of the traditional city . . . . outcasts without home or city could never be considered members of a citizen body" (Brown, 1992, p. 84; Veyne, 1976).

[6] Basil's *Second Homily on Psalm 14* (which actually exegetes Psalm 15) could also be considered one of Basil's sermons on poverty. This homily is about usury practices in the context of becoming impoverished. Because it repeats many of the themes found in Homilies VI and VII, it is not discussed here.

[7] While the themes of Nyssa's two-part sermon are similar, it is unlikely that they were delivered as a pair, given different manuscript traditions (Daley, 1999).

[8] It is not clear whether Nazianzus' oration builds from Gregory of Nyssa's second homily in his *On the Love of the Poor* or whether Nyssa works from Nazianzus' oration. Daley (1999) argues that Nazianzus works from Nyssa's homily while Holman (2001) presents evidence in the other direction.

[9] Vinson (2003, p. 59) translates 'primary equality of right" as "original egalitarian status."

[10] The Cappadocian Fathers are sometimes assessed as doing little to reform existing social structures that perpetuate poverty or oppression (Constantelos, 1991; Hol-

man, 2001). They continued to work within the existing patronage and gift economy systems, seeming to have little imagination for organizing society differently. Although Basil tried to use the power of his office at times to improve particular circumstances, "what is true is that he considered the state and the basic outlines of its political and social structures as given realities that he did not seek to change" (Gonzalez, 1990, p. 182). The practice of redemptive almsgiving extended charity, but the basic patronage system was left intact and the underlying causes of poverty were not challenged. Nor did the Cappadocian Fathers take on the task of dismantling the institution of slavery (although Nyssa comes closest to arguing for social reform in his Homily on Ecclesiastes 4). They seemed to view slavery as an economic necessity and part of the God-given social order (Phan, 1984).

[11] The notion of *philanthropia* as used by Basil and the Gregories was inherited from the ancient Greeks. In ancient Greece, *philanthropia* referred to the "love of the deity for man" and "man's love for man" (Constantelos, 1991, p. 3). The idea and practices imbedded in *philanthropia* notion were adopted by the early Christian community, although prior to the 3rd century, the term *agape* was more frequently used by New Testament writers, the Apostolic Fathers, and the early Greek apologists. Beginning with the 3rd century, *agape* was slowly replaced by *philanthropia*. Constantelos (1991) suggests that because Christianity was a syncretistic religion, absorbing both Hellenic values and practices with Hebrew morals, the adoption of *philanthropia* occurred because the idea of the love of the gods, or in this case, the love of God for human beings, was more familiar than *agape* to the Graeco-Roman world.

[12] This point cannot be fully developed here, but a few examples are illustrative. Isaiah 58:6-8 is regularly invoked as the kind of practical work that justice requires. Basil's Homily VIII begins with a comparison to the prophet Amos and the existing unjust social conditions. Nyssa does similar work in pointing to Daniel and Habakkuk. Nazianzus references Ezekiel's unjust shepherds who did not strengthen the weak, heal the sick, or bind up the injured (Ezekiel 34). Similarly, references to the Psalms (Psalm 10:12; 37:26; 41:1; 89:14; 112:5) and Proverbs (3:3, 27; 19:17; 28:14) point to God's concern with how the poor and needy are treated.

[13] Although all English translations of this passage refer to those who help as *righteous*, Wolterstorff (2006) argues that this is an incorrect translation of the Greek. The Greek word is the adjective *dikaios*. Although this word could be translated as either *just* or *upright*, given its context of following what the Hebrew Scriptures understand justice to be, the Greek adjective *dikaios* should have been translated with the adjective *just*. Says Wolterstorff, "It is the *just* who ask when they did what Jesus says they did; it is the *just* who enjoy eternal life. For what they did is exactly what Jesus and the Hebrew Scriptures say justice requires; they sought to undo the condition of the downtrodden and the excluded" (2006, pp. 129-130).

[14] Of course, this notion of redemptive almsgiving has a dark side. The idea of using the poor to secure one's place in the Kingdom is, in Christian traditions, bad theology. It denies that Jesus death was sufficient for salvation. And to people of all religious traditions, Christian or otherwise, the notion of passively using the poor to secure something for oneself is jarring, if not downright repulsive. One cannot help but wonder how the poor, whose voices have yet to be discovered in the 4th century, thought about their position and purpose. So what, if anything, can be said in defense of the Cappadocian Fathers on this count? First, they were not the first to come up with this idea. It was present already in the second century (and maybe earlier) when Christians realized that Christ's second coming was not coming any time soon. A pressing theological problem then was how to deal with the problem of post-baptism sin, that is, how to atone for sins committed after Christians had been baptized. Martyrdom and alms-giving became the main strategies (Garrison, 1993). Second, the Cappadocian Fathers were first of all preachers, not theologians, trained as first-class rhetoricians, and practically-focused. They needed to address an overwhelming

crisis in a particular cultural context. They developed a theological language out of their classical training and a patronage system and put it to use to address human need.

[15] It might also be called "social justice; " Wolterstorff calls it primary justice because it is basic justice. If this sort of justice is violated, then retributive justice is needed.

[16] Wolterstorff distinguishes between the *concept* of justice and the *contours* of justice. The concept of justice has to do with rights. The contours of justice addresses what a just social order might look like. It is possible, for instance, that people might agree on the concept of justice as having to do with rights, but disagree about the implications of this.

[17] In fact, as Nyssa and Nazianzus often describe, to care for and feed the poor is to care for and feed God incarnate. And, by extension, to fail in caring for the poor is to fail God. Committing an injustice against the poor not only wrongs the poor, but also wrongs God.

[18] For further development of this idea, see Basil's ascetical homily *On Mercy and Justice* (Wagner, 1950).

[19] The theory and practice of almsgiving is complex, and we cannot give it sufficient attention here. While modern notions of almsgiving often equate it with mercy or charity, almsgiving in the Hebrew Scriptures and as appropriated by Greek Christians is grounded in justice. Almsgiving emerges from the Hebrew word *tsedeqa*, meaning *the right thing* or *doing right* (Donahue, 1977). Concern for one's neighbor, says Donahue, is not just an excess of charity or compassion for others "but is rooted in claims of justice, i.e., how one can be faithful to the Lord who has given the goods of the earth as common possession of all and be faithful to others in the human community who have equal claim to these goods" (84-85). Almsgiving is expected of a just person, and is expressed in the care of the stranger and the poor (Countryman, 1980; Veyne, 1976).

[20] Oration 43 is Basil's funeral eulogy, delivered by Nazianzus, most likely on the two-year anniversary of Basil's death.

[21] This project was likely conceived by Basil around the time the famine began and completed in 371 or 372, built on land donated by Emperor Valens. It was funded by Basil's inheritance, by donations from those moved to action in the sermons of the Cappadocian Fathers, and through tax exemptions and financial aid sought by Basil from Governor Elias.

[22] While there are earlier antecedents of the *Basileias*, none address all three of the essential features of the *Basileias* (i.e., inpatient care, professional care, and an institutionalized system to benefit the sick in general). See Crislip (2005), Holman (2001), Miller (1985) for a more detailed discussion of services to each of these populations.

[23] Ironically, says Daley (1999), Basil's new city came to be a new city as well in a geographical sense. In the century following the erection of the Basileias, other buildings were constructed around the Basileias. This became the center of the city's later development, now known as the modern Turkish city of Kayseri.

References

Brown, P. (1995). *Authority and the sacred: Aspects of the Christianisation of the Roman world*. Cambridge: Cambridge University Press.

Brown, P. (2002). *Poverty and leadership in the later Roman Empire*. Hanover, NH: University Press of New England.

Constantelos, D. J. (1981). Basil the Great's social thought and involvement. *The Greek Orthodox Theological Review, 26*, 81-88.

Constantelos, D. J. (1991). *Byzantine philanthropy and social welfare*, 2/e. New Rochelle, NY: Aristide D. Caratzas, Publisher.

Countryman, L. W. (1980). *The rich Christian in the Church of the early empire: Contradictions and accommodations*. New York: The Edwin Mellen Press.

Crislip, A. (2005). *From monastery to hospital: Christian monasticism and the transformation of health care in late antiquity*. Ann Arbor, MI: The University of Michigan Press.

Daley, B. E. (1999). 1998 NAPS Presidential Address; Building a new city: The Cappadocian fathers and the rhetoric of philanthropy. *Journal of Early Christian Studies, 7*, 431-461.

Donahue, J. R. (1977). Biblical perspectives on justice. In J. C. Haughey, *The faith that does justice: Examining the Christian sources for social change*. New York: Paulist Press.

Garrison, R. (1993). *Redemptive almsgiving in early Christianity*. Sheffield, England: Sheffield Academic Press.

Gonzalez, J. L. (1990). *Faith and wealth: A history of early Christian ideas on the origin, significance, and use of money*. San Francisco: Harper and Row, Publishers.

Holman, S. (2000). The entitled poor: Human rights language in the Cappadocians. *Pro Ecclesia, 9*, 476-489.

Holman, S. (2001). *The hungry are dying: Beggars and bishops in Roman Cappadocia*. New York: Oxford University Press.

Horden, P. (2005). The earliest hospitals in Byzantium, Western Europe, and Islam. *Journal of Interdisciplinary History*, xxxv, 3, 361-389.

Ierley, M. (1984). *With charity for all: Welfare and society, ancient times to the present*. New York: Praeger Publishers.

McCauley, L., Sullivan, J., McGuire, M., & Deferrari, R., trans. (1953). *Funeral orations by Saint Gregory Nazianzen and Saint Ambrose*. Washington, DC: The Catholic University of America Press.

Miller, T. (1985). *The birth of the hospital in the Byzantine Empire*. Baltimore: John Hopkins University Press.

Phan, P. (1984). *Social thought: Message of the Fathers of the Church*. Wilmington, Delaware: Michael Glazier, Inc.

Reichart, E. (2003). *Social work and human rights: A foundation for policy and practice*. New York: Columbia University Press.

Rousseau, P. (1994). *Basil of Caesarea*. Berkeley: University of California Press.

Siepierski, P. (1988). Poverty and spirituality: Saint Basil and Liberation Theology. *Greek Orthodox Theological Review, 33(3)*, 313-326.

Stark, R. (1996). *The rise of Christianity: A sociologist reconsiders history*. Princeton, NJ: Princeton University Press.

Sterk, A. (2004). *Renouncing the world yet leading the church: The monk-bishop in late antiquity*. Cambridge, MA: Harvard University Press.

Toal, M. F., trans. ed. (1959). *The Sunday Sermons of the Great Fathers: A manual of preaching, spiritual reading and meditation*. Volume Three. Chicago: Henry Regnery Company.

Toal, M. F., trans. ed. (1963). *The Sunday Sermons of the Great Fathers: A manual of preaching, spiritual reading and meditation*. Volume Four. Chicago: Henry Regnery Company.

Van Dam, R. (2002). *Kingdom of snow*. Philadelphia: University of Pennsylvania Press.

Van Dam, R. (2003). *Families and friends in late Roman Cappadocia*. Philadelphia: University of Pennsylvania Press.

Veyne, P. (1976). *Bread and circuses: Historical sociology and political pluralism* (B. Pierce, trans.). London: Penguin Books.

Vinson, M., trans. (2003). *St. Gregory of Nazianzus: Select orations*. Washington, DC: The Catholic University of America Press. The Fathers of the Church – A New Translation. Vol 107.

von Campenhausen, H. (1998). *The Fathers of the Church*. Peabody, MA: Hendrickson Publishers, Inc.

Wagner, M., trans. (1950). *St. Basil: Ascetical works*. Washington, D. C: The Catholic University of America Press.

Way, A. C., trans. (1951). *The Fathers of the Church: St Basil letters 1-185*. Washington, D.C: The Catholic University of America Press.

Way, A. C., trans. (1955). *The Fathers of the Church: St Basil letters 186-368*. Washington, D.C: The Catholic University of America Press.

Wolterstorff, N. (2006). Justice, not charity: Social work through the eyes of faith. *Social Work and Christianity, 33(2)*, 123-140.

CHAPTER 6

SOCIAL WORK'S LEGACY
THE METHODIST SETTLEMENT MOVEMENT[1]

Sarah S. Kreutziger

Walter Trattner in his social welfare history From Poor Law to Welfare State, critically asserts that religious settlements were little more than "modified missions....bent on religious proselytizing, rigorous Americanization, and the imposition of social conformity on lower class clientele" (1976, p. 17). I believe he vastly underestimates the scope and positive impact of religious settlements on the more highly publicized Social Settlement Movement and on social work itself. Starting in the mid-nineteenth century, in response to the demands of the industrialization of American cities and towns, the religious settlement workers created, financed, and staffed outreach programs to the most marginalized inhabitants of the inner cities. They formed Bible classes, kindergartens, industrial schools, clubs, loan banks, job bureaus, dispensaries, reading rooms, and other programs that laid the groundwork for later social reforms. In the process, they created the foundation for the beginning of modern social work. Religious settlements strengthened the cause of women's rights and paved the way for women to enter careers in social welfare. And, in the South, religious settlers led the campaign for racial and ethnic equality.

Many denominations sponsored these specialized city missions, but perhaps none was as well organized and tenacious as the Methodist Episcopal Church (now the United Methodist Church) in spearheading this form of mission outreach. For that reason, an examination of the Methodist Religious Settlement Movement not only shows the work of religious settlers as part of the religious settlement movement, but highlights as well the tension between the ideologies of Christianity and the emerging tenets of enlightenment liberalism. This tension forms social work values today.

Origins of the Methodist Religious Settlement Movement

City Missions

The religious settlement movement in American Methodism began in New York City "on the 5th of July, 1819, [when] 'a number of females' met at the Wesleyan Seminary... for the purpose of forming an Auxiliary Society to the Missionary Society of the Methodist Episcopal Church, which had been formed the previous April" (Mason, 1870, p. 82). While their original purpose was to support missionaries to the North American Indians, their work gradually focused on problems closer to home. By 1850, "the ladies of the mission," united in evangelistic pragmatism, began their work in the notorious Five Points of New York City surrounded by:

> ...miserable-looking buildings, liquor stores innumerable, neglected children by scores, playing in rags and dirt, squalid-looking women, brutal men with black eyes and disfigured faces, proclaiming drunken brawls and fearful violence (Mason, 1870, p. 33).

The Five Points Mission was the earliest city mission and the precursor of later settlement homes and community centers in the United States (Leiby, 1978; Magalis, 1973; Riis, 1962).

Led by evangelist Phoebe Palmer, one of the most famous women of her day, the ladies raised money for a building, appointed a paid missionary, and volunteered to conduct Sunday schools, church services, and a nursery for working women. Later, they opened a reading room as an enticement for men who habitually sought solace in taverns, started a medical dispensary, installed public baths for the tenement dwellers, and provided emergency food and shelter for the poor.

Another project of the Missionary Society was "rescue work." In 1833, the women formed the Moral Reform Society to help women who "were victims of sin and shame" (Ingraham, 1844, p. 39) find ways to support themselves other than prostitution. The Society hired city missionaries who were some of the first female social workers. The first and most famous was Margaret Pryor whose descriptions of her "walks of usefulness" became a best-selling book and did much to publicize their work.

Pryor's and Palmer's pleas to move into social reform were spoken in language of the "woman's sphere of action." This language can be appreciated best when we consider the assigned roles and relationships of that era. As homemakers whose responsibility was to build a "sanctified" (holy) society, women were exhorted by religious leaders to protect their homes and others' homes by instilling spiritual values and righteous living in their children and other members of the household. Their special providence was to take care of other women and children who did not have similar resources or religious beliefs. It followed then, that other rescue work was directed at children. Charles Loring Brace, founder of a massive foster care system for destitute children, began his career at Five Points Mission. His work there convinced him that "effective social reform must be done in the source and origin of evil,—in prevention, not cure" (Brace, 1973, p. 78). He founded the Children's Aid Society in 1853; an organization that relocated more than fifty-thousand children to rural homes to remove them from the real and perceived dangers of city life.

The Five Points Mission and similar agencies were part of a broader effort known as the City Mission Movement which had its roots in the New York Religious Tract Society. The tract societies distributed religious literature to convert the inner-city poor. In the 1830s, members of the Tract Society began holding prayer meetings and establishing Sunday schools for the children marked for evangelism (Smith-Rosenberg, 1971). As the volunteers became familiar with the living conditions of the residents, they carried food and clothing with them on their rounds and set up emergency funds. In time, they organized their welfare work into wards for distribution and created a new organization, the Society for the Relief of the Worthy Poor. This became the New York Association for Improving the Condition of the Poor. By 1870, forty full-time salaried missionaries were pioneering model tenements, summer camps for children, industrial training schools, and systematic "outdoor" relief. The Association was a forerunner of the New York Charity Organization Society, a pioneer of early professional social work.

The Institutional Churches

The rapid replication of the programs of the Five Points Mission was inspired by the challenge of the industrial age and the difficulties experienced by the men and women who immigrated to the United States to work in its factories. "Between 1860 and 1900, some fourteen million immigrants came to America and about another nine million, mainly from southern and eastern Europe... arrived between 1900 and 1910" (Trattner, 1979, p.135). The massive crowding, illnesses, and social problems created by the influx of largely unskilled, illiterate, foreign-speaking individuals was unparalleled in our history. In New York City, two-thirds of the population lived in tenements in 1890, while Chicago, then the fastest growing city in the world, packed inner-city residents near the putrid-smelling, unsanitary stockyards where slaughtered animal carcasses fouled water and air. Gangs and petty criminals, fortified by alcohol and other drugs, preyed on the new arrivals. The "urban frontier, like the rural frontier, was a dangerous place" (Seller, 1981, p. 50).

To the native born Americans, the newcomers were dangerous in other ways. Their political attitudes, born out of feudal societies in which government was an agent of social control, provided a challenge to American democracy. In the slums, the immigrants turned to old-world political traditions such as the "padrone," or political boss, who would manipulate the system for personal gain in exchange for votes. American ideals of patriotic civic action on the basis of self-denial and responsibility clashed with these attitudes (Hofstadter, 1955).

Americans were also concerned about the breakdown of traditional Protestant religious customs and beliefs founded on Puritanism which portrayed the United States as a "holy experiment" destined to create a new society as a beacon to the rest of the world (Winthrop, 1960; Woodbridge, Noll, & Hatch, 1979). Living sin-free, disciplined, temperate, hard-working lives was crucial to this cause. The immigrants, mostly Roman Catholic, drank, brought "continental ideas of the Sabbath" with them, displayed nomadic living habits, and wore fancy dress (Strong, 1893, p. 210). These practices severely distressed city evangelists. Even worse for their cause was the reality that many in the mainline denominations were becoming indifferent to the plight of the poor and abandoning the inner city churches.

The solution to these changes was to set up a specialized form of city missions in these abandoned churches to Americanize, and hence Christianize, the new arrivals by offering them resources and support. These citadels against the onslaught of massive social problems were called Institutional Churches. Programs and activities developed in these "open" or "free" churches (because there was no charge for the pews) were adopted by the social settlers and others following in their footsteps (Bremner, 1956). These churches viewed themselves as "institutions" that ministered seven days a week to the physical and spiritual wants of all the people within their reach. They sponsored clinics, free Saturday night concerts, self-supporting restaurants and lodging houses, wood yards for the unemployed, "fresh air work" for women and children, and "gold-cure" establishments for drunkards. There was a marked emphasis on practical education. Institutional churches sponsored libraries and literary societies and carried on kindergartens, trade schools, and community colleges (McBride, 1983, p. xi).

Although these churches have been described as similar to the secularized social settlements because they adopted many methods and educational theories of the "new charity" (Abell, 1962, p. 164), there is much evidence that the primary mission of the institutional churches was evangelism. While their programs were similar to non-sectarian charities, their ideology was quite different. The Methodist women who supported institutional work were motivated by Scripture. They were to feed the hungry, care for the sick, and clothe the poor (Tatum, 1960). Methodist women carried these ideals into their work with the religious settlements and supported all of these missions through the structure and activities of the Home Missionary Societies.

The Home Missionary Societies

Almost without exception, the Home Missionary Societies were made up of white, middle-class women, better educated than most of their female contemporaries and freed from time-consuming house chores by the same industrial revolution that was creating the massive social problems in the cities and towns. While many other denominations were ministering to poor and oppressed individuals, the Methodists were the most zealous and well-organized. By 1844, when the Methodist Episcopal Church separated into the southern and northern branches over slavery, there were already 360 missionaries in the United States and one mission in Liberia supported by these societies (Norwood, 1974).

After the Civil War, the local mission societies joined together to build national organizations within the two divisions. The northern church established its missionary societies first in 1869, followed by the southern church nine years later, to aid foreign missions. The Woman's Home Missionary Society was founded in 1880 in the northern Methodist Episcopal Church to support missions within the United States. Their support of missions in the South, especially for the recently freed slaves, led to the founding of the southern church's Home Mission Society in 1880 (*Home Missions*, 1930).

Much of the philosophy undergirding the mission societies' work came from a societal view of women as the moral guardians of the home. In the North, missionary society members organized under the banner of "evangelical domesticity," the notion that the natural spiritual superiority of women gave them the authority to protect their homes and children from the evil influences of society (Lee, 1981). Countless women echoed the belief that "in every well-regulated family their [sic] mother is the potent influence in molding the little ones committed to her sacred guidance" (*Women's Missionary Society*, 1884, p. 4). Much of the reform activity therefore, was directed toward helping other women and children create barriers against the evils that would destroy the sanctity of the home.

In the South, the drive to purify homes was made more difficult by an-tebellum ideology. The plantation mentality that enslaved black women kept white women in bondage as well. A rigid, tightly-knit, hierarchical social order demanded obedience and submissiveness. As a result, religious activities for women stressed personal piety rather than the "social holiness" of evangelical service that northern women had channeled into abolition, women's rights, and other reforms (Thompson, 1972; Scott, 1970). The Civil War, despite its devastation, liberated southern women for reform activities previously denied them. Consequently, they poured their energies into "their appointed sphere": the churches. In time, the wives, daughters, and sisters of former slave hold-ers joined with the wives, daughters, and sisters of slaves to establish agencies and organizations that promoted racial harmony and reinforced the cause of women's rights (Hall, 1979; Scott, 1984). A significant product of their work was the Methodist Religious Settlement Movement.

The Religious Settlements

Activities and Staffing

Methodist settlements, like their predecessors, often began as child care facilities for working mothers and expanded into kindergartens, sewing clubs, domestic labor training, homemaker clubs, rescue work for prostitutes, boys' athletic clubs, classes in cooking, play grounds, and religious services. Although they also included reading rooms, public baths, English classes, night school, dispensaries, lectures, concerts, music lessons, bookkeeping and banking classes, military drills, gymnastics, milk stations, saving associations, libraries, and "improvement clubs for men,"—they were primarily geared to the needs of mothers and children (Woods & Kennedy, 1911).

The settlement houses were originally sponsored as an expanded mission project of the Women's Home Missionary Society (WHMS), the Chicago Train-ing School for City, Home and Foreign Missions (CTS), and several independent associations. While the goal of the leaders of these organizations was still the sanctification of society through the changed lives of individuals, their work among the poor enlarged their vision of the difficulties that these individuals faced. City missionaries realized that society as a whole must be changed if their goal to evangelize the world was to be reached. Fed by the theology of the social gospel, which saw sin as systemic as well as individual, the city missionaries and their supporters created a broader, more far-reaching attack upon the barriers that kept all people from realizing their God-given potential.

Volunteers from the missionary societies and churches, along with a few paid city missionaries, ran many of the early missions; but the need for better training and education for their expanding work prompted missionary society leaders such as Lucy Rider Meyer, Jane Bancroft Robinson, and Belle Harris Bennett to advocate for biblically-trained women who would live in the neighborhoods among the disadvantaged in the same manner that foreign missionaries lived with citizens in the lands they served. After much planning, hard work, and many setbacks, the efforts of these women and others were realized by the 1880's in a new version of the home missionary: the deaconess.

Deaconesses were distinguished from the city missionaries by the clothing they wore, their communal living arrangements, their formal connection to the church, and their unsalaried service (*Deaconess Advocate*, February 1901). Easily recognized because of their dark dresses, starched bonnets tied with a large white bow, and brisk manner, the deaconesses took their calling seriously. Their task was to "minister to the poor, visit the sick, pray for the dying, care for the orphan, seek the wandering, comfort the sorrowing, [and] save the sinning..." (Thoburn & Leonard in Lee, 1963, p. 37). With the biblical deaconess Phoebe as their model, deaconesses went into the inner cities of the North and the factory towns and rural communities of the South as part of the twentieth century vanguard for the religious settlement movement. In the first thirty years of the Methodist diaconate, the Chicago Training School, founded by Lucy Rider Meyer, sent nearly 4,000 deaconesses and city missionaries to work in hospitals, schools, settlements, rescue homes, and churches. Forty of these institutions were started by CTS graduates (Brown, 1985).

In the Southern states, Methodist settlements constituted from 30% to 100% of all settlements when the first national listing was compiled in 1911 (Woods & Kennedy, 1911). Settlements that served white populations were called Wesley Houses, after Methodism's founder John Wesley, and settlements that served African-Americans were known as Bethlehem Houses (Tatum, 1960). Settlement leaders worked with white American cotton mill employees in Georgia, French-Arcadians families and Italian immigrants in Louisiana, African-American farms workers in Tennessee and Georgia, European seafood workers in Mississippi, and Hispanic migrant workers in Texas and Florida (Nelson, 1909). Many of the settlements were headed by deaconesses who lived in the neighborhoods they served. In 1910, there were six Methodist deaconess training schools and ninety social agencies staffed by 1,069 deaconesses (Glidden, in Dougherty, 1988).

The Deaconess Mother Heart

The religious basis of the beliefs and values of the deaconess sisterhood was the Puritan vision of America's spiritual manifest destiny: America as the beacon to the rest of the world. Deaconess values were also formed from Wesleyan ideals of "perfecting" society through service and mission, cultural definitions of women's position and place, enlightenment views of scientific reasoning, and the emerging social gospel. Their declared goal was the salvation of the "household of faith": American society. The evils of unchurched people, drunkenness, pauperism, and negative influences from foreigners could be wiped out, they believed, with a return to Christian ideals based on the earlier promise of God's covenant with the "New Jerusalem," the United States. This heavenly pattern, imprinted upon America, would ensure the salvation of the world. As deaconess educator Belle Horton declared, "we must 'save America for the world's sake'" (Horton, 1904, p. 41).

Justification for women's entry into this noble endeavor came from church tradition and the Bible as expressed through the metaphor of the Mother Heart. The Mother Heart, as described by Meyer, was the nurturing, caring, feminine side of God understood and possessed by women. Deaconess sisterhood, re-inforced by communal living arrangements and church connection, readily integrated the holistic social gospel tenets into their ideological center. Since building the Kingdom of God on earth required the sanctification of each home, it was important for churches to include the work of women: those whose specific mission was the care of God's "unmothered children". This allowed the deaconesses, and by extension—all females—greater authority to be ministers to the whole of society. This expanded vision of women's role in the church and community helped set the stage for the ordination of women, suffrage, and other forms of women's rights. It also helped pave the way for women to enter paid careers as the profession of social work emerged from its two pioneer branches: the Charity Organization Societies and the Settlement Movements.

Religious Settlements and Social Settlements

The women who staffed the settlement homes and institutions were on the front lines of the home mission field. Because the early city mission and institutional churches had provided the model for service and intervention in the lives of the dispossessed for non-sectarian settlements and associated charities just as they had for the religious settlements, there was a great deal of exchange of information, ideas, education, and services. Meyer was a friend of social settlement leader Jane Addams and each knew and respected the other's work. Addams helped Meyer select the site for the CTS and was involved in the early plans. Meyer had wanted to put Addams on the School's Board of Trustees in 1892, but was voted down. Hull-House was just then drawing the fire of the churches because it had been thought necessary to eliminate any direct religious teaching from its program and one or two members of the Training School Board protested against the presence of this "unChristian enterprise" (Horton, 1928, p. 182).

Addams discussed this experience in *Twenty Years at Hull-House* (1981) and the embarrassment it caused, in her words, to "the open-minded head of the school" (p. 72). Addams compared the Training School favorably to the activities of the social settlements. Meyer and Addams continued to be friends throughout their careers and Meyer frequently spoke of Addam's work in the *Deaconess Advocate*, the journal of the CTS.

Despite opposition from church members who objected to the non-religious atmosphere of the social settlements, social settlement leaders continued to lecture regularly at the CTS and the students' field work included living as residents at Hull-House and other social settlements (Brown, 1985). By 1913, Meyers had supplemented the biblically-oriented lectures with textbooks by charity organization pioneers Edward J. Devine and Amos Warner (*Bulletin CTS,* January, 1914). By 1918, her students were working in the United Charities and Juvenile Protection Associations as "visitors" (*Bulletin CTS,* December, 1918), and were learning to think in the codified, scientific methods of the "new charity." Although religious motivation and language continued to be part of the curriculum, the new field of sociology and its promise of "perfecting" society through social engineering gradually supplanted the earlier emphasis on evangelism and proselytization in all the training schools. In time, it would become increasingly difficult to distinguish between the ideology and practices of those who graduated from the deaconess training schools and those who graduated from the university-based schools of social work. As deaconess education and values became less and less distinguishable from the values and methods of early professional social work, deaconess organizations began to lose the sponsorship of the church and other financial backers. Consequently, deaconess training schools were merged into schools of theology or schools of social work (Tatum, 1960; Nola Smee, telephone interview, July, 1995; address by Walter Athern, April 26, 1926, Boston University School of Theology Archives).

The Decline of the Methodist Religious Settlement Movement

While the movement toward non-sectarian liberalism characterized by scientifically-trained workers was initially moderated by the religious training of the settlers and other mission workers, the increasing centralization of reform activities and governmental intervention in social reform tipped the balance in favor of secularism. Additionally, "the spontaneous will to serve," so evident in earlier church volunteers, was subverted by the drive for professionalization. Previous values that had stressed compassion, emotional involvement, and vigorous love of humanity, according to social work historian Roy Lubove (1965), were "educated out" in preference for a "scientific trained intelligence and skillful application of technique" (p. 122). This new climate of professionalism at the beginning of the twentieth century changed the relationship between helper and those helped. Agencies became bureaucratic rather than evangelical, more contractual than spontaneous, and more removed from their clients.

One of the defining and continuing differences between the social settlements and the religious settlements was the pressure by churches on sectarian settlements to use their work for proselytizing (Doris Alexander, telephone interview, July, 1995; Davis, 1967). This pressure caused many of the settlements begun under religious auspices to sever their ties with their parent organizations. This was done to solicit community-wide support and to appeal to wealthy industrialists interested in ecumenical charities (Dubroca, 1955; Trolander, 1987).

After World War I, with the rise of the Community Chest and other centralized social service funding, social settlement leaders were forced to answer to an organizational hierarchy that could dictate policy and programs. The net result was less emphasis on controversial community action (Trolander, 1987) and religious instruction. Funding from these centralized agencies also reinforced the drive to replace sectarian-trained workers with professional social workers.

Compounding these trends was social work's move into individual treatment and away from community development. Veterans of World War I suffering from battle-fatigue and shell shock required more than friendly neighborly relationships to help them cope with their personal and health-related problems. Red Cross workers treating military families discovered that Freudian psychoanalytic approaches and casework techniques developed by Mary Richmond, pioneer leader of the Charity Organizational Societies, were better suited to their needs. "Friendly visiting" gave way to therapeutic intervention as settlements were changed from community centers into mental health clinics.

This trend continued until by the early 1960's, professional social workers had replaced volunteers and religious settlement workers in many of the centers. The consequences of the move, according to one historian, led to greater emotional detachment between residents and the workers and less mutual concern and care. As she explained:

> In place of spontaneity and being available around the clock, [social workers] made appointments and 'treatment plans.' Instead of seeking to do *with* the neighborhood, they sought to do *for* the neighborhood. Their 'professional' detachment from the neighborhood was not only physical, it was psychological (Trolander, 1987, p. 39).

While Methodists followed similar practices related to staffing, there were some differences. Methodist deaconesses continued to reside in the settlements until the mid 1980's (Nola Smee, telephone interview, July, 1995) which helped to maintain the physical as well as the symbolic presence and sense of involvement in the neighborhoods that is part of the settlement legacy. Even when the settlers moved out, it was not so much because of their lack of dedication as it was from church policy and changing attitudes. The decline of religious settlers paralleled the decline of the deaconess movement as deaconesses began to retire and fewer and fewer women were willing to expend the level of commitment required for the diaconate as other opportunities for ministry and employment opened to women. The success of the deaconess crusade, the right of women to participate fully in the church and community, in other words, contributed to its decline (Betty Purkey, telephone interview, July, 1995).

Implications for the Future

While the history of religious settlements has remained in the shadows of the highly publicized work of social settlements such as Jane Addam's Hull-House (Addams, 1981; Davis, 1967; Leiby, 1978), the fact remains that these sectarian-sponsored organizations contributed much to the origins and success of early social work. Overlooked by most social work chroniclers were the hundreds of religiously-committed women, backed by an army of loyal supporters, who also moved into inner-city and rural neighborhoods to share their talents and service with the less fortunate. Methodist settlement leaders were typical examples of these women and their dreams.

The Methodist religious settlers' vision of society began with evangelical hopes for a holy nation undergirded by mutual concern for each other and love of God. This vision inspired the work that built hundreds of social welfare institutions and provided the support and financial resources to run them. When these front-line city missionaries were forced by the overwhelming task and changing times to create new ways of thinking and practice, they lost part of the religious underpinning that defined their vision. Despite these challenges and the decline of the deaconess movement, many of the original settlement houses survive as community centers and urban outreach stations for the churches. As such, they serve as reminders of what the church is capable of doing when the call for commitment, dedication, and sacrifice is answered. When, in the words of Bellah et al., (1985), we seek "the recovery of our social ecology [that] would allow us to link interests with the common good" (p. 287).

The religious and social settlers faced a society reeling from the effects of "wrecked foundations of domesticity" (Addams, 1972, p. 47) and other problems of societal dislocation and despair. Many contemporary people would agree that this century's end brings similar challenges. Family disorganization, international disruptions, population shifts, some with tragic consequences, and continuing disagreements over race, class, and gender create disunity and loss of purpose. Our country, like religious institutions and other social service professions, seems to be searching for a renewed vision and mission. Social work leaders Harry Specht and Mark Courtney (1994) join others calling for the profession of social work to return to its defining mission in the tradition of the settlement movements and the strong belief in the improvement of society. The history of the Methodist Religious Settlement Movement offers one avenue to reclaim that charge.

Note

[1] This chapter was rewritten from information from the author's unpublished dissertation research for Tulane University and research from a paper submitted to the School of Divinity at Duke University.

References

Abell, A. I. (1962). *The urban impact on American Protestantism 1861-1900*. Hamden: Archon.

Addams, J. (1981). *Twenty years at Hull House*. Phillips Publishing Co., 1910; reprint, New York: Signet Classic.

Addams, J. (1972). *The spirit of youth and the city streets.* New York: MacMillan Co., 1909; reprint, Urbana: University of Chicago Press.

Bellah, R. N., Madsen R., Sullivan W. M., Swidler A. & Tipton S.M. (1985). *Habits of the Heart: Individualism and commitment in American life.* Berkeley: University of California Press.

Brace, C. L. (1973). *The dangerous class of New York.* New York: Wynkoop & Hollenbeck, Publisher, 1872; NASW Classic reprint, Washington, DC: NASW.

Bremner, R. H. (1956). *From the depths: The discovery of poverty in the United States.* New York: New York University Press.

Brown, I. C. (1985). *"In their times": A history of the Chicago Training School on the occasion of its centennial celebration, 1885-1985.* Evanston: Garrett Evangelical Theological Seminary.

Bulletin of the Chicago Training School for City, Home and Foreign Missions. (1914). 15(4).

Bulletin of the Chicago Training School for City, Home and Foreign Missions. (1918). 18(4).

Davis, A. F. (1967). *Spearheads for reform: The social settlements and the progressive movement 1890-1914.* New York: Oxford University Press.

Deaconess Advocate. Vols. 14-29, 1898-1914.

Dougherty, M. A. (1988). *The Methodist Deaconess, 1885-1918: A study in religious feminism.* Ph. D. diss., University of California, Davis.

Dubroca, I. (1955). *Good neighbor Eleanor McMain of Kingsley House.* New Orleans: Pelican Publishing Co.

Hall, J. D. (1979). *Revolt against chivalry: Jessie Daniel Ames and the women's campaign against lynching.* New York: Columbia University Press.

Hofstadter, R. (1955). *The age of reform.* New York: Alfred A. Knopf

Home Missions. (1930). Nashville: Woman's Missionary Council, Methodist Episcopal Church, South.

Horton, I. (1904). *The burden of the city.* New York: Fleming H. Revell Company.

Horton, I. (1928). *High adventure—life of Lucy Rider Meyer.* New York. Methodist Book Concern.

Ingraham, S. R. (1844). *Walks of usefulness or reminiscences of Mrs. Margaret Prior.* New York: American Female Moral Reform Society.

Ladies of the Mission. (1854). *The old brewery and the new mission house at the Five Points.* New York: Stringer & Townsend.

Lee, E. M. (1963). *As among the Methodists: Deaconesses yesterday today and tomorrow.* New York: Woman's Division of Christian Service, Board of Missions, Methodist Church.

Lee, S. D. (1981). Evangelical domesticity: The Woman's Temperance Crusade of 1873-1874. In H. Thomas & R. S. Keller, (Eds.), *Women in new worlds,* (pp. 293-309). Nashville: Abingdon Press.

Leiby, J. (1978). *A history of social welfare and social work in the United States.* New York: Columbia University Press.

Lubove, R. (1965). *The professional altruist: The emergence of social work as a career 1880-1930.* Cambridge: Harvard University Press.

Magalis, E. (1973). *Conduct becoming to a woman.* New York: Women's Division, Board of Global Ministries, The United Methodist Church.

Mason, M. (1870). *Consecrated talents: Or the life of Mrs. Mary W. Mason.* New York: Carlton & Lanahan.

McBride, E. B. (1983). *Open church: History of an idea.* U.S.A.: By the author.

Nelson, J. (1909). *Home mission fields of the Methodist Episcopal Church, South.* Home Department, Board of Missions, Methodist Episcopal Church, South.

Norwood, F. A. (1974). *The story of American Methodism.* Nashville: Abingdon Press.

Riis, J. A. (1962). *How the other half lives: Studies among the tenements of New York.* 1890. Reprint, American Century Series. New York: Hill & Wang.

Scott, A. Firor. (1970). *The southern lady: From pedestal to politics 1830-1930.* Chicago: University of Chicago Press.

Scott, A. Firor. (1984). *Making the invisible woman visible.* Urbana: University of Illinois Press.

Seller, M. S. (1981). *Immigrant women.* Philadelphia: Temple University Press.

Smith-Rosenberg, C. (1971). *Religion and the rise of the American city: The New York City Mission Movement, 1812-1870.* Ithaca: Cornell University Press.

Specht, H. & Courtney M. E. (1994). *Unfaithful angels: How social work has abandoned its mission.* New York: The Free Press.

Strong, J. (1893). *The new era or the coming kingdom.* New York: Baker & Taylor Co.

Tatum, N. D. (1960). *A crown of service: A story of women's work in the Methodist Episcopal Church, South, from 1878-1940.* Nashville: Parthenon Press.

Thompson, E. (1972). God and the southern plantation system. In Samuel Hill, (Ed.), *Religion and the solid South,* (pp. 57-91). Nashville: Abingdon Press.

Trattner, W. I. (1979). *From poor law to welfare state.* (2nd. ed.), New York: Free Press.

Trolander, J. A. (1987). *Professionalism and social change.* New York: Columbia University Press.

Winthrop, J. (1960). A model of Christian charity. In H. S. Smith, R. T. Handy, & L. A. Loetscher (Eds.), *American Christianity,* (pp. 98-102). New York: Charles Scribner's Sons.

Woman's Missionary Society of the Methodist Episcopal Church, South. (June): 1884.

Woodbridge, J. D., Noll M. A., & Hatch N. O. (1979). *The gospel in America.* Grand Rapids: Zondervan Publishing House.

Woods, R. A. & Kennedy A.J., (Eds). (1911). *Handbook of settlements.* New York: Charities Publication Committee.

Archives

Boston University School of Theology.
Special Collections, University Libraries,
Boston, Massachusetts

CHAPTER 7

EXPLORING THE FILTERING ROLE OF CHRISTIAN BELIEFS AND VALUES IN THE INTEGRATION OF CHRISTIAN FAITH AND SOCIAL WORK PRACTICE

Rick Chamiec-Case

Bob was a new member of the North American Association of Christians in Social Work (NACSW), as well as new to the Christian faith. Shortly after joining NACSW, Bob called the association's executive director with a pressing question. Bob explained that he had been a social worker for many years, and wanted to know how becoming a Christian might have an impact on his work as a social worker. Misunderstanding his question, NACSW's executive director explained that social work and the Christian faith shared much in common, including a commitment to service, social justice, the dignity and worth of persons, the importance of human relationships, and integrity and competence (Code of Ethics, 1999). Bob listened respectfully for a while, but at his first opportunity politely interrupted saying: "I wasn't asking if social work and my Christian faith have much in common. I am already convinced of this. What I really want to know is this: how will my Christian faith contribute to and shed new light on how I understand and carry out my social work practice!"

Behind Bob's question rests a conviction shared by many people of faith—as well as many that do not necessarily consider themselves people of faith. This conviction is that persons' most deeply held beliefs and values about what is ultimately real and meaningful unavoidably shape how they understand every aspect of their lives. As such, many Christians in social work believe that their most deeply held Christian beliefs and values *can and should* inform, impact, and shape how they understand and practice social work. Yet how should this work? What should this process of integration look like? How can social workers tap the resources of their Christian faith to energize and meaningfully inform their work, and at the same time retain a healthy respect for and reliance on the integrity and value of the knowledge base and practice wisdom that has been developed by the social work profession over the years?

The Filtering Role Model of Integration

In his short book entitled *Reason within the Bounds of Religion* (1984), Nicholas Wolterstorff offers an insightful approach to the integration of Christian faith and learning that focuses on the role of what he calls "Christian control beliefs."

The next part of this chapter explores Wolterstorff's approach as a model for the integration of Christian faith and social work practice.

As social workers, we are called upon to evaluate a variety of claims every day, from relatively small, mundane statements of fact, to large, substantive theories and philosophical suppositions. For example, in a recent issue of *Social Work*, the article entitled, "Mental Illness Stigma: Problem of Public Health or Social Justice" (Corrigan, Watson, Byrne, & David, 2005) makes a variety of claims within its pages, including two that will be examined in this paper:

1. Stigma harms people with mental illness.
2. All people (including people with mental illness) are fundamentally equal and share the right to respect and dignity.

When social workers are called upon to evaluate the veracity of such claims, they tend to weigh them against beliefs and values they hold that are related to the claims being made. Many of the beliefs social workers hold are based primarily on their immediate experience, observation, and/or empirical investigation (Wolterstorff calls these "data beliefs.")

For example, related to the first claim that stigma harms people with mental illness, a social worker might have observed firsthand how landlords and employers often summarily dismiss her clients' applications for apartments or jobs as soon as they become aware that her clients are persons with a mental illness. As a result of these experiences, this social worker comes to believe that often persons are denied apartments or jobs for which they are otherwise qualified merely because they are mentally ill. When weighing the credibility of the claim that stigma harms people with mental illness, this particular data belief lends this claim a good deal of support.

Of course, other data beliefs related to this claim might be brought to bear in evaluating this claim as well. For example, this same social worker might have recently read an article by an author she respects arguing that (based on his research) because people with mental illness have access to publicly-funded case management services to help them find jobs and places to live, persons with mental illness actually have an easier time acquiring apartments and housing than persons who are not mentally ill. A belief based on this research would at least on the surface conflict with the first belief (that people with mental illness often do not get apartments of jobs solely because they are mentally ill), and with the claim that stigma harms people with mental illness.

The fact that we often hold many conflicting data beliefs partly explains why weighing claims is often a complicated, difficult process. Still, for claims like this one (that stigma harms people with mental illness), beliefs based on our immediate experience, observation, and/or empirical investigation are often most effective in helping a person decide whether or not to embrace such claims.

There are other claims, however, for which beliefs based on our immediate experience, observation, and/or empirical investigation are not likely to be as decisive in persuading a person whether or not they are true and/or ought to be embraced. Examples of such claims might include broad philosophical or metaphysical claims (like "God exists" or "persons have free will"), value claims (like "society should ensure that all persons regardless of race, age, or gender, etc. have access to adequate housing and health care"), and the claims of major theories (like "Bandura's concept of reciprocal determinism is a more complete explanation of human behavior than Skinner's concept of operant conditioning").

The statement that all people, including people with mental illness, are fundamentally equal and share the right to respect and dignity appears to be such a claim. For although data beliefs are not irrelevant to the task of weighing whether or not all people, including people with mental illness, are fundamentally equal and share the right to respect and dignity, there are other considerations that play an even more critical role here—what Wolterstorff calls "control beliefs."

According to Wolterstorff, control beliefs are "beliefs as to what constitutes an acceptable sort of claim on the matter under consideration" (Wolterstorff, 1984, p. 63). He goes on to explain that control beliefs either lead us to reject certain *types* of claims because they contradict or do not comport well with our control beliefs, or lead us to support (or develop) other types of claims or theories that do comport well with these beliefs. In this way, our core beliefs act as filters that lead us to reject or support certain types of claims based on their fit with these core beliefs and values. Wolterstorff argues further that the core religious beliefs of Christians can, do, and should function as filters in this way—since core religious (and non-religious) beliefs and values unavoidably do for all persons.

But what does it mean to say that core religious beliefs and values can, do, and should lead Christians in social work to reject or support certain *types* of claims they come across in their work as social workers? It might be helpful to take a look at a hypothetical example to illustrate this more fully.

Let's say, for example, that a Christian in social work (let's call her Jane) has been recently transferred to an interdisciplinary team in a hospital providing medical services for a person with a mental illness (let's call him Joe, and label his mental illness as a bipolar disorder) who is in desperate need of a kidney transplant. The hospital doctors have determined that Joe will not likely live for more than 6-9 months without a new kidney. However, according to hospital policy (which is in compliance with state law), persons with a mental illness may be (but don't necessarily have to be) excluded from consideration for a place on the hospital's kidney transplant waiting list—or receive a downgraded priority status—because of their mental illness. Aside from having a bipolar disorder, Joe meets all of the other criteria for being given a priority place on the waiting list, particularly because of his serious medical condition. The number of persons needing kidney transplants in the community served by the hospital is extremely large. The hospital committee which makes decisions about placement on the waiting list will be meeting next week with Joe's interdisciplinary team to evaluate the team's request that Joe be given a priority place on the waiting list in light of his serious medical condition.

As Jane begins to grapple with the various issues raised by this situation, she astutely discovers that there are be two broad, competing claims vying for her acceptance that will significantly impact how she understands and acts with regard to the situation at hand. The first claim is the one presented earlier in this article, that is, that all people, including people with mental illness, are fundamentally equal and share the right to respect and dignity. A competing claim has been articulated by philosopher Peter Singer, who in the context of a discussion about abortion, infanticide, and euthanasia, has argued that all persons are not in fact equal—but rather that the worth of human life *varies* depending on a person's life circumstances (Singer, 1993). As such, Singer maintains that we should view and treat persons:

> ...in accordance with their ethically relevant characteristics including consciousness, the capacity for physical, social and mental interaction with other beings, having conscious preferences for continued life, and having enjoyable experiences. Other relevant aspects depend on the relationship of the being to others, having relatives for example who will grieve over your death....All of these things make a difference to the regard and respect we should have for a being (1995, p. 191).

For Singer then, it is not the case that all persons are fundamentally equal. Rather, the worth of persons is more properly based on several considerations related to the *quality* of a person's life rather than on anything inherent in all persons.

Granting for the sake of argument that there is no way to reconcile these two competing claims, how might Jane go about deciding which of these claims, if either, to embrace—knowing that her decision will have a significant impact on how she understands and acts with regard to Joe's situation? It seems clear that because these competing claims are broadly philosophical and/or value-based in nature (that is, they deal with whether or not all persons are fundamentally equal in terms of worth and value, and whether the decisions about Joe's place-ment on the kidney transplant waiting list *should* or *should not* take into account the quality of his life as impacted by his mental illness), is not likely that *factual* beliefs based on Jane's immediate experience and/or empirical investigation will be decisive in arguing why she would embrace one claim versus the other. Factual beliefs at best *describe* some facet of the world around us. They do not, at least by themselves, provide us with clear direction regarding what a person *ought* to do in a moral or ethical sense (Sherwood, 2002). It is when weighing claims of this sort that Wolterstorff argues persons will and should draw upon their core beliefs and values to help them decide "what constitutes an acceptable sort of claim...on the matter under consideration" (Wolterstorff, 1984, p. 63).

So, what might be an example of a core Christian belief or value that Jane might draw upon to help decide what would be an acceptable type of claim in a situation like Joe's? One that comes readily to mind is the belief embraced by most Christians through the centuries that all persons are made in the image of God, and as a result, all human life is sacred (*"Catholic social teaching", n.d.*), and all persons are of infinite worth (Keith-Lucas, 1985).

So if Jane, then, was to use this core Christian belief/value as a filter for deciding the *types* of claims she would actively consider on the matter under consideration, she would likely: a) rule out claims that assign differing levels of worth or value to people depending on their quality of life, life circumstances, or other related criteria; b) view favorably claims that endorse the view that all persons are equal in terms of ultimate worth and value.

In this case, then, given the two specific claims she is weighing, Jane would be much more likely embrace that first claim that all people, including people with mental illness, are fundamentally equal and share the right to respect and dignity, and rule out the second claim that the worth of persons varies depending on considerations related to the *quality* of a person's life circumstances rather than on anything inherent in all persons.

It is important to note here that this is *not* the same as saying that the first claim is a uniquely *Christian* position on this issue. Instead, it would be more precise to say that this first claim is *congruent* or *comports well* with core Christian beliefs/values, whereas the second claim is/does not. Translating this decision to embrace the first claim into action, Jane would likely feel compelled to argue with a firm conviction before the hospital's kidney transplant committee that the team's petition for a priority place on the kidney transplant waiting list should not in any way be discounted or negatively affected by Joe's mental illness, and that to do so would be tantamount to saying that Joe's life was of less value and worth than persons who are not mentally ill.

Importantly, Wolterstorff argues that Christians in social work should not be apologetic about allowing the content of their core Christian beliefs to function as a filter when weighing claims and theories because they—like all persons regardless of their worldviews—ought to seek integrity, authenticity, wholeness, and continuity between their overall body of beliefs on the one hand, and their commitments and actions on the other. For all persons, Christians or not, are in the same epistemological boat:

> [The] lives that we live and the knowledge we possess are based crucially on sets of basic assumptions and beliefs...[that are] starting points, trusted premises, postulated axioms, presuppositions 'below' which there is no deeper or more final justification, proof, or verification (Okundaye, Smith, & Lawrence-Webb, 2001, p. 46).

For Christians in social work, their core beliefs and values about and commitment to the Christian faith should be ultimately decisive in their lives, beliefs to which the rest of their lives and thinking are appropriately brought into harmony (Wolterstorff, 1984).

Healthy Cautions Regarding the Use of Core Christian Beliefs and Values as Filters

The focus of the chapter thus far has been to describe a model illustrating how Christians in social work can tap their core Christian beliefs and values to support their efforts to weigh the variety of claims they come across each day in their work. Yet there are several points that need to be mentioned to interject some healthy caution into the discussion about what core Christian beliefs and values can (should)—and cannot (should not)—do.

1. *Core beliefs and values are filters, not prescriptions.*

First, with regard to most important issues in social work, there is invariably more than one claim that comports satisfactorily with core Christian beliefs and values. Put another way, for the most part, core Christian beliefs and values do not spell out exactly which specific claims Christians in social work should embrace. Instead, the main contribution of these core beliefs and values is that they act as filters, leading Christian social workers to reject certain *types* of claims or theories which are inconsistent with core beliefs and values. However, once a certain *type* of claim has been shown to comport well with core Christian beliefs and values, Christians in social work in most cases will still have to weigh or evaluate *particular* claims with "the same capacities of imagination" (Wolterstorff, 1984, p. 74) as any other social worker. That is, they must make use of critical thinking, rigorous research (such as that embodied in evidence-based practice), and sober reflection on the world around them. For this reason, different Christians in social work, even when they share the same core Christian beliefs and values, will not all necessarily embrace the same *particular* claims.

Let's look at two examples to illustrate this point. First, take two particular claims: 1) All persons (when they are born) are fundamentally equal in terms of worth and value, and maintain their worth and value regardless of how they live their lives; and 2) All persons (when they are born) are fundamentally equal in terms of worth and value, but some, by indiscriminately taking the lives of others, forfeit at least some measure of the inherent worth and value with which they were originally born.

Arguably, both of these claims are congruent with the core Christian belief that all persons are made in the image of God, and as a result, all human life is sacred and all persons are of infinite worth and value. The key difference is that the latter claim contends that the inherent worth and value with which all persons are born can—at least in extreme cases—be diminished (for example, when a person indiscriminately takes the innocent lives of others). No doubt other particular claims congruent with the core Christian belief that all persons are of infinite worth and value can be found as well. And so it is entirely possible that Christians in social work who hold the same core Christian beliefs and values might embrace significantly different *particular* claims consistent with these core beliefs and values.

Alternatively, it is also possible that social workers who do not hold core Christian beliefs and values might embrace the same particular claims as many Christians in social work (for example, that all persons are born equal in terms of ultimate worth and value, and maintain their worth and value regardless of how they live their lives), even if they embrace these claims for different reasons (that is, based on different core beliefs and values).

In fact, it is even possible that some Christians in social work will agree with their non-Christian colleagues on particular claims (for example, that persons are born equal in terms of ultimate worth and value, and maintain their worth and value regardless of how they live their lives) while disagreeing with the particular claims held by their Christian colleagues (for example, that all persons are born equal in terms of ultimate worth and value, but some, by indiscriminately taking the lives of others, forfeit at least some measure of the inherent worth and value with which they were born).

Let's look at a second example illustrating this point. Take the following claims: 1) Persons with mental illness, because they are fundamentally equal (that is, equal to persons who are not mentally ill), should have equal access to placement on kidney transplant waiting lists; and 2) Persons with mental illness, although they are fundamentally equal (to persons who are not mentally ill), should not have equal access to placement on kidney transplant waiting lists because of their decreased ability to provide the level of medical self-care (taking their medication, following through with medical appointments, etc.) necessary to maximize the chances of a successful kidney transplants.

Again, arguably, both of these particular claims are congruent with the core Christian belief that all persons are made in the image of God, and as a result, all human life is sacred and all persons are of infinite worth and value. The key difference is that the latter claim contends that differences in the abilities of persons with mental illness to maintain a high level of medical self-care after a kidney transplant (differences that are empirically testable) trump other considerations when making the determination about appropriate access to kidney transplant waiting lists.

Since arguably both of these claims are consistent with core Christian beliefs and values, Christians in social work would have to evaluate these disparate claims with "the same capacities of imagination" (Wolterstorff, 1984, p. 74) as any other social worker by making use of critical thinking as well as rigorous research and empirical investigation. Again, it is entirely possible that after weighing the relevant considerations, some Christians in social work would end up embracing the former claim, and some the latter.

2. Core beliefs and values may not be exclusively Christian.

Second, not all of the core beliefs and values held by Christians in social work will be derived solely or even primarily from their Christian faith. For no person is just a Christian. She or he also belongs to a particular ethnic group, is a member of a particular socio-economic class, and likely affiliates with a particular political party, and so on. Identifying with and belonging to different groups typically involves embracing different sets of core beliefs and values, many of which will also function as filters when weighing claims relevant to social work (Wolterstorff, 1984).

3. Core Christian beliefs and values do make a difference.

Third, someone might object that this focus on core Christian beliefs and values as filtering beliefs is only trivially important, since the majority of social work's core values as expressed in the NASW Code of Ethics (commitment to service, social justice, the dignity and worth of persons, the importance of human relationships, integrity and competence) are highly correlated with core Christian beliefs and values anyway. As David Sherwood notes, a Christian worldview "is the soil out of which much of the Code has sprung" (2002, p. 27). Yet while there is a high degree of agreement with regard to these central social work values as cited in the NASW Code of Ethics, there are core Christian beliefs and values that potentially relate to other areas of concern to social workers as well. This last part of the chapter will discuss several additional examples of core Christian beliefs and values that might be used as filters in the weighing of relevant social work claims or theories.

Examples of Core Christian Beliefs and Values from the Literature

Keith-Lucas' Examples of Core Christian Beliefs
Alan Keith-Lucas is one of the earliest (and most prolific) Christians in social work to write about the integration of faith and social work practice. In his *Giving and Taking Help* (1994) and *So You Want to Be a Social Worker: A Primer for the Christian Student* (1985), Keith-Lucas outlines several "basic assumptions" from the Judeo-Christian tradition that are excellent examples of filtering beliefs relevant to social work practice. A small sample of Keith-Lucas' examples includes:

1. Human beings are of infinite worth, irrespective of gender, race, age or behavior. At the same time, humans are created beings, one of whose problems is that they act as if they were not and try to be autonomous.
2. Human beings have been endowed with the faculty of choice and are responsible for the consequences of their choices.
3. Human beings are fallible, but at the same time, sometimes capable, with appropriate help, of transcending themselves and showing great courage or unselfishness.
4. Love is the ultimate victor over evil, including force. Love, understanding and compassion are the source of well-being and acceptable behavior, rather than the reward for them.

Bowpitt's Examples of Core Christian Beliefs
Graham Bowpitt, in his *Social Work and Christianity* (1989) and "Working with Creative Creatures: Towards a Christian Paradigm for Social Work Theory, with Some Practical Implications" (2000), outlines what he calls a "Christian theological anthropology" consisting of a number of core Christian beliefs that are relevant to social work. Several of these include:

1. People are the climax of God's creativity and therefore the result of a purposeful act of will, not mere outcomes of an impersonal evolutionary process with all its deterministic implications.
2. A facet to the Christian view of human nature that social workers have traditionally found particularly hard to stomach is the sinfulness of humankind, particularly the understanding that sin affects every aspect of our humanity at every level (individual, family, community, and society).
3. Because people are made in God's image, they possess many of the attributes of the Creator - intellectual, moral and aesthetic. Of greatest importance

to social work, being made in God's image means people have capacity for self-determination and moral responsibility. They can make moral choices, and are held accountable for them.

4. All persons are potentially redeemable by a re-creative act on the part of the Creator. All persons can be restored by the power of God's grace by a process in which we are active participants, and which transforms every aspect of our beings.

Core Christian Beliefs in Catholic Social Teaching

Catholic social teaching represents a body of social and moral principles articulated in a variety of documents and writings from the Roman Catholic Church. Some core Christian beliefs from Catholic social teaching (*"Catholic social teaching", n.d.*) include:

1. Every person has a fundamental right to life and a right to those things required for human decency including food, shelter and clothing, employment, health care, and education. Human dignity can be protected only if human rights are protected and responsibilities are met with respect to one another, to our families, and to the larger society.

2. The goods of the earth are gifts from God, and are intended for the benefit of everyone. We have a responsibility to care for these goods as stewards and trustees; how we treat the environment is a measure of our stewardship, a sign of our respect for the Creator.

3. The deprivation and powerlessness of the poor in a society wounds the whole community, which can only be healthy if its members give special attention to those who are poor and on the margins of society.

4. Persons are social beings who realize their dignity and rights in relationship with others in community. The obligation to "love our neighbor" includes both an individual dimension, but also a responsibility to contribute to the good of the whole society.

Implications of Core Christian Beliefs for Christians in Social Work

Based on some of these examples of core Christian beliefs and values gleaned from Keith-Lucas, Bowpitt, and Catholic social teaching, what would be some of the *types* of claims—and by extension, social work interventions—that might not be congruent with a Christian perspective? Or put alternatively, what types of claims, theories, or interventions might core Christian beliefs and values tend to filter out? The following represent a few brief illustrations:

1. Claims or theories (or aspects of theories) that view people as *completely* determined by physical, psychological, social or economic forces outside their control do not comport well with basic Christian belief that persons are creative, morally responsible agents accountable to God and each other at the individual as well as societal/structural levels. The implication of the Christian belief here is that even though it may be true that persons are *regularly* constrained in their choices, it is important to maintain that

they are not *completely* so. So for instance, while B.F. Skinner's behaviorism has a great deal to teach us about shaping and changing human behavior, to the degree that it claims all behavior can be exhaustively explained by environmental and genetic factors alone, it remains incompatible with core Christian beliefs and values. It is important to note that such claims are also rejected by the general social work profession, which recognizes persons as bio-psycho-social-emotional-spiritual agents capable of meaningful choice as well.

2. When providing support and services for people in need, there is enormous value in focusing on the strengths, assets, and potential of individuals, groups, and communities. At the same time, claims or theories that presuppose unrealistically high expectations regarding the human ability to prevail over persistent individual and social struggles without acknowledging the deep and pervasive influence of the human condition do not comport well with a Christian understanding of human finitude as well as the effects of persons' profound estrangement from and disrupted relationships with each other and with their Creator. So for instance, Rogers' humanism has a great deal to teach us about the value of treating others with unconditional positive regard when building relationships with and engendering the trust of our clients; to the degree, however, that it claims "if individuals...are accepted for what they are, they will turn out 'good" and live in ways that enhance both themselves and society" (Rowe, 1996, p. 75), it remains in tension with some of our core Christian beliefs and values.

3. Claims that presuppose a clear-cut distinction between worthy/deserving persons and unworthy/undeserving persons do not comport well with the Christian belief that because all persons are made in God's image, all persons have inherent dignity and worth and are therefore deserving of social workers' respect, support and services.

4. Claims or theories that are based on the position that some people in society are beyond all hope for help or a better life (as, for instance, characterized by the expression, "once a user, always a user") do not comport well with a Christian belief that God's love makes possible the healing and transformation of even the most destitute, desperate, and destructive in our communities.

This chapter started by posing the question, "How does the faith of a Christian in social work potentially contribute to and shed new light on how she understands and carries out her social work practice?" This article argues that at least one answer to this question is that to be a Christian in social work means to be thoughtfully engaged in tapping the resources of one's core Christian beliefs and values to help sort out the types of claims and theories one can faithfully embrace as a professional social worker.

It is important to note, however, that this is only *one* answer to the question. For the emphasis of the filtering model of integration described in this paper is clearly *cognitive* in orientation. Of course, persons are not just cognitive beings, but also emotional, psychological, volitional, social, and spiritual beings as well, and each of these dimensions has something important to say about what it means to be a Christian social worker. It would be misleading to leave the impression that what is relevant about being a Christian in social work has *only* to do with one's Christian *beliefs and values*. It's not *only* about one's Christian beliefs and values. But it still is *significantly* about Christian beliefs and values and the role they play in filtering the claims that shape the professional practice of Christians in social work.

References

Bowpitt, G. (1989). *Social work and Christianity*. Handsel.

Bowpitt, G. (2000). Working with creative creatures: towards a Christian paradigm for social work theory, with some practical implications. *British Journal of Social Work*, 30(3), 349-364.

Catholic social teaching. (n.d.). Retrieved December 31, 2005, from http://www.osjspm.org/cst/doclist.htm

Code of ethics of the National Association of Social Workers. (1999). Washington, D.C.: NASW.

Corrigan, P. W., Watson, A. C., Byrne, P., & David, K. E. (2005). Mental illness stigma: Problem of public health or social justice? *Social Work, 50*(4), 363-368.

Keith-Lucas, A. (1985). *So you want to be a social worker: A primer for the Christian student*. St. Davids, PA: NACSW.

Keith-Lucas, A. (1994). *Giving and taking help* (Revised ed.). St. Davids, PA: NACSW.

Okundaye, J. N., Smith, P., & Lawrence-Webb, C. (2001). Incorporating spirituality and the strengths perspective into social work practice with addicted individuals. *Journal of Social Work Practice in the Addictions, 1*(1), 65-82.

Rowe, W. (1996). Client-centered theory: A person-centered approach. In F. Turner (Ed.), *Social work treatment: Interlocking theoretical approaches* (pp. 69-93). New York: The Free Press.

Sherwood, D. (2002). The relationship between beliefs and values in social work practice: Worldviews make a difference. In B. Hugen & L. Scales (Eds.), *Christianity and social work: Readings on the integration of Christian faith and social work practice* (2nd ed., pp. 9-30). Botsford, CT: NACSW.

Singer, P. (1993). *Practical ethics* (2nd ed.). Cambridge: Cambridge University Press.

Singer, P. (1995). *Rethinking life and death: The collapse of our traditional ethics*. Oxford: Oxford University Press.

Wolterstorff, N. (1984). *Reason within the bounds of religion* (2nd ed.). Grand Rapids, MI: Eerdmans.

CHAPTER 8

GOOD NEWS FOR THE POOR: CHRISTIAN INFLUENCES ON SOCIAL WELFARE

Mary Anne Poe

For The United States of America, the wealthiest and most powerful country in the world, the question of what to do about the poor in our midst is a haunting question. How do the poor impact our economy and political system—our freedom and well-being—our rights and privileges? How does American prosperity affect the poor? The United States has to address the problem because of concern for the very ideals that are American. It also has to address the problem because widespread poverty leads inevitably to social unrest.

For Christians, the question of what to do about the poor raises even more critical concerns. How does God want the poor to be treated? What does the Bible say? What is our responsibility as individuals and as part of the church to our poor neighbors? How should Christians try to influence the political and economic systems?

Social welfare programs and policies are a response to questions that arise in each generation. Why should we care about the poor? How do we determine who deserves help and who does not? Should we attempt to change individual hearts or change social structures in order to alleviate poverty? Who is responsible for the poor? Programs and policies always reflect our values about the nature of poor people and our responsibility to them. What we do as a society about poverty, what programs and policies we develop, depends on how we answer these questions.

Like music in a symphony, there have been recurring themes in the relationship between programs and policies serving the poor and the belief systems that inform them. The political, economic, and social context gives shape to particular programs and policies emphasizing specific beliefs that vary across historic periods. Political, economic, and social conditions interact with belief systems in unpredictable ways at various times to influence views of poverty (Dobelstein, 1986). This chapter highlights some of those recurring in history and describes how Christian faith and practice have intersected with the public arena to address needs.

Biblical Principles Regarding the Poor

The Bible records God's revelation to people and how humans have responded to God. The biblical record, taken as a whole, supports specific principles about what it means to be human and how humans should relate to God, to other people, and to the environment. Some of the fundamental premises in the biblical record set the stage for social welfare history. These basic premises have been described in more detail by others (Keith-Lucas, 1989; Sider, 2007), but generally include the following:

- Humans are created beings designed for relationship with others. They are interdependent.
- God is concerned for justice and right relationships among people.
- In these relationships humans can do great good or great harm.
- Humans have the ability and responsibility to choose, perhaps not their particular life circumstances, but how they will respond to their life circumstances.
- Humans have value and dignity.
- Work is a natural part of human nature and contributes to one's sense of worth and dignity.
- The ability to create wealth is a gift.
- Material and environmental resources should be shared. They do not "belong" to any one person or group. Stewardship is the human responsibility to share resources fairly.
- God has a special concern for those who are disadvantaged.

The earliest biblical records reveal distinctive guidelines for the care of the poor. The guidelines are shaped by the covenant relationship of a people with their God who represented love and justice. If God is Creator, then all human life should be treated with respect and care. This is a way to honor God. The guidelines apply not only to individuals and families, but also to the larger community and society.

The ancient Hebrew idea of charity, *tsedekah*, is directly related to the concept of justice (Morris, 1986). The helper benefited from the act of charity as well as the one receiving help. It was a reciprocal benefit that balanced relationships between people. In the Scriptures, God specified the need for interdependent relationships, and charity was an aspect of this. The prophet Micah summed up this principle by stating, "He has showed you, O people, what is good. And what does the Lord require of you? To act justly and to love mercy and to walk humbly with your God" (Micah 6:8). God intended that society benefit by sharing resources among all its members in a just and equitable way.

The Old Testament law specified how the community should provide care and to whom. God's people were supposed to be hospitable to strangers and foreigners (Exodus 22:21; Hebrews 13:2). The Sabbath and Jubilee years restored property and maintained a more equitable distribution of resources (Leviticus 25; Exodus 21: 1-11; Deuteronomy 15: 12-18). Those with wealth were supposed to leave grains in the fields for the poor (Leviticus 19: 9-10; Ruth). Communities and families cared for widows and orphans (Deuteronomy 14: 28-29; 26:12). They were to offer kind treatment to slaves and debtors and provide a means for them to gain their freedom (Deuteronomy 15). Lenders were to make loans without charging interest (Exodus 22: 25; Deuteronomy 15: 1-11).

God is known for avenging the mistreatment of the weak (Psalm 9:8, 12, 16; 10: 17-18). The prophets railed against the people and nations that failed to behave mercifully and justly with the poor. They voiced words of judgment when the laws were ignored (Isaiah 59: 15; Ezekiel 34: 1-6; Amos 4: 1-3; Amos 5: 21-24; Zechariah 7: 8-14; Malachi 3:5). Those who could work were expected to do so, but the laws were aimed at the community and required the kind of compassion toward the poor that God himself had demonstrated. God's word strongly asserts that God is just and wants people to behave in a just and caring way toward one another, and especially toward the weak (Sider, 2007).

The New Testament added a new and more challenging idea to the care of the poor. Jesus' life serves as a model for all to follow. The four Gospels record the behavior of Jesus toward those who were disenfranchised. The message to those who will hear it is to "follow Jesus," do what Jesus did. Jesus asked his followers to love others as he loved. The reason to care about the poor is not simply the reciprocal benefit of charity or obedience to the Old Testament laws, but one's commitment to God. One cares about others, especially the poor, not because it brings benefit but because that person in need is made in the image of God: "Whatever you do for one of the least of these, you did for me" (Matthew 25:40).

The New Testament also proclaims God's concern for justice. Jesus announced his mission in his first public message in the synagogue in Nazareth. He read from the prophet Isaiah,

> The Spirit of the Lord is on me, because he has anointed me to preach good news to the poor. He has sent me to proclaim freedom for the prisoners and recovery of sight for the blind, to release the oppressed, to proclaim the year of the Lord's favor (Luke 4:18-19).

His ministry was characterized by attention to the weak and helpless and oppressed. The early church adopted the same standard of care so that "there was no poverty among them, because people who owned land or houses sold them and brought the money to the apostles to give to others in need" (Acts 4:34). The apostle James warned the church about unequal distribution of material resources (James 5: 1-6) and about prejudicial treatment based on one's social class (James 2: 1-17).

The Bible supports the value of work and the accompanying idea that one's ability to create wealth is a gift. Adam and Eve worked in the Garden even before their fall into sin. The story of Job shows that wealth can be transitory and is subject to God's control. Jesus himself worked as a carpenter. The apostle Paul admonishes believers to "settle down and get to work and earn your own living," and "whoever does not work should not eat" (II Thessalonians 3. 10-12).

Social Welfare History in Western Cultures

Biblical principles about human relationships and God's will for humans have had a profound impact on social welfare history in the Western Hemisphere. The earliest records of church life reveal radical efforts to be sure that material and spiritual needs were met. The book of Acts states that material resources were shared in the community so that none were needy. The early church stressed the need to provide help to the poor even if some that were helped were not deserving of it. The church was a "haven of vital mutual aid within the pagan environment" (Troeltsch, 1960, p. 134).

The charity of the early church was formulated in small Christian communities that had little or no influence on the state in the early years under Roman rule. Christianity began with many, but not all, members from the poorer classes because most people were from these ranks (Stark, 1996). The aim was to show God's love. The church was not a political movement and thus not necessarily directed at prompting social reform.

The human tendency of those with sufficient means to try to distinguish the deserving from the undeserving emerged regularly and in contrast to the earliest biblical teachings. Some early Christian leaders responded to this human tendency toward judgment. Chrysostom of Antioch in the fourth century was a strong advocate for charity based on the need of the giver to share. He was concerned with the heart of the giver and the need for those who had sufficient means to share with those who did not. Gregory of Nanzianus believed that a lack of care for the poor was a greater sin than giving to the undeserving poor (Keith-Lucas, 1989). The tension between the idea of charity as a need of the giver's soul and charity to simply meet the needs of the poor has existed throughout social welfare history.

As Christianity spread through the Roman Empire and beyond, it began to exert more influence on political, economic, and social policies. Thus, by the time Constantine institutionalized Christianity as the "state" religion, biblical ideas of justice and charity held some political power. By the Middle Ages, the church and state were enmeshed with the church taking the lead role in the care of the poor as well as many other matters of political or economic interest. Over time the church's initial interest in showing God's care for the poor was overshadowed by interest in maintaining a seat of power in the political arena. After the Middle Ages, the church's power diminished. The Renaissance, the Industrial Revolution, the Enlightenment, and the Modern Era all had the effect of shifting political and economic power from the church to more secular entities. The locus of control for social welfare shifted as well.

Who Is Responsible for the Social Welfare?

A major theme through history has addressed the question of who is responsible for the poor. As Christianity developed and became more institutionalized, the social welfare system also developed. The church provided social services —not always with compassion or justice- but nevertheless motivated by biblical imperatives. It amassed an enormous amount of property after Constantine's rule and through the Middle Ages, some of which was used to benefit of the poor. The bishop of each diocese was the patron for the poor (Troeltsch, 1960). Hospitals, hospices and sanctuary were typical services provided by the church for those who did not get aid through the feudal system (Keith-Lucas, 1989). Tithing was a prominent aspect of life in the church. Usually one-third of the tithe was designated for the care of the poor (Dolgoff & Feldstein, 2006). The giving of charity became a way to earn one's salvation.

The state was reluctant to assume responsibility for the poor early in western history. In England, The Statute of Labourers in 1349 was the first law enacted that gave government the responsibility. The value of work and a person's responsibility to provide for a family dominated its formulation. The law was less about being charitable and more a means of controlling labor and the behaviors of poor people (Dolgoff & Feldstein, 2006). A series of Poor Laws followed the Statute of Labourers from its passage in 1349 to the mid-1800s. The shift had begun from church responsibility for the poor to government responsibility. Beginning with the Poor Laws, the state gradually accepted a role in oversight. The church and its biblical understandings, though, helped to shape the laws because the bishops sat in the House of Lords and government officials were drawn from the clergy. As government involvement increased, church acceptance of responsibility slowly abated (Popple & Leighninger, 2005). However, individual church members or clergy continued to provide leadership and personnel for the actual work of relief.

Social Control

The need for order has had great popularity during certain periods of time as a way to control the poor. Reasons and motives for helping the poor are numerous. On one extreme is the biblical imperative to love as God loved. Christian believers have Jesus as a model for how to care about the most marginalized and oppressed people. Biblical injunctions include doing justice, showing mercy, valuing every life regardless of circumstances, and personal responsibility and freedom to behave in a manner that contributes to the good of all. At the same time a reason for helping the poor developed out of a need to regulate the social and economic order, to encourage productive work and discourage dependency. The Poor Laws were, in part, designed to regulate labor and the migration of people from one community to another. Minimum wage laws and various tax laws are also a means to regulate poverty through control of the economic system (Piven & Cloward, 1993).

Reasons for helping the poor and efforts toward that end can begin with the best of intentions and after time become sidetracked. The poor can be hurt by the very efforts designed to help. Assistance given in the name of Christ but not in the spirit of Christ is perhaps capable of doing the greatest harm (Keith-Lucas, 1989; Perkins, 1993). Those who profess to help, yet are judgmental, patronizing, or cruel, do not reflect the manner of help prescribed by God. Some would argue that the emergence of state-operated "help" for the poor tended to shift the emphasis from one of charity as outlined by the model of Jesus to one of social control.

Personal Responsibility

During the period of the Protestant Reformation in the church, the culture changed from an agrarian one built on a communitarian spirit to an industrial society focused on individual rights and responsibility. Families were more isolated and less interdependent. Understanding of many biblical principles was shifting as well. Rather than the one Holy Catholic Church representing the biblical tradition and having authority to interpret biblical principles, the reform movement sanctioned individual responsibility to God for understanding and interpreting scripture and for how to live one's faith. Martin Luther, John Calvin, and the Anabaptists stressed personal salvation, and church authority became less hierarchical. Anyone who had faith could relate to God and interpret the Bible. Though all Christian groups continued to give consideration to the poor, the emphasis on personal responsibility meant that the poor, too, were responsible to live holy lives. God would bless faithful believers (Keith-Lucas, 1989).

The reformers were outraged at the abuses of power perpetrated by the church. They decried the greed of the ecclesiastical establishment and sought to restore biblical concern for individual dignity and faith (Couture, 1991). The perspective on social welfare was also shifting. Biblical imperatives to show compassion and mercy had ebbed in relation to the need to urge the poor toward personal responsibility and labor. The "principle of less eligibility" established in the Poor Laws continued to ensure that those who labored would not have less material resources than those who received aid (Dolgoff & Feldstein, 2006). Rigorous scrutiny and early means tests prevented those who were considered "undeserving" from enjoying the benefits of aid. The theology of the Protestant Reformation focused on personal salvation and holiness, challenged church authority as it had been practiced by Roman Catholics, and encouraged hard work and thriftiness. The Protestant work ethic became the standard applied to poor people and to social welfare programs.

The English Poor Laws crossed the Atlantic and shaped the social welfare system in the American colonies (Trattner, 1998; Axinn & Stern, 2004). Still, the Judeo-Christian tradition provided the philosophical basis for treatment of the poor (Hugen & Scales, 2002). Biblical principles, though often misconstrued in actual practice, remained the rationale for the system that existed. The biblical belief in the value of work and the responsibility to care for one's family became the dominant philosophical basis for almost all social welfare programs. Principles that were powerfully informed by the life and work of Jesus and the early church, however, were weakened by the traditions of church and society.

Personal Regeneration and Social Change

Two religious movements of the nineteenth century had particular influence on the administration of social welfare. The first of these was revivalism. The periods of the Great Awakenings stressed personal regeneration and holiness. Those transformed by the power of God were called to service in the world.

The goal for the revivalist was dynamic Christian faith that would change society as a whole. George Whitefield and George Muller established orphanages. Jonathan Edwards advocated for American Indians who were being exploited by settlers. Many leaders of the abolitionist movement were products of revivals, including Harriet Beecher Stowe, John Woolman, and Charles Finney (Cairns, 1986). Numerous social ministries emerged as a result of spiritual revivals. These included urban mission centers, abolitionist societies, the Salvation Army, the Young Men's Christian Association (YMCA), the Women's Christian Temperance Union (WCTU), and Volunteers of America (Smith, 2004; Maguson, 1977; Cairns, 1986). The revivals sparked concern for the spiritual salvation of souls and also for the overall welfare of society (Cairns, 1986; Poe, 2002).

The second religious trend affecting social welfare practices in the nineteenth century was the social gospel movement (Trattner, 1998). Theological liberalism of the nineteenth century was an attempt to make the Christian tradition congruent with the prevailing scientific naturalism of the day. Theologians like Walter Rauschenbusch and Washington Gladden articulated this theology for the academy. Charles Sheldon popularized it with his novel, *In His Steps*. Interestingly, a phrase from this book, "What would Jesus do?" re-emerged in evangelical Christian circles in the last decade of the twentieth century (Poe, 2002). The social gospel focused on building the kingdom of God on earth. It adopted the popular scientific methodologies of the day and hoped for social change based on humanitarian ideals rather than regenerate hearts.

This more liberal theology called into question long-standing "fundamentals" of the faith. The nature of Scripture and the doctrines of creation and Christology were subjected to scientific analysis. Liberal theologies minimized the supernatural aspects of faith while more conservative theologies emphasized them. The divergent theologies caused the two groups to disassociate from each other in their works of service in the world. Whereas liberal theologies contributed to the rise of the profession of social work and increased governmental oversight of social welfare (Wenocur & Reisch, 2001), conservative theologies focused on church growth, evangelism and the future kingdom of God, and distanced themselves from secular attempts to reform society by good works.

Philosophies dominant in the twentieth century in the United States — naturalism, materialism, and capitalism— do not necessarily reflect a Christian worldview that demands care for others because they are valued creations of God. These philosophies emphasize productivity, the value of work and wealth, and order in society. The profession of social work, though, espouses values of celebrating the worth and dignity of every person regardless of their circumstances. As David Sherwood asserts, it is only fair to ask of the profession "where did these values come from and what gives them moral authority?" (Sherwood, 1997, p. 122).

Social Casework and Social Reform

The growth of the profession of social work in the late nineteenth century illustrates another recurring dilemma. Can poverty be eliminated by helping one person at a time—the social casework method. Or is poverty best fought by social reform as reflected in the settlement house movement. Through history, both approaches have been used by church and state. The early church functioned as a community in which no one had need (Acts 4:32-34). The Great Awakenings of the nineteenth century resulted in organized efforts to change aspects of the social order such as abolishing slavery. At other times, the focus was on one individual poor person at a time. For many Christians, poverty is simply a spiritual matter healed by spiritual regeneration. As people are converted, society itself will be transformed. This thinking especially dominates some forms of evangelicalism. For other Christians, poverty is a reflection of an unjust society that needs reform. Conversion of individual souls is not the focus for these Christians, but rather social action.

The state also has approached aid to the poor by addressing individual needs for change as well as changing social structures. Income transfer programs are directed at individual poor people who deserve aid to enable them to rise above poverty level. Programs such as Head Start, though, reflect a broader institutional effort to change the nature of the poor community to allow more equal opportunity in the market place. The Personal Responsibility and Work Opportunity Reconciliation Act (PRWORA) of 1996 captured both of these methods to some extent, though the emphasis is clearly individual reform. In this Act, assistance is time-limited with expectations that the poor will enter the labor market quickly. Individuals can lose benefits if they do not comply with certain lifestyle rules. For example, a mother under age eighteen must live at her parents' home or in another adult-supervised setting and attend school. Welfare mothers must identify the fathers of their children and convicted drug felons need not apply. To encourage steady employment, states can use funds for employment supports like childcare. Tax laws and minimum wage laws are examples of addressing the economic system in order to reduce poverty. The Earned Income Tax Credit is an example of a policy that "helps the poor, rewards work, strengthens the family, and discourages welfare" (Sider, 2007, p. 126).

The Welfare State

The early twentieth century was a period of growth and prosperity for the nation, which was still relatively young. As the free market economy matured, the United States clearly represented the land of opportunity. Immigrants flooded the borders. Natural resources abounded for the consumption of the relatively small population and a political system based on liberty and justice for all created an environment in which anyone supposedly could succeed. By the twentieth century the state was established as the primary caretaker for the poor and in this role often overlooked the contributions made by faith-based organizations (Vanderwoerd, 2002).

A prosperous nation or person tends to have little tolerance for those who cannot or do not succeed. Though Judeo-Christian ideology was still a strong undercurrent for most American life at this time, the increasing strength of liberalism, materialism, and capitalism deeply impacted public welfare policy (Dobelstein,

1986). The American ideals of rugged individualism and hard work suggested that the poor simply needed the influence and advice of those who had succeeded. Material relief was viewed as more handicap than aid. Many felt that material relief and ill-informed charity promoted laziness and pauperism (Wilson, 1996).

The Depression of the 1930's presented an occasion to question views that held individuals alone responsible for their poverty. American society confronted the reality that poverty often was a consequence of the condition of the economic system rather than simply believing that poverty resulted from immoral living or unwise personal decisions. Congress responded with the Social Security Act in 1935 and other New Deal legislative acts that addressed economic needs. The Social Security Act assured aid to the elderly, the needy, the blind, and dependent children. The New Deal established responsibility for the poor firmly in the seat of government (Trattner, 1998; Levitan, Mangum, Mangum, & Sum, 2003).

While faith-based groups continued to provide much relief, the ultimate authority in American society for developing social welfare programming was given to government. What had begun to happen in the latter part of the Middle Ages and during the Industrial Revolution with the Poor Laws was complete. Certainly the philosophical basis for society paying attention to the poor still had some connection with the Judeo-Christian tradition of charity, but in reality the principle of stabilizing the economy and maintaining social order guided policy making. Government had decided that poverty would always be an issue and that it was the role of government to give oversight (Levitan et al., 2003).

Government policies and programs established rigorous means tests to determine a person's eligibility for aid. The presumption persisted that many recipients of aid were out to defraud the generosity of others. The "principle of less eligibility" remained. Aid provided subsistence support but nothing more. Processes for accessing aid were often designed to protect the system rather than serve the needs of the poor. Social welfare had changed quite dramatically from that demonstrated by early Christian believers of the first few centuries after Christ.

Welfare policies since World War II have tended to sway back and forth in levels of generosity. During the Johnson era, the War on Poverty had the lofty vision of eradicating poverty. While its goals were hardly attained, there is some evidence that this era established a safety net for most of the poor (Trattner, 1998). At least most could be assured of having food and basic medical care. In this period, solving the problem of poverty involved adjusting social and economic systems and providing services to support families.

The Reagan/Bush years of the 1980's emphasized different priorities. Poverty was still a problem, but the goal was to eradicate dependency. Programs and services were designed to relieve the federal government of responsibility for the poor and to turn welfare recipients into full participants in the regular market economy. When Clinton became President the goal was to "end welfare as we know it." Welfare reform legislation passed in 1996 with the Personal Responsibility and Work Opportunity Reconciliation Act (PRWORA). This act essentially ended the federal guarantee of help for poor families with dependent children and signaled massive change in the structure and scale of the American social welfare system (Mink, 1999; Dolgoff & Feldstein , 2006; Boyer, 2006; Ozawa & Yoon, 2005). It shifted the administration of relief from the federal government to states in block grants. The act was predicated on the belief that poor relief could be better managed closer to home. The 1996 welfare reform legislation also assumed that the free market system was a level playing field where the poor could be motivated toward self-sufficiency (Wilson, 1996).

The Importance of Social, Political, and Economic Context

By the later twentieth century, the Depression years that prompted the nation to establish a federalized system of public welfare had faded out of memory. Many people believed that the welfare system created in the 1930's spawned a different and dangerous set of values from the American ideals of work, independence, and family. Much in the United States had changed since the earliest European settlements. The economic system was mature and now dominated worldwide markets. Society had evolved from an agrarian one to an industrial one to a tech-nological and global one. Furthermore, the nation that had begun with decidedly Judeo-Christian values had become more and more pluralistic and postmodern. These changes in culture influenced the treatment of the poor and the programs and policies formulated to address their needs. The evangelical Christian focus on personal salvation and holiness reinforced the American belief system that each person must be independent and self-sufficient. Conservative political and economic analysts, such as Charles Murray and Lawrence Mead, ascribed the ills of poverty to the "negative effects of welfare" (Wilson, 1996, p. 164).

The devolution of welfare policy administration from the federal to the state level that occurred in 1996 with PRWORA demonstrates on another level the power of context to influence how people experience the system. Constituent characteristics, such as race, ethnicity and economic well-being, and available resources that vary by state are factors that impact policies and programs of aid. Different approaches by the different states since 1996 reflect a wide range of values and priorities that drive social welfare policy. The combination of variables related to context create distinct and unique policies and services (Fellowes & Rowe, 2004).

The twentieth century had ushered in welfare states, both in the United States and in Europe. A difference in the social welfare systems is found in the fundamentally different premises of American and European thought and the very different political and economic contexts. The two contexts illustrated by the United States and Europe after World War II demonstrate the power of the political, economic, and social context in shaping social welfare policies. After World War II, Europe was devastated. The entire society needed rebuilding. The United States, in contrast, had not experienced as much loss during the war. The Depression that preceded the war had ended and American values of independence and productivity dominated. American welfare has tended to focus on particular groups, such as the aged, blind, disabled, or orphaned. The "doctrine of less eligibility" prevails and the valuing of rugged individualism dominates. The European system places more emphasis on a communitarian belief system. Consequently, social welfare in Europe tends to be more generous and more inclusive. Social benefits related to health care, housing, child care, employment, and income support tend to be applicable to the entire population rather than limited benefits targeted to particular groups as in the United States (Wilson, 1996; Pedersen, 2006).

Faith-Based Initiatives

George W. Bush came into office as President in 2000 with a call for "compassionate conservatism." Those with biblical faith have always been concerned for the poor, but with the rise of the modern welfare states in the United States and Europe, the church has not prioritized a corporate responsibility for social welfare policies and programs. Since welfare reform in 1996 and the election of George W. Bush, the state revisited the idea of collaboration. Charitable Choice provisions in the welfare reform legislation of 1996 opened possibilities again for partnerships between church and state in caring for the poor (Sider, 2007; Sherwood, 1998; Hodge, 2000).

In January 2001, President Bush established the White House Office of Faith-Based and Community Initiatives (OFBCI). He appealed to the old Judeo-Christian tradition of compassion and care for the poor and to the old economic and political view that the poor are often best helped by non-governmental services. The assignment for this office was to strengthen the collaboration of government with faith-based organizations providing social services. The Charitable Choice provisions of the PRWORA of 1996 had opened the doors to partnership between government and faith communities that had essentially been closed since the New Deal of the 1930's (Vanderwoerd, 2002; Sherwood, 1998; Sider, 2007; Hodge, 2000; Sherman, 2003). This raised again the question of who is responsible to care for the poor and how is help best given, whether the state or faith-based initiatives should be the driving force behind social welfare policy (Belcher, Fandetti, & Cole, 2004).

Global Context

While economic prosperity and tax cuts, education reform, and faith-based initiatives were Bush's emphases upon taking the oath of office in January 2001, the terrorist events of September 11, 2001 radically changed the political and economic landscape. Global realities and needs took center-stage and displaced concern for domestic social welfare policy. Attention on the war in Iraq and Afghanistan, extreme poverty in much of the world, and the continuing ravages of AIDS and other diseases has diverted much public attention away from the "compassionate conservatism" directed at domestic policy that carried Bush into office. The American public has struggled to find a balance between concern for safety from terrorism and engagement with world problems and concern for the social and economic well-being of its own citizens in need.

Christians believing the call to follow Jesus should be very concerned about global social welfare. For the richest and most powerful nation on earth to continue living in its ease while having knowledge of devastating poverty, disease, and war in some nations evokes the prophetic voice of the Old Testament: "Away with your hymns of praise! They are only noise to my ears. I will not listen to your music, no matter how lovely it is. Instead I want to see a mighty flood of justice, a river of righteous living that will never run dry" (Amos 5:23). "I despise the pride and false glory of Israel, and I hate their beautiful homes. I will give this city and everything in it to their enemies" (Amos 6:8).

Biblical faith calls Christians to practice good citizenship by being engaged in the public discourse about social welfare policies and programs and the impact of all policies on the poor in the world. The reality for the twenty-first century is a global economy. It is this political and economic context that will shape U.S. policy in the years ahead. Today, social welfare policies are inevitably linked to the global marketplace. Minimum wage laws, immigration laws, labor and trade laws will all influence how the poor are treated in the United States as well as around the world. The relationship of faith-based organizations and their provision of social services with the government system of social services will also continue to be a dominant theme.

Conclusion

The biblical narrative primarily challenges the non-poor to create conditions for the poor that are just and caring. God does not allow the prosperous to simply wallow in their comfort. In so doing, they become oppressors. Rather, God wants people to have open hands and hearts to the poor, to overflow with generosity and concern. The responsibility is given to family, friends, and community to offer "a liberal sufficiency so that their needs are met" (Sider, 2007, p.86).

Details of time and place vary dramatically. Social, political, religious, and economic systems create contexts that warrant a variety of methods and approaches to dealing with poverty and influence understanding of the poor. The Bible says that we will have the poor with us always (Deuteronomy 15:11; Matthew 26:11). The biblical imperative to care for the poor and the weak in a manner that empowers them and values their worth and dignity as persons has not changed. What distinguishes followers of Christ is a fundamental commitment to continually work to support the most vulnerable members of society, for all are God's children and made in God's image. Whether it is organizing a soup kitchen or challenging tax policies, the call of God for Christians is to bring good news to the poor. This is the mission for social workers as well.

References

Axinn, J., & Stern, M. (2004). *Social welfare: A history of the American response to need* (6ᵗʰ ed.). Boston: Allyn and Bacon.

Belcher, J. R., Fandetti, D., & Cole, D. (2004). Is Christian religious conservatism compatible with the liberal social welfare state? *Social Work, 49(2),* 269-276.

Boyer, K. (2006). Reform and resistance: A consideration of space, scale, and strategy in legal challenges to welfare reform. *Antipode, 38(1),* 22-40.

Cairns, E. E. (1986). *An endless line of splendor: Revivals and their leaders from the Great Awakening to the present.* Wheaton, IL: Tyndale House.

Couture, P. D. (1991). *Blessed are the poor? Women's poverty, family policy, and practical theology.* Nashville, TN: Abingdon Press.

Dobelstein, A. W. (1986). *Politics, economics, and public welfare.* Englewood Cliffs, NJ: Prentice-Hall, Inc.

Dolgoff, R., & Feldstein, D. (2007). *Understanding social welfare : A search for social justice (7ᵗʰ ed.).* Boston, MA: Allyn & Bacon Publishers.

Fellowes, M. C., & Rowe, G. (2004). Politics and the new American welfare states. *American Journal of Political Science, 48(2),* 362-373.

Hodge, D. R. (1998). Welfare reform and religious providers: An examination of the new paradigm. *Social Work and Christianity, 25(1),* 24-48.

Hugen, B. & Scales, T.L. (Eds.). (2002). *Christianity and social work: Readings on the integration of Christian faith and social work practice.* Botsford, CT: North American Association of Christians in Social Work.

Hurst, C. E. (2006). *Social inequality: Forms, causes, and consequences* (6ᵗʰ ed.). Needham Heights, MA: Allyn and Bacon.

Keith-Lucas, A. (1989). *The poor you have with you always: Concepts of aid to the poor in the western world from biblical times to the present.* St Davids, PA: North American Association of Christians in Social Work.

Levitan, S. A., Mangum, G. L., Mangum, S. L., & Sum, A.M. (2003). *Programs in aid of the poor* (7ᵗʰ ed.). Baltimore: Johns Hopkins University Press.

Magnuson, N., & Magnuson, B. (2004). *Salvation in the slums: Evangelical social work, 1865-1920.* Eugene, OR: Wipf & Stock Publishers..

Mink, G. (Ed.). (1999). *Whose welfare?* Ithaca, NY: Cornell University Press.

Morris, R. (1986). *Rethinking social welfare: Why care for the stranger?* New York: Longman.

Ozawa, M. N., & Yoon, H. (2005). "Leavers" from TANF and AFDC: How do they fare economically? *Social Work, 50(3),* 239-249.

Pedersen, S. (2006). *Family, dependence, and the origins of the welfare state: Britain and France, 1914-1945.* New York: Cambridge University Press.

Perkins, J. (1993). *Beyond charity: The call to Christian community development.* Grand Rapids, MI: Baker Books.

Piven, F., & Cloward, R. (1993). *Regulating the poor: The functions of public welfare.* New York: Random House.

Poe, M. A. (2002). Christian worldview and social work. In D. S. Dockery & G. A. Thornbury (Eds.), *Shaping a Christian worldview: The foundations of Christian higher education* (pp. 317-334). Nashville, TN: Broadman & Holman.

Popple, P. R., & Leighninger, L. (2005). *Social work, social welfare, and American society.* (6ᵗʰ ed). Boston: Allyn and Bacon.

Sherman, A. L. (2003). Faith in communities: A solid investment. *Society, 40(2),* 19-26.

Sherwood, D. A. (1997). The relationship between beliefs and values in social work practice: Worldviews make a difference. *Social Work and Christianity, 24(2)*, 115-135.

Sherwood, D. A. (1998). Charitable choice: Opportunities and challenge for Christians in social work. *Social Work and Christianity, 25(1)*, 1-23.

Sider, R. J. (2007). *Just generosity: A new vision for overcoming poverty in America*. Grand Rapids, MI: Baker Books.

Smith, T. L. (2004). *Revivalism and social reform: American Protestantism on the eve of the Civil War.* Gloucester, MA: Peter Smith Publishing.

Stark, R. (1996). *The rise of Christianity: A sociologist reconsiders history*. Princeton, NJ: Princeton University Press.

Trattner, W. I. (1998). *From Poor Law to welfare state: A history of social welfare in America.* New York: The Free Press.

Troeltsch, E. (1960). *The social teaching of the Christian churches*. Chicago: University of Chicago Press.

Vanderwoerd, J. R. (Spring, 2002). Is the newer deal a better deal? Government funding of faith-based social services. *Christian Scholar's Review, 31(3)*, 301-318.

Wenocur, S., & Reisch, M. (2001). *From charity to enterprise: The development of American social work in a market economy*. Urbana, IL: University of Illinois Press.

Wilson, W. J. (1996). *When work disappears: The world of the new urban poor.* New York: Alfred A. Knopf.

CHAPTER 9

"I AM MAKING EVERYTHING NEW!" BIBLICAL THEMES FOR MACRO PRACTICE

Jim R. Vanderwoerd

Social workers of all stripes are familiar with the "person-in-environment" perspective and how it provides a framework and justification for social work practice across a breadth of contexts ranging from individuals, couples, and families through groups, organizations, communities, all the way to institutions and even entire societies (Timberlake, Farber & Sabatino, 2002, pp. 10-14). The latter end of that continuum is often called macro practice and is broadly defined as planned change by professional social workers within community, organizational, administrative, and policy contexts in which the focus is on improving the social well being of particular individuals and groups, especially focusing on those who are most vulnerable and disadvantaged. As Popple and Leighninger (2004) note, in an individualistic society, the macro end of the continuum is often a tough sell; aspiring social work students often resist learning about change efforts directed beyond individuals, and much of the emphasis in professional circles still leans towards individual practice.

This challenge may be just as problematic for Christians in social work. Faith seems to be a personal matter to many Christians, and there is a tendency among some evangelical, Protestant Christians in particular, to focus excessively on one's personal relationship with Jesus at the expense of broader social concerns (Sider, 2005). Social work educators have had to be intentional and persistent to maintain macro perspectives in the curriculum and find ways to inspire and challenge new generations of social workers. This is no less true in Christian social work programs. This chapter provides a rationale for the place of macro practice as an appropriate and essential element of social work practice that is rooted in a biblically informed worldview (see Sherwood, chapter 2). Three broad biblical themes are discussed: 1) the person and work of Jesus Christ and his death and resurrection; 2) the overarching framework of the biblical story from creation through human disobedience in the fall and God's design to restore and renew his creation; and, 3) the biblical story as a drama that we not only read as observers, but place ourselves within as actors in the drama. Drawing on these three themes, the chapter then discusses the implications of these themes in two areas. Our understanding of the biblical story shapes first how we view ourselves as individuals doing social work macro practice, and second, how we view social problems and our attempts to resolve them.

Three Biblical Themes

The late Harry Specht, respected social work educator and author, stirred up a controversy within the profession in 1990 by boldly claiming:

> Social work has been diverted from its original vision, a vision of the perfectibility of society, the building of the 'city beautiful', the 'new society', and the 'new frontier' (Specht, 1990, p. 354).

Specht was not the first or the last to lament the trend in the profession of focussing on individual problems rather than the broader conditions which lead to such problems. For most of its history, in fact, the social work profession has been conflicted and ambivalent about the appropriate balance between micro and macro emphases (Haynes & Mickelson, 2003, ch. 3). Specht followed up this argument with the even more controversial book *Unfaithful Angels: How Social Work Abandoned Its Mission* in which he and co-author Mark Courtney argued that the social work profession had sold out to the "popular psychotherapies" and had abandoned its mission to address the larger structural and systemic injustices of poverty and discrimination that were at the root of most social problems (Specht & Courtney, 1994).

A small but important detail was lost in the controversy. In the first chapter of the book, based largely on the earlier 1990 article, the same passage appears, but this time, Specht dropped the phrase 'city beautiful' from the description of social work's original vision. Christians (and perhaps others) immediately recognize the 'city beautiful' image from Revelation 21:

> Then I saw "a new heaven and a new earth," for the first heaven and the first earth had passed away, and there was no longer any sea. I saw the Holy City, the new Jerusalem, coming down out of heaven from God, prepared as a bride beautifully dressed for her husband. And I heard a loud voice from the throne saying, "Look! God's dwelling place is now among the people, and he will dwell with them. They will be his people, and God himself will be with them and be their God. 'He will wipe every tear from their eyes. There will be no more death or mourning or crying or pain, for the old order of things has passed away." He who was seated on the throne said, "I am making everything new!" (Revelation 21: 1-5, Today's New International Version).

Is this what the social work profession has in mind when it envisions the "perfectibility of society"? Although most social workers would welcome a world with no more death, mourning, crying, or pain, it strains belief to imagine that the social work profession today would ever endorse such an explicit biblical, Christian vision, despite the fact that Christians, motivated by the biblical call to show love to their neighbors, to provide for the "least of these", and right the injustices arising from urbanization and industrialization, were instrumental in establishing the profession of social work in the 19th and early 20th centuries (Christie & Gauvreau, 1996; Cnaan, Wineburg & Boddie, 1999; Marty, 1980).

I would submit that the biblical vision of the city of God is not just one among several images for the "perfectibility of society," but is precisely at the heart of what it means for Christians to engage in social work practice at the macro level. In fact, Specht's inadvertent inclusion of this explicitly biblical image captures the grand vision of renewal, redemption, restoration, and reconciliation—everything made new—that goes far beyond any possibility evoked by the "new society" or the "new frontier." Christian social workers have our hope in a future without pain, hurt, illness, or tragedy that simply is not possible outside the transforming work of God our Father, through Christ's victory over sin and death on the cross and the power of the Holy Spirit.

Christ and the Cross

Christians across time and space confess that the starting point for understanding our world through God's revelation in scripture is Jesus Christ, God's Son, Messiah, and Lord over all. As eloquently put in John 1 and Revelation 21:6 everything begins and ends with Jesus:

> In the beginning was the Word, and the Word was with God, and the Word was God. He was with God in the beginning (John 1:1-2).

> I am the Alpha and the Omega, the Beginning and the End (Revelation 21:6).

The implications of this confession are fleshed out in poetic style in Paul's letter to the Colossians, where the essence of Christ's identity as the Origin, Reconciler, and Ruler over all things is made startlingly clear:

> The Son is the image of the invisible God, the firstborn over all creation. For in him all things were created: things in heaven and on earth, visible and invisible, whether thrones or powers or rulers or authorities; all things have been created through him and for him. He is before all things, and in him all things hold together. And he is the head of the body, the church; he is the beginning and the firstborn from among the dead, so that in everything he might have the supremacy. For God was pleased to have all his fullness dwell in him, and through him to reconcile to himself all things, whether things on earth or things in heaven, by making peace through his blood, shed on the cross (Colossians. 1:15-20).

Brian Walsh and Sylvia Keesmaat (2004), in their contemporary restatement of this poem, emphasize that Christ's victory on the cross is not simply a victory over individual death and sin, but over all the powers and principalities that stand against God and his Kingdom. Jesus' death and resurrection, therefore, have implications far beyond the forgiveness of individuals' sins, but reach to every part of the universe. When in macro social work we seek to change structures and systems that are unjust and oppressive, we are participating in

Jesus' redemptive work for all creation. Christians understand that the person and work of Jesus Christ are the singular dominant focal point through which we understand, not just our own past, present and future, but all of history.

Creation – Fall – Redemption

Jesus Christ and his victory over sin and death on the cross stand at the fulcrum of the biblical story. This story begins with creation's origin in God's spoken word, continues through humankind's disobedience and the distortion of God's goodness in creation through sin, and moves on through God's redemption plan in Jesus. Social work deals with human hurt and brokenness, and the bible provides a compelling account of God's mighty work to restore the brokenness that distorted his good creation. In an individualistic culture, North American Christians too quickly limit God's work of salvation to a one-time act directed only to individual souls. As Eugene Peterson (2005, pp. 137-148) notes, however, salvation is the entire, monumental undertaking that God orchestrated to reverse a creation spiralling down into sin, and steer it, instead, back in the direction He intended. Salvation, therefore, is far more than that your and my sins are forgiven and that we are right before God. Instead, salvation is the relentless creep of God's plan reaching into all the nooks and crannies of what He made to restore creation to its original goodness. Social work is a human profession that seeks to bring healing to human pain, and the biblical drama of God's salvation plan shows unequivocally that the work of healing cannot be limited to individuals. Sin is much more than individual failing (Gauer, 2005), and salvation, therefore, is much more than forgiveness of individual sins.

Within this overarching framework is the idea that God's work of creation includes not only the physical and material world of nature, but also the social and cultural developments throughout history. Wolters (1985) describes this by noting the distinction between laws, which cover the proper ordering of the physical world, such as laws of gravity, thermodynamics, temperature, and so on, and *norms* which set forth God's intentions for various social and cultural arrangements, such as the family, marriages, schools, the state, art, and music. The main difference is that while the nonhuman aspects of God's creation cannot choose to disobey God's laws, the human aspects of creation can: thus, people can disobey God's norms in marriage, art, politics, schools, and so on.

Of course, just saying this does not tell us exactly what those norms are. The Bible does not give precise or specific norms for most social and cultural institutions and developments in the 21st century. For example, we cannot simply take biblical examples (like Paul's admonition against women keeping their heads uncovered, or the proper treatment of slaves) as providing detailed norms for what it means to be obedient regarding issues of women's behaviors or slavery. This admittedly moves us into very shaky ground, because we do not have perfect insight into God's norms, and thus need to be very humble about what we propose is "right" or "wrong" in any given social or cultural arrangements (Mouw, 1992). Nevertheless, this understanding opens the way to see that social and cultural arrangements cannot simply be labelled as "pagan"or "worldly," but fall fully under the claims of Jesus' authority, and are subject to God's work of reconciliation and redemption.

Following from this understanding of creation, the bible's account of Adam and Eve's disobedience and the fall of creation into sin also informs our understanding of current social arrangements (and particularly how we understand when they go wrong—which they often do). The bible tells us that sin is not simply an individual breakdown of the relationship between God and humans, or even of a break in relationships between people, but also includes all of God's creation (Romans 8:20-22). The grand inclusive sweep of God's hand in all of creation also means that sin has permeated all of creation as well. Nothing is untouched or unscarred. Accordingly, the reach of sin extends into social institutions and cultural arrangements as well, such that we recognize that these represent something less than what God intended. Human agency in realizing and developing social and cultural practices and arrangements has occurred in the context of a sin-tainted world in which all is not what God meant it to be (Plantinga, 1995). Humans have devised these arrangements as sinful beings, and, being entwined within the social institutions, they have developed a sinful character, even while God's active hand in creation ensures their goodness.

Fortunately, God did not leave sin to run its course. Rather, from the moment sin entered his creation, God set off on a course to head it off and ultimately conquer it. Not that this was without its rough moments along the way. For example, early on, the biblical story provides an astonishing revelation of the mind of God, showing our God to be personally invested in His creation. Genesis 6 recounts that when God saw the mess that humans had made in His world, "The LORD regretted that he had made human beings on the earth, and his heart was deeply troubled" (Gen. 6: 6). Lawrence Ressler, in an eloquent devotion, summarizes God's response as follows:

> But God did not destroy his creation. He began a process of reconciliation—taking individuals one at a time, groups one at a time and remaking them. First there was Noah, then Abraham, Isaac, Jacob—on and on throughout history. God cared enough to not give up on his creation. He cared enough to send his son, God incarnate, to live among us, suffer for and with us, that we might live again" (1994, p. 1).

We see in God's work that His redemption vision goes far beyond only personal, individual sin. Isaiah 65 and Revelation 21 both provide dramatic and heart warming images of God's intent to restore and renew his entire creation. In Romans 8 Paul speaks of *all* creation groaning and waiting for God's salvation. It is clear in this passage that God's redemption plan is not restricted to individual human sin but to the entire breadth of creation. What is also revealed in the biblical account of God's plan to bring about the renewal and redemption of his creation is the particular means which God chooses to use: God works his plans through human actions and in the context of human history, including social workers working to bring about healing in individuals and families, and seeking change in neighborhoods, communities, and organizations.

Putting Ourselves in God's Story

To fully grasp God's redemption plans realized through humans in history we need to step back from the bible's details and read the bible as the all-encompassing story of God and his work (Bartholomew & Goheen, 2004; Wolters, 1985). Bartholomew and Goheen, in *The Drama of Scripture* (2004), suggest that the bible is a drama that can be told in six acts: Act I: creation, Act II: fall, Act III: redemption initiated through the people of Israel, Act IV: redemption accomplished in Jesus' death and resurrection, Act V: the spreading kingdom of God through Christ's body, the church, and Act VI: the final establishment of the kingdom of God in the return of Christ.

Of course, it is not just Christians who live by and in stories; everybody does. As sociologist Christian Smith (2003) makes so clear, telling stories and using them as a way of understanding who one is and how one ought to live is a fundamental characteristic of virtually every human community. According to Smith (2003):

> ...we not only are animals who make and tell narratives but also animals who are told and made by our narratives. The stories we tell are not mere entertainment. Nor do they simply suggest for us some general sense of our heritage. Our stories fully encompass and define our lives. They situate us in reality itself, by elaborating the contours of fundamental moral order... Our individual and collective lives come to have meaning and purpose insofar as they join the larger cast of characters enacting, re-enacting, and perpetuating the larger narrative. It is by finding ourselves placed within a particular drama that we come to know our role, our part, our lines in life—how we are to act, why, and what meaning that has in the larger scheme of reality (p. 78).

In addition to the Christian narrative, Smith also identifies several other narratives that shape current Western civilizations (for example, the American Experiment, Capitalist Prosperity, Progressive Socialist, Scientific Enlightenment) as well as others from non-western cultures (for example, Militant Islamic Resurgence, or Divine Life and Afterlife associated with eastern religions and cultures).

One of the contributions of postmodernist thinking has been to draw explicit attention to the way narratives are used to justify the imposition of one group's culture and way of life onto others in patterns that are oppressive (Middleton & Walsh, 1995). For example, aboriginal peoples around the world have challenged their colonization at the hands of white European cultures which interpreted their conquest of native lands as the story of the advancement of progress and civilization. The postmodern solution has been to make space for *every* narrative and favor none. Ironically, postmodernists seem not to recognize that their plea to just let everyone have their own story is itself based on a narrative which they impose on everyone else.

The fact that postmodernism itself tells a story which it imposes on others does not by itself deflect the postmodern critique. The Christian narrative *has* been used in oppressive ways at least as much as (and, according to many, more than) other narratives to silence minority voices and cultures. As Middleton and Walsh (1995) point out, "the problem, from a postmodern point of view, is that the Scriptures ... constitute a metanarrative that makes universal claims.... [T]he biblical story has, in fact, often been used ideologically to oppress and exclude those regarded as infidels or heretics" (p. 83- 84).

A quick tour through the six acts of the drama of scripture demonstrates that the biblical story is *not*, despite the postmodern critique, a story that oppresses, but rather—in the long run—one which identifies with the suffering of the vulnerable and that liberates them from oppression. The story begins with a God who is introduced as the creator of a world he called good, crowned with humans who were *very* good. No sooner dubbed good, however, humans attempt to seize control, taking their God-given authority and turning it immediately to their own selfish aims. These dramatic events (Acts I and II) occur in the first three chapters of the Bible, followed by a long and often convoluted story of how God set about to work through human means and in human history to restore the good in creation that humans had poisoned. Act III tells of how God chooses Abraham to establish the people of Israel as a means of bringing blessing to all nations (Gen. 12:1-3; Gen. 18:18). Act III is a long act with many scenes; the gist of it is that God remains faithful to his promise to use Israel as his means for bringing blessing, even though Israel continues through seemingly endless cycles of disobedience from the repeated refrain in Judges—"again the Israelites did evil in the eyes of the Lord"—all the way through the exile. Act IV reveals the central thrust for how God uses Israel as a means to bring right from wrong; namely, in the person and work of Jesus Christ, who is descended from and born into the context of the nation of Israel.

Perhaps here we might expect the Hollywood ending, where the good guy defeats the enemy, runs him out of town, and everyone lives happily ever after. But, that is not how God chose to act. Rather, Jesus' ministry is one of service and humility leading to death; after his resurrection, he leaves behind a tiny band of demoralized followers. But, Act V shows how Jesus sent his Spirit—as he promised—to move mightily among his followers and equip them for the task of spreading the news of the victory of Jesus' resurrection over sin and death.

If the first scene of Act V is the early church spreading throughout the Roman Empire, then we could view the story of the church since then as Scene Two (Bartholomew & Goheen, 2004). For Christians, the Bible is not simply a collection of inspiring stories about other people; this is *our* story. We can understand our place in the world and make sense of the events of our time and place in terms of this drama, in which we join with the "cloud of witnesses" (Hebrews 12:1) and are now part of God's unfolding plan to reclaim and renew his creation by using humans to accomplish his purposes. The final act of this drama has not yet occurred, but we know with absolute certainty from the biblical story that it *will* come. In Revelation, and in several of the Old Testament prophets, we get glimpses of what Act VI will look like, although it seems clear that there is much more we don't know. To the postmodern critique that our story oppresses others, we must first acknowledge and confess those times when we have performed our part in the story in ways that have been oppressive. But then, we can point out that the God-authored story is consistently one where the weak and the vulnerable are not oppressed but lifted up and liberated, in much the same way that Jesus declared the launch of his ministry on earth:

> The Spirit of the Lord is on me, because he has anointed me to proclaim good news to the poor. He has sent me to proclaim freedom for the prisoners and recovery of sight for the blind, to set the oppressed free, to proclaim the year of the Lord's favor (Luke 4:18-19).

In that Spirit, we can confidently take our place in God's story, looking ahead to the promised time when "there will be no more death or mourning or crying or pain" (Revelation. 21:4).

Implications for Social Work Macro Practice

So what does this all mean for macro social work practice? How do these biblical themes shape a Christian understanding of social work with communities, organizations, and larger systems? What implications do these themes have for the way we understand our work as Christians in social work seeking to be agents of change in our neighborhoods, churches, agencies, towns, cities, and countries?

It is my contention that the implications of a biblical vision for macro practice in social work are mostly invisible. For the most part, it is not so much in the specific strategies, tactics, and actions where one clearly sees a "Christian" approach to macro practice as compared to a so-called "secular" approach. Suppose a visitor arrives right in the middle of a neighborhood association planning meeting. Would that visitor be able to tell from the way the community worker ran the meeting whether she was a Christian or not? I doubt it. But, imagine if the visitor interviewed the community worker extensively about her motivations, her goals, and how she understood the challenges and particularities of her work. I would guess that it would only be a matter of time before it would start to become clear what that worker's fundamental convictions were.

That became clear to me in my own experience as a community worker working alongside colleagues, community residents, and social service agency representatives from all walks of life. I do not think that my work stood out as uniquely distinctive from my fellow community participants because I was a Christian. But, I recall clearly a discussion at one meeting where fundamental differences—often submerged—poked through the surface. The neighborhood association and the community project staff were planning to join a province-wide "Women's March Against Poverty" to protest a 22% reduction of income assistance rates for single mothers on welfare. Some of the neighborhood women were despairing about whether any good would come out of participating in a protest, to which the community worker, a seasoned veteran, replied:

It may feel hopeless now, but look back at how far we've come. Women in this country have made a lot of gains, and it's because people like us have stood up and fought back. Maybe it won't be tomorrow or next month or even next year, but I just know that this will make a difference, and that things can get better for poor women and children in this country. I just picture in my mind my own great-grandkids looking back on the 20th century and being amazed at how backward we were then. And that's because of the difference that *we* made. We can do it. What we do *will* make a difference. Someday—I don't know when—but someday, this country will treat poor women and families with respect, and we won't have the kind of poverty we see around us now, and *it will be because of us*. I know in my heart that this will happen.

I remember the glow in the room as her words sunk in. The women around the table were visibly moved and uplifted by the worker's passionate encouragement, and I nodded fervently in agreement. But, something bothered me about it, something I couldn't quite put my finger on at the moment. Over the next several days it continued to niggle at the back of my mind, and then it became clearer: This was not my story. When I peered into the future and imagined what my own great grandchildren might say about the state of the world in their day compared to mine, I didn't imagine them patting themselves on the back because of social workers' victories that led to their current golden age. No, I pictured the biblical vision: "See, I will create new heavens and a new earth, says the Lord" (Isaiah 65: 17, 25; emphasis added).

Later, I asked my colleague about her impassioned speech. We had a relationship of mutual trust and respect, and she knew I was a Christian. So I asked her point blank: "What do you think the future holds and how will we get there?" We talked at length about our respective visions of the future, and what we were really talking about is the different stories that each of us was living in, and how those stories reflected and shaped our understanding of ourselves and our work. Her story was essentially what I would characterize as the modern progress myth; more specifically, the one shaped by conflict, Marxist and feminist theorists, as well as by the social gospel movement: society's ills can be attributed to the lack of compassion of the rich (i.e., male capitalists) for the poor, and through the concerted efforts of citizens and enlightened professionals, we will one day (sooner or later, although it's not clear when) eliminate every form of oppression and create, in the words of former USA President Lyndon B. Johnson, the "great society". Added to this modern story was a healthy dose of postmodern sensibility that oppression originates in anyone attempting to foist their reality on others; therefore, the prescription for the great society is not just the march of progress envisioned by the socially enlightened, but also involves liberating the voices of those who have been excluded and marginalized.

Two things need to be said about this story. First, of course, is that it is oversimplified: in reality there are a great many variations (see Smith, 2003, chapter 4), and there is as much disagreement as agreement. Even in this simplified version, however, my colleague grudgingly admitted that this was a reasonable depiction of what she sees down the road. Second, I agree with a lot of it. I *do* think that citizens and professionals can make a difference, that oppression of the powerful should be challenged, and that the voiceless need to be given a space to have their say. What kind of a social worker in macro practice would I be if I disagreed with any of this? But it's the ultimate end of the story where I part ways with my colleagues who live in (a) different stories(y). As I've already described earlier, as a Christian, I live in God's story, told (in part) in His revealed Word (although much is yet to be revealed and still being told). When I look ahead in the story, I definitely do not see a future where we social workers, together with other enlightened activists, have figured out just the right way to build communities, lobby governments, regulate corporations and do whatever else it takes to manufacture with human hands some version of a perfect world. In fact, left to human devices, I would, frankly, be in despair about our collective future. But God's story is one of hope wrought from brokenness; where God inserts himself into human life by sending His Son to walk among us and turn the whole thing around and upside down.

Living in that story is what makes me most different from my colleagues who live in different stories. What we each do in the living / telling, as I noted above, may look quite similar, if not, at times, exactly the same. I still participated in that women's march against poverty. I still lobbied my provincial legislators. I still strategized with my fellow citizens to promote local businesses in my city and block the preferential treatment of big box retailers. I still joined with others on my campus to raise awareness of the plight of immigrant trailer park dwellers being forced out of their homes by university administrators. True, there are times when certain tactics or activities themselves might be viewed as being "unchristian." In my experience, however, the line between acceptable and unacceptable tactics is as much in evidence among Christians as it is between Christians and others.

But living in the biblical story does have other implications for how we work and how we understand our work in macro practice. I contend that to be a Christian in macro social work practice is not so much a matter of identifying particular Christian tactics or activities, but rather of highlighting several themes that flow from living within the biblical story. One theme centers around our understanding of ourselves as individuals, while the second major theme concerns how we view our work.

Who We Are

Living in the biblical story provides an important way to understand our identity, and therefore shapes our thinking, our behavior and actions, and our relationships. A central aspect of our identity as humans is an ironic paradox: compared to the all-powerful, all-knowing God, we humans are really quite inconsequential. Psalm 8 asks, "What are mere mortals that you are mindful of them?" (Psalms 8: 4). It turns out that in the biblical drama humans don't play the hero's role. True, human characters are involved in all parts of the story, but their conduct leaves much to be desired. The humans in the biblical story mostly make mistakes, act selfishly, are prone to violence, lack good judgment, and otherwise thwart God's good designs even when they intend otherwise or claim to be advancing God's plan. And if we place ourselves as actors in later acts of this story, we must acknowledge that our conduct isn't much better than the biblical characters. Recognizing our sin through confession and repentance is a fundamental part of the Christian life, and I would submit that the primary stance we ought to adopt in seeking change is one of humility. We ought to temper our arrogance and remind ourselves that we don't always know what is best, that our prescription for this policy, or that program, or the other community initiative may be just plain wrong. But, recognizing our human limits should not stop us from trying; it certainly does not stop God from choosing to use us.

Through God's grace, weakness and failure are only part of being human. Psalm 8 doesn't end with a lament for human smallness, but goes on to the more amazing side of the paradox: that despite our weakness, God elevates us to special status and gives us unparalleled authority and responsibility:

> You have made them a little lower than the heavenly beings
> and crowned them with glory and honor.
> You made them rulers over the works of your hands;
> you put everything under their feet (Psalms 8: 5-6).

When we place ourselves within the biblical story, we see repeatedly that God chooses to use humans to advance his designs. Psalm 8 uses royal language to describe how important we are to God, and this language is echoed in Paul's second letter to the Corinthians where he describes us as "ambassadors" of reconciliation (II Corinthians 5:17-20). Webster's Dictionary defines an ambassador as "the *highest-ranking* diplomatic representative appointed by one country or government to represent it in another" (Webster's, 2002; emphasis added). As Paul describes it, in God's plan to reconcile all things to himself, he appointed us as the primary agents to carry out his plans. This is a high calling indeed, and one that carries enormous responsibility and authority.

So to be human means to be both weak and strong; to be cognizant of our limits and failures, but rather than be immobilized by this awareness, to respond eagerly to God's appointment of us as his representatives to do his work. To seek change in the communities, organizations, and systems of which we are a part means to be both humble and confident. Recognizing that we are human entails acknowledging that we are the *created*, not the *Creator*. Thus, our role as ambassadors is an important calling and a responsibility, but ultimately not a necessity in God's designs. To put it starkly, God uses us, but he doesn't need us. He could accomplish his purposes without us—in fact, he could do it more easily and quickly without us. Just as a parent allows a toddler to sweep the kitchen floor, God allows us to carry out his work, even though, as a parent, he could do it easier and quicker himself.

Two corollary insights are worth mentioning here. First, the quality of our work and our willingness to do it will not make the difference between the success or failure of accomplishing God's "new heavens and new earth" vision.

The new heavens and the new earth are coming sooner or later, and nothing we do is going to stop it, or even hurry it or slow it. God's kingdom will come through his work in his time, not ours. Second, the quality of our work and our willingness to do it will not make any difference in whether or not we get to be in the new city. In other words, our salvation does not depend on our works; we can't earn our way into the city of God by working harder or better or smarter. As we well know, this is indeed a good thing, because if the membership of the new city includes only those who earned it, it would be a very lonely city.

Recognizing our human limits and weaknesses compared to God raises some troubling implications of understanding ourselves as humble servants of God. If our participation makes no difference in whether God's plan is accomplished or whether we are included as members of the new city, why should we even bother to work for social change if we confess that God will do it all anyway? First, because we are called to love our neighbor as ourselves, which means that we must do all we can to seek the best interests of others, not just eternally, but right here and now. Jesus made this abundantly clear when he described God's final judgment in Matthew 25 as one which sorts out the sheep and the goats by how they showed compassion for the "least of these."

But apart from our daily work of compassion for the least of these, we also are called to lives of obedience and discipleship (Peterson, 1980). Paul's injunction to the Romans suggests the outcome of a life of obedience: "Do not conform any longer to the pattern of this world, but be transformed by the renewing of your mind" (Romans 12:2). The renewing of our minds undoubtedly can be taken to mean many things, but includes at least developing the virtue of discernment, which I would describe as combining the wisdom and knowledge of God with critical thinking skills. When we live in obedience to God, we are doing the work of transformation and renewal that Paul calls us to; becoming a disciple of Christ means developing the discipline and habits of obedience. So, whether or not our work as God's ambassadors makes any difference to God's reconciliation plan, we are assured that our work will most certainly transform us. Thomas Merton advised, in his "Letter to a Young Activist":

> Do not depend on the hope of results. When you are doing the sort of work you have taken on, essentially an apostolic work, you may have to face the fact that your work will be apparently worthless and even achieve no result at all, if not perhaps results opposite to what you expect.... The big results are not in your hands or in mine (1978).

We become who God intends us to be through grateful and disciplined obedience to his invitation to be his co-workers (I Corinthians. 3:9); in addition, God uses our efforts to accomplish His purposes in ways that we intend or do not intend, and in ways that we may see or not see, because, as Merton makes clear, the "big results" are not in our hands, but in God's.

To summarize, our work as social workers in macro practice is fundamentally shaped by how we understand our identity as humans in God's story. The central figure of the story is God and the hero is Jesus Christ. Humans, through God's grace, are given important but not necessary roles. We are called, therefore, to seek change in humble confidence that through our weakness God will take our actions and turn them to his own good uses. Of course, God can and does turn all human actions to his own uses, even those who do not acknowledge him. This implies that what is important in working for social change is not whether certain persons or groups or methods are Christian or not, but rather whether the work is consistent with God's design and plan. But who is to judge, and how?

When we see Scripture as an unfolding and unfinished drama, then we notice, as described above, that the story is not yet finished, and that we are part of the story. Middleton & Walsh (1995) suggest an analogy in which actors discover a new Shakespeare play in which the second last act is missing. The actors would then have to immerse themselves in the beginning acts and the final act, and attempt to develop their own response for the missing act in such a way that their rendering of the story is consistent with what has come before and what they know to be the ending. In a similar way, we can see ourselves as actors in the biblical drama in which we are given the responsibility and opportunity to interpret the story up to the point we have it, and then seek to live out the unfinished part in a way that is consistent with God's story up to the time of the early church, and in a way that faithfully and consistently leads to the conclusion. Middleton & Walsh (1995) describe it this way:

> Like the experienced Shakespearean actors immersing themselves in the script, Christians need to indwell the biblical drama by serious, passionate study of the Scripture. This indwelling requires us to become intimately familiar with the biblical text in order to gain a deep, intuitive sense of the story's dramatic movement and the Author's plot intentions.... The church's praxis or "performance" must be faithful to the thrust, momentum and direction of the biblical story. Any action that is inappropriate to the story must be judged in the light of the story (p. 184).

According to this analogy then, it is clear that our participation in the story is important and necessary, even though the end of the story is already known. Further, we see again the paradox of being human: compared to God we are small, weak, and insignificant, yet despite this, God empowers and equips us to *live and act* in his story, and not to be mere passive observers.

What and How We See

Canadian singer/songwriter Bruce Cockburn (1991) captures the importance of a way of seeing in his song "Child of the Wind":

> Little round planet / In a big universe
> Sometimes it looks blessed / Sometimes it looks cursed
> Depends on what you look at obviously
> But even more it depends on the way that you see.

The way we understand the world—as blessed or cursed—and the way we diagnose, assess, and evaluate social problems and design strategies and tactics to solve them is shaped fundamentally not only by *what* we see, but *how* we see. How we see ourselves as humans is obviously included, as we've already discussed, but it goes further than this. Here we consider how our understanding of God's redemption / reconciliation story and our place in it shapes how we see the world around us; more particularly, for macro practice, how we understand social problems and their solutions.

Understanding the problem is one part of what and how we see. We social science professionals have developed a dizzying array of jargon-laden concepts and terminology for the social problems we face: dysfunction, conflict, deviance, pathology, disorganization, oppression, disequilibrium, and so on. Each of these and other terms is rooted in particular theoretical perspectives and traditions, the vast majority of which rest on non-biblical understandings. At the risk of oversimplifying, I would argue that the two dominant worldviews that characterize contemporary helping professions are the modernist and postmodernist. As described by David Sherwood in Chapter 2 of this volume, each of these has a different take on the social problems we face. According to the modernist view, social problems arise because of impediments to progress, which is understood to be the advancements in technological prowess through human ingenuity, science, and rationality. Postmodernists view social problems as rooted in the tendency for individuals, groups, even societies, to assume that their own perspective is universal, and therefore imposing it on others in ways that dehumanize and oppress.

For Christians, of course, the real problem is neither the lack of scientific progress and technology nor the imposition and oppression of one group over another, but rather, sin. Or, put differently, human disobedience to God profoundly altered his creation and marred every aspect and dimension of what God had originally called good (and, in the case of humans, *very* good). The social problems we see and experience are not due to some extraneous force, but rather arise directly from our own culpability and disobedience. But, as we have seen, the brokenness of sin is much more than simply individual failings; all parts of God's creation, including neighborhoods, organizations, communities, governments, and every other institution and social system is in one way or another less than what God intended.

The biblical view of social problems, therefore, stands as distinct from other secular perspectives. Alan Keith-Lucas (1994, chapter 9) describes two dominant understandings of social problems in social work. In the "capitalist-puritan" perspective, individual human moral failures and irresponsibility are the primary cause of social problems, while in the "humanist-positivist-utopian" perspective, social and environmental forces are to blame (see also Smith, 2003, p. 70). Currently the second perspective is most dominant in the helping professions, although we have seen a resurgence in the past decade or so to the first position (for example, it is no coincidence that the 1996 legislation to substantially alter the welfare system in the USA was entitled the "the *Personal*

Responsibility and Workplace Opportunity Reconciliation Act; emphasis added). The biblical perspective we have outlined above clearly rejects either of these distortions: social problems are a combination of *both* individual and personal failings *and* social, organizational, and institutional brokenness. For Christian social workers in macro practice, this means that we must acknowledge that seeking change in larger social systems must include attention to individual responsibility, but also to the way in which larger systems are broken and need to be released from the bonds of sin.

As every social policy student learns, understanding the underlying assumptions of social problems has a direct impact on how and what solutions are generated (see Popple & Leighninger, 2004, chapter 5). The biblical themes sketched above have implications as well for how and what we do as Christians in social work attempting to solve social problems. Perhaps it goes without saying that the most obvious implication is that we don't have the solutions, God does. In line with our earlier point that we ought to adopt an attitude of humility and recognize that God chooses us but doesn't need us, we can be released from shouldering the ultimate responsibility for the problems we see around us. The ultimate resolution will not come about through our work, but rather through God's. While this is reassuring, it does not provide useful details about exactly *what* solutions we ought to develop and support. It is important to acknowledge that understanding the bible as a story of God, his work, and the way he used humans in the centuries before and immediately after Christ's life on earth does not provide the level of detail that can be readily adapted to 21st century social problems. As we've already noted above, therefore, we have to be both cautious and humble in our attempts to make the two-millenia leap between biblical contexts and our own particular situations. To put it simply, the bible cannot tell us exactly *what* to do, but it does say quite a bit about *how* to do it.

If we read the bible as the story of God's work through humans to restore his creation, then rather than looking to the bible for direct instructions about *what* to do about social problems, we can draw more meaningful implications about *how* to live in ways that are consistent with our understanding of ourselves as God's co-workers and ambassadors. I would submit that there are at least three characteristics that can be derived from the biblical story and guide *how* we practice as social workers seeking change in larger social systems. These three characteristics—weakness, uncertainty, and subversive engagement—emerge from what the biblical story says but also from what it does not say.

One of the primary responses of the Jewish people to Jesus' ministry among them was surprise and dismay. Expecting a king, the Jewish religious elite consistently interpreted the Torah and the prophets as pointing towards a Messiah made in the image of man: that is, as a conquering and powerful ruler. When Jesus turned out to be quite the opposite, the vast majority of the Jewish people simply could not accept and believe that Jesus could be a Messiah by being a servant and laying down his life. Jesus turned the whole concept of leadership upside down. In his various letters and writings, Paul consistently focuses on how Jesus' power and authority came from surrender and weakness (see especially Philippians 2: 1-11), and how that ought to guide how we become made new in the likeness of Christ. This suggests that one central characteristic for how we are to work for change is not through exercising our own power, but rather through servanthood marked by gentleness and meekness. For example, the approach in the locality development model for community organizing (Rothman, 2001) seems particularly apt to this style of organizing, wherein the organizer intentionally takes a back seat and allows and equips others—notably those from disadvantaged or vulnerable communities—to acquire the power and get the credit.

A second characteristic of how we seek change in social systems as actors in the biblical story is uncertainty. As we've already seen, the biblical story provides absolute certainty about *the* end: namely, that God will definitely "make everything new". Beyond that, however, we can't be sure what God's restored order for our social and communal life will look like. Given that uncertainty, we must take a cautious stance when it comes to specific policy options, community initiatives, or institutional programs. Instead of certainty about these specifics, the biblical story points us to the importance of living our lives together within diverse and vibrant communities where there is harmony and thriving in the humdrum of daily life. The prophet Isaiah paints a beautiful picture of what such a life together might look like by describing not a garden scene, but rather, the God-made-new city of Jerusalem (Isaiah 65: 17-25). Earlier, Isaiah provides a description of the kind of community in which justice reigns and even the weakest are cared for by the community:

> If you do away with the yoke of oppression, with the pointing finger and malicious talk, and if you spend yourselves in behalf of the hungry and satisfy the needs of the oppressed, then your light will rise in the darkness, and your night will become like the noonday.... Your people will rebuild the ancient ruins and will raise up the age-old foundations; you will be called Repairer of Broken Walls, Restorer of Streets with Dwellings (Isaiah. 58: 9-12).

Could this be one of the first references to a community social worker? Eugene Peterson's translation of this passage in *The Message* suggests a similar understanding:

> You'll use the old rubble of past lives to build anew, rebuild the foundations from out of your past. You'll be known as those who can fix anything, restore old ruins, rebuild and renovate, *make the community livable again* (Peterson, 2002, p. 1324, emphasis added).

I would suggest that "making the community livable again" ought to be a primary focus of social work macro practice.

A final characteristic of how we work within God's redemptive plan I would call "subversive engagement" and can be gleaned from Brian Walsh's notion of "subversive Christianity" (Walsh, 1992; Walsh & Keesmaat, 2004). Walsh describes how the Israelites in captivity in Babylon were instructed to live out their lives as God's people in the context of a thoroughly God-rejecting culture in Babylon. Paradoxically, God called his people not to isolate themselves from Babylonian life, nor to seek to tear down or oppose Babylonian life, but to live "normally" by having children, growing crops, carrying out their work and business and seeking the welfare of the city (Jeremiah 29:4-7; Gornick, 2002, p. 103). At the same time, they were to be subversive: to live in such a way that it was clear that they marched to a different drummer; not the gods of Babylon, but the God and Creator of heaven and earth. Thus, the subversive act was to live and tell a story completely opposite to the dominant culture's story. This story confronts head-on the challenge of the Kingdom of God to the abnormality of the current culture (Hiemstra, 2005).

Not only were the Israelites to carry out the routines of a normal life, but God's instructions go farther: the Israelites were commanded "to seek the peace and prosperity of the city to which I have carried you into exile" (Jeremiah. 29: 7). In a similar way, social workers are called both to support the welfare of our city and country, by honoring and supporting its institutions and authority (see also Romans 13:1-6). But, we are also to regard our current culture as profoundly abnormal, that is, not in keeping with God's vision for shalom. Thus, we are to challenge the ways in which society's structures vary from God's will. Subversive engagement means that we challenge the God-denying culture in which we live not by isolating ourselves from it, or by attacking it, but by engaging with it; that is, by working within its systems, with and among many different groups of people, seeking to be the salt and yeast that God mixes through his kingdom dough to change it from within.

Conclusion

To be a social worker is to keep one eye on the hurting person before us, while at the same time keeping the other eye on the big picture. In the social work profession, we have somewhat artificially divided these two views into separate micro and macro practices. But, unlike horses or birds, most of us humans can't truly divide the world into separate views from each eye. For Christians in social work, the hurting person before us is a fellow human, created in the image of God, declared by him as very good, but unable without God to escape the clutches of sin. The big picture is the grandest story imaginable, the God-authored drama in which God sees to it that everything eventually turns out well. As Christians in social work seeking change in our agencies, neighborhoods, communities, governments, and nations, we can rest in the assurance that no matter our methods, no matter the challenges, and no matter our failings, God declares, "See, I am making everything new!"

References

Bartholomew, C. & Goheen, M. (2004). *The drama of scripture: Finding our place in the story of the Bible.* Grand Rapids, MI: Baker.

Christie, N. & Gauvrea, M. (1996). *A full-orbed Christianity: The protestant churches and social welfare in Canada, 1900-1940.* Montreal, PC / Kingston, ON: McGill – Queen's University Press.

Cnaan, R., Wineburg, R. & Boddie, S. (1999). *The newer deal: Social work and religion in partnership.* New York, NY: Columbia University Press.

Cockburn, B. (1991). *Child of the wind, nothing but a burning light.* Toronto, ON: True North.

Gauer, L. (2005). A Christian perspective on poverty and social justice: Sin is more than just flawed character. *Social Work & Christianity, 32,* 4, 354-365.

Gornick, M. (2002). *To live in peace: Biblical faith and the changing inner city.* Grand Rapids, MI: Eerdmans.

Haynes, K. & Mickelson, J. (2003). *Affecting change: Social workers in the political arena,* (5th Ed.). Boston, MA: Allyn & Bacon.

Hiemstra, J. (2005). Section I. church, state and the kingdom of God, an overview. Reconciling all things to himself: Reflections on the kingdom of God, the church and the state's role in plural societies. *Reformed Ecumenical Council Focus, 5*(2), 3-49.

Keith-Lucas, A. (1994). *Giving and taking help, (Revised Edition).* St. Davids, PA: North American Association of Christians in Social Work.

Merton, T. (1978). Letter to a young activist (a letter to James H. Forest, February 21, 1966), *Catholic Agitator, 8*(4).

Marty, M. (1980). Social service: Godly and godless. *Social Service Review, 54*(4), 463-481.

Middleton, R. & Walsh, B. (1995). *Truth is stranger than it used to be: Biblical faith in a postmodern age.* Downer's Grove, IL: InterVarsity Press.

Mouw, R. (1992). *Uncommon decency: Christian civility in an uncivil world.* Downer's Grove, IL: InterVarsity Press.

Peterson, E. (1980). *A long obedience in the same direction: Discipleship in an instant society.* Downer's Grove, IL: InterVarsity Press.

Peterson, E. (2002). *The message: The bible in contemporary language.* Colorado Springs, CO: NavPress.

Peterson, E. (2005). *Christ plays in ten thousand places: A conversation in spiritual theology.* Grand Rapids, MI: Eerdmans.

Plantinga, N. (1995). *Not the way it's supposed to be: A breviary of sin.* Grand Rapids, MI: Eerdmans.

Ressler, L. (1994). *Hearts strangely warmed: Reflections on biblical passages relevant to social work.* St. Davids, PA: North American Association of Christians in Social Work.

Rothman, J. (2001). Approaches to community intervention. In Rothman, J., Erlich, J. & Tropman, J. (Eds.) *Strategies of Community Organization,* (6th Ed.), pp. 27-64. Itasca, IL: F.E. Peacock.

Sider, R. (2005). *The scandal of the evangelical conscience: Why are Christians living just like the rest of the world?* Grand Rapids, MI: Baker Books.

Smith, C. (2003). *Moral, believing animals: Human personhood and culture.* New York, NY: Oxford University Press.

Specht, H. (1990). Social work and the popular psychotherapies. *Social Service Review, 64*(3), 345-357.

Specht, H. & Courtney, M. (1994). *Unfaithful angels: How social work abandoned its mission.* New York, NY: Free Press.

Timberlake, E., Farber, M. & Sabatino, C. (2002). *The general method of social work practice: McMahon's generalist perspective.* Boston, MA: Allyn & Bacon.

Walsh, B. (1992). *Subversive christianity: Imaging God in a dangerous time.* Bristol, GB: The Regius Press.

Walsh, B. & Keesmaat, S. (2004). *Colossians remixed: Subverting the empire.* Downer's Grove, IL: InterVarsity Press.

Webster's new world college dictionary, (4th Edition). (2002). Cleveland, OH: Wiley.

Wolters, A. (1984). *Creation regained: Biblical basics for a reformational worldview.* Grand Rapids, MI: Eerdmans.

CHAPTER 10

SOCIAL WORK FOR SOCIAL JUSTICE: STRENGTHENING SOCIAL WORK PRACTICE THROUGH THE INTEGRATION OF CATHOLIC SOCIAL TEACHING

Mary Ann Brenden

During the past decade, there has been a trend in higher education to provide encouragement to articulate and demonstrate the primary commitments of institutional mission in the disciplines and professional programs offered at a given university. At the College of St. Catherine and University of St. Thomas (CSC/UST) School of Social Work (St. Paul, Minnesota), this has provided an opportunity to consider how the social work program responds to and reflects the Catholic identity and mission of its sponsoring institutions. This has presented both opportunity and challenge. Prior to 2006, some faculty had recognized Catholic Social Teaching as a valuable resource and incorporated it into courses (particularly those addressing social policy) in a meaningful but unsystematic matter.

This is the story of how the CSC/UST School of Social Work responded to this "opportunity-challenge" and call to "teach to mission." Recognizing Catholic Social Teaching (CST) as a rich resource of social justice, the School has made a commitment to strengthen the social justice content of our programs through the integration of CST. This is a comprehensive project which addresses faculty development, student engagement, and curriculum development. Much more than a series of tasks, this process has been a transformative journey focused on our School's commitment to social justice and its identity as a program sponsored by Catholic institutions.

What is Catholic Social Teaching?

"...Action on behalf of justice and participation in the transformation of the world..."
Synod of Catholic Bishops, Rome, 1971

Catholic Social Teaching (CST) represents a comprehensive tradition of social ethics derived from multiple sources within Catholic Church tradition, including scripture, papal encyclicals, episcopal statements, and writings of theologians. CST, which addresses the challenges of economic/political life and global harmony, defines standards that universally apply to all human beings and provides guidance as to how people should interact and treat one another within the economic and political spheres of our communities and world. As such, these social teachings provide direction on how to live out the Christian mandate to 'love one another.'

The first Church document addressing social teaching, *Rerum Novarum* (*On the Condition of Labor*), was issued by Pope Leo XIII in 1891. Twelve key documents, published since (including *Rerum Novarum*), are commonly recognized as the primary sources of CST (Massaro, 2000). The concerns addressed in these various documents correspond to the time of publication and include world peace, progress, poverty, equality, the environment, and global justice. These timely social concerns were not addressed to or intended for Catholics alone. Rather, the teachings were issued with a global perspective and address universal human needs of our global community.

The Office of Social Justice of the St. Paul/Minneapolis Archdiocese has identified ten key principles that emerge from CST (www.osjspm.org/cst.2006):

1. **Human Dignity:** "…human life is sacred and … the dignity of the person is the foundation of a moral vision of society…"

2. **Community and the Common Good:** "… how we organize society—economics and politics, in law and policy—directly affects human dignity and the capacity for individuals to grow in community….the role of government and other institutions is to protect human life and human dignity and promote the common good."

3. **Rights and Responsibilities:** "…every person has a fundamental right to life and a right to those things required for human decency. Corresponding to these rights are duties and responsibilities—to one another, to our families, and to the larger society."

4. **Option for the Poor and Vulnerable:** "… a basic moral test is how our most vulnerable members are faring… our traditions…instruct us to put the needs of the poor and vulnerable first."

5. **Participation:** "All people have a right to participate in the economic, political and cultural life of society. It is a fundamental demand of justice and a requirement for human dignity that all people be assured a minimum level of participation…"

6. **Dignity of Work and Rights of Workers:** "…the economy must serve people, not the other way around. If the dignity of work is to be protected, then the basic rights of workers must be respected—the right to productive work, to decent and fair wages, to organize and join unions, to private property and to economic initiative."

7. **Stewardship of Creation:** "…We are called to protect the people and the planet."

8. **Solidarity:** "…we are our brothers' and sisters' keepers, wherever they live. We are one human family… Solidarity means that 'loving our neighbor' has global dimensions in an interdependent world."

9. **Role of Government:** "… the state has a positive moral function. It is an instrument to promote human dignity, protect human rights, and build the common good….According to the principle of subsidiarity, the functions of government should be performed at the lowest level possible…"

   10. Promotion of Peace: "…There is a close relationship between peace and justice. Peace is the fruit of justice and is dependent upon right order among human beings."

While there are numerous frameworks describing CST, there is much consistency across them in that they reflect the principles listed above.

   Upon examining the numerous source documents as well as the various analyses and summaries of CST, an over-arching theme of social justice is readily apparent. In a nutshell, CST is about social justice. While *human dignity* and *the common good* emerge as the two most fundamental cornerstones of CST and are consistently evident in each and every principle/theme, social justice is the resilient and unifying message. This two-pronged vision of social justice (human dignity and the common good) is relevant to all social settings (family, workplace, economy, and government) and all levels of human relationship (community, nation, world). As a comprehensive framework of social ethics, CST presents a solid foundation for social work education and practice.

Rationale: Why is Catholic Social Teaching Relevant for Social Work?

Rationale from the Social Work Perspective: The NASW Code of Ethics

   Social work is a regulated profession in the United States. In addition to state laws that establish boards of social work which, in turn, set policies for social work practice, the primary authority on social work practice is the National Association of Social Workers (NASW).

   Perhaps the most important leadership function provided by NASW is the provision of a code of ethics. The *NASW Code of Ethics* is "…a guide to the everyday professional conduct of social workers" (NASW, 1999). The *Code of Ethics* identifies six core values of social work practice: service, justice, dignity and worth of the person, importance of human relationships, integrity, and competence. Frequently, the overarching commitments of the profession are identified as the first two of these core values: service and justice. In relation to justice, the *Code* (NASW, 1999, p. 5) states that "social workers challenge social injustice" as follows:

> Social workers pursue social change, particularly with and on be-
> half of vulnerable and oppressed individuals and groups of people.
> Social workers' social change efforts are focused primarily on is-
> sues of poverty, unemployment, discrimination, and other forms of
> social injustice. These activities seek to promote sensitivity to and
> knowledge about oppression and cultural and ethnic diversity. Social
> workers strive to ensure access to needed information, service and
> resources; equality of opportunity; and meaningful participation in
> decision-making for all people.

   The *NASW Code of Ethics* outlines the "social workers' ethical responsibilities to the broader society" i.e. to the social justice function of the profession.

The following responsibilities are specified in relation to social justice (1999, pp. 26 – 27, emphasis mine):

- **General Welfare:** Social workers should promote the general welfare of society, from local to global levels, and the development of people, their communities, and their environments…
- **Participation:** Social workers should facilitate informed **participation** by the public in shaping social policies and institutions.
- **Public Emergencies:** Social workers should provide appropriate professional services in public emergencies to the greatest extent possible.
- **Social and Political Action:**
  - Social workers should engage in **social and political action that seeks to ensure that all people have equal access** to the resources, employment, services, and opportunities they require to meet their basic human needs and to develop fully….
  - Social workers should act to **expand choice and opportunity for all** people with special regard for the vulnerable, disadvantaged, oppressed, and exploited people and groups.
  - Social workers should promote conditions that **encourage respect for cultural and social diversity**….
  - Social workers should act to **prevent and eliminate domination of, exploitation of, and discrimination** against any person, group, or class on the basis of race, ethnicity, national origin, color, sex, sexual orientation, age, marital status, political belief, religion, or mental or physical disability.

The *Code* also emphasizes the social workers' responsibility to clients, colleagues, practice settings and the profession. While the ethical principles set forth on these pages support the profession's commitment to human dignity, they do not specifically address social justice and the common good. Thus, while the *Code* very specifically identifies detailed standards of ethical practice in relation to its *service* function, ethical standards related to its *social justice* function are limited, brief, and general in nature.

It is important and useful to step back and examine the profession's historical track record relative to its two overarching purposes, service and justice. While social work has a rich history in both areas over the last 100 years, the profession's priority and strength, has been clearly to service. While we have shining moments relative to our justice functions, such as the Settlement Movement, Progressive Era reforms, and extensive contributions to the New Deal and the War on Poverty, our preferential focus has consistently been that of service (Specht & Courtney, 1994; Reisch & Andrews, 2001). The social work profession stands to benefit from more specific direction as to how to pursue our responsibilities for advancing social justice. CST is a rich resource that lends itself to this use, particularly in the context of an educational program that is sponsored by Catholic institutions.

Rationale from the Catholic Perspective: Ex Corde Ecclesiae and Institutional Mission/Identity

Social work education programs sponsored by Catholic colleges and universities are strategically positioned to employ and build upon the rich tradition of CST. The characteristics of the Catholic tradition of higher education present an environment well-suited to social work education. Catholic-sponsored education has historically placed a strong dual emphasis on the liberal arts and the helping professions. Accordingly, social work's foundation in the liberal arts makes a Catholic institution a natural fit for social work. Furthermore, Catholic higher education has a legacy of linking education to moral and ethical considerations. Social work's strong emphasis on ethics makes a Catholic institution a logical and fitting sponsor for the value-centered enterprise of social work.

In recent years, the Church has called upon Catholic institutions of higher education to more clearly articulate and demonstrate their Catholicity. Pope John Paul II regarded Catholic colleges/universities as primary players in his vision of world transformation and he articulated this in *Ex Corde Ecclesiae* (*From the Heart of the Church*), the Apostolic Constitution issued in 1990. Social justice and service to those who are vulnerable are just two of the compelling calls put forth to Catholic higher education in this document (Trainor, 2006).

The contemporary "mission-driven" culture facing American business, not-for-profits, and education poses yet another prompt for colleges and universities to articulate clear vision and mission statements. In an environment which is competitive for both resources and students, institutions can gain and maintain their niche in the marketplace only if they clearly articulate who they are and ensure that their 'walk matches their talk.' Articulating and consistently demonstrating Catholic identity is essential for institutions that wish to maintain relationships of vitality with their alumnae base and other Catholic constituents in the community.

CST is a rich resource that comes to us from the larger Catholic intellectual tradition and presents a valuable legacy to inform and provide specificity to the social justice goals of social work education and practice. CST provides direction on how to live out the Christian mandate to 'love one another.' CST is relevant to all people, not just Catholics. While all faith traditions make a contribution to social justice, the thoroughness, articulateness, and timeless quality of the CST as a body of social doctrines makes it an especially valuable resource. The Minnesota Joint Religious Legislative Coalition (JRLC), an interfaith advocacy organization representing Jewish, Christian, and Islamic traditions, looks to CST to guide its policy analysis and advocacy activities. In the words of Brian Rusche, JRLC Executive Director:

> Catholic Social Teaching is the most systematic and thorough attempt by a religious faith to articulate its positions on social policy. For JRLC's interfaith work, it provides a first lens to look at nearly every social justice issue and seriously influences all our position statements. Catholic Social Teaching is a gift to the world and people of all faiths.

The Catholic Church's tradition and expectation in relation to the pursuit of justice is three-fold: seeing, judging and acting. Seeing entails the study of social problems. Judging involves the use of ethics to discern alternatives to the problem. Action follows as problems are addressed utilizing the insights gained through study and judgment. Hence change (transformation) is pursued (Kammer, 2004). This cyclical model interfaces effectively with social work's planned change process which identifies the steps of engagement, assessment, planning, implementation, and evaluation/termination (Kirst-Ashman, 2003). CST provides a framework of social justice principles that enables social workers to fulfill their professional responsibilities and equips social work education programs with a means to address the profession's commitment to social justice.

The Church's commitment to social justice is evident in the mission statement of both of our host institutions. Institutional commitments to "Prepare students to demonstrate ethical leadership grounded in social responsibility" (CSC) and "To educate morally responsible leaders who think critically, act wisely, and work skillfully to advance the common good" (UST) are addressed in the strategic plan of each institution. In its strategic plan, the College of St. Catherine articulates a commitment to make its "Core mission elements—Catholic, women and liberal arts—explicit throughout the curriculum and co-curriculum [by]... integrating the Catholic intellectual tradition and social teaching." Likewise, the University of St. Thomas commits to engaging "its Catholic identity by exploring the meaning and heightening the understanding of Catholic intellectual traditions throughout its curricular and co-curricular activities [through]... the integration of Catholic tradition, ethics and social justice."

The mission of the School of Social Work reflects its sponsors' missions in its pledge to educate social workers to "...promote social justice and human rights." The School's strategic plan further explicates this with a commitment to "...make explicit the central components of the SSW [School of Social Work] identity—Catholic, joint, liberal arts, generalist and clinical" through the "integration of Catholic Social Teaching into all aspects of the School of Social Work."

The connectedness and flow between and among the mission, vision and strategic goals of the program's host institutions and those of the School are evident in the following chart.

Chart 1: Mission, Vision, and Strategic Direction

College of St. Catherine	University of St. Thomas	School of Social Work
Mission: The College of St. Catherine educates women to lead and influence. Founded by the Sisters of St. Joseph of Carondelet in 1905, the College integrates liberal arts and professional education within the Catholic traditions of intellectual inquiry and social teaching. Committed to excellence and opportunity, the College engages students from diverse backgrounds in a learning environment uniquely suited to women. Education at the College of St. Catherine prepares graduates to demonstrate ethical leadership grounded in social responsibility.	**Mission:** To education morally responsible leaders who think critically, act wisely, and work skillfully to advance the common good.	**Mission:** Drawing from the Judeo-Christian traditions of social caring, we prepare students to use social work knowledge, values and skills to demonstrate the intrinsic value of all human kind as they serve those in need and promote social justice and human rights.
Vision: To be the world's pre-eminent Catholic college educating women to lead and influence.	**Vision:** To be a recognized leader in Catholic higher education that excels in effective teaching, active learning, scholarly research and responsible engagement with the local community as well as with the national and global communities in which we live.	**Vision:** To be a premier Catholic School of Social Work offering outstanding BSW and MSW programs while maintaining close connections to the practice community.
Strategic Direction: Make St. Catherine's core mission elements—Catholic, women and liberal arts—explicit throughout the curriculum and co-curriculum. Integrate the Catholic intellectual tradition and social teaching within the curriculum and co-curriculum.	**Strategic Priority: Catholic Identity** The University of St. Thomas will further engage its Catholic identity by exploring the meaning and heightening the understanding of Catholic intellectual tradition throughout is curricular and co-curricular activities. In curricular and co-curricular activities, evidence of the integration of Catholic tradition, ethics, and social justice is prized. New employee and student orientations include information on Catholic identity with special emphasis on ethics and social justice. Search committees provide information on the Catholic identity and mission of the University to candidates and consider their potential contributions to the mission of the University.	**Strategic Direction:** Through the curriculum and co-curriculum, strengthen and make explicit the central components of the SSW identity—Catholic, Joint, Liberal Arts, Generalist and Clinical. Integrate Catholic Social Teaching into all aspects of the School of Social Work.

Conceptual Framework: Project Components

This project is focused on the integration of CST into BSW and MSW curricula. Project goals/outcomes include the following:

- Enhance social work faculty's understanding of commitment to institutional religious identity and mission, particularly of CST.
- Increase faculty's and students' understanding of the congruence between CST and values and ethics of the social work profession.
- Strengthen the social justice component of the social work curricula in order to prepare and empower students to effectively pursue justice in their social work practice.
- Increase students' understanding of the difference between faith-based and secular social work education and practice and provide an environment which encourages them to clarify and incorporate their personal values, including faith-based values, into their lives and social work practice.
- Enhance faculty and student understanding of social work as a call to service/vocation.

The project is comprised of three primary components: faculty development, student engagement, and curriculum development. Each of these three arenas of activity has been critical to the project and each has informed the others.

Faculty Development

Faculty development has been the centerpiece of this project. This component has engaged faculty in becoming familiar with the themes of CST, discovering the congruence between CST and social work ethics, and recognizing CST as a rich resource for curriculum development.

Two faculty development retreats were undertaken to lay the foundation of our work. In January, 1999 and 2005, the social work faculty convened to explore the *Catholic Intellectual Tradition and Social Work* and *Social Work: Called beyond Career to Vocation*. Both of these programs were important in setting the context for the project and preparing faculty to understand and appreciate CST.

Through a series of readings and discussions, the first retreat familiarized faculty with the Catholic Intellectual Tradition and facilitated an understanding of how the social work program articulates and serves the institutional missions of its Catholic sponsors. This experience was instrumental in helping faculty to recognize attributes of our institutional culture (such as emphasis on teaching, liberal arts, values/ethics, and service) as distinctive characteristics related to the institutions' Catholic identity.

The second retreat focused on social work as a calling/vocation and provided an opportunity for faculty to reflect on the development of their own personal "call" to the profession, the definition and evolution of their "vocation of social work" over time, and the way in which we, as professors and advisors, support and encourage our students to recognize and respond to their own personal calling to the profession. This retreat was a highly spiritual experience for faculty as they reflected on the role the social work profession has played in their personal development and the important role we, as faculty, play in the training of students as they explore and discern their own professional calling/vocation.

While this project is focused on utilizing the long and rich tradition of CST, it has been important in our faculty development efforts to acknowledge that all faith traditions espouse beliefs and teachings addressing love for others and social justice. In order to recognize and celebrate the diversity of faith-inspired justice teachings, our faculty participated in a series of faculty development seminars featuring the social teaching of various traditions, including Muslim, Jewish, Buddhist and Protestant perspectives. These experiences enhanced faculty understanding of the diverse religious perspectives about social justice and reinforced the universality of the social teaching themes. An interest in developing course activities which provide students with an opportunity to learn about social justice perspectives of diverse faith traditions also emerged from this component of our work.

In order to launch the segment of this project directly focused on the integration of CST into the curriculum, a retreat format was used once again. In preparation, the faculty read *Living Justice: Catholic Social Teaching in Action* by Thomas Massaro (2000). This primer provides an overview of the sources, methods and themes of CST as well as an articulate discussion of its application to contemporary times. This text inspired the title and theme of our retreat, *Teaching Justice: Catholic Social Teaching in Action*. The retreat provided an opportunity for faculty to examine and discuss a variety of frameworks that organize CST themes. The faculty considered potential contributions of CST by identifying barriers and obstacles which might be encountered during integration into the BSW and MSW curricula. Faculty participated in a preliminary brainstorming session about ways in which CST might be integrated into the various content areas of the BSW and MSW curriculum.

Perhaps the most inspiring activity of the retreat involved the faculty sharing stories about individuals who have inspired their own passion for justice. This activity culminated in the establishment of the CSC/UST School of Social Work Social Justice Hall of Fame, featuring 24 individuals including Jesus, Gandhi, Dorothy Day, Jane Addams, and Paul Wellstone, as well as local heroes/ heroines.

While the retreat afforded an opportunity for the faculty to launch this project and garner understanding, momentum, and commitment for the work ahead, it is important to acknowledge that it also included struggle. Ours is a religiously diverse faculty which includes Catholics, Protestants (numerous denominations), Jews, and Buddhists, as well as diversity across other dimensions including race/ethnicity, sexual orientation, and practice expertise. Some aspects of the dialogue were challenging and difficult. This was the case especially in relation to Church practices that are inconsistent with social work values (such as those related to inequality of women and discrimination against GLBT persons) and perceived as incongruent with the social justice principles of CST.

An important outcome of the retreat, especially in light of this struggle, was the articulation of the following points of consensus by the faculty:

- CST has potential as a framework/tool for teaching social justice content in the social work curriculum. CST is a fluid, not static, statement of values principles. Since the first encyclical informing CST was written (Rerum Novarum, 1891), CST has evolved over time to address concerns of the times.
- By virtue of our Catholic sponsorship, it is logical to use CST to inform the curriculum. In doing so, it is important to acknowledge its origins in Church history.
- As there are numerous and varying statements of CST, it is crucial that we clearly articulate a statement of CST principles that informs our curriculum. This statement of principles must be informed by and congruent with the *NASW Code of Ethics* (1999). This statement of principles must be approved by the faculty and used consistently for purposes of integration.
- As we as social work educators, bound by the *NASW Code of Ethics* (1999) and teaching within Catholic institutions of higher education, integrate CST into our curriculum, it is incumbent upon us to carefully and clearly delineate the convergence and divergence between the two commitments (CST and the *Code of Ethics* (1999). These points of convergence and divergence must be clearly articulated in a way that demonstrates the challenges faced and the opportunities for us to assist in living out the values presented in CST.
- The integration of CST principles into the curriculum will recognize and acknowledge the universality of these principles across numerous other faith traditions. Likewise, we recognize that the *NASW Code of Ethics* (1999), a bedrock of principles for the profession, emerges from greater universal ethical principles that speak to how all people should interact and treat each other.
- As social work educators, we are bound by the *NASW Code of Ethics* (1999) and therefore responsible to teach our students to become professionals dedicated to service and justice. Principles of CST provide a framework for strengthening the way in which we educate for justice, a link that has been historically weak in social work education and in the profession.

These points of consensus were an important outcome of our work in that they helped us to realize and acknowledge that difficult dialogues, despite their inherent struggles, can be avenues of discovery of common ground and shared insights. It became clear to us that even challenging discussions, which may seem to focus on divergent perspectives, hold the potential for the discernment of consensus.

The next faculty development activity following the *Teaching Justice* retreat focused on a comparative analysis of the *NASW Code of Ethics* (1999) and CST. The social work faculty was divided into 10 subgroups and each subgroup was assigned one of the CST themes identified by the Office of Social Justice, Archdiocese of St. Paul-Minneapolis (listed previously). Each subgroup was asked to examine its assigned principle in relation to the *NASW Code of Ethics* and to identify convergence and divergence between the two, as well as emergent 'flashpoint' issues. A greater number of points of convergence were found which led to a realization that there is much common ground between social work professional ethics and CST.

The primary "flashpoint" issues were equality of women, reproductive policy, and gay rights. The emergence of these issues surprised no one; tension related to their existence had been lurking since the very early stages of the project. Naming the issues was important, for this acknowledged the reality that there are instances when social work values and Church teachings may collide and diverge. Nor was there surprise when discrepancy between Church teaching and Church practice emerged, particularly in relation to the Church's Social Teaching relating to human dignity and the Church's practice of less than equal treatment of women and lack of full affirmation of GLBT persons.

There was surprise, however, when it became clear that the social work profession also has a record of disparity between its ethics and practices, as is evident in its historical role in relation to social control and its stronger commitment to service over justice. This parallel insight relating to the Catholic Church and the social work profession and ways in which the "walk" falls short of the "talk" provided much food for thought.

This examination of the convergence and divergence between social work ethics and CST led to a synthesis and formulation of a statement entitled *Social Work for Social Justice: Ten Principles* (Appendix I). This amalgamation of social work ethics with CST has become the focus of our integration project. It represents both our identity as a social work program sponsored by Catholic institutions and the social justice commitments of the Church and the profession. The faculty has felt strongly about distinguishing between the parts that are informed by CST (connoted by italics) and those which represent the social work perspective (connoted by non-italics) so that both the convergence and divergence between the two are explicit. This statement evolved naturally out of continuous faculty dialogue. The statement represents a milestone in our project since it has become the heart of our work and the defining focus of our project.

Now, when we talk of *the integration of CST into the curriculum*, we are speaking of the integration of these principles. The *Ten Principles* define our program's 'brand' of social justice—one that is informed both by social work ethics and Catholic social ethics. They have become our hallmark of social justice. Formulation of the justice principles created a component useful for curriculum development, another integral aspect of this project which is explored below.

As faculty development continued through the activities described above, considerable progress was apparent. Faculty members were discussing social justice in new and deeper ways and forging a new familiarity with and appreciation for the Catholic heritage of its sponsor institutions. At the same time, it is again important to acknowledge that the process was complex and, at times, the dialogue was difficult and tense. It was clear to us that oppressive practices of the Church in relation to women and gay persons has resulted, for some, in a reluctance, and, at times, a resistance, to integrate Catholic social ethics for fear that this would simultaneously engender the incorporation of attitudes of oppression and/or discriminatory practices. There were times when it was difficult to know how to discuss these difficult topics and maintain forward momentum.

In order to address these challenges, the *Catholic Common Ground Initiative Principles of Dialogue* outlined in *Called to be Catholic: Church in a Time of Peril* were adapted to the purposes of this project to guide faculty interaction and set norms of communication for the challenging discussions at hand (National Pastoral Life Center, 1996). Our *Finding Common Ground Guidelines* are presented in Appendix II. While these *Guidelines* have been described as "ingenious and inspired" by those with whom we have shared our work, what we have learned is that *introducing* the *Guidelines* is the *easy* task. Remaining true to new habits of dialogue and interaction that depart substantially from conduct typical within academe constitutes the real challenge with which we continue to struggle.

Student Engagement

In order to engage student participation in this project, all undergraduate and graduate social work students were invited to participate in focus groups to explore and discuss the proposed integration of CST into the curricula. In order to strengthen the student perspective of the focus group, an MSW student employed as a research assistant assumed the primary role in planning, convening, and recording the findings of the student focus groups.[1]

A total of 31 individuals responded to our invitation and participated in the focus groups or, when unable to do so, provided input via email: 6 BSW students, 20 MSW students, 2 MSW students who are also alumnae of the CSC/UST BSW program, and 3 MSW alumnae. Student response to the proposed integration of CST (CST) into the social work curriculum reflected three areas: perceived advantages, concerns, and ideas about how to go about integration.

Advantages of Integrating Catholic Social Teaching into the Social Work Curriculum

Students identified a number of potential advantages to integrating CST into the social work curriculum. Five themes emerged: the congruence between CST and social work values and ethics, the Catholic identity of the schools, the need for greater emphasis on social justice, the importance of integrating spirituality in social work education and practice, and an increased attractiveness of the program to prospective students.

Congruence between CST and Social Work Values and Ethics. All of the students except two concurred that there is a high degree of congruence between CST and social work values and ethics. Several students initially confused CST and Catholic doctrine. However, once they received clarification, they were quite enthusiastic about its inclusion due to its strong connection to social work

---

[1] The following summary is an abbreviation of a summary written by graduate research assistant, Stephanie Spandl, SSND. The author is grateful to Sr. Stephanie for her fine work and contribution to this project.

values. The students spoke of the CST principles as "universal to all people," and as able to "provide a universal base/common frame of reference for ethical/ moral considerations for social workers." Related to the observations regarding the universality of CST were comments connecting CST to the NASW Code of Ethics. Several students noted that CST can potentially enrich the Code of Ethics with "more depth, specificity and richness."

Catholic Identity of the Schools. Numerous students agreed that the Catholic identity of the institutions makes CST a desirable addition to the social work curriculum, while several others acknowledged that its inclusion is logical and appropriate for this reason. Some students indicated that they came to a Catholic institution specifically for a values-based education in which spirituality and faith are considered both legitimate and important. Given the Catholic identity of CSC and UST, several students felt that marketing the integration of CST in the social work curriculum would enhance the attractiveness of the program for many students seeking "to integrate the richness of spirituality and faith traditions into their practice of social work." They felt that CST "could serve to further differentiate the CSC/UST program from other Twin Cities social work programs."

Emphasis on Social Justice. The participants expressed the importance of social workers participating in efforts for justice and were enthusiastic about the ways CST could enhance this awareness and effort. On a practical level, students of color believed that use of these principles in the curriculum would prepare students to work more effectively with diverse populations and at-risk groups. Another response, typical of the student discussion, observed, "It [CST] would broaden a social worker's perspective of what they can do for a client as well as how to work with and empower a client. It would increase awareness of how social workers can advocate for their clients at many levels in society."

The Importance of Integrating Spirituality into Social Work Education and Practice. Although the topic was CST, numerous students brought up the integration of CST as a means to increase the inclusion of spirituality in general in the social work curriculum and social work practice. Students recognized, "[The] principles [as] a 'bridge' to the discussion of religious/spiritual beliefs in the classroom and practice setting [that] could help students become more comfortable talking about religious beliefs/spirituality, important because many clients have religious/spiritual beliefs that need to be considered." Students also noted that spirituality is gaining recognition as an important part of social work/ therapy and that the inclusion of CST would better prepare graduates "to see their clients as whole persons and meet their needs—body, mind, soul, spirit—as a person in an environment and in relationship to family, neighbors, etc."

Increased Attractiveness of the Program to Prospective Students. Several students felt that marketing the integration of CST in the social work curriculum would enhance the attractiveness of the program for many students seeking "to integrate the richness of spirituality and faith traditions into their practice of social work." They felt that CST "could serve to further differentiate the CSC/ UST program from other Twin Cities social work programs." At the same time, other students noted that the "Catholic" label might deter some students who might misunderstand what CST is all about. In response to this concern, one student pointed out, "While we might fear losing some students due to such integration, it is important to consider that we might also be losing students for not having it."

Concerns about Integrating Catholic Social Teaching into the Social Work Curriculum

Three primary concerns were identified in regard to the proposed integration: the importance of the distinction between CST and other aspects of Catholic doctrine, the potential risk of alienating or excluding non-Catholic and/or non-Christian students, and the importance of faculty "buy-in"/consistency.

Several students expressed the opinion that, "it is very important to distinguish between Catholic Social Teaching and [other] Catholic doctrine to avoid student resistance," observing that, "…some people have allergic reactions to anything that comes from a church" and noting that "the political environment is very volatile in relation to religion right now."

The majority of students named potential feelings of alienation or exclusion by non-Catholic and/or non-Christian students as a concern. There was much discussion about this issue, and it was clear that students are aware of the diversity of the student body. However, with the exception of one student, students expressing this concern did not suggest that this should prevent the school from integrating CST, but rather that it should be done with care. Students offered the following insight about the inclusion of values in general, "Any place you go to school there will be a values set. I prefer to know them up front. This [CST principles] could identify our values/philosophy. The principles are universal. They are not about conversion." Another noted, "At a Muslim university, I would expect to discuss Islam content in my classes. One doesn't have to believe everything that is said. CST gives you something to respond to."

While some students suggested that the integration of CST might attract students and assist in marketability of the program, other students noted that the "Catholic" label could deter some students who might misunderstand what CST is all about. They noted that it would be crucial to be absolutely clear in any program promotional materials that it is Catholic *social* ethics that are addressed and to distinguish this from other aspects of Catholic teaching/doctrine.

Students also noted that it is crucial that all members of the faculty be "on board" with this project if it is implemented, and suggested that faculty development will be *very* important. Presentation/integration of the principles consistently throughout the curriculum was considered essential for it to be effective in strengthening the program. One student noted that faculty will need to be truly invested in the process and comfortable with "facilitating the emotions and variety of opinions that are likely to come up in discussion."

In summary, there was substantial support and enthusiasm for integrating CST into the social work curriculum and some specific concerns that need to be addressed if it is to be done. Students are especially enthusiastic about the strong social justice component of CST as well as its potential to deepen exploration of professional social work values. While enthusiastically supporting integration, students feel strongly that the integration needs to be done so as to avoid the alienation or exclusion of students identifying with other faith traditions. They suggest that it be sensitively and carefully done in a way which is respectful of religious/spiritual diversity. They encourage a classroom climate that would allow for open discussion and exploration of diverse perspectives. They also indicate that the program should be careful in how it advertises this in light of the potential to confuse CST with other elements of Catholic doctrine. Students identified consistency among the faculty and faculty development as strategies to minimize these potential risks. Overall, students consider the richness that CST could bring to their social work education greater than potential risks. They believe that the potential risks can be addressed and they supported the program in moving forward with this endeavor.

Curriculum Development

Formulation of our hallmark *Social Work for Social Justice: Ten Principles* and faculty development laid the groundwork necessary for the curriculum development component of this project which includes two phases: curriculum review and analysis, and integration.

Curriculum Review and Analysis

Consistent with the social work dictum of "starting where the client is," curriculum development began with an assessment of present practices. This process focused on the question, "How are we presently teaching social justice content in the BSW and MSW curriculum?" Standing committees exist within the BSW and MSW program which are responsible for curriculum in each of the following content areas: policy, human behavior and the social environment, research, practice, and fieldwork. Each of these ten content committees (5 BSW and 5 MSW) reviewed the present curricula and identified ways in which social justice/injustice content was already addressed through readings, class activities, assignments, and so on. An inventory for each course was completed, outlining present content and activities related to justice.

This process resulted in a litany of strengths which detailed ways in which social justice was already being addressed in the classroom and through assignments. Current examples were shared, awareness was raised and more content than initially anticipated was identified. This discussion 'got the juices flowing' in that it generated ideas and creativity for new opportunities to incorporate content on social justice.

Next, each committee was asked to consider the *Social Work for Social Justice: Ten Principles*, the goals and objectives of the content area, and to select the *Justice Principles* that relate to each specific content area. This exercise was framed as an opportunity to build upon present strengths of the curriculum. A grid summarizing the *Justice Principles* which relate most pertinently to each content area was compiled. These grids will be instrumental in guiding faculty as they begin to integrate the *Justice Principles* into the curriculum. Another important outcome of this phase of the process was a detailed inventory of current practices addressing justice content.

Integration of Social Justice Content

Once faculty completed the assessment of current practices, compiled an inventory of current inclusion of social justice content, and identified the *Justice Principles* pertinent to each curricular content area, the stage was set for comprehensive integration of social justice content.

The first step in the integration process asked curriculum content committees to creatively brainstorm in response to the following question: "Considering the *Justice Principles* identified as relevant for the content area, what are logical points of intersection where the *Justice Principles* could be integrated into a current activity or assignment to enhance how "justice" is taught in this content area?"

While the emphasis of this exercise was to *integrate* our *Justice Principles into* existent *course* activities, faculty also generated innovative ideas of new ways to both broaden and deepen the integration of justice content related to the identified *Justice Principles*. These brainstorming sessions were creative discussions in which faculty were encouraged to think big about transforming the curriculum to balance and reflect both the service and justice functions of the social work profession. This exercise resulted in lists of ideas about how to enhance and integrate justice content in course syllabi through integration in existent activities as well as adding new activities. These lists will serve as a "resource menu" for the next phase of integration and revision of course syllabi.

Courses have been identified in the BSW and the MSW programs as starting points for the integration of social justice content, and this process of integration is currently underway. A series of instructional modules have also been developed to serve as resources for faculty as they go about integrating the *Justice Principles* into course syllabi. Many of the modules are assignments and class activities that integrate the *Justice Principles* and are used in BSW and MSW courses. These instructional modules have been made available to serve as models or for actual use or adaptation, according to faculty preference.

**Accessing Campus and Community Wisdom and Support:
Convening an Advisory Committee**

An advisory committee was formed at the outset of the project to support and guide this work. Membership includes experts on CST and theology from our college/university communities, a representative from the Archdiocesan Office of Social Justice, a parish priest, the executive director of a local interfaith advocacy organization, and students. These individuals have made themselves available as consultants and have been an invaluable source of wisdom and support as they have been called upon through the various components and phases of this project. Their wise insights, strategic advice and enthusiastic support have been crucial to project momentum and success.

Concluding Reflections

As we step back and take stock of the progress of our efforts to strengthen the social justice content of our program through the integration of CST, it is clear that much has been accomplished… and that much work remains. It is, as the dean insightfully observes, "The end of the beginning." While the many tasks of integration lie ahead, it is important to note and celebrate our progress. The faculty, student, and curriculum activities we have experienced have resulted in:

- **A renewed commitment to social justice**, our profession's commitment to it, and an increased awareness of social justice content in our BSW and MSW curricula. We have assessed our curricula, inventoried present practices related to the inclusion of social justice content and identified opportunities, as well as strategies, to systematically integrate social justice content throughout the curricula.
- **A keener sense of understanding of our host institutions' Catholic identity** as well as their respective missions and strategic commitments for the future.
- **A deep appreciation for CST** and the rich resource that it presents to social work education and practice.
- **Humility** in response to the struggles endured through difficult dialogues that have compelled us to embrace complexity.
- **Resolve** as we commit to the tasks which lay ahead.

What was initially seen as primarily a task and curriculum project has been recognized as a process, a transformative process which has had a profound impact on our faculty and our program. The effect on faculty has been at both the personal and collective level. Each individual faculty member has been called upon to consider at a newer, deeper level, what it means to be a faculty member at Catholic institutions and how being Catholic informs our roles as educators and social workers. We are building a new vocabulary as we talk with one another and begin to introduce these discussions to students in the classroom.

Along with increased awareness of and connection to our Catholic identity, this project has also heightened faculty awareness of and commitment to the social justice mission of social work. We have had the opportunity to acknowledge and celebrate the extent to which we are already "teaching justice" and we have responded to a call to strengthen our program and more effectively prepare students to "practice justice." We have developed a keen sense of appreciation for our Catholic heritage and the incredibly rich resource of social justice found in CST.

As for the curriculum, it has just begun to reflect the outcomes of this project. As faculty move forward, some with reticence and some with eagerness, to undertake the next steps of the integration process, there is a sense of both accomplishment and anticipation. Our work has generated many outcomes— some tangible such as discussion guidelines and *Justice Principles*—and others intangible, such as a deeper sense of our Catholic mission and renewed commitment to social justice. These accomplishments are accompanied by a sense of anticipation and the knowledge that the next steps are likely to be as transformative, satisfying, *and* challenging as those already accomplished.

References

Boileau, D. A. (Ed.). (1998). *Principles of Catholic social teaching.* Milwaukee, WI: Marquette University Press.

Chambers, C. (1980). Social service and social reform: A historical essay. In *Compassion and Responsibility: Readings in the History of Social Welfare Policy in the United States* (pp. 14-28). Chicago: University of Chicago Press.

Curran, C. E. (2002). *Catholic social teaching, 1891-present: a historical, theological, and analysis.* Washington D.C.: Georgetown University Press.

DeFerrari, P. (1998). Proclaiming justice: Women and Catholic social teaching. In NETWORK,

Kammer, F. (2004). *Doing faith justice: An introduction to Catholic social thought.* Mahwah, NJ: Paulist Press.

Kirst-Ashman, K. (2003). *Introduction to social work and social welfare: Critical thinking perspectives.* Pacific Grove, CA: Brooks/Cole-Thomson Learning.

Massaro, T. (2000). *Living justice: Catholic social teaching in action.* Franklin, WI: Sheed & Ward.

National Association of Social Workers. (1999). *Code of Ethics of the National Association of Social Workers.*

National Pastoral Life Center. (1996). *Called to be Catholic: Church in a time of peril.* Retrieved June 6, 2006 from http://www.nplc.org/commonground/calledcatholic. htm.

Office of Social Justice, Archdiocese of St. Paul and Minneapolis. *Major themes from Catholic social teaching.* Retrieved June 6, 2006 from http://www.osjspm.org/cst/themes.htm.

Reisch, M., & Andrews, J. (2001). *The road not taken: A history of radical social work in the United States.* Ann Arbor, MI: Sheridan Books.

Rerum Novarum (*On the Condition of Labor*), 1891.

Specht, H., & Courtney, M. (1994). *Unfaithful angels: How social work has abandoned its mission.* New York: The Free Press.

Trainor, S. (2006). A delicate balance: The Catholic college in America. *Change,* March/April, 14-21.

Appendix I

❧ Social Work for Social Justice: Ten Principles ❧

Human Dignity	Dignity of Work and the Rights of Workers
Dignity of the human person is the ethical foundation of a moral society. The measure of every institution is whether it threatens or enhances the life and dignity of the human person. Social workers respect the inherent dignity and worth of all individuals. Social workers treat each person in a caring, respectful manner mindful of individual differences and cultural and ethnic diversity. Social workers seek to promote the responsiveness of organizations, communities and social institutions to individuals' needs and social problems. Social workers act to prevent and eliminate domination of, exploitation of, and discrimination against any person or group on any basis.	In a marketplace where profit often takes precedence over the dignity and rights of workers, it is important to recognize that the economy must serve the people, not the other way around. If the dignity of work is to be protected, the basic rights of workers must be respected—the right to productive work, to decent and fair wages, to organize and join unions, to private property and to economic initiative. Social workers challenge injustice related to unemployment, workers' right and inhumane labor practices. Social workers engage in organized action, including the formation of and participation in labor unions, to improve services to clients and working conditions.
Community and the Common Good	**Solidarity**
All individuals by virtue of their human nature have social needs. Human relationships enable people to meet their needs and provide an important vehicle for change. The family, in all its diverse forms, is the central social institution that must be supported and strengthened. The way in which society is organized—in education, economics, politics, government—directly affects human dignity and the common good. Social workers promote the general welfare and development of individuals, families and communities. Social workers seek to strengthen relationships among people at all levels to promote the well being of all.	We are our brother's and sister's keeper. We are one human family, whatever our national, racial, ethnic, economic, and ideological differences. An ethic of care acknowledging our interdependence belongs in every dimension of human experience — including the family, community, society and global dimension. Social workers understand that relationships between and among people are an important vehicle for change. Social workers engage people as partners in the helping process and seek to strengthen relationships among people to promote well being at all levels.
Rights and Responsibilities	**Stewardship**
People have a right and a responsibility to participate in society and to work together toward the common good. Human dignity is protected and healthy community can be achieved only if human rights are protected and responsibilities are met. Accordingly, every person has a fundamental right to things necessary for human decency. Corresponding to these rights are responsibilities—to family, community and society. Social workers, mindful of individual differences and diversity, respect and promote the right of all individuals to self-determination and personal growth and development. Social workers provide education and advocacy to protect human rights, and to end oppression. Social workers empower individuals/groups to function as effectively as possible.	It is incumbent upon us to recognize and protect the value of all people and all resources on our planet. While rights to personal property are recognized, these rights are not unconditional and are secondary to the best interest of the common good especially in relation to the right of all individuals to meet their basic needs. Stewardship of resources is important at all levels/settings: family, community, agency, community and society. Social workers strive to ensure access to needed information, services and resources; equality of opportunity; and meaningful participation for all people. Social workers promote the general welfare of people and their environments.

Priority for the Poor and Vulnerable	**Governance/Principle of Subsidiarity**
A basic moral test of any community or society is the way in which the most vulnerable members are faring. In a society characterized by deepening divisions between rich and poor, the needs of those most at risk should be considered a priority. Social workers advocate for living conditions conducive to the fulfillment of basic human needs and to promote social, economic, political, and cultural values and institutions that are compatible with the realization of social justice. Social workers pursue change with and on behalf of vulnerable and oppressed individuals and groups to: address poverty, unemployment, discrimination and other forms of social injustice; and to expand choice and opportunity.	Governance structures in all levels/settings have an imperative to promote human dignity, protect human rights, and build the common good. While the principle of subsidiarity calls for the functions of government to be performed at the lowest level possible in order to insure for self-determination and empowerment, higher levels of government have the responsibility to provide leadership and set policy in the best interest of the common good. Social workers engage in social and political action in order to promote equality, challenge injustice, expand opportunity and empower individuals, families and groups to participate in governance structures at all levels.
Participation	**Promotion of Peace**
All people have a right to participate in the economic, political and cultural life of society. Social justice and human dignity require that all people be assured a minimum level of participation in the community. It is the ultimate injustice for a person or a group to be excluded unfairly. Social workers strive to ensure access to equal opportunity and meaningful participation for all. Social workers empower individuals and groups to influence social policies and institutions and promote social justice. Social workers advocate for change to ensure that all people have equal access to the resources and opportunities required to meet basic needs and develop fully.	In light of the human dignity and worth of all and the ethical imperatives of solidarity and stewardship, we are called to promote peace and non-violence at all levels -within families, communities, society and globally. Peace is the fruit of justice and is dependent upon the respect and cooperation between peoples and nations. Social workers promote the general welfare of society from local to global levels.

Copyright © July 2006 CSC/UST School of Social Work
Sources: NASW Code of Ethics; *US Conference of Catholic Bishops, Office of Social Justice – Archdiocese of St. Paul and Minneapolis*

Appendix II

Finding Common Ground...
as we work together to build a program and a profession
which more strongly articulate a commitment to social justice

1. We will recognize that no single voice/view has a monopoly on the truth. We will remind ourselves that solutions to our challenges will emerge from dialogue that embraces diverse perspectives.

2. We will not envision ourselves or anyone as 'having all the answers.' No one person/group will judge itself alone to be possessed of enlightenment or spurn others as wrong or misguided.

3. We will test all ideas/proposals for their truth, value and potential impact on our program, on our students and on the clients they will serve. This is our responsibility as ethical social work educators.

4. We will presume that those with whom we disagree are acting with good intentions. We will extend civility, courtesy and genuine effort to understand their concerns. We will not diminish nor trivialize their ideas or concerns with labels, abstractions or blanket terms (such as she/he 'just doesn't get it', 'is a sellout', 'has been led astray', 'is misguided', etc). Instead, we will embrace the complexity of the realities we face and examine their various and multiple dimensions.

5. We will put the best possible construction on differing positions, addressing their strongest points rather than seizing upon the most vulnerable aspect in order to discredit them. We will detect the valid insights and legitimate worries that may underlie even questionable arguments.

6. We will be cautious in ascribing motives. We will not impugn another's motives, loyalties, opinions or comprehension. We will not rush to interpret disagreements as conflicts of starkly opposing principles rather than as differences in degree or in prudential judgment about the relevant facts.

7. We will embrace the realities of our institutional cultures, not by simple defiance nor by naïve acquiescence, but acknowledging both their valid achievement and real dangers.

Adapted from *Called to be Catholic: Church in a Time of Peril*
Published by the National Pastoral Life Center, New York, NY, 1996.

CHAPTER 11

FAIRNESS IS NOT ENOUGH: SOCIAL JUSTICE AS RESTORATION OF RIGHT RELATIONSHIPS

Mary Anne Poe

When my two daughters were young, I heard the refrain regularly, "But that's not fair!" Usually, this exclamation occurred over some rather trivial distribution of goods or punishments, like cookies or "time out." Their innate sense of justice had been violated and thus the appeal to fairness. Distribution of resources, retribution for wrongs, and concern for fairness have dominated the discussion about social justice through the ages. These approaches to social justice have directed attention away from the most fundamental meaning of justice—the restoration of right relationships.

Though the human reaction to perceived injustice often defaults to an appeal to fairness, as my daughters' reactions suggest, fairness is simply not adequate to satisfy the human spirit and longing for justice. Additionally, strategies for determining fairness are multiple and complex, including random selection, greatest merit, or first-come, first-served. Both the processes for promoting and attaining justice and the final outcome are occasions for discontent in the human spirit.

Social justice is an ideal that has captured the imagination of people from the beginning of recorded history. Philosophers, theologians, and political leaders from every historic era have grappled with this most elusive virtue. Justice is one of the most sought after notions, with most every society invoking it as a worthy goal. John Rawls' classic work, *A Theory of Justice*, claims that it is the "first virtue of social institutions, as truth is of systems of thought" (Rawls, 1971, p. 3). The concept is deeply rooted in cultural and religious traditions and beliefs. Because people exist within culture, their understanding of justice is shaped by their cultural context. American revolutionaries had a quite different perspective on the justice of their times than either the American Indians or the British loyalists. This relativity of perspectives does not mean the ideal does not exist. Theologian Miroslav Volf (1996, p, 199) explains that we have to distinguish between the idea of justice and justice itself. Evidence of the efforts to make this distinction pervades the history of law, economics, and politics.

The Christian faith is deeply rooted in the idea of justice. The Old and New Testaments relate both conceptual themes about justice and narratives that describe its application in practice. Scholars have debated whether the two testaments describe different concepts of justice and its application or whether the Bible as a whole has one continuous theme of justice. Understanding the language of justice and the various meanings and applications of the Scriptures has been a major occupation through Christian history (Dunn & Suggate, 1993; McGrath, 1986; Solomon & Murphy, 1990).

In the twentieth century, the profession of social work claimed the promotion of justice as a core value in its code of ethics (NASW, 1996). To some extent, the profession emerged out of the mission of the church in the context of theological debates about the language and meaning of justice (Poe, 2002b). Defining social justice has been elusive for the profession of social work just as it has been for the Christian faith and for philosophers (Pelton, 2001; Scanlon & Longres, 2001). Banerjee (2005) conducted a literature review that revealed very little agreement among social workers about the meaning of social justice and how to achieve it.

This paper identifies through a broad overview various historical definitions and approaches to thinking about justice and gives consideration to some of the linguistic and philosophical difficulties. Since social justice represents a foundational construct for both social work practice and Christian faith, I will explore both challenges and points of congruence that arise for Christians in social work practice who wish to integrate their biblical faith with current understandings of social justice. Justice as a legal term connoting distribution of resources or fairness in court proceedings has been the dominant conceptual framework for thinking about justice in both historic Christianity and the profession of social work. This paper presents a conceptual framework that goes beyond justice as fairness to justice as an ideal that reflects the human longing for wholeness and harmony in human relationships.

Historic Understandings of Justice

Definitions of social justice abound, as do descriptions of various types of social justice. The most common idea of justice is distributive in nature. Distributive justice is concerned with how resources, material goods, influence, and power are shared among people. Sometimes this is summed up by the classic phrase, *suum cuique*, "to each what is due" (Hollenbach, 1977, p. 207). Retributive justice is concerned with punishing wrongdoers, commonly represented by the idea of "an eye for an eye." The American criminal justice system is largely based on retributive justice. In recent years, the criminal justice system has experimented with restorative justice, a form of justice that goes beyond punishing wrongdoers and strives to reconcile criminals and victims (Burford & Adams, 2004; Colson, 2001; Wilson, 2000). Commutative justice refers to a balanced and fair system for agreements or contracts, such as wage laws.

Historically, justice was seen as supreme among all the virtues. It was one of the four cardinal virtues. Socrates posed the question "What is justice?" to Plato in *The Republic* and launched the centuries-long philosophical discourse that has shaped much of western philosophy (Solomon & Murphy, p. 13). Cicero asserted two principles that defined justice. The first was to "do no harm, unless provoked by wrong." The second was to contribute to the common good or overall social welfare (as cited in Langan, 1977, p. 157).

For the ancient Greeks, justice was linked to human well-being, but it accepted class differences and inequality. Plato's conception of justice was one of harmony in the community, but within the community of one's natural status or class. Aristotle followed Plato's lead. He did not believe that people were equal. For him, justice was the single virtue that was directed at "the other" but justice did not require a redistribution of resources in order to arrive at a more fair distribution with the other. Rather, justice entailed accepting one's position in life in the hierarchical scheme established by one's birth (McGrath, 1986; Reisch, 2002).

The Greek philosophers reflect an enduring tension between the retributive principles of just deserts or vengeance that characterize some ideas of justice with the civic virtues of harmony and peace. The ideal of justice that Plato describes as a virtue has to be worked out in the practicalities of life. How do we achieve a just society?

In ancient religious and political practices, both in the East and the West, the appeal for justice is to a divine or singularly authoritative being, such as an emperor. Both the Bible and the Koran appeal to divine authority. The idea of "an eye for an eye" is balanced with appeals to divine and human mercy (Solomon & Murphy, 1990) and suggests the limitations of retribution, an "eye" and no more than an "eye." In ancient China and in Greece, Confucius and Plato assert the authority of the state in settling issues of justice (Solomon & Murphy, 1990). This early acknowledgement of the need for a standard bearer in identifying and upholding justice is a critical point for contemporary discussion of justice.

In *The Republic*, Plato asserts that "the just man and the just city will be no different but alike as regards the very form of justice." The way to identify or define justice is "when each one of us within whom each part is fulfilling its own task will himself be just and do his own work" (as cited in Solomon & Murphy, 1990, 36). The question of whose justice and what standard establishes justice endures to contemporary times. One modern effort to offer a global standard for basic human rights and justice is the United Nations' 1948 *Universal Declaration of Human Rights*. The use of this document, though, requires interpretation about whether in fact justice exists in a given society and begs the question about what privileges this document more than others to define human rights.

The idea of justice in the West bore the imprint of the ancient philosophers' questions about the nature of existence coupled with the theology of the church. Discussion about justice tended to be focused on civil order. In *Summa Theologica*, Aquinas joined the Christian faith and the metaphysics of the philosophers, especially Aristotle, to articulate a theology that dominated the life and thought of the Church until the eighteenth century. Regarding justice, Aquinas emphasized distributive principles.

By the eighteenth century, Thomas Hobbes, John Locke, and Jean-Jacques Rousseau had given shape with various new twists to the idea of justice as a social contract (Solomon & Murphy, 1990). John Stuart Mill advocated utilitarianism as a means to arbitrate the social contract in the nineteenth century and, in doing so, further undermined the idea that justice is an ideal inherent in nature (Solomon

& Murphy, 1990). The social contract idea has pervaded the discussion about justice until modern times and is reflected in documents such as the Declaration of Independence and the Universal Declaration of Human Rights.

In the twentieth century, John Rawls' *A Theory of Justice* became the central and dominant voice about the meaning of justice (Banerjee, 2005; Solomon & Murphy, 1990). His theory is a version of the social contract but added the idea of social responsibility to those who are disadvantaged. By this time the idea of justice as an ideal or virtue, or as something more than mere distribution or retribution, had virtually disappeared from the conversation about justice. Justice was linked with the social contract and with the idea of fairness, whether in distribution of resources or in response to wrongdoing. The ancient Hebrew belief in an ideal state of harmony, peace, equality, virtue, and right relationships called justice had been set into a legal and rationalistic framework of contractual law. The essence or character of justice had given way to the practicalities of how to do it.

Biblical Backgrounds

The ancient Hebrew concept of justice appears in the earliest biblical records. The idea of justice is a central theme throughout the Old Testament as it gives an account of the history of the revelation of God's justice. In the Hebrew Bible, two words are translated justice: *sedaqah* and *mishpat*. These two terms are often used in combination for emphasis. *Sedaqah* is about God's plan to build community, to establish right relationships. Some older meanings connect the idea to victory and to the right ordering of affairs (McGrath, 1986). It is not used in the Old Testament in a legal sense to refer to punishment. *Mishpat* is commonly a legal term or claim on an individual. (Mott, 1982; Ripley, 2001).

Emil Brunner noted that the modern age restricted the original meaning of justice and its immense scope and reduced it to mean "giving to each what is due" (as cited in Lebacqz, p. 114). Mott (2000) claims that justice in the Hebrew mind was closer in meaning to "love" than to the distributive meaning of the modern age. Ripley (2001) asserts that the "root of God's justice, no matter how exacting, is always in the context of God's desire for a loving relationship."

McGrath (1986) analyzes the etymology for the Hebrew word *sedaqah* and asserts the fundamental meaning connects the idea to covenantal relationships and in that context to "conformity to a norm." The basic idea of *sedaqah* had meaning for the ancient Hebrews in the law court where the standard for the court was the covenant law with God, the Torah. Thus, being just was being in conformity to the covenant with God (Wright, 2006). It was bound to the idea of wholeness and harmony in relationships.

The New Testament treatment of justice continues the Hebrew focus on right relationships. *Dikaiosune* is the Greek word in the New Testament generally translated "justice" or "righteousness." According to Vine (1996, p. 298), it is the "character or quality of being right or just" or whatever has been appointed by God as right. It designates a relationship rather than an inherent personal quality (Williams, 1980). The word reflects the Hebraic concept of covenant, the establishment of a loving, faithful, and true relationship. A covenant is a binding commitment, with reciprocal benefits and responsibilities. The biblical sense of justice is one of hope and promise, salvation and victory, so that people will thrive in social relationships (Ripley, 2001). Wolterstorff (1983) connects justice with *shalom*. Shalom is the "human being dwelling at peace in all his or her relationships" (p. 70). Justice is fundamental to *shalom*.

The grand narrative of the Bible relates the story of justice. God created people who fractured their relationship with the Creator in an act of rebellion. The rebellion resulted in broken relationships, not only with God, but also in the family and throughout society. Human history provides the evidence of pervasive brokenness and records human efforts to create systems, structures, and laws that reach toward the establishment of justice, or a restoration of right relationships. The incarnation of Jesus, his death and resurrection, and redemption for believers provides a way to restore justice in all relationships.

Christian justice is not dependent on context or culture or individuals. It is founded on the very nature and character of God. The two great commandments, "to love God with all your heart, soul, strength, and mind, and to love your neighbor as yourself" express this nature in a succinct fashion (Kunst, 1983, p. 111).

The Essence of Justice

When conflicts arose between my two daughters and their sense of justice was violated, I sometimes had them sit at a table together and take turns saying kind things to the other. They despised this discipline at the time, but the eventual result was usually laughter, their recognition of the many positive traits of the other, and a realization that good relationships were valuable. They had wanted me to be fair and punish the one who had wronged the other, but trying to arrive at "fairness" seemed to exacerbate the problem.

I could rarely assess who was at fault because I often had not directly observed the contested interaction. I also could not judge them equally responsible because they were not equal. Oliver Wendell Holmes once observed that "there is no greater inequality than the equal treatment of unequals" (as cited in Rosado, 1995). One child was three years older, thus bigger, stronger, and more verbally adept. How could I determine fairness between the two?

I found trying to assess fairness frustrating and it did not produce the outcome that I actually desired. I wanted my daughters to grow old together, be lifelong friends, and enjoy genuine harmony and peace. What I wanted was a peaceful and loving relationship to develop between them and within the household. I wanted the *shalom* of the Bible.

A value such as social justice only has meaning for a culture if everyone has a similar understanding of what that value is. For example, love is a value esteemed in American society, but love means many different things to people. For one person, love is self-sacrifice. For another, it is a romantic liaison. Love may mean "never having to say you are sorry" or it may be "do unto others as you would have them do unto you." Americans have not settled on a standard definition for love. Regardless of the number of definitions for love, the value is fundamentally social in nature. Justice, like love, is also fundamentally social in nature, and, like love, how it is understood depends on one's perspective.

Justice is dependent on the connections between and among persons. Justice is often associated with love or contrasted with charity or mercy (Sider, 1999). Augustine defined justice in terms of love in his essay, *De Moribus ecclesiae catholicae* (as cited in Langan, 1977, p. 173). Volf (1996, p. 223) asserts, "If you want justice without injustice, you must want love." Cassidy (1989, p. 442) suggests that justice is about "putting love into structures." If love establishes right relationships, then just structures serve to ensure the desired outcome; justice defines the laws or means that result in loving relationships. The apostle John captures this connection, especially in relation to distributive justice, "But whoever has the world's goods, and beholds his brother in need and closes his heart against him, how does the love of God abide in him?" (I John 3:17, NASB).

It is much easier to identify justice by what it is not than by what it is. Injustice is easily recognized when it happens to us or to "our group." We are much less adept at identifying injustice when it happens to groups of others outside our familiar social categories. Only when we are well connected with others can we recognize when they are experiencing a sense of injustice. Thus, assessing justice requires a level of intimacy in relationships that acknowledges the experienced reality of others. We "enlarge our thinking" by listening to others, especially those with whom we differ, and allowing them to help us see from their perspective (Volf, 1996, p. 213).

Dorothy Day, a Christian activist in the Catholic Workers' Movement, voiced concern for justice in the 1930s. She said, "We need always to be thinking and writing about [poverty], for if we are not among its victims, its reality fades from us. We must talk about poverty because people insulated by their own comfort lose sight of it" (as cited in Kauffman, 2003). Dr. Martin Luther King, Jr. in his *Letter from a Birmingham Jail* extended the responsibility to know the experience of others far beyond the immediate family or neighborhood relationships. He said, "Injustice anywhere is a threat to justice everywhere" (King, 1963, p. 77). Concern for social justice requires knowledge and understanding beyond one's own small circle of friends, extending to the world.

The Social Work Profession and Social Justice

The social work profession has its own history and claim on the concept of social justice. *The Social Work Dictionary* defines justice as "an ideal condition in which all members of a society have the same basic rights, protection, opportunities, obligations, and social benefits," (Barker, 2003, p. 404). This definition suggests a distributive principle in which resources and opportunities are spread about the entire population in a fair manner. Rawls' work has shaped the contemporary landscape for the profession of social work as well as for the larger society (Banerjee, 2005; Rawls, 1971). His development of the idea of the social contract rests on a definition of justice as relational, but based on fair distribution. He is also concerned that the least advantaged are helped in any process of redistribution. Other contemporary social work voices emphasize various dimensions of the concept of justice. Young (1990) argues for a relational type of social justice that includes more than simply a just distribution of goods, but also insists upon fair representation, participation, and influence in decision-making. Others have linked social justice with structures that lead to oppression and thus connected social justice to diversity and multiculturalism (Finn & Jacobsen, 2003; Reisch, 2002). In a more recent and radical step, Reichert (2001, 2003) believes that the lack of a clear definition for social justice begs for a shift in social work thought to that of a "rights-based perspective" utilizing the *Universal Declaration of Human Rights* as a guide or standard.

The social work profession mandates that social workers challenge injustice. It is one of the six core values and ethical principles of the profession as written in the *Code of Ethics* of the National Association of Social Workers (NASW). The Council on Social Work Education (CSWE, 2003) mandates in its *Educational Policy and Accreditation Standards* that curriculum includes social justice content "grounded in an understanding of distributive justice, human and civil rights, and the global interconnections of oppression." Though social justice is not defined explicitly by the CSWE in this document, it does assert that social work practice should entail "strategies to promote social and economic justice" and "advocacy for nondiscriminatory social and economic systems."

Wakefield (1988a) views social justice as the primary mission of social work and insists upon fairness and access to resources. Reid and Popple (1992) argue for a moral foundation to social work, an objective rule that supplies a standard for measuring what is right. They do not offer a source or basis for their moral foundation or describe the standard apart from the ethical assertions of the profession. Even though no clear agreement exists regarding the components of justice or appropriate strategies for achieving justice, the profession's conversation continues. Questions about whose rights trump the others' and how goods should be distributed seem to change with the winds of culture and political realities. Countless others in social work have written about social justice with the usual emphasis on distribution of resources and access to them (Pelton, 2001; Scanlon & Longres, 2001).

Standards of Justice

Defining justice in social terms suggests the possibility that "right" or just relationships can happen, that a standard for right relationships exists. The challenge begins with describing what right relationships are like and is fulfilled with achieving them. Metaphors and symbols serve an important function as societies strive to achieve the ideal. Perhaps the most common symbol for justice is a scale. This symbol confines justice to the idea of distribution. It was used for measurements of goods until recent times. The scale as a metaphor illustrates the push and pull of often opposing voices striving for justice. It demonstrates the power of perspective and social location. In the construction industry a plumb line serves as a symbol of what is just. A wall is straight, or just, if the plumb line measures it as straight. The plumb line functions because of the law of gravity that establishes a universal standard of perpendicularity to the ground. Modern computers can "justify" margins either to the left or the right or the middle of a page. Accountants "justify" or reconcile the debits and credits for a business, bringing the account into balance. The ancient mythological image of Justitia, an angelic, blindfolded woman with a sword in one hand and scales in the other, represents an ideal justice that holds no special interest, is blind to the objects of justice and thus can render justice fairly and truly. All of these metaphors for justice rely on the idea that a standard exists by which justice can be assessed. The standard varies from a natural law such as gravity, to a balance between two existing products such as debits and credits.

From ancient time to the present, a system of measurements ensured a common and reliable standard for measurements of tangible materials. This system is gaining precision. In ancient times, the measurement of a foot, or twelve inches, was roughly equivalent to the length of a man's foot. In the present time, scientists can measure distance to sub-atomic precision in nanometers or to galactic proportions in light years. If justice is by its nature relational, it must be evaluated in relation to something, or someone, that is consistent across time and space. When measuring social relationships, the standard has to be a social relationship. Societies have produced social standards for justice, all of which have been declared obsolete or have changed over time. The emperor or king may have set the standard in some cases. When one king died, his standard of justice died with him. The new king had a different set of standards. In other cultures, laws and rules arose, but laws and rules change. Some cultures created and lived by mythologies or religious beliefs about gods who ruled the world. Whatever happened was at the will of the gods. People accepted the "justice" of the gods.

The incarnation of God in Jesus Christ poses an entirely different kind of standard. C.S. Lewis sums up his view of all the fundamental myths that have dominated human literature and culture in a 1931 letter to his friend Arthur Greeves: "Now the story of Christ is simply a true myth: a myth working on us in the same way as the others, but with this tremendous difference—that *it really happened*" (Hooper, 2004, p. 977). Christian faith offers an unequivocal and unchanging standard of justice—God in the person of Jesus Christ. If Jesus, the incarnation of God on earth, serves as the standard, then the acquisition of justice is dependent on a right relationship to this person.

Justice is not ever going to be satisfied by a set of rights or laws or moral principles or anything less than that encompassed in the story of relationship. Other approaches to justice lack a standard that is consistent over time and space by which to evaluate what is just. Jesus Christ is an historical figure. He lived, died, and was resurrected in history. He sets a standard for just relationships unparalleled in any other mythological or philosophical system. Christians, then, accept Jesus himself as the model and standard for justice. He was the bearer of a new possibility of human, social, and therefore political relationships (Scott, 1980; Yoder, 1972). How believers behave in social relationships is "just" based only on its likeness to the way that Jesus would have behaved. Jesus states it this way in Matthew 25: "to the extent that you did it to one of these brothers of Mine, even the least of them, you did it to me" (Mt. 25:40, New American Standard Bible).

Two Streams of Christian Tradition

The Christian tradition is rooted in the grand narrative of the Bible, but Christian tradition is not pure. It represents coalescence of multiple cultures and times interpreting the Scriptures and the traditions in various ways. Volf (1996) argues that the church should not, even if it could, attempt to develop one "coherent tradition." Rather, the church should be interested in "affirming basic Christian commitments in culturally situated ways" (pp. 210-211).

The historic Christian tradition has produced two dominant streams of thought about social justice; one emphasizes the common good or institutional well-being, and the other the rights and responsibilities of the individual. Both offer a pathway toward a just and caring society, though with different means to the end. Many variations of these two themes have emerged through the years depending on the political, economic, and social context for the church.

The Catholic Church has a long tradition of Christian social teaching and represents an emphasis on the institutional community of faith and the common good. This tradition is marked by three fundamental values or premises: 1) All people are created in the image and likeness of God and thus have value and dignity; 2) God created people to live in community together; we are social creatures and need each other, and 3) Each person has a right to share in the abundance of nature, though this right is accompanied by responsibilities (Lebacqz, 1986).

For many centuries the Catholic Church dominated the western Christian landscape. The vision for justice was set in a worldview that understood individual rights, for each person was uniquely made by God, but the emphasis was on the social nature of our condition. It is for the welfare of individuals that society, and especially Christians, should be concerned for the common good. The emphasis in Catholic social teaching on the common good serves as a harness to runaway individualism. It keeps in check the human tendency toward seeking one's own interests at the expense of others. In the nineteenth and twentieth centuries, Catholic teaching understood Hebrew Scriptures to suggest that God gave preferential treatment to the poor and so should the church. The Bishop's Letter of 1971 asserts that the "justice of a community is measured by its treatment of the powerless in society" (as cited in Lebacqz, 1986, p. 72).

The second stream of Christian teaching emerged significantly during the years of the Protestant Reformation. As Martin Luther challenged the bureaucracy and practices of the Catholic Church, he ushered into Christian teaching what became a more privatized and personalized religious life. "Faith alone" became the theme of Protestant thought and eternal salvation the goal, not by works, but by faith. The phrase in Romans 1:17 (NASB), "the righteousness (*dikaiosune*) of God is revealed from faith to faith," served as a basis for Luther's stand that human effort could not achieve what the work of God could in the heart of a person (Ripley, 2001).

Each person had the ability and responsibility to stand before God with his eternal destiny in the balance. The kingdom of God and his justice (*dikaiosune*) described a future kingdom. Justice in this present age was beyond reach. According to some, the influence of the church to shape civil society decreased and interest in social justice declined as a result of the Protestant Reformation (Dulles, 1977; Emerson & Smith, 2000; Haughey, 1977; Lebacqz, 1986; Roach, 1977). However, other influences such as the breakdown of the feudal system with its social contract and the rise of urbanization and industrialization also had significant impact on how church and state both viewed social welfare.

How society approaches social justice depends somewhat on the starting place for discussion. The two streams of Christian thought represented by Catholic thought and Protestant thought are not as simple as described above. They are much more complex based on the particularities of the historical context and the multitude of voices that have articulated differing positions along the continuum. Catholic tradition certainly has not always emphasized the common good, nor has Protestant tradition neglected the pursuit of the common good. What began with Constantine as an attempt to Christianize the western world and serve the general social welfare devolved into a pursuit of political power and status among the clergy and systems of indulgences and penances that strapped the common folk. These two streams can serve, though, as a picture of the dichotomy, or tension, which exists between an emphasis on the common good and that of individual rights and responsibilities.

Linguistic Challenges

The ancient Greeks had two words commonly translated as justice. They are *isotes*, which means equality, and *dikaiosune* which is translated as righteousness (Solomon & Murphy, 1990). The selection of words used in translation suggests nuances of meaning, and over time translations can alter the original intent of the user. Though *isotes* means equality, the ancient Greeks hardly espoused an egalitarian society. On the other hand, *dikaiosune,* when translated as righteousness, suggests a connection with the idea of personal and civic virtues that were so important to the ancient Greek philosophers. Language translation reflects the persistent difficulty in capturing the meaning of justice through history and across cultures and also within cultures.

The translation of the Bible has played an important, though subtle, role in how Christians have thought about justice. New Testament translations have a particularly powerful impact on current understanding.

The Latin Vulgate, used in the early life of the church, translated the Greek word *dikaiosune* into the word *justitio* (McGrath, 1986). Early English translations, such as the King James Version, translated the Latin Vulgate's *justitio* as "justice." After the powerful influence of the Reformation, and more translations developed, the New Testament rendering of *dikaiosune* often became "righteousness." With the Protestant emphasis on personal faith and individual rights and responsibilities, righteousness began to be connected commonly with personal regeneration and likeness to Christ.

The connotation of social justice, that is right relationships between and among people, was subsumed by the drive toward personal morality and piety.

Interestingly, modern English translations seldom translate *dikaiosune* as justice. However, *dikaiosune* is the central theme in Jesus' Sermon on the Mount in the Gospel of Matthew. It is used at every juncture to signify the mission of Jesus to usher in the kingdom of God. For his inaugural sermon in the synagogue at the beginning of his public ministry, Jesus draws on the prophet Isaiah's rendering of the future kingdom, "The spirit of the Lord is upon me, because he anointed me to preach the Gospel to the poor. He has sent me to proclaim release to the captives, and recovery of sight to the blind, to set free those who are downtrodden, to proclaim the favorable year of the Lord" (Luke 4: 18-19, NASB). This seems to indicate that Jesus saw his own mission in "justice" terms as Isaiah had foretold. The coming kingdom was to establish "justice to the nations" (Isaiah 42:1, NASB). In fact, Jesus is announcing that he is justice incarnated (Haughey, 1977).

When *dikaiosune* is translated as righteousness, as it is in most modern English translations, it is commonly understood as doing what is right or holy and faithful to the promises of God as an individual. A pardon from sin "interiorizes the meaning too much and fails to account adequately for the dimension of practical social justice" (Scott, 1980, p. 85). This translation fails to evoke the "powerful social transformation" that the word suggests in the original language. Reconciled and restored relationships identify the central motif in all justice issues (Bader-Saye, 2003). Luther's reformation, though probably not intended by Luther himself, taught that God expects believers to be just, or righteous by their faith alone, an interior state of being. Belief in Jesus will ensure that people will have God's righteousness, but it can be a highly individualized and compartmentalized faith that has little relevance to social relationships and the larger social order (Ripley, 2001). Personal conversion and piety with a view toward the afterlife become paramount rather than the present social order.

In contemporary society, the word "justice" inevitably draws one's attention to the legal aspects of the word. Distribution of resources, fairness in law, crime, and its consequences, and the system that executes "justice" over wrongs are the images that emerge. Justice and judgment are inextricably linked. The affirmation that "God is just" suggests that God is the great judge who will bring punishment and condemnation for wrongdoers.

The original linguistic intentions of *sedaqah* and *dikaiosune* that reflect a positive image of restoration of covenant relationships have been lost. The connection of justice with love and mercy has disappeared. Mercy and justice serve as contrasting approaches to wrongs committed rather than as a picture of restoration of wholeness.

Church and State

Since Constantine, the church in the West had assumed major responsibility for addressing social problems such as poverty, illness, and abuse. Understanding of the new life in Christ and biblical mandates, as well as tradition, suggested that the church was responsible for alleviating pain and suffering and providing for the needy. The poor and needy were offered help as an act of worship of God, not because they had a "right" to it. The church and synagogue were the standard bearers for social services (Leiby, 1985). The early church teachings, including the *Didache*, *The Shepherd of Hermas*, as well as teachings of Polycarp, Clement, Cyprian, and many others, asserted the rights of the poor and the responsibility of the rich. They exhibited a radical sense of community across economic strata (Walsh & Langan, 1977). The poor were seen as entitled to care because they are made in the image of God.

These teachings persisted through the history of the church, though the implementation of justice was certainly not always in accord with this ideal (Poe, 2002b). As Protestantism developed and the church and state became less bound together in the eighteenth and nineteenth centuries, the nature of care for the needy changed; understanding of social justice shifted as well. Which social institution, the church or the state, was the keeper of social justice? Increasingly, the state alone became the arbiter of social justice. The rule of law articulated the standard for social justice and the means for executing it.

The profession of social work emerged largely from the impetus of the faith community and its adherents (Poe, 2002a). The motivation toward promoting social welfare was one's faith and the societal belief that God was concerned for all. In the early twentieth century as the social work profession was developing credibility, practice models, leadership, and relevance, its relationship with the faith community began to change. In the twentieth century, the social work profession bought into state jurisdiction of social welfare while evangelical and mainline churches largely relinquished it. The Catholic Church persisted with a strong emphasis on social justice in such efforts as the Catholic Workers' Movement, but it had lost a considerable amount of political power. Under the influence of the Enlightenment, mainline Protestant churches reacted to an evangelical emphasis on personal regeneration and bought into a rationalistic and empirical emphasis during the nineteenth and twentieth centuries (Poe, 2002a). The state became accepted as the arbiter of social welfare and all issues of justice.

With the church as the entity giving meaning and direction for social justice, the standard for justice and indeed for all social relationships was Jesus. The aim was the kingdom of God. When the state became the defining institution for implementing social welfare services, the standard became the rule of law and human rights. The goal of social welfare shifted to following welfare policies, "regulating the poor," or controlling protest against injustice rather than eliminating injustice (Burford & Adams, 2004; Leiby, 1985; Piven & Cloward, 1971).

The modern evangelical church has largely missed its opportunities to promote justice during seasons of great social upheaval. Two examples may illustrate the impact that the privatization of faith and righteousness may have had on the role of the church as champion of social justice.

In the United States, the Civil Rights movement of the 1960s had little support from White, evangelical churches. The battle was fought primarily in the public and political arenas and the courts. The Catholic Church and more liberal, mainline Protestant churches had more representation, but, generally, the fight for social justice was dependent on the legal and political systems of the state. The Black church with its limited power embraced the idea of systemic change and provided leadership to advocate for it. It understood that the arbiter of justice was the state but they appealed to the witness of the church. King's *Letter from a Birmingham Jail* (1963) illustrates his dismay at the inability of White clergymen to connect social justice and Christian living. The White evangelical voice was not engaged as an advocate for social justice.

Likewise, in the 1970s and 1980s, evangelical leaders were not concerned with apartheid in South Africa. The "talk was of justification, personal, wonderful justification by faith, but never of justice" (Cassidy, 1989, p. 73). Individual church leaders, such as Archbishop Desmond Tutu, were advocates for biblical justice. The South African ship of state, though, hearkened for many long years to a rule of law that was undergirded by an entrenched but flawed theological system that privatized faith and left social justice out of the equation. Both of these social movements reflect the power of the state to shape social welfare policy. The voice of the church was mediated by individuals through governmental structures, leaving the true witness of the institutional church for social justice to be compromised.

Contemporary Challenges

A challenge exists for both the social work profession and biblical Christianity when defining and promoting social justice. For the profession, the challenge is to identify what standard can be used to evaluate the attainment of justice. Reichert's suggestion to move the profession away from the concept of social justice to one of human rights does not solve this problem (Reichert, 2001, 2003). In fact, to abandon a foundational value of the profession due to its elusiveness seems irresponsible. The profession has to grapple with its roots in the Judeo-Christian tradition that provided a philosophical and ethical basis for the values that shaped its development (Sherwood, 1996). It surely cannot be satisfied if each person has their portion and their rights, but relationships between and among people are still fractured and strained.

The *NASW Code of Ethics* asserts in another of its six core ethical principles that social workers are to recognize the central importance of human relationships. The *Universal Declaration of Human Rights*, while extremely valuable as a guide toward distributive justice, does not give guidance to restore broken relationships and establish *shalom*. And though it is used as a standard, measuring alignment with the standard is elusive. How much education or health care does one have a right to claim? While grounded in the belief that being human merits certain rights and deems one worthy of value, it simply aims at freedom from harm and a minimal fairness in material distribution and access to resources. It does not in fact offer a universal standard for determining when the claims of justice have been met. The profession separates social justice and human relationships into two separate core values. These two values are inextricably linked and undergirded as well by the NASW core value of the worth and dignity of the each person.

Christians do have a universal and objective standard for measuring justice, though Christians themselves do not have the capability of fully attaining or even assessing alignment with the standard with precision. This poses a challenge.

Another challenge is to restore the balanced, biblical understanding of justice that includes both the individual and the social dimension of the concept. Personal faith has to be accompanied by an engagement in the social dimensions of righteousness as reflected through orthodox Christian belief and tradition. Not doing justice is not an option for Christian discipleship. Consider the multiple appeals of the prophets to "do justice" (Micah 6:8, NASB); to "establish justice" (Amos 5:15, NASB); to "preserve justice" (Isaiah 56:1, NASB). The justice of the Bible is not simply fairness. It includes an "embrace of the other" (Volf, 1996, p. 221). What matters is the relationship. This is ultimately what defines justice for a Christian believer. Martin Luther King, Jr. said that social advance in history does not "roll on the wheels of inevitability. Every step towards the goal of justice requires...tireless exertions" (as cited in Cassidy, 1989, p. 463).

The exertions promoting social justice suggest personal responsibility and engagement in the social order. The triumph of early Christianity was its radical sense of community, that everyone would be brought into the fellowship and cared for (Walsh & Langum, 1977). Christians are called to faith and works that lead to a restoration of right relationships, whether an individual's relationship with a neighbor, the relationship of one tribe to another, or one nation to another. Fairness simply does not satisfy the demands of justice.

Societies have constructed elaborate systems of laws and rules, and in the process have settled for fairness as the ultimate expression of justice. The distributive principle of justice has dominated the thinking. The Christian concept of justice, based on biblical principles, involves much more than fairness in the distribution of resources. It is fundamentally a restoration of relational harmony.

Jesus serves as a model for demonstrating justice by the manner in which he related to different people and different societal institutions. He did not treat everyone the same, as though some law or guidebook instructed him. Rather, Jesus demonstrated the capacity to make nuanced judgments, informed by laws but not restricted by the merely human standards or customs of the day. Jesus touched the untouchables, breaking the rules but offering a possibility of restored relationships to a community. He challenged the religious leaders, again violating the customs of the day, but in so doing, offered to the community a chance for *shalom*. Jesus crossed ethnic and gender barriers that produced oppressive environments in efforts to demonstrate what a just and caring world might require. Ultimately, Jesus' death and resurrection give hope to the Christian faithful and a vision for a community of wholeness.

Christian social workers must struggle along with the profession regarding how justice plays out in the world. Christians should be concerned about the distribution of resources and power and access to these resources. They should be concerned about legal systems and human rights. Christians should also strive to understand the biblical concept of social justice, grounded in the very nature of God, and the implications for a just society that is guided by Christian faith. As Christians in social work, the ultimate goal for practice entails a much deeper and richer reality for the nature of human relationships than fairness. The movement in criminal justice settings toward restorative justice is one example of the yearning for this approach.

The prophet Micah proclaims for all time the requirements of God for his people, "to do justice, to love kindness, and to walk humbly with your God" (Micah 6:8, NASB). In the poetic literary tradition of the Hebrew language, this is not three requirements, but one. Doing justice, loving kindness, and walking with humility are rhyming thoughts in Hebrew. They are all part of a unified endeavor that brings wholeness to relationships in the community.

Thus the radical call of God for justice is more than just an even distribution of goods or a fair retribution for wrongs. It is concerned with the quality and nature of the relationships between and among people. This is what I wanted my daughters to experience together in their simple experiences of injustice and this is what I desire for Christians who give their lives to promoting social justice in their social work practice.

References

Bader-Saye, S. (2003). Violence, reconciliation, and the justice of God [Electronic version]. *Crosscurrents, 52*(4), 536-542.

Banerjee, M. (2005). Social work, Rawlsian social justice, and social development [Electronic version]. *Social Development Issues 27*(1), 6-24.

Barker, R. (2003). *The Social Work Dictionary* (5th ed.). Washington D. C.:NASW Press

Burford, G. & Adams, P. (2004). Restorative justice, responsive regulation and social work. *Journal of Sociology and Social Welfare, 31*(1), 7-26.

Cassidy, M. (1989). *The passing summer: A South African's response to White fear, Black anger, and the politics of love.* London: Hodder & Stoughton.

Colson, C. (2001). *Justice that restores.* Wheaton, Il.: Tyndale House Publishers, Inc.

Council on Social Work Education. (2003). *Handbook of accreditation standards and procedures, (5th ed.).* Alexandria, VA: CSWE.

Dulles, A. (1977). The meaning of faith considered in relationship to justice. In J. C. Haughey, (Ed.). *The faith that does justice: Examining the Christian sources for social change.* New York: Paulist Press.

Dunn, J. D. G & Suggate, A. M. (1993). *The justice of God: A fresh look at the old doctrine of justification by faith.* Grand Rapids, MI: Wm. B. Eerdman's Publishing Co.

Emerson, M. O. & Smith, C. S. (2000). *Divided by faith: Evangelical religion and the problem of race in America.* Oxford: Oxford University Press.

Finn, J. & Jacobsen, M. (2003). *Just practice: A social justice approach to social work.* Peosta, IL: Eddie Bowers Publishing Co.

Haughey, J. C. (Ed.). (1977). *The faith that does justice: Examining the Christian sources for social change.* New York: Paulist Press.

Hollenbach, D. (1977). Modern Catholic teachings concerning justice. In Haughey, J. C. (Ed.) *The faith that does justice: Examining the Christian sources for social change.* New York: Paulist Press.

Hooper, W. (Ed.). (2004). *The collected letters of C. S. Lewis, volume 1.* NY: Harper San-Francisco.

Kauffman, R. A. (2003). Justice. *Christianity Today, 37*(3), 70.

King, M. L. Jr. (1963). *Why we can't wait.* New York: The New American Library-Mentor Books.

Kunst, T. J. W. (1983). The kingdom of God and social justice [Electronic version]. *Bibliotheca sacra 140 (April-June),* 108-116.

Langan, J. P. (1977). What Jerusalem says to Athens. In Haughey, J. C. (Ed.) *The faith that does justice: Examining the Christian sources for social change.* New York: Paulist Press.

Lebacqz, K. (1986). *Six theories of justice: Perspectives from philosophical and theological ethics.* Minneapolis, MN: Augsburg Publishing House.

Leiby, J. (1985). Moral foundations of social welfare and social work: A historical view. *Social Work, 30*(4), 323-330.

McGrath, A. (1986). *Justitia Dei: A history of the Christian doctrine of justification.* Cambridge: Cambridge University Press.

Mott, S. C. (2000). Foundations of the welfare responsibility of the government. In S. W. Carlson-Thies & J. W. Skillen (Eds.). *Welfare in America: Christian perspectives on a policy in crisis.* Grand Rapids, MI: Wm. B. Eerdman's Publishing Co.

Mott, S. C. (1982). *Biblical ethics and social change.* New York: Oxford University Press.

National Association of Social Workers. (1996). *NASW code of ethics.* Washington D. C: NASW Press.

Pelton, L. H. (2001). Social justice and social work [Electronic version]. *Journal of Social Work Education. 37*(3) 433-439.

Piven, F. F & Cloward, R. A. (1971). *Regulating the poor: The functions of public welfare.* New York: Vintage Books.

Poe, M. A. (2002a). Christian worldview and social work. In D. S. Dockery & G. A. Thornbury (Eds.). *Shaping a Christian worldview: The foundations of Christian higher education.* Nashville, TN: Broadman & Holman Publishers. Pp. 317-334.

Poe, M. A. (2002b). Good news for the poor: Christian influences on social welfare. In B. Hugen & T. L. Scales (Eds.). *Christianity and social work: Readings on the integration of Christian faith and social work practice* (2nd ed.). Botsford, CT: NACSW.

Rawls, J. (1971). *A theory of justice.* Cambridge, MA: Harvard University Press.

Reichert, E. (2003). *Social work and human rights.* New York: Columbia University Press.

Reichert, E. (2001). Move from social justice to human rights provides new perspective. *Journal of Professional Development, 4*(1), 5-11.

Reid, P. & Popple, P. (1992). *The moral purposes of social work.* Chicago, IL: Nelson-Hall Press.

Reisch, M. (2002). Defining social justice in a socially unjust world [Electronic version]. *Families in Society, 83*(4), 343-354.

Ripley, J. I. (2001). Covenantal concepts of justice and righteousness, and Catholic-Protestant reconciliation: Theological implications and explorations [Electronic version]. *Journal of Ecumenical Studies, 38*(1) 95-109.

Roach, R. R. (1977). Tridentine justification and justice. In J. C. Haughey, (Ed.). *The faith that does justice: Examining the Christian sources for social change.* New York: Paulist Press.

Rosado, C. (1995). God's affirmative justice, *Christianity Today, 39*(13) 34-35.

Scanlon, E. & Longres, J. F. (2001). Social work and social justice: A reply to Leroy Pelton [Electronic version]. *Journal of Social Work Education, 37*(3) 441-444.

Scott, Waldron (1980). *Bring forth justice.* Grand Rapids, MI: Wm. B. Eerdman's Publishing Co.

Sherwood, D. (1996). Asking the impertinent question: Why should I care? *Social Work and Christianity,* 23(2) 79-85.

Sider, R. (1999). *Just generosity: A new vision for overcoming poverty in America.* Grand Rapids, MI: Baker Book House.

Solomon, R. C. & Murphy, M. C (1990). *What is justice? Classic and contemporary readings.* New York: Oxford University Press.

United Nations. (1948). *Universal Declaration of Human Rights.* Retrieved June 13, 2006 fromhttp://www.unhchr.ch/udhr/lang/eng.htm.

Vine, W. E. (1996). *An expository dictionary of New Testament words with their precise meanings for English readers.* Old Tappan, NJ; Fleming H. Revell Co.

Volf, Miroslav (1996). *Exclusion and embrace.* Nashville, TN: Abingdon Press.

Wakefield, J. C. (1988a). Psychotherapy, distributive justice, and social work. Part 1: Distributive justice as a conceptual framework for social work [Electronic version]. *Social Service Review,* 62(2), 187-210.

Walsh, W. J. & Langan, J. P. (1977). Patristic social consciousness: The church and the poor. In J. C. Haughey (Ed.). *The faith that does justice: Examining the Christian sources for social change.* New York: Paulist Press.

Williams, S. K. (1980). The "righteousness of God" in Romans [Electronic version]. *Journal of Biblical Literature,* 99(2), 241-291.

Wilson, J. (2000). Crying for justice: When victims in grief meet offenders in shame, profound new healing takes place. HOPE, 3-8.

Wolterstorff, N (1983). *Until justice and peace embrace.* Grand Rapids, MI: Wm. B. Eerdman's Publishing Co.

Wright, N. T. (2006, May 1). Righteousness. *New Dictionary of Christian Theology.* Retrieved on 5/1/2006 from http://www.ntwrightpage.com/right_NDCT_Righteousness.htm

Yoder, J. H. (1972). *The politics of Jesus.* Grand Rapids, MI: Wm. B. Eerdman's Publishing Co.

Young, I. M. (1990). *Justice and the politics of difference.* Princeton, NJ: Princeton University Press.

CHAPTER 12

WHO CARES?
SOCIAL WELFARE IN A DIVERSE SOCIETY

James R. Vanderwoerd

It is easy for most Christians to agree on how to answer the question "Who is my neighbor?" It is far more difficult to reach consensus on the specific implications of the principle that every person in need has a claim on the resources of others simply by virtue of being in need, or the corollary principle that each one of us has an obligation to surrender (or volunteer) our resources for others' welfare.

One answer to these questions has been to institutionalize and formalize the responsibility for the care and welfare of others via the establishment of the welfare state. At the beginning of the 21st century, however, the idea of the welfare state came under question in many industrialized societies (Gilbert, 2004), and there have been increasing critiques of the welfare state and whether its advancement can even be considered a success. This debate has important implications for the legitimacy, role, and authority of social work, since it is a profession that depends to a large extent on the welfare state for its existence.

Should Christian social workers defend the welfare state? Should trends such as devolution, faith-based initiatives, and for-profit services be interpreted as threats to be resisted, or do these trends portend an appropriate return to a limited government that makes room for the charitable impulse of voluntary, church-based helping? Foundational to these questions is the question of who is responsible, in a diverse, technologically advanced, multi-cultural society, for the welfare and well-being of those who are most disadvantaged and vulnerable. Past answers no longer suffice—neither the 19th century version, in which individuals were responsible to exercise their charitable obligations to their needy neighbors, nor the 20th century version, in which the state was responsible.

This chapter identifies several key biblical principles that provide a foundation from which to understand a Christian vision for 21st century social welfare. First, a brief discussion of the nature of societies will be described, followed by some implications and principles for how individual Christians, particularly social workers, understand their role in such societies. Next follows a discussion of the mutual rights and responsibilities that flow from this view and its understanding of the nature of humans as God's image-bearers. Finally, the chapter explores the implications of this vision for three social welfare policy issues: the role of faith-related social service organizations; the rights of persons who are gay, lesbian, bi-sexual or transgendered (GLBT) to adopt or foster children; and the social welfare roles and responsibilities of business corporations.

Complex Societies

The Salvation Army, Rosie O'Donnell, and Enron—mention any of these names in mixed company and one quickly gets a sense of the complexity of 21st century North American society and the widely disparate perspectives that exist among different people. How are we to understand such variation and complexity? Nostalgic hearkening to the "good old days" often portrays a mythical simple society that everyone understood and about which most people (it was assumed) agreed about right and wrong. But today, people hold different beliefs about different things at different levels. Society is complex, if not downright confusing.

One way Christians have made sense of this confusion and complexity has been to start with an understanding of creation informed by the biblical story. For example, Wolters (1985), working from within the neo-Calvinist tradition, describes in his book *Creation Regained* how God created all of existing reality, including different societies, and continues to uphold it all. This biblical understanding of society posits that social structures were not created exclusively by humans, but rather were established by God as part of the created order. However, humans do have a unique role in developing, establishing, and refining these structures in response to God's created order, and can thus choose to do this in obedience or in rejection of God. Further, according to Wolters, these structures have characteristics and properties, similar to the laws that govern physical reality, which God built into them and that establish parameters for their functioning (Wolters, 1985; 1995).

The overall purpose of social structures is to facilitate God's intent for humans in His creation, which is the abundant flourishing of human relationships in harmony—what the Hebrews in the Old Testament called *shalom* (Gornick, 2002). One of our tasks as humans is to seek understanding and knowledge about the characteristics and properties of various social structures so that we might discern God's intent and purpose for them—and for us (MacLarkey, 1991).

To be sure, however, this is tricky business, in part because the Bible is not a social science reference book that provides simple formulas for universal application. God has given humans considerable latitude in developing social structures that are appropriate to specific times and places. It would be too simplistic to suggest that the Bible provides blueprints for particular social arrangements that are universal across the breadth of historical and cultural variation.

Nevertheless, humans are called to develop and utilize social arrangements in a way that is consistent with God's commands and in a way which either contributes to or detracts from shalom. That is, social reality, unlike physical reality, can stray from adherence to God's norms because social structures are established and realized by human effort, and humans, unlike rocks, water, and other inanimate matter, can be obedient or disobedient.

Creation, however, is not static, but is continually changing, not least through the work of humans, who are empowered by God to work in the world to develop it. Humans not only build physical things, but also develop social organizations, practices, and institutions. Societies evolve and change over time through human imagination and intervention; social forms and entities that exist today did not exist yesterday and may not tomorrow. Such variation is understood to be part of God's plan for his creation—albeit distorted and stunted by sin and human failing. Nevertheless, the evolution of societies from agrarian rural to industrial and post-industrial are not seen as diverging from God's will, but rather as the unfolding history of God's kingdom in which humans play a primary role (Kalsbeek, 1975; Koyzis, 2003).

Not all humans, however, acknowledge God, and some outright reject or disobey Him. What are Christians to do about such people? Few would advocate that they be forced to obey God or become Christians, even if this was possible (sadly, this has not stopped some Christians in the past from resorting to coercion, even violently so). We take it for granted that not all citizens in a given nation are Christians, and that even if they were, wide differences of opinion about how things ought to be would exist. Further, we recognize that citizens have a right to believe what they want, and to express that belief freely. Indeed, this right is enshrined as the First Amendment in the Constitution of the United States and in the Canadian Charter of Rights and Freedoms.

The idea of pluralism is often used to recognize the religious diversity within societies. There are at least two types of pluralism. The first, variously labeled as *confessional pluralism* (Skillen, 1994) or *spiritual or directional diversity* (Mouw & Griffioen, 1993), addresses diversity based on spiritual beliefs, religion, or confessions. This type of pluralism recognizes that individuals and groups within society may legitimately hold varying beliefs and, within the rules of law, act on these beliefs. It is this type of pluralism that makes space for differences in spirituality and religion, and provides guidance for how persons from different religious and confessional (including belief systems that are not explicitly religious) belief systems treat one another.

People also take for granted that the Salvation Army, Rosie O'Donnell and her lesbian partner's relationship with their children, and Enron are very different types of social entities, among many more: we attend churches, play on soccer teams, volunteer at the public library, sit on school boards, serve Thanksgiving dinners at the downtown soup kitchen, visit art galleries and museums, enroll our children (and their animals) in 4H clubs, hold memberships in the American Automobile Association, and send donations to Bread for the World.

These and a virtually infinite number of other ways in which people can associate and interact are a second type of pluralism referred to as *structural pluralism* or *associational diversity*. Regardless of the specific labels, the underlying idea is a recognition that society consists of a wide variety of types of organizations, and that individuals are free to join and associate together according to their own voluntary choices. Together, these two types of pluralisms capture the idea that people organize themselves and their lives both in terms of their fundamental beliefs about the world (i.e, confessional/directional) and in terms of the purpose or function of the grouping (i.e., structural/associational). While we may disagree with other individuals and their choices, we recognize that in a diverse society, coercion or force is not a legitimate response when we encounter individuals who make choices different from our own, unless such choices violate established rules of law.

Sociologists use the term *institutions* to make sense of all the different ways in which people associate together within society. Institutions are the major building blocks of society and can be understood as the basic ways in which humans organize themselves to meet their needs. Commonly identified institutions include family, marriage, religion, law or justice, government and politics, education, and health.

The idea that society is more than simply individuals pursuing their own self-interests within a set of minimal government regulations (what Enlightenment liberals have called "the social contract"; see Nisbet, 1982) has led to much renewed interest in how individuals work together to offset the alienation and bureaucracy that arise in large institutions, along with the sense of helplessness that comes from simply acting on one's own. *Civil society* and *mediating structures* are terms that are used increasingly to refer to the many ways in which people live, work, play, and relate to one another other than as individuals or as units within large institutions (Berger & Neuhaus, 1996; Wuthnow, 2004).

Of particular interest is how these numerous and different social entities relate to one another and how the overlapping, multiple, and sometimes contradictory claims of these entities can be sorted out. For example, who is responsible for teaching children about sexuality—parents or schools? What role should government have in sorting out such a question? Is government to be "above" parents and schools, telling them what they may or may not do? Or, are parents, schools (and other social entities) independent of government, and thus allowed to do as they wish?

Two prominent Christian theories address these questions: the Catholic concept of subsidiarity, and the neo-Calvinist concept of sphere sovereignty (Chaplin, 1995; Koyzis, 2003; McIlroy, 2003). According to both positions, God's work of creation includes an ordering of the social relationships and organizations of society such as families, marriages, schools, business corporations, unions, sports teams, neighborhood associations, and consumer groups. Both subsidiarity and sphere sovereignty assert that these various social entities exist not simply at the behest of the state, but have a legitimacy and authority that ultimately comes from God.

Further, both positions claim that these entities possess autonomy appropriate to their social space and function. The concept of proximity is an important principle of subsidiarity. According to this idea, it is always preferable for decision-making and control to be held and exercised at the level that is closest (i.e, most proximate) to the situation. Local organizations and institutions, therefore, have the right to govern their own affairs. For example, churches do not need to get government approval over their doctrines, nor do parents need government to tell them what to feed their children. In other words, these various organizations have the right to make decisions without interference from government.

At the same time, however, Catholics and Calvinists both assert a role for government that is, in slightly different ways, overarching of these many other social organizations. Catholic social thought appeals to the idea of the common good and argues that government must provide the context and regulatory framework to ensure that other organizations contribute to, or at least do not directly detract from, the common good (Weigel, 1993). Thus, according to subsidiarity, the key criterion is not protecting the interests of particular organizations or entities, but rather, to ensure the best possible achievement of the common good. In other words, the common good as a principle is more important than the rights of organizations or individuals. Therefore, Catholic social thought always allows—indeed, demands—that higher and more distant entities, such as government, are entitled and have the responsibility to intervene when the common good is threatened by more local organizations.

Similarly, sphere sovereignty argues that each social organization has a specific and central role that is inherently attached to that organization as part of God's creation plan. The term *norm* refers to this role as the ideal standard to which organizations must aspire. Whether a specific organization identifies itself as Christian or not matters less than whether that organization conducts itself consistent with God's norms. The norm for government—that is, its central role and fundamental purpose—is to uphold public justice, that is, to encourage other organizations under its jurisdiction to fulfill their respective obligations and to adjudicate and protect the rights of other citizens and organizations to just and fair treatment in keeping with their unique, God-created norms (Koyzis, 2003; Sherrat, 1999; Skillen, 1994).

The key similarity in both subsidiarity and sphere sovereignty is an understanding that government has a unique, overarching—but also limited—role with respect to all the other types of social organizations. Government is not simply one among other entities, but has special responsibilities and obligations toward all of the citizens and residents within its jurisdiction. All other types of organizations can limit their memberships and therefore can choose whom to serve or include.

While the specifics of each of these viewpoints is beyond the scope of this paper, the key difference is that subsidiarity tends to a more vertical and hierarchical ordering of social institutions, whereas sphere sovereignty views various social entities as being arranged horizontally (Chaplin, 1995; Koyzis, 2003).

Individuals within Complex Societies

A Christian worldview also provides an understanding of the nature of humans and their roles and characteristics within diverse, pluralistic, and complex societies. The fundamental characteristic of humans, according to this view, is that we are created as image-bearers of God (see Genesis 1 -2; Middleton & Walsh, 1995, ch. 6). Exactly what that means has been a matter of much debate, but it includes at least that we image God's "we-ness" and his creativity. God said, "Let *us* make man in *our* image, in *our* likeness" (Gen. 1:26). God's plural self-identification alludes to his three-in-one personhood as Father, Son, and Holy Spirit. We can infer from this that God is relational and social, and that we, as His image-bearers, are also relational and social. To be human—to image God—is to be in mutual, harmonious, independent relationships with others; the reverse is also true: when we are isolated from others or when our relationships are constrained, limited, or broken, then we are in some way less than fully human as God intended. The various types of social entities discussed above are an indication of the many ways in which we humans have lived out our relational character.

We are also creative beings with the capacity to envision and imagine. We mirror God by harnessing our talents, gifts, and resources to build and establish physical structures and social arrangements and to make something of ourselves and the world. Further, our being made in God's image as creative beings also carries with it the responsibility to use our creative energy for God's purposes and for others' benefit. Neil Plantinga (1995) describes this as follows:

> [W]e are to become *responsible* beings: people to whom God can en-
> trust deep and worthy assignments, expecting us to make something
> significant of them—expecting us to make something significant of
> our lives. None of us simply finds himself here in the world. None of
> our lives is an accident. We have been called into existence, expected,
> awaited, equipped, and assigned. We have been called to undertake
> the stewardship of a good creation, to create sturdy and buoyant
> families that pulse with the glad give-and-take of the generations. We
> are expected to show hospitality to strangers and to express gratitude
> to friends and teachers. We have been assigned to seek justice for our
> neighbors and, whenever we can, to relieve them from the tyranny of
> their suffering (p. 197; emphasis added).

As image bearers of God, we carry both responsibilities and rights. We are responsible, as Plantinga argues, to both God and others. But, we have the right to basic treatment and conditions, not because we deserve them, or only because of our worth as humans, but also so that we have what we need in order to carry out those responsibilities. Responsibility cannot be exercised without adequate resources to enable us to fulfill our calling. Part of what it means to image God's creativeness is that we participate in creation and its unfolding. The capacity to participate is therefore a fundamental ingredient in our life together (Coffin, 2000; Mott, 1996).

What role do individual Christians have in complex societies? Christian sociologist Brad Breems (2001) argues that we must be "critical—curative." To be critical is to be discerning about our contemporary culture and its spirits, and how these complement and diverge from God's intentions. It requires keen observation into the world around us, as well as a regular rootedness in God's ways via Scripture, prayer and meditation. But, to be critical alone is not sufficient. Breems argues we must also be curative—that is, we must use our discernment and insights as a call to action to bring healing (or *shalom*, see Gornick, 2002) where there is brokenness and pain.

To be critical and curative is not only to bring healing to individual hurt and pain, but also to apply God's word of redemption to the structures of society as well. We know that all of creation groans under the weight of sin (Romans 8:21-22), and thus that God's redemption plan includes not only people, but all other parts of creation, including the social organizations and institutions within which we humans live out our social lives together. The apostle Paul says God makes us ambassadors in his reconciliation plan (II Cor. 5: 17-20). This means that we are appointed as God's representatives to carry out his work to fix the brokenness. A lofty mandate, to be sure, but not one that tempts us to conclude that our way is best or right. Richard Mouw (1992) reminds us of the need to avoid triumphalism and take on an attitude of humility and civility, even as we carry on with confidence the work to which we have been called.

Implications in Three Areas

In sum, a Christian worldview provides a framework for understanding humans and their place in an increasingly complex post-industrial society (Poe, 2002; Walsh & Middleton, 1984). Further, this worldview provides a way for Christians to make sense of the conflicting claims in a diverse culture, particularly when so many of these claims are counter to, if not outright inimical to God's claims. Directional and associational pluralism recognizes that there must be space and allowance for people to associate and conduct themselves in accordance with their own worldview, beliefs, or doctrine, even if others would view such conduct as unacceptable. We also recognize that the impulse we witness in ourselves and our neighbors to associate and gather together for an infinite number of reasons and ascribing to a wide variety of beliefs is evidence of our being made in God's image, even if we believe others' choices to be disobedient to God's will.

Three social welfare policy issues serve as examples of the implications of this framework: the role of faith-based groups in addressing social problems, the rights of persons who are gay, lesbian, bisexual or transgendered (GLBT) to adopt or foster children, and the social welfare responsibilities of business corporations. Although each of these issues merits more attention to be addressed adequately, the purpose here is to show how the Christian worldview sketched above helps us to think about complex social welfare issues.

Faith-based Organizations

Christians disagree about the extent to which faith groups, especially churches, should be responsible for social problems and in particular, whether religion should replace government as the primary social institution responsible for addressing the needs of our most vulnerable citizens (Wuthnow, 2004).

Fundamental to these issues is an understanding of the role of government vis-à-vis other social institutions. According to the framework described in the first part of this paper, government has a special responsibility to uphold justice. Mott (1996) elaborates on this by distinguishing between government's obligation to protect people from bad things (what he calls negative justice) and ensuring that people have access to good things (positive justice) in order to allow individuals to fulfill their obligations and responsibilities. Government, therefore, must not surrender its responsibility for the welfare of its citizens, particularly toward those who are most vulnerable. With respect to religious organizations' role in social welfare, government must provide a context that encourages their participation, but does not offload a social welfare responsibility onto religion (Bane, Coffin, & Thiemann, 2000; Daly, 2005).

On the other hand, the practice in both the USA and Canada in the last half of the 20th century has been to marginalize and exclude some religious organizations from social welfare participation unless those organizations are willing to give up some aspect of their faith in order to adhere to a secular, allegedly value-free perspective that is often the price of participation in social welfare provision, especially with public funding (Donaldson & Carlson-Thies, 2003; Monsma, 1996).

Legal and regulatory practice regarding the limitation of public funding of religious organizations in the USA, and similar practices in Canada (despite the lack of an explicit principle of church-state separation; Hiemstra, 2002) has been until recently based on a separationist principle that restricts religious organizations' access to public funding. The implication of structural and confessional pluralism, however, is that a new relationship between government and faith-based organizations becomes possible (Vanderwoerd, 2002). Rather than regarding government aid to faith-based organizations as a violation of the First Amendment, this kind of pluralism would mean that faith-based organizations be given the same opportunity for access to public dollars as other nonprofit organizations.

In other words, organizations should not be prevented from accessing public funding on the basis of their religious beliefs, or because the services for which they seek funding are explicitly religious. Rather, the principle of structural and confessional pluralism would enable various organizations to maintain the integrity of their particular religious beliefs and still participate in particular aspects of public life.

Some legal scholars have suggested that the concept of neutrality (sometimes also referred to as "equal treatment") provides a legal interpretation that acknowledges this pluralism compared to earlier separationist interpretations that operated according to a "no aid to religion" principle (Esbeck, 1997; Monsma, 1993, 2000). The neutrality principle allows for individuals and groups to participate fully in the public square without having to leave their personal religious or secular viewpoints at home. Esbeck (1997), for example, in support of government funding for faith-based social service organizations, suggests that,

> ...the neutrality principle rejects the three assumptions made by separationist theory: that the activities of faith-based charities are severable into "sacred" and "secular" aspects, that religion is "private" whereas government monopolizes "public" matters, and that governmental assistance paid to service providers is aid to the providers as well as aid to the ultimate beneficiaries (p. 21-22).

With the rejection of these first two assumptions, neutrality theory is consistent with the concept of structural and confessional pluralism. Further, this principle suggests an approach which does not violate the intentions of the First Amendment, namely, that government neither advance nor restrict religious belief, but allow its citizens and groups autonomy regarding religious conviction and practice.

Finally, in the interest of protecting religious autonomy, the neutrality principle improves on the separationist interpretation that attempted to divide religious organizations' activities into secular and "pervasively sectarian" categories. Recognizing that religious beliefs are expressed across the spectrum of human life—and not just constrained to either private life or to the church—the neutrality principle allows FBOs to receive public money and still maintain their religious integrity in the particular work they do. The concept of neutrality, therefore, is seen to provide a legal framework that opens the way for government funding of faith-based organizations while remaining true to the intentions of the First Amendment.

The legislative and regulative changes associated with the White House Office of Faith-Based and Community Initiatives represent a level of recognition and space for religious expression in public life that is overdue. Reducing the religious barriers to accessing government funds acknowledges that faith is more than just the private beliefs of individuals, but that it also centrally directs a society's public life. Further, in a diverse country, space must be allowed for the public expression of many faiths, rather than the imposition of either the majority's faith perspective, or an allegedly neutral secular perspective. On this basis alone, the "newer deal," as these developments have been called (Cnaan, 1999), is a welcome advance in social welfare policy.

Despite this promise, unanswered questions remain. First, the claims of superior effectiveness of faith-based organizations in addressing social problems compared to secular alternatives must be subjected to more rigorous evaluation. Appropriate social science techniques must be employed to identify and test the unique characteristics of faith-based services. Such evaluation is particularly necessary to avoid uncritically favoring faith-based organizations over secular services absent other criteria for effectiveness.

Second, it would be a grave mistake to imagine that increasing the participation of faith-based providers with government funds can substitute for a governmental responsibility. Social problems have never been due solely to personal failures or personal sin, and individually focused solutions will never solve the deeper-seated structural and systemic failures that are also implicated in social problems. When God calls his people to be ambassadors of reconciliation it is clear that this reconciliation is not reserved just for personal and individual brokenness, but for *all* creation. Government-faith partnerships should be part of the solution, but can never be the whole solution.

Same Sex Adoption and Fostering

The right of persons who are gay and lesbian to adopt or foster children is even more controversial and contested than the role of religion in social welfare. However, just as associational and directional diversity allow space for religious organizations to participate in social welfare with public funding and support, so also does this principle provide space for gays and lesbians to live out their choices without discrimination.

Many Christians find this position unsettling because it appears to condone or even encourage behavior and practices that they believe are fundamentally contrary to God's intent. It is important to note at the outset that Christians disagree about what God's will is for same-sex relationships (Christian Scholar's Review, 1997; Zahniser & Cagle, 2007). Regardless of one's position on the legitimacy of same-sex relationships, however, the issue here is what government's role ought to be with respect to two other types of social structures: marriage and the family.

The concepts of confessional and structural pluralism, as described above, suggest that we must be willing to accord others the right to live their lives according to their fundamental assumptions and beliefs (whether explicitly religious or otherwise) and for these beliefs to be allowed expression not only in people's choices about religious activities and expression (i.e., confessional pluralism), but also in the way they participate in other social entities (i.e., structural pluralism). Skillen (1994) argues this point as follows:

> The Constitution does not give government the right to confound religion with, or to confine religion to, institutional churches.... If...citizens are given legitimate protection under the Constitution to practice their religions freely (confessional pluralism), then all citizens should be free to conduct family life, schooling, and other social practices (structural pluralism) in ways that are consistent with the obligations of their deepest presuppositions and faiths (pp. 86-87).

The principle of sphere sovereignty provides further parameters on what authority different spheres should or should not exercise. In this case, government's authority is to provide the context for individuals and groups to exercise their responsibilities according to their convictions. Thus, government should not limit or constrain individuals or groups unless there is some direct reason connected to the general welfare or, in Catholic social thought, the common good. The neutral stance that government takes with respect to religious organizations in social welfare is also called for here: government cannot implicitly or explicitly endorse a particular arrangement or structure for families unless and only if there is a compelling reason to do so to serve the common good (Van Geest, 2002).

The issue here is for government to act in such a way as to enhance public justice and further the common welfare or good of all without infringing on the rights of individuals or groups to live according to their own beliefs. In particular, it is important for government to protect minority groups from having the will of the majority imposed upon them. Indeed, in the Netherlands, both Protestants and Catholics combined their numbers and argued for space and protection from secular perspectives, arguing their position on the basis of sphere sovereignty and subsidiarity. In that country, religious groups get full access to public funding for schools, agencies, media outlets, and many other institutions (Glenn, 2000); as well, the Netherlands also provides greater freedom for same-sex couples to marry.

The importance of the public justice principle becomes apparent if we imagine if Christians were no longer in the majority and we envision several scenarios in the next one hundred years:

- Jews have become the dominant religion in the US, and most of them have concluded that all boys and men should be circumcised; or,
- Muslims have become the majority, and most of them believe that wives must not work outside the home, but be available at all times to provide for their husbands, children, and guests; or,
- Christians who interpret the bible literally are in the majority, and most of them have concluded that women must keep their hair long.

Now imagine that a couple with a short-haired wife, or a working mom, or an uncircumcised dad wants to adopt or foster a child. If the appropriate child welfare professionals have determined that the family would be suitable, are there any grounds for a state government, in any of the three scenarios above, to pass a law to prevent short-haired women, working moms, or uncircumcised dads from fostering or adopting? Unless there is some compelling evidence to conclude that short-haired women, working mothers, or uncircumcised fathers present a clear danger or harm to children, the answer clearly would be "no."

No matter how much we as individuals might strongly disagree with these couples' choices about hair length, occupation, or circumcision, we would hardly expect the government to pass laws to restrict such choices, even if we find them morally repugnant according to our faith beliefs. The same is true for gay or lesbian partners who wish to adopt or foster children. There is compelling (Patterson, 2004)—though disputed (Dailey, 2001)—research evidence that homosexual parents are no better or worse than heterosexual parents, and that children of homosexual parents are no more or less likely to become homosexuals or to develop sexual identity problems.

The role of the state is not to attempt to define and enforce morally correct behavior or choices unless it can be clearly demonstrated that such behavior threatens the common good or limits public justice. It is the role of the state to provide safe alternatives for neglected, abused, and troubled children whose own parents or families have failed them. Whether homosexuality or working moms or circumcision or hair length is morally right or wrong is not a matter for public laws, but for churches, synagogues, temples, families, and couples to determine. Governments must provide the liberty and capacity for these groups to make these choices for themselves, not pass laws that impose the choices or beliefs of one group over others.

The task for Christians in social work is to attempt to discern God's norms for the social entity called the family. If our ultimate goal is to facilitate the development of healthy relationships, then that overrides our faith conviction about the morality of same sex partners as adoptive or foster parents. In the three hypothetical examples above, it is clear that appealing to a higher norm leads one to see past the convictions of other groups with whom we disagree about women's hair length or career paths, or about male circumcision as criteria by which to assess the suitability of an adoptive or foster placement.

Business Corporations

People seldom think of business corporations when thinking about social welfare policy or social problems. Nevertheless, the corporation has become a major provider of social welfare benefits in most post-industrial economies, and even further, has enormous influence—both negative and positive—over many people's lives, both directly and indirectly, via its economic activity and decisions. Even aside from the substantial role that private corporations play in social welfare, the Christian worldview articulated here leads to the inclusion of this somewhat unusual example.

Business corporations tend to fly under the radar when social welfare is discussed, but here, too, the concept of sphere sovereignty asserts that business corporations are not autonomous, but have their authority and legitimacy in God's creational design for social life. Further, God's creational order provides parameters for how business corporations function in relationship to other social organizations (such as families, schools, unions, nonprofits, and so on) and to government. Antonides (1978) develops this as follows:

> A business enterprise must respond to a broader variety of social norms than merely the economic; it must take into consideration a broader variety of interests than merely the financial yardstick of profit. A business enterprise—also a multinational corporation—must take into account the interests of investors, but also the interests of the suppliers of natural resources, of the workers, of the consumers, and of persons and social structures—especially families—that are directly or indirectly affected by the enterprise's productive activity. An economic enterprise is never closed off from its social environment and the slogan "free enterprise" should not blind us to this fact. An economic enterprise must display its own normative structuration—"sphere sovereignty"—in the context of societal/interdependence and intertwinement (p. 178).

A business corporation is one among many types of social structures, with its own unique characteristics and properties or norms. What, then, is the purpose or function of a business corporation? How does a business corporation represent obedience or disobedience to God's norms? The vast majority of Christians who have wrestled with these questions tend to focus exclusively on the ethical behavior of the persons who own or run the company (Rae & Wong, 2004). Here the emphasis is on developing a set of ethical principles or guidelines which are presumed to distinguish between a Christian or biblical and a so-called secular way of managing a business (Novak, 2004). None of these, however, gets at the underlying question of *what* a business corporation is, and what its purpose is other than to generate wealth or profit.

As with the previous two issues, the foundation laid from the perspective outlined in the first part of this paper provides the basis for understanding the underlying and fundamental aspects of business corporations. Vandezande (1984), drawing on the concept of sphere sovereignty, distinguishes between the business corporation and the business enterprise:

I view the *corporation* as the entity that legally "owns" and adminis-
ters the financial investments of the shareholders. I view the business
enterprise as the human work-community that has the organizational
obligation to develop and implement stewardly aims and activities.
While the corporation is the legal trustee of the shareholders' financial investments, such as land, buildings, machinery, and equipment,
it does not own the enterprise. A human work-community and its
talents cannot be owned (p. 72).

Bob Goudzwaard (1979), a Dutch Christian economist, in his analysis of
capitalism, shows how the biblical emphasis on humans as stewards (Genesis
1-2; Psalm 24) of God's creation provides the origins for the term *economics*.
This concept of stewardship is identified as the key characteristic for the business corporation (or *enterprise*, using Vandezande's term) as a social structure.
Antonides (1978) develops this further by drawing on the Dutch philosopher
Herman Dooyeweerd, whose Christian philosophical framework identified fifteen fundamental aspects of creation and their key characteristics. Included is
the economic aspect, for which the key characteristic is the management—or
stewardship—of scarce resources (Kalsbeek, 1975; Skillen, 1979).

As Antonides (1978) makes clear, the key criterion on which to evaluate
the performance of a business corporation, therefore, is according to the biblical
principle of stewardship, rather than profit.

> The norm for a business enterprise as an economically qualified
> societal structure is stewardship. This must be the key guideline in
> all its activities. The realization of the norm of stewardship entails
> a careful use and allocation of natural resources, labor, managerial
> talent, capital, etc., so that an economic surplus is attained as a
> result of economic productive activity. This economic surplus can
> be measured in a financial manner in terms of profit. But, as soon
> as we mention the word profit, a warning is in order because of the
> loaded history of that term. A business enterprise must respond to
> a broader variety of social norms than merely the economic; it must
> take into consideration a broader variety of interests than merely
> the financial yardstick of profit (p. 178).

Indeed, many in the secular business world have become increasingly aware
that profit as "the bottom line" is no longer adequate, and, in the end, has become counterproductive to sound business practice (Batstone, 2003; Norman
& MacDonald, 2004). As well, some Christians have begun to acknowledge that
the concept of stewardship is fundamental to understanding business corporations and discerning whether their activities and performance are consistent
with God's will (Krueger, 1997; Stackhouse, 1995).

A Christian worldview that recognizes the God-created diversity of social
structures and their norms also brings into focus business corporations when
social workers consider the question of who ought to care. The acronym

TINA—There Is No Alternative—has been used by critics of globalization to draw attention to the way in which the role of corporations and the structures and arrangements of a free market economy are presumed to be off limits when debating such controversial policy issues such as free trade, worker rights, minimum wages, and social benefits. As Christians who confess that Christ's lordship extends to all his creation, we reject TINA and boldly assert instead that "…there are thousands of alternatives" (Kang, 2005, p. 10), and that discerning these means careful examination of business corporations, not simply according to the dominant norm of profitability, but to a broader assessment of how corporations measure up to God's norms.

Conclusion

Social workers operating from the perspective sketched here can no longer afford to focus entirely on the role of government as the sole provider of social welfare, or, in the other extreme, argue that individuals and churches acting charitably are solely responsible. The simple answer to the question "who cares?" should, of course, be all of us.

In complex, diverse societies, it is far more difficult to put that into practice. In small, homogenous, self-contained, and independent communities, the practice of being a neighbor and sharing the responsibility for others' welfare is comparatively easy. As modern, industrialized and capitalist nation-states emerged in the 18th and 19th centuries, however, needs born of new social problems outstripped the capacity of the welfare community, welfare family, or welfare tribe (Chatterjee, 1996). The welfare state filled the gap, and by the mid-20th century had all but replaced the family and the community as the primary institution responsible for social welfare.

Under pressure from neo-conservative governments, reduced revenues, and soaring costs, cracks appeared in the welfare state in the closing decades of the 20th century. As a result, social workers, along with other left-leaning groups—reacted predictably by advocating nearly unanimous calls to shore up the welfare state (Mishra, 1999). In fact, advocating for social justice has become nearly synonymous with support for government-driven and financed welfare state expansion (Schneider & Netting, 1999), and questioning this is viewed as heresy and abandonment of social work values (Belcher, Fandetti, & Cole, 2004; Chatterjee, 2002; personal communication, October 31, 2002).

At the same time, public support for an advanced welfare state has waned substantially since the 1970s, and there is widespread sentiment that the welfare state has produced an "entitlement" society that fails to reward or encourage responsibility. It is no coincidence that the 1996 welfare reform legislation signed into law by former president Bill Clinton was named the "Personal Responsibility and Work Opportunity Reconciliation Act."[1]

As well, many evangelical Christians have become increasingly vocal in their resistance to the perceived domination of the welfare state, and particularly the way in which the welfare state as an institution has been part of what is perceived as a sustained "liberal" attack on the traditional structures of society, particularly marriages and families. Thus, we have an impasse where social workers and other professions associated with the "liberal elite" support the welfare state, pitted against conservatives and many religious persons who support a reduced government role and renewed support for traditional approaches to solving compelling social problems (Hodge, 2003 2004; Olasky, 1992; Schwartz, 2000)

The understanding of society described in this paper—drawing on Catholic social thought and Protestant Reformed thinking, particularly in the neo-Calvinist tradition—provides a way to circumvent this standoff and point us in a direction where Jesus' admonition that anyone in need is a neighbor can be implemented realistically in complex, diverse societies. Sphere sovereignty (and the similar Catholic concept of subsidiarity) suggests that society consists of multiple social structures, and that each has a unique function and a legitimate area of responsibility commensurate with its characteristics and in obedience to God's norms.

Although it is true that we can never be absolutely confident that we fully understand these structures and their norms (Mouw, 1992; Wolterstorff, 1995), that should not stop us from trying. A long tradition of Christian scholarship and practice has established public justice and the pursuit of the common good as the special purview of government (Hiemstra, 2005). This means that government has the responsibility to ensure that all persons and groups under its jurisdiction are encouraged and supported to participate and fulfill their responsibilities. This does *not* mean, however, that government has the only responsibility for social welfare.

Confessional and structural pluralism entail a social order in which persons are able to associate both according to their fundamental beliefs (whether explicitly religious or not) across the full spectrum of social structures, and not simply within the social structure of formal religion via churches, synagogues, mosques, and other bodies of worship. Faith-based organizations, therefore, should have the same access to public funding for social welfare services as secular organizations.

In a similar way, if two persons of the same sex, on the basis of their fundamental beliefs about the world, seek to partner to adopt or foster children, government ought not to restrict such persons from that choice, or at least, from the legal, regulative, and welfare benefits that are available to heterosexual persons who adopt or foster.

Finally, Christians in social work can participate with others to draw attention to the ways in which corporations, as one of many God-created social structures, live up not simply to the norms of the market, but to the higher obligations to which God calls them.

Christians in social work must develop increasing sensitivity to the wide variety of confessions out there, especially when they differ from our own. We know too well our own substantial rifts even within the body of Christ. Our task is to attempt to discern the sources of social brokenness and seek to bring healing by facilitating and equipping other social entities to fulfill the obligations and expectations which God has set for them. Our call as social workers is to exercise compassion—not coercion—in pursuit of shalom.

Note

[1] The "reconciliation" part of the name was added as a compromise from an earlier bill whose name was identical but for that added word; see Karger & Stoesz, 2002 for details.

References

Antonides, H. (1978). *Multinationals and the peaceable kingdom.* Toronto, ON: Clarke, Irwin.

Bane, M., Coffin, B., & Thiemann, R. (Eds.). (2000). *Who will provide? The changing role of religion in American social welfare.* Boulder, CO: Westview Press.

Batstone, D. (2003). *Saving the corporate soul & (who knows?) maybe your own: Eight principles for creating and preserving integrity and profitability without selling out.* San Franciso, CA: Jossey-Bass.

Belcher, J., Fandetti, D., & Cole, D. (2004). Is Christian religious conservatism compatible with the liberal social welfare state? *Social Work,* 49(2), 269-276.

Berger, P., & Neuhaus, R. J. (1996). *To empower people: From state to civil society, 20th Anniversary Edition.* Washington, DC: American Enterprise Institute.

Breems, B. (2001). The service of sociology: Providing a lighter cloak or a sturdier iron cage? In J. Kok (Ed). *Marginal Resistance,* (pp. 253-272). Sioux Center, IA: Dordt College Press.

Chaplin, J. (1995). Subsidiarity and sphere sovereignty: Catholic and reformed conceptions of the role of the state, In *Confessing Christ in Doing Politics: Essays on Christian Political Thought and Action,* (pp. 104-129). Potchefstroom, RSA: Institute for Reformational Studies, Potschefstroom University.

Chatterjee, P. (1996). *Approaches to the welfare state.* Washington, DC: NASW Press.

Christian Scholar's Review. (1997). *Theme issue: Christianity and homosexuality,* 26(4).

Cnaan, R. (1999). *The newer deal: Social work and religion in partnership.* New York, NY: Columbia University Press.

Coffin, B. (2000). Where religion and public values meet: Who will contest? In M. Bane, B. Coffin, & R. Thiemann (Eds.). *Who Will Provide? The Changing Role of Religion in American Social Welfare,* (pp. 121-146).

Boulder, CO: Westview Press.

Dailey, T. (2001). Homosexual parenting: Placing children at risk. *Insight Issue* No. 238. October 30, 2001. [Available: http://www.frc.org/get.cfm?i=IS01J3].

Daly, L. (2005). Compassion capital: Bush's faith-based initiative is bigger than you think. *Boston Review,* 30, April / May 2005. [Available: http://bostonreview.net/BR30.2/daly.html].

Donaldson, D., & Carlson-Thies, S. (2003). *A revolution of compassion: Faith-based groups as full partners in fighting America's social problems.* Grand Rapids, MI: Baker Books.

Esbeck, C. (1997). A constitutional case for governmental cooperation with faith-based social service providers. *Emory Law Journal,* 46(1), 1-41.

Gilbert, N. (2004). *Transformation of the welfare state: The silent surrender of public responsibility.* New York, NY: Oxford University Press.

Glenn, C. (2000). *The ambiguous embrace: Government and faith-based schools and social agencies.* Princeton, NJ: Princeton University Press.

Gornick, M. (2002). *To live in peace: Biblical faith and the changing inner city.* Grand Rapids, MI: Eerdmans.

Goudzwaard, B. (1979). *Capitalism and progress: A diagnosis of western society.* Grand Rapids, MI: Eerdmans / Toronto, ON: Wedge.

Hiemstra, J. (2005). Section I. church, state and the kingdom of god, An overview, *REC [Reformed Ecumenical Council] Focus,* 5(2), 3–49.

Hiemstra, J. (2002). Government relations with faith-based non-profit social agencies in Alberta. *Journal of Church & State,* 44(1), 19-44.

Hodge, D. (2004). Who we are, where we come from, and some of our perceptions: Comparison of social workers and the general population. *Social Work,* 49(2), 261-268.

Hodge, D. (2003). Differences in worldviews between social workers and people of faith. *Families in Society,* 84(2), 285-295.

Kalsbeek, L. (1975). *Contours of a Christian philosophy: An introduction to Herman Dooyeweerd's thought.* Toronto, ON: Wedge Publishing.

Kang, Y. (2005). Global ethics and a common morality. Paper presented at the International Symposium of the Association for Reformational Philosophy, Hoeven, The Netherlands, August 16-19, 2005.

Karger, H., & Stoesz, D. (2002). *American social welfare policy: A pluralist approach,* 4th Ed. Boston, MA: Allyn & Bacon.

Koyzis, D. (2003). *Political visions & illusions: A survey & Christian critique of contemporary ideologies.* Downer's Grove, IL: InterVarsity Press.

Krueger, D. (1997). *The business corporation & productive justice.* Nashville, TN: Abingdon Press.

MacLarkey, R. (1991). Reformational social philosophy and sociological theory. *Perspectives on Science and Christian Faith,* 43, 96-102.

McIlroy, D. (2003). Subsidiarity and sphere sovereignty: Christian reflections on the size, shape and scope of government. *Journal of Church and State,* 45(4), 739-763.

Middleton, R., & Walsh, B. (1995). *Truth is stranger than it used to be.. Biblical faith in a postmodern age.* Downer's Grove, IL: InterVarsity Press.

Mishra, R. (1999). *Globalization and the welfare state.* Northampton, MA: E. Elgar Press.

Monsma, S. (1993). *Positive neutrality: Letting religious freedom ring.* Grand Rapids, MI: Baker Books.

Monsma, S. (1996). *When sacred and secular mix: Religious nonprofit organizations and public money.* Lanham, MD: Rowman & Littlefield.

Monsma, S. (2000) Substantive neutrality as a basis for free exercise - no establishment common ground. *Journal of Church and State,* 42(1), 13-35.

Mott, S. (1996). Foundations of the welfare responsibility of the government. In S. Carlson-Thies & J. Skillen (Eds). *Welfare in America: Christian Perspectives on a Policy in Crisis.* Grand Rapids, MI: Eerdmans.

Mouw, R. (1992). *Uncommon decency: Christian civility in an uncivil world.* Downer's Grove, IL: InterVarsity Press.

Mouw, R., & Griffioen, S. (1993). *Pluralisms and horizons: An essay in Christian public philosophy.* Grand Rapids, MI: Eerdmans.

Nisbet, R. (1982). *The social philosophers: Community and conflict in western thought.* New York, NY: Washington Square Press / Harper & Row.

Norman, W., & MacDonald, C. (2004). Getting to the bottom of "triple bottom line". *Business Ethics Quarterly,* 14(2), 243-262.

Novak, M. (2004). A theology of the corporation, In S. Rae & K. Wong, (Eds). *Beyond Integrity: A Judeo-Christian Approach to Business Ethics,* (pp. 216-222). Grand Rapids, MI: Zondervan.

Olasky, M. (1992). *The tragedy of American compassion.* Washington, DC: Regnery Gateway.

Patterson, C. (2004). Lesbian and gay parents and their children: Summary of research findings. In *Lesbian and Gay Parenting: A Resource for Psychologists*. Washington, DC: American Psychological Association.

Plantinga, N. (1995). *Not the way it's supposed to be: A breviary of sin*. Grand Rapids, MI: Eerdmans.

Poe, M. A. (2002). Christian world view and social work, In D. Dockery & G. Thornbury, (Eds). *Shaping a Christian Worldview: The Foundations of Christian Higher Education*. (pp.317-334). Nashville, TN: Broadman & Holman,

Rae, S., & Wong, K. (Eds). (2004). *Beyond integrity: A Judeo-Christian approach to business ethics*. Grand Rapids, MI: Zondervan.

Schwartz, J. (2000). *Fighting poverty with virtue: Moral reform and America's poor, 1825-2000*. Bloomington, IN: Indiana University Press.

Schneider, R., & Netting, E. (1999). Influencing social policy in a time of devolution: Upholding social work's great tradition. *Social Work*, 44(4), 349-357.

Skillen, J. (1979). Herman Dooyeweerd's contribution to the philosophy of the social sciences. *Journal of the American Scientific Affiliation*, 20-24.

Skillen, J. (1994). *Recharging the American experiment: Principled pluralism for genuine civic community*. Grand Rapids, MI: Baker Books.

Sherrat, T. (1999). Rehabilitating the state in America: Abraham Kuyper's overlooked contribution. *Christian Scholar's Review*, 29(2), 323–346.

Vanderwoerd, J. (2002). Is the newer deal a better deal? Government funding of faith-based social services. *Christian Scholars Review, 33*, 300-318.

Vandezande, G. (1984). *Christians in the crisis*. Toronto, ON: Anglican Book Centre.

Van Geest, F. (2002). Homosexuality and public policy: A challenge for sphere sovereignty. *Perspectives: A Journal of Reformed Thought*, 17(10), 5-10.

Walsh, B., & Middleton, R. (1984). *The transforming vision: Shaping a Christian world view*. Downer's Grove, IL: InterVarsity Press.

Weigel, G. (1993). *Building the free society: Democracy, capitalism, and Catholic social teaching*. Grand Rapids, MI: Eerdmans and Washington, D.C.: Ethics and Public Policy Center.

Wolters, A. (1985). *Creation regained: Biblical basics for a reformational worldview*. Grand Rapids, MI: Eerdmans.

Wolters, A. (1995). Creation order: A historical look at our heritage, in B. Walsh, H. Hart, & R. Vander Vennen, (Eds). *An Ethos of Compassion and the Integrity of Creation*, (pp. 33-48). New York, NY: University Press of America.

Wolterstorff, N. (1995). Points of unease with the creation order tradition, In B. Walsh, H. Hart, & R. Vander Vennen, (Eds). *An Ethos of Compassion and the Integrity of Creation*, (pp. 62-66). New York, NY: University Press of America.

Wuthnow, R. (2004). *Saving America? Faith-based services and the future of civil society*. Princeton, NJ: Princeton University Press.

Zahniser, J., & Cagle, L. (2007). Homosexuality: Toward an informed compassionate response. *Christian Scholar's Review*, 36(3), 323-348.

CHAPTER 13

SPIRITUAL DEVELOPMENT

Hope Haslam Straughan

Within the social work profession, there is a growing movement that affirms that spirituality and religious beliefs are integral to the nature of the person and have a vital influence on human behavior (Hugen, 1998). Canda (1988) identifies spirituality as a basic aspect of human experience, both within and outside the context of religious institutions. If a social worker is going to approach a person in a holistic manner, he or she must be willing to consider each person as a wondrous combination of bio-psycho-social-spiritual elements. In this way, workers will have an extremely broad base from which to approach the strength and resiliency in the people with whom they interact. Spiritual development, a component of this broad understanding of a person, seems to occur both in a measurable, outward, predictable manner, as well as in a less tangible personal journey. These complex and intertwined spiritual growth markers will be explored within this chapter, primarily from a Christian point of view.

Smith (1997-1998) claims that Christians are 'meaning makers,' taking "the raw material of lived experience—the gladness and the sorrows—and trying to seek the deeper meaning, see the larger picture, understand the levels and layers of life in all its fullness and intensity. We live, and then in faith we try to discover meaning" (p. 2). Faiver, Ingersoll, O'Brien, and McNally (2001) note:

> Spirituality may be described as a deep sense of wholeness, connectedness, and openness to the infinite . . . We believe spirituality is an innate human quality. Not only is it our vital life force, but at the same time it is also our experience of the vital life force. Although this life force is deeply part of us, it also transcends us. It is what connects us to other people, nature and the source of life. The experience of spirituality is greater than ourselves (p.2).

Spiritual deepening, or development then, is about becoming more consciously aware—being attentive, present in the moment, and paying attention to life as we seek meaning.

The Council on Social Work Education (2000) added the concept of spirituality to the list of content areas to be addressed within the curriculum of accredited schools of social work in 2000. There are many important ways in which to incorporate this information in the overall social work curriculum. For instance, the role of religious institutions in society can be investigated, while considering the impact of their presence, and the potential natural support networks such entities might lend for some persons. In addition, techniques utilized by social workers that value a variety of possible religious experiences or spiritual beliefs might be explored in a practice course (Cascio, 1998). One aspect of the growing self-awareness of social work students might be focused on their personal faith or spiritual experiences, including awareness of their own beliefs, and the impact of these on the people and their environments with which students will interact. Finally, one might argue that spiritual development content must be included in a course in which community is considered, as many religious traditions feature a strong cultural and communal identity and experience.

Incorporating spirituality within the Human Behavior and Social Environment life span content is a foundational attempt to honor holistic personal development. One can consider the development of an individual's spirituality from gestation through the years of life to death, while considering the socio-economic, political, racial, ethnic, and greater societal influences impacting a person's faith journey. This approach is based on a clear assumption that an individual's spiritual capacity and awareness is not stagnant, but indeed develops, changes, and potentially increases. This type of thinking immediately causes us to consider whether spiritual information is best presented utilizing a traditional stage-based theoretical approach, or if the concepts lend themselves to a more fluid consideration in which particular themes are revisited throughout life. James Fowler (1981) has drawn from a deep psychological understanding of human development and crafted a model of spiritual development containing a pre-stage, and six subsequent stages of faith, which holds true to many of the assumptions of the traditional stage-models. Joan Borysenko (1998) and others have proposed more fluid approaches to spiritual development and have recognized that spiritual themes may be re-occurring throughout the life span. This concept is consistent with the spiral approach to growth and development. These ideas, often building upon the familiar concepts of the stage-based developmental patterns, will be presented in a later portion of this chapter.

Social workers commonly work within community-serving agencies, while seeking to help people who often have few choices about the conditions under which essential human needs are met. In this role, we must ensure that every protection is given the client and that his or her helplessness is not exploited (Spencer, 1961). "Certainly, in the light of the high value the social work profession has always placed upon the client's right to solve his [or her] own problems in the way that seems right to him [or her], it is assumed that any considerations of the social worker's role in the area of religion would be set in this context" (pp. 519-520).

In order to accomplish this, a level of spiritual competency must be developed. This competency is based upon the workers' own awareness of his/her spirituality and belief systems, an acknowledgement of the spiritual nature of all persons, an open stance when hearing the stories of clients, and paying attention to the language used and the meaning the client attributes to spiritual components of their lives (Guadalupe, 2005). In addition, spiritual competency demands a level of growing knowledge and understanding of the spiritual experiences of diverse populations.

Definitions

The roots of social work contain many religious and spiritually based components, lending motivation, direction, foundation, and location for social service provision. When approaching the issue of spiritual development and the impact of this on an individual, family, group, community or organization, it is crucial to define the terms that create the backbone for this important discussion. Sue Spencer (1961) was one of the first to attempt to define religion and spirituality from the perspective of a social worker. She identified three major hurdles experienced by those desiring to discuss spirituality and social work. "The first of these is the wide variety of religious beliefs held by individuals and by organized church bodies" (p. 519). The second hurdle is the difficulty of looking at the issue of religion and spirituality in an objective, yet comfortable and sympathetic way, as any discussion of religion is likely to be colored by considerable feeling and emotion that often stem from one's early experiences with organized religion. The third difficulty is found in our cultural bias, which celebrates the freedom to express religious impulses and to meet religious needs as persons see fit. This hurdle cautions persons against infringing upon the right of spiritual or religious freedom of others.

"From the rain dances of Native Americans to the celebratory dances of Hasidic Jews, from the whirling dervishes of Islam to the meditating monks of Zen Buddhism, from the ecstatic worship services of charismatic churches to the solemn, silent meetings of the Quakers, spirituality takes on many expressions" (Elkins, 1999, p. 45). Given the hurdles identified by Spencer, and the rich descriptions of spiritual expression listed by Elkins, it is crucial that when discussing spirituality and social work practice, we define terms consistently and clarify what is meant by spirituality. Edward Canda (1988), a social work educator who has made significant contributions to conversations about spirituality and practice has provided a definition that will serve as the cornerstone for this chapter and be continually integrated with our discussion of spiritual development. Canda suggests an understanding of spirituality that encompasses human activities of moral decision making, searching for a sense of meaning and purpose in life, and striving for mutually fulfilling relationships among individuals, society, and ultimate reality (however that is conceptualized by the client). "In that these aspects of human activity are common to all people, they are necessarily relevant to all areas of social work practice" (p. 238). Canda further delineates this spiritual component, by stating that the "professional helping relationship must be a genuine expression of the social worker's spiritual commitment to compassion and social justice—an 'I' who empathically relates with a 'Thou'" (p. 245). Though Canda does not limit his approach to a particular religious tradition, such as Christianity, the focus of this chapter is that of Christian faith and a Christian understanding of God.

Approaches to Thinking about Spiritual Development

Schriver (2004) utilizes a very helpful delineation of traditional and alternative paradigms as a way to structure thinking about people and their environments.

The traditional paradigm, characterized in this chapter as those theories based on stage-based, predictable, ladder-oriented development, has sometimes led to a belief in only one route to only one answer rather than many routes to many answers. These theories have offered very important concepts that are often utilized and expanded within broader or alternative ways of thinking about development. "Alternative ways of viewing the world such as interpretive, consensual, non-Eurocentric, and feminist perspectives can add much to what we know and what we need to know to *do* social work" (p. xix). Building on these assumptions, the remainder of the chapter will be organized in such a way as to demarcate particular spiritual development approaches. These approaches will be divided between those which seem to follow traditional paradigms, and those which lend themselves to alternative processes of understanding the spiritual journey of people, all the while acknowledging the crucial and unique role of their environments.

Traditional Ways of Thinking about Spiritual Development

Many researchers have found that a stage-based model of development, whether psychosocial, cognitive, spiritual, or moral, is descriptive and informative when considering the normal development of human beings. The work of two such researchers, Erik Erikson and Lawrence Kohlberg, will be considered in this chapter in relation to James Fowler's proposed stages of spiritual development. Erik Erikson (1950) proposed a theory of psychosocial development comprising eight stages. These established eight stages were later expanded to include a ninth stage by his wife, Joan, after Erikson's death (Erikson, 1997). In reviewing their life's research and writings, as well as experiencing life into her 90's, she found cause to expand to a ninth stage which encompasses the realities of persons living into their eighth and ninth decade into very old age. The key component in Erikson's work is the development of the sense of self by going through a series of crises. He proposes that the society within which one lives makes certain psychic demands at each stage of development, and that the individual must adjust to the stresses and conflicts involved in these crises in order to move to the next stage of development. Lawrence Kohlberg (1969) proposed a series of six stages through which people progress as they develop their moral framework. A summary of the stages presented by Erikson, Kohlberg, and Fowler can be seen in Table 1. A summary of James Fowler's (1981) stages of faith development across the lifespan will be utilized as a point of reference for a discussion of spirituality as it relates to Erikson's and Kohlberg's research.

James Fowler: Stages of Faith

Perhaps the most recognized contributor to the stage-theory approach to considering spiritual development is James Fowler (1981). A theologian and religious psychologist, Fowler set off a new wave of thinking about faith based on the work of such renowned developmental psychologists as Erik Erikson, Jean Piaget and Lawrence Kohlberg. "He claimed that faith, like life itself, goes through distinct stages as a person matures" (Kropf, 1991, p. 12). Fowler's term 'faith' is closely linked to the concepts Canda (1988) presents in his definition of spirituality. Canda's definition is broad enough to allow us to subsume Fowler's concept of 'faith' as connected to a sense of meaning and purpose in life, as well as the belief in an ultimate reality. Fowler considers the interface of the religious/spiritual dimension with other psychosocial aspects of the person (Joseph, 1988). Marra (2000) describes this phenomenon as developing sequentially. As in other stage-based developmental theories, it is possible to accelerate growth, or impede it, but steps cannot be skipped. Fowler (1981) discerns six stages in faith development. A pre-stage called Undifferentiated Faith is reflective of the infant up to about one and a half years of age, and is unavailable to empirical research (see Table 1). The faith of early infancy is characterized by the mutuality between infant and nurturers (Helminiak, 1987). "The emergent strength of faith in this stage is the bond of basic trust and the relational experience of mutuality with the one(s) providing primary love and care" (Fowler, p. 121). Looking at Table 1, we can see obvious similarities in the descriptions of Erikson's Stage-1 of psychosocial development, Basic Trust versus Basic Mistrust, and Fowler's pre-stage. Both researchers identify the most important task during the first 18 months of life as the development of trust due to the infants' needs being met by nurturers. Erikson discusses religion and notes that children may not need a religious upbringing. But, says Erikson (1950), they do need a sense of basic trust, a feeling not only that their fundamental bodily needs will be met and that their parents love them and will take care of them, but also that they have not been abandoned to the empty haphazardness of existence. The trust of the infant in the parents finds its parallel - and takes its mature form - in the parents' trust in God (Brandt, 1991).

Fowler (1986) states that "faith begins in relationship. Faith implies trust in-reliance upon another; a counting upon or dependence upon another" (p. 16). If one is to accept the basis for Erikson's stage progression, crisis completion, it raises a basic question related to spiritual development. At this early point in one's life, what impact would a child's inability to successfully reach basic trust or mutuality have on his or her spiritual development? Canda (1988) and Guadalupe (2005), also define spiritual development partially as striving for mutually fulfilling relationships among individuals, society, and ultimate reality.

For Fowler, transition to Stage-1 begins with the convergence of thought and language, opening up the use of symbols in speech and ritual play. Stage-1 Faith, called Intuitive-Projective Faith, typical of the child of three to seven, involves a child thinking of God only in literal terms. For example, if an adult says "God is always with us," then the child sitting at the table may want to move over and give God half of his/her seat. Kohlberg (1969) describes the moral development of children at this age as motivated by avoidance of punishment. In many Protestant religious traditions, children are taught that God is love and lives in heaven with those that love God, while persons not loving God will go to hell. Due to a child's literal understanding at this age, he or she is often concerned with avoiding hell, or ultimate punishment.

Stage-2 Faith, Mythic-Literal Faith, is normative for children from the age of six to twelve, but as with all the subsequent stages of faith, they may remain in that stage throughout life. Robert Coles (1990) asked a class of fifth graders

Table 1: Stages of Psychosocial, Moral, and Spiritual Development Erikson, Kohlberg, and Fowler

Erik Erikson's Eight Stages of Man (Psychosocial Development) *Ninth Stage contributed by Joan Erikson		Lawrence Kohlberg's Six Stages of Moral Development		James Fowler's Six stages of Faith Development	
Stage/Age	Description	Stage/Age	Description	Stage/Age	Description
Stage 1: Basic trust vs. basic mistrust Birth-12/18 months	Infant develops trust, as he or she understands that some people or things can be depended on.			Pre-Stage: **Undifferentiated Faith** Birth-1 ½ years	Faith characterized by mutuality between infant and nurturers. First pre-images of God are formed prior to language & are feeling-oriented, not reason-oriented.
Stage 2: Autonomy vs. Shame & Doubt 18 months – 3 yr.	Accomplishing various tasks/activities provides children with feelings of self-worth and self-confidence.				
Stage 3: Initiative vs. Guilt 3-6 years	Preschoolers encouraged to take initiative to explore & learn are likely to feel confident in initiating relationships, & pursue career objectives later in life. Preschoolers consistently restricted, or punished, are more likely to experience emotional guilt, & most often follow the lead of others.	Level 1-Preconventional 4-10 years Stage 1: **Punishment & Obedience Orientation** Controls are external. Behavior governed by receiving rewards/punishments. Decisions concerning what is good/bad are made in order to avoid receiving punishment. Stage 2: **Naïve Instrumental Hedonism** Rules are obeyed in order to receive rewards. Often favors are exchanged.		Stage 1: **Intuitive-Projective Faith** 3-7 years	Child constructs ever-shifting world of imitation, fantasy, & imagination. Child thinks only literally. Sees God as person yet realizes imagery falls short.
Stage 4: Industry vs. Inferiority 6-12 years	These children need to be productive & succeed in play and school activities.	Level 2 – Conventional 10-13 years Stage 3: **"Good Boy/Girl Morality"** Behavior governed by conforming to social expectations. Good behavior is considered to be what pleases others. Stage 4: **Authority-Maintaining Morality** Belief in law & order is strong. Behavior conforms to law & higher authority. Social order is important.		Stage 2: **Mythic-Literal Faith** 6-12 years	Emergence of concrete operational thinking precipitates the transition to this stage, as a child is able to see the world from more than 1 perspective. Child's world is simple, orderly, temporally linear, and dependable.

Erikson's Psychosocial Stages	Kohlberg's Moral Development	Fowler's Faith Stages	
Stage 5: Identity vs. Role Confusion Adolescence This transition period from childhood to adulthood is when a person examines the various roles they play, and integrate these roles into a perception of self, or identity.	Level 3 – Post Conventional (many persons never move to Level 3) Late adolescence **Stage 5: Morality of Contract, of Individual Rights, and of Democratically Accepted Law** Moral decisions internally controlled. Morality involves higher level principles beyond law and self-interest. Laws considered necessary, subject to rational thought and interpretation.	Emergence of formal operational thinking allows critical reflector on myths central to Stage 2. See God as personal & relational, holding great value to religious symbols.	**Stage 3: Synthetic-Conventional Faith** 12-beyond
Stage 6: Intimacy vs. Isolation Young adult Young adulthood is characterized by a quest of intimacy. Persons not attaining intimacy are likely to suffer isolation, and were likely to resolve some of the crises of earlier psychosocial development.		Physical separation from home and encounter with new environment; authority moves from outside to inside person. Perception of God similar to Stage 3.	**Stage 4: Individuate-Reflective Faith** Young adulthood or beyond (many persons stay between Stage 3 & 4)
Stage 7: Generativity vs. Stagnation Maturity People are concerned with helping, producing for, or guiding the following generation. People lacking generativity become self-absorbed and inward.	Adulthood **Stage 6: Morality of Individual Principles & Conscience** Behavior based on internal ethical principles. Decisions made according to what is right vs. what is written into law.	Person must have known life experiences of grief/confusion; deepest truths are inconsistent; sweeter spirit than Stages 3 & 4; lives with ambiguity; views faith from perspective of others; open to change.	**Stage 5: Conjunctive Faith** mid-life or beyond
Stage 8: Ego Integrity vs. Despair Old Age People look back over life and reflect, taking stock in their decisions. For some this leads to a sense of peace (ego integrity) and for others a sense of sadness and despair.		Characterized by brotherhood of all; focus on love, peace & justice; religion is relational, not conceptual; a radical absorption with unity of all people.	**Stage 6: Universalizing Faith** Adulthood (exceptionally rare)
* **Stage 9: Basic Mistrust vs. Trust:** <u>Hope</u> Shame & Doubt vs. Autonomy: <u>Will</u> Guilt vs. Initiative: <u>Purpose</u> Inferiority vs. Industry: <u>Competence</u> Identity Confusion vs. Identity: <u>Fidelity</u> Isolation vs. Intimacy: <u>Love</u> Stagnation vs. Generativity: <u>Care</u> Despair & Disgust vs. Integrity: <u>Wisdom</u> Eighties and Nineties People enter their late 80's and 90's and experience new demands, reevaluations, and daily difficulties. Despair is a close companion due to intense multiples losses, failing physical and cognitive abilities, and lessening autonomy. Old age is a circumstance which places the dystonic elements in a more prominent position than in earlier stages, with syntonic qualities having less potency. The underlined characteristics are possible outcomes of a person in their 80's or 90's struggling with each paired element, which can lead to growth, strength and commitment.			

to respond to the following question: "Tell me, as best you can, who you are" (p. 308). One boy wrote that "I was put here by God, and I hope to stay until He says OK, enough, come back" (p. 312). A Puerto Rican girl who usually did not say much responded with "Well, how *does* He decide? How can He possibly keep track of everyone? I asked our priest, and he said all kids want to know, and you just have to have faith, and if you don't, then you're in trouble, and besides, you'll never know, because that's God's secret. . . But I still can't see how God can keep His eyes on everyone, and my uncle says it's all a lot of nonsense" (p. 312). These children were focused on the very concrete issue of God keeping track of so many persons, and could not get beyond that incomprehensible idea without the stories and words of their families, faith communities, and spiritual leaders.

Stage-3 Faith, Synthetic-Conventional Faith, can begin to evolve at adolescence. Persons in this stage tend to see God as personal and relational, and in a more spiritual sense than before, assigning great value to religious symbols. A teen in this stage of faith may find great attachment to a cross necklace, as a symbol of his or her beliefs. A teen might find value in the Lord's Supper or communion, even if he or she is unable to specify the deep connection through words.

Fowler's Stage-3 corresponds with Erikson's Stage-5, identity versus role confusion, at least in terms of possible age identified as adolescence, or twelve and beyond. Erikson (1950) describes adolescence as a transition period from childhood to adulthood, when people examine the various roles they play, and integrate these roles into a perception of self, or identity. Fowler assumes that the teen has an ability to think abstractly which allows for a new level of thinking critically in relation to the stories and myths that one has been told in relation to one's belief. In Kohlberg's (1969) Stage-5, Morality of Contract, of Individual Rights, and of Democratically Accepted Law, the adolescent is moving to an internally controlled morality which parallels Fowler's and Erikson's stages. A person at this stage in life is making the significant shift from looking to others to define him or herself, to identify what is right or wrong, and to lead out in appropriate expressions of faith, to a more internally driven, and personally informed way of living. As a teen engages in critical thinking over time, he or she is able to move into a space that allows his or her own motivation and understanding to direct decisions, actions, and faith activities.

Consequently, developmental factors that lead to Stage-4 Faith include beginning to clash with external authority (most often parents in this case); encounters with life experiences and perspectives that force persons to examine belief structures; leaving home physically and/or emotionally, causing the examination of self and theology; and the influence of adult models at Stage-4. The optimum time to enter Stage-4 is during the traditional college years, age 18-22. Typically, life situations encountered during these years cause a person to think about his or her religious and spiritual identity and beliefs. Cognitively, the power of reason and critical analysis comes to the forefront, and this often is the case in a person's quest for understanding related to his or her spiritual self as well. Persons in this stage are often open to seriously consider the views of others through study (reason), but not be open to being changed by them.

In Stage-4 Faith, Individuate-Reflective Faith, both the interruption of reliance on an external authority and the relocation of authority within the self, the "executive self" are required (Fowler, 1981, p. 79). Concurrently, Kohlberg (1969) identifies the center for moral decision making during adulthood, Stage-6, Morality of Individual Principles and Conscience, as internal ethical principles. Decisions made from this perspective are made according to what is right versus what is written into law, honoring this newly relocated authority within the self, as Fowler described.

Reaching Stage-5 Faith, Conjunctive Faith—formerly called Paradoxical-Consolidative Faith—is rare before middle age. This is largely due to an emerging awareness that reality is more complex than what one's Stage-4, highly rationalized view can contain (Helminiak, 1987). Externally, Conjunctive Faith realizes the validity of systems other than one's own and so moves away from seeing a situation as a dichotomy, as seen in Stage 4's either-or thinking. Persons using Conjunctive Faith realize that the deepest truths are inconsistent, resulting in what is often described by others as a sweeter spirit than previous stages. Erikson (1950) describes Stage-7, Generativity versus Stagnation, which is concurrent in the lifespan with Fowler's Stage-5, as a time when a person is concerned with helping, producing for, or guiding the following generation. Both researchers emphasize the external focus of this stage of life. During this stage of life, this search for meaning and purpose often culminates in the extension of oneself for the support and development of others (Canda, 1988). Still, a person in Stage-5 "remains divided" (Helminiak, p. 198). People in Stage-5 faith are living in an untransformed world while experiencing visions of transformation. In some few cases this division leads to radical actualization called Stage 6 faith.

During later adulthood, changes associated with psychological and cognitive development impel a person to focus on the inner or spiritual self (Mulqueen, & Elisa, 2000). Exceedingly rare, according to Fowler, Stage-6, Universalizing Faith, incarnates and actualizes the spirit of an inclusive and fulfilled human community, drawn to the familihood of all people (Marra, 2000). This stage constructs an ultimate environment that includes and cherishes all beings (Fowler, 1981). For persons reaching this rare stage of faith development, Fowler suggests that they would be beyond mid-life. Erikson (1950) describes persons of old age as being in a crisis of Ego Integrity versus Despair. Persons in this stage, Stage-8, are looking back over their lives, reflecting, and taking stock of their decisions. For some persons this review leads to a sense of peace, but for others, to a sense of sadness and despair. As people are living longer, more persons are entering into the final stage of development posed by Joan Erikson (1997), Stage-9, and are finding that hope and trust are no longer the firm support they were found to be in previous stages, and that perhaps facing down despair with faith and appropriate humility is the wisest course. One of the greatest concerns in this stage is how to remain engaged with community as persons are losing autonomy, physical and cognitive functioning, and experiencing the more dystonic potentials of all the previous stages of development. Joan Erikson suggests that 'transcen*dance*' might be the "regaining of lost skills, including play, activity, joy, and song, and above all, a major leap above and beyond the fear of death" (p. 127). The components of relationship and unity might suggest some further parallels to Fowler's Stage-6 Faith described above.

Therefore, traditional ways of considering spiritual development draw on the assumptions of general human development. According to stage-based theorists, this growth in authentic self-transcendence that results from the individual's taking responsibility for him or herself, "moves from infant, impulse-dominated self-centeredness to a conformist identity with one's social group and finally to post-conventional self-determination and integration of internal and external reality" (Helminiak, 1987, p. 77). Helminiak proposes Fowler's extensive work around stages of spiritual development as *the* stages of spiritual development, "at least within middle-class American and equivalent cultures" (p. 84). As has been demonstrated above, it can be useful to consider Fowler's stages of faith in light of other types of development across the lifespan, in order to gain a greater understanding of the common crises, cognitive abilities, conceptual frameworks, and worldviews.

One of the "criticisms leveled at general stage theories is that such theories are merely descriptions of how specific people change, and that such models are only valid for the one culture out of which they have emerged. The patterns are chiefly due to cultural factors, expectations, roles, and conditioning, or else economics, and do not reflect universal tendencies of human nature outside of the society portrayed" (Irwin, 2002, p. 30). Erikson himself conceded that what a man adds up to must develop in stages, but no stage explains the man (Coles, 1970). Other specific critique of Kohlberg's and sometimes Erikson's work includes potential cultural biases inherent in categorization, limitations imposed by children's developing vocabulary and expression of their ideas, the lack of clear-cut divisions between one category and another, and the idea that the stages must occur in an absolute order.

Dykstra (1981) questions the very foundation of Kohlberg's work. Though he finds Kohlberg to be quite clear about what he thinks morality is and what it takes to be a moral person, Dykstra questions the judgment-based or juridical ethics upon which this image of a moral person is derived. Dykstra contrasts Kohlberg's form of ethics, which provide a clear guide for action through its rules and principles for decision making, with 'visional ethics'. Dykstra's visional ethics focuses on questioning what we see and what it is that enables human beings to see more realistically. For visional ethics, action follows vision, and vision depends upon character—"a person thinking, reasoning, believing, feeling, willing, and acting as a whole" (p. 59). Fowler (1986) himself contends that the contributions of Kohlberg and others are useful only to a point when addressing conceptually the last relational step of faith. This is primarily because Kohlberg favors an objectifying, technical reasoning, which has no room for freedom, risk, passion, and subjectivity, all central in Fowler's final stage of faith development.

Alternative Ways of Thinking about Spiritual Development

As social workers, concerning ourselves with "what and how we actually live in this world" can lead to a variety of approaches for defining and understanding spiritual development within ourselves and for those with whom we work (Marra, 2000, p. 72). While recognizing the worth and unique contribution of the stage-based approaches, a number of researchers have proposed expanded or additional ways of considering spiritual development. Carol Gilligan, Joan Borysenko, Matthew Fox and others have approached development from a largely feminist perspective and offer some additional useful ideas for thinking about spiritual development. Further, Wendy Haight incorporates some broader cultural implications for considering the importance of the role of spirituality within the lives of children and all individuals. And, finally, Craig Dykstra's unique process critique, which focuses on the practices and behaviors that he identifies as inherent in spiritual development, will be discussed.

Gilligan, Borysenko, & Fox: Feminist Approaches to Development

An alternative way of thinking invites the participation of voices of those persons often unheard, including persons other than the young, white, heterosexual, Judeo-Christian, able-bodied, male, with sufficient resources and power (Schriver, 2004). Carol Gilligan and others (Taylor, Gilligan, & Sullivan, 1985) have examined the research and findings of many traditional theorists, and concluded that generally the experience of girls and women at best are treated with curiosity, and a brief description inferring 'otherness' in comparison to the 'norm,' defined as or assumed to be boys and men. Gilligan proposes a look at girls as "'different,' mainly to hold it apart from its common mistranslation, 'deficient'" (p. 2). She suggests that to listen to the voices of women is to learn a great deal about what is necessary for more completely understanding the meaning of individual development for both women and men (Gilligan, 1982). Additionally, persons in many minority groups hold a worldview emphasizing the inter-relatedness of the self or the individual with other systems in the person's environment such as families, households, communities, and the ethnic group as a whole, often embracing 'story' as legend, myth and metaphor. "In addition to and in conjunction with the family, religious and spiritual institutions hold and pass along the philosophical standpoints or worldview of the people" (p. 355). Therefore, it is useful to review approaches that embrace a communal spiritual developmental process.

In her bio-psycho-*spiritual* model, Joan Borysenko (2004; 1998) expands the more traditionally accepted bio-psycho-social understanding of individual development. Borysenko's work builds on the assumption that a person's spiritual development is integrally connected to his/her cognitive, physical, and psychosocial learning and transformation. Utilizing the bio-psycho-spiritual feedback loop, she describes this spiral-formation of development through 12 seven-year cycles of renewal and metamorphosis, each one preparing for the next (See Table 2). There are three such cycles in each 'quadrant.' The four quadrants

Table 2: The Feminine Life Cycle – in Seven Year Cycles Joan Borysenko	
Quadrant One: Childhood and Adolescence	Early Childhood 1st Period: Ages 0-7 From Empathy to Interdependence
	Middle Childhood 2nd Period: Ages 7-14 The Logic of the Heart
	Adolescence 3rd Period: Ages 14-21 Snow While Falls Asleep, But Awakens to Herself
Quadrant Two: Young Adulthood	A Home of One's Own 4th Period: Ages 21-28 The Psychobiology of Mating and Motherhood
	The Age 30 Transition 5th Period: Ages 28-35 New Realities, New Plans
	Healing and Balance 6th Period: Ages 35-42 Spinning Straw into Gold
Quadrant Three: Midlife	The Midlife Metamorphosis 7th Period: Ages 42-49 Authenticity, Power, and the Emergence of the Guardian
	From Herbs to HRT 8th Period: Ages 49-56 A Mindful Approach to Menopause
	The Heart of a Woman 9th Period: Ages 56-63 Feminine Power and Social Action
Quadrant Four: Elder Years	Wisdom's Daughters 10th Period: Ages 63-70 Creating a New Integral Culture
	The Gifts of Change 11th Period: Ages 70-77 Resiliency, Loss, and Growth
	Recapitulating Our Lives 12th Period: Ages 77-84 and Beyond Generativity, Retrospection, and Transcendence
Death	The Ultimate Act of Renewal & Growth

are broadly defined as childhood and adolescence, young adulthood, midlife, and late adulthood. The thirteenth part of the life cycle, death, is perhaps the ultimate act of renewal and growth.

Borysenko explains the evolving capacities of each period, traces the waxing and waning of feminine consciousness, and assures women that midlife is a stage, not a crisis. Thomas (2001) cites similar findings, as she describes a "renewal of spirituality" for many women, as their lives changed the moment they gave birth (p. 93). Though Borysenko's work is grouped within linear age-related stages, her approach is largely focused on the recurring themes of inter-connectedness between people, nature, and things. A person living in such a way as to embrace the ideals set out by Borysenko would recognize that true intimacy based on respect and love is the measure of a life well lived. This often plays out in a person's choices related to work, leisure, living arrangements, and social com-mitments, as well as forming the underlying motivation for all relationships. As the person grows older, Borysenko (1998) suggests that "this innate female spirituality underlies an often unspoken commitment to protect our world from the ravages of greed and violence" (p. 3). This presentation gives a wonderful example of the spiral-model of spiritual development (see Table 2).

A spiritual metaphor for traditional and alternative paradigms may be found in the familiar themes of 'Climbing Jacob's Ladder' and 'Dancing Sarah's Circle.' Climbing Jacob's ladder, as defined by Fox, is a metaphor based on Jacob's dream recorded in the twenty-eighth chapter of Genesis, interpreted through the lens of a Western-Christianity, male-dominated perspective (Fox, 1999). This Biblical text has been utilized to describe the faith journey as one symbolic of fleeing the earth in an upward climb to God. In this model or metaphor, Fox suggests that "we climb to God by contemplation and descend to neighbor by compassion. Thus compassion is descent; it is also an after-thought, a luxury that one can afford only after a very long life-time of contemplative ascending" (p. 40). According to Fox, a spiritual developmental understanding based on this traditional, hierarchical, competitive, independent, and linear approach to growth will necessarily embrace distinct, clearly defined, and restrictive patterns. Openness to the visual and theoretical under-standing of dancing Sarah's circle allows for a wide variety of spiritual experiences, explanations, and attachments of meaning for persons on this journey.

Borysenko (2000) replaces the heroic model of step-by-step progress up Jacob's ladder with the image of women walking and dancing Sarah's circle. She suggests that, like all women, the mother of Isaac came to know herself in the deep, intui-tive way through the medium of her relationships rather than strictly in terms of a relationship with a transcendent God (2004). Dancing Sarah's Circle is based on the biblical text found in Genesis 18-21, culminating in Sarah, at the age of ninety, giving birth to a surprise son she named Isaac, meaning "God has smiled, God has been kind" (Fox, 1999, p.44). Thus, a spirituality of Dancing Sarah's circle is one of wonder and joy. Sarah could be surprised, filled with unexpected wonder, and able to laugh. Sarah, then, is a symbol of laughter, creativity, and shalom.

A spiritual developmental understanding based on this alternative notion including a shared experience/ecstasy, interdependence, nurture, circle-like welcome of others, culminating in a love of neighbor that *is* love of God, will necessarily embrace a broader, fluid, circular, dynamic, shared pattern of spiritual growth. Jesus' supper times with his disciples can be seen as a Sarah circle kind of intimacy and his Last Supper experience rings especially true to this dynamic. The sacrament of washing the feet that meant so much to Jesus the night before he died is a patent example of a Sarah circle dynamic. Jesus both washed his disciples' feet *and* had his feet washed with ointment by a woman willing to dry them with her long hair. "All of Sarah's circle dynamic is as much receiving as giving" (Fox, 1999, p. 56).

Within alternative approaches to understanding spirituality and spiritual development, certain concepts are central, such as mutuality, cooperation, harmony between persons, the earth, and God, and participating in significant life events. These are the main tenets of Sarah's Circle. One example of persons working together within this understanding of spirituality is a liberation group. Persons in these groups come together to share their pain of oppression and discrimination thus building a bond, and striving for mutual empowerment. Person's embracing the Sarah-Circle dynamic might take part in cooperatives such as food or clothing or housing, expanding the options, resources and flexibility of all involved. Living in harmony with the environment through interest in solar, wind and water energy systems is another example of people living Sarah's Circle within society. Finally, parents who insist on natural childbirth wherein their child will be welcomed eye to eye by a circle of fully conscious and celebrating, wonder-struck family, offer another way in which persons may choose to live out the tenets held within Sarah's circle, in full participation of important life events.

Borysenko (1998) acknowledges in the introduction to her book that although it is written primarily for women, she hopes that it will be equally enlightening to men. For whether we are biologically male or female, each of us contains aspects of the other. Her focus is the critical factor that unites women in a deeply spiritual perspective, transcending differences in religious beliefs. "From a spiritual vantage point our major life task is much larger than making money, finding a mate, having a career, raising children, looking beautiful, achieving psychological health, or defying aging, illness, and death. It is a recognition of the sacred in daily life—a deep gratitude for the wonders of the world and the delicate web of inter-connectedness between people, nature and things" (p. 3). Borysenko's description of the spiritual realm of a person's life parallels nicely with Canda's (1988) emphasis on seeking a sense of meaning and purpose in life, and striving for mutual fulfilling relationships among individuals, society, and ultimate reality. Both authors focus on the relational aspects of persons, including connections with other persons, nature, things, and ultimate reality.

A significant difference between the growth of persons in Borysenko's understanding and Fowler's is that each previous type of interaction, personal experience, and belief process is cherished and viewed as critical, remaining part of a person's whole, rather than an emphasis on leaving a particular stage behind for another, higher one. Bohannan (1992) comes to a similar conclusion. She states that women experience the sacred as immanent rather than as transcendent, living their lives in the awareness of the sacred around them, and practicing grace and love in the here and now. This rhythmic approach to the understanding of a woman's body, mind, and spirit, is interdependent, creative, and dynamic (Borysenko, 2004).

Wendy Haight: Cultural Implications for Spiritual Development
Spiritual socialization can be central to children's healthy development. Haight (1998) found that for some African American children, this foundation is directly tied to resiliency. Despite profound, ongoing stressors, her research recognized significant strength within African American children, their families and communities, often tied to the role of the church in their lives, and of a generally shared spiritual connection. Neumark (1998) suggests that spiritual development cannot be taught or managed, but "children can be encouraged to develop spiritually through being given the opportunity to consider, reflect, dream, and challenge" (p. 22).

Ancestral worldviews are reflected throughout the social institutions responsible for imparting the beliefs and values of the group such as the family, and religious and spiritual institutions (Schriver, 2004). The African-American community, like others, has a rich traditions and history that uplifts the hurt, comforts the struggling, and celebrates the soul (Hudley, Miller, & Haight, 2003). Church leaders rise to significance in the daily moral life of families and communities. "Individuals, families, and neighborhoods seek their counsel and support, guidance and inspiration. The church is also a fulcrum of much of the social life in the community and exists as a staging area for political and social activism" (Saleebey, 2001, p. 315).

A rabbi working as a community organizer found that the lives of many low- to moderate-income people of color and working-class ethnic whites revolve around their religious and spiritual beliefs (ben Asher, 2001). Many African Americans hold a worldview with roots in an African philosophical position that stresses collectivism rather than individualism. The worldviews of many Native Americans perceive all aspects of life as interrelated and of religious significance although there is no single dominant religion among the many Native American cultures. Asian/Pacific American families stress a belief system in which harmony is a core value. Latino religious beliefs reinforce a belief system in which the role of the family is a central tenet (Guadalupe, 2005; Harrison, Wilson, Pine, Chan, & Buriel, 1990). Such worldviews as these suggest much more in common with the core concerns of social work. The principles of social systems and ecological thinking found in these worldviews compliment the growing emphasis on spirituality and religion within social work practice (Schriver, 2004).

The church often plays an important and supportive role for families of color. Church provides a sense of community and inter-relatedness for many individuals and families. Family and church are so intertwined for some African Americans, for example, that church members may refer to other members as their 'church family.' One's church family may provide such important supports as role models for young family members and assistance with child rearing (Hudley,

Miller, & Haight, 2003). Even for African American families that do not belong to a formal church, spirituality may play a significant role. This spirituality is often a strength and a survival mechanism for African American families that can be tapped, particularly in times of death and dying, illness, loss, and bereavement (Boyd-Franklin, 1993; Hudley, Miller, & Haight). It is important to acknowledge the cultural implications of spiritual development, and the unique roles, meaning, and expectations found within each faith community.

Craig Dykstra: A Process Critique of Spiritual Development

Craig Dykstra (1999) embraces a certain 'strangeness,' a 'peculiarity' of Christian practice, as an asset, not a handicap. He accents the role of families, however defined, and youth, however attracted, in such settings which is a similar focus to Haight's findings related to some African American communities. This openness to 'strangeness' or other ways of thinking about and understanding certain life events, and ascribing meaning to them, fits well within an alternative approach to thinking about spiritual development. Dykstra's approach leaves more room for less traditional ways of expressing one's spiritual journey, which can include meditation, the acknowledgement of a particular geographic space which serves as a spiritual oasis, and the honoring of the God-given life and worth in all living beings.

Dykstra (1999) believes that the development of Christian nurture, rather than following formal 'stages,' relates to themes integral to the Christian story itself, focusing on ways of being and thinking and doing. If one considers spiritual development as a spiral-shaped experience, drawing from the recurring realities of a circle, but honoring the assumed growth and movement that a ladder suggests, it is possible to begin to understand a more thematic approach to this process. Dykstra identifies hunger, life, practices, places, and signs as broad themes recurring in our lives, embracing the mystery or depth of Christian faith, and a variety of methods for practicing this faith.

William Hull (1991) describes Christian salvation as a dynamic process—we were saved, we are being saved, and we will be saved. This somewhat subtle shift from the ladder image to a re-visiting process in cyclical form is quite profound, as the spiral-formation of growth allows one to re-engage with themes throughout life. This approach mirrors our own yearly reliving of the significant events on the liturgical calendar including communion, Lent, Easter, Pentecost, Advent, Christmas, and Epiphany. The process of re-experiencing these pivotal celebrations allows us to find the extraordinary in the 'ordinary.' As we continue to grow, change, understand ourselves, others, and God in different ways, our experiencing of these events is repetitive, yet new.

These alternative approaches to understanding spiritual development allow for the impact of greater societal, political, racial, ethnic, socioeconomic, physical, and emotional factors throughout this life process. Helminiak (1996) argues that if the needs of organisms are not met, the higher levels of psyche and spirit are adversely affected. Inversely, a sick spirit impacts psyche and organism negatively. Young, Cashwell, and Shcherbakova (2000) conclude that spirituality seems to provide a buffer from stressful life events that are perceived as negative, further supporting the value of the spiral-formed developmental impact which sustains the connections to previous life experiences.

Conclusion

The spiritual development approaches discussed in this chapter support the central tenet that "important religious beliefs, rituals, and social structures can play key roles as individuals and families move through the life cycle" (Hugen, 2001, p. 13). Some of the elements identified as significant dimensions of spiritual development are creativity, contemplation, wholeness, connectedness and quest or search for meaning (Guadalupe, 2005). In short, "spirituality is essential to human happiness and mental health" (Elkins, 1999, p. 44).

What occurs between the client and the social worker involves not only the traditional interventions, methods, and skills the social worker applies, but also a two-way exchange of ideas, feelings, beliefs, and values that may or may not be directly addressed or acknowledged. "Whether professionals are 'believers' in the spiritual dimension is important. 'Nonbelievers' may not be fully able to accept clients who consider spirituality and religion to be meaningful and useful within the context of their life experiences" (Sermabeikian, 1994, pp. 178-79). Social workers, therefore, should develop self-understanding regarding personal biases, their own experiences that lead to strong assumptions about others, existential issues and spiritual growth (Canda, 1988; & Cascio, 1998). "Self-inquiry must be a disciplined and consistent process of personal and professional growth. Social workers should examine their beliefs, motivations, values, and activities and consider the impact of these factors upon the client's spirituality" (Canda, p 245)

A spiritual bias can be just as harmful as racism or sexism. When consider- ing the issue of spirit, spiritual, and spirituality, a social worker must also consider his or her assumptions about the process of growth, deepening awareness, and the language and meanings attached to this spiritual development. Whether the philosophical tenets of climbing Jacob's ladder or those supporting dancing Sarah's circle are embraced, social workers must enter into an awareness of the sacred for themselves and for the persons with whom they work.

References

ben Asher, M. (2001). Spirituality and religion in social work practice. *Social Work Today, 1*(7), 15-18.

Bohannan, H. (1992). Quest-tioning tradition: Spiritual transformation images in women's narratives and 'housekeeping.' *Western Folklore, 51*(1), 65-80.

Borysenko, J. (1998). *A woman's book of life: The biology, psychology, and spirituality of the feminine life cycle.* New York: Riverhead Books.

Borysenko, J. (2000). *A woman's journey to God: Finding the feminine path.* New York: Riverhead Books.

Borysenko, J. (2004). *A woman's spiritual retreat: Teaching, meditations, rituals to celebrate your authentic feminine wisdom*. Louisville, CO: Sounds True Publishing.

Boyd-Franklin, N. (1993). Race, class and poverty. In *Normal family processes*, Walsh, F. (Ed.). New York: Guilford.

Brandt, A. (1991). Do kids need religion? *Utne Reader*, 43, 84-88.

Canda, E.R. (1988). Spirituality, religious diversity, and social work practice. *Social Casework: The Journal of Contemporary Social Work*, 238-247.

Canda, E.R., & Furman, L.D. (1999). *Spiritual diversity in social work practice: The heart of helping*. New York: Free Press.

Cascio, T. (1998). Incorporating spirituality into social work practice: A review of what to do. *Families in Society: The Journal of Contemporary Human Services*, 79(5), 523-531.

Coles, R. (1990). *The spiritual life of children*. Boston: Houghton Mifflin.

Coles, R. (1970). *Erik H. Erikson: The growth of his works*. Boston: Little, Brown and Company.

Council on Social Work Education. (2000). *Curriculum policy statement for master's degree program in social work education*. Alexandria, VA: Author.

Dykstra, C. (1999). *Growing in the life of faith: Education and Christian practice*. Louisville, KY: Geneva Press.

Dykstra, C., & Parks S. (Eds.). (1986). *Faith development and Fowler*. Birmingham, AL: Religious Education Press.

Dykstra, C.R. (1981). *Vision and character: A Christian educator's alternative to Kohlberg*. New York: Paulist Press.

Elkins, D.N. (1999). Spirituality. *Psychology Today*, 32(5), 44-50.

Erikson, E. (1997). *The life cycle completed: Extended version with new chapters on the ninth stage of development*. New York: Norton.

Erikson, E. (1950). *Childhood and society*. New York: Norton.

Faiver, C., Ingersoll, R.E., O'Brien, E., & McNally, C. (2001). *Explorations in counseling and spirituality: Philosophical, practical, and personal reflections*. Belmont, CA: Wadsworth/Thomson Learning.

Fowler, J. (1981). *Stages of faith: The psychology of human development and the quest for meaning*. San Francisco: Harper Collins.

Fowler, J. (1986). Faith and the structuring of meaning. In C. Dykstra, & S. Parks (Eds.), *Faith development and Fowler* (pp. 15-44). Birmingham, AL: Religious Education Press.

Fowler, J. (1986). Dialogue toward a future in faith development studies. In C. Dykstra, & S. Parks (Eds.), *Faith development and Fowler* (pp. 275-301). Birmingham, AL: Religious Education Press.

Fox, M. (1999). *A spirituality named compassion*. San Francisco: HarperCollins.

Gilligan, C. (1982). *In a different voice: Psychological theory and women's development*. Cambridge: Harvard University Press.

Guadalupe, J.A. (2005). Spirituality and multidimensional contextual practice. In K.L. Guadalupe & D. Lum (2005). Multidimensional contextual practice: Diversity and transcendence, (pp. 146-163). Belmont, CA: Thomson Brooks/Cole.

Haight, W.L. (1998). "Gathering the Spirit" at First Baptist Church: Spirituality as a protective factor in the lives of African American children. *Social Work*, 43(3), 213-21.

Harrison, A., Wilson, M., Pine, C., Chan, S., & Buriel, R. (1990). Family ecologies of ethnic minority children. *Child Development*, 61, 347-362.

Helminiak, D.A. (1987). *Spiritual development: An interdisciplinary study*. Chicago: Loyola University Press.

Helminiak, D.A. (1996). *The human core of spirituality: Mind as psyche and spirit.* Albany, N.Y.: State University of New York Press.

Hudely, E.V.P., Miller, P.J., & Haight, W. (2003). *Raise up a child: Human development in an African-American family.* Chicago: Lyceum Books.

Hugen, B., (Ed.). (1998). *Christianity and social work: Readings on the integration of Christian faith and social work practice.* Botsford, CT: North American Association of Christians in Social Work.

Hugen, B. (2001). Spirituality and religion in social work practice: A conceptual model. In Van Hook, M., Hugen, B., & Aguilar, M. (Eds.), *Spirituality within religious traditions in social work practice* (pp. 9-17). Pacific Grove, CA: Brooks/Cole.

Hull, W.E. (1991). *The Christian experience of salvation.* Nashville: Broadman & Holman Publishers.

Irwin, R.R. (2002). *Human development and the spiritual life: How consciousness grows toward transformation.* New York: Kluwer Academic/Plenum Publishers.

Joseph, M.V. (1988). Religion and social work practice. *Social Casework: The Journal of Contemporary Social Work,* 443-449.

Kohlberg, L. (1969). *Stages in the development of moral thought and action.* New York: Holt, Rinehart & Winston.

Kropf, R. (1991). Faith's last stage may well be leap in the dark. *National Catholic Reporter, 28*(9), 12.

Marra, R. (2000) What do you mean, "spirituality"? *Journal of Pastoral Counseling, 22,* 67-79.

Mulqueen, J., & Elias, J.L. (2000). Understanding spiritual development through cognitive development. *Journal of Pastoral Counseling, Annual,* 99-113.

Neumark, V. (1998). Hole makes whole. *Times Educational Supplement,* 4272, pp. 22-24.

Saleebey, D. (2001). *Human behavior and social environments: A biopsychosocial approach.* New York: Columbia University.

Schriver, J.M. (2004). *Human behavior and the social environment: Shifting paradigms in essential knowledge for social work practice* (4th ed.). Boston: Allyn & Bacon.

Sermabeikian, P. (1994). Our clients, ourselves: The spiritual perspective and social work practice. *Social Work, 39*(3), 178-83.

Smith, M.H. (1997-1998). Embodied wisdom, embodied faith: Bio-spirituality. *Hungryhearts,1*(3-4), 1-7.

Spencer, S.W. (1961). What place has religion in social work education? *Social Work,* 161-170.

Taylor, J.M., Gilligan, C., & Sullivan, A.M. (1985). *Between voice and silence: Women and girls, race and relationship.* Cambridge, MA: Harvard University Press.

Thomas, T. (2001). Becoming a mother: Matrescence as spiritual formation. *Religious Education, 96*(1), 88-105.

Van Hook, M., Hugen, B., & Aguilar, M. (2001). *Spirituality within religious traditions in social work practice.* Pacific Grove, CA: Brooks/Cole.

Young, J.S., Cashwell, C.S., & Shcherbakova, J. (2000). The moderating relationship of spirituality on negative life events and psychological adjustment. *Counseling and Values, 45*(1), 49-60.

CHAPTER 14

SPIRITUAL ASSESSMENT: A REVIEW OF COMPLEMENTARY ASSESSMENT MODELS

David R. Hodge and Crystal R. Holtrop

Assessment is considered by many to be an underdeveloped area in social work (Mattaini & Kirk, 1991). The lack of development is particularly acute in the area of spiritual assessment (Bullis, 1996; Sherwood, 1998). For instance, numerous studies have found that most social workers have received no training in the area of spiritual assessment (Bullis, 1996; Canda & Furman, 1999; Derezotes, 1995; Sheridan & Amato-von Hemert, 1999; Furman & Canda, 1994). The lack of attention devoted to spiritual assessment represents a significant oversight. Four issues, ontology, ethics, strengths, and autonomy will be discussed in brief to highlight the importance of spiritual assessment in social work.

Spirituality is often central to clients' personal ontology, meaning it may be the essence of their personhood. Spirituality may inform attitudes and practices in such areas as child rearing, diet, marriage, medical care, military participation, recreation, schooling, social interactions, as well as many other dimensions of life (DiBlasio, 1988; Rey, 1997). For one third of the general population, religion is the most important facet of their lives and over 50% consider it to be a very important aspect of their lives (Gallup & Lindsay, 1999; Walsh, 1999). Further, for African Americans, Hispanics, women, the elderly, the poor, and many other populations of significance to social workers, spirituality is even more salient (Gallup & Lindsay, 1999; Pargament, 1997). The provision of respectful services to these groups is often contingent upon practitioners' awareness of clients' spiritually based beliefs and practices. In order to provide effective services, social workers must develop some understanding of clients' spiritual worldview.

A second factor stems from the profession's ethical mandates. Spirituality is often expressed in distinct traditions or faith-based cultures (Fellin, 2000; Talbot, 2000). The NASW Code of Ethics (1999) stipulates that social workers are to demonstrate competence and sensitivity toward faith based cultures (1.05b) and recognizes the strengths that exist among such groups (1.05a). Ethically sound practice entails obtaining the knowledge to exhibit spiritual sensitivity to clients.

Social workers are increasingly recognizing the importance of strengths (Cowger, 1994; Hwang & Cowger, 1998; Saleebey, 1997). Reviews have consistently found a generally positive association between spirituality and a wide number of beneficial characteristics (Ellison & Levin, 1998; Gartner, Larson & Allen, 1991; Koenig, McCullough & Larson, 2001; Pargament, 1997). More specifically, various dimensions of spirituality have been associated with recovery from addiction (Turner, O' Dell & Weaver, 1999), depression (Propst, 1996), divorce (Nathanson, 1995), homelessness (Lindsey, Kurtz, Jarvis, Williams & Nackerud, 2000; Montgomery, 1994), serious mental illness (Sullivan, 1997), sexual assault (Kennedy, Davis & Talyor, 1998) as well as empowerment (Calhoun-Brown, 1998; Maton & Salem, 1995) and healing (Maton & Wells, 1995; McRae, Thompson & Cooper, 1999). While spirituality is often an important client asset, unfortunately, these strengths often lie dormant (Saleebey, 1997). To tap clients' spiritual assets for the purposes of ameliorating problems, practitioners must use methods designed to identify clients' strengths (Ronnau & Poertner, 1993).

Finally, there is the issue of client autonomy. Many clients desire to integrate their spiritual beliefs and values into the helping relationship (Privette, Quackenbos & Bundrick, 1994). According to Gallup data reported by Bart (1998), 66% of the general public would prefer to see a professional counselor with spiritual values and beliefs and 81% wanted to have their own values and beliefs integrated into the counseling process. Further, research suggests that spirituality tends to become more salient during difficult situations (Ferraro & Kelley-Moore, 2000; Pargament, 1997), when individuals may be more likely to encounter social workers.

In sum, spiritual assessment provides social workers with a means to understand clients' spiritual strengths, beliefs, and values—in short—their worldview. Not only is such knowledge often critical for culturally competent practice, in many instances it is an ethical imperative. Spiritual assessment provides a mechanism to identify clients' spiritual resources and honor their desire to integrate their beliefs and values into the clinical dialogue.

In light of the importance of spiritual assessment, this chapter reviews a number of recently developed assessment approaches and provides examples of how they may be applied in practice with Christian clients. Our intent is not to provide an exhaustive review of various assessment methods, but rather to review a specific series of assessment instruments. These four instruments were developed to complement one another in the hopes of providing social workers with a set of assessment tools for use in numerous settings with a variety of clients. Rather than being interchangeable, one approach may be ideal in one context while another tool may be better suited to address a different client-to-practitioner interface. Readers are encouraged to obtain the original articles in which the instruments first appeared and to become familiar with the strengths and limitations of each assessment instrument. The assessment tools may be used with a variety of different religious traditions, but here we will be applying a Christian point of view and using examples from practice with Christian clients.

After defining spiritual assessment, spirituality, and religion, four assessment instruments are reviewed: spiritual genograms (Hodge, 2001b), spiritual lifemaps (Hodge, in press), spiritual histories (Hodge, 2001a), and spiritual eco-maps (Hodge, 2000; Hodge & Williams, in press). A brief overview of the assets and limitations of each method is provided and, for the three diagrammatic instruments, case examples are provided to familiarize the reader with the instrument. A brief discussion on conducting an assessment concludes the chapter.

Definitions

Spiritual assessment is defined as the process of gathering and organizing spiritually based data into a coherent format that provides the basis for interventions (Hodge, 2001a; Rauch, 1993). The subsequent interventions may or may not be spiritually based. As implied above, a spiritual assessment may be conducted for the purposes of using traditional, non-spiritual, interventions in a manner that is more congruent with clients' beliefs and values.

Spirituality is defined as an existential relationship with God (or perceived transcendence) (Hodge, 2001a). Religion flows from spirituality, expressing the spiritual relationship in particular beliefs, forms, and practices that have been developed in community with other individuals who share similar spiritual experiences (Hodge, 2000). Accordingly, spirituality and religion are overlapping but distinct constructs (Canda, 1997; Carroll, 1997).

Spiritual Genograms

In a manner analogous to traditional genograms, spiritual genograms provide social workers with a tangible graphic representation of spirituality across at least three generations (Hodge, 2001b). Through the use of what is essentially a modified family tree, they help both practitioners and clients understand the flow of historically rooted patterns through time. In short, spiritual genograms are a blueprint of complex intergenerational spiritual interactions.

In keeping with standard genogram conventions (McGoldrick, Gerson & Shellenberger, 1999; Stanion, Papadopoulos & Bor, 1997), the basic family structure is commonly delineated across at least three generations. Typically, squares represent males and circles denote females. In some cases, triangles or other geometric shapes can be used to designate individuals who have played major spiritual roles but are not members of the immediate biological family (Hodge, 2001b).

To indicate clients' spiritual tradition, colored drawing pencils can be used to shade in the circles and squares (Hodge, 2001b). Color coding provides a graphic "color snapshot" of the overall spiritual composition of the family system (Hardy & Laszloffy, 1995). Various colors can be used to signify religious preference (Buddhist, Christian, Hindu, Jewish, Muslim, New Age, none, etc.), or more specifically when the information is known, denomination (Assemblies of God, Brethren, Catholic, Southern Baptist, Presbyterian, etc.). For example, a circle representing a female Southern Baptist could be colored red, a member of the Assemblies of God might be colored orange, a Muslim might be colored brown, and an individual whose affiliation and beliefs are unknown could be left uncolored. A change in an adult's religious orientation can be signified by listing the date of the change beside a circle which is drawn outside the figure and filling in the space between the circle and the figure with the appropriate color, a procedure which indicates the stability or fluidity of the person's beliefs over time. Using a similar approach, changes in orientation might also be noted by coloring the vertical segment connecting the child with the parents.

If needed, the color scheme can also be used to incorporate information on commitment (devout vs. nominal) and theology (conservative vs. liberal) (Hodge, 2001b). For example, yellow might be used to signify a devout, conservative Methodist while gray could be used for a nominal Methodist. Alternatively, symbols, which are placed beside the appropriate circle or square, could be used to indicate the degree of commitment or theological orientation. An open set of scriptures, for instance, might be used to indicate a devout person. Social workers should explain the options to clients and allow them to select the colors and symbols that they perceive best express their worldview.

Spiritually meaningful events should also be incorporated, such as water and spirit baptisms, confirmations, church memberships, and bar mitzvahs (Hodge, 2001b). Symbols drawn from the client's spiritual journey can be used to signify these events. For instance, a cross might be used by a Christian to indicate reaching a point of conversion, a dove might be used by a Pentecostal to depict a deeper work of the Holy Spirit, or a sunbeam might used by a New Age adherent to symbolize a time of profound spiritual enlightenment. In addition, short summary statements can be used to denote significant events or personal strengths.

In addition to depicting religious beliefs, it is also possible to include an affective component (Hodge, 2001b). In other words, felt spiritual closeness between family members can be illustrated on spiritual genograms. Lines with double-headed arrows [◄——►] can be used to symbolize a relationship in which individuals experience a close reciprocal spiritual bond. The thickness of the line can indicate the intimacy or strength of the relationship. In situations where the relationship is more hierarchical and less reciprocal—as might occur with a grandparent mentoring a grandchild—a single arrowhead can be used to depict the flow of spiritual resources. Finally, spiritual conflict can be portrayed with a jagged line, similar to a lightening bolt, drawn between the two individuals.

Case Example

Diagram 1 (following page) indicates what a relatively straightforward spiritual genogram might look like for a couple, Mark and Beth, who are experiencing marital problems. In place of the colors that would normally be used with a spiritual genogram, patterns (for example, dots, diagonals, waves) are employed to depict various denominations.

After three years of marriage, Mark, 26, and Beth, 23, requested counseling after the recent birth of their daughter, Megan. Her birth renewed their interest in church attendance as they both desired to raise Megan with spiritual values and to have her baptized. However, they disagreed on practically everything else—how to spend money, parent their daughter, where to go to church, and how to accomplish household tasks. Mark and Beth's inability to resolve conflict was due to a power struggle over whose family of origin's rules they were going to follow. Due to their conflict over which church to attend, the therapist developed a spiritual genogram to enhance their traditional genogram.

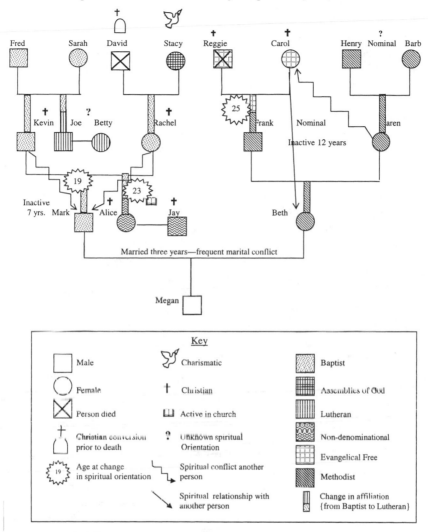

Diagram 1.

During Mark's childhood, his nuclear family and his paternal grandparents attended the Baptist church that was three blocks away from their house. His family shared a tradition of going to Mark's paternal grandparents' house every Sunday after church. Although Mark knew that Aunt Betty and Uncle Joe attended a Lutheran church regularly, he had never heard them talk openly about their faith at family gatherings and was unsure how important it was to them. His maternal grandmother attended an Assemblies of God church before she was placed in the nursing home. He recalled his grandmother sharing a story about how she prayed for 30 years that her husband would become a Christian, and that her prayers were answered shortly before her husband died.

During his adolescence, Mark perceived his parents' rules as old-fashioned and rigid and rebelled against them. As soon as he left home, Mark stopped attending church, much to his parents' chagrin. His sister, Alice, left the Baptist church when she was 23 years old and started attending a non-denominational church where she met her husband, Jay. Alice and Jay are still actively involved in this church and frequently share information with Mark and Beth about family activities that are occurring there. As Mark shared this information, the therapist drew a cross by the names of his parents, paternal grandparents, maternal grandmother, sister, and brother-in-law to indicate that they were Christians. She put a question mark next to his aunt and uncle due to Mark's lack of clarity about their level of commitment to their faith. In order to signify Alice and Jay's devout faith and active participation in their church, the therapist drew an open Bible near their names. She colored their circles and squares different colors to indicate the various denominations represented in Mark's family. Uncle Joe's and Alice's rectangles that attach them to their respective parents have two colors, indicating that they switched from attending the Baptist church to a different denomination.

Beth's family attended a Methodist church when she was young. However, their attendance dwindled to Easter and Christmas as Beth became active in school activities. She knew that her parents both believed in God, but did not see this belief influencing their lives. However, Beth had fond memories of sitting on her paternal grandmother's lap as she listened to her grandmother, Carol, read Bible stories to her. She also recalled attending Vacation Bible school which was sponsored by the Evangelical Free church her grandmother attended. She assumed that "Grandma Carol" was a committed Christian because she overheard her mother complain about "how religious Grandma Carol was" and observed her mother rebuff Grandma Carol whenever she offered to pray for the family. To signify Beth's mother's underlying conflict towards Grandma Carol over spiritual matters, the therapist drew a jagged arrow between their circles. Although her paternal grandfather died before Beth was born, she recalled her Grandma Carol fondly referring to her husband as "a fine man who loved people and the Lord."

Although Beth stated she believes in God, she acknowledged that she presently refers to God primarily when she is swearing angrily at Mark. However, as the conflict between Beth and Mark continued to escalate, she started contemplating "giving God a try." She was open to attending a church as long as it was not Mark's parents' church. She thought his mother already interfered with their marriage far too much. The therapist colored Beth's maternal grandparents' and parents' circles and squares red to represent the Methodist denomination. Due to their nominal interest in spiritual matters, Beth and Mark agreed that the therapist should not draw a cross by their names. She did draw a cross by Grandma Carol's name and by her paternal grandfather's name, and also drew an arrow from her Grandmother Carol to Beth, indicating the spiritual influence she had on Beth.

With the multi-colored spiritual genogram directly in front of them, Mark and Beth were struck by the diversity of denominations represented in their extended families. This new perspective helped them see beyond their original, narrowly defined choices of Baptist vs. Methodist that Mark and Beth clung to out of loyalty to their families of origin. The therapist encouraged the couple to interview members of their extended family, asking questions concerning their faith, their religious practices, and the strengths and limitations of their church and denomination. Beth and Mark discovered that the new perspectives gained from the interviews helped them be more evaluative in their decision-making process and moved them beyond their stalemate.

Assets and Limitations

Although spiritual genograms can be effective assessment instruments in a number of situations, they may be particularly useful when the family system plays an especially salient role in the client's life or when the client presents with problems involving family members or family of origin issues (Hodge, 2001b). For example, spiritual genograms might be used with interfaith couples experiencing spiritually based barriers to intimacy to expose areas of difference and potential conflict as well to highlight the respective spiritual strengths each person brings to the relationship. Similarly, spiritual genograms could also be used with couples from similar backgrounds to increase their level of intimacy.

Conversely, spiritual genograms may be an inappropriate assessment instrument in situations where historical influences are of minor importance. Further, even in situations where generational influences are pertinent, many clients do not connect past events with current difficulties. Accordingly, clients may view genogram construction and between-session tasks as an ineffective use of time. As Kuehl (1995) notes, proceeding with such interventions before clients appreciate their usefulness can reduce treatment adherence and jeopardize outcomes. Consequently, in some contexts it may be best to use assessment approaches that do not focus on the generational aspects of spirituality.

Spiritual Lifemaps

While spiritual genograms chart the flow of spirituality across at least three generations, spiritual lifemaps depict clients' personal spiritual life-story (Hodge, in press). More specifically, spiritual lifemaps are a pictorial delineation of a client's spiritual journey. In a manner analogous to renowned African writer Augustine's (354-430/1991) *Confessions*, spiritual lifemaps are an illustrated account of clients' relationship with God over time: a map of their spiritual life.

At its most basic level, a drawing pencil is used to sketch various spiritually significant life events on paper (Hodge, in press). The method is similar to various approaches drawn from art and family therapy in which a client's history is depicted on a "lifeline" (Tracz & Gehart-Brooks, 1999). Much like road maps, spiritual lifemaps tell us where we have come from, where we are now, and where we are going.

To assist clients in the creative expression of their spiritual journeys, it is usually best to use a large sheet of paper (e.g., 24" x 36") on which to sketch the map (Hodge, in press). Providing drawing instruments of different sizes and colors are also helpful as is offering a selection of various types and colors of construction paper and popular periodicals. Providing these items, in conjunction with scissors, glue sticks, and rulers, allows clients to clip and paste items onto the lifemap.

Spiritually significant events are depicted on a path, a roadway, or a single line that represents clients' spiritual sojourn (Hodge, in press). Typically, the path proceeds chronologically, from birth through to the present. Frequently the path continues on to death and the client's transition to the afterlife. Hand drawn symbols, cut out pictures, and other representations are used to mark key events along the journey. In keeping with many spiritual traditions, which conceive material existence to be an extension of the sacred reality, it is common to depict important lifestage events on the lifemap (for example, marriage, birth of a child, death of a close friend or relative, or loss of a job). While it is often necessary to provide clients with general guidelines, client creativity and self-expression should be encouraged.

To fully operationalize the potential of the instrument, it is important to ask clients to incorporate the various crises they have faced into their lifemaps along with the spiritual resources they have used to overcome those trials (Hodge, in press). Symbols such as hills, bumps and potholes, rain, clouds, and lightning can be used to portray difficult life situations. Delineating successful strategies that clients have used in the past frequently suggests options for overcoming present struggles.

Case Example

Diagram 2 (folowing page) provides an example of what a spiritual lifemap might look like on a smaller scale. Tyrone, a 42 year-old black male, was recently diagnosed with terminal cancer. The doctor confirmed his worst fears that the cancer was inoperable, and predicted that Tyrone had approximately 6 months to live. A medical social worker on the oncology ward met with Tyrone to help him process the shock of his prognosis and prepare for what appeared to be a premature death. Shortly into their conversation, the social worker discovered that Tyrone was actively involved in the Third Missionary Baptist Church. Tyrone's eyes lit up as he shared that he began playing guitar in the church's music ministry 10 years ago, a couple of years after he became a Christian. It soon became clear to the social worker that Tyrone's faith was a significant strength and could help him cope with his present crisis. In order to help Tyrone identify effective coping strategies, the social worker encouraged Tyrone to develop a spiritual lifemap. Tyrone's creativity and musical interests seemed to indicate that this assignment would be a good fit for his personality.

Tyrone's parents divorced when he was 9 years old. He and his 2 older sisters lived with his mother and periodically visited his father. His mother was actively involved in a Pentecostal church and sang in the church choir. When Tyrone reached adolescence, his anger toward his absent father began to mount and was acted out in rebellion toward his mother. Out of desperation, his mother arranged guitar lessons for Tyrone to creatively redirect his anger and build his self-esteem. Tyrone established a lifelong mentoring relationship with his guitar teacher, Jerome, who consistently believed in him and spawned a passion for a variety of musi-

Diagram 2.

cal styles including blues, jazz, gospel, and rock. When he graduated from high school, he joined a band and played in clubs for the next 9 years. Disillusioned with God for not answering his childhood prayers for his father, Tyrone started experimenting with drugs and alcohol to numb his emptiness inside.

By age 27, Tyrone had successfully recorded a CD with his band and was gaining local notoriety. Life was good. He was doing well financially and he enjoyed dating several different women. However, this season was short-lived. By age 30, he was significantly in debt and was emotionally broken. After three years of dating, Tyrone's girlfriend, Janet concluded that Tyrone was more committed to his band than to her and she broke up with him. He coped by increasing his alcohol consumption, which hurt his performance and created conflict with his band members. After a particularly heated argument, Tyrone sought solace from Jerome, his former guitar teacher. Through this renewed friendship, Tyrone began examining his life, his priorities, and the source of his emptiness and bitterness. He forgave God for what he perceived to be abandonment (a replication of his father's abandonment) and he experienced a profound sense of God's love and acceptance. Tyrone soon realized that it was he, not God, who had abandoned divine and human love out of bitterness and despair.

Tyrone started attending the Third Missionary Baptist church. Upon Jerome's advice, Tyrone took a break from playing guitar and immersed himself in Bible study, prayer, and Christian books to help him sort out his unresolved hurts, develop effective anger management skills, and evaluate his life goals. He also developed significant relationships with other men in a Promise Keepers group. He watched several men in the group weather severe trials by clinging onto God's promises and by receiving love and support from their friends. He gradually learned that no matter what happens in life, God is good, faithful, and in control. After a 2-year hiatus, Tyrone began playing guitar in church. Using his talents to worship God gave him a sense of meaning and joy that was deeper than any he had experienced before. Completing the spiritual lifemap helped Tyrone reflect on his life, his pit and peak experiences, the lessons he had learned, and the people who had blest him. Most importantly, he identified key people that would support him through his present illness and pray for God to heal him. While discussing the lifemap with his social worker, Tyrone began to clarify the goals he still wanted to accomplish, like mentoring some young boys in church who were growing up in single parent homes. Through this reflective assignment, he also made the decision to write some songs as a creative way to express his pain, cry out to God, and receive strength and comfort.

Assets and Limitations

Of the assessment methods reviewed in this chapter, spiritual lifemaps are perhaps the most client-directed. Consequently, there are a number of unique advantages associated with the use of this diagrammatic model (Hodge, in press). By placing a client-constructed media at the center of assessment, the message is implicitly communicated that the client is a competent, pro-active, self-directed, fully engaged participant in the therapeutic process. Additionally, individuals who are not verbally oriented may find pictorial expression more conducive to their personal communication styles (McNiff, 1992).

The relatively secondary role that social workers play during assessment also offers important advantages. For many clients, spirituality is a highly personal, sensitive, and important area. Most social workers have had limited training about various spiritual worldviews, in spite of the central role spirituality plays in human behavior. (Canda & Furman, 1999). Consequently, there is the distinct risk that social workers may offend clients and jeopardize the therapeutic relationship through comments that are inadvertently offensive, especially with the use of more practitioner-centered, verbally-based assessment approaches. The pictorial lifemap affords practitioners the opportunity to learn more about the client's worldview while focusing on building therapeutic rapport by providing an atmosphere that is accepting, nonjudgmental, and supportive during assessment (Kahn, 1999).

In terms of limitations, some social workers may feel so removed from the process that this assessment approach makes poor use of therapeutic time. Indeed, in the time constrained, managed care world in which many practitioners work, in some cases it may be advisable to use the lifemap as a homework assignment (Hodge, in press). Another significant limitation is that many clients, such as those who are more verbal, those that are uncomfortable with drawing, or those who prefer more direct practitioner and client involvement, may find the use of a largely non-verbal, pictorial instrument to be a poor fit.

Spiritual Histories

A spiritual history represents a narrative alternative to a spiritual lifemap (Hodge, 2001a). Instead of relating the client's spiritual sojourn in a diagram made format, the client's spiritual story is related verbally. In a process that is analogous to conducting a family history, the client is provided an interactive forum to share his or her spiritual life story.

To guide the conversation, a two-part framework is used (Hodge, 2001a). As can been seen in Table 1 (following page), the first part consists of an initial narrative framework. The purpose of these questions is to provide practitioners with some tools for structuring the assessment. The aim is to help clients tell their stories, typically moving from childhood to the present.

It should also be noted that the questions delineated in Table 1 are offered as suggestions (Hodge, 2001a). Social workers should not view them as a rigid template that must be applied in every situation, but rather as a fluid framework that should be tailored to the needs of each individual client. In other words, the questions provide a number of possible options that can be used to facilitate the movement of the narrative and to elicit important information.

The second part of Table 1 consists of an interpretive framework (Hodge, 2001a) based on the anthropological understandings of Chinese spirituality writer Watchman Nee (1968). In addition to soma, Nee envisions a soul, comprised of affect, will, and cognition, and a spirit, comprised of communion, conscience, and intuition. Although human beings are an integrated unity and, consequently, the six dimensions interact with and influence one another, it is possible to distinguish each dimension. As is the case with other human dimensions, such as affect, behavior, and cognition, the dimensions of the spirit also can be discussed individually.

Communion refers to a spiritually based relationship. More specifically, it denotes the ability to bond with and relate to God. Conscience relates to one's ability to sense right and wrong. Beyond a person's cognitively held values, conscience conveys moral knowledge about the appropriateness of a given set

Table I. Guidelines for conducting spiritual histories

Initial Narrative Framework

1.   Describe the religious/spiritual tradition you grew up in. How did your family express its spiritual beliefs? How important was spirituality to your family? Extended family?

2.   What sort of personal experiences (practices) stand out to you during your years at home? What made these experiences special? How have they informed your later life?

3.   How have you transitioned or matured from those experiences? How would you describe your current spiritual/religious orientation? Is your spirituality a personal strength? If so, how?

Interpretive Anthropological Framework

1.   Affect: What aspects of your spiritual life give you pleasure? What role does your spirituality play in handling life's sorrows? Enhancing its joys? Coping with its pain? How does your spirituality give you hope for the future? What do you wish to accomplish in the future?

2.   Behavior: Are there particular spiritual rituals or practices that help you deal with life's obstacles? What is your level of involvement in faith-based communities? How are they supportive? Are there spiritually encouraging individuals that you maintain contact with?

3.   Cognitive: What are your current religious/spiritual beliefs? What are they based upon? What beliefs do you find particularly meaningful? What does your faith say about trials? How does this belief help you overcome obstacles? How do your beliefs affect your health practices?

4.   Communion: Describe your relationship to the Ultimate. What has been your experience of the Ultimate? How does the Ultimate communicate with you? How have these experiences encouraged you? Have there been times of deep spiritual intimacy? How does your relationship help you face life challenges? How would the Ultimate describe you?

5.   Conscience: How do you determine right and wrong? What are your key values? How does your spirituality help you deal with guilt (sin)? What role does forgiveness play in your life?

6.   Intuition: To what extent do you experience intuitive hunches (flashes of creative insight, premonitions, spiritual insights)? Have these insights been a strength in your life? If so, how?

Table from Hodge (2001)

of choices. Intuition refers to the ability to know—to come up with insights that by-pass cognitively based, information-processing channels.

As is apparent in Table 1, the questions in the interpretive anthropological framework are designed to elicit information about each of the six dimensions. The questions are not meant to be asked in any specific order. Rather, they are provided to help social workers draw out the richness of clients' spiritual stories. As clients relate their spiritual narrative, they may tend to touch upon some of the dimensions listed in the interpretive anthropological framework. Social workers can pose questions drawn from the framework to more fully explore clients' spiritual reality in the natural flow of the therapeutic dialogue.

Assets and Limitations

There is a considerable amount of evidence that information is stored and organized narratively in the mind (Strickland, 1994). Accordingly, assessment methods that are congruent with this reality work with, rather than against, clients' mental thought processes. Indeed, for verbally oriented persons, spiritual histories may provide the best assessment method. The non-structured format allows clients to relate their stories in a direct, unfiltered manner. For example, whereas genograms require clients to circumscribe their spiritual reality upon a generational chart, assessment with spiritual histories allows clients to choose the relevant material to be shared.

However, not all clients are verbally oriented and some may find that a narrative assessment places too much attention on them in light of the sensitive, personal nature of spirituality. Some clients find it helpful to have a specific framework. Given the amorphous, subjective nature of spirituality, physical depiction may help concretize the client's strengths (Hodge, 2000). In other words, the process of conceptualizing and depicting one's spiritual journey may help to focus and objectify spiritual assets, which can then be discussed and marshaled to address problems. Still another limitation is the time spent exploring portions of the client's spiritual history that may have limited utility in terms of addressing the present problem the client is wrestling with.

Spiritual Eco-maps

In contrast to the above assessment tools, spiritual eco-maps focus on clients' current spiritual relationships (Hodge, 2000; Hodge & Williams, in press). The assessment instruments previously are united in the sense that they all are designed to tap some portion of clients' spiritual story as it exists through time. Spiritual genograms, lifemaps and histories typically cover one to three generations of a client's spiritual narrative. Spiritual eco-maps, on the other hand, focus on that portion of clients' spiritual story that exists in space. In other words, this assessment approach highlights clients' present relationships to various spiritual assets.

In keeping with traditional eco-gram construction (Hartman, 1995) the immediate family system is typically portrayed as a circle in the center of a piece of paper. Household family members can be sketched inside the circle, with squares depicting males and circles representing females (Hodge, 2000). Alternatively, separate eco-maps can be drawn for each individual (Hodge & Williams, in press).

Significant spiritual systems or domains are depicted as circles on the outskirts of the paper, with the names of the respective systems written inside the circles. The circles are placed in a radius around the family circle, which may consist of a single figure representing the client. While clients should be encouraged to depict the domains that are most relevant to their spiritual worldviews, there are a number of spiritual systems that are strengths in particular spiritual traditions.

More specifically, social workers should generally seek to explore clients' relationships with God, rituals, faith communities and encounters with angels, demons, and other spiritual visitations (Hodge, 2000). One's relationship with God is widely regarded as a key strength, as are rituals, or codified spiritual practices such as devotional reading, meditation, prayer, scripture study, singing hymns, worship, "practicing the presence" of God by focusing on God's presence and active involvement in daily affairs. Faith communities refer to various church and para-church communities that individuals may associate with on a regular basis, such as church services, fellowship groups, mid-week Bible studies, youth groups, and singles associations.

As suggested above, social workers should also seek to incorporate into the eco-map any spiritual system that has meaning to the client (Hodge, 2000). For example, one may wish to explore clients' relationship to their parents' spiritual traditions or their relationship to individuals who hold a position of significant spiritual leadership in their lives, such as a pastor, spiritual mentor or elder. The goal should be to delineate on the eco-map all the spiritual systems that are relevant to the client's present spirituality.

The heart of the spiritual eco-map is the depiction of relationships between the family system and the spiritual systems, which are represented by various types of sketched lines (Hodge, 2000). Thicker lines represent stronger or more powerful relationships. A dashed line represents the most tenuous relationship, while a jagged line denotes a conflicted one. An arrow is drawn on the line to indicate the flow of energy, resources, or interest. As is the case with the other diagrammatic instruments profiled above, short, descriptive encapsulations, significant dates, or other creative depictions, can also be incorporated onto the map to provide more information about relational dynamics.

When using eco-maps with individuals, the appropriate type of line is drawn in between the family system (the figure representing the client) and the spiritual systems. When working with families, lines are drawn to the family system as a unit when the family shares a particular relationship in common, or more frequently, connections are drawn to individual family members depicting the various unique relationships between each family member and various spiritual systems.

A Case Example

In an abbreviated manner, Diagram 3 (following page) depicts how a spiritual eco-map might be used with the Martinez family, consisting of Miguel and Maria, and their two children, Angie, 16, and Tony, 10. The Martinez family sought counseling as part of a relapse prevention plan for Angie who had recently been released from an in-patient alcohol treatment program. The goal of counseling was to reduce the conflict and distrust that existed between Angie and her parents. Angie thought her parents were overly strict, and her parents felt betrayed by Angie's chronic lying. In addition, Miguel and Maria removed Angie from public school and enrolled her in a Christian school in an attempt to prevent her from associating with her peer group that frequently abused alcohol.

Angie and her parents were embroiled in a heated conflict as Angie complained that the Alcoholic's Anonymous (AA) groups that her parents insisted she attend were "stupid and a waste of time." Due to Angie's prior deceitfulness and poor decision-making, her parents did not trust Angie's assessment of the AA groups and were adamant that she needed to continue attending two groups per week to help her maintain her sobriety. In order to address this dilemma, the therapist developed a spiritual eco-map with the family to explore the family's spiritual worldview and resources and identify spiritually based alternatives to AA attendance. The family was receptive to this because AA had substantiated the benefits of spirituality in treating alcoholism.

The Martinez family was currently attending St. Vincent's parish. Maria had grown up in this parish and knew many of the parishioners. She and Miguel had attended Cursillo, a weekend retreat that guided participants as they explored a deeper relationship with God, and they continued to participate in Cursillo's on-going groups. Maria, in particular, stated that she had received a great deal of support and prayer from this group when she and Miguel discovered Angie's struggle with alcoholism. Tony had been an altar boy for a couple years and looked forward to seeing his friends at his Christian education class. In the past, Angie had viewed attending mass with disdain and thought that her peers at their parish were "stale." However, after attending in-patient treatment and switching to the Christian school, Angie slowly began to develop an interest in spirituality. Upon invitation from her new friends at school, Angie attended several local youth groups. Specifically, she enjoyed the "cool music" at Solid Rock Gospel Church, and liked the youth pastor, Dan, and his wife, Karen, at Victory Faith Temple. The therapist asked Miguel and Maria if they would be comfortable replacing the AA groups with the youth groups. Although they both wished Angie would attend the Catholic youth group at their parish, they agreed to give it a try and the family contracted to evaluate the youth groups' effectiveness in two months.

The therapist asked the Martinez family if they practiced any family rituals at home. Maria stated that she and Miguel each individually spent some time reading scripture and praying. Angie surprised her parents by stating that, after a conversation with Karen, she had recently started reading a devotional book when she felt upset and praying when she felt tempted to drink. Miguel

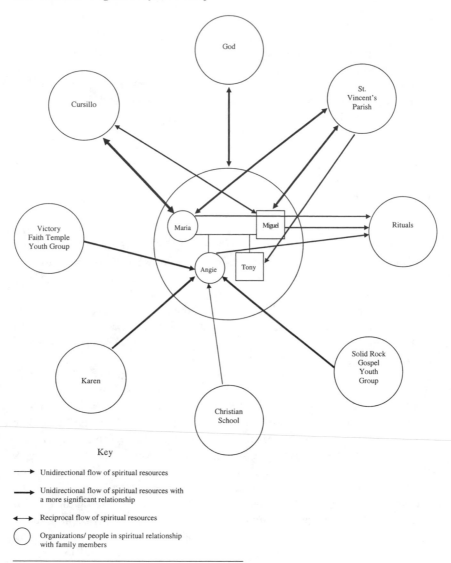

Diagram 3.

shared that they discontinued their attempt at family devotions a year ago after a major fight arose between Angie and him. The therapist asked if they would be interested in initiating family devotions again. However, in order to break the conflictual pattern of the parents lecturing and Angie bristling at their rigid rules, the therapist encouraged structuring the family devotional time as an open forum in which all family members would be free to share their perspectives and struggles. Miguel and Maria might share how their faith guides their decision-making and helps them deal with life's pain and hardships. Angie and Tony might share what they were learning in youth group, school, and Christian education class. This weekly ritual could potentially reassure Miguel and Maria that Angie was learning productive coping skills, build trust between family members, and help them forgive past grievances.

In congruence with the AA model, the therapist asked Angie if she could identify anyone on the spiritual eco-map that she respected and would like to be her sponsor who would provide support, guidance, and accountability for her. Angie stated that Karen had shared her life story in youth group, and was sure that Karen would be understanding, nonjudgmental, and helpful to her.

By developing the spiritual eco-map, the therapist was able to use the Martinez family's current spiritual resources to help them identify new solutions to their problems. Before this counseling session, Miguel and Maria had briefly heard Angie mention Karen's name, but their distrust and concern that the youth groups were not Catholic had prevented them from hearing the positive influence Karen and the groups were having in Angie's life. The process of developing the spiritual eco-map allowed Angie to openly share for the first time that her new-found faith was helping her stay sober and that the youth groups were helping her grow spiritually. As a result, the family moved past their stalemate, broke down barriers to communication, and began establishing trust.

Assets and Limitations

The main asset of spiritual eco-maps is that they focus upon clients' current spiritual strengths (Hodge, 2000). For social workers seeking to operationalize clients' spiritual assets to help clients solve their problems, this assessment approach may be ideal. The time spent in assessment is focused upon tapping into present spiritual resources.

In some cases, clients may find it less threatening to have a concrete object that functions as the focus of subsequent conversation. As is the case with all diagrammatic instruments, spiritual eco-maps provide an object that can serve as the focal point of discussion. The design of eco-maps, however, with their focus on environmental systems rather than, for example, clients' life stories, helps remove the emphasis from the client as an individual. In short, while other approaches may implicitly emphasize clients, devoid of their contexts, spiritual eco-maps explicitly stress the spiritual systems in clients' environments (Hartman, 1995).

Spiritual eco-maps suffer from the same limitations as other diagrammatic instruments relative to verbally based spiritual histories. In addition, in at least some situations, the focus on current spiritual assets may result in a limited assessment that overlooks salient historical factors. In other words, in some contexts an approach that allows social workers to explore current and historical resources may be useful.

Conducting an Assessment

Knowledge in terms of how to conduct an assessment is also important. Developing familiarity with assessment tools is only part of the assessment process. Practitioners must also know how to use these tools in an appropriate, spiritually sensitive manner. Although a detailed discussion of the mechanics of conducting a spiritual assessment is beyond the scope of this chapter, a few important points will be highlighted.

Social workers should be aware that many clients may be hesitant to trust practitioners due to concerns that practitioners will not treat with honor that which is held to be sacred (Furman, Perry & Goldale, 1996; Richards & Bergin, 2000). Consequently, due to the highly personal nature of spirituality, it is appropriate to procure clients' consent before engaging in a spiritual assessment. Additionally, social workers should explain a particular assessment instrument to ensure that the client is comfortable with the particular approach before engaging in an assessment.

To a great extent, clients' apprehension can be alleviated by expressing genuine support. Adopting an attitude of interest and curiosity toward the client's belief system is an appropriate therapeutic stance (Patterson, Hayworth, Turner Christie & Raskin, 2000).

Social workers can also demonstrate spiritual sensitivity by obtaining knowledge of common spiritual traditions. For example, if one works in an area where Mormons and Pentecostals are prominent spiritual traditions, then seeking out information on Mormonism (Ulrich, Richards & Bergin, 2000) and Pentecostalism (Dobbins, 2000) can assist social workers in exhibiting spiritual sensitivity with these populations. Ideally, in the process of attempting to understand clients' spiritual worldviews, social workers should seek to envision life through the particular worldview of the client.

In their attempts to understand the worldviews of clients, social workers should develop their understanding of the oppression people of faith often experience in the largely secular culture. It is important for social workers to recognize that the dominant secular culture often marginalizes or otherwise de-legitimizes devout faith in such influential forms as television (Skill & Robinson, 1994; Skill, Robinson, Lyons & Larson, 1994), popular periodicals (Perkins, 1984), and high school (Sewall, 1995; Vitz, 1986; Vitz, 1998) and college level textbooks (Cnaan, 1999; Glenn, 1997; Lehr & Spilka, 1989). Social workers should reflect on how living in a culture that often ignores, devalues, and even ridicules believers' most cherished beliefs and values affects the psychology of people of faith.

Developing their understanding of clients' worldviews can assist social workers in respecting clients' spiritual autonomy. The focus of practice should not be on determining whether clients' spiritual beliefs are right or wrong, but rather on how their values animate their lives and assist them in coping with difficulties. The social worker's job is not to accept or reject clients' spiritual values but to understand them and help them use their beliefs and practices to assist clients in overcoming their problems (Fitchett & Handzo, 1998).

In some cases, however, social workers may perceive that clients' spiritual beliefs may be problematic. In such situations, social workers should not attempt to change clients' values in an area that lies outside the realm of their professional competence. Rather, practitioners should collaborate with or refer such clients to clergy (Johnson, Ridley & Nielsen, 2000). Given that this is the clergy's area of professional competency, pastors, priests, and other spiritual specialists are better equipped to ascertain the appropriateness of a given set of beliefs and practices. It is critical, however, that practitioners respect clients' spiritual autonomy by forming collaborative relationships with clergy that share the same denominational and theological orientation as the client. It would be unethical to covertly attempt to subvert clients' values by, for example, referring a client who holds conservative beliefs to a liberal pastor.

In keeping with their roles as social workers, practitioners should remain focused on empowering clients to address their problems. During the assessment process, social workers should keep two questions in mind. First, during past difficulties, how have clients culled from their spiritual frameworks, various resources to address their problems? Second, what types of unaccessed resources are available in this framework that can be marshaled to address current problems? Social workers can attempt to link clients with untapped resources to help them solve their problems. Practitioners might, for example, suggest particular interventions either drawn from, or consistent with, clients' spiritual worldviews.

More specifically, social workers might employ a modified form of cognitive therapy in which unhealthy beliefs are identified and replaced with positive beliefs drawn from the individual's spiritual belief system (Backus, 1985; Propst, 1996). Similarly, practitioners may explore the possibility of reframing current problems as opportunities for spiritual growth (Pargament, 1997). In attempting to foster the adoption of more productive patterns of behaviors, spiritual rituals may be employed as "exceptions" to unproductive behavioral patterns (Hodge, 2000). Decision-based forgiveness interventions may be useful in some contexts (DiBlasio, 1998) while existential, brevity of life interventions may be appropriate in other situations (Hodge, in press). In each individual setting, the unique spiritual beliefs of the clients and the theoretical orientation of the social worker will indicate which interventions are selected. In any setting, however, the goal should be to help clients use their spiritual strengths to address their issues and concerns.

Conclusion

In order to provide services that are sensitive to clients' spiritual worldviews, social workers must conduct spiritual assessments to have some awareness of clients' spiritual realities. Similarly, to help clients tap into their spiritual strengths to address the problems they wrestle with, it is necessary to undertake an assessment of clients' strengths. A single assessment approach, however, is unlikely to be ideal in all situations; diverse needs call for a variety of approaches. If the profession of social work is to take seriously its mandate to provide culturally sensitive services that build upon clients' unique strengths, then in many cases performing a spiritual assessment is an imperative.

References

Augustine. (354-430/1991). *Confessions* (H. Chadwick, Trans.). New York: Oxford University Press.

Backus, W. (1985). *Telling the truth to troubled people.* Minneapolis, MN: Bethany House.

Bart, M. (1998). Spirituality in counseling finding believers. *Counseling Today, 41*(6), 1, 6.

Bullis, R. K. (1996). *Spirituality in social work practice.* Washington, DC: Taylor & Francis.

Calhoun-Brown, A. (1998). While marching to Zion: Otherworldliness and racial empowerment in the black community. *Journal for the Scientific Study of Religion, 37*(3), 427-439.

Canda, E. R. (1997). Spirituality. In R. L. Edwards (Ed.), *Encyclopedia of social work* (19th ed., pp. 299-309). Washington, DC: NASW Press.

Canda, E. R., & Furman, L. D. (1999). *Spiritual diversity in social work practice.* New York: The Free Press.

Carroll, M. M. (1997). Spirituality and clinical social work: Implications of past and current perspectives. *Arete, 22*(1), 25-34.

Cnaan, R. A. (1999). *The newer deal.* New York: Columbia University Press.

Cowger, C. D. (1994). Assessing client strengths: Clinical assessments for client empowerment. *Social Work, 39*(3), 262-268.

Derezotes, D. S. (1995). Spirituality and religiosity: Neglected factors in social work practice. *Arete, 20*(1), 1-15.

DiBlasio, F. A. (1988). Integrative strategies for family therapy with Evangelical Christians. *Journal of Psychology and Theology, 16*(2), 127-134.

DiBlasio, F. A. (1998). The use of a decision-based forgiveness intervention within intergenerational family therapy. *Journal of Family Therapy, 20*(1), 77-94.

Dobbins, R. D. (2000). Psychotherapy with Pentecostal Protestants. In P. S. Richards & A. E. Bergin (Eds.), *Handbook of psychotherapy and religious diversity* (pp. 155-184). Washington, DC: American Psychological Association.

Ellison, C. G., & Levin, J. S. (1998). The religion-health connection: Evidence, theory, and future directions. *Health Education and Behavior, 25*(6), 700-720.

Fellin, P. (2000). Revisiting multiculturalism in social work. *Journal of Social Work Education, 36*(2), 261-278.

Ferraro, K. F., & Kelley-Moore, J. A. (2000). Religious consolation among men and women: Do health problems spur seeking? *Journal of the Scientific Study of Religion, 39*(2), 220-234.

Fitchett, G., & Handzo, G. (1998). Spiritual assessment, screening, and intervention. In J. C. Holland (Ed.), *Psycho-oncology* (pp. 790-808). New York: Oxford University Press.

Furman, L. D., & Canda, J. M. (1994). Religion and spirituality: A long-neglected cultural component of rural social work practice. *Human Services in the Rural Environment, 17*(3/4), 21-26.

Furman, L. D., Perry, D., & Goldale, T. (1996). Interaction of Evangelical Christians and social workers in the rural environment. *Human Services in the Rural Environment, 19*(3), 5-8.

Gallup, G. J., & Lindsay, D. M. (1999). *Surveying the religious landscape.* Harrisburg, PA: Morehouse Publishing.

Gartner, J., Larson, D. B., & Allen, G. D. (1991). Religious commitment and mental health: A review of the literature. *Journal of Psychology and Theology, 19*(1), 6-25.

Glenn, N. (1997). *Closed hearts, closed minds: The textbook story of marriage.* New York: Institute for American Values.

Hardy, K. V., & Laszloffy, T. A. (1995). The cultural genogram: Key to training culturally competent family therapists. *Journal of Marital and Family Therapy, 21*(3), 227-237.

Hartman, A. (1995). Diagrammatic assessment of family relationships. *Families in Society, 76*(2), 111-122.

Hodge, D. R. (2000). Spiritual ecomaps: A new diagrammatic tool for assessing marital and family spirituality. *Journal of Marital and Family Therapy, 26*(1), 229-240.

Hodge, D. R. (2001a). Spiritual assessment: A review of major qualitative methods and a new framework for assessing spirituality. *Social Work, 46*(3), 203-214.

Hodge, D. R. (2001b). Spiritual genograms: A generational approach to assessing spirituality. *Families in Society, 82*(1), 35-48.

Hodge, D. R. (In press). Spiritual lifemaps: A client-centered pictorial instrument for spiritual assessment, planning, and intervention. *Social Work.*

Hodge, D. R., & Williams, T. R. (In press). Assessing African American spirituality with spiritual eco-maps. *Families in Society.*

Hwang, S.-C., & Cowger, C., D. (1998). Utilizing strengths in assessment. *Families in Society, 79*(1), 25-31.

Johnson, W. B., Ridley, C. R., & Nielsen, S. L. (2000). Religiously sensitive rational emotive behavior therapy: Elegant solutions and ethical risks. *Professional Psychology: Research and Practice, 31*(1), 14-20.

Kahn, B. B. (1999). Art therapy with adolescents: Making it work for school counselors. *Professional School Counseling, 2*(4), 291-298.

Kennedy, J. E., Davis, R. C., & Talyor, B. G. (1998). Changes in spirituality and well-being among victims of sexual assault. *Journal for the Scientific Study of Religion, 37*(2), 322-328.

Koenig, H. G., McCullough, M. E., & Larson, D. B. (2001). *Handbook of religion and health.* New York: Oxford University Press.

Kuehl, B. (1995). The solution-oriented genogram: A collaborative approach. *Journal of Marital and Family Therapy, 21*(3), 239-250.

Lehr, E., & Spilka, B. (1989). Religion in the introductory psychology textbook: A comparison of three decades. *Journal for the Scientific Study of Religion, 28*(3), 366-371.

Lindsey, E. W., Kurtz, P. D., Jarvis, S., Williams, N. R., & Nackerud, L. (2000). How runaway and homeless youth navigate troubled waters: Personal strengths and resources. *Child and Adolescent Social Work Journal, 17*(2), 115-140.

Maton, K. I., & Salem, D. A. (1995). Organizational characteristics of empowering community settings: A multiple case study approach. *American Journal of Community Practice, 23*(5), 631-656.

Maton, K. I., & Wells, E. A. (1995). Religion as a community resource for well-being: Prevention, healing, and empowerment pathways. *Journal of Social Issues, 51*(2), 177-193.

Mattaini, M. A., & Kirk, S. A. (1991). Assessing assessment in social work. *Social Work, 36*(3), 260-266.

McGoldrick, M., Gerson, R., & Shellenberger. (1999). *Genograms: Assessment and intervention* (2nd ed.). New York: W.W. Norton & Company.

McNiff, S. (1992). *Art as medicine.* Boston: Shambhala.

McRae, M. B., Thompson, D. A., & Cooper, S. (1999). Black churches as therapeutic groups. *Journal of Multicultural Counseling and Development, 27*(1), 207-220.

Montgomery, C. (1994). Swimming upstream: The strengths of women who survive homelessness. *Advances in Nursing Science, 16*(3), 34-45.

NASW Code of Ethics. (1999). Available: www.naswdc.org/Code/ethics.htm (Accessed 1/20/00).

Nathanson, I., G. (1995). Divorce and women's spirituality. *Journal of Divorce and Remarriage, 22*(3/4), 179-188.

Nee, W. (1968). *The spiritual man.* (Vols. 1-3). New York: Christian Fellowship Publishers.

Pargament, K. I. (1997). *The psychology of religion and coping.* New York: Guilford Press.

Patterson, J., Hayworth, M., Turner Christie, & Raskin, M. (2000). Spiritual issues in family therapy: A graduate-level course. *Journal of Martial and Family Therapy, 26*(2), 199-210.

Perkins, H. W. (1984). Religious content in American, British, and Canadian popular publications from 1937 to 1979. *Sociological Analysis, 45*(2), 159-165.

Privette, G., Quackenbos, S., & Bundrick, C. M. (1994). Preferences for religious and nonreligious counseling and psychotherapy. *Psychological Reports, 75,* 539-547.

Propst, L. R. (1996). Cognitive-behavioral therapy and the religious person. In E. P. Shafranske (Ed.), *Religion and the clinical practice of psychology* (pp. 391-407). Washington, DC: American Psychological Association.

Rauch, J. B. (1993). *Assessment: A sourcebook for social work practice.* Milwaukee: Families International.

Rey, L. D. (1997). Religion as invisible culture: Knowing about and knowing with. *Journal of Family Social Work, 2*(2), 159-177.

Richards, P. S., & Bergin, A. E. (Editors). (2000). *Handbook of psychotherapy and religious diversity.* Washington, DC: American Psychological Association.

Ronnau, J., & Poertner, J. (1993). Identification and use of strengths: A family system approach. *Children Today, 22*(2), 20-23.

Saleebey, D. (Editor). (1997). *The strengths perspective in social work practice* (2nd ed.). White Plains, NY: Longman.

Sewall, G. T. (1995). *Religion in the classroom: What the textbooks tell us.* New York: American Textbook Council.

Sheridan, M. J., & Amato-von Hemert, K. (1999). The role of religion and spirituality in social work education and practice: A survey of student views and experiences. *Journal of Social Work Education, 35*(1), 125-141.

Sherwood, D. A. (1998). Charitable choice: Opportunity and challenge for Christians in social work. *Social Work and Christianity, 25*(3), 1-23.

Skill, T., & Robinson, J. D. (1994). The image of Christian leaders in fictional television programs. *Sociology of Religion, 55*(1), 75-84.

Skill, T., Robinson, J. D., Lyons, J. S., & Larson, D. (1994). The portrayal of religion and spirituality on fictional network television. *Review of the Religious Research, 35*(3), 251-267.

Stanion, P., Papadopoulos, L., & Bor, R. (1997). Genograms in counseling practice: Constructing a genogram (part 2). *Counseling Psychology Quarterly, 10*(2), 139-148.

Strickland, L. (1994). Autobiographical interviewing and narrative analysis: An approach to psychosocial assessment. *Clinical Social Work Journal, 22*(1), 27-41.

Sullivan, W. P. (1997). On strengths, niches, and recovery from serious mental illness. In D. Saleebey (Ed.), *The strengths perspective in social work practice* (pp. 183-199). White Plains, NY: Longman.

Talbot, M. (2000, February 27). A mighty fortress. *The New York Times Magazine,* 34-41, 66-8, 84-5.

Tracz, S. M., & Gehart-Brooks, D. R. (1999). The lifeline: Using art to illustrate history. *Journal of Family Psychotherapy, 10*(3), 61-63.

Turner, N. H., O' Dell, K. J., & Weaver, G. D. (1999). Religion and the recovery of addicted women. *Journal of Religion and Health, 38*(2), 137-148.

Ulrich, W. L., Richards, P. S., & Bergin, A. E. (2000). Psychotherapy with Latter-day Saints. In P. S. Richards & A. E. Bergin (Eds.), *Handbook of psychotherapy and religious diversity* (pp. 185-209). Washington, DC: American Psychological Association.

Vitz, P. C. (1986). *Censorship: Evidence of bias in our children's textbooks.* Ann Arbor, MI: Servant Books.

Vitz, P. C. (1998). *The course of true love: Marriage in high school textbooks.* New York: Institute for American Values.

Walsh, F. (1999). Religion and spirituality. In F. Walsh (Ed.), *Spiritual resources in family therapy* (pp. 3-27). New York: Gilford Press.

CHAPTER 15

CHRISTIANITY AND THE TREATMENT OF ADDICTION: AN ECOLOGICAL APPROACH FOR SOCIAL WORKERS

Jason Pittman and S. Wade Taylor

Most people can describe at least one instance of how alcohol and drug addiction has had a negative impact on their own lives or the lives of people they love. Children today, regardless of age or ethnicity, grow up in a society where access to drugs and alcohol is extremely easy. Parents who misuse these potentially addictive substances also influence how their children perceive and understand the use of alcohol and drugs. At a recent Christian ministry conference, participants were asked to share how drugs and alcohol had personally affected their lives, or the lives of people they know. Nearly everyone in attendance shared stories about their sons and daughters, aunts and uncles, mothers and fathers, and grandparents whose lives were negatively affected by addiction.

In 1999, Gallup suggested that addiction is a common issue involved in most of the following social problems: "murder and lawlessness, highway deaths, suicides, accidental deaths, injustices, hospitalizations, poor school performance and dropout, job absenteeism, child and spouse abuse, low self-esteem, and depression" (p. xi). According to the National Center for Health Statistics (2005), in 2003 the number of induced deaths contributed to alcohol excluding homicides and accidents was 20,687. In a recent press release by the National Institutes of Health (2004), the National Epidemiological Survey on Alcohol and Related Conditions found that "the number of American adults who abuse alcohol or are alcohol dependent rose from 13.8 million (7.41 percent) in 1991-1992 to 17.6 million (8.46 percent) in 2001-2002." In addition, the Department of Health and Human Service's Substance Abuse and Mental Health Services Administration in 2005 concluded that approximately 19.7 million Americans over the age of 11 (8.1% of the population) were current users of illicit drugs in the past month (Office of Applied Studies, 2005). We all know alcohol abuse and illicit drug use are habit forming behaviors that often result in addiction. It is a serious and increasing problem, so it is imperative that we continue trying to understand its impact, not only in the U.S., but in the entire world.

Professionals working in the field of addiction treatment and laypersons helping from a Christian perspective have struggled with how best to assist addicts. For example, Gray (1995) noted that most people dealing with addiction are also struggling in many other areas of life. Social workers need to advocate for an eclectic approach that involves the contributions of many disciplines. An eclectic approach includes "models of intervention strategies and approaches, modalities of intervention, organized conceptualizations of client problems or of practice, sets of practice principles, practice wisdom, and even philosophies of practice" (Abbott, 2000, p. 27).

This chapter attempts to provide insight into the main issues regarding an informed eclectic approach. In the first section, we discuss the general field of addiction treatment, define addiction for the purpose of this chapter, provide a summary of addiction etiology theories, and discuss relevant treatment interventions. The second section is a discussion concerning the interaction of Christianity and addiction historically, with particular emphasis on the contribution of pastoral theology and Christian treatment programs. The chapter concludes by emphasizing that social workers should utilize an eclectic approach when helping addicts, while integrating the contributions of addiction etiology theories and treatment interventions.

Addiction Treatment Field

Brief History

In the U.S., the nation's first settlers had to deal with issues related to drug and alcohol abuse. They drank more beer than water because of the lack of safe drinking water (Van Wormer, 1995). In the eighteenth century, distilled spirits became available to the masses and contributed to the drunkenness at all class levels. People viewed alcohol and drug addiction as a moral problem, resulting from sinful behavior and moral weakness in the individual. Society treated addicts very poorly, and they faced condemnation, guilt, shame, and many times ostracism (Morgan, 1999, p. 4). The term "alcoholic" was first used by the Swedish physician Magnus Huss in 1849. He defined alcoholism as "the state of chronic alcohol intoxication that was characterized by severe physical pathology and disruption of social functioning" (White, 1998, p. xiv).

Within the last hundred years, we have seen a major shift in how society perceives addiction. During the temperance and prohibition movements people tried to eliminate alcohol completely, believing that if alcohol were illegal, then addiction would cease to exist. Later, with the help of scientific research, the medical field began identifying addiction as a disease, considering the etiology to be strictly biological (Van Wormer, 1995). It was during the early 1900s when Huss's term "alcoholic" began to be circulated within professional circles, and in the 1930's, Alcoholics Anonymous (AA) launched the term into widespread use.

By 1944, the U.S. Public Health Service identified addiction as the fourth largest health concern in the nation (Strung, Priyadarsini, & Hyman, 1986). The professional, medical, and research communities began to mobilize and to create the new field of addiction treatment through the following: work of pioneers like E.M. Jellinek and Mark Keller; organizations such as the National Committee for Education on Alcoholism, Research Council on Problems of Alcohol; the Summer School of Alcohol Studies at Yale University; and volunteers like Marty

Mann and her National Council on Alcoholism (Morgan, 1999; White, 1998; Royce, 1981). The first major step in shaping the field of addiction treatment and counseling occurred when the American Medical Association accepted the disease concept of alcoholism in 1956. One year later, the World Health Organization accepted the concept of alcoholism as a pathological condition.

By 1960, society began debating how best to define alcoholism while over 200 definitions circulated in various helping arenas (White, 1998). Professionals began to include other drugs and behaviors besides alcohol in the field of addiction, causing the debates to continue through the end of the 20th century. The American Psychiatric Association (APA) uses the term "substance related disorders" to be inclusive of a broad range of problems associated with alcohol and drug usage (APA, 2000). In this chapter, we will use the term addiction earlier defined by APA as the state of being "compulsively and physiologically dependent on a habit-forming substance" (McNeece & DiNitto, 1998, p. 23).

Addiction Etiology Theories

The 1960s-1980s was a time of growing research and development concerning addiction studies in the broad areas of psychology, psychiatry, and social work. A number of theories explain addiction, and these theories are as varied as the number of definitions of addiction (McNeece & DiNitto, 2005). Below, we provide a brief summary of the following five broad areas of etiology theory: moral, biological, psychological, sociocultural, and multi-causal.

Historically, the moral theory has described addiction as a result of "humankind's sinful nature" (McNeece & DiNitto, 2005). Fingarette and Peele (as cited in McNeece & DiNitto) provide the contemporary equivalent of the moral theory. These theorists, however, do not suggest that addiction is caused by sinful nature; instead, addiction is a result of bad choices within one's lifestyle. We place these theorists in the moral model because their primary premise is that addiction is cured by the simple choice of abstinence.

Biological theories assume addicts are "constitutionally predisposed to develop a dependence on alcohol or drugs" (McNeece & DiNitto, 2005, p.29). These theories emphasize the physiological sources of addiction such as genetics or neurochemistry. Genetic research is not suggesting that people are genetically determined to be addicts. Instead, it points toward people as being predisposed to addiction. Neurochemistry is divided into two theories: brain dysfunction and brain chemistry. These theories argue that biochemical changes taking place in addicts may cause irreversible loss of control during the use of alcohol or drugs. Research suggests that certain people have the propensity to be unable to control their usage once they start. This lack of control may be due to heredity or actual changes that occur within the body because of the drug interacting with the brain (Clinebell, 1990; Leshner, 2001).

Psychological theories include a broad range of theories that have very different outlooks on the cause of addiction. For example, cognitive-behavioral theories suggest several reasons for addicts taking drugs: to experience variety, desire to experience pleasure, or avoidance of withdrawal symptoms (McNeece & DiNitto, 2005). In addition, psychodynamic and personality theories look to underlying personality issues, hoping to explain the causes of addiction. These explanations vary greatly and may consist of coping with painful experiences, guilt, loneliness, conflict, or low self-esteem (Clinebell, 1990).

Sociocultural theories emphasize the importance of social attitudes toward addiction and link those attitudes surrounding alcohol and drugs as being the cause of many people's decision to start abusing drugs or alcohol (Ciarrocchi, 1993). Theorists categorize sociocultural theories into areas that focus on different environmental factors found in society and culture (McNeece & DiNitto, 2005). For example, theorists argue that European countries have a much lower rate of alcoholism as compared to the U.S. because of their tolerant views on drinking and intolerant views on drunkenness.

Addiction is a very complex disorder that affects all aspects of one's life. Professionals in the last 60 years have provided extensive research and literature in the field, attempting to explain the root causes of addiction. Unfortunately, research does not provide one simple cause of addiction. Theorists have proposed two models, however, that attempt to include multiple etiology theories of addiction. Pattison and Kaufman (as cited in McNeece & DiNitto, 1998) offered a multivariate model in the early 1980s that encompassed a multitude of causes of addiction. Health care and human service professionals, however, have advocated for the public health model. This model attempts to encompass many different possible causes of addiction and involves looking at the interaction of the agent, host, and environment.

Addiction Treatment Interventions

A variety of interventions are available to treat individuals suffering from addiction. For this chapter, intervention is conceptualized in three ways: self-help groups, professional treatment programs, and counseling techniques. Results from the 2005 National Survey on Drug Use and Health (Office of Applied Studies, 2005) indicate that approximately 2.1 million people aged 12 or older received treatment through self-help groups. Alcoholic Anonymous (AA) is an example of a spiritually based self-help group. AA attempted to bypass the problems of etiology and move into offering to alcoholics and helpers a pragmatic program of recovery that is based on the person's spiritual life and understanding of a higher power. Therefore, many people today mistakenly refer to AA as a treatment program instead of a self-help group. AA started in the 1930s with two alcoholics trying to help each other stop drinking. It was one of the pioneering self-help groups and quickly became a widespread movement. In addition, AA was instrumental in promoting the labeling of alcoholism as a disease. However, AA itself did not advocate a strict disease model. It was simply a fellowship of people with a common desire to stop using alcohol and drugs and finding sobriety by "working" through a twelve-step program. As of January 2007, AA reported over 105,000 groups worldwide with membership totaling over 2 million people (General Service Office, 2007). Although one of the hallmarks of AA is non-professional treatment, most professional treatment centers have integrated AA's ideas into the core of their addiction treatment programs (Van Wormer, 1995).

Interventions can also include professional treatment programs such as outpatient or inpatient clinics or hospitals as well as long-term residential facilities. Results from the National Survey on Drug Use and Health (Office of Applied Studies, 2006) also indicated that 23.2 million persons 12 and older needed illicit drug use or alcohol abuse treatment, and of these persons, 23 million received treatment at a specialty facility, which included inpatient hospitals, rehabilitation centers or mental health centers. These treatment programs may include a number of bio-psycho-social-spiritual theories and interventions that facilitate positive treatment. The Minnesota model of treatment, introduced by the Hazelden Treatment Center in Minnesota in the 1940s, combined AA's twelve-steps with psychologically based group therapy (Van Wormer, 1995). This model gained popularity in the 1970s and is the predominant model used in treatment centers today.

There is a multitude of interventions available to clinicians treating addicts based on counseling techniques and theories, many which are based on the etiology theories discussed in the previous section. Similar to how researchers have proposed that one etiology theory is not sufficient, they also have suggested that there are strengths in many of the counseling interventions. In fact, Miller and Ester (2003) argued in their methodological analysis of outcome studies that "there is no one tried and true, state-of-the art treatment of choice for alcohol problems" (p. 10). Furthermore, they propose that future research and practice be directed by an informed eclecticism while considering a number of methodologies guided by empirical evidence.

Transtheoretical Model

Prochaska, DiClemente, and Norcross (1992) investigated how people change in psychotherapy. They realized that the hundreds of outcome studies did not offer insight into the common principles that were allowing the change to occur. These researchers spent years analyzing and researching the processes that people go through when they change and the corresponding processes therapists use to facilitate that change. They developed the Transtheoretical Model that consists of two important interrelated theories for practice: the stages of change and the processes of change. The magnitude of literature written on this model is immense, as researchers from multiple disciplines utilize its structure to facilitate behavioral and social change.

In the first part, Prochaska et al. (1992) suggested that the stages of change (see table 2.0) do not necessarily progress in a linear nature, but because of how common relapse is in addiction, addicts usually follow a spiral pattern of change. Abbott (2000) noted that, "not every one completes the cycle. Some recycle numerous times; others stay in one or more stages of change, never exiting"

(p. 117). Prochaska et al. explained that "the stage of change scores were the best predictors of outcome; they were better predictors than age, socioeconomic status, problem severity and duration, goals and expectations, self-efficacy, and social support" (p. 1106).

The Transtheoretical Model also stresses the importance of matching the processes of change to the stage of change. Prochaska et al. (1992) noted that past addiction treatment's poor success rates were in part due to treatment centers not having tailored their therapeutic approach to match the clients' stage of change (see table 2.0). Abbott (2000) suggested that when the social worker is choosing a process of change and accompanying methods and techniques, it is best to consider the client's "age, personality characteristics, cultural factors, lifestyle, previous experiences with therapy, the severity of the ATOD [alcohol, tobacco, other drugs] problem, and available environmental resources" (p. 120).

Table 2.0
Stages of Change in Which Particular Change Processes are Most Useful

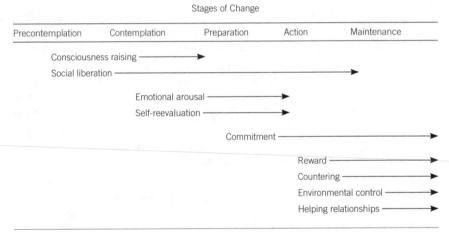

Source: Table 3 from Changing for Good (1994) by James O. Prochaska and John C. Norcross and Carlo C. Diclemente. Reprinted by permission of Harper Collins Publishers Inc.

Christian Approaches to Etiology and Intervention

This section explores the development of Christian approaches to etiology and treatment of addiction. We also highlight the significance of Christianity in the development of Alcoholic Anonymous. Christianity has struggled with the topic of addiction, because it has historically characterized addiction as simply a sinful choice. This has created barriers between Christians attempting to provide a theological contribution to the field of addiction treatment and the secular community.

In the late 1800s, a religious experience was viewed as the antidote for addiction (White, 1998). Many addicts were proclaiming that God took away their addiction in religious revivals. These revivals provided entrance for addicts into other social groups such as lodges, churches, tent meetings, missions, and informal helping resources. The emergence of an urban society significantly contributed to the increase in the numbers of Christian approaches to alcoholism recovery. The areas in cities where vagrants and destitute alcoholics made their homes were labeled "Skid Rows" (White, p. 72). These areas were becoming major problems for civic leaders, and chronic addiction was seen as the primary problem.

In 1826, David Nasmith started a "rescue mission" in Glasgow, Scotland. The name rescue mission implied that the organization would rescue persons from "Skid Rows" by providing temporary shelter, food, and other assistance. Jerry McAuley and Samuel Hadley started similar rescue missions in the U.S. to address the problems associated with addiction and "Skid Rows" (White, 1998). These pioneers were heavily influenced by Protestant evangelists who preached that addiction was a sin and emphasized the conversion experience as the cure for addiction. By the early 1900s, the rescue mission movement had spread to most of the major cities in the U.S. (Bakke, 1995).

Salvation Army became the most extensive urban Christian organization helping addicts (White, 1998). William Booth started Salvation Army in 1865 in London, England, and the organization expanded to the U.S. in 1880. Booth attracted addicts by providing them with food and shelter and suggested that the cure for addiction would involve "Christian salvation and moral education in a wholesome environment" (White, p. 74). By 1900, Salvation Army had spread to over 700 U.S. cities. In 2003, Salvation Army had 9,027 units of operation centers in the US that served 206,502 persons for substance abuse rehabilitation (Salvation Army, 2003).

The early 20th century also saw an emergence of professional views on religion and addiction recovery. In 1902, William James, a Harvard psychologist and medical doctor, wrote *The Varieties of Religious Experiences* (White, 1998). This book explored the role of religious conversion as the cure for addiction, describing religious transformation as being either a sudden or a gradual process. James wrote about the power that conversion has on removing the cravings for alcohol and providing a new perspective or outlook for the addict's life. These ideas highly influenced the later developments of AA.

Another example of a Christian presence in the addiction field was seen when the Emmanuel Church Clinic in Boston opened in 1906 for the treatment of various psychological disorders (White, 1998). These early clinicians attempted to integrate religion, medicine, and psychology in their treatment for addiction. This program was quite different from Salvation Army or rescue missions. Emmanuel's treatment was the first to focus on psychologically based group and individual counseling. White suggested that this program "foreshadows the current use of spirituality in addiction treatment" (p. 100). Their use of self-inventory and confession was influential in the development of the Oxford Group, a Christian evangelical group, and later AA. The Emmanuel clinic discontinued its treatment program after the death of one of the primary founders, Rev. Dr. Elwood Worcester, in the 1940s.

Alcoholics Anonymous is one of the most influential approaches rooted in Christianity. AA does not align itself with any religious group, church, or organization. It understands addiction to have biological, psychological, and social influences, but primarily offers a spiritual approach to recovery (Miller & Hester, 2003). Christian concepts, however, are inherent in AA's twelve steps, and these concepts have had a large impact on the development of various twelve-step programs.

The founders of AA, Bill Wilson and Dr. Bob Smith, began as members of the Oxford Group (White, 1998). The Oxford Group movement began on college campuses in England and spread quickly in the U.S. Clinebell (1998) suggested "it was an attempt to bring vital, first-century Christianity into the lives of people, challenging them to live by certain ethical absolutes and mo- tivating them to change others" (p. 273). The Oxford Group used six steps to accomplish this purpose. In 1939, Wilson and "Dr. Bob" took the ideas from these six steps and adapted them specifically to the needs of alcoholics, thereby, creating the Twelve Steps of AA.

The idea of AA's Twelve Steps is that alcoholics cannot overcome addiction on their own. They must turn their lives over to a higher power and seek a spiritual path to recovery as the only way to gain control of their addiction (Miller & Hester, 2003). It is important to note that the Twelve Steps are not a require- ment for AA membership; they are the steps the founding AA members took to obtain and maintain sobriety and are "suggested as a program of recovery." In addition, AA stresses that these principles are primarily "guides to progress" and members "claim spiritual progress rather than spiritual perfection" (Alcoholics Anonymous, 2001, pp.59- 60).

Step one suggests that alcoholics should admit they are "powerless over alcohol—that [their] lives had become unmanageable." Step two begins the process of believing that a Higher Power can help them, while Step three suggests they need to make a "decision to turn [their] will and [their] lives over to the care of God as [they] understand Him." In Step four, alcoholics make a "searching and fearless moral inventory of [themselves]" (Alcoholics Anonymous, 2001, p. 58). Then, Step five suggests that alcoholics should admit to "God, to themselves and to another human being the exact nature of their wrongs." Step six asks alcohol- ics to be ready for God to help them with their character defects, and Step seven encourages alcoholics to ask "Him to remove [their] shortcomings." In Step eight, alcoholics make "a list of all persons we had harmed, and become willing to make amends to them all" (Alcoholics Anonymous, pp. 58-59). Subsequently, Step nine encourages members to make amends with those people.

The final three maintenance steps provide suggestions for alcoholics to maintain sobriety. Step ten requires alcoholics to be continually responsible for their negative behavior and promptly admit when they are wrong. Step eleven emphasizes that alcoholics must continue in spiritual growth through prayer and meditation with the goal of being knowledgeable of God's will for their lives and the "power to carry that [will] out." Finally, in Step twelve, once alcohol- ics have completed the other steps and have had a "spiritual awakening," they are encouraged to help other alcoholics through that same process (Alcoholics Anonymous, 2001, pp. 58-60).

When Wilson and "Dr. Bob" created the Twelve Steps, they purposely avoided any direct reference to Jesus Christ, and this omission upset many Christians (Hardin, 1994). They thought that the anonymity of God in the Twelve Steps was strategically important. This generic form of spirituality and the traditions of AA have kept it from being an organized religion. However, it is important to note that both AA and organized religions share a "moral and transcendent perspective, an emphasis on repentance, ultimate dependence and conversion experience; scriptures and a creed; rituals; and a communal life" (Peteet, 1993, p. 263-267). Christians should not let the lack of direct references deter them from utilizing AA.

The success and rapid growth of AA had an effect on the development of Salvation Army's addiction treatment programs. By the 1940s, Salvation Army began to separate their addiction treatment centers from their homeless shelters (White, 1998). They changed their programs in order to include "a broadening approach to treating alcoholism that integrated medical assistance, professional counseling, Alcoholics Anonymous, and Christian Salvation" (White, p. 75). Salvation Army officers were also involved in the initial Summer School of Alcohol Studies at Yale University, and, by the 1950s, Salvation Army was hiring social workers to help implement a more professional structured therapy program (White).

Rescue missions and Salvation Army historically have received the most criticism for their moralistic views on addiction, viewing that addicts just need to "get saved" (Clinebell, 1998). As described above, however, Salvation Army has attempted to integrate clinical models with a Christian perspective. Furthermore, research has shown that Salvation Army has comparable success rates to other secular treatment centers (Bromet, Moos, Wuthmann, & Bliss, 1977; Gauntlett, 1991; Katz, 1966; Moss, 1996; Zlotnick & Agnew, 1997).

In recent years, rescue missions have also begun to integrate clinical models with their Christian perspective. Rescue missions, overall, still emphasize Christian conversion as the primary solution to recovery more than does the Salvation Army. Additionally, Salvation Army primarily uses AA while the association of rescue missions is a sponsor of Alcoholics Victorious, a network of explicitly Christian twelve-step support groups. Unfortunately, little research has been conducted on the evaluation or treatment approach of rescue missions (See Fagan, 1986).

In 1958, David Wilkerson, a Pentecostal preacher, started Teen Challenge, a more explicitly Christian salvific approach to addiction treatment. In his book, *The Cross and the Switchblade,* Wilkerson shares his experiences in ministering to the youth and the gangs in New York City. Teen Challenge views addiction as primarily an issue of sin, and the solution is a conversion experience where the person is "'born again' by accepting Jesus Christ as 'personal Savior'" (Muffler, Langrod, & Larson, 1997, p. 587). A University of Tennessee study reported in 2002 that Teen Challenge operated 120 centers in the U.S. (Teen

Challenge, 2002), and today, the organization boasts having 230 centers and 180 outreaches in 90 countries (Global Teen Challenge, 2007). Ironically, very few Teen Challenge centers serve teenagers exclusively. Many programs also have changed their name to be more inclusive for all ages (e.g., Life Challenge in Dallas, TX). Interestingly, Muffler, Langrod, and Larson (1997) argued that the rates of success for Teen Challenge have been grossly over stated; instead of 86%, they suggest that success rates are closer to 18.3%, similar to the 15% success rates of secular therapeutic communities.

Other arenas of Christian treatment have developed over the years. Saint Marr's Clinic in Chicago, the Christian Reformed Church's Addicts Rehabilitation Center in New York, Episcopal Astoria Consultation Service in New York, and East Harlem Protestant Parish's Exodus House (White, 1998) are some examples. Muffler, et al. (1997) noted that Protestants and Catholics address addiction at the denominational or diocesan level through organizations like Catholic Charities or Lutheran Social Services. Also, there are Christian treatment programs located within hospital settings (e.g., Rapha) or outpatient clinics (e.g., New Life Clinics or Minirth Myer Clinics) designed for individuals with insurance or other means to pay for treatment.

In addition, there are thousands of smaller Christian treatment programs throughout the US. In the state of Texas, for example, of the approximately 115 registered faith-based providers the larger Christian organizations mentioned in the paragraph above account for fewer than ten of the providers. The majority of the remaining organizations are local Christian treatment facilities. Furthermore, the Christians in Recovery's (2002) database contains over 2500 Christian ministries, organizations, local groups and meetings worldwide that deal with addiction. The Substance Abuse and Mental Health Services Administration, a government agency, does not track faith-based or Christian programs in their database of over 15,000 treatment facilities. In fact, they claimed it was difficult even to define faith-based programs because a facility may be funded by a religious organization, but not have inherently religious teachings (L. Henderson, personal communication, April 15, 2002).

Pastoral Theology's Contribution

Christian approaches to addiction treatment vary based on particular theological interpretations of Biblical passages which led to a dichotomy of Christian approaches to addiction treatment. Some approaches have focused on addiction simply as sin, and "getting saved" was the primary solution. Other groups took a more liberal approach to addiction as some theologians were beginning to shift their thoughts to what the Bible says about human nature, our relationship with God, and God's purpose for our lives and applying it to addiction treatment. A full historical account of the development of pastoral theology's contribution to the addiction treatment field is not within the scope of this section. However, a brief historical summary is provided with particular emphasis on several theologians' contributions to the understanding of addiction.

Protestant pastoral theology began in the 1800s in Germany, but the American pastoral theology movement, which focused more on the psychology of religion, emerged in the 1930s with pioneers such as Anton Boisen, Richard Cabot, and Russell Dicks (Burck & Hunter, 2005). They provided insight into the relationship between religion and health, and contributed to the field a large amount of literature concerning psychological pastoral care and counseling to the field. These pioneers drew from the work of Paul Tillich and other neo-orthodox theologians.

Clinebell's (1998) textbook presented his pastoral approach to addiction. Originally published in 1956, it was the first major work on addiction by a pastoral theologian. Clinebell (1994) argued that religious factors rooted in the addicts' handling of existential anxiety are crucial to understanding both the etiology and the treatment of addiction. He suggested that addicts are trying to "satisfy religious needs by a nonreligious means—alcohol" (p. 267). A Christian holistic view of addiction, from a pastoral theological view, does not suggest that people are "sinful because they are addicted . . . rather, disharmonious existence is a state of being indigenous to the human condition and requires intervention by a power greater than ourselves" (Morgan, 1998, p. 27).

One can trace this theology back to existential philosophers and theologians such as Heidegger, Kierkergaard, Tillich, and Moore (Morgan & Jordan, 1999). Existentialism is primarily concerned with questions regarding the meaning and value of human life (Evans, 1984). Existentialists argue that all humans are finite beings, and we all experience "a sense of limits, restlessness, and estrangement" (Morgan & Jordan, p. 265). Tillich (1991) described estrangement as separation from God and said it was a part of our "essential nature" (p. 187).

Clinebell (1998) applied this theology to understanding addiction and argued that this estrangement causes us to have anxiety, and we seek to soothe our anxiety in inappropriate ways. Hunter (2005) suggested that this anxiety leads to inner conflict that cuts off the person from growth and development. This experience of aloneness and feeling isolated, not just from others, but also from self, makes us vulnerable to addiction. Clinebell (1998) wrote that as we begin to crave the "anxiety-deadening effects" of drugs and alcohol we are attempting to soothe the anxiety through artificial means (p. 30).

It is important to understand that dealing with issues of meaning and the finite nature of human life is basic to everyone. We all struggle with who we are psychologically and spiritually (Morgan & Jordan, 1999). For addicts, coping takes the form of addiction and has the psychological function to "compensate for missing or inadequately developed psychological functions of self-care, self-soothing, and self-regulation" (Hopson & Moses, 1996, p.10). Temporarily, this form of coping will suffice to numb the anxiety. Eventually, however, it is not enough to stop the deep psychological and spiritual need for meaning and purpose. In fact, as addicts continue to use drugs and alcohol, life becomes even more meaningless, hopeless, and spiritually empty (Clinebell, 1998). The American Psychiatric Association (as cited by Miller, 1998) described addiction as "a phenomenon that slowly takes over a person's life, displacing all else"

(p. 34). Addicts position alcohol and drugs in the place of God, attempting to fill the void of estrangement. The theological term for this process is idolatry (Romans 1; Isaiah 42:8).

Surrender and Sanctification

Continuing with pastoral theology's contributions to the addiction field, we take the next step to see how confronting the idolatry helps in the recovery process. Addicts begin to deal with the idolatry in their lives when they confront and deal with their existential anxiety (i.e., the void of not knowing what the purpose in life is). As they begin to ask for help, a Christian spirituality can offer addicts a "nonchemical means" of soothing their anxiety (Clinebell, 1998, p. 283). This process of spirituality begins with surrendering, a process that addicts go through when they begin to realize they cannot control their addiction. AA identifies this process as, "hitting bottom." It may occur during different points in life for each addict, and the common thread between addicts is a realization that they have lost their freedom in addiction, realizing that alcohol and drugs are not God.

Christians have a rich theological history from which they can draw ideas relating to this idea of surrender. Saint Augustine, an early theologian, wrote that until the human heart rests in God, the restlessness in our lives would not cease (Morgan & Jordan, 1999). Writing about human pursuit of happiness and the need to soothe the anxiety, Augustine argued that people would only find emptiness until they come to a place of surrender, allowing God to fill the void that only God can fill. Augustine emphasized the bondage of the will by describing it as "the force of habit, by which the mind is swept along and held fast even against its will" (Stone & Clements, 1991, p. 260).

Dietrich Bonhoeffer (1995), a twentieth century theologian, wrote that the first step for maturing Christians is to cut off ties from the previous life. He added that single-minded obedience is how God calls people in the Scripture; one only needs to deny oneself in order to be a disciple of Christ. Jurgon Moltmann (1999), a contemporary theologian, said that when Christians deny themselves, they become weak, but it is in this weakness where they will find their strength. As they surrender, they find meaning and purpose in God.

Albers (1997) described the process of surrender as "experienced, but never totally explained; accepted for what it is, but never totally accounted for; observable, but not objectively definable in conventional scientific categories" (p. 25). Interestingly enough, secular scientists have some understanding and appreciation of this process. Tiebout, a pioneer psychiatrist in the field of addiction, looked at this process of conversion in alcoholics involved in AA and concluded that surrender and the process of spiritual transformation is the key to change for addicts (Tiebout, 1951, 1994).

Let it be noted that surrender is not an instantaneous event that cures addiction. Addicts may not be seeking to soothe the anxiety with drugs, but addicts are still "addict(s) in the therapeutic sense" (Limeta, 1993, p. 40). In many ways, this is when the difficult work begins; Christian theology terms this process sanctification. Once addicts surrender and begin a relationship with the divine, the process of sanctification assists the believers as they seek to mature in their faith.

Discussion of Theories and Treatment Interventions

McNeece and DiNitto (1998) noted, "a significant advance in the study of addiction is the realization that it is probably not a unitary disease" (p. 32). However, practitioners may become very dogmatic in their application of one theory for all types of cases. This approach of taking from only one theory is not supported by the literature, and therefore, it has the possibility of not providing the best treatment. Abbott (2000) warned that the wrong use of theory in social work practice could lead to ineffective treatment for clients.

The National Association of Social Workers (as cited in Abbott, 2000) suggested that social workers should take into consideration that "social, economic, and environmental factors contribute to alcohol, tobacco, and other drug abuse." (p. xi). Goodman (1995), a psychiatrist, wrote that one of the problems in addiction treatment is that it encompasses biological, behavioral, social-interpersonal, and psychodynamic issues; and most treatment providers are only trained in one or two of those areas. Social workers are trained in all of these areas and bring valuable skills and education to the addiction treatment field.

Van Wormer (1995) noted that the ecological framework provides the best paradigm in capturing the complexities of addiction and offers assistance when conceptualizing and treating addiction. A major advantage of the ecological framework is that "it can subsume within its framework other theoretical models and treatment orientations. There is not an either-or with this formulation— viewing the person in the situation includes the total biopsychosocial reality" (Van Wormer, 1995, p. 18). Social workers need to appreciate the contributions each of the etiological theories of addiction provides to understanding the problem, while realizing that only one model is insufficient for total recovery.

Illustrative Case Scenario: Jorge Gonzales

In order to review a concrete application of the transtheoretical model we will present a case scenario from practice.

Jorge was a 24 year old male struggling to keep steady employment and maintain a positive relationship with his girlfriend. Alcohol seemed to be the precipitating factor for his struggles. Jorge had been fired one week prior to his arrest, because he came to work multiple times still intoxicated from the night before. Jorge's girlfriend also told him he had to do something about his drinking and get things "right" with God before she would consider marrying him. Jorge's girlfriend thought there was a person who could help him and asked Jorge to go see the social worker at Mission Detroit, a faith-based organization associated with First Baptist Church that offers twelve-step groups, employment programs, mentoring services, and other programs, all in a Christian context.

Jorge went to see the social worker, Chris, and told him that he wanted help finding employment. During the conversation with Chris, Jorge blamed various people in his life for the fact that he was struggling with steady employment. He explained that his previous employers fired him because they did not understand the pressure of supporting his girlfriend and her daughter. He suggested that his girlfriend did not understand him and did not see how hard he worked to be successful.

Chris asked Jorge if he thought that he drank too much. Jorge very quickly said his drinking did not affect his work performance or his family. He said he enjoyed a drink or two to let off steam and to relax a little after a hard day at work. When Chris suggested that he thought his drinking might be a problem, Jorge abruptly changed the subject, denying that alcohol had anything to do with his problems.

Jorge described himself as "a good guy" and said he was a Christian. "I'm not perfect, but I am trying," he explained. He also questioned aloud why his girlfriend didn't think he was 'right' with God. Chris explored deeper what Jorge's faith meant to him and asked him how he thought someone who was 'right' with God lived. Chris felt like there was a slight breakthrough with Jorge. When Jorge began to talk about his faith journey, he described going to church in the past and feeling close to God. But now, he felt empty and alone.

Just as Chris began to feel like he was getting through, Jorge again abruptly changed the subject and argued that he didn't think these things had anything to do with his current situation.. Chris observed that Jorge did not take responsibility in the session for the problems associated with his drinking; rather he blamed other people in his uncontrolled life. Chris was concerned that if Jorge did not deal with these problems effectively, he could end up in a worse condition or even dead. Chris also was concerned about entering Jorge in the employment training program when he thought there were underlying substance abuse issues that needed primary attention.

Perspectives on Jorge's Situation

Social workers who strictly ascribe to the AA model might say Jorge needs to "hit bottom" before he can begin the healing process. Enough bad things must happen to him, making him terribly miserable, so that he could break through his denial. Upon this breakthrough, the long and arduous recovery process could begin. Those following the AA model most likely would not suggest an intervention during this waiting process that is painful for everyone involved, including the professional who is allowing Jorge to possibly destroy everything that is important to him.

The Transtheoretical Model, however, provides an alternative perspective for understanding that the stage of denial is crucial in helping Jorge make immediate improvements in his life. This is a comfortable place for Jorge; in this stage, he does not have to take responsibility for his problems. He feels invincible.. He does not feel guilty for the problems because he perceives they are not his fault. Jorge would be in the precontemplation stage. Intervention would need to be tailored to this stage and therapy should focus on consciousness raising and self-revelation. The social worker would need to focus on providing appropriate feedback for Jorge to help him see how his drinking behavior is affecting other areas of his life. Education would be geared toward helping Jorge see he is not alone in his problems and that others have struggled with similar issues (Prochaska & Norcross, 1994).

Furthermore, Neff and MacMaster (2005) concurred with the opinion that the stages of change idea has become the dominant conceptual framework for addiction treatment. However, they point out that the model adequately describes in detail the mechanisms that drive the stage process. They suggested that "empathy, forgiveness, and acceptance are important elements of engaging the individual in a change from 'pre-contemplative' to 'contemplative' stages" (p. 48). Furthermore, they go on to suggest that role modeling, social reinforcement and support provided by communal settings are all critical factors in assisting individuals to move through the stages.

Therefore, Chris' role in this case could be to assist Jorge in finding a place where his faith could be nurtured in ways he had experienced in the past. A church could provide Jorge with role modeling and social reinforcement needed to help Jorge through the stages of change.

The Transtheoretical Model, a good example of an ecological model, is one of the most promising and helpful research and practice tools in the addiction field. Dunn (2000) suggested that social workers should adopt this model for addiction treatment not only because of the strong empirical research supporting it, but also for its "compatibility with the mission, values, and problem solving orientation of social work practice" (p. 143). The Transtheoretical Model provides the tools necessary to assess the client's stage of change, as well as the means to select and implement an eclectic counseling intervention. It also will allow social workers to be effective in their pursuit of helping addicts through the problem solving process. Furthermore, the model lends itself to effective social work practice that is designed and tested to work with diverse client populations.

Although the Transtheoretical Model is not inherently based upon Christian principles, many of the techniques and processes can be adapted to and integrated with Christian beliefs. For example, the model is very insistent about the idea that change from addiction occurs over time and should not always be construed as a one-time event; surrender is just the beginning of the process of healing for addicts (Velicer, Prochaska, Fava, Norman, & Redding, 1988). In fact, all the stages of change can be applied to assisting addicts in changing or maturing in their spiritual lives.

Despite the clear congruence between social work and proven empirical evidence for the Transtheoretical Model, it is not the only tool social workers should be utilizing. Social workers must be committed to looking at whole persons in their environments. One of the most powerful tools to help addicts is to provide them with the opportunity to build a community of support and fellowship. Churches can help fill this void for addicts. Many times, however, there is the need to be around people struggling with the same issues; addicts can find this encouragement and support in AA.

Clinebell (as cited in Albers, 1999) positively stated, "in all the long, dark, dismal history of the problem of alcoholism, the brightest ray of hope and help is Alcoholics Anonymous" (p. 1). Davis and Jansen (1998) argued that there is a gap in recent social work literature regarding AA. Researchers have debated the efficacy of AA, but Emerick's (as cited in Davis & Jansen) recent review of AA studies and outcome evaluations suggested that AA is successful in treating addiction, at least for a large number of addicts. In response to this success, social workers need to be aware of the workings of AA and how many of the concepts of AA can be understood through Christian theology. According to Haller (1998), social workers need to understand the spiritual nature of AA because it allows social workers to be better listeners and helpers when they recognize popular AA terminology.

Social workers also should assist in translating these concepts for other social workers. Our dual roles can be used to assist in educating others about the spirituality emphasis in AA, dispelling the prevalent myths (e.g., Davis & Jansen, 1998). Social workers must make the connection that both the profession of social work, in regard to the NASW Code of Ethics, and AA "embrace empowerment, connectedness, and interdependence, and most important, the principle that people can change, regardless of how oppressed they find themselves by their circumstances" (Davis & Jansen, p. 180).

In addition, there is mounting evidence that AA's emphasis on surrender and powerlessness are problematic for African Americans (Morgan & Jordan, 1999). Critics believe these flaws are because of the influence of the founders of AA, white middle class men heavily influenced by the conservative evangelical Oxford Group. The work of the Black Extended Family Project, a partnership with Haight Ashbury Free Clinics and Cecil Williams at Glide United Methodist Church (as cited in Smith & Seymour, 1999) has helped to bridge this gap. They offer an alternative and innovative Christian spiritual program for African Americans that take into consideration these legitimate concerns.

Feminists have been especially critical of AA for these reasons and for AA's use of a male God (Van Wormer, 1995). Others have countered that AA encourages a personal understanding of a Higher Power that does not dictate a male or female God. Sanders (2004) investigated through mixed-methods how alcoholic women empowered themselves through the 12-step program using feminist phenomenology as a theoretical framework and a gender-sensitive perspective. She noted that within a therapeutic milieu of a 2-1 ratio of men to women, women continued to "hold strong gender-role attitudes, maintain feminist beliefs, and actively participated in feminist activities" (p. ii).

Some social workers have resisted the disease theory implications of addiction because it contradicts the strengths perspective or systems framework (Rhodes & Johnson, 1996; Spense & DiNitto, 2002). Van Wormer (1995) argued that the disease model is simply "a mere explanation and not a theory or framework at all" (p. 18). Furthermore, social workers have suggested that the disease concept emphasizes the pathological nature of addiction and assumes that addicts do not accept responsibility for their addiction.

However, the disease model is particularly useful in moving society's view of addiction from a previous moralistic stance to encompass a broader understanding of addiction. It allows addiction to be understood as a progressive and potentially life-threatening problem, if it is not treated. In addition, Morgan (1998) suggests that the disease model assists in reducing "the church's tendency to objectify evil as external to itself" (p. 36). Although the disease theory should not be used exclusively, it does provide a tool for the clinician when working with addicts.

Many Christian treatment programs attempt to integrate the addiction etiology theories and treatment interventions previously discussed with Christian teaching. Good research on these organizations, however, is not present at this time. The literature is lacking in both empirical outcome studies and descriptive studies on Christian treatment interventions. We have just a few studies on Christian treatment programs such as Salvation Army, Teen Challenge, and rescue missions (Neff & MacMaster, 2005). Although these studies, at a basic level, suggest Christian programs are successful, most of those conducted, and particularly the Teen Challenge studies, do not hold up to empirical standards.

Furthermore, we have only limited information on what individual centers do in their programs. Neff, Shorkey, and Windsor (2005) provided one of the first studies of multiple faith based treatment programs utilizing both qualitative and quantitative methods. Their research provides insight into the unique and common elements of faith-based and traditional treatment programs. In a small study conducted by Wolf-Branigin and Duke (2007) in the Salvation Army Harbor Light Center in Washington, D.C., the researchers found that those addicts involved in spiritual activities during their treatment program where more likely to complete the program. These church program activities included "Bible study, fellowship meetings, religious services, music programs, youth activities, and pastoral counseling" (p.241). This Salvation Army faith-based program is helping clients complete treatment programs, resulting in a lower chance of abusing addictive substances again.

There are several reasons for the lack of research literature on Christianity and treatment of addiction. The rigors of science have long ignored the efficacy of Christian approaches, and even the very popular AA has not received the rigorous studies that other treatment modalities have received. Most secular sources categorize AA in the moral category, when in reality it is a spiritually based program. In addition, there is difficulty in empirically testing such concepts as estrangement or idolatry. It may not be easy, but that does not mean that the ideas are invalid.

Conclusion

McNeece and DiNitto (2005) note that "the major definitional issue concerning addiction is whether it is a bad habit, a disease, or a form of moral turpitude" (p. 7). On one end of the spectrum, we have addiction treatment programs that have built their intervention model around the idea that "faith is both the starting and end point in recovery. It is the healing power of Jesus Christ, in the Church, and not the intervention of behavioral science, that brings about and maintains the individual's rehabilitation" (Muffler et al., 1997, p. 587). On the other end of the spectrum, we have addiction treatment programs that have moved so far away from their evangelical roots that their programs are hardly distinguishable from secular programs.

Christian social workers, drawing on their ecological framework, should advocate for an approach to addiction that attempts to balance theological beliefs regarding addiction with the growing scientific knowledge and theories available. Social workers should provide leadership in developing, evaluating, and implementing holistic models for addiction treatment. Social workers practicing in a Christian addiction treatment environment need to embrace all that theology and science have to offer in order to provide the best care possible for those suffering from addiction.

References

Abbott, A. A. (Ed.). (2000). *Alcohol, tobacco, and other drugs: Challenging myths, assessing theories, individualizing.* Washington, DC: National Association of Social Workers.

Albers, R. H. (1997). Transformation: The key to recovery. *Journal of Ministry in Addiction & Recovery,* 4(1), 23-37.

Albers, R. H. (1999). Editorial: The spirit and spirituality of twelve step groups. *Journal of Ministry in Addiction & Recovery,* 6(1), 1-7.

Alcoholics Anonymous. (2001). *Alcoholics anonymous: The story of how many thousands of men and women have recovered from alcoholism* (4th ed.). New York: Alcoholics Anonymous World Services.

American Psychiatric Association. (2000). *Diagnostic and statistical manual of mental disorders* (4th ed.). Washington, DC: American Psychiatric Association.

Bakke, R. (1995). New faces of rescue missions [Electronic version]. *City Voices, Summer.*

Bonhoeffer, D. (1995). *The cost of discipleship* (1st Touchstone ed.). New York: Touchstone.

Bromet, E., Moos, R., Wuthmann, C., & Bliss, F. (1977). Treatment experiences of alcoholic patients: An analysis of five residential alcoholism programs. *International Journal of the Addictions,* 12(7), 953-958.

Brown, H. P., Peterson, J. H., & Cunningham, O. (1988). A behavioral/cognitive spiritual model for a chemical dependency aftercare program. *Alcoholism Treatment Quarterly,* 5(1-2), 153-175.

Burck, J. R., & Hunter, R. J. (2005). Pastoral theology: Protestant. In R. J. Hunter (Ed.), *Dictionary of pastoral care and counseling* (pp. 867-872). Nashville, TN: Abingdon Press.

Christians in Recovery. (2002). *Recovery ministry database.* Retrieved April 24, 2002, from http://christians-in-recovery.org/db

Ciarrocchi, J. (1993). *A minister's handbook of mental disorders.* New York: Paulist Press.

Clinebell, H. J. (2005). Alcohol abuse, addiction, and therapy. In R. J. Hunter (Ed.), *Dictionary of pastoral care and counseling* (pp. 18-21). Nashville, TN: Abingdon Press.

Clinebell, H. J. (1994). Philosophical-religious factors in the etiology and treatment of alcoholism. *Journal of Ministry in Addiction & Recovery, 1*(2), 29-46.

Clinebell, H. J. (1998). *Understanding and counseling persons with alcohol, drug, and behavioral addictions: Counseling for recovery and prevention using psychology and religions* (Rev. ed.). New York: Abingdon Press.

Davis, D. R., & Jansen, G. G. (1998). Making meaning of Alcoholics Anonymous for social workers: Myths, metaphors, and realities. *Social Work, 43*(2), 169-182.

Dunn, P. C. (2000). The stages and processes of change model: Implications for social work ATOD practice. In A. A. Abbott (Ed.), *Alcohol, tobacco, and other drugs: Challenging myths, assessing theories, individualizing* (pp.111-143). Washington, DC: National Association of Social Workers.

Evans, C. S. (1984). *Existentialism: The philosophy of despair and the quest for hope.* Grand Rapids, MI: Zondervan.

Fagan, R.W. (1998). Religious nonprofit organizations: An examination of rescue missions and the homeless. *Social Thought, 18*(4), 21-48.

Gallup, G. H. J. (1999). Preface. In O. J. Morgan & M. R. Jordan (Eds.), *Addiction and spirituality: A multidisciplinary approach* (pp.xi-xii). St. Louis, MI: Chalice Press.

Gauntlett, S. L. (1991). Drug abuse control and the Salvation Army. *Bulletin on Narcotics, xiii*(1), 17-27.

General Service Office. (2007). *AA fact file.* Retrieved January 13, 2007, from http://www.alcoholics-anonymous.org/en_pdfs/m-24_aafactfile.pdf

Global Teen Challenge. (2007). Welcome to Global Teen Challenge. Retrieved February 23, 2007, from http://www.globaltc.org/pages/FrontPAGE2.html.

Goodman, A. (1995). Addictive disorders: An integrated approach: Part one - An integrated understanding. *Journal of Ministry in Addiction & Recovery, 2*(2), 33-75.

Grant, B. F., & Dawson, D. A. (2006). Introduction to the national epidemiological survey on alcohol and related conditions. *Alcohol Research & Health, 29*(2), 72.

Gray, M. C. (1995). Drug abuse. In Richard L. Edwards (Ed.), *Encyclopedia of social work* (Vol. 1, pp. 795-803). Washington, DC. National Association of Social Workers.

Haller, D. J. (1998). Alcoholics Anonymous and spirituality. *Social Work and Christianity, 25*(2), 101-114.

Hardin, M. (1994). Let God be God: A theological justification for the anonymity of God in the 12 step program. *Journal of Ministry in Addiction & Recovery, 1*(2), 9-22.

Hopson, R. E., & Moses, M. J. (1996). Theology of paradox: A Pauline contribution to the understanding and treatment of addictions. *Journal of Ministry and Addiction, 3*(1), 7-47.

Hunter, R. J. (2005). *Dictionary of pastoral care and counseling.* Nashville, TN: Abingdon Press.

Katz, L. (1966). The Salvation Army's men's social center. *Quarterly Journal of Studies on Alcohol, 27*(4), 636-547.

Leshner, A. I. (2001). Addiction is a brain disease: Issues in science and technology online. Retrieved November 10, 2001, from http://www.nap.edu/issues/17.3/leshner.htm.

Limeta, M. (1993). *A guide to effective rescue mission recovery programs.* Kansas City, MO: International Union of Gospel Missions.

McNeece, C. A., & DiNitto, D. M. (2005). *Chemical dependency: A systems approach* (3nd ed.). Boston: Allyn and Bacon.

McNeece, C. A., & DiNitto, D. M. (1998). *Chemical dependency: A systems approach* (2nd ed.). Boston: Allyn and Bacon.

Miller, W. R., & Hester, R. K. (2003). Treating alcohol problems: Toward an informed eclecticism. In R. K. Hester and W. R. Miller (Eds.). *Handbook of alcohol treatment approaches: Effective alternatives* (3rd ed., pp. 1-12). Boston: Allyn and Bacon.

Miller, W. R. (1998). Researching the spiritual dimensions of alcohol and other drug problems. *Addiction, 93*(7), 979-990.

Moltmann, J. (1999). *God for a secular society: The public relevance of theology.* London: SCM Press.

Morgan, O. J. (1998). Practical theology, alcohol abuse and alcoholism: Methodological and biblical considerations. *Journal of Ministry in Addiction & Recovery, 5*(2), 33-63.

Morgan, O. J. (1999). Addiction and spirituality in context. In O. J. Morgan & M. R. Jordan (Eds.), *Addiction and spirituality: A multidisciplinary approach* (pp. 3-30). St. Louis, MI: Chalice Press.

Morgan, O. J., & Jordan, M. R. (Eds.). (1999). *Addiction and spirituality: A multidisciplinary approach.* St. Louis, MI: Chalice Press.

Moss, B. G. (1996). Perceptions of church leaders regarding the role of the church in combating juvenile delinquency in San Antonio, Texas: Implications for church and community-based programs. *Dissertation Abstracts International: Section B: The Sciences and Engineering, 57*(6-B), 4036.

Muffler, J., Langrod, J. G., & Larson, D. B. (1997). There is a balm in Gilead: Religion and substance abuse treatment. In J. W. Lowinson (Ed.), *Substance abuse: A comprehensive guide* (pp.584-595). Baltimore: Williams &Wilkins.

National Center for Health Statistics. (2005). Health, United States, 2005: With chartbook on trends in the health of Americans. Retrieved February 6, 2007, from http://www.cdc.gov/nchs/data/hus/hus05.pdf#068

Neff, J. A., MacMaster, S.A. (2005) Spiritual mechanisms underlying substance abuse behavior change in faith-based substance abuse treatment. *Journal of Social Work Practice in Addictions, 5*(3), 33-54.

Neff, J.A., Shorkey, C.T., Windsor, L.C. (2005) Contrasting faith-based and traditional substance abuse treatment programs. *Journal of Substance Abuse Treatment, 30*, 49-61.

Office of Applied Studies. (2005). National survey on drug use and health: National findings. Substance Abuse and Mental Health Services, DHHS. Retrieved February 22, 2007, from http://www.drugabusestatistics.samhsa.gov/NSDUH/2k5NSDUH/2k5results.htm#1.1

Office of Applied Studies. (2004). National survey on drug use and health: National findings. Substance Abuse and Mental Health Services, DHHS. Retrieved February 6, 2007, from http://www.oas.samhsa.gov/NSDUH/2k4NSDUH/2k4results/2k4results.htm#ch7

Uniform facility data set (UFDS). Washington, DC: Substance Abuse and Mental Health Services, Department of Health and Human Services.

Peteet, J. (1993). A closer look at the role of a spiritual approach in addictions treatment. *Journal of Substance Abuse Treatment, 10*, 263-267.

Peters, T. K. (1980). *An investigation into the role of religious experience and commitment as a therapeutic factor in the treatment and rehabilitation of selected drug addicts from Teen Challenge: A follow up study.* Unpublished doctoral dissertation, New York University, New York.

Prochaska, J. O., DiClemente, C. C., & Norcross, J. C. (1992). In search of how people change: Applications to addictive behaviors. *American Psychologist, 47*(9), 1102-1113.

Prochaska, J. O., Norcross, J. C., & DiClemente, C. C. (1994). *Changing for good: The revolutionary program that explains the six stages of change and teaches you how to free yourself from bad habits.* New York: W. Morrow.

Rhodes, R., & Johnson, A. D. (1996). Social work and substance abuse treatment: A challenge for the profession. *Families in Society, 77*(3), 182-185.

Royce, J. E. (1981). *Alcohol problems and alcoholism: A comprehensive survey.* New York: Free Press.

Salvation Army. (2003). *What we do.* Retrieved February 20, 2002, from http://www.salvationarmyusa.org/usn/www_usn.nsf

Sanders, J. (2004). Twelve-step recovery and feminism: A study of empowerment among women in Alcoholics Anonymous. *Dissertation Abstracts International, 54* (7-A), 2663.

Smith, D. E., & Seymour, R. B. (1999). Overcoming cultural points of resistance to spirituality in the practice of addiction medicine. In O. J. Morgan & M. R. Jordan (Eds.), *Addiction and spirituality: A multidisciplinary approach* (pp.95-110). St. Louis, MI: Chalice Press.

Spense, R. T., & DiNitto, D. M. (2002). Introduction. *Journal of Social Work Practice in the Addictions, 1*(3), 1-5.

Stone, H. W., & Clements, W. M. (1991). *Handbook for basic types of pastoral care and counseling.* Nashville: Abingdon Press.

Strung, D. L., Priyadarsini, S., & Hyman, M. M. (Eds.). (1986). *Alcohol interventions: Historical and sociocultural approaches.* New York: The Haworth Press.

Teen Challenge. (2002). *About Teen Challenge.* Retrieved January 15, 2007, from www.teenchallenge.com

Tiebout, H. (1951). Surrender as a psychological event. *American Journal of Psychoanalysis, 11,* 84-85.

Tiebout, H. M. (1994). The ego factors in surrender in alcoholism. Northvale, NJ: Jason Aronson Inc.

Tillich, P., & Taylor, M. I. (1991). *Paul Tillich: Theologian of the boundaries.* Minneapolis, MN: Fortress Press.

U.S. Department of Health and Human Services National Institutes of Health. (2004, June 10). *Alcohol abuse increases, dependence declines across decade.* Retrieved January 8, 2007, from http://www.nih.gov/news/pr/jun2004/niaaa-10.htm

Van Wormer, K. (1995). *Alcoholism treatment: A social work perspective.* Chicago: Nelson-Hall Publishers.

Velicer, W. F., Prochaska, J. O., Fava, J. L., Norman, G. J., & Redding, C. A. (1988). Applications of the transtheoretical model of behavior change [Electronic Version]. *Homeostasis, 38,* 216-233.

White, W. L. (1998). *Slaying the dragon: The history of addiction treatment and recovery.* Bloomington, IL: Chestnut Health Systems/Lighthouse Institute.

Wolf-Branigin, M., & Duke, J. (2007). Spiritual involvement as a predictor to completing a Salvation Army substance abuse treatment program. *Research on Social Work Practice, 17*(2), 239-245.

Zlotnick, C., & Agnew, J. (1997). Neuropsychological function and psychosocial status of alcohol rehabilitation program residents. *Addictive Behaviors, 22*(2), 183-194.

CHAPTER 16

THE ROLE OF RELIGIOUS ORIENTATION IN THE RECOVERY PROCESS OF PERSONS WITH A SEVERE MENTAL ILLNESS

Beryl Hugen

Today a sizable amount of literature documents the positive relationship between religious commitment and health (Johnson, 2002; Koenig, McCullough, & Larson, 2001; Plante & Sherman, 2001). Research on the relationship between religious commitment and mental health is not as plentiful or clear. In fact, mixed and contradictory findings appear to be the rule (Gartner, Larson & Allen, 1991). While some have long argued that religious commitment contributes to emotional disturbance (Ellis, 1973, 1980), others point to the beneficial effects of religious commitment on individual coping and psychological well-being (Fitchett, Burton, & Sivan, 1997; Miller, 1999; Williams, 2004; Pargament, 1997).

Fewer studies have examined the role of religious commitment for persons with severe and persistent mental illness such as schizophrenia, major depression, bipolar, and schizoaffective disorders. This may be in part because historically many mental health practitioners regarded the role of religious commitment among persons with severe and persistent mental illness as particularly challenging—citing the religious content of delusions and hallucinations, the use of religious motives as well as religious language in self-injury, and the perceived rigidity of religious beliefs and spiritual practices which may exacerbate symptoms. To some degree this was understandable, given the confusion and difficulty persons with a severe mental illness have in organizing their thoughts.

The tensions or differences between religious and secular perspectives on the helping process run deep. From the humanistic point of view, religious or spiritual pursuits are simply reflections of more basic psychological and social motives. There really are no distinct religious or spiritual motives. A religious perspective offers a very different understanding, building on the belief that what is spiritual or sacred is real, and that spiritual desires can't be reduced to a matter of psychological needs. Additionally, most religious traditions hold that the search for the sacred takes priority over the secular (Van Hook, Hugen, & Aguilar, 2001).

Even so, recent studies indicate persons with a severe mental illness closely resemble the general population in their tendency to find meaning and support through spirituality and religion (Bremer, 2004; Fitchett, Burton & Sivan, 1997; Corrigan, McCorkle, Schell & Kidder, 2003; Neeleman & Lewis, 1994; Lindgren & Coursey, 1995). Growing support also exists for the importance of religion and spirituality in psychosocial rehabilitative efforts with this population (Corrigan, McCorkle, Schell & Kidder, 2003; Bremer, 2004, Fallot, 2001). Additionally, efforts to incorporate a religious perspective into psychoeducational programs for persons with a severe mental illness show promising results (Fallot & Newburn, 2000; Lindgren & Coursey, 1995).

Building on these studies, efforts now are beginning to focus on the development of conceptual frameworks and theoretical models related to how religious commitment contributes to, sustains, and enhances the social and psychological well-being of persons with a severe and persistent mental illness. For example, one conceptual framework seeks to understand spirituality as a "protective factor" related to the course and prognosis of a severe mental illness (Brekke & Slade, 1998). A related theoretical model considers spirituality and religion as an important resource in coping with a severe mental illness, providing persons with the capacity or strength to survive and transcend their illness (Bremer, 2004; Pargament, 1997).

One particularly promising approach with this population is what is commonly referred to as recovery, or the recovery process (Anthony, 1991, 1993). An examination of the relationship between religious commitment and the recovery process is the focus of this chapter. Specifically, the chapter offers a beginning conceptual framework or model as to how religious commitment contributes to the recovery process for persons with a severe and persistent mental illness.

To this end, the chapter addresses six areas of special significance related to the role of religious commitment and the recovery process. These include: (1) changes in professional standards to include religion; (2) the recovery process; (3) a definition of religious orientation; (4) the unique contributions a religious orientation brings to the recovery process; (5) a conceptual framework linking the recovery process and religious orientation in the lives of persons with a severe mental illness; and (6) first-person accounts illustrating the relationship between religious orientation and the recovery process.

Professional Standards

One impetus for this line of research comes from the renewed awareness and interest in spirituality and religion within the helping professions. This includes changes within the field of psychology, namely, the inclusion of religion as a category of human diversity within the *Ethical Principles of Psychologists and Code of Conduct* (2002), which requires practitioners to have knowledge of issues related to religiosity, as well as an ability to effectively address clients' religious concerns in treatment. Similarly, the DSM-IV (American Psychiatric Association, 2000) now includes a V-Code entitled "Religious or Spiritual Problem" that recognizes that people with severe mental illnesses may indeed present similar spiritual or religious concerns to those with no mental disorder—concerns "include distressing experiences that involve loss or questioning of faith, problems associated with conversion to a new faith, or question of spiritual values that may not necessarily be related to an organized church or religious institution" (p. 741). In the same way, the social work profession's *NASW Code of Ethics* (1999) now includes four standards that explicitly affirm the role of religion in practice. Likewise, two standards in the *NASW Standards for Cultural Competence in Social Work Practice* (2001) emphasize the importance of religious cultures and communities in work with clients.

The Recovery Process

The beginnings of the recovery movement lay in the aftermath of deinstitutionalization during the 1970s. In the necessary effort to understand severe mental illness and address the devastating effects of the illness, helping approaches frequently lost touch with the person who had the illness, the person trying to make sense of his/her life and survive on a day-by-day basis. For many persons with a severe mental illness, the illness easily became the central characteristic of their identity, contributing to a painful stigma. Difficulties in the implementation of the policy of deinstitutionalization highlight the realization that persons with a severe mental illness want and need more than just symptom relief and case management (Davidson, Hoge, Godleski, Rakfeldt, et al, 1996).

The concept of recovery, quite common in the field of physical illness and disability, emerged in the field of severe mental illness principally through a consumer driven movement. Anthony (1993) describes this recovery process as:

> a deeply personal, unique process of changing one's attitudes, values, feelings, goals, skills, and/or roles. It is a way of living a satisfying, hopeful, and contributing life even with limitations caused by illness. Recovery involves the development of new meaning and purpose in one's life as one grows beyond the catastrophic effects of mental illness (p. 15).

Such an understanding of the recovery process is integral to the mental health consumer movement's conceptualization of recovery, commonly described as "the ongoing process of learning to live with one's disability and gradually rebuilding a sense of purpose, agency, and meaning in life despite the limitations of the illness" (Davidson & Strauss, 1992, p.166; Deegan, 1992, 1993; Weingarten, 1994, 1997).

Recovery is a common human experience. Everyone encounters tragic events in life and faces the challenge of recovering from such events. To recover from a tragic experience or personal calamity (illness, death in the family, disability) does not change the fact that the tragic event occurred, or that the heartbreaking effects of the experience are still present—or that one's life may be forever different. Successful recovery means simply that the meaning of a tragic experience or event has changed for the person. No longer is the catastrophic event the primary focus in one's life. One learns to move ahead, to go on to new activities, assimilate new attitudes, and embrace alternative social roles. The notion of recovery significantly and directly challenges the concept of chronicity, a previously accepted feature of life for persons with a serious mental illness.

Recovery is a multi-dimensional concept. The process involves recovering *from* the stigma of mental illness—the negative side effects of unemployment, the pain of loneliness, and a sense of lack of control and self-determination in one's life. The process also involves *seeking and searching for* outcomes in life that approximate "normalcy." One such outcome is a sense of psychological well-being, where a person with a mental illness experiences the present, both its satisfactions and its limitations, as a meaningful and acceptable condition. Another outcome involves the development of a sense of hope, to look towards the future with the promise of continued satisfaction and achievement, despite the limitations life may bring. Psychological well-being and hope, along with self-esteem, empowerment, community connectedness, social support, and self-determination are all considered indicators or markers for success related to the recovery process (Anthony, 1993).

Research efforts to understand and examine a variety of these recovery indicators in the lives of persons with a severe and persistent mental illness are growing (Corrigan, Calabrese, Divan, Keogh, Keck, & Mussey, 2002; Corrigan, Faber, Rashid, & Leary, 1999; Corrigan & Gorman, 1997; Davidson & Strauss, 1992; Fallot & Harris, 2002; Herth, 1991; McDermott, 1995; Rogers, Chamberlin, Ellison, & Crean, 1997; Rudnick & Kravetz, 2001; Weingarten, 1994). These research studies clearly lend support to the importance and salutary efforts of fostering and nurturing these recovery outcomes in the lives of persons with a severe mental illness. Many of the studies, however, encounter methodological limitations, using quantitative survey scales as sole indicators for what are fairly subjective recovery outcomes.

Definition of Religious Orientation

Spirituality and religion, common concepts in the social work literature, are defined in a wide variety of ways within this literature. Spirituality is seen as involving a sense of ultimate purpose, meaning, and value, principally nurtured through a relationship with a transcendent reality or higher power. Religion is recognized as involving an institutional context, including a shared set of beliefs, practices, and an identifiable community of believers (Canda & Furman, 1999). The social work profession has tended to see spirituality as the central and more inclusive concept, with religion limited to the institutional and social dimensions of religious communities. Outside of social work and particularly in the field of religious studies, religion is more often seen as the central and overarching concept, with spirituality being more narrowly related to the way a person develops a personal relationship with God or a higher power.

For many people, spirituality and religion function as a single entity (Van Hook, Hugen & Aguilar, 2001). One prominent researcher, Kenneth Pargament, combines the two, seeing spirituality and religion as one process, which he labels religion. He defines religion as "a process, a search for significance in ways related to the sacred" (Pargament, 1997, p. 32). For Pargament, the significance one searches for is what is of utmost value in life, that which offers and gives life ultimate meaning and purpose. Also important is that the search involves being in a relationship with the sacred. The sacred may be a spirit, the divine, a transcendent being, God, or whatever may be associated with a higher power. It may also include objects, people, and activities that become sanctified by virtue of their association with the sacred.

Pargament (1997) further describes this search for significance as involving a set of sacred destinations or end points, along with an array of pathways or means to reach or attain these destinations. Common religious ends include the search for meaning (an ordered and structured world) or self-identity and purpose (who am I and why am I here). Other religious ends or destinations include health and mental health, being in community with others, comfort, and hope. Each of these religious ends or destinations may vary depending on a person's particular understanding of the sacred.

All religions offer their members the means or paths to follow in the pursuit of these religious ends. The pathways are not always easy and can be different, even contradictory, in different religious traditions. Religious means include an assortment of objects, personal characteristics, and activities. This could include time and space (Sabbath, synagogue); events and transitions (birth... to...death); materials (crucifix, wine, incense); religious literature and music; people (saints, priest, and pastor); practices and rituals; psychological attributes (patience, long suffering, courage); social attributes (compassion, justice); and roles (wife/husband, parent, vocation). For many people, these religious destinations and pathways are learned, developed, and nurtured within congregations, denominations, and religious traditions.

When an individual seeks a sacred destination in life, or takes a pathway directed toward the sacred, that individual expresses a religious orientation (Pargament, 1997). Religious orientations are general dispositions that use particular means to attain particular ends—in the search for significance related to the sacred. Religious orientations engage our senses, thoughts, actions, and relationships with others.

A religious orientation may serve as a "cognitive schema," a mental representation of the world that helps one to filter and make sense of the events and circumstances of one's life. It provides a framework that "allows for the integration of tragic or difficult experiences into one's view of self, helping make such experiences more understandable by infusing them with meaning and helping preserve a sense of personal cohesiveness and control" (Koenig, 1995, p. 32; Antonovsky, 1979).

Lindgren and Coursey (1995) consider a religious orientation as both a cognitive and affective spiritual support. They describe a religious orientation as "the perceived, personally supportive components of an individual's relationship with God" (p. 94). For persons with a mental illness this is manifest through two ways. The first is through cognitive mediation, the interpretation and meaning that religious beliefs give to events. The second they refer to as emotional support, the feeling of being cared for and valued, attained either from the support of others, a higher power, or through belonging to a religious community.

Ventis (1995) maintains that an important aspect of a religious orientation for persons with a mental illness includes involvement in a religious community.

A religious community provides opportunity to "share common beliefs—which may serve as central organizing principles in one's life—as well as providing human contact and emotional support" (p. 40). Similarly, Idler (1987) argues that for persons with a mental illness, participation in a religious community offers "access to a unique system of symbols, providing cultural resources in the form of a consistent body of knowledge and set of meanings that allow individuals to make sense of and cope with their experience, reducing uncertainty in ordinary life and at moments of crisis alike" (p. 229). Walsh (1995) documents that a person's religious disposition tends to persist despite the onset of schizophrenia, with religion allowing the person "to identify with a community that transcends the self" (p. 553).

In summary, a religious orientation may assist individuals with a mental illness to make sense of their experience by providing specific religious coping methods, help construct personal narratives that take into account transcendent and sacred realities, and provide both emotional and social support. For example, a woman with a severe mental illness who has lost her job may use her Christian religious orientation to find strength through prayer, seek guidance or comfort by reading the Bible, accept social support from her congregation, understand the work she seeks to re-establish as a vocation, or identify her unemployment as an opportunity to develop a closer relationship with God—to depend on Him more. Each of these means and ends emanate from her religious orientation.

Unique Aspects of a Religious Orientation

A religious orientation is one of several orientation systems people with a mental illness bring to the coping process. Other orientation systems common to mental health consumers and within the behavioral sciences include rational choice, catharsis, and behaviorism. How does a religious orientation differ from these orientation systems? Are there unique and distinctive features that a religious orientation brings to the recovery process? If so, what are these unique features?

Although the goals or aims of religious and secular orientation systems have much in common, there are several differences. First of all, the goal of secular helping orientations is focused on helping clients gain control of their thinking, affect, and behavior. The focus is on identifying and developing client strengths and facilitating client empowerment. In contrast, a unique goal of a religious orientation is to appreciate what one cannot control—to learn to live with human limitations. The focus is on the limits of human agency, and the specific practices and processes that help persons adapt to a harsh environment or circumstances in life over which they may have little control (Pargament, 1997). The religious concepts and processes of surrender, suffering, hope, transformation, and forgiveness are all rooted in the awareness and conviction of human limitations and insufficiency (Miller, 1999). This is not to say a religious orientation is only focused on helping people learn to live with human limitations. Religious orientations are interested in both—the ways to gain control and the ways to live with human insufficiency.

A second unique or distinctive feature of a religious orientation is that it provides a framework of beliefs, practices, and experiences that help people go beyond the self as a means to come to grips with human limitations. Religious orientations insist on the reality and significance of a power beyond the self, a power superior to individual human capacity and which transcends human sensory experience. Secular help tends to place the self at the center of the helping process. Personality change is the healing of the self. Religious orientations, in contrast, see healing and health related to being in a right relationship with the sacred, a power beyond the self.

Recovery Process and Religious Orientation—Common Assumptions

The recovery process and a religious orientation share several common assumptions. First, both the mental health and religious helping literature recognize that people and problems are most malleable during hard times, times of crisis, illness, and tragedy. Second, religious orientations and the recovery process both envision times of crisis as constructed in terms of their significance (Pargament, 1997). In other words, although a tragic event in a person's life may remain the same, the personal meaning of the event changes. It is this alteration in significance that is central to both persons who use a religious orientation in coping and those involved in the recovery process.

Third, both the recovery process and a religious orientation emphasize the need to recognize personal limitations as a key principle in the helping process. Recovery is "a way of living a satisfying, hopeful, and contributing life even with limitations caused by illness" (Anthony, 1993, p. 15). GROW, an international spiritually based recovery program for persons with mental illness operates on the principle that participants admit "that we were inadequate or maladjusted to life" (GROW, p. 5). This principle is not meant to suggest that persons with serious mental illness are less effectual than others. On the contrary, the humble admission of having problems, or limitations, is acknowledged to be an important and positive initial step in the recovery process.

Last, the recovery process and a religious orientation seek very similar outcomes. Studies suggest that spiritual motivation is not inconsistent with other psychological and social purposes (Pargament, 1997). Most faiths put forward a way to reconcile the spiritual and the human. People have worth in the Christian tradition because they have been created in God's image. Since human need and desire are part of God's creation, they too are worthwhile. Human drives related to justice, love, kindness, and self-actualization can become spiritual motives when associated with religious commitment.

The recovery process identifies several outcomes for persons with a severe mental illness, including self esteem, self-determination, personal and community support, empowerment, and a sense of identity and purpose (Anthony, 1993; Emotions Anonymous, 1980; Recovery, Inc., 2006). These outcomes serve as indicators that a person is in recovery. Similarly, religion offers a variety of religious ends or destinations for persons with a severe mental illness in their search for significance related to their illness. These include, but are not limited to, spiritual support, self esteem, hope, comfort, empowerment, and a sense of personal meaning and purpose (Fallot, 1998; Fallot & Newburn, 2000; GROW, 1982; Lindgren & Coursey, 1995).

Consumer Voices

The following section is based upon the personal accounts that individuals offered the author to illustrate specific ways a religious orientation helped in the recovery process.

These consumers of mental health services participated in a semi-structured interview of approximately one hour. Each informant matched the criteria for severe and persistent mental illness depicted by the basic dimensions of diagnosis, duration, and disability (American Psychiatric Association, 2000). All the informants were white, with 8 being female and 2 male. Eight of the informants preferred to be interviewed in a group (2-3 persons) format, with two choosing an individual interview.

Each informant came from a Judeo-Christian background. Seven of the informants were members of North Presbyterian Church in Kalamazoo, Michigan and/or of the Togetherness Group, a support and socialization group for persons with a severe and persistent mental illness, sponsored by North Presbyterian Church.[1] Three informants were involved in the Ministry with Persons with Disabilities through the Catholic Diocese of Kalamazoo.[2] One informant was Jewish (a member of the Togetherness Group).

All informants voluntarily chose to participate in the project. Interviews were conducted at North Presbyterian Church and the Catholic Diocese of Kalamazoo, locations convenient to participants. The underlying assumption informants brought to the interview was that their religious orientation, including an institutional religious affiliation, is and has been important in their recovery process. Informants were asked to share how their religious orientation influences and shapes their coping with a severe mental illness.

All interviews were tape recorded and transcribed. Interview responses were analyzed employing the processes of Spradley's (1979) ethnographic interviewing methodology. The use of this qualitative methodology was purposefully chosen in order to obtain information wholly from the informant's perspective. This ethnographic interview process recognizes the consumers as the experts, in this case, as the experts in their own recovery process, and captures the consumers' religious orientation in their own words.

Interview analyses identified five dimensions of support or areas of growth (recovery outcomes) that were influenced by their religious orientation. These areas or dimensions relate to self-esteem, empowerment, hope, community connections and relationships, and comfort. Drawing on first-person accounts, the following section portrays each of these five areas.

Religious Orientation Areas/Recovery Outcomes

Self-esteem

Respondents indicated their religious orientation helps them accept themselves as having value, believing that no matter how bad their physical, mental, social, or spiritual condition, they are always accepted and loved by a transcendent being. In addition to feeling a sense of being valued, they report that their life has a purpose—experiencing a unique place and part in God's healing and transforming work in the world.

One respondent commented, "disability doesn't mean inability. "I'm still a human being, we are all children of God... and He doesn't love any of us less than he loves others." Another stated:

> Everybody has adversity in their life; some people have more than others. If you can come up through your adversity in life without being bitter, mean-spirited and nasty, you've done a pretty good job with your life, no matter what you've been through. I've been able to do that and I thank God for that because if I hadn't had Him in my heart and with me all the time walking hand-in-hand, I couldn't have made it. I would be a bitter person, but I'm not. I'm a caring and giving person, and I try to do as much as I can. I have the ability to spot discomfort or pain or uneasiness in people.

Several respondents described discovering a positive identity for themselves through their experience with mental illness.

> My sister pointed out to me, 'Have you ever thought that God did this to make you a better person?' ... and I think I am. I'm more generous, I think more about the poor, and I worry about if people are hungry.
>
> In my faith, they say that 'for every hardship comes a blessing.' So we look for those hardships and embrace them because if you have a hardship, you are closer to God. It is like someone saying, 'you are the blessed one, look at all that you've been through; we envy you.' So often others express the opposite.

Empowerment

Most respondents voiced a motivation to gain control over their life, to overcome barriers, and to determine what happens in their life. This includes the ability to influence the organizational and societal structures in which they live, to believe that a problem can be solved by taking action, and that working together can have an effect on one's community.

Several consumers described how their religious orientation provides a sense of personal strength and courage.

Mental illness does not stop you from doing anything you wanted to do. I do get frustrated with myself because I am not able to do some things I would like to, but the things I can do are a heck of a lot more than I can't do.

My faith has got me through some tough times in my life. There were times that I didn't think I could make it, but then God shows me, you know, ways that He can help ... me through it.

Other respondents shared how their religious orientation helps facilitate personal discipline.

I have learned about good stewardship and it's my responsibility to pay for my bills ... that's my responsibility, it's what I need to do to take care of myself.

My religion stresses obedience and self-discipline, and was something I needed. Now it helped me as far as my thinking, and self-control as far as some spending habits that were out of control. I feel more in control and less a victim.

For others, their religious orientation empowers them to survive the circumstances that accompany their illness.

My faith is like, 'through God, I can do all things who strengthens me' and if I didn't believe in the Lord, if I didn't have Him on my side, I probably wouldn't be able to cope with life itself, but with the power of the Lord, ... greater is He in me than is in the world, you know. And he promised never to leave me nor forsake me, and I believe that.

My spirituality is what kept me alive. When I was in the state hospital for 18 years, I'd be in seclusion quite a lot ... solitary confinement if you want to call it that. I would pull a nail out of the door and I would draw a rosary on the wall, because you could draw on walls with metal, and I would see the rosary on the wall.

I would get my prayer book at night, it was locked up in the cabinet and it was the only time they would let me have it. And I would read the night prayers, and I would always pray for a miracle, 'dear God, let things just get better.' And you know what, they are, God has made things better. So I am glad to have them answered.

Hope

Hope encompasses looking toward the future with the promise of continued satisfaction. It involves believing that time heals, that there is a future and meaningful purpose to the difficulties of living with a mental illness. Two informants illustrate this religious end.

It is helpful to know that there is a God, a higher source that takes care of things. And that we go through what we go through for a reason, to make us stronger, wiser, to make us what we are today.

I may not always understand it … the trials He puts us through. But there is always a reason, there is always a purpose for being put in that position and why you have to go through that… that struggle.

For others hope is experiencing a sense of achievement despite the limitations that life may bring. It is to perceive the positive within life's circumstances—to persevere even when hurt and discouraged.

If there were no afterlife, if there were no God, I don't see the point in continuing my life; I would end it … I wouldn't put up with this all the time if I didn't believe that. I believe I'm eventually going home to God; mental illness is not fun no matter what stage you are in.

It's like the difference of going down a corridor without a flashlight, and going down a dark corridor and having a flashlight. You know the difference really. And sometimes, in my life I really didn't know I had a flashlight, to tell you the truth. It was there, it has always been there, you know. But in the depths of it all, sometimes I really didn't realize it. And then later, I looked and I did realize that I had it. It's always been there.

Community Connections and Relationships

To be a part of community means to both seek and receive help, to resolve to get well and co-operate with assistance that is offered. Overall one recognizes the need to be in a relationship with others.

I can still reach out and talk to somebody and help somebody else along the way. My faith has shown me that … there is a way around and a way to get through, you know.

You're not ever going to be alone, and through the Togetherness Group, and through God, I reached out more and more to other people than I ever thought possible."

And so, I'm like going down this road. I'm not scared to go down this road, but yet I'm stumbling down a little bit… but God is like pushing me… I want you back in the people. You know, and keep saying, 'I can read the Word, I can hear you on the TV,' but He's like saying, 'that's not the same, you have to be amongst people,' and I'm like, 'I don't really want to be amongst people,'… but you were happy among the people. Yeah I was happy; I don't understand your Word that well, but you got to stay among people in order to get better.' This is God talking to me.

Informants also describe the motivation to help others, to share their life experiences with others, and to experience the satisfaction of reaching out to others.

> If I'm struggling and somebody comes along ... I can walk with somebody and say, alright, I'm having a hard time too. So it gets them up and helps me also. We carry each other along the way. It's like God coming along and saying ... well you are struggling a little bit, and I'm going to help you along this way.

> There was one of our fellow members that lost a friend, and he was going through a rough time, and we just gathered together and prayed with him. He's still struggling with it, but we do help each other.

Comfort

Comfort, perhaps a unique outcome to the recovery process, is particularly pertinent for those who bring a religious orientation to the process. For those from a religious orientation, comfort means to console, to ease grief and trouble, primarily through mitigating the sense of loss, rather than experiencing full relief. It often involves the lifting of spirits from loneliness or boredom as well as from pain and grief. Several informants illustrated comfort by stating things like this:

> Sometimes I go in my room and just cry out to God, 'I need you now. I can't do it alone, I need you.' Sometimes I am in bed and can't sleep, I say a prayer and it's like ... I just go right back to sleep and wake up the next morning and say, "thank you God for a peaceful night.

> I think that where spirituality helps me the most is when I'm alone at night and the medication is not working. Or the last time I got put in crisis housing, which was months ago, all I did was pray. I think you almost have to have a walk with God when you are mentally ill. You know, because mental illness can make you feel so lonely anyway, and having that walk with Christ, in my case, have me a little bit more sociable because I'm a little bit less lonely. It is hard to explain, but that is what it about comes down to.

One informant found solace in the Biblical verse from Psalm 94: 19 (ASV), "In the multitude of my thoughts within me thy comforts delight my soul." ("When anxiety was great with me, your consolation brought joy to my soul"—NIV)

Discussion and Implications

First person accounts illustrate the ways a religious orientation may serve as a resource in a consumer's recovery process. Most importantly, they demonstrate how a religious orientation, with a focus on human limitations and decentralization from self, provides a compelling way of coping for many persons who struggle with a serious and persistent mental illness. Each informant's religious orientation provides a powerful mechanism by which they are able to alter the appraisal of their situation, thus allowing them to adapt more successfully to a harsh environment over which they may have little control. In addition, given that the recovery process is not entirely understood and highly subjective in nature, these personal accounts offer a valuable glimpse into the process.

How can these insights into the recovery process best be integrated into practice? First, social workers and mental health practitioners need to increase their sensitivity and knowledge regarding the religious needs of persons with a severe mental illness. Secondly, increased effort is needed to encourage programs, which work with this population, to develop relationships and work collaboratively with congregations and faith communities (Walters & Neugeboren, 1995). This includes helping congregations and faith communities reach out to and seek to be more inclusive of persons with severe mental illness. Informants in the study clearly convey how the communal and social aspects of religious life foster adaptation to stress by providing human contact and emotional support.

A third important focal point is to increase the visibility and accessibility of self-help groups for persons with a severe mental illness (Emotions Anonymous, 1980; GROW, 1982; Recovery, Inc., 2006). These self-help groups offer help to combat isolation and offer consumers a socially valued role of providing support to others. These groups frequently operate within the framework of a religious orientation or ideology. The religious orientations of these groups not only counteract assumptions and attitudes that maintain problems for participants, but offer a "cognitive antidote" that positively facilitates the recovery process (Antze, 1976).

This research, like much of the research today that demonstrates a positive relationship between mental health and religious belief or activity, is conducted with persons predominantly from Christian religious traditions. The Judeo-Christian religious tradition's focus on suffering and coping with adverse life events provides a rich framework for integrating and working through such experiences. It is not appropriate to generalize these findings to other religious traditions.

Cultural competence is an important element in social work practice. Culture is understood as "the way of life followed by a particular group, including their worldview, structures of behavior, perspectives on life, and a concept of the essential nature of the human condition" (Devore & Schlesinger, 1991, p. 4). Clients and practitioners alike see the world through "cultural filters" of values and assumptions. Typically, cultural competence or cultural sensitivity has meant ethnic or racial sensitivity. Religious orientations function, for many persons with a mental illness, as a significant element of their culture. Cultural competence in working with persons with a severe mental illness requires sensitivity and knowledge about a client's religious orientation. For many persons with a severe and persistent mental illness, their religious orientation is the core element of the road to recovery.

Notes

[1] North Presbyterian Church is an informal, diverse, inclusive, 90 member urban church on the north side of Kalamazoo, Michigan. Approximately one half of its parishioners are people with a severe and persistent mental illness. For fifteen years North Church has had a special ministry with and for people with a mental illness. People with a mental illness are represented on all the groups and boards of the church. The church sponsors the Togetherness Group, a weekly activity and enrichment group for people of the church and the community who have a mental illness. For additional information visit North Church's website at: http://www.northchurchpcusakalamazoo.org.

[2] Ministry with Persons with Disabilities of the Catholic Diocese of Kalamazoo seeks to assist individuals and parish to fully include everyone in the life of the church. Activities focused on mental illness include a weekly spirituality sharing group, an annual retreat, information, referral and other assistance to individuals and families, and advocacy with public systems. For additional information visit the Diocese of Kalamazoo's website at: http://www.dioceseofkalamazoo.org.

References

American Psychiatric Association. (2000). *Diagnostic and statistical manual of mental disorders* (4th ed.). Washington, DC.

Antonovsky, A. (1979). *Health, stress, and coping.* San Francisco: Jossey-Bass.

Anthony, W. (1991). Recovery from mental illness: The new vision of services researchers. *Innovations and Research, 1*(1), 13-14.

Anthony, W. (1993). Recovery from mental illness: The guiding vision of the mental health service system in the 1990's. *Psychosocial Rehabilitation Journal, 16*(4), 11-23.

Antze, P. (1976). The role of ideologies in peer psychotherapy organizations: Some theoretical considerations and three case studies. *Journal of Applied Behavioral Science, 12*(3), 323-346.

Brekke, J. & Slade, E. (1998). Schizophrenia. In Williams, J. & Ell, K. (Eds.), *Advances in Mental Health Research, Implications for Practice,* (pp. 157-181). NASW Press.

Bremer, L. (2004). Spirituality as a moderating variable in facilitating the association between coping and social functioning among the severely mentally ill. *Dissertation Abstracts International: Section B: The Sciences and Engineering, 64*(9-B), 4604.

Canda, E., & Furman, F. (1999). *Spiritual diversity and social work practice: The heart of helping.* New York: Free Press.

Corrigan, P., Calabrese, J., Divan, S., Keogh, C., Keck, L., & Mussey, C. (2002). Some recovery processes in mutual-help groups for persons with mental illness; I: Qualitative analysis of program materials and testimonies. *Community Mental Health Journal, 38*(4), 287-301.

Corrigan, P., Faber, D., Rashid, F., & Leary, M. (1999). The construct validity of empowerment among consumers of mental health services. *Schizophrenia Research, 38,* 77-84.

Corrigan, P., & Gorman, A. (1997). Considerations for research on consumer empowerment and psychosocial interventions. *Psychiatric Services, 48*(3), 347-352.

Corrigan, P., McCorkle, B., Schell, B., & Kidder, K. (2003). Religion and spirituality in the lives of people with serious mental illness. *Community Mental Health Journal, 39*(6), 487-499.

Davidson, L., Hoge, M., Godleski, L., Rakfeldt, J., et al. (1996). Hospital or community living? Examining consumer perspectives on deinstitutionalization. *Psychiatric Rehabilitation Journal, 19*(3), 49-58.

Davidson, L. & Strauss, J. (1992). Sense of self in recovery from mental illness. *British Journal of Medical Psychology, 65,* 131-145.

Deegan, P. (1992). The independent living movement and people with psychiatric disabilities: Taking back control over our own lives. *Psychosocial Rehabilitation Journal, 15,* 3-19.

Deegan, P. (1993). Recovering our sense of value after being labeled mentally ill. *Journal of Psychosocial Nursing, 31,* 7-11.

Devore, W. & Schlesinger, E. (1991). *Ethnic-sensitive social work practice* (3rd ed.). New York: Merrill.

Ellis, A. (1973). *A guide to rational living.* N. Hollywood, CA: Wilshire Book Co.

Ellis, A. (1980). Psychotherapy and atheistic values: A response to A.E. Bergin's psychotherapy and religious values. *Journal of Consulting and Clinical Psychology, 48*(5), 635-639.

Emotions anonymous. (1980). Revised Edition. Emotions Anonymous Ltd.

Ethical principles of psychologists and code of conduct. (2002). Retrieved 9/21/06, from: http://www.apa.org/ethics/code2002.html.

Fallot, R. (1998). Spiritual and religious dimensions of mental illness recovery narratives. *New Directions for Mental Health Services, 80*(1), 35-44.

Fallot, R. (2001). Spirituality and religion in psychiatric rehabilitation and recovery from mental illness. *International Review of Psychiatry, 13*(2), 110-116.

Fallot, R. & Harris, M. (2002). The trauma recovery and empowerment model (TREM). Conceptual and practical issues in a group intervention for women. *Community Mental Health Journal, 38*(6), 475-485.

Fallot, R. & Newburn, J. (2000). *A spirituality and trauma recovery group for women with co-occurring disorders.* Washington, DC: Community Connections.

Fitchett, G., Burton, L., & Sivan, A. (1997). The religious needs and resources of psychiatric inpatients. *Journal of Nervous & Mental Disease, 185*(5), 320-326.

Gartner, J., Larson, D., & Allen, G. (1991). Religious commitment and mental health: A review of the empirical literature. *Journal of Psychology and Theology, 19*(1), 6-25.

GROW. (1982). *The program of growth to maturity.* Sydney, Australia: GROW Publications.

Herth, K. (1991). Development and refinement of an instrument to measure hope. *Scholarly Inquiry for Nursing Practice, 5*(1), 39-51.

Idler, E. (1987). Religious involvement and the health of the elderly: Some hypotheses and an initial test. *Social Forces, 66*(1), 226-238.

Johnson, B. (2002). *Objective hope: Assessing the effectiveness of faith-based organizations: A review of the literature.* Philadelphia, PA: Center for Research on Religion and Urban Civil Society.

Koenig, H. (1995). Religion as cognitive schema. *The International Journal for the Psychology of Religion, 5*(1), 31-37.

Koenig, H., McCullough, M., & Larson, D. (2001). *Handbook of religion and health.* New York: Oxford University Press.

Lindgren, K. & Coursey, R. (1995). Spirituality and serious mental illness: A two-part study. *Psychosocial Rehabilitation Journal, 18*(3), 93-111.

McDermott, B. (1995). Development of an instrument for assessing self-efficacy in schizophrenic spectrum disorders. *Journal of Clinical Psychology, 51*(3), 320-331.

Miller, W. (1999). (Ed.), *Integrating spirituality into treatment*. Washington DC: American Psychological Association.

NASW Code of Ethics. (1999). Retrieved September 21, 2006, from http://www.social-workers.org/pubs/code/code.asp.

NASW Standards for Cultural Competence in Social Work Practice. (2001).

Retrieved September 21, 2006, from http://www.socialworkers.org/sections/credentials/ cultural comp.asp.

Neeleman, J. & Lewis, G. (1994). Religious identity and comfort beliefs in three groups of psychiatric patients and a group of medical controls. *The International Journal of Social Psychiatry, 40*(2), 124-134.

Pargament, K. (1997). *The psychology of religion and coping*. New York: The Guilford Press.

Plante, T., & Sherman, A. (2001). Research on faith and health: New approaches to old questions. In Plante, T., & Sherman, A. (Eds.), *Faith and Health: Psychological Perspectives*, (pp. 1-13). New York: New York.

Recovery, Inc. (2006). Retrieved September 21, 2006, from, http://www.recoveryinc.com/ resources.html.

Rogers, S., Chamberlin, J., Ellison, M., & Crean, T. (1997). A consumer-constructed scale to measure empowerment among users of mental health services. *Psychiatric Services, 48*(8), 1042-1047.

Rudnick, A., & Kravetz, S. (2001). The relation of social support-seeking to quality of life in schizophrenia. *The Journal of Nervous and Mental Disease, 189*, 258-262.

Spradley, J. (1979). *The ethnographic interview*. New York: Holt, Rinehart & Winston.

Van Hook, M., Hugen, B., & Aguilar, M. (2001). *Spirituality within religious traditions in social work practice*. Pacific Grove, CA : Brooks/Cole.

Ventis, W. (1995). The relationships between religion and mental health. *Journal of Social Issues, 51*(2), 33-48.

Walsh, J. (1995). The impact of schizophrenia on client's religious beliefs: Implications for families. *Families in Society, 76*(9), 551-558.

Walters, J. & Neugeboren, B. (1995). Collaboration between mental health organizations and religious institutions. *Psychiatric Rehabilitation Journal, 19*(2). 51-57.

Weingarten, R. (1994). The on-going process of recovery. *Psychiatry, 57*, 367-375.

Weingarten, R. (1997). How I've managed chronic mental illness. In Spaniol, L. & Cagne, C. (Eds.), *Psychological and Social Aspects of Psychiatric Disability*, (pp. 123-129). Boston: Boston University Center for Psychiatric Rehabilitation.

Williams, N. (2004). Spirituality and religion in the lives of runaway and homeless youth: Coping with adversity. *Journal of Religion and Spirituality in Social Work, 23*(4), 47-66.

Acknowledgement: I wish to thank Rev. Linda McDonald, North Presbyterian Church, and Ann Sherzer, Director of Ministry with Persons with Disabilities, Diocese of Kalamazoo, along with Becky Herdick, Coordinator for the Togetherness Group, for their support and assistance. Special thanks go to each of the persons who willingly shared with me how their faith supports and sustains their recovery process.

CHAPTER 17

SPIRITUALITY, END-OF-LIFE CARE, AND AGING

Cheryl K. Brandsen

Social workers interested in spirituality, palliative and end-of-life care, and gerontology no doubt find this to be a thought-provoking and demanding moment in the profession.[1] Each of these three areas presently receives much attention in the social work profession and literature.[2] The work is stimulating and energizing, yet difficult and, at times, overwhelming. In this chapter, I will do three things: First, I will identify several challenges social workers face in their efforts to integrate spirituality into end-of-life care for older adults. Second, I will review models of human development, of spirituality, and of end-of-life care with an eye toward understanding the needs and experiences of dying older adults with respect to spirituality. These models of spirituality are congruent with Christian faith. Third, given the challenges Christian social workers face, I will propose a model for practice.

Conceptual and Pragmatic Challenges for Social Work Practitioners

Social workers who take seriously the challenge to address spirituality with aged and dying persons encounter large conceptual and pragmatic difficulties. Conceptual challenges include the heterogeneity of older adults, lack of conceptual models for end-of-life care, and ambiguity about definitions of spirituality and religion. Pragmatic challenges include concerns with delivery of care in nursing homes, hospices, and acute care hospitals.

Heterogeneity of older adults: Conceptually, older adults are not easily defined. Given entitlement criteria attached to Social Security and Medicare policies, we often think of older adults as being about 65 years of age or older. However, there is tremendous heterogeneity of aging with respect to physical and psychological variables. Consequently age tells us little about who is an older adult. When speaking of frail elders, older persons with significant physical and mental health problems, Kaufman (2005) notes that no cultural or normative models exist for slow decline and its concerns and sufferings. In American society, says Kaufman, "there is no narrative about what is good for the patient when the patient is an old person in decline" (1999, 2000, p. 81).

Frameworks for end-of-life care: Delivering quality end-of-life care is hampered by the lack of a conceptual model for what constitutes such care. Singer, Martin, and Kelner (1999) observe that only experts have been included in conceptualizing end-of-life care while models based on patients' perspectives are missing.[3] Furthermore, clarity is lacking about when the dying process begins. Physicians have far less prognostic confidence than the general public realizes, and lack accurate prediction models for the multi-system diseases and declines of older adults. Deaths that have a clear terminal diagnosis, a staged trajectory of dying (such as AIDS or cancer), and an aware and expressive person making complex health care decisions are not typical in later life (Kaufman, 2005; Seale, 1998). Rather, a trajectory of slow and uneven decline shaped by various chronic diseases result in a sense that death will not happen *this time*; another hospitalization and further life-prolonging treatments can always be tried. Thus, until we begin to pay attention to the "living-dying interval," that is "the period of time between the knowledge of one's impending death and death itself" (Engle, 1998, p. 1172), we are without useful practice models for supporting or assisting the dying process when older adults are frail, cognitively impaired, and unable or unwilling to direct treatment decisions.

Defining spirituality: Defining spirituality in a way that is useful to practitioners is also challenging. The health care and social science literature, including social work, does not lack thoughtful deliberations with respect to defining spirituality. Such considerations often contrast spirituality with religion, and to a lesser extent, faith.

For the purposes of this chapter, Canda and Furman's (1999) understanding of religion and spirituality form the basis for our discussion. These social workers have spent much of their professional lives addressing these issues, and their definitions build from and on the work of others. In their review of definitions, Canda and Furman identify six common attributes of spirituality. These include:

1. An essential or holistic quality of a person that is considered inherently valuable or sacred and irreducible.
2. An aspect of a person or group dealing with a search for meaning, moral frameworks, and relationships with others, including ultimate reality.
3. Particular experiences of a transpersonal nature.
4. A developmental process of moving toward a sense of wholeness in oneself and with others.
5. Participation in spiritual support groups that may or may not be formally religious.
6. Engagement in particular beliefs and behaviors, such as prayer or meditation, in a spiritual or religious context (pp. 44–45).

In coming to a working definition of spirituality, Canda and Furman (1999) suggest that spirituality "relates to a universal and fundamental aspect of what it is to be human—to search for a sense of meaning, of purpose, and moral frameworks for relating with self, others, and the ultimate reality... Spirituality may express through religious forms, or it may be independent of them" (p. 37). In contrast, religion is "an institutionalized pattern of beliefs, behaviors, and experiences, oriented toward spiritual concerns, and shared by a community and transmitted over time in traditions" (p. 37).

While these understandings of spirituality and religion underlie the discussion here, it is important to recognize that at the practice level, the clients with whom we work may hold very different understandings of these terms. Thus the challenge for practitioners is not only to arrive at explicit definitions so that further research about the impacts of spirituality and religion can occur, but also to assess carefully and respectfully the multiple meanings clients attach to these terms (Eisenhandler, 2003; McFadden, Brennan & Patrick (2003); Zinnbauer, Pargment, Cole, Rye, et al., 1997).

Nursing home care: In addition to conceptual challenges, social workers also face serious pragmatic difficulties in addressing spirituality with clients. Some of these are related in part to the site of death, and in particular, when sites of death are nursing home facilities, hospice care, or acute care hospitals. With respect to nursing homes, the Omnibus Budget Reconciliation Act of 1987 (OBRA 1987) contained within it nursing home regulations that emerged from a series of nursing home reforms in the 1980s. Among other things, OBRA 1987 mandated the development and use of the Resident Assessment Instrument (RAI) to collect uniform data about each resident for individualized care planning. The RAI includes both the Minimum Data Set (MDS) for resident assessment and the Resident Assessment Protocols (RAPs) for standardized care planning that are triggered by selected MDS items. While in theory, this process makes sense, the RAI has been criticized for several significant shortcomings. The 500-question MDS administered to new residents contains only one question assessing religious needs, and residents' responses to that question do not trigger further formal care planning through the Resident Assessment Protocol (RAP). Thus spiritual needs may well be overlooked in formal care planning even though other studies report that nursing home residents find religion and spiritual care to offer much comfort and assistance in coping (Engle, 1998; Engle, Fox-Hill, & Graney, 1998; Koenig, 1994).

Hospice care: Difficulties in addressing spirituality with Hospice clients are well documented in the professional literature. Hospice practitioners, like social workers in general, are unclear about how to define spiritual care. McGrath (1997) notes that in spite of the centrality of spirituality in hospice ideology, it is the ignored dimension. Individual programs tend to make their own decisions about the role of spirituality (Millison, 1995). Although recognized as an important aspect of patient services in the Medicare code, the federal guidelines for spiritual care are vague and unclear. The regulations do not define what is within the parameters of the requirements made. Specifications such as what spiritual counseling is to address, how it is to be delivered, and how it is to be reimbursed, are not discussed (Babler, 1997).

Additional documented challenges with addressing spirituality in hospice sites include uncertainty about disciplinary domains, lack of knowledge among staff, and lack of clarity about assessment. Although clergy receive the most intentional training in spiritual care, no consensus exists that this domain belongs to clergy alone (Derrikson, 1996; Reese & Brown, 1997; Welk, 1998). With respect to staff knowledge, hospice staff, like many other social workers and health care personnel, report they lack knowledge of how to assess and address spirituality concerns (Canda & Furman, 1999; Hay, 1989; Piles, 1990). Definitional, domain, and knowledge concerns about spirituality result in lack of clarity about meaningful criteria on which to base spiritual assessment (Millison, 1995). No standard spiritual assessment exists except for a lengthy list of over 50 triggers that might indicate the possible existence of a spiritual need. Timing issues are also a concern. Spiritual assessment is emphasized at intake, but no ongoing assessment mechanisms are in place. Furthermore, addressing spiritual care assumes a time period of up to six months, but in reality the median hospice stay is 15 days.

Acute care hospitals: A large body of empirical research documents serious shortcomings in end-of-life care with respect to comfort, communicating with patients and families, honoring preferences for treatment or lack thereof, and basic medical care (Field & Cassell, 1997; Hawkins, Ditto, Danks & Smucker, 2005). The Study to Understand Prognosis and Preferences for Outcomes and Risks of Treatments (SUPPORT), a major investigation into end-of-life care in prestigious teaching hospitals found that pain and physical suffering among dying patients was inadequately assessed and treated; family members reported moderate to severe pain for at least half of the time for 50 percent of patients who died in the hospital. Furthermore, patient preferences for care, including do-not-resuscitate orders, were routinely ignored. Additionally, families incurred devastating financial bills. One-third of families of dying persons reported losing most or all of the family's major source of income, one-third reported losing life savings, and one-fifth of families had to delay or cancel significant personal events, such as a job, an education, or needed medical care (Knaus, Lynn, & Teno, 1995).

Conceptual Models for Social Workers

Given the challenges social workers face in addressing spirituality with older adults in end-of-life care, it is useful to remind ourselves of existing human development models that include older adults, explicit models for understanding spirituality, and models for understanding end-of-life care. From these we glean understanding about the tasks and themes that need to be explored.

Human development theories: Erik Erikson's psychosocial development theory is familiar to most social workers. Focusing on his eighth and final stage of life for person's age 65 and older, Erikson suggests that the last task to be completed is achieving integrity. Erikson defines integrity as certainty about the meaning and order of life, a love of the human ego (not of the self) that demonstrates "some world order and spiritual sense," and an "acceptance of one's one and only life cycle as something that, by necessity, permitted no substitutions" (1950, p. 232). Despair points to a lack of ego integration resulting in fear of death, a rejection of one's life accomplishments and practices, and a feeling that no further time is available for achieving integrity. The central process by which one achieves integrity, says Erikson, is through a process of life review.

Lars Tornstam (1999), in collaboration with Joan Erikson (1997), Erik Erikson's widow, and Erikson himself before death, identifies a ninth stage of development for Erikson's theory. This stage, called gerotranscendence, explores how "aged people face the deterioration of their bodies and faculties" (Erikson, 1997, p. 123). Tornstam describes this stage as a "shift in metaperspective from a materialistic and pragmatic view of the world to a more cosmic and transcendent one, normally accompanied by an increase in life satisfaction" (p. 178). It differs from Erikson's stage of ego integrity in that it is more forward moving and focused on the cosmic or transcendent dimensions of life. These dimensions include a preoccupation with generational interconnections, relations between life and death, reflections on the mystery of life, and may include a decreased interest in material things and a greater need for solitude.

Critiques of these developmental theories abound. Yet their continued utility in the professional literature, in case studies, and as frameworks for research in emotional and cognitive changes as we age suggests that the themes and tasks of achieving integrity, of redefining oneself in the face of decline, of connections with other people and with a higher Being, and of writing a coherent story with our lives requires that we pay attention to these perspectives.

Models for conceptualizing spirituality: In addition to these theories of human development, explicit frameworks for conceptualizing spirituality also exist. Here, several social work-based models are summarized.

Ellor, Netting, and Thibault (1999) present a holistic model—a Whole Person model—for conceptualizing spirituality grounded in what is meaningful to the client (in contrast to a particular theoretical paradigm or personal theology of a given practitioner). This model pays attention to the physical, emotional, social, and spiritual self. Each self can be understood as a separate domain in theory, and perhaps treated separately in practice, but to do so is reductionistic, say the authors. The Whole Person model consists of parallel spheres. The lower sphere constitutes traditional clinical distinctions of emotional, social, and physical domains. The overlay of the spiritual sphere consists of affective, behavioral, and cognitive sub-domains. These sub-domains "overlap and interact in a dynamic interplay which results in the person's unique religious or spiritual identity" (p. 117). In addition, the spiritual sphere is conceptualized as a potentially integrative structure with the sphere of traditional clinical dimensions. The authors affirm that the model is:

> highly dynamic.... The correlation between the various subdimensions of spirituality will be different from one person to the next and within the same individual over time. Like a top spinning on a platter, the spiritual domain can touch other single domains, but most frequently it moves, encompassing some or even all of the several domains in the holistic views of the person (p. 118).

Canda and Furman (1999) present both a holistic model and an operational model for conceptualizing spirituality. The holistic model is conceptualized as three concentric circles. In the center circle, spirituality is understood as the center of a person, "a quality of a human being that is not reducible to any part" (p. 47). The second circle is divided into four quadrants each describing a particular aspect of human beings: biological, psychological, sociological, and spiritual. The outer circle, spirituality as wholeness of the person in relation with all, moves one beyond a sense of personal integrity and wholeness to a transpersonal self—one that is "in relation to other people, other beings, and the ground of being itself" (p. 48).

Canda and Furman's (1999) operational model of spirituality can help support more precise operationalization of concepts for practice and research. They identify six interrelated categories of manifestations: spiritual drives; spiritual experiences; functions of spirituality; spiritual development; contents of spiritual perspectives; and religious expressions in individuals and groups. Operationalization of spirituality here, they claim, "is much less murky" (p.56).

Moving closer to conceptualizations of spirituality and end-of-life care, Dona Reese (formerly Ita, 1995) proposes a causal model of death acceptance using a theoretical framework based on Erik Erikson's work where dying is seen as an additional life stage with its own psychosocial tasks, and spiritual issues are central to these tasks. Reese (1999) defines spirituality as a two-dimensional construct: transcendence in purpose in life and transcendence in sense of connection to an ultimate reality. Each construct raises important issues that dying persons consider. Concerns that illustrate the sense of purpose in life construct include (1) a search for meaning about why one has become ill and the meaning of one's life; (2) death anxiety and fears of the unknown, of suffering, of loneliness, and of extinction; and (3) unfinished business that keeps one from recognizing the positive purposes fulfilled in life and meeting unrealized goals. Concerns that map onto the sense of connection construct include (1) facing one's relationship with God and understanding how God works; (2) isolation and the interpersonal and structural factors that contribute to this as one is dying; and (3) paranormal experiences such as visions of deceased loved ones and religious visions. These are viewed as a connection with an ultimate reality and generally are not disturbing to dying persons.

There are also conceptual models for addressing spirituality at the end-of-life that are less developed, but nevertheless useful in recognizing important themes and tasks in dying. Dunbar, Mueller, and Medina (1998) present a model of psychological and spiritual growth at the end-of-life that includes five components important for growth: reckoning with death, life affirmation, creation of meaning, self-affirmation, and redefining relationships. Derrikson (1996), based on work with hospice patients, suggests four tasks that frame spiritual care: (1) remembering, where patients come to understand the meaning of their lives; (2) reassessing, where patients consider how they have defined themselves and their worth in the world; (3) reconciliation, where patients consider unfinished business with others; and (4) reunion, where patients report visions of deceased loved ones who come to accompany their passing from this world to the spirit world.

From this brief discussion of spirituality models, it is important that the reader remember the following points as we move forward. First, the notion of spirituality is wholistic; it is not an "add-on" but rather foundational to whom we are as unique human beings. Metaphorically, spirituality is akin to roots that nourish a tree, or a network of capillaries that course through our bodies and sustains life. Second and closely related, although not stated as such in the models summarized above, is the idea that spirituality is embodied in human beings. When we suffer, when we are isolated, or when we experience forgiveness and reconciliation with a loved one, for instance, we experience these through our bodies. Third, spirituality is dynamic. It is not something we understand in linear, cause-and-effect terms; rather "the working of spirituality in motion is dynamic, nonlinear, and multilevel" (O'Brien, 1992, p. 4). Fourth, spirituality is understood, experienced, and expressed by human beings in particular and unique ways. Ellor, Netting, and Thibault (1999) are especially clear about this, and recognize that practitioners must find ways to assess clients' unique understandings of spirituality grounded in what is meaningful to clients, not practitioners. Finally, all of these models are compatible with Christianity. Themes of finding purpose and meaning in life, making connections and experiencing a sense of belonging with others and to someone greater than ourselves, and giving and receiving forgiveness are central Biblical themes.

Models for conceptualizing end-of-Life care: Earlier the point was made that delivering quality end-of-life care is hampered by the lack of a conceptual model for what constitutes such care from the perspectives of patients (Singer, Martin, & Kelner, 1999). Working from a developmental perspective, physician Ira Byock (1996) conceptualizes dying as the last stage in a continuum of developmental stages. Like other stages of life, dying has its own "characteristic challenges, or developmental landmarks" that "may develop a sense of completion, satisfaction, and even a sense of mastery within areas of life that are of subjective importance (p. 247). Paying attention to these themes and addressing them as they arise reduce suffering. These developmental landmarks include:

(1) sense of completion with worldly affairs;
(2) sense of completion in relationships with the community;
(3) sense of meaning about one's life (through life review, telling on one's stories, and transmission of knowledge and wisdom);
(4) experience love of self (self-acknowledgement, self-forgiveness);
(5) experiencing love of others and being able to express love and gratitude;
(6) sense of completion in relationship with family and friends;
(7) acceptance of the finality of one's life, including total dependency through finding a connection with some enduring construct;
(8) sense of new self beyond personal loss;
(9) sense of meaning about life in general; and
(10) letting go, including for some surrender to the Transcendent (Staton, Shuy, & Byock, 2001, p. 260).

These developmental landmarks in dying are congruent with developmental tasks in models of human behavior and themes in constructs of spirituality discussed earlier.

How Best to Help: A Model for Practice Congruent with Christian Faith

This brief review highlights that bringing spirituality, end-of-life care, and older adults together as a focus for social work assessment and intervention is complex and multi-layered, mediated broadly by practice settings and related organizational and public policies, culture, the experiences we have, and the meanings we attach to our experiences. Furthermore, the developmental and spiritual themes that are relevant for aging and dying seem to be, for many, all-encompassing, dynamic, and particularistic. Consequently, competent social workers need a practice model that can accommodate such variability and diversity.

Competent, Christian practitioners also require such a practice model. Additionally, they are concerned that the work they do with aging, dying persons is faithful to God. Working from Bouma, Diekema, Langerak, Rottman, and Verhey (1989) in the context of health care, I suggest three guidelines for Christian social workers to keep in mind; these three suggestions have implications for practice models selected by practitioners.

Bouma et al. (1989) suggest that having faith in God the Provider means, in large part, that "God's care is the world's constant companion" (p. 9). When people suffer, as they often do in later life, Christian people respond by being present with those who suffer, thereby assuring them that they do not suffer alone and are not abandoned in their suffering. A caring response to suffering will include competent medical and non-medical care, recognizing that suffering can be greater than physical pain, and may well include spiritual suffering. The practice model Christian social workers use should be one that communicates a willingness to suffer with aged, dying persons.

Also, because God's care is the world's constant companion, we must treasure and preserve the freedom in life. Working from an Augustinian understanding of freedom, Bouma et al. (1989) define freedom not as the option to do one thing one moment and another the next, but rather "the freedom to establish an identity and to maintain integrity" (p. 15). God invites us to establish ourselves in faithfulness to God and there find our freedom. Paradoxically, being free means that some will establish an identity apart from God. God's providence:

> respects and preserves it [freedom] even when that freedom is culpably and paradoxically used against God and its own fulfillment. And faithfulness to God the provider will dispose us to respect and preserve the freedom God gives even when, in terrifying mystery, it denies God's claims and cause (p. 14).

Subsequently, practice models used by Christian practitioners must be ones that, even in old age, assist clients to make choices congruent with identities constructed over a lifetime and preserve integrity.

Finally, what makes life "fundamentally good is caring relationships—relationships with God, with other people, with creation, and with ourselves" (Bouma et. al., 1989, p. 274). These relationships shape our identities, mold our commitments and responsibilities, and allow us to be with others in authentic ways. Subsequently, the practice model used by Christian practitioners must be one that values the importance of relationships in the lives of aged, dying persons.

Social Constructionism

Given what competent, Christian social workers must pay attention to with respect to spirituality and older persons who are dying, social constructionism provides a helpful theoretical framework. As a theoretical perspective, social constructionism questions modernist assumptions that knowledge is gained objectively and mirrors reality. Instead, social constructionism holds that our sense of what is real, and the meanings we attach to our experiences, is constructed in and through interactions with others, and is deeply influenced by the social, political, and historical contexts in which we live our lives (Allen, 1993; De Jong & Berg, 2002; Thayne, 1997; Weick, 1993). We create ways to understand the world, and these interpretations become part of the frameworks that govern everyday practices, seemingly unrecognized as structures that could be changed. Implicit here is the notion that we construct meaning not only as an individual exercise, but also with regard for and to others.

Given developmental tasks and themes of achieving integrity and gerotranscendence, of understanding the role and function of spirituality in one's life, and of negotiating quality end-of-life care, practice models grounded in social constructionism are well-suited to explore intersections between spirituality, aging, and end-of-life care. Together practitioner and client can co-construct the next stage of life, a stage congruent with one's identity over the lifespan, and which maintains one's integrity.

Narrative Practice. Narrative practice models are one example of practice models that emerge from social constructionist frameworks. Narrative methods, borrowed from literary fields, pay attention to life stories, how the story is told (structure), key themes, and ascribed meanings. Mohrman (1995), a physician, notes that "there is much to be learned from the way patients tell their own tales of suffering: What they emphasize, the chronology as they have experienced it, the side events that sound unrelated to us but clearly are not to them, what they fear it all means" (p. 67). Through attentive listening to patient stories, we restore the sufferer to "full personhood," and help them complete their lives in a way that is congruent with their identity and with the way in which they have lived their lives thus far.

Narrative assessment occurs frequently in the social science literature, and includes addressing issues related to end-of-life care, spirituality, and aging.[4] Although practitioners can simply invite clients to tell their stories, certain framing questions can be useful for telling the story. Ellor, Netting, and Thibault (1999) offer the following basic components for completing a spiritual assessment. In summary form, these include:

(1) taking a spiritual life history;
(2) determining how important religion and spirituality are to the client;

(3) determining how spiritually autonomous or institutionally or commu-
nity-connected the client is;

(4) determining whether the client's spiritual and religious beliefs and practices are positively transformative, adaptive, or maladaptive;

(5) determining whether spiritual or religious pathology exists;

(6) determining if and why the client's spirituality is in conflict with the
spirituality of his or her significant others;

(7) determining how spiritual and religious beliefs are translated into or
influence the physical, psychological, interpersonal, societal, and environmental activities of daily life;

(8) determining how spirituality helps or hinders the client when thinking
about or experiencing suffering and dying;

(9) determining what the client's spiritual goals are;

(10) determining what part spirituality plays in the overall therapeutic process;
and

(11) determining whether the provider is the most appropriate source of
intervention or if the client should be referred (p. 93).[5]

Strengths-based, Solution-focused Practice: Strengths-based, solution-
focused (SBSF) practice is also congruent with social constructionist perspectives.[6] Although used in a wide variety of practice settings, its use in working
with dying persons or with respect to spirituality does not appear in the professional literature.

Broadly, SBSF questions help persons create well-formed goals within their
own frames of reference and develop solutions out of existing strengths and
successes (De Jong & Berg, 2002). Solution-focused conversations often begin
with asking persons, "How can I be useful to you?" What follows is often a
description of problems. Rather than exploring the who, what, where, when,
and why of these concerns in detail, solution-focused interviewers respectfully
turn the conversation toward developing goals, listening carefully for who and
what is important to a person, and what that person wants different in his or
her life. A question such as "When things are better for you, what will be different?" invites persons to think about future possibilities and what they would
like different when current problems do not exist.

What follows are excerpts from an initial interview with a hospice client
where SBSF practice is employed. The client did not request this interview;
rather it is part of the intake process, so it cannot be assumed that the client
has any interest in meeting, or has anything that he wishes were different in his
life. The interview was conducted by an MSW; a hospice nurse was also present.
The client was an 80-year old man, Joe, who moved into a hospice residence
about 48 hours before the interview was conducted. Joe's spouse of 53 years
had died two years before, and only one of his seven children lived nearby.
Joe had chronic obstructive pulmonary disease (COPD). He had pneumonia
and lung infections frequently over the past 5 years. Joe lived several months
longer than anticipated after his move into the residential program. Having his

oxygen levels and medications monitored more closely than he was able to do at home alone resulted in an increased level of energy and quality of life. While unknown at the time of the interview, Joe lived for nearly six months in the hospice residence.

Pieces of the initial interview relevant to spirituality are transcribed below. We join the interview after introductions have been made and roles have been explained.

Social Worker (SW): So Joe, we understand from speaking with your doctor that this decision you made to move to the residence was a difficult one for you to make. How are you finding things to be here?

Joe: It was a huge decision. I didn't know what to do. I didn't want to burden my kids. And at first doing this felt like I was walking out on life. I'm not a quitter, and making this decision felt like quitting at first.

SW: I can only imagine how huge a decision this must have been for you, especially if it seems like walking out on life. How did you go about making this decision?

Joe: Mostly I did a lot of thinking. I talked to my doctor a bit. But mostly I sat on my porch and just thought.

SW: So you're a thinker, huh? How is thinking helpful to you? What's different after you spend time thinking?

Joe: (long pause) Well, I just sort things out in my head and things get clearer. I talk to my wife, who passed two years ago, and ask her what she thinks. Of course, she doesn't really answer me... I'm not going crazy and hearing voices... don't worry (laughs). But I imagine what she would say to me.

SW: So when you talked in your head with your wife about what you should do about coming here, what did your wife say?

Joe: She said, "Joe, don't be such a stubborn cuss. You're 80 years old. You had a good life and you worked hard. You took good care of me and the family. You served your country. You were kind and generous, even if you did drink too much and watch a few too many football games. There's no shame in dying, and there's no shame in needing some help now."

SW: Wow, she had lots of good things to say to you... a good husband and father, that you weren't a quitter...

Joe: (nodding and laughing) Yes, I married a smart lady. I made a good choice there.

SW: Sounds like it. It seems like you are really good at facing these big decisions that need to be made in life—who to marry, how to decide about moving here. Have you always been good at that, or did you have to work hard at learning that along the way?

Several things are happening here. First, the practitioner is exploring how Joe made the decision to come to the hospice residence. With COPD, the disease trajectory toward death is not clear cut, and there were several times earlier in Joe's life where he could have chosen to receive hospice care but did not. He has entered the "living–dying interval" discussed earlier (Engle, 1998). Second, the practitioner is working toward identifying strengths and resources. Several emerge quickly: Joe is a thinker; he is not a quitter; he is a hard worker and a good provider; and he has been a good husband. The practitioner compliments him about these. Third, Joe introduced his wife into the discussion. The worker uses this opportunity to ask relationship questions and better understand the context of Joe's life. Recall that relationship questions are central for Christian practitioners to explore, integral to social constructionism, and a key theme in spirituality models summarized earlier. A few minutes later, the conversation returns to how Joe is a thinker.

SW: You mentioned earlier that thinking is helpful to you in making big decisions because it helps you sort things out in your head. You talked with your wife about moving here. Did you talk with anyone else in your head about this?

Joe: I talked to God about this too. I asked him whether things were enough in order for me to have a spot in heaven. God said they could find room for even a defunct Catholic like me. Somewhere I remember someone telling me that you didn't need to be perfect to get into heaven, because heaven is where you get perfected. But I don't know if that's right. . .

SW: So how was this for you when you imagined God's response to whether you should come here now?

Joe: I'm not a feeling type of person. Never have been. But I cried a little bit when I thought about God saying that to me. It made me feel real good. But I don't know if it's true. I wish I knew if it was true. If I knew it was true, then I could go in peace. It's ok with my wife to go. She doesn't see me as a quitter. I'm just not sure about God and whether God would take me in.

SW: So being sure about God is a big thing to you? (Joe nods). Help me understand this. What will be different for you if you were sure about God—if you were sure God had a place in heaven for a defunct Catholic like yourself?

Joe: I could go in peace.

SW: Ah, and if you were going in peace, what would we notice about you that says "Joe is going in peace."

Joe: I would be sleeping better at night. Right now I wake up in a sweat, and get all confused about whether I am living or whether I've died. I'd sleep better.

SW: So you would be sleeping better. What else would we notice that tells us you are going in peace?

Joe: Hmmm (long pause). I would read my Bible again, and maybe even call a priest to talk with me. I don't do either of those things now because I keep thinking I *will read something or the priest will say something that tells me there is no hope for me. So I just avoid those things… you know, what do you people call it, denial?*

SW: So if you were reading your Bible or talking with a priest, we would know then that you were at peace? Anything else?

In these interactions, the practitioner continues to understand the meanings Joe attaches to his move to the residence. Notice how smoothly spirituality issues enter the conversation. In discussing how he made the decision to move, Joe offers some poignant commentary on his relationship to God, and it becomes clear that he is anxious about dying because he is not sure God will accept him into heaven. If he had such assurance, he could "go in peace." Practitioners using Ellor, Netting, and Thibault's (1999) spiritual assessment (summarized earlier) already have useful data for further exploration. The practitioner and Joe are also discussing themes noted earlier in models of spirituality. Notice also how the practitioner works toward preserving Joe's identity. Being a thinker and not being a quitter have emerged as qualities Joe values. The practitioner could have, at several points, offered assurances and given advice. She refrains from doing this, honoring Joe's ability to think this through. Finally, notice how the practitioner uses Joe's words and works at getting as clear an understanding as possible about what she and other staff would notice if Joe were "going in peace." This clear picture of going in peace will be useful in caring for Joe in the way he wishes to be cared for, for figuring out what needs to happen so that Joe can "go in peace," and for evaluation purposes, that is, to what extent Joe did "go in peace."

After a few more minutes of discussion on this subject (including a series of relationship questions about what other people would notice), the practitioner asks a scaling question.[7] Note that the practitioner could have returned to asking whether Joe talked with anyone else about the move to the hospice residence. Instead, she chooses to follow the idea of dying in peace.

SW: Here is an odd question for you, Joe. On a scale of 1 to 10, where one stands for you being in the worst kind of turmoil and fear about where you stand with God, and 10 stands for perfect peace knowing that you stand on solid ground with God, what number would you give yourself today?

Joe: A three, no, a four… a three. Three. Definitely a three.

SW: Ok, definitely a three. Now, with all you are going through—the COPD, moving here to this place—why a three? Why not a one or a two? How did you get to a three?

Joe: (looking puzzled). I don't usually think this way. (laughing). But this is better than all those damn paper and pencil tests you people seem so fond of giving… Well, things were a lot worse right after my wife died. I think she died because taking care of me was such hard work. I went through a really bad spell about 3 or 4 years ago, and could hardly get around. The doctor suggested hospice then, but I couldn't see it. Chrissy took good care of me, never complained, and then one night, she died in her sleep. A heart attack. I couldn't help but think that if I hadn't been such a stubborn cuss, as Chrissy called me, and gone into hospice back then, that she wouldn't be dead. I was feeling really guilty.

SW: That is a lot to live with. How did you cope with all that guilt?

Joe: Lots of thinking again. I knew Chrissy wouldn't want me feeling guilty. She would have said, "Joe, I married you for life, in sickness and health. There's no better way I would want to pass than taking care of you."

SW: It sounds like Chrissy loved you a lot.

Joe: That she did, and I loved her too, but one thing else I do know that Chrissy would tell me to do. Get things straightened out with Kate, our daughter. She's the youngest, always been a devil. Got pregnant at 16, moved out, lived with the bum, kicked him out, raised the baby on her own. She was doing a damn good job of it too, but I was just always too stubborn to be nice to her again. It always bothered Chrissy that I was so mad at Kate. So I knew when Chrissy died, I had to get things right with Kate. For Chrissy's sake, and for my sake, because then I was really scared I might die in my sleep too, and then I was really sure I wasn't right with God because of how I treated Kate. That is why I'm not at a 1 or 2 now.

SW: You are not a 1 or 2 now because you got things right with Kate? (Joe nods). Wow, was that hard for you to do? (Joe nods). How did you do this—get things right with Kate?

Joe: Kate did most of it. A week or so after the funeral, she came over to get a ring that was Chrissy's. I'm not a big talker, but I did say, "Kate, I'm sorry for everything." Kate took over from there. She's got a big heart, which is why she probably got into trouble in the first place. She didn't make me grovel. She said, "I know you're sorry. You're just a stubborn old man."

SW: So you got things worked out?

Joe: Sort of. We didn't ever talk about anything. But I started to act differently— talk to her when she came over—and she started to come over more. Danny, her boy, came over too. We'd watch football together. It's comfortable now. No, it's good, very good now.

SW: This is amazing. You wanted to get things right with Kate and you took the first step. And now things are very good. Some people find apologies very hard. And yet you did it.

Joe: I'm not a quitter. At my core, I'm a family man. It had to happen.

In the process of scaling, the practitioner here learns a great deal about what Joe has already done to lessen his fears about dying and get right with God. Again, returning to themes of importance noted earlier in spirituality (Byock, 1996; Derrikson, 1996; Dunbar, Mueller, & Medina, 1998; Reese, 1999; Smith, 1995) and spiritual assessment (Ellor et al, 1999), several have unfolded. Notice also how certain themes about his life re-merge: a family man, devoted to his wife, and not being a quitter. These qualities, in addition to the importance Joe attaches to his ability to think things through and then act, helps the practitioner understand the way Joe makes sense of his life. Finally, while difficult to grasp from a textual narrative, notice the way in which the practitioner suffers with Joe in re-telling painful experiences of past mistakes. Guilt over Chrissy's death and Joe's treatment of Kate are faced squarely without false assurances; Joe's attempts at making things right are affirmed. The interview continues:

SW: So you are at a 3 right now with knowing where you stand with God, and dying in peace. So Joe, what do you think needs to happen so that you can move up just one step on the scale, to a 4. What would it take to be a 4?

Joe: (long pause). I don't know… I have no idea.

SW: This is a very hard question. Dying in peace and being right with God seems very important to you. Take your time thinking about it. This is very hard.

Joe: This is bigger than I thought. I kind of forgot about how hard it was to take the first step with Kate. But I did, and now I can honestly say that there are no left-overs with any of my kids.

SW: Wow, really? That is amazing. You have a lot of kids, and to have no left-overs, that is something!

Joe: (laughing). It sure is… (long pause). Thinking out loud here, I am almost ready to say that to move to a four, I would read my Bible again, at least parts of it. But I'm not sure.

SW: If you were to decide that reading your Bible would be helpful to you, what will be different for you when you do that? What will you notice?

Joe: It's been a long time since I opened that book—maybe 20 years—except at Easter. I think there are some stories that would give me peace. I remember some of them sort of, or maybe I've just remembered them the way I want to remember them. A son who runs off and spends his father's inheritance and then comes home and the father loves him. Isn't that one? (SW nods). And one of those prophets, talking about how God can't let go of him, just like a husband loves a wife even though she is a prostitute. I think those would give me comfort. Maybe I would sleep better. . .

SW: So maybe you would sleep better if you read some of those stories? How is it that those stories would help you sleep better, do you think?

Joe: Well, if the stories are as I remember, they would give me peace that even though I have been gone from God for a long time, I can still come back. There would be room for me…

SW: So knowing that there is room for you—that brings peace? (Joe nods). On a scale from 1 to 10, Joe, where 1 means there is no way you will ever read the Bible, and 10 stands for I will do it as soon as you leave me alone (Joe laughs), how likely are you to decide that reading your Bible would be a good thing for you?

Joe: I am an 8.

SW: Oh my, an 8. That is very high—almost a 10. What tells you are an 8?

Joe: I don't know. Thinking about Chrissy dying and how I got through that guilt, and thinking about Kate and how we got things right after lots of ugly years. . . makes me think I can do this thing too. It doesn't seem so big right now, to pick up that Book and read it, or at least parts of it. But I need to think about it more. (Joe is getting tired. The nurse signals it would be best to stop.)

SW: Of course you do. You are a thinker, and from what you are telling me today, the decisions you make when you think them through carefully are wise and hard decisions. You don't take the easy way out. You thought hard about coming to this hospice. You thought hard about how to deal with your guilt when Chrissy died. You thought hard about getting right with Kate. And probably lots of other things in your life. And now you are thinking very hard about this big thing of getting right with God and dying in peace. So I would like for you keep thinking hard about this very big thing. (Joe nods). And if it is ok with you, I would like to talk with you again to hear about what you are thinking.

Joe: That's good. Come back.

SW: OK, when would you like me to stop by again?

Joe: Tomorrow?

SW: Tomorrow it is.

In this set of interactions, the practitioner and Joe begin to move toward figuring out what it would take for Joe to get right with God and die in peace. From a practice perspective, an interesting shift occurs when Joe thinks about this question. Earlier he stated that reading his Bible would be an indicator that he is dying in peace. Here he identifies reading his Bible as the necessary step to move from a three to a four; it now becomes a means to dying in peace. Notice too how earlier discussion of how he faced difficult decisions gives him encouragement to do something that he is very much afraid to do, and which in fact he has avoided for a number of years. The conversation with Joe ends with the practitioner giving Joe modified "end-of-session" feedback. The worker compliments previous difficult decisions that Joe has made, offers a bridging statement congruent with Joe's perception of himself as a thinker, and gives an assignment that Joe has already identified as being congruent with the thinker that he is. With respect to spiritual assessment, Joe is discussing concerns about "left-over" business with loved ones, and also his large fears about once again reading the Bible.

This interview in its entirety lasted about 40 minutes, ending because of Joe's fatigue. Clearly not all issues related to spirituality were addressed here. Several good things happened here, however. Joe had the opportunity to tell part of his story in a way that made sense to him. He moved easily between physical concerns (not sleeping), social and psychological concerns (guilt and relationship with Kate), and spiritual concerns (dying in peace and being right with God). His ability to figure out how best to deal with spiritual concerns was affirmed by remembering how he faced difficult decisions in the past, and was done in a way that respected his way of working and the way in which he defined himself (being a thinker).

Subsequent conversations with Joe using SBSF interviewing continued until his death. On difficult days, coping questions uncovered a number of interventions staff could use that would be helpful to Joe: sitting on the porch and watching the birds and squirrels; listening to music, including hymns he learned as a child; sharing a blueberry pie with Kate and Danny; looking forward to and being able to witness a great-grandchild's first communion (in tandem with going to Mass for the first time in more than 20 years); watching football on television; being outdoors in his wheelchair with the help of his children; and reading or having someone read his Bible to him.

Conclusion

A practice model drawing from narrative and SBSF practice, grounded in social constructionism, offers the Christian practitioner a way, first of all, to embody God's care and suffer with those who suffer. This model is sufficiently flexible and broad to bring together, rather than reduce, the complexities of human experience and emotion over the course of a life. Elders can tell their stories in a way fitting to them and in doing so, work toward maintaining both identity and integrity. Second, this model offers Christian practitioners a way to embody the notion of treasuring and preserving freedom. This model is persistent in its efforts to be respectful toward and affirming of clients' capacities to make decisions, or write the next chapter, in a manner that maintains integrity and preserves identities constructed over a life time. Yet is does not let just "anything go." SBSF interviewing, for instance, offers practitioners a way to affirm the importance of community in shaping who we are and become. The model, particularly through the use of relationship questions, is sufficiently inclusive to allow connections with significant others, who help shape, challenge, confront, and sustain our lives with meaning.

Notes

[1] For ease of communication, I use the term "end-of-life" care in this paper. I mean for it to include the care one thinks of when someone is given a terminal diagnosis and also palliative care, that is, symptom relief or comfort care and psychosocial care earlier in the trajectory of expected death.

[2] I point to just a few examples. Attention to aging in social work education has received a large boost the John A Harford Foundation. These monies have funded the Council on Social Work's National Center for Geronotological Social Work Education through the Gero-Ed Center. The role of social work in end-of-life care is being re-defined as evidenced by the Social Work Summit on End-of-Life and Palliative Care in March 2002 (Stoesen, 2002) and various funding initiatives such as the Robert Wood Johnson State-Community Partnership grants and the Project on Death in America. Terry Altilio, social worker at Beth Israel Medical Center, began the Social Work Network in Palliative and End of Life Care listserv (an outcome of the Project on Death in America). This is a lively and useful venue for social workers to network and discuss multidimensional issues related to palliative and end of life care. *The Journal of Social Work in End-of-Life*

and Palliative Care, edited by Ellen Csikai, is the first of its kind in social work and is dedicated to publishing empirical and practice-related articles for social workers.

   [3] Field and Cassell, 1997.

   [4] For examples, see Black 1999; Fallot, 1998; Kaufman, 2005; Zlatin 1995.

   [5] For examples of other spiritual assessments compatible with narrative social work practice, see Boyd, 1998; Canda and Furman, 1999; Hodge, 2001a; Hodge 2001b.

   [6] For a helpful discussion of social constructionism, solution-focused interviewing, and the intersection between the two, see Berg and De Jong, 1996. To sum, social constructionism and solution-focused interviewing strategies both posit the social construction of reality and emphasize that change occurs through the discovery of new meanings perceptions of others.

   [7] Scaling questions assess persons' perceptions of many things, including "self-esteem, pre-session change, self-confidence, investment in change, willingness to work hard to bring about desired changes, prioritizing of problems to be solved, perception of hopefulness, and evaluation of progress" (Berg, 1994, pp. 102 –103; cited in DeJong and Berg, 2002, p. 108). Persons are asked to put their observations on a scale from one to ten, where one stands for the worst possible scenario and ten represents the best possible scenario.

References

Allen, J. (1993). The constructivist paradigm: values and ethics. In J. Laird, (Ed.) *Revisioning social work education: A social constructionist approach*. New York: Haworth Press.

Babler, J. E. (1997). A comparison of spiritual care provided by hospice social workers, nurses, and spiritual care professionals. *The Hospice Journal*, 12 (4), 15 – 27.

Berg, I. K. & De Jong, P. (1996). Solution-building conversations: Co-constructing a sense of competence with clients. *Families in Society*, 77, 376 – 391.

Black, H. K. (1999). Life as gift: Spiritual narratives of elderly African-American women living in poverty. *Journal of Aging Studies*, 13 (4), 441 – 455.

Bouma, H., Diekema, D., Langerak, E., Rottman, T., & Verhey, A. (1989). *Christian faith, health, and medical practice*. Grand Rapids, MI: William B. Eerdmans Publishing Company.

Boyd, T. A. (1998). Spiritually sensitive assessment tools for social work practice. In B. Hugen (Ed.) *Christianity and social work: Readings on faith and social work practice*. Botsford, CT: NACSW.

Byock, I. (1996). The nature of suffering and the nature of opportunity at the end of life. *Clinics in Geriatric Medicine*, 12 (2), 237 – 252.

Canda, E. R. & Furman, L. D. (1999). *Spiritual diversity in social work practice: The heart of helping*. New York: The Free Press.

De Jong, P. & Berg, I. K. (2002). *Interviewing for solutions*, 2/e. Pacific Grove, CA: Wadsworth Thomson Learning.

Derrikson, B. S. (1996). The spiritual work of the dying: A framework and case studies. *The Hospice Journal*, 11 (2), 11 – 30.

Dunbar, H. T., Mueller, C.W. & Medina, C. (1998). Psychological and spiritual growth in women living with HIV. *Social Work*, 43 (2), 144 – 154.

Eisenhandler, S. (2003). K eeping the Faith in Later Life. New York: Springer Publishing Company.

Ellor, J. W., Netting, F. E., & Thibault, J. (1999). *Religious and spiritual aspects of human service practice*. Columbia, South Carolina: University of South Carolina Press.

Emmanuel, E. J. & Emmanuel, L. L. (1998). The promise of a good death. *Lancet*, 351 (supplement II), 21 –29.

Engle, V. Care of the living, care of the dying: Reconceptualizing nursing home care. *Journal of the American Geriatric Society*, 46, 1172 – 1174.

Engle, V. F., Fox-Hill, E., & Graney, M. J. (1998). The experience of living-dying in a nursing home: Self-reports of black and white older adults. *Journal of the American Geriatric Society*, 46, 1091 – 1096.

Erikson, E. (1950). *Childhood and society*. New York: W. W. Norton.

Erikson, J. (1997). *The life-cycle completed: Extended version*. New York: W.W. Norton.

Fallot, R. D. (1998). Spiritual and religious dimensions of mental illness recovery narratives. *New directions for mental health services*, 80, 35 – 44.

Field, M. J. & Cassell, C. K. (1997). *Approaching death: Improving care at the end of life*. Institute of Medicine, Committee on Care at the End of Life. Washington, D.C: National Academy Press.

Hawkins, N. A., Ditto, P. H., Danks, J. H., and Smucker, W. D. (2005). Micromanaging death: Process preferences, values, and goals in end-of-life medical decision making. The Gerontologist, 45 (1), 107-117.

Hay, M. W. (1989, September/October). Principles in building spiritual assessment tools. *The American Journal of Hospice Care*, 25 – 31.

Hodge, D.R. (2001a). Spiritual assessment: A review of major qualitative methods and new framework for assessing spirituality. *Social Work*, 46 (3), 203 – 214.

Hodge, D. R. (2001b). Spiritual genograms. A generational approach to assessing spirituality. *Families in Society*, 82, 1, 35 – 48.

Ita, D. J. (1995). Testing of a causal model: acceptance of death in hospice patients. *Omega*, 32 (2), 81 – 92.

Kaufman, S. R. (1999/2000). The clash of meanings: medical narrative and biographical story at life's end. *Generations*, 23 (4), 77 – 82.

Kaufman, S. R. (2005). *And a time to die: How American hospitals shape the end of life*. New York: Scribner.

Knaus, W.A., Lynn, J., & Teno, J. (1995). A controlled trial to improve care for seriously ill hospitalized patients. *Journal of the American Medical Association*, 274 (20), 1591 – 1598.

Koenig, H. G. (1994). *Aging and God: Spiritual pathways to mental health in midlife and later years*. New York: Haworth Pastoral Press.

McFadden, S., Brennan, M., and Patrick, J. H. eds. (2003). New Directions in the Study of Late Life Religiousness and Spirituality. Binghamton, N.Y: Haworth Press.

McGrath, P. (1997). Putting spirituality on the agenda: Hospice research findings on the 'ignored' dimension. *The Hospice Journal*, 12 (4), 1 – 12.

Measuring quality of care at the end of life: A statement of principles. (1997). *Journal of the American Geriatric Society*, 45, 526 – 527.

Millison, M. B. (1995). A review of the research on spiritual care and hospice. *The Hospice Journal*, 10 (4), 3 – 19.

Mohrman, M. E. (1995). *Medicine as ministry*. Cleveland, Ohio: The Pilgrim Press.

Neill, C. M. & Kahn, A. S. (1999). The role of personal spirituality and religious social activity on the life satisfaction of older widowed women. *Sex Roles*, 40 (3/4), 319 – 329.

O'Brien, P. J. (1992). Social work and spirituality: Clarifying the concept for practice. *Spirituality and Social Work Journal*, 3 (1), 2 – 5.

Piles, C. L. (1990). Providing spiritual care. *Nurse Educator*, 15 (1), 36 – 41.

296 Cheryl K. Brandsen

Reese, D., J. (1999). Spirituality conceptualized as purpose in life and sense of connection: major issues and counseling approaches with terminal illness. *Healing Ministry*, 6 (3), 101 – 108.

Reese, D. J. & Brown, D. R. (1997). Psychosocial and spiritual care in Hospice: Differences between nursing, social work, and clergy. *The Hospice Journal*, 12 (1), 29 – 41.

Seale, C. (1998). *Constructing death: the sociology of dying and bereavement.* Cambridge: Cambridge University Press.

Singer, P. A., Martin, D. K., & Kelner, M. (1999). Quality end-of-life care: Patients' perspectives. *Journal of the American Medical Association*, 281 (2), 163 – 168.

Smith, E. (1995). Addressing the psychospiritual distress of death as a reality: A transpersonal approach. *Social Work,* 40 (3), 402 – 413.

Staton, J., Shuy, R., & Byock, I. (2001). *A few months to live: Different paths to life's end.* Washington, D.C: Georgetown University Press.

Stoesen, L. (2002). Role in end-of-life care examined. *NASW News*, 47 (5), 4.

Thayne, T. R. (1997). Opening space for clients' religious and spiritual values in therapy: A social constructionist perspective. *Journal of Family Social Work*, 2 (4), 13 –23.

Tornstam, L. (1999). Late-life transcendence: A new developmental perspective on aging. In Thomas, L. E. & Eisenhandler, S. A. (Eds.) *Religion, belief, and spirituality in later life.* New York: Springer Publishing Company.

Weick, A. (1993). Reconstructing social work education. In J. Laird, (Ed.) *Revisioning social work education: A social constructionist approach.* New York: Haworth Press.

Weick, A. (1999). Guilty knowledge. *Families in Society*, 80, 327 – 332.

Zinnbauer, B. J., Pargament, K. I., Cole, B., Rye, M. S., Butter, E. M., Belavich, T. G., Hipp, K. M., Scott, A. B., & Kadar, J. L. (1997). Religion and spirituality: Unfuzzying the fuzzy. *Journal for the Scientific Study of Religion*, 36 (4), 549 – 564.

Zlatin, D. M. (1995). Life themes: A method to understand terminal illness. *Omega*, 31 (3), 189 – 205.

Further Resources

Angell, G. B., Dennis, B. G., & Dumain, L. E. (1998). Spirituality, resilience, and narrative: Coping with parental death. *Families in Society*, 79 (6), 615 – 630.

Armer, J. M. & Conn, V. S. (2001). Exploration of spirituality and health among diverse rural elderly individuals. *Journal of Gerontological Nursing*, 27 (6), 28 –37.

Brooks, S. (1996). What's wrong with the MDS (Minimum Data Set)? *Contemporary Long Term Care*, 8, 18 – 25.

Bullis, R. K. (1996). *Spirituality in social work practice.* Philadelphia, PA: Taylor and Francis.

Cantwell, P., & Holmes, S. (1994). Social construction: A paradigm shift for systemic therapy and training. *The Australian and New Zealand Journal of Family Therapy*, 15, 17 – 26.

Carr, E. W. & Morris, T. (1996). Spirituality and patients with advanced cancer: A social work response. *Journal of Psychosocial Oncology*, 14 (1), 71 – 80.

Carrol, M. M. (1998). Social work's conceptualization of spirituality. In E. R. Canda, (Ed.) *Spirituality in social work: New directions.* Binghampton, NY: Haworth Pastoral Press.

Csikai, Ellen L. and Chaitin, E. (2006). Ethics in End-of-Life Decisions in Social Work Practice. Chicago: LyceumBooks, Inc.

Derezotes, D. S. (1995). Spirituality and religiosity: Neglected factors in social work practice. *Arete*, 20 (1), 1 – 15.

Derezotes, D. S. & Evans, K. E. (1995). Spirituality and religiosity and practice: In-depth interviews of social work practitioners. *Social Thought*, 18 (1), 39 – 56.

De Vries, P. (1984). *Slouching towards Kalamazoo*. New York: Penguin Books.

Erikson, E. (1982). *The life-cycle completed*. New York: W.W. Norton.

Fowler, J. W. (1981). *Stages of faith*. San Francisco: Harper and Row Publishers.

Franklin, C. & Jordan, C. (1995). Qualitative assessment: A methodological review. *Families in Society*, 76, 281 – 295.

Fry, P. S. (2000). Religious involvement, spirituality and personal meaning for life: existential predictors of psychological wellbeing in community-residing and institutional care elders. *Aging and Mental Health*, 4 (4), 375 – 387.

Graney, M. J. & Engle, V. F. (2000). Stability of performance of activities of daily living using the MDS. *The Gerontologist*, 40, 582 – 586.

Hanesbo, G. & Kihlgren, M. (2000). Patient life stories and current situation as told by carers in nursing home wards. *Clinical Nursing Research*, 9, 260 – 279.

Ingersoll, R. E. (1994). Spirituality, religion, and counseling: Dimensions and relationships. *Counseling and Values*, 38, 98 – 111.

Koenig, H. G. (1999). The healing power of faith. *Annals of Long-Term Care*, 7 (10), 381 – 384.

Koenig, H. G., George, L. K., & Siegler, I. C. (1988). The use of religion and other emotional-regulating coping strategies among older adults. *The Gerontologist*, 28 (3), 303 – 310.

Levin, J. S. (1994). *Religion in aging and health: Theoretical foundations and methodological frontiers*. Thousand Oaks, CA: Sage Publications, Inc.

MacKinlay, E., Ellor, J.W., and Pickard, S., eds. (2001). Aging, Spirituality, and Pastoral Care: A Multi-National Perspective. Binghamton, NY: 2001.

Kimble, M. A., McFadden, S. H. and Park, M. (2003). Aging, Spirituality, and Religion: A Handbook, vol.2. Minneapolis: Augsburg Fortress Press.

Neill, C. M. & Kahn, A. S. (1999). The role of personal spirituality and religious social activity on the life satisfaction of older widowed women. *Sex Roles*, 40 (3/4), 319 – 329.

Ouslander, J. G. (1994). Maximizing the Minimum Data Set. *Journal of the American Geriatrics Society*, 42, 1212 – 1213.

Ouslander, J. G. (1997). The Resident Assessment Instrument (RAI): Promises and pitfalls. *Journal of the American Geriatrics Society*, 45, 975 – 976.

Ramsey, J. L. & Blieszner, R. (1999). *Spiritual resiliency in older women: Models of strength for challenges through the life span*. Thousand Oaks, CA: Sage.

Schoenbeck, Sue L. (September 1994). Called to care: Addressing the spiritual needs of patients. *The Journal of Practical Nursing*, 19 – 23.

Sheridan, M. J. & Bullis, R. K. (1991). Practitioners' views on religion and spirituality. *Spirituality and Social Work Journal*, 2 (2), 2 – 10.

Sherwood, D. (1998). Spiritual assessment as a normal part of social work practice: Power to heal and power to harm. *Social Work and Christianity*, 25 (2), 80 – 99.

Simmons, H. C. (1998). Spirituality and community in the last stage of life. *Journal of Gerontological Social Work*, 29 (2/3), 73 – 92.

Stuckey, J. C. (2001). Blessed assurance: The role of religion and spirituality in Alzheimer's disease caregiving and other significant life events. *Journal of Aging Studies*, 15 (1).

Teresi, J. A. & Holmes, D. (1992). Should MDS data be used for research? *The Gerontologist*, 32, 148 – 149.

Thomas, L. E. & Eisenhandler, S. A. (Eds.). *Religion, belief, and spirituality in later life.* New York: Springer Publishing Company.

Van Hook, M., Hugen, B., & Aguilar, M., (Eds.) (2001). *Spirituality within religious traditions in social work practice.* Pacific Grove, CA: Brooks/Cole Thomson Learning.

Wink, Paul. (1999). Addressing end-of-life issues: Spirituality and inner life. *Generations,* 23 (1), 75 – 80.

Wuthnow, Robert. (1998). *After heaven: Spirituality in America since the 1950s.* Los Angeles: University of California Press.

CHAPTER 18

CHRISTIANITY IN CHILD WELFARE PRACTICE [1]

Jill Mikula and Gary R. Anderson

Christianity has impacted formal child welfare practice since Western society began to recognize the need for a system of child protection (Garland, 1994). Whether through the orphanages and asylums administered by various Christian (and other) religious faith communities in the late 1800's, or the current resurgence of social work service provision through faith-based organizations, Christian principles put into action have helped to shape the landscape of child welfare practice. Indeed, as one considers the role of Christianity in child welfare, the current local Catholic Charities, Baptist Children's Homes, or Lutheran Social Services organizations seem the most obvious examples. But the manifold expressions of Christianity are far more deeply interwoven with child welfare. How for example, does the identified religious orientation of an organization affect its relationship with its community? How does faith impact the nonreligious foster child placed with devoutly religious foster parents? How does a social worker's faith impact his or her well-being when feeling the daily strain of the work? How do Christian principles guide the social services organization charged with balancing the state and federal guidelines with a faith-based mission statement? And how does this affect the steps a nation has taken to guide its government toward a balance of public and private responsibility for the care and well being of its children?

In this chapter we examine the history of child welfare as well as the impact of Christian faith, religious practices, and institutions on child welfare organizations, children in the child welfare system, parents and care providers in the child welfare system and child welfare social workers, including contextual considerations related to community, state, and federal policy. We will place special emphasis on the role of Christianity in foster care. We will review some tensions between child welfare and Christianity, and close with a vision for the positive role of Christianity in child welfare practice.

First, a few clarifications should be made. For the purposes of this chapter, *Christian organizations* may refer to churches, dioceses, denominational associations, outreach services, agencies, in other words, any formal, organized service provider, or network of service providers designed to strengthen or promote the well being of children and families within the context of a faith tradition. *Christian religious practices* will refer to the religious habits and actions of Christians as expressed in both worship and daily activity. These practices may include prayer, Bible study, church attendance, communion, etc. *Christian faith* refers to an individual's identified belief in the basic tenets of Christianity, or self-identification as a Christian.

It is important to note that the terms listed above are not considered exclusive of each other; for some, it naturally follows that self-identification as a Christian necessitates engagement in Christian religious practices and participation in Christian organizations. As we explore the various levels upon which Christianity impacts child welfare, however, such distinctions become important. For example, a faith-based organization which forms its mission statement based on Christian teachings of "love thy neighbor" but otherwise delivers religion-neutral services may take very different approaches to integrating Christianity into service provision than a faith-based organization which actively proselytizes and requires certain religious practices.

A Brief History of Child Welfare

The beginning of child welfare in the early days of the United States is found primarily in adult-supervised congregate care facilities (orphanages) for abandoned children or those without living parents. Rudimentary attempts at foster/adoptive placement began with Charles Loring Brace's Orphan Trains, developed as a means of placing urban children with rural farm families of the West and Midwest who would potentially adopt them (Anderson & Mikula, 2002; Cook, 1995). By 1873, a child protection system had begun to develop in New York City, spurred by the controversial case of an abused child, Mary Ellen. It was not until the mid-1900's that state agencies began providing child protection services (Anderson & Mikula, 2002; Costin, 1991).

The early 1900s saw a shift away from orphanages to volunteer foster families in an effort to provide a more home-like environment for children. Since that time, foster care has remained the primary form of out-of-home placement for abused and neglected children. Research, however, has shown that long placements out-of-home and frequent moves between families have affected children negatively, leading to "drift" (Anderson & Mikula, 2002). As debate and professional opinion shifted throughout subsequent decades, legislation such as the federal Permanency Planning Law of 1980 (PL96-272) and the Adoption and Safe Families Act (ASFA) of 1997 was enacted with the intent of strengthening the system's focus on locating and maintaining permanent placement and ultimately adoption for children placed out-of-home. These programming emphases give evidence of the dilemma of all child welfare policy: that of finding a balance between preserving the biological family as much as possible, yet serving the best interests of children by finding an alternative permanent home placement within a relatively short timeframe.

Today, child welfare services include family support services, child maltreatment prevention programs, family preservation services, crisis nurseries and respite care, emergency shelters, foster care, group homes, residential treatment facilities, and adoption services. Among these, hundreds of private, faith-based organizations provide programming, funded at community, state, and federal levels (Anderson & Mikula, 2002). And while each organization may conform to program standards established in the public sphere, each brings its own perspective, mission statement, and Christian-based values that provide the mandate and justification for the support and protection of children and families.

Role of Faith in Child Welfare Organizations

Modern Christian social services organizations abound, and among the most recognizable are the child welfare organizations associated with foster care, adoption, and supportive services to children and families. Christian denominations and nondenominational Christian organizations administer large networks of national and international social organizations. Notable are the (Roman) Catholic Charities, Lutheran Child and Family Services, Lutheran Social Services, Baptist's Children's Home, and the nondenominational Bethany Christian Services. Other examples of Christian organizations include Christian faith-based shelter services, child care programs, and health/clinic services.

While some organizations maintain a "name only" approach to integration of Christian religious practices into their organizational structure, some may strongly encourage their employees to adhere to Christian religious practices or make statements of Christian faith. Still others directly address Christian religious practices and encourage Christian faith in their services, whether through counseling sessions, religious outreach services, or mandating that consumers engage in Christian practices in exchange for concrete items, shelter, etc. Such requirements are far less likely if the organization is a grantee of state-funded programs, (such as foster care or family preservation programs), but the organization's right to retain its religious personality is protected. The Clinton-era Personal Responsibility and Work Opportunity Reconciliation Act (PROWRA) of 1996 contained a "charitable choice" provision, requiring that "states treat religious organizations as any other non-government provider when contracting for services funded under this legislation," and further specified that the religious identity of such an organization could be maintained, so long as consumers retained their own religious freedom (Pipes & Ebaugh, 2002). In practice, this legislation has been applied primarily to general welfare services. While it was intended to apply to child welfare organizations, this has not yet fully developed. Given the range of adherence to general or specific Christian religious practices among organizations, it is the consumer who must, at times, determine in advance his or her comfort level with seeking assistance from an organization whose practices or requirements are as-yet unknown.

People of faith have different perceptions of the role of faith in a social service organization. In fact, evidence suggests that the religious orientation of an organization may override its reputation of quality when being considered by members of the clergy as a place to refer churchgoers in need (Collett et al., 2006). When clergy were asked whether they would refer an individual to an organization of unknown quality or an organization of high quality, 100% of respondents chose the organization of high quality. But when the organization of unknown quality was identified as a religious organization, 28% of respondents chose the religious organization over the organization that they knew to be of high quality. More surprising, however, were the results when an organization of high quality was assigned a religious orientation versus an organization of unknown quality. Seventeen percent of clergy stated they would avoid the religious organization, *despite* knowing it was of high quality. Follow up interviews suggested that their reasoning included a discomfort with the practices of some religious organizations, such as openly proselytizing to clients or promoting religious beliefs that could potentially differ from the clergy member's (Collett et al., 2006). Wuthnow, Hackett, and Yang Hsu (2004), in examining client perceptions about various organization types found that mean effectiveness and trustworthiness scores are higher for faith-based organizations than they are for non-sectarian organizations or government agencies, though evidence did not suggest that the faith-based organizations were actually more effective. In practice, while a faith-based organization may have formed their mission around universal service provision without religious instruction or proselytizing, the perception by a potential client that these components *might* be included may still prevent services being provided. Faith—even perceptions of faith—makes a difference.

Children in the Child Welfare System

What, then, of the children served by child welfare agencies? How does Christianity impact the experiences of a child moving through the child welfare service delivery system? The experiences of the child, placed out-of-home through the foster care system, with Christianity via biological parents, foster parents, and outward religious practices are explored later in this chapter. Here, however, we examine the nature of children's inner spirituality and faith, and the factors which affect it.

There exists in the literature a difference of opinion regarding the spiritual nature of children, specifically, whether children's spirituality exists in stages similar to development in other areas, or whether it is 'whole' in childhood just as it is in adulthood. Erikson believed that childhood attention to "existential concerns" is unique only to some individuals, who later develop into deeply spiritual beings (citing examples such as Martin Luther or Mohandas Ghandi) (Robbins et al, 1998). James Fowler outlined stages of faith throughout the human lifespan. These stages include in childhood, *primal faith* in infancy (in which the presence or absence of nurturance affects the child's trust in the universe and in God), *intuitive-projective faith* in early childhood (in which "imaginative fantasy about the mysterious" blends with instruction and modeling from adults), *mythical-literal faith* during middle childhood (in which the child's beliefs and understanding of "stories, morals and values" are based on the child's community) and *synthetic-conventional faith* in adolescence (in which the meaning of life and relationships help to shape one's sense of identity) (Robbins et al., 1998). Bosacki and Ota (2000) (citing various studies), observed that, while some researchers view preadolescents as "innately spiritual and self aware," others point to concern of a spiritual "numbness" suggested by observed apathy, boredom, and more alarmingly, school and youth violence. Bosacki and Ota, however, understood spirituality in children not as an unfinished shadow of adult spirituality, but rather as being whole in and of itself in childhood, being in a state of constant growth and development, and being deeply important to the child's overall development. Ota interviewed 135 9-11 year olds over a two year period regarding their worldviews and the role of "religious education," and he shared resulting narratives in which preadolescents not only identified themselves as believers in Jesus, but demonstrated conceptual understanding of religious tolerance as well. Bosacki and Ota challenged adults to actually listen to the voices of children regarding their worldviews, understanding of self, and understanding of spirituality, rather than presuming knowledge of childhood spirituality based solely on developmental stages similar to those described above (Bosacki & Ota, 2000).

Bosacki and Ota are not alone in their call for children's voices to be heard concerning their religious or spiritual selves. As cited by Scott (2003), "the United Nations Convention on the Rights of the Child (UNCRC) (1991) and the Association for Child and Youth Care Practice's document: *Competencies for Professional Child and Youth Work Practitioners* (Mattingly & Stuart, 2001) indicate that spiritual development is a factor in children's lives," with the UNCRC specifically identifying such as a "category of human development and health worthy of rights protection...." In other words, children have the right to have their spiritual and religious beliefs protected from forced alteration or negative consequences. The UNCRC specifically differentiates religion as "a matter of mind, belief, and practice" and spirituality as "an aspect of human development and overall health." (Scott, 2003).

The effects of religion and spirituality in a child's sense of self continue into adulthood. While one study suggests that religious practices as a child are not a predictor of continued church involvement as an adult, *personal* spirituality (defined by the authors as attending a prayer meeting or Bible study, reading the Bible, listening to Christian programming or reading a religious book other than the Bible) was affected by experiences during one's childhood (O'Connor, Hoge, & Alexander, 2002). In addition, "(1) the culture of the denomination in which the person was raised, including its teaching and habits; and (2) the amount of involvement in church youth programs" had the "most long-lasting effects on the personal adult religious involvement" of the youth (O'Connor, Hoge, & Alexander, 2002). While the study was limited by its longitudinal nature (not all adults who participated as youth could be contacted), and its primary focus on middle class youth in the suburbs of Washington DC (O'Connor, Hoge, & Alexander, 2002), it brings to bear a question directly related to child welfare practice: How critical is the role of religion when determining placement of children in foster, kinship, or adoptive homes? Literature clearly indicates that religion and spirituality in children has a lifelong effect.

Parents and Care Providers in the Child Welfare System

The role of Christianity in parenting and other forms of child care provision is complex. Christianity in this sphere ranges from the impact of the parent or care provider's personal faith on his or her resiliency during times of parenting difficulty to the impact of Christian religious practices on the parent, child, and family.

It is understandably difficult to measure the impact of Christian faith on parents in the child welfare system, largely because faith can only be quantified by measurable behaviors or through subjective self-analysis of how strong one's faith is. One study attempted to determine whether stronger Christian or Mormon faith in fathers related to higher levels of parental involvement as compared to "fathers for whom faith is not central." No significant relationship was found, although there was a "marginally significant correlation between being a Mormon and being an involved father." [2] In another study, 20% of grandparents struggling to raise grandchildren reported that religious faith was a coping strategy, including "prayer and meditation" which led to "inner strength and direction in times of trouble" (Waldrop & Weber, 2001). In their examination of spirituality and religion in preadolescents, Bosacki and Ota (2000) cited one study that suggests that parental religion and spirituality "contribute to substantial variation in adult reaction to and interpretation of childhood fantasy activities." A fourth study found that high levels of religious fundamentalism among college students were associated with a preference that their (in some cases, future hypothetical) children display obedience rather than displaying autonomy. The second part of the same study found that high levels of fundamentalist religious orientation in parents predicted a heightened desire for their children to adhere to the parent's religious faith. Corporal punishment as a form of child discipline was also positively associated with fundamentalist beliefs (Danso, Hunsberger, & Pratt, 1997). While corporal punishment and child abuse are not one and the same, research is unclear about whether there is a link between approval of corporal punishment and incidence of child abuse.

The Role of Faith in Foster Care

The examples given above highlight ways in which Christianity affects the parenting practices of various groups. There is at least one group of care providers to be examined more closely as we discuss the impact of Christianity on child welfare practice. These care providers are the biological parents and foster parents (and, perhaps, future adoptive parents) of children served in the child welfare system.

In order to ethically deliver services, the child welfare foster care worker and the child welfare organization have to balance a number of rights and responsibilities. In out-of-home placements, this balance includes weighing the rights and wishes of biological parents, respect for the rights and wishes of the foster parents, and respect for the foster child's cultural and family ties and self-determination.

These rights and perspectives raise a variety of complex dilemmas for child welfare agencies in responding to the needs and preferences of the biological parent, the foster child, and the foster parents and their family. When there are religious differences between any of these parties, maintaining sensitivity to the religious choices of each party becomes difficult. Particularly challenging issues are raised when one of the parties prefers that religion not be a part of the foster placement, or when the biological and foster families embrace two distinctly different religious views (Schatz & Horejsi, 1996b).

For the last twenty years, determining placement matches on the basis of culture has been one of the most controversial issues surrounding foster care. One of the most notable controversies in the media and the field is the practice of matching children to foster parents on the basis of race (which has been legally forbidden in recent years.) Experts on culture, racial issues, and child welfare differ sharply on the appropriate method for placing children, particularly minority children, with foster parents of a different race. For some time, the attention to cultural matching appeared to end here. Religion was less frequently noted as a significant factor in out-of-home placements (Schatz & Horejsi, 1996a). With the recent and increasing attention to religion in social work practice, religion is now being examined as a significant cultural factor in foster care placement.

In the past, it was considered preferable to place a child in a home with religious values matching those of the biological parents' stated preference. In many cases, however, the biological parent does not indicate officially a preference of religion in the foster home,. In such situations, who is to make the decision of the appropriateness of a foster home in the context of religion?

There are a variety of concerns that foster parents, caseworkers, and biological parents have with regard to foster care placement and religion. Rarely is the foster care placement process so convenient that Presbyterian children are automatically placed with Presbyterian foster parents at the biological parents' request. Instead, due to an ever-present need for available foster homes for children coming into placement, the closest possible fit is attempted. Oftentimes, locating a home—any foster home—is difficult. Also, other variables in placement decision are prioritized, for example, finding a home that will accept a large sibling group or children with special needs.

Some of the major dilemmas that arise in this placement process are outlined in the Colorado *Fostering Families* training manual authored by Schatz & Horejsi (1992):

1. *The biological parent has no religious persuasion, and prefers that her child not be raised in a religious atmosphere.* In this (not uncommon) circumstance, clearly it is preferable to place the child with a foster family that is not affiliated with a religion. But given the high numbers of foster families who have some religious affiliation, there is a significant possibility that attempts to find a nonreligious home could delay placement of a child. The dilemma for the caseworker and for the foster parents is finding an ac-

ceptable means of both respecting the biological parents' wishes while not forcing the foster family to alter their own private religious practices.

2. *The biological family has significantly different religious beliefs than the foster family.* Currently, the procedure for addressing this type of placement is for the foster placing organization to request that the foster family make every possible effort to allow their foster child to continue practicing his or her religious beliefs. In the Colorado Department of Social Services Staff Manual this includes a foster child being encouraged and allowed to practice religious holidays, arranging attendance at the former church or religious institution of the foster child, and receiving written approval from the biological parents for any type of religious intervention used with the child.

   However, when viewing religion as part of the culture of a family, it becomes clear that church service attendance and religious holidays are not the only ways in which a child experiences religion. If, for example, a child of a non-Christian affiliation is placed with a Christian family, in what ways does this affect the foster family's practice of their own religion? What are the implications for such traditions as mealtime prayers or family Bible study? What are the implications for the foster family's biological children's religious practices? How does the foster child avoid feeling isolated in a family in which everyone else participates in faith-related expressions that the foster child does not? He or she can choose to participate, and enjoy accord with the family, or be excluded from several of the family's activities. This can hardly be helpful in a setting where a child is likely to feel some isolation already.

3. *The foster child chooses not to participate in the foster family's religious activities, or ridicules them.* In part this follows from the previous section, as an example of dilemmas that arise when placing a child of one religion (or no religion) with a family of another (or no religion). What is the appropriate response of the foster parent in this situation? By what means does the foster parent address these issues so that no religious views are imposed on the child?

4. *The biological parents object to or ridicule the foster parents' beliefs.* Assuming that this is a separate dilemma from the preceding issue, it could result that a foster child in placement is torn between two parental figures, one that practices a certain religion and one that derides it. To which authority figure does the child listen?

5. *The foster child chooses to participate in or embrace the foster family's religious beliefs, against the biological parents' wishes.* Most states maintain that the biological parent retains the right to choose the religion of their minor child. Is the child then not allowed to choose his or her own religion? (See notes above regarding the right of children to practice a religion.) How does an organization safeguard against foster parents, consciously or unconsciously, using their position to attempt to convert their foster children?

6. *The foster child undermines the religious beliefs of the foster family's birth children.* Whether the foster child practices a different religion, no religion at all, or simply does not agree with the religious teachings of his or her biological parent(s), the potential exists for their foster child to affect the religious beliefs of the foster parents' biological children. Matters become quite delicate when attempting to address issues such as this in a family unit without advocating for a specific religious belief.

Practically speaking, it is not difficult to find examples of value conflicts arising in the foster home. For instance, it may be the preference of a foster family to send all of their biological children to a Christian school. Once a foster child enters the home, several decisions must be made. Does the biological parent have a preference about the type of school attended (or can the child continue to attend the school he or she previously attended before placement out of home?) If the preference is for public schools, how does attending a different school than the other children in the home affect the foster child's integration into the foster family? Even simpler decisions, such as involvement in mealtime prayer, pose the risk of imposing values on a child unaccustomed to such rituals, or risking the child feeling a sense of alienation from the foster family.

Child Welfare Social Workers

The impact of Christianity on social workers in the child welfare system may also begin with the social worker's Christian faith. We highlight three areas in which Christian principles and perspectives influence the child welfare social worker: spiritual resources, social supports, and a sense of calling and purpose. *Spiritual resources* for the Christian social worker are drawn from the belief that the worker has been placed in a certain position for a purpose, and with certain safeguards. These include comfort and direction from God, as well as a meaningful personal relationship with God—in which prayer is central—designed to support the Christian worker. *Social supports* for the Christian worker include participation in Christian religious institutions, such as churches or other faith communities, with which come encouragement and support from others, and opportunities to participate in teaching and expression that can potentially enhance the worker's ability to cope with the challenges experienced during social work practice. Concrete needs provision and access to resource networks may be included in the social support system of the Christian social worker as well. Finally, *a sense of calling and purpose* may be felt by the Christian social worker as he or she draws upon a number of beliefs that could support work with maltreated children and their families. This could be derived from Scriptural reference to the well-being of children, or references to Biblical commitments to individual and social justice.

Setting aside their own personal experiences of faith or religion, as it concerns the client (either child or adult) in the child welfare system, caseworkers are encouraged to view religion as a cultural characteristic of a child or family, much as ethnic background or socioeconomic status shape one's experiences and beliefs. As a cultural part of one's life, the impact of religion extends beyond formal religious practices and rituals. Values, decisions, moral codes, and behavioral expectations can be influenced by a set of basic beliefs that are essential to one's religious practices. Examining one's own values and being cognizant of areas in which there might be a conflict with those of a foster child or a biological parent is a useful tool for a child welfare worker in the process of becoming culturally competent.

Social workers, in consultation with their supervisors and other organizational personnel, are encouraged to address the issue of religious practices in the foster home. This may be difficult as workers may think this crosses the boundary separating church and state, or fear that they may be perceived as promoting their own religious values. Religion is to be addressed with caution and neutrality by caseworkers, but should not be ignored; it is an important part of the personal makeup of foster children and their biological or foster parents.

While most professional social workers are trained to address religious matters only as a function of the client's identified needs, support networks, and perspectives, child welfare organizations are not comprised only of professional social workers. Paraprofessionals and community volunteers contribute enormously to service provision, especially in the area of concrete needs, such as volunteer transportation, shelters, and food or clothing banks. [3] While agencies may take steps to prevent volunteers or paraprofessionals from discussing religion, in one study, a director of one organization commented, "I just don't feel like we can hand out food and money and then neglect the spiritual. From a personal viewpoint, that's where we know the change is going to happen."(Pipes & Ebaugh, 2002). It rests upon the organization's administration and supervisors to promote respect for the religious practices and faiths of its consumers, both through instruction and by example.

Tensions Between Child Welfare and Christianity

Dilemmas related to the relationship between faith and child welfare have been noted throughout this chapter, particularly as they relate to service delivery, placement decisions, the rights of consumers, and the appropriate inclusion of religious practices in the assessment and intervention process. We feel that it is also important to discuss broader tensions between what many consider Christian doctrine and the values and beliefs of social workers in child welfare.

Genuine Christian compassion for the well being of children seems natural based on the compassionate example of Jesus, the Christian ethic of love, and specific scriptural admonitions to care for children without parents or basic necessities. However, historically there have been a number of areas in which there has been tension between the child welfare community and religion. Topics of tension include (1) *the definition of child abuse and neglect*; (2) *the causes of child maltreatment*; and (3) *perceptions of Christianity in the national and global community*.

(1) *Definition*: In the United States there is no nationally accepted definition of child abuse or child abuse and neglect law. Instead, definitions of abuse and neglect vary from state to state, and are often general and vague, allowing multiple interpretations of conditions described as "harm" and "injury". Such lack of clarity reflects a conflict of values, or at least differing viewpoints, with regard to parenting and discipline. The sanctity of the home and parents' rights to raise their children in the manner they choose may be in conflict with the value of protecting children from harm, and society's obligation to protect children and monitor parenting on behalf of children. For example, while for some parents it is considered traditional and normal to use physical discipline to correct a child, to Child Protective Services workers, any discipline which leaves a visible mark on a child might be considered child abuse. "Spare the rod and spoil the child" is a frequently cited Biblical reference to discipline, interpreted literally by not a few parents. It is, however, viewed with concern by some child welfare professionals, particularly if religious teachings support physical punishment and fail to sufficiently warn against excessive punishment (Dobson, 1970; Lovinger, 1990, Wiehe, 1990). Defining only extreme, life endangering physical harm as abuse (particularly combined with a belief that child abuse could not occur in a Christian family) could lead to the failure to recognize and respond to potentially harmful situations (Pagelow & Johnson, 1988).

(2) *Causes of Maltreatment*: Broader than the issue of physical punishment, religion has been portrayed as providing the context or belief system that contributes to child abuse and neglect. A number of theories of child abuse point to the role of an authoritarian or patriarchal family structure in creating an atmosphere in which children (and sometimes women) are viewed as subservient to fathers or husbands (Horton and Williamson, 1988; Peek, Lowe, & Williams, 1991). Equating patriarchy with authoritarian parenting styles, some express concern about physical abuse of children, emotional abuse or neglect, and a climate in which child maltreatment is justified or allowed. The child is expected to be obedient to the parent (Alwin, 1986), and not display a "willful" spirit (Fugate, 1980; Hutson, 1983). The parent is charged with shaping the child's will (sinful nature) and spirit, and discipline required for achieving maturity in the child needs to be firmly enforced by the parent (Hyles, 1974; Rice, 1982). Parental actions may be justified through these arguments, to the extent that the perceived religious mandate for discipline may override caution against causing harm to the child.

(3) *Perceptions:* A final area of tension concerns the general perception of Christianity by consumers or the community at large. This is complicated by the potential negative contributions of distorted religious beliefs and practices to child and family well being. Due to revelations, particularly in the past several years, of harmful abuse of children perpetrated by religious leaders, the connection between religious faith, parenting, and maltreatment has become more complicated. Even the connotation with Christian practices suggested by the name of a faith-based organization can affect a consumer or referring individual's willingness to pursue services (Danso, Hunsberger, & Pratt, 1997).

Conclusion

This chapter has offered analysis of the interaction of Christian institutions, practices, and faith with child welfare. We have, within historical and current contexts, examined the impact of Christianity on child welfare organizations, clients, social workers, and child welfare policy and practice. In understanding these issues, one may choose as a professional to view the impact of this religion from a scientific or sociological perspective, attending to the impact it has on stakeholders in child welfare both internally and externally, from micro- to macro-level systems of interaction. The reader may alternately or concurrently choose to view the impact of Christianity from a religious perspective, acknowledging the social and personal effects while also considering the role of faith in child welfare on a more spiritual or theological level. From any angle, the importance of acknowledging the role of Christianity and religion in child welfare practice cannot be denied.

We challenge those working in the field to assess well the role of religion in the lives of clients, and to genuinely examine it as a potential social and spiritual need of the children, parents, and care providers served. We challenge agencies and policymakers to affirm the spiritual and religious freedom of the child welfare service recipient, and to work to counteract negative perceptions of Christianity, either through education or intervention. Finally, we challenge the child welfare system, as individuals and as a whole, to conscientiously consider the best interests of those it serves—not only socially, economically, or psychologically, but spiritually as well.

Notes

[1] Portions of this chapter were included in the previous edition of *Christianity and Social Work*, in the chapter titled "Spirituality and Religion in Child Welfare."

[2] In this study, "Christian faith" was measured by the participant's engagement in 19 religious behaviors as identified on the *Religious Behavior Survey*, which include activities described as Christian religious practices. Bollinger & Palkovitz acknowledged that these religious behaviors are not a measure of "faith per se," but rather a measure of "the extent to which one enacts Christian teachings," (Bollinger & Palkovitz, 2003).

[3] While none of these are strictly child welfare services in and of themselves, transportation services are often affiliated with visitation arrangements between foster child and the biological parent; families in need may find themselves in need of shelter, etc.

References

Alwin, D. (1986). Religion and parental child-rearing orientations. *American Journal of Sociology*, 92, 412-440.

Anderson, G. R. & Mikula, J. (2002). Spirituality and religion in child welfare practice. In B. Hugen & T. L. Scales (Eds.), *Christianity and social work: Readings on the integration of the Christian faith and social work practice, 2nd Ed.* (pp. 251-268). Botsford, CT: NACSW Press.

Bollinger, B. & Palkovitz, R. (2003). The relationship between expressions of spiritual faith and parental involvement in three groups of fathers. *The Journal of Men's Studies*, 11(2), 117-129.

Bosacki, S. & Ota, C. (2000). Preadolescents' voices: a consideration of British and Canadian children's reflections on religion, spirituality, and their sense of self. *International Journal of Children's Spirituality*, 5(2), 203-219.

Collett, J. L. et al. (2006). Faith-based decisions? The consequences of heightened religious salience in social service referral decisions. *Journal for the Scientific Study of Religion*, 45(1), 119-127.

Cook, J. F. (1995). A history of placing out: The orphan trains. *Child Welfare*, 74, 181-199.

Costin, L. (1991). Unraveling the Mary Ellen legend: Origins of the "cruelty" movement. *Social Service Review*, 65, 203-223.

Danso, H., Hunsberger, B., & Pratt, M. (1997). The role of parental religious fundamentalism and right-wing authoritarianism in child-rearing goals and practices. *Journal for the Scientific Study of Religion*, 36, 496-511.

Dobson, J. (1970). *Dare to discipline*. New York: Bantam Books.

Fugate, R. (1980). *What the Bible says about child training*. Tempe, AZ: Aletheia.

Garland, D. (1994). *Church agencies: Caring for children and families in crisis*. Washington D.C.: Child Welfare League of America.

Horton, A. & Williamson, J. (1988). *Abuse and religion: When praying isn't enough*. Lexington, MA: Lexington.

Hutson, C. (1983). *The why and how of child discipline*. Murfreesboro, TN: Sword of the Lord.

Hyles, J. (1974). *How to rear children*. Hammond, IN: Hyles-Anderson.

Lovinger, R. (1990). *Religion and counseling: The psychological impact of religious belief*. New York: Continuum.

Mattingly, M. A. with Stuart, C. (2001). *Competencies for professional child and youth work practitioners*. Retrieved January 8, 2007 from http://www.acycp.org.

O'Connor, T. P., Hoge, D. R., & Alexander, E. (2002). The relative influence of youth and adult experience on personal spirituality and church involvement. *Journal for the Scientific Study of Religion*, 41(4), 723-732.

Pagelow, M. & Johnson, P. (1988). Abuse in the American family: The role of religion. In *Abuse and religion: When praying is not enough*. Lexington, MA: Lexington.

Peek, C., Lowe, G., & Williams, L.S. (1991). Gender and God's word: Another look at religious fundamentalism and sexism. *Social Forces*, 69, 1205-1221.

Pipes, P. F. & Ebaugh, H. R. (2002). Faith-based coalitions, social services, and government funding. *Sociology of Religion*, 63(1), 49-68.

Rice, J. (1982). *God in your family*. Murfreesboro, TN: Sword of the Lord.

Robbins, S., Chaterjee, Pl, Canda, E., & Hussey, D. (1998) Theories of Cognitive and Moral Development. In *Contemporary Human Behavior Theory: A Critical Perspective for Social Work*. Needham Heights, MA: Allyn & Bacon.

Schatz, M.S. & Horejsi, C. (1992). Religion and the foster home. *Fostering Families*. Colorado State University, Fort Collins, Colorado. Designed in consultation with the Colorado Department of Social Services.

Schatz, M.S. & Horejsi, C. (1996a). From moral development to healthy relationships: The role of religion in out-of-home placement. ERIC Clearinghouse on Counseling and Guidance (ERIC-CASS) CG02. University of North Carolina at Greensboro, 1999. Presented at the 24th Annual Child Abuse and Neglect Symposium, Keystone, Colorado, May, 1996.

Schatz, M.S. & Horejsi, C. (1996b). The importance of religious tolerance: A model for educating foster parents. *Child Welfare*. Vol. LXXV, #1, 73-85.

Scott, D.G. (2003). Spirituality in child and youth care: Considering spiritual development and "relational consciousness". *Child & Youth Care Forum*, 32(2), 117-130.

Waldrop, D. P. & Weber, J. A. (2001). From grandparent to caregiver: The stress and satisfaction of raising grandchildren. *Families in Society*, 82(5), 461-472.

Wiehe, V. (1990). Religious influence on parental attitudes toward the use of corporal punishment. *Journal of Family Violence*, 5, 173-186.

Wuthnow, R., Hackett, C., & Yang Hsu, B. (2004). The effectiveness and trustworthiness of faith-based and other service organizations: A study of recipients' perceptions. *Journal for the Scientific Study of Religion*, 43(1), 1-17.

CHAPTER 19

THE HELPING PROCESS AND CHRISTIAN BELIEFS: INSIGHTS FROM ALAN KEITH-LUCAS[1]

Helen Wilson Harris

"Helping is not a technique. It is an investment of one's self" (Keith-Lucas, p. 17). That statement begins our journey into understanding the nature and approach of our professional helping according to one who has written most practically and profoundly about the nature of the helping relationship in social work. Clinician, consultant, and author Alan Keith-Lucas devoted much of his professional life to understanding and communicating what actually makes a difference when "professional helpers" encounter those we call clients and patients and consumers. The buzz word today is "evidence based practice." How do we as social workers engage our clients in ways that produce change? Alan Keith-Lucas taught that there are principles of helping that are essential to effectiveness and to positive outcomes. "This is a difficult and skilled business. If we are going to attempt it, we need to have some skill in helping." (Keith-Lucas, p. 31).

I first met Alan Keith-Lucas more than 30 years ago. I was a caseworker at the South Texas Children's Home where "Keith" (as he asked to be called) was a consultant who was invited by our administrator to the campus periodically to help us figure out this thing called faith based residential child care. Dr. Keith-Lucas (I know, Keith) was, on first inspection, an odd looking man with his thin brushy goatee, his tweed jacket with the patched pockets, and his unlit pipe in one hand. His "older adult" look and his British accent gave him a distinguished air though he never seemed formidable to me. I went to the first meeting with him more than a little skeptical that this "outsider" could offer any insight of value to those of us who lived and worked among these children every day. He captured my imagination and my respect by the end of our first five minutes together. Here was a man who read and wrote widely, thought deeply, and loved children simply and completely. He was able in a few days on the campus to connect with the most intractable of the children. He delivered with kindness insights into the attitudes and behaviors of the staff (including me, I confess) that allowed us to look with new eyes into the hearts and potential of children instead of the scars from their damaged lives. He drew as much from Uncle Remus stories as he did from scripture. He, like another great teacher and minister to children, communicated through stories the most amazing truths. He was unorthodox in many ways. Keith saw and responded to the wounded child inside each of us. Remarkably, he left us with the tools to do the same for every child in our care as well as their parents and families.

I continue to regularly read what Alan Keith-Lucas wrote and left behind and I ask my students to do the same. He was a visionary, prophetic social worker, and educator. He wrote, in some cases 50 years ago, about concepts beginning to be understood and used in child care and in social work practice today. Keith's understandings and articulations are life changing. His understandings of the helping relationship, of the importance of the whole person with all of his or her history, of the value of concrete services, of the lifelong impact of separation and loss, of the Biblical mandate to love and respect others including (perhaps especially) those different than we are changed me and continues to change others more than ten years after his death.

I do not propose in this chapter to improve on what Keith has written about the helping relationship. I propose to gather from his works clarifying insights that provide the reader with both a glimpse and deep baptism into the wisdom Alan Keith-Lucas offers us as we discover more about being a helper in a relationship with those in the world who are wounded and to whom we are called.

In his book, *Giving and Taking Help*, Alan Keith-Lucas asks us to consider anew our motivation and our preparation for entering into a helping relationship with others. He asks us to move away from formulaic helping and tells us that focusing on the application of a particular technique can result in poor outcomes if we have forgotten the main thing, the client. That, more than anything, sums up his central premise: The client is the expert of his/her own experience. The client is the specialist in the helping relationship, the person who must, in the end, make the decisions and be invested in the process. Keith explains that we begin as helpers by respecting our client's right and ability to make the choices that lead to change. It is the client who must live out the choices that are made and the results that are set in motion. So the client must be engaged in making active choices. An active, willing choice is one that brings with it commitment and the energy and potential to deal with life's circumstances. What then is the helping person's role? It is in relationship and in remembering that the relationship is mutual; the helper and the "helped" are mutually engaged in a relationship focused on choice and change. But having a helping relationship does not mean a having a social relationship like a friendship or a relationship that is focused on being pleasant. Yes, effective helping professionals care deeply about their clients; but that caring means both not prescribing what the other person should do and being willing to stay engaged in the helping relationship even when the circumstances and the decisions are difficult.

Keith-Lucas tells us: "The defined purpose of the helping relationship is to help a person or group to make choices about a problem or situation and about the help they are willing to take about it." (p. 51) This by necessity means learning how to hear what the client is saying to us and believing that only the client can make a real choice about what course of action will have meaning to him or her. Even in situations where the social worker also represents the "agenda" or interests of the agency, there can be no significant helping without the client's engagement and involvement. It is possible through effective helping to secure that engagement and involvement, to break through the barriers of distrust and agency power and prescription. It works when we let go of the notion of social control and engage in the kind of helping in which clients understand their own responsibility for their lives and the impact of their decisions on the lives of others. Keith-Lucas compares helping a client to trying to move a stalled trolley up against a coiled spring. All of the pushing in the world will only increase the "resistance" and likelihood of ending up further away from the stated goal. Instead, our role as helpers, according to Keith, is to help "uncoil the resistance" or in effect, address the negative experiences and negative feelings that may be keeping the client from being able to make progress. Keith presents a fascinating model for working with clients who have experienced loss of all kinds. He addresses the most important question in helping those who have experienced loss: What makes the difference in coming out of the crisis or loss experience with resilience and mastery instead of despair and lifelong disengagement? Every client encounters tragedy and loss. Keith adapts the "standard" grief and loss model to clarify that those who overcome and are able to turn tragedy into triumph are those who are empowered to address the loss and the feelings that come with it, a phenomenon he calls "protest." The helping person is then, not the person who makes everything seem fine, but the person who permits, even facilitates, the expression of the pain and outrage generated by the loss. The theme again of the helping relationship is authenticity and acceptance of clients even when they are crying or angry or tired or unpleasant.

What follows is the substantive text from Chapter 5 and Chapter 10 from the 1994 revised edition of *Giving and Taking Help*, in Dr. Keith-Lucas' own words. Some of the original text has been abridged in order to make space for materials from both chapters. My comments and reflections are in italics. I do this in the belief that Keith's work will be transforming in the life of the social worker who is called of God to professional helping. I'm not sure anyone can improve on Keith's words. My reflections are intended to lift up the concepts and add my own voice and experience to his.

Keith has much more to say about the nature of helping than I have been able to capture here. This material has been chosen because it captures one of his core ideas—that all good helping involves the skillful use of reality, empathy, and support—and that these dimensions of helping reflect the very nature of God.

The Helping Factor (*Giving and Taking Help*, Chapter 5)

Various Theories

There must be something which the helping person brings into the relationship through which help is actually given. The relationship we have discussed cannot do this by itself. It is resultant and not something that can be created apart from what goes on between helper and helped. We cannot set up such a relationship and then sit back and expect help to flow from it without some positive action or contribution on our part. Helping happens when we invest ourselves in the lives of others, when we are engaged with them in the "here and now" as they understand it. We bring ourselves to the process understanding that we may well be changed as much as the person we are committed to helping. This active participation is the key to effective helping.

Quite clearly too the helping factor is something more than the material things with which help often deals, such as money, a job, housing or medical care, although it is a mistake to think that these things are unimportant. It was one of the misapprehensions of many nineteenth-century helpers that to give material things was wrong, or at best a necessary evil. Many helping persons today seem to miss the tremendous importance of "concrete helping." The model of Jesus as helper includes many examples of his provision of material needs, his ability to meet the needs presented to him in the moment.

A job, a house, an opportunity are very important to people. They may be completely necessary to the solution of their problems. Yet, there is something more to helping than this. While there are obvious situations in which they are all that are needed, in which case helping would seem to consist solely in their provision, in the majority of situations something else has to happen, either in the actual giving or possibly before it, if a person is to make full use of them. And even then their mere provision can be done in such a way that their use is enhanced or limited. The dignity of the application procedure, the concern shown for details, the promptness of their provision, even the setting in which they are given, all contribute to or deduct from their helpfulness.

There have been many attempts to isolate or define the primary helping factor. The nineteenth century, by and large, relied on moral exhortation, friendliness, and encouragement. Later a more rationalist approach relied on careful case study and appropriate treatment, which in general meant manipulation of the environment and the supplying of influences which the helped person was thought to lack. A little later, in the late twenties and early thirties of this century, it was believed that listening alone was perhaps the primary helping factor. The helper became little more than a mirror against which the helped person projected his concerns.

Knowing "Why"

With the advent of psychoanalysis, interpretation of unconscious motives was given first place. It was believed that the rationality of the conscious brain, brought face to face with the apparently infantile reasoning which the unconscious seems to employ—its tendency, for instance to identify wholly unlike things—would reject this irrationality in favor of sensible behavior. Insight would lead to change.

So deeply is this concept ingrained that many people will uphold that one cannot modify one's behavior unless one knows exactly why one has misbehaved in the first place, which is clearly not always so. Some understanding of one's motives may be very helpful in coming to a decision but many of a person's most fruitful decisions and commitments are made without knowing exactly why.

The belief that understanding motive is critical to behavior change once caused a class of mine to insist that the purpose of an interview with a delin-

quent girl [called Mary Ann] we were studying could be no other than to find
out "why" she ran away from home. They were quite shocked when I said that
this might be quite helpful, if it could ever be known, although I doubted that
it would ever tell us more than the precipitating factor. The actual causality
would be probably almost infinitely complex and involve many factors outside
both their and Mary Ann's control, a recognition which is being increasingly
made by students of epidemiology. If they were interested in trying to create
conditions in the community which would minimize delinquency, such an
analysis might have value.

But this was not the purpose of the interview as it was held. It could have
only one purpose. That would be to find out ways by which Mary Ann would
be able to handle her impulse to run away again.

I do not mean that the epidemiological approach, the desire to control
or alter conditions so that other Mary Anns might not need to run away, is
something with which a social worker should not be not be concerned. I do
mean that to help Mary Ann in the here and now the knowledge of her action's
complicated causality is probably not enough. Even if Mary Ann could say, and
even be convinced, that she ran away because of any number of factors, there
is still her will, her image of herself, her fears, and the reality of her present
situation to take into account. Humans are not simple rational creatures, and a
fourteen-year-old girl perhaps not always an exemplar of logical thinking.

If Mary Ann were a very sick child, or if her impulse was such that it was
uncontrollable by any conscious act on her part even with some change of attitude on the part of her parents, psychotherapy with interpretation might have
been necessary. The need for this would have shown up, perhaps, in a more total
disorganization than this girl was presenting, or in her failure to make use of the
helping process that most people can use to some extent. Even here her problems
might have been solved by psychiatric treatment not involving interpretation.

Her particular behavior might be amenable to conditioning or to drug
therapy. This solution would involve a "why" or a sort knowledge at least
that her condition could become manageable if certain tensions were relieved,
which is not so much a "why" as a "how." Sometimes by handling one factor in
a complex situation a person may be brought to a condition below, as it were,
the critical point at which symptoms appear.

However, a preoccupation with causality would have failed to engage Mary
Ann's capacity to face her situation and to do something about it herself. It is all
very well to know that one behaves badly because one has been rejected or unloved.
There is no doubt that to be rejected makes it harder to behave well. But it does
not remove the responsibility of a person to do something about his behavior.

Reality, Empathy, and Support

Doing something about her impulse to run away is what Mary Ann needs
to struggle with now. To help Mary Ann do this the worker must start with
the reality of the situation, the fact that she has done something illegal; the

possibility that the judge might send her to a correctional school, or let her go home only under supervision, which she might find difficult to bear; even the fact that she might find it impossible not to run away again. In order to decide what she wanted, what she could bear, what use she could make of whatever was decided, and what help she needed to do this, Mary Ann would need to be held to facing these facts and possibilities.

She would also need to be free to discuss and explore her feelings about them, and in fact be reassured that her expression of these feelings would not get her into trouble. Part of these feelings might be anger, at her parents, at the judge or at the probation officer. The last is particularly true if the worker has done her job in holding Mary Ann to the reality of the situation; but since this anger is something which Mary Ann cannot help feeling about the situation, and since to repress it, or "bottle it up" will only make it more important and harder to deal with, it may need to be expressed.

Lastly, if Mary Ann is to take help in her situation, she must know that the worker will be available to her, will not turn against her when she is troubled, and will provide as far as she can what Mary Ann needs to carry out her decisions.

This situation may serve, despite its particularity, to help us see what it is that the helping person must convey to any person in trouble. What has to be conveyed can be phrased as a "statement" which the helping person makes, although it is much more than this. It is not simply something said. It is something conveyed by words, feeling, and action. But in terms of a statement it could be phrased in three sentences, as follows:

"This is it." (Reality)
"I know that it must hurt." (Empathy)
"I am here to help you if you want me and can use me," or more succinctly, "You don't have to face this alone." (Support)

These three sentences in turn may be expressed in terms of what is actually offered through them. In this form the helping factor is composed of three complex, interrelated and important elements which we may call reality, empathy, and support.

These three elements are always necessary in any helping process and the three together do in fact constitute the helping factor. I know of no piece of helping that cannot be analyzed in these terms, and no piece of unsuccessful helping that does not show a weakness in at least one of these elements. Reality has been partial or empathy and support conditional.

We will examine first each principle by itself and then try to bring them together. The order in which they are presented here does not necessarily mean that one introduces them, in helping, serially or in this order. One may start with an expression of empathy or even of support, and in any case they are interwoven. One does not stop where another starts. But if there is an order, reality often does come first.

Reality

Reality means a number of things, some of which have already been touched on. It means, first, not discounting another's problem, not taking it away from him by believing it unimportant. This is a thing we are particularly likely to do to children, whom we cannot believe, for some reason, feel as deeply as we do. How often we say, "Oh, they'll soon forget it," or "They're too young to be affected much," when everything that we really know about them points to the fact that their despair, their fear, and their anger are not only intense but can leave permanent scars. To be real, on the other hand, means to face the problem with someone in all of its ugliness or terror. It means doing him the honor of taking his problem seriously. And, with children, in particular, but with adults also, this is the first requirement if a relationship is to grow.   Another form of taking away a person's problem is to solve it for him or to insulate him from it. We either produce a quick solution or we help him to evade it, to forget it, not to come into contact with it often to spare him the pain or disturbance.

But, while it might be necessary to allay some forms of disturbance temporarily, disturbance has about it some of the qualities that are now recognized in a fever. It used to be good medical practice to allay all fevers. Now there is growing understanding that a fever is the body's way of fighting an infection. A child once, in a Children's Home, was very much disturbed by her mother's visits. The social worker suggested solving the problem by restricting the mother's visits. The child said, with a good deal of anger, "What you don't understand is that this is something I need to get disturbed about."

People need their problems if they are to solve them for themselves. Sometimes they need to be disturbed. Not to permit them to become so, when they are trying to tackle their problems, is to encourage nonchoice.

False Reassurance as "Nonreality"

A common form of nonreality is reassurance. False reassurance, is an attempt to palliate reality by telling the person in trouble that "things will be all right" when there is no reason to think that this will be so, or when the present hurts so much that this is wholly unimportant. We can recognize obvious cases of it. No wise parents today would tell their child that the dentist won't hurt. The dentist very well may hurt, and the parent be proved a liar. But we still, some of us, will tell a child that he will be happy in a foster home when this may not be so and when in any case all he can think of at the moment is his pain at leaving his own parents.

We use this kind of reassurance for two reasons. In the first place, we cannot stand the child's present unhappiness and are willing, although we may not know it, to try to dispel it even at the cost of greater unhappiness later. And, in the second, we are apt to be a little defensive because a foster home, in this case, or some other service, is what we have to offer him and we do not like the idea that he might not like the only thing that we have to give him. It makes us feel very inadequate. I have seen a welfare worker "reassure" a client that the termination of her grant does not really matter, since she ought to be able to get support from a recently located absent husband, when her lights and gas were to be turned off that afternoon. False or unrealistic reassurance does not strengthen a person's ability to handle his problem. It effectually disarms him and robs him of the anger or despair he may need to deal with it.

Another reason for false reassurance is our natural protectiveness toward those we consider vulnerable or lacking in real strength. We feel that the person we are helping would be hurt by coming face to face with the truth. There may be some instances in which the helped person could not possibly face the truth, but more often the helping person is only too glad to have a good reason not to face the helped person with the truth. The genuine cases where the truth is so horrible that it would be more harmful than helpful are rather rare.

Protecting People from the Truth

To protect someone from the truth is to make a very serious judgment about him. It is to say that he is incapable of being helped with his real problem. As a minister expressed it to me once, it is to deny him his chance for an "abundant life," fully experienced.

The truth, too, is often much less harmful than what the imagination puts in its place. Some years ago I was approached by a teacher who was concerned about a fifteen-year-old boy, the adopted son of an apparently stable and loving family, who had begun to run away. There seemed to be nothing in the home to suggest a need to escape from it, and although the boy was adolescent, he did not appear to be particularly rebellious. The boy was plainly running "to" rather than "from," and when I was told that the town he was running to was his birthplace, I was fairly safe in assuming at least tentatively that he was doing what so many children away from their own parents have to do, which was the answer the question, "Why did my parents give me up?

I therefore asked the teacher why the boy's parents had done so and was told that the boy was illegitimate. It was quite hard for her to take when I suggested that if she wanted to help the boy, someone had better tell him the truth. To her surprise the boy was greatly relieved. As the boy expressed it, "Of course she had to find another home for me." Later the boy confessed that he had been for several years tortured by two alternative fantasies, one that his parents were murderers; the other that he had an unbearable odor. We are much too ready to assume that another person cannot bear the truth. Only when an untruth has become so necessary to a person that he or she cannot live without it is it wise not to face the truth. We must remember, however, that reality is only one of the three helping elements. It cannot be introduced without empathy and support.

Reality as Difference

We sometimes call a piece of reality deliberately introduced into a helping situation a piece of difference. It may be a fact. It can conceivably be an opinion, although we need to be careful that it is not a prejudice or a personal point of view irrelevant to the helped person's need. Unskilled workers are, as we have said, full of inappropriate difference, and they introduce pieces of difference in inappropriate ways. We do this when we blame others for their situations and preempt their problem solving with advice and with prescriptive instruction. Inappropriate difference is what happens when we set ourselves up as good and moral and imply that others could be too if they were just like us.

How do we know when difference is appropriate? I would suggest at least four criteria for appropriate difference. The first, and perhaps the most important, of these is that there is sufficient likeness—understanding, common purpose— to assure the helped person that the difference is not a personal attack. People can, after all, say things to other people who know that they love them that they could not possibly say to a stranger.

Secondly, the difference must be expressed in the helped person's terms. Often the most useful little bits of difference can be expressed by using the helped person's own words. A welfare worker was interviewing a deserting father, who rather naturally was trying to excuse his desertion. His statement was that he could not bear not being master in his own house. "You know," said the worker, "that's the strangest way I've ever heard of being master in your own house, to run away from it."

Thirdly, there is a somewhat elusive quality about the person who is ready to accept difference. There is an element of challenge, of projecting an image and watching to see how you are going to respond to it. This was very obvious in the deserting father's words. This is perhaps the least concrete of our criteria. It is a sense one gets, an understanding of the process of image projection, a knowledge that a projection is being made for a purpose. The helped person is really saying, "Will you buy this image of me?" and if you do, you only strengthen the image and make the real self less accessible.

The last criterion has to do with empathy and support. It is briefly that one has no right to introduce difference or reality unless one is prepared to help the person one is helping with the shock. Reality by itself is harsh. It is only reality approached with empathy and support that is a true helping process. Indeed we might restate the whole method of help as "facing people with reality with empathy and support." To face someone with reality and leave them to handle it alone is cruelty, not help.

Problems in Using Reality

The fear of not being able to handle the repercussions is one of the chief obstacles to introducing appropriate difference. Obviously to tell even a small percentage of those one is trying to help that they are unpleasant people would be a poor rule in practice. In most cases it would result in the very reverse of helping. It could only be done when the worker is sure that the client recognizes her desire to help. Just as people can tell "home truths"- in itself an interesting term- to those who are sure of their love and interest, so a helper can risk difference with someone who trusts her. Sometimes one can pick up an inherent contradiction in what the seeker for help may say or do. Sometimes one many have to say to someone, "You say you enjoy doing this but you don't sound like it." Body language, too, often betrays what a person is feeling. So does tone of voice. The classic example is that of the counselor who told a mother that her child needed more loving if he were to behave better. The mother came to the next session dragging the child into the office and said, "You were wrong. I've half killed this brat loving him and it hasn't helped a bit."

Playing Devil's Advocate

Another form of difference which can sometimes be of help, providing again that it is kept within a framework of likeness, consists in the speculative assumption of exactly the opposite of what the helped person is asserting, so that he may gain strength in demolishing your argument. This is in fact the function of the devil's advocate in a canonization procedure. What a devil's advocate says is, in effect, "Have you considered the possibility that we're on the wrong track altogether? Let's look at that possibility." This is a form of difference that can only be used when the helped person is fairly sure of himself; when, in fact, all that he needs is to move from a tentative statement to a forthright claiming of what he knows and believes.

Reality and "Tact"

Reality also means being direct. Helping persons, unfortunately, have acquired something of the reputation of being rather "wily birds" who tread delicately and never quite say what they mean. This is sometimes described as "tact" or "consideration" but so easily becomes either evasion or a way of gently manipulating someone else to do what you want him to do and at the same time think that it was his own idea. One area in which the reality of the situation needs to be very clearly expressed is that of the helping relationship itself. It includes what will or may happen, the probable consequences of actions, the authority and rights each person has in the situation, who can tell whom to do what, and the conditions under which help is being offered. Concealed power is both unfair and generally unhelpful. The worker from the juvenile court who minimizes its authority and presents it only as wanting to be "of help" without making clear that it will enforce this "help" is trying to buy relationship at the cost of the truth, and she will end up having neither.

Do Not Justify Reality

A further requirement of reality is that it must be presented as it is, without attempts at justification. The moment one does this to reality, one robs it of its primary helping value, which is that it exists outside both helper and the helped person and is something that they can both look at together, as a fact, and without a predetermined mental attitude toward it. To justify, or to explain, means that one claims the reality as "good" and that the helped person is wrong in being angry at it. It raises the possibility that it could be different and nearly always ends in a wrangle between the helped and the helping person about what might be instead of about what is. Helper and helped person need to be on the same side of reality.

The Right to Fail

But there is one use of the word "reality" which helpers should avoid. Unfortunately, the word is often used in professional social work literature to mean the social worker's estimate of the client's capabilities. A course of action is seen to be unreal if, in the social worker's opinion, the client is attempting something beyond his power. But this assessment, although it may be common sense, is not reality for the client. It is merely a judgment on him. What is real is what such plans would cost him and the very real possibility that he might fail As David Soyer points out, people have the right to fail and may not in fact be satisfied with a second best until the impossible has been attempted. Sometimes, too, people surprise one. To elevate into reality a diagnosis, however careful, is presumptuous and is in all too many cases a disguised form of protectiveness.

Being Nice

Reality is perhaps the hardest of the three elements to hold to for any sensitive person. None of us likes to be the bearer of bad news. We do not like seeing people hurt, and reality often hurts. Americans in particular find great difficulty with it, since American culture puts a high premium on considerateness and on not "hurting people's feelings," which makes plain speaking very difficult. If anyone doubts this— and paradoxically many Americans think of themselves as outspoken—one need only compare American and British book reviews or political comment. There is a deep tradition in our culture of being "nice." Really to face reality with someone often feels like being "mean," although it can be tremendously helpful. Even professions which have something of a tradition of "toughness" and no nonsense" about them have apparently developed a need to show themselves gentle and understanding.

Empathy

In order to help someone else with reality one has to show empathy for him. Empathy is the ability to know, or to imagine, what another person is feeling and, as it were, to feel it with him without becoming caught in that feeling and losing one's own perspective. It is not, let us be very clear, a way of softening reality. Empathy needs to be clearly distinguished from two other responses to people in trouble, sympathy and pity. The three responses have sometimes been described as feeling "like" someone (sympathy), feeling "with" someone (empathy), and feeling "for" someone (pity), but I find these prepositions somewhat difficult. The real difference between them lies in the amount and the kind of difference from the helped person that the helping person maintains.

In sympathy there is little difference. The helping person feels as does the person she is helping. She shares the same feelings, identifies herself with his interests, becomes aligned with him, loves and hates the same things. The helper who feels empathy on the other hand, understands the feelings that the other has about the situation, knows, as we have said, that "it must hurt," but does not claim these feelings herself. The helper who feels pity also retains her difference. She does not get overwhelmed by the troubled person's feelings. Emphasis is on the difference between her and the person she is helping, and the likeness, or understanding, is for the most part lost. Sympathy, as we have described it, is not entirely useless. There is some value in the precept to "rejoice with those that do rejoice and weep with those who weep." It is good to know that one is not alone and there are others who feel as you do. This may seem like an exaggerated sympathy. But this is one of sympathy's problems. We often hear it said that one can have too much sympathy for such and such a person (or such and such a group of persons). This is perfectly true. Sympathy can very easily become a weak emotion, and it can confirm a weak person in his weakness. Empathy is both a strong and a strengthening emotion. Because of the difference that the person who has empathy retains, she never condones or confirms weakness but enlists the troubled person's feelings in the attempt to overcome it. One cannot have too much empathy. But—and here, perhaps is the rub—empathy very easily slops over into sympathy. Sympathy is much the easier emotion. It is very easy to get caught in someone else's feeling system and to begin to identify with it.

An Act of the Loving Imagination

I have spoken of empathy as an emotion, and purposely so. It is, of course, formally an act, but an act based on feeling. The best description I know of it is an "act of the loving imagination."

Both "act" and "imagination" are important words here. Empathy is much more than knowing intellectually what another must be feeling. It always involves the ability to enter into this feeling, to experience it and therefore to know its meaning for the other person and the actions that are likely to flow from it.

There is in fact a paradox here which it is very hard to explain in ordinary, rational terms. Both to feel and to know is necessary if the purposes of empathy are to be fulfilled. Nothing carries less conviction, or is likely to fall so wide of the mark, as an attempt at empathy that is purely intellectual. The purpose of empathy is to convey feeling, not knowledge. But because feeling is communicated by so much more than words—by gestures, tone of voice, facial expression, and bodily posture, which are too complex to be capable of dissimulation—an assurance of feeling can only be communicated if this feeling actually exists.

In my experience, the facility of empathy can be trained, if not fully taught. While there are certainly people who have a natural empathy for others, there are also those who can release a great deal of loving imagination once they can free themselves from stereotyped reactions to people and once they become aware of their tendency, in some situations, to respond negatively, or sympathetically rather than empathically.

To learn empathy one has to be free from the kind of blocks that are thrown in one's path by liking and disliking people, by lining oneself up either for them or against them, instead of just caring about them, whether one likes or dislikes them. And this comes largely from self-knowledge. It is not so much that a person stops liking and disliking as it is that he or she learns to control the consequences of such feelings. Empathy also depends on knowledge, and on encounters with people who are quite different from oneself.

Knowledge of social conditions and some of the causes of feeling can also be of help. But empathy does not in fact need to be too precise. There is always something of the tentative about it, an acknowledgment that feeling must be present, and probably within a given range, and an invitation to the helped person to express his feeling more precisely. That is why the statement which we have used to typify empathy is not, "I know how it hurts," but "I know that it must hurt."

The empathy which is needed, at least in the beginning of a relationship, is largely directed toward the struggle through which the helped person is going, his fear of help, his wanting and not wanting to get well, the frustrations of his efforts to solve his problem by himself, and this is common human experience, although not always recognized as such. There are times when one can convey empathy in a subverbal manner, but generally it needs to be expressed verbally. I find that many young helping people can feel empathically, but they find it difficult to put their feeling into words.

Support, No Matter What

The third element in the helping factor is support. This has two aspects, material and psychological. Material support, the means to accomplish the task, may or may not be present in the helping situation. It is not generally part of either psychotherapy or problem-related counseling. When it does occur in these, it takes the form of technical know-how of some kind, whether this be marital techniques or where to find a school for one's child. In some helping it is, however, the most visible part and is thought of by many people as all that there is to help. It is what helping gives, whether this be money, opportunity, or know-how. Nor, as we have said, can it ever be considered unimportant. People need money, opportunity, education, and technical assistance to implement their decisions.

But people also need psychological support. They need to know that they are accepted and that the helping person will not give up on them. She will not be shaken in her desire to help. Even if helping proves impossible, she will still care about the person she is helping, "no matter what."

Support Even When Help is Not Possible

Particularly she will not desert the person she is trying to help because that person disappoints her or makes what she believes to be an unwise or immoral decision. It is true that there are two or possibly three situations in which this decision or failure may mean an inability on the part of the helping person to go on being the primary helper. One situation occurs when the decision, or some limitation in the helped person, removes him from contact with the particular source of help with which he has been working. A student may fail and be required to leave a school; a child's behavior may be such that for the protection of others he must leave a Children's Home; or a client may no longer be eligible for assistance. There is also always the possibility that the helped person's problems may be such that no one knows at present how he can be helped. His resistance to help may be so strong or his ability to act so lacking that no skill that we have at present would be enough to provide any help. He may need, for his own protection or that of society, to be institutionalized, or control measures may have to be substituted for help. This decision would, however, have to be made with the greatest reluctance and with the knowledge that the helped person had not so much proved himself unhelpable as we unable to help him.

But even should one of these conditions separate helped person and helper, the principle of support means that the separation is not accompanied by rejection. The helping person still cares. She still respects and is concerned about what happens to the other. Sometimes indeed it is in this very act of separation that helping really begins.

I once knew a child in a Children's Home for whom all attempts to help her had seemed unsuccessful. When she faced trial in another city, the housemother, rather than rejecting her, asked the administrator to allow her to support the child through the trial. It was, not unnaturally, to the housemother who had shown concern for her at her worst that this child turned later in life. It was she whom she consulted over the problems of working and marriage. And six years later when her younger sister, who had remained at the Children's Home, became restless, she offered her sister a home and help.

It goes without saying that support is also hard to practice. It is very easy to reject those who have let one down, especially where this has been accompanied with anger, blame, or ingratitude. Hard, but possible

To Support is Not to Condone

It is extremely difficult for human beings to get away from the idea that to care about a person in trouble is to condone what he has done. It does not seem sufficient to allow someone to suffer the consequences of his act or to take his punishment for it. We seem to need to reinforce societal sanctions by disassociating ourselves from those who have offended against them, instead of seeing these people as those who need our help the most. Part of this is reaction against unrealistic helping. To be concerned about a delinquent is not to approve of delinquency. Nor is it to excuse it, to throw all of the blame onto conditions or onto society. Poor conditions, poor heredity, undoubtedly make it harder for acceptable decisions to be made, but not all people make such decisions under these strains. The helper whose support is a disguised form of exculpation, who believes that the delinquent had no choice but to act as he did, is being unrealistic. She is indulging rather than helping.

But in part our unwillingness to try to help rather than to punish the delinquent is our fear of ourselves. It is a strange reflection on how delicately balanced our "good" and "bad" decisions must be that we get so angry at the bad ones. This anger has its roots in fear. We fear that we too may be tempted. It has long been known to psychiatrists that those who are most violently opposed to some social ill are often those to whom it is secretly most attractive, and that the faults we see in others are often the ones we are most prone to ourselves.

Support may be indicated in a number of ways. Sometimes the mere fact of being there is sufficient. Sometimes it is indicated by physical contact, particularly with a child. Sometimes it includes a direct offer of help, or making clear that one is available. Sometimes it is a matter of giving someone an introduction, of "breaking the ice" for him in facing a new experience. One must, however, remember that the statement is not simply, "I am here to help you," but "I am here to help you if you want me and can use me." Support is at its best when it is consistent but unobtrusive and it must be always be unconditional.

Using the Elements

Reality, empathy, and support, then, are the three elements of the helping factor. They still do not tell us how to help in any given situation, which is perhaps something no one can tell another, but they do give us some idea of how we need to approach the problem. But even here they are not prescriptions. No one can go into a helping situation saying to herself, "I will be real. I will be empathic. I will offer support." The very effort would distract her from listening to the person she wanted to help.

But they do offer a way of looking at our own helping efforts. In every helping situation that has gone wrong, or been less than productive than one hoped, it is good to ask oneself three questions:

1. Have I been able to face reality with this person, or have I glossed over the truth or offered false reassurance?
2. Have I been able to feel and express real empathy, or has empathy been lacking, or limited ("You can share your feeling with me as long as you don't feel so and so")?
3. Have I offered real support, or has it been conditional support ("I will continue to try to help you as long as you don't do this or that")?

An honest answer to these three questions often shows us what has gone wrong.

All three elements are necessary to each other. Reality without empathy is harsh and unhelpful. Empathy about something that is not real is clearly meaningless and can only lead the client to what we have called nonchoice. Reality and empathy together need support, both material and psychological, if decisions are to be carried out. Support in carrying out unreal plans is obviously a waste of time. The three are in fact triune, and although in any one situation one may seem to be predominant, all three need to be present. Alan Keith-Lucas found significant connections between the concepts of reality, empathy and support and the roles of the Trinity in Father, Son and Holy Spirit. Effective helping requires all of the components of relationship with the God who provides ultimate helping.

The Triune God and Triune Helping

God the Father, the Creator, is in Christian thought certainly the author of reality—both the reality of things and that of the moral and natural law, as well as of the laws of causality and consequence. God is also the Wholly Other, the One who is different, who is "God, not man."

Biblical history, as Christians read it, certainly suggests that this reality was not enough. Human beings alone could not, of their own will, face reality and change in relation to it. There was needed an act of empathy, and there is no more characteristic or total act of empathy than that described in the Incarnation—God who became human and yet remained God, "who in every respect has been tempted as we are, yet without sinning." Indeed, the whole theology of "very God and very man," the refusal to consider Jesus as either less than God and not wholly human, or part human, or part God and part human, the insistence that he is a single person, is a struggle with the problem—how a person can feel another's pain and yet remain separate from it. Both require the concept that in doing two apparently different things at the same time, one does not do either less completely.

Again, the name given to the Spirit, both in the King James Version and in the Prayer Book, is the Comforter. Although the word "comfort" has suffered a weakening of meaning since the seventeenth century, its derivation is from cum, meaning " with" and fortis, meaning "strong." A comforter is therefore one who is "strong with you," and there is no better one-sentence definition of support.

Reality, empathy, and support—Father, Son, and Holy Spirit—the analogy may seem blasphemous at first. It is, however, logical that if the person asking for help is analogous to the recipient of grace, then the helping person must, as far as it is possible for a finite, fallible being to do so, model her helping on the actions of God. Help becomes in a new sense the expression of one's religion, not just as the term is often used, one's general but unspecified goodwill toward others, but what one actually believes. It follows too that the helping process is real, that it is not merely a collection of pragmatic principles, that it deserves much closer study than it has received to date, and that where we have got it right, it is much more than a set of useful techniques.

How Might We Distinguish a Christian Helper from A Secular One?

A Christian of Grace will not...
- Pass judgment because she is conscious of herself as a sinner dependent on grace.

- Practice direct evangelism or witness unless involved with members of her own faith or people who are seeking a Christian solution to their problems as witnessing is often not good helping. People rarely change and grow because they are told that they should. Most people one helps do not as yet trust the helper. The best witnessing occurs in service responding to the client when the client is ready to deal with spiritual matters. Many clients' life experience has been such that they have no reason to believe the Word of God. If one's only knowledge of having a father is that he beats one or deserts one, how can one believe in a Heavenly Father?
- Focus on spiritual help rather than tangible concrete help. Christianity is the only religion whose founder prayed for daily bread, and in Matthew 25, Jesus did not say, "I was in need of counseling and you counseled me," but "I was hungry, thirsty and naked."
- Ask if someone deserves to be helped. Jesus was more concerned with the character of the person who gives aid than the character of the person who receives aid.

Qualities of a Christian Helper...

- Looking for evidence of grace in those she helps
- Steadfastly standing by people and caring even when help seems impossible
- Standing by her values despite current culture
- Holding institutions accountable for justice, kindness, and walking humbly with God
- Staying tough enough to deal with reality with clients
- Continuing to exhibit true humility and willingness to learn, grow and discriminate new practice trends

Drawing it all Together

In the last several chapters of *Giving and Taking Help*, Alan Keith-Lucas helps us to understand that not everyone is called and gifted to helping, particularly professional helping as articulated here. Helping persons are human persons with our own needs and interests. This makes self awareness or "self knowledge" even more important as we consider our own areas of prejudice and personal challenge when working with clients. Awareness of our "similarities and differences" is the beginning of good helping. Helping persons use specific knowledge, values and skills, but not to the exclusion of spontaneity and natural helping. Keith identifies that helping persons particularly need courage to be real with clients, to take risks that they won't be liked, to give clients the right to fail. We also need the kind of humility, awareness of sameness, that lets us relate to clients without judging their differences and that keeps us grounded in serving others, knowing that ultimately our treatment of others as persons worthy of respect and care will bear fruit. It is not necessary that we "like" all of our clients. It is necessary that we care and that our concern includes respect rather than control.

Understanding the nature of the helping relationship and process allows us then to incorporate specific guidelines for our professional helping. Keith suggests that we always start with what the client is asking us for rather than what we think they should be asking for from us. We must tune in then to the feeling behind or underneath the words even before the client articulates them. Good helping means not taking the client's feelings personally and recognizing that feelings are neither good nor bad—they simply are. So we focus on the issues rather than denying the feeling by reframing the situation.

Real helping, according to Keith, means letting clients choose even when the choice includes failure and then continuing in the helping relationship to formulate the reality, the problem, the alternatives, and the opportunities. Clients can become overwhelmed by the enormity of their reality. Partializing the problem or concern allows them to focus on work that can be done now and in subsequent meetings when the helper and helped can explore how well the choices and resultant actions are working out. This evaluation of practice with the client allows modification of the plan of action in response to ongoing results. So the helper, rather than offering imperatives and control, may offer advice that the helped can consider and that can be modified as needed.

For Keith, helping another person is more like consultation than it is diagnosis and treatment. The helper comes alongside the person who is facing a difficult reality and helps the person figure out exactly what it is and what the available options might be, including what they each would take or cost to pursue. The helper tries to support the person in making what Keith calls "choice" rather than "non-choice" responses to the difficult situation. "Choice" responses come in two basic kinds: (1) To fight against the difficulty and to change it (when change is possible); or (2) To accept and constructively use the difficulty (when change is not possible). "Non-choice" responses come in two parallel basic kinds: (1) To deny the reality of the difficulty and seek ways to avoid it; or (2) To "accept" the difficulty in a way that leaves the person crushed. The helper can neither fully know when change is possible nor take responsibility for what the helped person is able to choose and do.

The key to helping is not the answer to "why?" but the answer to 'given your current circumstances, what next?" When we help clients to modify choices and decisions that aren't working and celebrate those that are, we bring with us movement toward long term success for those clients. Helpers cannot help everyone and must use self awareness and assessment to know when to refer clients for more specialized help. Even in those cases, the helper can often assist with immediate needs while the referral is being made. Keith-Lucas also identifies ways in which the principles of helping contribute to positive outcomes in more adversarial settings including court, business, arguments among colleagues and in therapeutic settings including work with children and families. His bottom line: "The helping process, in fact, works." (p. 157.)

The values that drive the helping process, according to Alan Keith-Lucas, are centered in the value of each person and the person's freedom to choose without being judged, leading to the use of feelings and relationship to help people find "their own way." He finds those values for himself grounded in and growing out of Judeo-Christian values, even as he acknowledges that the values of the helper have significant influence over the process. Helpers are frequently agents of social systems with power; the helper's willingness to empower clients rather than exacerbate the power differential is key to successful helping.

Alan Keith-Lucas describes God, the Father, as the author of reality; Jesus, the Son with us, as empathy; and the Holy Spirit as comforter and supporter. The use of the helping factors of reality through empathy and support sums up the professional use of self that is taught in so many helping programs and models the integration of Christian faith and professional helping practice.

Note

[1] Readers wishing to cite this work should do so understanding and noting that a substantive portion of this chapter is taken from the following work: Keith-Lucas, A. (1994). Chapters 5 and 10, *Giving and Taking Help* (Revised). Editor: David Sherwood. St. Davids, PA: The North American Association of Christians in Social Work. The original work was published in 1972.

CHAPTER 20

DOING THE RIGHT THING: A CHRISTIAN PERSPECTIVE ON ETHICAL DECISION-MAKING FOR CHRISTIANS IN SOCIAL WORK PRACTICE

David A. Sherwood

You are on the staff of a Christian Counseling Center and in the course of a week you encounter the following clients:

1. A minister who became sexually involved with a teen-age girl at a previous church several years ago. His current church is not aware of this. He says he has "dealt with his problem."
2. A Christian woman whose husband is physically abusive and who has threatened worse to her and their young child if she tells anyone or leaves him. She comes to your office with cuts and bruises, afraid to go home and afraid not to go home. She doesn't know what she should do or can do.
3. A single mother who is severely depressed and who is not taking adequate care of her two young children, both under the age of four. She denies that her personal problems are affecting her ability to take care of her children.

The list could easily go on. Helping professionals, Christian or otherwise, are daily confronted with issues that are immensely complex and which call forth judgments and actions that confound any attempts to neatly separate "clinical knowledge and skill," our preferred professional roles and boundaries, and, fundamentally, our world-view, faith, moral judgment, and character. Much as we would like to keep it simple, real life is messy and all of a piece. All kinds of things interconnect and interact. How would you respond to clients like the ones I just mentioned?

Christian social workers need to know who they are and what resources they have to do the right thing as children of God—personally, socially, and professionally. What are our resources and limits in choosing and acting ethically as Christians who are placed in helping relationships with others? I will try to review briefly a Christian perspective on:

- When we have a moral problem.
- Conditions under which we choose and act.
- Faith and the hermeneutical spiral (understanding God's will).
- How the Bible teaches us regarding values and ethics.

- The Principle/Practice Pyramid
- A decision-making model which integrates the deontological (ought) dimensions with the teleological (purpose and consequences) dimensions of a problem.
- The fundamental role of character formed through discipleship and the guidance of the Holy Spirit.

We cannot devise or forcibly wrench out of the scriptures a set of rules which will simply tell us what to do if we will only be willing to obey. It appears that God has something else in mind for us as He grows us up into the image of Christ. Ultimately, "doing the right thing" results from our making judgments which grow out of our character as we are "changed into his likeness from one degree of glory to another; for this comes from the Lord who is the Spirit" (II Corinthians 3:18).

When Do We Have a Moral Problem?

When do we have a moral "problem?" I would argue that value issues are so pervasive in life that there is virtually no question we face that does not have moral dimensions at some level. Even the choice regarding what brand of coffee to use (or whether to use coffee at all) is not a completely value-neutral question. However, for practical purposes I think it is helpful to realize that moral "problems" tend to be characterized by the following conditions:

1. **More than one value is at stake and they are in some degree of conflict.**
   This is more common than we would like to think. It need not be a conflict between good and bad. It is more usually differing goods or differing bads. A maxim that I drill into my students is "You can't maximize all values simultaneously." Which is to say life continually confronts us with choices, and to choose one thing *always* means to give up or have less of something else. And that something else may be a very good thing, so serious choices are usually very costly ones. A familiar, lighthearted version of this is the adage "You can't have your cake and eat it too." This is one of life's truisms which is very easy to forget or tempting to ignore, but which is at the heart of all value and moral problems. No conflict, no problem.

2. **There is uncertainty about what values are, in fact, involved or what they mean.**
   For example, what are all the relevant values involved in a decision regarding abortion? And what, exactly, is meant by choice, right to life, a person? Where do these values come from? What is their basis? How do they put us under obligation?

3. **There is uncertainty about what the actual facts are.**
   What is the true situation? What are the relevant facts? Are they known? Can they be known? How well can they be known under the circumstances?

4. **There is uncertainty about the actual consequences of alternative possible choices and courses of action.**

   Often we say that choices and actions should be guided by results. While it is true that their morality is at least in part influenced by their intended and actual consequences, Christians believe that God has built certain "oughts" like justice and love into the creation and that results always have to be measured by some standard or "good" which is beyond the naked results themselves. It is also crucial to remember that consequences can never be fully known at the time of decision and action. The best we can ever do at the time is to *predict*. We are obligated to make the best predictions we can, but we must be humbled by the limitations of our ability to anticipate actual results. However, unintended consequences turn out to be every bit as real and often more important than intended ones, especially if we haven't done our homework.

Under What Conditions Do We Have to Choose and Act?

Given this understanding of a moral "problem," it seems to me that real-life value choices and moral decisions are always made under these conditions:

1. **We have a problem.**

   An actual value conflict is present or at least perceived. For example, we want to tell the truth and respect our dying parent's personal rights and dignity by telling him the prognosis but we don't want to upset him, perhaps hasten his death, or create possible complications for ourselves and the hospital staff.

2. **We always have significant limitations in our facts, knowledge, understanding, and ability to predict the consequences of our actions.**

   What causes teen-age, unmarried pregnancy? What policies would lead to a decrease in teen-age pregnancy? What other unintended consequences might the policies have? Correct information and knowledge are very hard (often impossible) to come by. As Christians we know that human beings are both finite (limited) and fallen (liable to distortion from selfishness and other forms of sin). The more we can do to overcome or reduce these limitations the better off we'll be. But the beginning of wisdom is to recognize our weakness and dependence.

3. **Ready or not, we have to decide and do *something*, at least for the time being, even if the decision is to ignore the problem.**

   Life won't permit us to stay on the fence until we thoroughly understand all the value issues, have all the relevant data, conduct a perfectly complete analysis, and develop a completely Christ-like character. So, we have to learn how to make the best choices we can under the circumstances. ("You can't maximize all values simultaneously" but you have to give it your best shot!)

4. **Whatever decision we make and action we take will be fundamentally influenced by our assumptions, world-view, faith—*whatever* that is.**

"Facts," even when attainable, don't sustain moral judgments by themselves. They must be interpreted in the light of at least one faith-based
value judgment. Where do my notions of good and bad, healthy and sick,
functional and dysfunctional come from? Never from the "facts" alone
(Lewis, 1947, 1943).

5. **We would like to have definitive, non-ambiguous, prescriptive direction
so that we can be completely certain of the rightness of our choice, but
we never can.**
Not from Scripture, not from the law, not from our mother. We want to
know without a doubt that we are right. This has always been part of the
allure of legalism, unquestioning submission to authorities of various
stripes, and simplistic reduction of complex situations. The only way (to
seem) to be saved by the law is to chop it down to our own puny size.

6. **We may not have legalistic, prescriptive formulas, but we *do* have guidance and help.**
Doing the right thing is not just a subjective, relativistic venture. God
knows the kind of help we really need to grow up in Christ and God has
provided it. We need to be open to the kind of guidance God actually
gives instead of demanding the kind of guidance we think would be best.
What God has actually given is Himself in Jesus Christ, the story of love,
justice, grace, and redemption given witness in Scripture, the Holy Spirit,
and the community of the church, historically, universally, and locally.

7. **Ultimately, doing the right thing is a matter of identity and character.**
In the last analysis, our morality (or lack of it) depends much more on
who we are (or are becoming) than what we know or the procedures we
use. We must become persons who have taken on the mind and character
of Christ as new creations. And it turns out that this is precisely what the
Bible says God is up to—growing us up into the image of Christ, from one
degree of glory to another. The "problem" of making and living out these
moral decisions turns out to be part of the plot, part of God's strategy,
suited to our nature as we were created. Instead of fighting and resenting
the hardness of moral choice and action, maybe we should *embrace* it as
part of God's dynamic for our growth.

Faith and the Hermeneutical Spiral

Walking By Faith Is Not Optional

Christian or not, consciously or not, intentionally or not, we all inevitably
approach understanding the world and ourselves on the basis of assumptions
or presuppositions about the nature of things. Walking by faith is not optional.
All human beings do it. We do have some choice (and responsibility) for what
we continue to put our faith in, however. That's where choice comes in.

Is love real or a rationalization? Does might make right? Do persons possess inherent dignity and value? Are persons capable of meaningful choice and

responsibility? Are human beings so innately good that guilt and sin are meaningless or destructive terms? Is human life ultimately meaningless and absurd? Is the physical universe (and ourselves) a product of mindless chance? Is there a God (or are *we* God)? These are a few of the really important questions in life and there is no place to stand to try to answer them that does not include some sort of faith.

Interpreting the Facts

Like it or not, the world, life, and scripture are not simply experienced or known directly. Things are *always* interpreted on the basis of assumptions and beliefs we have about the nature of the world that are part of our faith position. Knowingly or not, we are continually engaged in hermeneutics, interpretation on the basis of principles.

My interpretation of the meaning of scripture, for example, is strongly affected by whether or not I believe the Bible is a strictly human product or divinely inspired. It is further affected by whether or not I assume the Bible was intended to and can, in fact, function as a legal codebook providing specific prescriptive answers to all questions. My beliefs about these things are never simply derived from the data of the scripture only, but they should never be independent of that data either. In fact, a good hermeneutical principle for understanding scripture is that our interpretations *must* do justice to the actual data of scripture (Osborne, 1991, Swartley, 1983).

The same is true regarding our understanding or interpretation of the "facts" of our experience. The same event will be seen and interpreted differently by persons who bring different assumptions and expectations to it.

On the day of Pentecost, the Bible records that the disciples "were filled with the Holy Spirit and began to speak in other tongues as the Spirit enabled them" (Acts 2.4). Some in the crowd didn't know anything about the Holy Spirit, but were amazed by the fact that they heard their own native languages. "Are not all of these men who are speaking Galileans? Then how is it that each of us hears them in his native tongue" (Acts 2:7-8). Some, however, heard the speech as drunken nonsense and said, "They have had too much wine" (Acts 2:13). Different interpretive, hermeneutical frameworks were in place, guiding the understanding of the "facts."

As a child, I occasionally experienced corporal punishment in the form of spankings from my mother (on one memorable occasion administered with a willow switch). The fact that I was on rare occasions spanked is data. But what did those spankings "mean" to me? Did I experience abuse? Was I experiencing loving limits in a way that I could understand? The experience had to be interpreted within the framework of the rest of my experiences and beliefs (however formed) about myself, my mother, and the rest of the world. And those "facts" continue to be interpreted or re-interpreted today in my memory. In this case, I never doubted her love for me or (at least often) her justice.

The Hermeneutical Spiral

We come by our personal faith position in a variety of ways—adopted without question from our families, friends, and culture; deliberately and critically chosen; refined through experience; fallen into by chance or default. Or, more likely, it comes through some combination of all of these and more. However it happens, it is not a static, finished thing. Our interpretation and understanding of life proceeds in a kind of reciprocal hermeneutical spiral. Our faith position helps order and integrate (or filter and distort) the complex overload of reality that we confront. But at the same time reality has the capacity to challenge and at least partially modify or correct our assumptions and perceptions (Osborne, 1991; Sherwood 1989).

Once the great 18th century English dictionary-maker, writer, conversationalist, and sometime philosopher Samuel Johnson was asked by his biographer Boswell how he refuted Bishop Berkeley's philosophical theory of idealism (which asserted that the physical world has no real existence). Johnson replied, "I refute it *thus.*" He thereupon vigorously kicked a large rock, causing himself considerable pain but gaining more than enough evidence (for himself, at least) to cast doubt on the sufficiency of idealist theory as a total explanation of reality.

This is a hermeneutical spiral. You come to interpret the world around you through the framework of your faith, wherever you got it, however good or bad it is, and however embryonic it may be. It strongly affects what you perceive (or even look for). But the world is not a totally passive or subjective thing. So you run the risk of coming away from the encounter with your faith somewhat altered, perhaps even corrected a bit, or perhaps more distorted. Then you use that altered faith in your next encounter (Osborne, 1991; Pinnock, 1984; Sire, 1980). Unfortunately, there is no guarantee that the alterations are corrections. But, *if* the Bible is true, and *if* we have eyes that want to see and ears that want to hear, we can have confidence that we are bumping along in the right general direction, guided by the Holy Spirit.

How Does the Bible Teach Us?

The Heresy of Legalism

For Christians, the desire for unambiguous direction has most often led to the theological error of legalism, and then, on the rebound, to relativism. Legalism takes many forms but essentially uses the legitimate zeal for faithfulness to justify an attempt to extract from the Bible or the traditions of the elders a system of rules to cover all contingencies and then to make our relationship to God depend on our understanding and living up to those rules (Sherwood, 1989).

It is theological error because it forces the Bible to be something that it is not—an exhaustive theological and moral codebook yielding prescriptive answers to all questions. It distorts the real nature and meaning of God's self-revelation in the incarnation of Jesus Christ, the Holy Spirit, the Scriptures, and even nature. Taken to its extreme, it effectively denies the gospel of justification by faith in Jesus Christ and substitutes a form of works righteousness. It can take the good news of redeeming, reconciling love and distort it into a source of separation, rejection, and condemnation.

The paradigm case in the New Testament involved some of the Pharisees. Jesus had some very strong words for them. When the Pharisees condemned the disciples for breaking the Sabbath by gathering grain to eat, Jesus cited the example of David feeding his men with the temple bread, also a violation of the law, and told them, in effect, that they were missing the point of the law. "The Sabbath was made for man, not man for the Sabbath" (Mark 2:23-28). In the parable of the Pharisee and the tax collector Jesus warned about those who "trusted in themselves that they were righteous and despised others" (Luke. 18:9-14). He talked of those who strain out gnats and swallow camels, careful to tithe down to every herb in their gardens but neglecting the "weightier matters of the law, justice and mercy and faith" (Mt. 23:23-24). When a group of Pharisees condemned the disciples because they didn't wash their hands according to the Pharisees' understanding of the requirements of purification, saying, "Why do your disciples transgress the tradition of the elders?" Jesus answered, "And why do you transgress the commandment of God for the sake of your tradition? . . . For the sake of your tradition you have made void the word of God. Hear and understand: not what goes into the mouth defiles a man, but what comes out of the mouth" (Matthew 15:1-11).

The Heresy of Subjective Relativism

If the Bible isn't a comprehensive lawbook out of which we can infallibly derive concrete, prescriptive directions for every dilemma, what good is it? Aren't we then left to be blown about by every wind of doctrine, led about by the spirit (or spirits) of the age we live in, guided only by our subjective, selfish desires? This is a good example of a false dichotomy, as though these were the only two alternatives. Either the Bible is a codebook or we land in total relativism. Yet this is the conclusion often drawn, which quite falsely restricts the terms of the discussion. Once we cut loose from the deceptively certain rules of legalism it is very easy to become the disillusioned cynic—"I was tricked once, but I'm not going to be made a fool again." If the Bible can't give me all the answers directly then it's all just a matter of human opinion. So the false dilemma is stated.

The Orthodoxy of Incarnation—What if God Had a Different Idea?

Such conclusions assume that, to be of any practical use, God's revelation of His will can only be of a certain kind, an assumption we are more likely to take *to* the Bible than to learn *from* it. It assumes that divine guidance must be exhaustively propositional, that what we need to be good Christians and to guide our moral lives is either specific rules for every occasion or at least principles from which specific rules can rationally be derived. What if such an assumption is wrong? What if it is not in keeping with the nature of God, the nature of human beings, the nature of the Bible, or the nature of the Christian life?

What if the nature of Christian values and ethics cannot be adequately embodied or communicated in a book of rules, however complex and detailed? What if it can only be embodied in a life that is fully conformed to the will of God and communicated through the story of that life and its results?

What if God had to become a man, live a life of love and justice, be put to death innocently on the behalf of others, and raise triumphant over death to establish the kingdom of God? What if the Bible were book about that? A true story of how to become a real person?

The point I am trying to make is that if we go to the Bible for guidance on its *own* terms, not deciding in advance the nature that guidance has to take, what we find is neither legalism nor relativism but precisely the kind of guidance that suits the kind of reality God actually made, the kind of creatures we actually are, the kind of God with whom we have to do.

We learn that ethical practice has more to do with our identity, our growth in character and virtue, than it does with airtight rules and that the Bible is just the kind of book to help us do this. It may not be as tidy as we would like. It may not be as easy as we would like to always tell the good guys from the bad guys. We may not always be able to act with the certain knowledge that we are doing just the right (or wrong) thing. But we will have the opportunity to get closer and closer to the truth of God, to grow up into the image of Christ. Growth is not always comfortable. But the Bible tells us *who* we are, *whose* we are, and *where* we're going.

God is Bigger Than Our Categories but the Bible is a Faithful Witness

The reality of God and biblical truth shatters our categories. At least, none of them, taken alone, can do the God of the Bible justice. Taken together, our categories have the potential to balance and correct each other. Human language can only carry so much divine freight in any particular car.

We are *all* susceptible to distorted use of Scripture. We need the recognition that we (*all* of us) always take preconditions to our Bible study that may seriously distort its message to us. In fact, we often have several *conflicting* desires and preconditions at work simultaneously. For example, we have the hunger for the security of clear-cut prescriptive answers ("Just tell me if divorce is always wrong or if I have a scriptural right to remarry") *and* a desire to be autonomous, to suit ourselves rather than submit to anyone or anything ("I don't want to hurt anyone, but my needs have to be met").

So, how do I think the Bible teaches us about morality? How does it guide us in making moral judgments in our professional lives? Struggling to rise above my own preconditions and to take the Bible on its own terms, to see how the Bible teaches and what the Bible teaches, I think I am beginning to learn a few things.

God's Project: Growing Us up into the Image of Christ

It seems to me that God is trying to reveal His nature and help us to develop His character. And it seems that the only way He could do that is in *personal* terms, creating persons with the dignity of choice, developing a relationship with a nation of them, becoming one of us Himself, revealing His love, grace, and forgiveness through a self-sacrificial act of redemption, and embarking on a process of growing persons up into His own image. The process requires us to be more than robots, even obedient ones. It requires us to make principled judgments based on virtuous character, to exercise wisdom based on the character of Christ. Neither legalism nor relativism produces this.

According to the Bible, growing us up to have the mind and character of Christ is an intrinsic part of God's redemptive project. We are not simply forgiven our sins that grace may abound but we are being rehabilitated, sanctified—being made saints, if you will. The theme is clear, as the following passages illustrate.

In Romans 6:1-2, 4 Paul says that, far from continuing in sin that grace may abound, we die to sin in Christ, are buried with him in baptism, and are raised that we too may live a new life. Romans 12:2 says that we do not conform to the pattern of this world but are to be transformed by the renewing of our minds which makes us able to test and approve what God's will is. II Corinthians 3:17-18 says that where the Spirit of the Lord is, there is freedom and that we are being transformed into His likeness with ever-increasing glory. Ephesians 4:7, 12-13 says that each one of us has been given grace from Christ to prepare us for service so that the body of Christ might be built up until we all reach unity in the faith and knowledge of the Son of God and become mature, attaining to the whole measure of the fullness of Christ. I John 3:1-3 marvels at the greatness of the love of the Father that we should be called children of God and goes on to affirm that, although what we shall be has not yet been made known, we do know that when Christ appears we shall be like him. In Philippians 2, Paul says that, being united with Christ, Christians should have the same servant attitude as Christ, looking out for the interests of others as well as ourselves. Then he makes this remarkable conjunction—"Continue to work out your own salvation with fear and trembling, for it is God who works in you to will and to act according to his good purpose."

And in I Corinthians 2 Paul says that we speak a message of wisdom among the mature, God's wisdom from the beginning, not the wisdom of this age, revealed to us by His Spirit. He explains that we have received the Spirit who is from God that we might understand what God has freely given us. He concludes, "Those who are unspiritual do not receive the gifts of God's Spirit for they are foolishness to them, and they are unable to understand them because they are spiritually discerned . . . But we have the mind of Christ."

A Key: Judgments Based on Wisdom Growing Out of the Character of Christ

It would seem that the key to integrating Christian values into professional practice (as in all of life) is making complex judgments based on wisdom growing out of the mind and character of God, incarnated in Jesus Christ.

In our personal and professional lives we face many complex situations and decisions, large and small. Real-life moral dilemmas confront us with having to make choices between (prioritize) values that are equally real (though not necessarily equally important—remember Jesus' comments on keeping the Sabbath versus helping a human being). Whatever we do, we cannot fully or equally maximize each value in the situation. (If the father embraces the prodigal son and gives him a party, there will be some who will see him as rewarding irresponsibility.) Whatever we do, we have to make our choices on the basis of limited understanding of both the issues involved and the consequences of our actions. Moreover, our decision is complicated by our fallen nature and selfish desires.

In situations like this, the answer is not legalism (religious or scientific) or relativism. The *mind* of Christ helps us to figure out *what* to do and the *character* of Christ helps us to have the capacity (i.e., character or virtue) to actually *do* it. It seems to me that in the very process of struggling through these difficult situations we are dealing with a principle of growth that God has deliberately built into the nature of things. The people of God are continually required to make decisions based on principles embodied in our very identity—the character of who we are, whose we are, and where we are going.

These virtues are not just abstract ones but rather they are incarnated in the history and *character* of Jesus Christ. Love and justice are the fundamental principles but we learn what they mean because Jesus embodies them. (Yes, keep the Sabbath but don't let that keep you from helping someone.)

How should a Christian social worker respond when a client says she wants an abortion? How should parents respond when an unmarried daughter tells them she is pregnant? How should a church respond to a stranger's request for financial aid? Should I be for or against our Middle Eastern policy? Should my wife Carol and I invite my mother to come and live with us? How much money can I spend on myself? It appears I have some complex judgments to make in order to live a life of love and justice.

So, one of God's primary dynamics of growth seems to be to place us in complex situations which require decisions based on judgment. These decisions require our knowledge of the character of Christ to make and they require that we be disciplined disciples at least beginning to take on the character of Christ ourselves to carry them out. It seems to me there is a deliberate plot here, daring and risky, but the only one that works, which fits the world as God made it.

Can the Preacher Have a Boat?

Permit me a personal example to illustrate the point. I remember a lively debate in the cafeteria as an undergraduate in a Christian College over whether or not a preacher (i.e. completely dedicated Christian) could have a boat. The issue, of course, was stewardship, our relationship and responsibility toward material wealth, our neighbors, and ourselves. How should faithful Christians spend money?

Being mostly lower middle class, we all easily agreed that a yacht was definitely an immoral use of money and that a rowboat or canoe was probably o.k. But could it have a motor? How big? Could it possibly be an inboard motor? How many people could it carry? It was enough to cross a rabbi's eyes. Since we believed the Bible to contain a prescriptive answer to every question, we tried hard to formulate a scriptural answer. But we found no direct commands, approved apostolic examples, or necessary inferences that would nail it down.

What we found was much more challenging—things like:

- The earth is the Lord's and the fullness thereof (Psalm 24:1).
- Give as you have been prospered (I Corinthians 16:2).
- What do you have that you did not receive (II Corinthians 4:7)?
- Remember the fatherless and widows (Jas. 1:27).
- Don't lay up treasures on earth (Mt. 6:19-20).
- Follow Jesus in looking out for the interests of others, not just your own (Phil. 2:1-5).

Plenty of guidelines for exercising love and justice, lots of examples of Christ and the disciples in action—in other words, no selfish relativism. But no iron-clad formulas for what to spend or where—in other words, no legalism.

Instead, every time I turn around I am faced again with new financial choices, fresh opportunities to decide all over again what stewardship means—plenty of chances to grossly rationalize, distort, and abuse the gospel, to be sure. But also plenty of opportunities to get it right this time, or at least better. To grow up into the image of Christ.

Gaining the Mind and Character of Christ

So, only persons of character or virtue can make the kind of judgments and take the actions required of us. To do the right thing we need to be the right kinds of persons, embodying the mind and character of Christ (MacIntyre, 1984; Hauerwas, 1981).

The most direct route to moral practice is through realizing our identity as Christ-Ones. In Galatians 2:20 Paul said, "I have been crucified with Christ and I no longer live, but Christ lives in me. The life I live in the body, I live by faith in the Son of God, who loved me and gave himself for me" and in Galatians 5:13-14 he said "You were called to freedom, brothers and sisters; only do not use your freedom as an opportunity for self-indulgence, but through love become slaves to one another. For the whole law is summed up in a single commandment, 'You shall love your neighbor as yourself.'"

The mind and character of Christ is formed in us by the Holy Spirit as we submit to God's general revelation in creation (Romans 1-2), written revelation in Scripture (II Tim. 3:15-17), and, ultimately, incarnated revelation in Jesus Christ (John 1:1-18; Col. 1:15-20). We can only give appropriate meaning to the principles of love and justice by knowing the God of the Bible, the Jesus of incarnation, and the Holy Spirit of understanding and power. This happens best (perhaps only) in the give and take of two living communities—Christian families and the church, the body of Christ.

What we have when this happens is not an encyclopedic list of rules that gives us unambiguous answers to every practical or moral issue we may ever encounter. Neither are we left in an uncharted swamp of selfish relativity. And, it should be noted well, we are not given a substitute for the clear thinking and investigation necessary to provide the data. The Bible and Christ Himself are no substitute for reading, writing, and arithmetic (or practice wisdom, theory, and empirical research)—getting the best information we can and thinking honestly and clearly about it.

Instead, what we have then is the enhanced capacity to make and carry out complex judgments that is more in harmony with God's love and justice than we could make otherwise (Hauerwas & Willimon, 1989; Adams, 1987). We are still limited. We still know in part and "see but a poor reflection as in a mirror" (I Corinthians 13:12).

We may be disappointed that the Bible or Christ Himself don't give us the kind of advice, shortcuts, or easy black-and-white answers we would like, but what they give us is much better—the truth. Do you want to live a good life? Do you want to integrate your Christian values and your professional helping practice? Do you want to do what is right? The only way, ultimately, is to know God through being a disciple of Christ. This doesn't mean that only Christians can have good moral character—God's common grace is accessible to all. But it really is *true* that Jesus is the way, the truth, and the life (John 14:6). God is the one who gives *content* to the idea of "good." The mind of Christ is really quite remarkable, filling up and stretching to the limit our humanity with God.

> Lord, help us to know
>> **who** we are,
>> **whose** we are, and
>> **where** we are going.

Applying Values in Practice: The Principle/Practice Pyramid

As I think about the relationship between basic faith (worldview assumptions and beliefs), core values or principles that grow out of our faith, the rules that we derive in order to guide our application of those principles to various areas of life, and the application of those values and rules to specific day-to-day ethical and practical decisions we must make, it helps me to use the image of a "Principle/ Practice Pyramid." The shape of the pyramid gives a rough suggestion of the level of agreement and certainty we may have as we go from the abstract to the concrete. You can turn the pyramid whichever way works best for your imagination—sitting on its base or balanced on its top. I put it on its base (Sherwood, 2002).

Fundamental Worldview and Faith-Based Assumptions

The base or widest part of the pyramid represents our fundamental worldview and faith-based assumptions about the nature of the world, human beings, values, and God. All persons, not just "religious" people or Christians, have no choice but to make some sort of faith-based assumptions about the nature of the world and the meaning of life. These are the basic beliefs that help us to interpret our experience of life. This is part of the "hermeneutical spiral" we spoke of earlier. It is on this level that Christians are likely to have the broadest agreement (There is a God, God is creator, God has given human beings unique value, values derive from God).

Core Values or Principles

On top of and growing out of the faith-based foundation sits our core values or principles. What is "good"? What are our fundamental moral obligations? As a Christian I understand these to be the "exceptionless absolutes" of love and justice (Holmes, 1984). God is love. God is just. There is no situation where these values do not apply. And we must look to God to learn what love and justice mean. The social work analogy would be the core values expressed in the Code of Ethics: service, social justice, dignity and worth of the person, importance of human relationships, integrity, and competence (NASW, 1999).

Moral or Ethical Rules

On top of and growing out of the "principle" layer are the moral rules that guide the application of the principles to various domains of life. These are the "deontological" parameters that suggest what we ought to do. Biblical examples would be the Ten Commandments, the Sermon on the Mount, and other Biblical teachings that help us to understand what love and justice require in various spheres of life. Tell the truth. Keep promises. Don't steal. In the Social Work Code of Ethics, these would be the specific standards relating to responsibilities to clients, colleagues, practice settings, as professionals, the profession itself, and the broader society. Each of these categories in the Code has a set of fairly specific and prescriptive rules. Don't have sexual relationships with clients. Maintain confidentiality. Avoid conflicts of interest. These rules are very important in giving us guidance, but they can never provide us with absolute prescriptions for what we should always do on the case level (Sherwood, 1999, Reamer, 1990).

Cases Involving Ethical Dilemmas

At the top of the pyramid sit the specific cases involving ethical dilemmas in which we are required to use the principles and rules to make professional judgments in the messiness of real life and practice. It is at this very concrete level that we will find ourselves in the most likelihood of conscientious disagreement with each other, even when we start with the same values, principles, and rules. The short answer for why this is true is found in what we have discussed before. It is that we are fallen (subject to the distortions of our selfishness, fear, and pride) and finite (limited in what we can know and predict). And even more challenging, our principles and rules start coming into conflict with each other on this level. We must maintain confidentiality; we have a duty to warn. Our ability to know relevant facts and to predict the consequences of various courses of action is severely limited, yet some choice must be made and some action taken, now.

An Ethical Decision-Making Model

Given this understanding of the human situation, how God is working with us to grow us up into the image of Christ and the proper role that the Bible plays in giving us guidance, I would like to briefly introduce an ethical decision-making model for Christian helping professionals. It is a simple "problem-solving" model that assumes and is no substitute for developing the mind and character of Christ. It is simple only in concept, not in application. And it is what we need to do in all of our lives, not just in our work with clients.

Deontological and Consequentialist/Utilitarian Parameters

Ethical judgments and actions can generally be thought of as being based on two kinds of criteria or parameters—deontological and consequentialist/utilitarian. These are philosophical terms for describing two types of measuring sticks of whether or not something is good or bad in a moral sense and either ought or ought not to be done.

Deontological Parameters—The "Oughts"
Deontological parameters or criteria refer to moral obligation or duty. What are the moral imperatives or rules that relate to the situation? What are the "oughts?" For the Christian, it can be summed up by asking "What is the will of God in this situation?" Understanding the deontological parameters of an ethical dilemma we face is extremely important. But it is not as simple as it may first appear. Some think that ethics can be determined by deontological parameters only or that deontological parameters operate without consideration to consequences in any way. For example, the commandment "Thou shalt not lie" is taken to be an absolute, exceptionless rule that is to be obeyed in all circumstances and at all times, regardless of the consequences. By this principle, when Corrie Ten Boom was asked by the Nazis if she knew of any Jews, she should have led them to her family's hiding place.

Trying to answer all moral questions by attempting to invoke a particular deontological principle in isolation, even if the principle is biblical, may wind up leading us into actions which are contrary to God's will. That is the legalistic fallacy that we discussed before. Normally we have an ethical dilemma because we are in a situation in which more than one deontological principle applies and they are in conflict to some degree. Do we keep the Sabbath or do we heal? The Ten Commandments or the Sermon on the Mount, for example, contain deontological principles that are vitally important to helping us understand the mind of Christ and doing the will of God. But they cannot be handled mechanistically or legalistically or we will become Pharisees indeed. Does "turning the other cheek" require us to never resist evil in any way?

Most Christians properly understand that God's will is fully embodied only in God's character of love and justice, which was incarnated in the person of Jesus Christ. Love and justice are the only "exceptionless absolutes" in a deontological sense. The moral rules and principles of scripture provide important guidelines to help us to understand what love and justice act like in various circumstances, but they cannot stand alone as absolutes nor can they be forced into a legal system which eliminates the need for us to make judgments.

Consequentialist/Utilitarian Parameters—The "Results"

For God and for us, moral reality is always embodied. Part of what this means, then, is that the deontological "oughts" can never be completely separated from the consequentialist/utilitarian parameters. The consequentialist/utilitarian parameters refer to the results. Christian ethical decisions and actions always have to try to take into account their consequences. What happens as a result of this action or that, and what end is served?

Many people (quite falsely) believe that moral judgments or actions can be judged exclusively on the basis of their results. Did it have a "good" or desired result? Then it was a good act. Many believe that if we value the end we implicitly accept the means to that end, no matter what they might be (say, terrorism to oppose unjust tyranny). This is just as much a fallacy as the single-minded deontological judgment. Pure utilitarianism is impossible since there must be some deontological basis for deciding what is a "good" result, and this can never be derived from the raw facts of a situation. And "goods" and "evils" must be prioritized and balanced against one another in means as well as the ends.

It is a fact that some adults engage in sexual activity with children. But so what? What is the moral and practical meaning of that fact? Is it something we should encourage or prevent? Without some standard of "good" or "health" it is impossible to give a coherent answer.

Another major limitation of consequentialist/utilitarian criteria in making moral judgments is that at best they can never be more than guesses or *predictions* based on what we *think* the results might be, never on the actual consequences themselves. If I encourage my client to separate from her abusive husband, I may think that he will not hurt her or the children, but I cannot be sure.

So, ethical and practical *judgments* are always required. They aren't simple.

And they always involve identifying, prioritizing, and acting on *both* deontological and consequentialist/utilitarian parameters of a situation (Sherwood, 1986).

The Model: Judgment Formed By Character and Guided By Principle

1. **Identify and explore the problem:**
   What issues/values (usually plural) are at stake?
   What are the desired ends?
   What are the alternative possible means?
   What are the other possible unintended consequences?
2. **Identify the deontological parameters:**
   What moral imperatives are there?
   What is the will of God, the mind of Christ?
   What are the principles at stake, especially in regard to love and justice?
   Are there any rules or rule-governed exceptions, biblical injunctions, commands, or codes of ethics which apply?
3. **Identify the consequentialist/utilitarian parameters:**
   What (as nearly as can be determined or predicted) are the likely intended and unintended consequences?
   What are the costs and benefits? How are they distributed (who benefits, who pays)?
   What must be given up in each particular possible course of action? What values will be slighted or maximized?
4. **Integrate and rank the deontological and consequentialist/utilitarian parameters:**
   What best approximates (maximizes) the exceptionless absolutes of love and justice?
5. **Make a judgment guided by character and act:**
   After gathering and analyzing the biblical, professional and other data, pray for wisdom and the guidance of the Holy Spirit.
   Make a judgment and act growing out of your character as informed by the character of Christ.
   Refusing choice and action *is* choice and action, so you must do the best you can at the time, even if, in retrospect it turns out you were "sinning bravely."
6. **Evaluate:**
   Grow through your experience. Rejoice or repent, go on or change.

Character Formed through Discipleship and the Guidance of the Holy Spirit

Ultimately, ethical Christian practice depends on one thing—developing the mind and character of Christ. It depends on our growing up into the image of Christ. This begins in the new birth as we become new creations in Christ. We are filled with the Holy Spirit and called to a life of discipleship in which we bring every thought and action in captivity to Christ (II Corinthians 10:5). We present our bodies "as a living sacrifice," not conformed to this world, but "transformed by the renewal of your mind" (Rom. 12:1-2). We hunger and thirst after righteousness. We seek to know God's will through scripture, the guidance of the Holy Spirit, and the community of the church. We identify with Jesus and the saints of God down through the ages. We daily choose to follow Christ as best we know and can. We repent and confess to our Lord when we fall. We thankfully receive his grace. We choose and act again.

Certainly piety is not a substitute for the discipline of professional training, careful research, and thoughtful analysis. Rather, the use of all of these is simply a complimentary part of our stewardship and discipleship. The most solid possible assurance that we will do the right thing in our personal lives and in our professional practice is our discipleship, growing to have more and more of the character of Jesus Christ, as we make judgments more in harmony with God's character and Spirit.

We become a "letter from Christ . . . Written not with ink but with the Spirit of the living God, not on tablets of stone but on tablets of human hearts, . . . ministers of a new covenant, not in a written code but in the Spirit; for the written code kills, but the Spirit gives life . . .Now the Lord is the Spirit, and where the Spirit of the Lord is, there is freedom. And we all, with unveiled face, beholding the glory of the Lord, are being changed into his likeness from one degree of glory to another; for this comes from the Lord who is the Spirit" (II Corinthians 3:3, 6, 17-18).

Note

A version of this chapter was previously published in *Social Work and Christianity*, 20(2), 1993.

References

Adams, R. M. (1987). *The virtue of faith*. New York: Oxford University Press.

Hauerwas, S. (1981). *A community of character: Toward a constructive Christian social ethic*. Notre Dame: University of Notre Dame Press.

Hauerwas, Stanley and Willimon, William H. (1989). *Resident aliens: Life in the Christian colony*. Nashville: Abingdon Press.

Holmes, A. (1984). *Ethics: Approaching moral decisions*. Downers Grove, IL: InterVarsity Press.

Lewis, C. S. (1947). *The abolition of man*. New York: Macmillan.

Lewis, C. S. (1943). *Mere Christianity*. New York: Macmillan.

MacIntyre, A. (1984). *After virtue: A study in moral theory*. 2nd Ed. University of Notre Dame Press.

NASW. (1999). *Code of ethics*. Washington, DC: National Association of Social Workers.

Osborne, G. R. (1991). *The hermeneutical spiral: A comprehensive introduction to biblical interpretation*. Downers Grove, IL: InterVarsity Press.

Pinnock, C. (1984). *The scripture principle*. New York: Harper and Row.

Reamer, F. (1990). *Ethical dilemmas in social service*. 2nd Ed. New York: Columbia University Press.

Sire, J. W. (1980). *Scripture twisting*. Downers Grove, IL: InterVarsity Press.

Sherwood, D. A. (Spring-Fall 1981). Add to your faith virtue: The integration of Christian values and social work practice. *Social Work & Christianity, 8*, 41-54.

Sherwood, D. A. (Spring 1989). How should we use the bible in ethical decision-making? Guidance without legalism or relativism. *Social Work & Christianity, 16*, 29-42

Sherwood, D. A. (Fall 1986). Notes toward applying Christian ethics to practice: Growing up into the image of Christ. *Social Work & Christianity, 13*, 82-93.

Sherwood, D. A. (1999). Integrating Christian faith and social work: Reflections of a social work educator. *Social Work & Christianity, 26*(1), 1-8.

Sherwood, David A. (2002). Ethical integration of faith and social work practice: Evangelism. *Social Work & Christianity, 29*(1), 1-12.

Smedes, Lewis. (1983). *Mere morality*. Grand Rapids: Eerdmans.

Swartley, Willard M. (1983). *Slavery, sabbath, war, and women: Case issues in biblical interpretation*. Scottsdale, PA: Herald Press.

Resources

Evans, C. S. (2004). *Kierkegaard's ethic of love: Divine commands and moral obligations*. New York: Oxford University Press.

Evans, C. S. (2006). Is there a basis for loving all people? *Journal of Psychology and Theology, 34*(1), 78-90.

Keith-Lucas, A. (1994). *Giving and taking help*. Botsford, CT: North American Association of Christians in Social Work.

Keith-Lucas, A. (1985). *So you want to be a social worker: A primer for the Christian student*. Botsford, CT: North American Association of Christians in Social Work.

Mott, S. C. (1982). *Biblical ethics and social change*. New York: Oxford University Press.

O'Donovan, O. (1986). *Resurrection and the moral order: An outline for evangelical ethics*. Grand Rapids: Eerdmans.

Sherwood, D. A. (2000). Pluralism, tolerance, and respect for diversity: Engaging our deepest differences within the bond of civility. *Social Work & Christianity, 27*(1), 1-7.

Sherwood, D. A. (2007). Moral, believing social workers: Philosophical and theological foundations of moral obligation in social work ethics. *Social Work & Christianity, 34*(2), 121-145.

Smith, C. (2003). *Moral, believing animals: Human personhood and culture*. New York: Oxford University Press.

Verhay, A. (1984). *The great reversal: Ethics and the new testament*. Grand Rapids: Eerdmans.

Wolterstorff, N. (2006). Justice, not charity: Social work through the eyes of faith. *Social Work & Christianity, 33*(2), 123-140.

CHAPTER 21

FAMILIES AND THEIR FAITH[1]

Diana R. Garland

Congregations often look to social workers as staff members or consultants to provide leadership for congregational ministries with families (Garland, 1999). Goals for family ministry include helping families strengthen the faith dimension of their family life, participate in a community where they are supported and provide support and service to others and to the larger community, and develop strength and resilience in their relationships so that they can face life challenges. These goals are mutually reinforcing. A significant body of research has demonstrated that families that are strong, especially in the face of adversity, have an active spiritual dimension to their life together. They are involved in a community of faith (Brody, Stoneman, & McCrary, 1994; Call & Heaton, 1997; Deveaux, 1996; McCubbin & McCubbin, 1988; Walsh, 1999).[2] For example, a group of researchers have discovered that regular attendance at religious services is inversely associated with domestic violence (Ellison, Bartkowski, & Anderson, 1999).

The research thus far has not described the variables of faith and religion in family life sufficiently for congregations to know *how* they can strengthen this dimension of family life, however. This question is not only of interest to social workers in congregations, but also to social workers in all kinds of settings whose work includes both preventing family distress by helping families to develop strength and resilience, as well as helping families in distress find effective coping strategies. Every crisis in life is by definition at some level a crisis of faith. Spirituality is a dimension of life that needs attention whatever the problem or circumstance that brings a family to seek help.

From a social systems perspective, it is commonly accepted that families have shared beliefs, values, and practices, although these frameworks of meaning have not been called "family faith." For example, Hamilton McCubbin and his colleagues studied the strength and resilience of families in many circumstances, including families in wartime who have lost loved ones or who have confronted the ongoing stressor of having a family member "missing in action." McCubbin concluded that families have what he called "a family schema." He defined a family schema as "a set of beliefs, values, goals, priorities, and expectations about themselves in relationship to each other, and about their family in relationship to the community and the social system beyond its boundaries" (McCubbin & McCubbin, 1993, p. 154). McCubbin has seen family schema as relatively stable, "a point of reference, a guide or standard against which situational and stressor level appraisals are compared and shaped" (McCubbin & McCubbin, 1993, p.

154). McCubbin's research describes families developing within the family unit a shared understanding, trust and acceptance, "usually with the assistance of their spiritual beliefs, thus making the difficulties comprehensible and meaningful" (McCubbin & McCubbin, 1986, p. 71). "Family faith" is an alternative definitional frame for studying family schema in Christian families.

Biblical Narratives and Family Faith

When working with a congregation, the effective social worker draws the connections from the social science research and theory to the language and concerns of the church, sometimes by connecting current concerns with the biblical themes and narratives of Christian faith. Bible stories provide a shared spiritual heritage that shapes our understanding of God, our world and ourselves. The meaning of biblical narratives is seldom transparent or uni-dimensional, providing rich opportunity for community conversation, conflict, and deeper understanding over time. Biblical texts that address the role of faith and spirituality in families provide such a framework for conversation about social work research and practice with families in congregations. The story of Lydia provides a fascinating place to begin this connection from social science research today to stories now 2000 years old.

When the head of the household became a Christian in the church of the first century, so did everyone else in the household. Lydia, a business woman and a household head, must have been remarkable in her patriarchal first-century Roman world. When Paul and Silas preached where the women in town gathered by the river to pray, Lydia was there and experienced God "opening her heart." In response, Lydia had the apostles baptize her whole household (Acts 16: 13-15). She then persuaded Paul and Silas to come eat and stay with her family.

Sometime later, Paul and Silas were arrested. While they were in prison, singing hymns and praying through the night, a violent earthquake shook the foundations of the prison and opened all the prison doors. The jailer, afraid that all the prisoners had escaped, prepared to run himself through with his sword, but Paul stopped him, shouting, "Don't harm yourself! We are all here!" (Acts 16:25-29). In response, the jailer asked what he must do to be saved. Paul's response was "Believe in the Lord Jesus, and you will be saved—you and your household" (Acts 16:31). In response, the jailer and his family were baptized "immediately" (Acts 16:33). The story concludes, like the story of Lydia, with Paul and Silas going home with the jailer for a meal with the family, the jailer "filled with joy because he had come to believe in God—he and his whole family" (Acts 16:34; see also 1 Cor. 1:16).

In the United States in the 21st Century, deciding to take up one religion or another is largely a personal choice. If a husband or wife makes a decision to become a Christian, we don't round up their spouse, children, sisters and brothers, and anybody else living in the household, and dunk or sprinkle them with baptismal waters (depending on the baptismal traditions of the particular faith community). Did Lydia's family take a vote about whether or not they wanted to be baptized? The jailer's family had not been at the prison to hear Paul and Silas' impromptu prayer meeting. What is more, Paul told the jailer that if *he* believed in the Lord Jesus, he *and his household* would be saved.

Clearly, cultural differences create these questions for us. In the patriarchal Roman culture of the early church, householders controlled the religious expression of the household. Households had their own gods and their own altars, and joining a household meant joining that household's religious practices. Christians adopted this household model for the early churches. Churches did not have land and buildings; they met in private houses. The earliest missionaries tried to win over one household, which then became the base for reaching out to other households in the community (Lampe, 1992; Straughan, 2002). We do not have any way of knowing the extent to which all members of the household understood, much less chose, the faith they were adopting (Osiek, 1996).

It is too easy to dismiss the concept of faith belonging to the household or family as a first-century cultural artifact, however. In a research project studying the faith of families, I conducted two-hour interviews with 120 Protestant Christian families for two hours each in four different regions of the country and in four different Protestant denominations: United Methodist, National Baptist, Presbyterian USA, and Southern Baptist (Garland, 2001; 2002a). The project used grounded theory methodology (Glaser & Strauss, 1967; Miles & Huberman, 1994; Rubin & Rubin, 1995; Weiss, 1994). The analysis of more than 240 hours of transcribed interviews has led to a model for understanding faith as a dimension of family life that has significance alongside and influencing the other dimensions of family life social workers consider in their assessment of families, such as communication, roles, power distribution, and subsystem boundaries. This model has grown from the study of a purposeful, nonrandom sample of Protestant Christian families and the generalizability to other Protestant Christian families and families of other religious traditions has yet to be explored. [3]

Religion, Spirituality, and Faith

The three terms religion, spirituality, and faith are interrelated but can be distinguished from one another. Religion refers to a *shared culture* of beliefs, values, and rules for behaving and relating to others and to God. Religion is thus an aspect of a group or a culture. Often that culture becomes formalized in organizations; in the Christian church, those organizations include congregations, denominations, and parachurch and ecumenical organizations.

Religious behaviors are often expressed in rituals that are rich with meaning because they express the beliefs and values shared by a people. The individual is not alone but is a part of and connected with a believing community that reinforces, challenges, and shapes individual faith. Prayers recited together, "passing the peace," baptism, and partaking of communion together are rituals rich with meanings that connect us to God and to the community of faith. Religion is for a community or culture, then, what faith is for the individual, and it is also in dynamic interaction and sometimes tension with individual faith when the individual is a part of a religious community or organization. For those persons who are part of a religious group or community, religion thus provides an environment in which faith develops and is nurtured and challenged. But religious organizations and communities are not any person's entire environment; many persons develop faith totally independent of and unrelated to formal religion. Even persons who are deeply religious—deeply committed to their church or religious traditions—are influenced by the other groups and cultures to which they belong. Faith develops in response to and in interaction with the person's whole physical and interpersonal environment, not just those contexts that are overtly religious. The nature of the faith of those who are significant to us also has an enormous influence on the shape of our own faith.

Spirituality refers to the individual, interpersonal, and transcendental *behaviors and experiences* through which we express and develop faith. Spirituality, then, is the behavioral component, that which we do because of our beliefs and understanding of God or the power that transcends our own. Sometimes spirituality is overtly religious, such as in rituals, and sometimes it is not. Persons can be spiritual without being a part of a religious group or tradition. In Christian religion, spirituality is often expressed in what have been called "practices" or "spiritual disciplines" These practice include such activities as worship, prayer, meditation, study of Scripture, singing, confession of failures to others, forgiveness of others, listening compassionately to others, hospitality, giving of one's financial and other resources, service to others, and working for social justice. (Anderson & Foley, 1998; Bass & Dykstra, 1997; Bender, 1995; Brother Lawrence of the Resurrection, 1977; Dykstra & Bass, 1997; Foster, 1978; Garland, 2002b; Lee, 1990; Nelson, 1990).

Because of the interrelationship and sometimes overlapping nature of religion and spirituality, people often do not distinguish between them (Zinnbauer & al., 1997). In fact, Charles Joanides found that Christians are uncomfortable with trying to discuss spirituality and religion as though they are separate entities, insisting that they are profoundly interrelated; "religion is likened to 'a bonding agent' that connected them to God, their neighbor (neighbor referring to people in their social network) and to their cultural and ancestral past" (Joanides, 1997, p. 72). He concluded that "faith" is a term that communicates more effectively with persons who are Christians than either religion or spirituality. As we are using the term, "faith" includes the highly individualized and internalized beliefs, sense of trust, actions, and experiences of individuals. It can also refer to the shared beliefs and behaviors of a group of people (a family) or a whole community (a congregation).

What is Faith?

David and Darlene have been married for ten years. They each brought a son and a different religious tradition to their marriage. David has continued to be involved in the Catholic church with his son Pete, and Darlene is active in the Presbyterian church with her son Paul. When I asked Darlene's family what faith means to them, she answered, "I guess faith is the belief that Jesus was here and real and died for us and we have eternal life through Him."

For Darlene, faith is *belief* about who God is and how God relates to persons. Faith has to do with the answers we have come to as we have wondered about the big questions of our lives. Faith is something that involves our minds, our thinking, our pondering and deciding on what we believe to be the truth.

Belief leads to *trust*, a second facet of faith. Another word for trust is *confidence*. The beliefs we hold increase our trust, our confidence that we can face life's challenges. Shamika is a young wife and only child of her widowed African-American mother and her deceased Anglo-American father. She answered the same question, "what does the word faith mean to you," by saying,

> It seems like faith is so much a part of me, but it's not conscious. It's inside me. It's like a thread in fabric. It's a thread that runs all through that you don't see but if you pull it out all the other threads fall out. My faith doesn't really hold my family together but I think it's definitely something that holds me together. I rely on it and then I don't worry so much about things that I can't control. I believe in God—that He loves me; that I can't control everything. I can't do everything by myself. I think my faith makes me stronger for the rest of my family.

Shamika not only *believes in God,* but she believes that *God loves her and acts* on that love by making her strong. She trusts God to hold her together. Her faith does not keep her from worrying, but it keeps her from worrying "so much." It also somehow prepares her for the demands of family life. If belief has to do with our thoughts and minds, then trust has to do with our emotions, our heart.

Beth and Tom have been married 40 years. Their daughter Misty is 25 and has always lived with them; their two grown sons live in other cities in the state. Misty works full time in a hospital and also is the youth minister for the youth in their church. She is carrying on what she has watched her parents do all her life—work in the church. Beth told me, "Most of our activities have been in the church; that's where we've met people and had friends." They have done renovation of the church building, carpentry and painting. And they have been leaders in various programs of their Methodist congregation, teaching adult Sunday School classes and leading children's groups. Misty said, "I can't remember ever a time in my life that the church was not there and a very active part of my life and our family's life." Currently, however, Beth is discouraged and angry over a conflict in their congregation and has not been attending. "It's the most traumatic experience I've ever been through," she said. Even so, they are still busy serving. Beth and Tom are running a food drive for an ecumenical community ministries agency. Tom repairs bicycles for the church to give to poor children. And they deliver Meals on Wheels. Here is how Beth defined faith for me:

Two things best describe God. One of them is a quick story about a little boy and little girl, and I'm this way about my faith. They are late for school and the little boy says, 'Let's stop and pray,' and the little girl says, 'Let's run and pray.' That's kind of my faith. I've got a faith that God is there. I talk to Him. I pray for the guidance. 'Just show me, guide me, and help me be aware that you are guiding me.' The other thing is that I guess my faith is too simple. To me there are just two verses in the Bible that are really important. "Love your neighbor as yourself" and "God so loved the world He gave his only son." And the third one is where Jesus said, "In my father's house are many mansions. I go to prepare a place for you." That's good enough for me.

Beth says her faith is "too simple;" she simply believes that God is there and listens to her prayers. She trusts that Heaven will be there and she does not have to worry about it. But she actually begins her definition of faith with action—she believes in running while she is praying. She does not simply leave it to God to work out problems. The three scriptures she refers to touch on three aspects of faith: belief ("God so loved the world...."), trust ("I go to prepare a place for you"), and action ("Love your neighbor as yourself").

People's actions flow from belief about what is real and what is important. Jesus taught us to be active, storing up treasures for ourselves in heaven, not on earth, where moth and rust destroy. "For where your treasure is, there your heart will be also" (Matt. 6:21). We treasure that which we value. That treasure is what we give our hearts to, what we trust. In other words, action not only grows out of our faith, but action also turns around and shapes our faith. What happens if we believe that God answers prayers when we believe and trust in him, and we do believe and trust, but still the sick child for whom we are praying so fervently and confidently dies? Sometimes the outcomes of our attempts to live faithfully deepen and confirm our faith. But other times, our faith is shaken and changed (Nelson, 1992). Faith is thus a cycle that begins with belief about God and our world and our place in it—the "meaning" of our lives and our experiences. Those beliefs lead to trust (or a lack of trust), which leads to actions, and the outcomes of those actions in turn have an impact on our understanding, our beliefs.

Figure 1. Faith as a dynamic cycle.

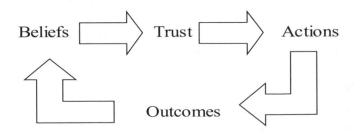

To truly understand a person's faith, we need to know more than a summary statement of beliefs, or even what that person values and trusts. We need to know how they are living their faith day by day in response to those beliefs. The stories of daily living are not simply illustrations; they *are* the embodied beliefs of persons, the lived experiences that are more than simple belief statements can say. Those actions are the person's identity as a person of faith. We need to know the stories of how they came to their beliefs, what they are committed to, and the stories of living those commitments. Craig Dykstra has argued that to study persons' faith, we need to look for the intentions that shape how they approach life. What are the person's life stories, the themes, events, and experiences that say "this is who I am?" Rather than assigning persons to stages of faith development, the approach James Fowler has taken (Fowler, 1981, 1991), this approach suggests that social workers need to learn about persons' faith biographies, the stories that represent persons' faith in all its complexity (Dykstra, 1986). Faith is particularly significant in social work practice because of the profession's focus on person-in-environment. Faith points us to the client's ultimate environment (Fowler, 1981). It identifies the powers and influences on persons' behavior that otherwise might be hidden to us. Viktor Frankl pointed out, for example, the unseen powers of hope and faith and meaning-in-the-midst-of suffering that had a significant impact on the survival of some concentration camp prisoners during the Holocaust (Frankl, 1969). The beliefs derived from one's faith identify the meaning of experiences, a meaning quite unlike what others would experience in similar situations. Stories provide a medium through which families develop and share their faith in the telling of their own family stories. These stories often tell more than the words and events used to tell the story; underneath and carrying the words are the meaning and purpose of their shared lives, and the faith they have—in one another, in what they value together, in God. Stories say to others and to the family itself, "This is who we are." Because of that underlying melody of meaning, stories give families a sense of identity and of belonging (Garland, 2003)

Family as the Crucible for Our Personal Faith

Family life provides a crucible for individuals to learn faith. For example, research has shown that parents directly and indirectly impact God-images in children. When parents are perceived as nurturing and powerful, especially when mother is perceived as powerful and father is perceived as nurturing, children perceive God as both nurturing and powerful (Dickie et al., 1997).

Adults, too, have their faith shaped by family life. Family experiences test, shape, and deepen our faith. A step-mother described faith to me this way:

> Real issues of living a Christian life are more difficult in an intimate relationship with your family than they are with anybody else. I mean, people can go out and serve food in a soup kitchen and think they're doing this Christian deed and then not understand how to

nurture or help somebody in their family who is starving for some other thing. I am not getting along with my step-daughter. Last Sunday, I sat in church and listened to the sermon and I just kept thinking, "This is horrible; I am not treating her in the way I would think of myself as a Christian." It tortured me to try to figure that out. I didn't get any further than that. A lot of people are looking for very simplistic guidance instead of having to suffer the pain of wrestling with things. The family represents a working path to get there.

Families Shape Personal Beliefs

Conversations about faith in families commonly take place in response to family life events or discussion of ideas and experiences to which members are exposed. Shamika's father worked at an automobile factory when he and Sheryl married. Because he was a white man marrying a black woman, other men at the plant began to harass him, and this continued for more than a year, until after Shamika's birth. Sometimes he ignored the taunts and threats, but when it got to him, he would lash back. Shamika's father ended up dead, his murder still unsolved. Shamika said:

> You never think that someone would be that prejudiced and that narrow minded that they would actually want to take another person's life. But it does happen. And it had happened in that town before. They knew of other cases where black men got together and killed a white person because they felt like you don't need to be with our women, or white men did it. It went both ways. When I was 13 or 14, it just hit me. I was looking through my photo albums one day. I don't know why, but I just couldn't handle it any more. I felt so alone. I was really depressed for a while, and my mom asked, "What's wrong?" I finally just broke down and started sobbing and she said, "You're not by yourself. Remember how I used to tell you when you were little that he's still watching you up there. He knows what's going on with you." She also told me that my dad was such a good person that he was just too good for the world. When I got married it came back again because I thought, 'Why can't I have my dad walk me down the aisle?' There are questions that come up that there is no answer for. There's no why. It's not something you can stop yourself from asking and it's very difficult for me."

Shamika went on to say that faith meant believing that she could leave justice in God's hands, as her grandmother taught: "My grandmother always used to tell my mother, 'What goes around comes around. Don't worry about it. God sees it.'"

Instead of thinking about revenge, she believes that God will dispense judgment on those who take care of people who don't do what they're supposed to do.

It's not up to me to decide it or find them or try and bring justice. That's not my job. God takes care of people who do things right and who do things wrong and I have to believe that. I have to let my hands not touch that one. It's almost evil hating something like that. I shouldn't be this angry. It's something I have to work through and I have to let it go and it's very hard. I think if I didn't have my faith, if I didn't believe in God, I don't think I would come out of it.

Growing up with the reality of her father's murder has created significant challenges for Shamika's beliefs about God and justice. The family has not just been the context for the challenge, however; it has also provided ways of thinking about it and emotional support for dealing with the challenge. Mother is there, sensitive enough to see through the moods of a 14-year-old that "something is wrong," and then offering presence and a comforting belief that her father is still with her. Grandmother offers a belief system that there will be justice, that Shamika can put her trust in God.

Families Teach People to Trust—or Not

Families also provide a context for persons—both children and adults—to learn to trust—trust one another and trust God. When family relationships are not trustworthy, then faith in God may also be shaken, for adults as well as for children. Erik Erikson describes the first task of human beings as the establishment of basic trust (Erikson, 1968). But this does not happen, if at all, merely once and for all (Parks, 1992). Persons repeatedly find anchors of trust shaken loose and then reestablished, often and especially in family relationships.

Jacob and Kate are parents of two sons David (age 9), and Douglas (age 7). Twenty years ago, Jacob and Kate met in college, fell in love, and married when they graduated. Both parents sing in their church choir. Also, Jacob directs and Kate plays the piano for their children's choir in which David and Douglas sing enthusiastically. They all go to Sunday School and worship every Sunday. It all sounds so "John and Mary Churchfamily," until they talk about the tragedy that has shaped their life together and their understanding of God's ways.

Kate grew up Catholic and Jacob grew up in a National Baptist church. Their different faith traditions were not important when they met and married, though, because church was not important to either of them. Kate remembers being one of only two African-American families in the church of her childhood, and how uncomfortable and unwelcome she felt there. Jacob became disillusioned with the church when his pastor's daughter became pregnant and, because of the pregnancy, the pastor refused to allow her a church wedding.

I thought to myself, "Here you're teaching us forgiveness. Are you really learning any of what you're telling us?" After a while I just found myself saying the heck with it. We'd read the paper in bed on Sunday mornings instead of getting up and going to church.

Their first son, Mark, was born when they had been married three years. Their lives revolved around him, a happy child with big smiles and dancing feet that entertained their extended family. He was the first grandchild. When Mark was three years old, Kate began having nightmares that something terrible was going to happen. "Does God send dreams?" she still wonders. Jacob describes what began as an average day, with Kate rushing to take Mark to the babysitter on her way to work.

> I remember the expression on Mark's face. He had his coat on and he looked at me and said, "Bye!" and he had this expression on his face like, "See ya. Everything's fine." I often wonder if children communicate with God more than adults do. He came back and gave me a kiss good-bye. He hadn't done that in a while. I still remember.

While they were both working, Kate told me, there was a fire at the babysitter's house and he died from acute carbon monoxide poisoning.

> "The flames didn't get him … "Jacob interrupted her, "Smoke inhalation. He was asleep at the time. They said that it was painless. He probably just took a deep breath and never woke up. Our pain never stops."

Their world fell apart. Both of them were angry—at God, at one another, at the world in general—because the loss was so terribly painful. They struggled to hold on to one another. Two more sons were born. But they were growing apart in their search for meaning in the seeming senselessness of Mark's death. Kate was desperate:

> I went to see spiritualists and they said, "You need to pray more." They gave me some suggestions and I went to the library and I was looking at different books. I came across the dream books and I came across meditation and one thing just led to another. I was into searching, so I looked at a lot of different things. Channeling, and all that. What is everything about? This was my thing. Strictly my thing. I tried to share it a little bit with Jacob, but he wasn't into it. I didn't want to impose.

As Jacob said, "We just took different paths." They occasionally visited churches together, because Jacob was looking for more "traditional" answers to his grief. No place felt right, and they never attended the same church twice. Seven years after their son's death, the pastor of a little Baptist church in their community came to visit them and asked something they had never heard before from a church leader, "Is there anything we can do for you?" He held their hands and prayed with them, and they went to church with him to find a delightful mix of Anglo and African-American families worshipping together. They felt at home. The congregation did not try to salve their grief or tell them why their son had died but gave them a safe place to grieve and struggle together. It has been almost ten years since their son's death, and even today it is still difficult for them to talk about.

They still don't agree on what it means. Jacob believes that somehow God needed his son:

> When Mark passed, I'd just get up every morning and think, "Well, there's a plan out there. Nobody consulted me when He thought it up, but there must be a plan out there for something like this to happen." He was three. At every family gathering he'd dance. And I just believe that there must be somebody out there that needed whatever that spirit could provide more than us. I have to think that there's a reason why. It's got to be because somebody else must have been going through some serious deprivation in their life and it was time for them to feel good too. I think I'm a much better parent now.

Kate disagrees.

> I don't have the same feelings. Mark was an extremely intelligent little boy. I was just beginning to teach him to read and spell words and he could do it. I'll never forget that. I remember a couple of days before he passed away, I was bragging to somebody at work about how smart my boy was. It just blows me away. I think everybody is part of a plan. His death pushed me to grow spiritually. I don't know if he was still here if we would be going to church. I really don't know.

Jacob added, "I've never thought about that, but it's true."

Kate continued:

> I like to think I would have. God doesn't give you burdens that you can't bear. It was real traumatic when that happened. We survived it. We've moved on. We've progressed. We did not go backwards.

Clearly, their faith has been shaped by their shared experience, and they both think they have grown spiritually as a consequence. The account of their son's death that they had shared earlier is a family story, told to me in the typical tag team story-telling of families. It is clear, however, that they have not talked much about their attempts to understand the *meaning* of their son's death, indicated when Jacob says, "I've never thought about that." They do agree about trusting that God allowed this tragedy to occur for a reason, though they do not agree on what that reason is. They both describe the resulting spiritual growth they have experienced, but they use the word "me" not "we." Although they do not necessarily agree on the meaning of their son's death, putting their lives together afterwards has clearly been a family experience, expressed as something "we" have done.. As Kate says, "We survived it. We did not go backwards."

With all their unanswered questions and even fundamental differences in their understanding of God's ways, they celebrate their survival. They had lived in their house three months when Mark died. For Jacob, the house has come to symbolize their life since his death:

I think this house pictures the way that things have been with us. It looks great now. But if you had seen what it was like before we got hold of it, you wouldn't have believed it. I put the floor down. Kate and I patched and sanded and primed and painted those walls. I put the moldings up. Whatever you see here is because we did it. Sometimes people come in those rooms and say, "Oh this is beautiful"! and I feel like saying, "Do you want to see the scars? Do you want to see how it got to look beautiful"?

Their family is "beautiful" because they have survived. They may never agree on the meaning of their son's death. Many in their church community probably would not agree with either one of them. Does God cause the death of children because their spirits are needed elsewhere? Or to shake their parents into a spiritual journey? Perhaps senseless, evil things happen outside of God's control, and God grieves with us and is present to us as we grieve. But if God does not cause such things to happen, then is God not in control? Why do bad things happen?

No one who loves others is spared such questions. Every family has or will someday face life-shaking tragedy. Perhaps it will not be Kate and Jacob's kind of tragedy, but it will be a tragedy nevertheless. In families, we confront the most fundamental issues of life and death and faith. We learn faith here, and we are shattered here, and we struggle—whether together or in isolation—to make sense of it all here. Often the families whom social workers serve are dealing with such fundamental issues; death, unemployment, disabling illness, addictions, and all the other crises of family life are fundamentally crises of life's meaning and thus of faith. For Kate and Jacob, this has been a lonely path because they found different answers. And yet they did so in one another's arms, and in the arms of a community of faith. They held on to one another, gave one another room to struggle and, at the same time, did not leave one another alone in the struggle. They remodeled their house—together.

Family as the Context for Action

Families provide multiple opportunities in both the mundane and the extraordinary experiences of life for acting on faith. Parents overwhelmed by the responsibilities of parenting pray and find strength greater than what they believe they could muster without God's help. The actions of reading the Bible and praying provide a sense of peace even in the most difficult times. In a time of great financial crisis, the community of faith provides help that carries a family through and deepens their trust in God and the people of faith. At other times, however, the expected outcomes of their faith-based action are not forthcoming. Faith is challenged and sometimes reshaped. Corrine described the crisis of faith she experienced that began with a routine surgery on one of her sons shortly after her conversion.

I had my newborn faith. I felt like I had been born again and was trying to be a little bit too rigid in my behavior. I thought, "I'm not going to cuss and I'm not going to think bad thoughts." I had my little checklist and thought if I did all these things I would be okay with God. And I prayed every day for 45 minutes for all these people on my list. I thought if I did this, I would be okay with God. Kurt (the younger son) had all these warts on his hand. They said they could remove them with laser surgery, and just give him a general anesthesia. That's pretty traumatic to give a little seven-year-old. So while Kurt was in recovery and I looked across the street and I saw the cross and I started praying. I said, "God I know that this is a sign that everything is going to be just fine. Thank you Lord that you protected my child just like I had been praying so hard for. And thank you for letting him come out and they say everything will be fine."

Everything was not fine, however. Her son developed a rare infection and almost died. Afterward he developed other major problems that have continued to threaten his health and have challenged his mother's faith:

Some churches teach that if you pray those prayers of protection and if you do everything right things will be right in your life. And I thought, "Why?" I even went to a Bible study called "Trusting God." My next door neighbor took me. She said, "I think this will help you." It left me even more spiritually devastated because I felt like they were pointing a finger at me: "This must have happened for a reason. Did God do this to you to bring you closer to Him?" And I thought, "He would not use a child! These things don't happen to bring me or my husband to the Lord." I will never go back to that. I don't try to fit theology in little neat boxes any more. I just say that I don't understand. We're just supposed to help each other through it. I will never go back to those churches again. I love my church because they would soothe, they would comfort, but they weren't pushy like we had to get in and solve this today. They were just there.

This family experience challenged her beliefs about how God responds to faith practices. In fact, she rejected those beliefs. In the resulting crisis of faith, she sought out and joined a new faith community and, in the process, redefined her understanding of God. When the results of being faithful have are not what we expect, our beliefs often change and the cycle of belief, trust, behavior and outcomes continues.

Up to this point, we have been looking at ways that families provide a context for shaping, challenging, and reshaping the faith of individuals. In addition, however, families have sacred stories that tell about their experiences *as a family*.

Narratives of Family Faith

James and Marianne brought four children to their marriage from their previous marriages. James' son Corey has severe developmental and physical challenges and uses a wheel chair. Corey works part-time at a sheltered workshop.

Marianne has two daughters, Sasha (16) and Sandi (11). Last year, the "ours" baby, Ariah, was born. They live on the edge of poverty, both economically and geographically. Both of them are working at low-wage jobs to support their four children. The two-story home they proudly own is located in the inner city on a quiet street but not far from the public housing projects where James works as a maintenance man. The area is inhabited by gangs and has a high rate of violence. James sees the projects as his mission field. Whenever he goes into an apartment to fix a leaky faucet or broken appliance, he prays. He doesn't pray for protection. He prays instead that he will care for the resident as he would care for Jesus. It is Marianne who is praying for protection for him!

It has not always been this way. Soon after their marriage, James became unemployed and, in discouragement, slipped into alcohol and drug abuse, sometimes not coming home at night. Marianne hung on, praying for God to help her husband. Now he is recovering and has had a profound conversion experience. They are proud that they are becoming an anchor family in their struggling community. James loves their congregation and their pastor, and he is in training to become a deacon. As we talked about their faith, Marianne told me that she identifies with Moses' wife:

> She just stuck with him with him being gone up to the mountain and coming back down. That's how I look at myself. Through thick and thin. That's my husband. It got close, because I kept thinking when we were going through it, "I'm just going to tell him to get out, to leave." And then I thought, "No, because if I tell him that, he'll really do it. If I tell him to leave, he won't come home." Through all of what was happening, I kept praying and praying and praying. It just made me stronger. It was something that I needed to increase my faith and to make me strong.

Sandi, the eleven-year old, picked up on the earlier statement that her mother identifies with Moses' wife. Sandi said her favorite Bible story is of the boy David,

> Because he fought Goliath with only five stones. And Goliath had a sword and shield, and David killed Goliath with just one stone. I think I'm as strong as David and I can do anything with Christ.

This is a story of strength, and a child learning strength from parents who have "been through" and persevered.

Family Belief and Trust

Peggy and Bill are in their 70s, married more than 50 years. They raised four sons, and the story of their life that overshadows all others is that of losing Chris. Chris was in the military, stationed in Puerto Rico. They knew that Chris and his wife were have marital troubles, but they didn't know how serious. Chris became depressed. As they told the story to me, they interrupted and verbally tumbled over one another, both of them with tears in their eyes through most of the story. First, they received a call that Chris was "missing in action" from his military unit. During those same days, Bill's elderly mother became ill and died. The funerals were in the same week.

As Bill began to relate how, that same weekend, one of their grown sons came for a visit, Peggy interrupted "Let me tell this," she said. "The Lord just takes care of you because Grant (oldest son) was here and the day that they came to tell us that Chris' body had washed ashore. Grant and his wife came."

Bill picked up the story again,

He said "Daddy we have some folks here." It was about this time in the afternoon. He said, "We have some folks here that want to see you; are you up to seeing them?" I said, "Sure I want to see them." He said, "They're from the military." I said, "Are they here to tell me they found Chris' body?" He said, "Yes, sir." I don't believe there is any way you can do something like this without the Lord. For three days, knowing your son is missing and not knowing where he is, all you do is pray and talk to God about it every waking minute and you wonder how you sleep, but I slept like a baby.

Peggy interrupted him,

On Tuesday—that's the day that they came out to tell us that they had found his body—well, by that time all of us were getting anxious and didn't know what to do. Thousands of miles away and he's missing. So each one, Bill and all three of our other sons, had gone to see their pastors.

Bill explained,

I went to talk to Brother Tim and said, "Preacher I don't know how to take it." I just told him about Chris being missing and I just talked to him about 30 minutes. Well, Grant in (another town) went and talked to his preacher that day, Marty in (another town) talked to his preacher that day and Bart over in (another state) went and talked to his preacher that day. All four of us talked to our preachers that day.

Peggy said,

A kind of peace came over me, and I just sort of relaxed and when they came and told us the news you know, I was still calm. I didn't go to pieces or anything. I guess we had been prepared. Bill told me that he went and talked to his preacher and they mostly prayed for me. So I felt like that's what happened.

Bill agreed,

A peace comes over you that is unexplainable. During this time we have a swing that is on the back lot and in the four days time—I wasn't working because I had just had a heart attack—and I'd just sit in that swing and mope and dread and cry my heart out and talk to the Lord. In it I told the Lord that day if he'd help me find Chris (crying), I'd try to live my life to suit him. And I'm trying to do it.

Peggy went on with the story: "The lady that came from the base, she was a psychologist that came and talked to us. She had told us that if a storm had not come up his body would never have washed ashore."

The details of Peggy and Bill's story turn what seems like a senseless tragedy into a story of God at work in their lives during this terrible time. Their oldest son happened to be in their home because of his grandmother's death when the news came of his brother's body being found. Peggy cited this detail as evidence that "the Lord takes care of you"; Grant was there to support and comfort them. They credit Peggy's sense of peace to the fact that the three remaining sons and Bill all independently consulted their pastors on the same day and prayed for her, and it was at that time that she found a new sense of peace in the midst of the crisis. The father had prayed for searchers to find his son, presumed dead by that point, pledging to live a more "suitable life" if God would help. When he adds, tears rolling down his face, that he's "trying to do it," his wife explains. A storm washed their son's body ashore, or he would never have been found. She implies that God sent the storm as an answer to the father's prayer. They have suffered tremendous grief. But the story is one that communicates not chaos and meaningless but quite the opposite. Through the presence of others orchestrated by God, and through a storm many miles away, they trace orderliness and experience these events as God's care for them. Together, telling the story confirms the meaning they have found together in these events.

You met Darlene and her second husband David earlier. They have two sons from previous marriages, his son Pete (age 14) and her son Paul (age 11). When were talking about what faith means to them, Paul said that for him,

Faith means living the life that I think God would want me to live and believing that He is our creator and nothing happens without God having a plan. I was talking to my mom about it in the car just a few days ago about how every bad thing ends up with a good thing. When my mom moved here, she probably thought it was going to be the end of the world because she didn't know anybody or about anything that goes on down here [in the Deep South]. But if she hadn't done that she wouldn't have met my dad and chances are she wouldn't have had me. And another example is if my mom hadn't gotten divorced, I wouldn't have Pete [stepbrother] or my Dad [stepdad].

Paul takes two crises in his mother's life—her move to the South and her divorce—and traces how God used them for good. These must be family stories he has been told, because all of this happened before he was born or can remember. He does not simply tell the story but further develops it, pointing out that without the move, she would not have met his father (and had him!), and without the divorce, he would not have his stepfather and stepbrother. Notice, too, that he had this conversation with his mother "in the car just a few days ago." Conversation about faith and other matters of importance often come when families are on our way to somewhere else, not when they plan for them.

Family faith stories are not all sweetness and good feelings. Paul later recounts a rather frightening incident for him. I had asked the family if they had ever experienced a time when God seemed absent. Paul began hesitantly, casting his eyes at his parents,

> Paul: I don't know if I should say this about this cause it was a real bad time.
>
> Mom: Go for it. That you felt God's absence? When?!
>
> Paul: Well I know He wasn't absent but I remember one time at our old house my mom had accidentally sat some of my dad's file papers next to the water, the sink and I think I might have bumped them into the sink and the water dripped all over them. . .
>
> Dad (interrupting): At the old house?
>
> Paul continues: And you got real mad cause your case was tomorrow.
>
> Everyone began talking at once, and Paul said, louder than the others, "I remember this one."
>
> Dad. Did they get really wet?
>
> Paul: The ink went all over and you couldn't read anything.
>
> Dad: (laughing) I don't remember this.
>
> Paul pressed on: You thought Mama did it and she didn't and I kept trying to tell you that and you were so mad that you got Mamas' jewelry box and threw it out the door.
>
> Pete: I remember that.
>
> Mom: I don't remember this.
>
> Pete: I remember that. I don't know if it was papers, though.
>
> Paul, steadily eying his stepfather: I felt like, "God why didn't you....."
> I tried to tell you that but you were too busy yelling at Mom.

The parents agree in not remembering this incident and seem to be considerably embarrassed at the telling of it. It is a poignant scene as the older stepbrother powerfully sides with the younger child by affirming over and over that he also remembers this event his parents claim to have forgotten, yet at the same time softening the tension of the moment just a bit by questioning one of the details of the story (whether or not it was papers that got wet). Paul frames his story as a time when he felt God's absence, even though he "knew" God was still there. His trust was shaken, even though his belief did not change. He had been through the divorce of his parents, although he did not remember it because he was a baby. But here is his stepfather, the man he knows as father, throwing his mother's most precious things out the back door. Perhaps Paul saw this as a frightening warning. He is the other precious "thing" in his mother's life, and if his stepfather knew that he had caused the wet papers, he might be thrown away, too.

It is doubtful that the parents would have considered this to be a faith-shaping experience for their children. But now they cannot escape it, because the story has been told, affirmed by the older stepbrother and told in the context of the son's understanding of God. The story is now a part of the family's narrative about God and faith and themselves.

Stories often take on a life and develop meanings that were not apparent when they "actually" happened. In fact, they are continuing to "actually happen" as the family tells the story as an illustration of their life together. The story of the angry stepfather above is such a recollection. The story "happens" all over again as the 11-year-old links this memory to his understanding of God, bringing the past into the present as they process it together and frame it as a story of faith. As frightening as this event is, it is a story of faith and trust. The stepson feels secure and trusting enough to tell it these years later, with his mother's encouragement, and the family has survived what may have felt like a rending of relationships at the time. It was just a jewelry box after all. The family survived. And now they can laugh about it, although the parents are clearly unsettled at this revelation of what their children remember. Even so, what once felt so shaky is now secure, now trustworthy. What does that mean to this child's understanding of God?

Family Outcomes

Families have stories of how "things work out"—or not—as a result of their shared faith. Jan and Harold live in the back of a very large old home in a downtown neighborhood in a Southern city. Their divorced daughter and their two grandsons live upstairs. They are not totally happy about this arrangement, but they are trying to help their daughter through some difficult times. They have a large sitting area and living space in their bedroom. These are their "private" quarters; the rest of the house is shared. Jan is a schoolteacher and takes care of her daughter's two sons in the after school hours. In addition, her elderly mother lives about three houses away. They also have three other grown children and several other grandchildren. Their son Martin has been a particular source of challenge and grief, having been involved with using and selling drugs for almost a decade. Their relationship with their son has been the most significant context in which their faith has been tested and shaped. Harold said,

> I figured if I set him down and tried to talk to him the way you and
> I are talking, I could convince him. You can't do it. The drugs are

stronger. Lying upstairs, I said my prayers, I said, "All right God, he's yours. I've done all I can do." God intervened. I had taken out a $40 a month insurance policy on him, kept it for a year and it paid $12,000 for treatment. That took care of the whole thing for a while, then he got back into it and he disappeared. God intervened again. Martin went to the beach, found a friend, and the friend said, "If you stay drug-free, you can live with me until you get on your feet." He met his wife, and she straightened him out. God has come in so many times.

Jan added, "That's the only time we ever had results. It was when we told God that he was no longer ours anymore."
Harold went on,

Jan said he got a child on drugs and he was working right over there by the school. I wanted him in a pine box in the ground. (Their son sold drugs to a schoolchild, and Harold wanted him dead as a consequence.) We got to the point that, although we didn't plan the funeral, we knew that if it happened, we were all right. When I turned him over to God that night you cannot imagine the doors that started opening.

This story began as Harold's but quickly became a family story of faith as Jan added her thoughts. When Harold said, "I said my prayers, I said, "All right God, he's yours," Jan responded, "It was when *we* told God that he was no longer ours anymore." She has broadened the story; this is no longer simply the story of a grief-stricken father. This is *their* story. He is not alone in it. And he affirms what she has just said, by continuing, "We know…" Undoubtedly, they have talked over these experiences many times before. Each of them has thought about it, trying to make sense of it. But they have also talked it over together, constructing this shared understanding of their experience. Even so, Harold ends this segment by returning to his private prayer, "And when I turned him over to God that night…." The individual's faith experience is not lost in the family's experience. Rather, the two interact with one another.

Implications for Social Work

Every family provides a context in which faith develops and is challenged. Family life may provide the context for the individual's faith experience, such as Shamika's struggle to trust God to deal justly with those who murdered her father. Both children and adults have their faith shaped in the transactional life of families, as these family stories demonstrate. The family's life offers multiple crises that challenge and/or affirm the faith of family members. In turn, as these stories are told and retold, they become family stories, stories in which individuals participate in a story of faith that belongs to the family group, such as the story of Jan and Harold's wrestling with their son's drug addiction. As social workers listen to the stories of families who are wrestling with different life circumstances, they need to tune into how family's understand and find meaning in those experiences, what they believe to be "truth" and how they make sense of their life experiences both as individuals and as a family.

Belief and trust lead to actions based on faith, and those actions have consequences. In turn, the consequences give us more to ponder, confirming, challenging, and sometimes modifying beliefs and trust. When Corrine's prayers for her son's safety during minor surgery were met instead with life threatening illness that is still affecting his health, her beliefs and trust were thrown into disarray. When their infant son died in a fire, Jacob and Kate spent years struggling to find answers for themselves. Family life can be a safe haven, but it can also present faith-threatening challenges.

Social workers often find themselves thrust into the stream of client family's experiences and need to learn much more about that family than whether they are Catholic or Lutheran or Buddhist or Unitarian Universalist. They need to know the faith stories of their lives, and the crisis that concurrently confronts them in the context of that narrative. Families need to tell their stories to one another, and social workers can provide that safe haven for telling their stories, sometimes for the first time. Stories are how families say who they are; they deepen family celebrations; and give families ways to cling to one another in hard times. As important as it is to tell stories to one another in families, families also need to share their stories with others, to pass them on and share them and compare them with those of a larger community of people who confirm, challenge, and deepen the narratives of a family's faith journey, connecting the family's story to the great stories of religious faith. If a congregation is truly a community of faith, then it is a place where people and families know one another not just by name but also by their stories.

Notes

[1] Adapted from Garland, D. (2003) *Sacred stories of ordinary families: Living the faith everyday.* San Francisco: Jossey-Bass.

[2] See also Brigman, Schons, & Stinnett, 1986; DeFrain, DeFrain, & Lepard, 1994; Knaub, Hanna, & Stinnett, 1984; Stinnett, Sanders, DeFrain, & Parkhurst, 1982; Stinnett & Stinnett, 1995.

[3] For more details about the research, see (Garland, 2002a, 2003)

References

Anderson, H., & Foley, E. (1998). *Mighty stories, dangerous rituals: Weaving together the human and the divine.* San Francisco: Jossey-Bass.

Bass, D. C., & Dykstra, C. (1997). Growing in the practices of faith. In D. C. Bass (Ed.), *Practicing our faith: A way of life for a searching people* (pp. 195-204). San Francisco: Jossey-Bass.

Bender, C. (1995). *The meals are the message : The growth and congestion of an AIDS service in organization's mission multiple institutional fields*. New Haven, CT: Program on Non-Profit Organizations, Institution for Social and Policy Studies, Yale University.

Brother Lawrence of the Resurrection. (1977). *The practice of the presence of God*. Garden City, NY: Doubleday.

Dickie, J. R., Eshleman, A. K., Merasco, D. M., Shepard, A., Vander Wilt, M., & Johnson, M. (1997). Parent-child relationships and children's images of God. *Journal for the Scientific Study of Religion, 36*(1), 25-43.

Dykstra, C. (1986). What is faith?: An experiment in the hypothetical mode. In C. Dykstra & S. Parks (Eds.), *Faith development and Fowler* (pp. 45-64). Birmingham: Religious Education Press.

Dykstra, C. & Bass, D.C. (1997). Times of yearning, practices of faith. In D. C. Bass (Ed.), *Practicing our faith: A way of life for a searching people* (pp. 1-12). San Francisco: Jossey-Bass.

Ellison, C. G., Bartkowski, J.P., & Anderson, K.L. (1999). Are there religious variations in domestic violence? *Journal of Family Issues, 20*(1), 87-113.

Erikson, E. H. (1968). *Identity: Youth and crisis*. NY: W.W. Norton & Co.

Foster, R. (1978). *The celebration of discipline*. New York: Harper & Row.

Fowler, J. W. (1981). *Stages of faith: The psychology of human development and the quest for meaning*. San Francisco: Harper & Row.

Fowler, J. W. (1991). *Weaving the new creation: Stages of faith and the public church*. San Francisco: Harper.

Frankl, V.E. (1969). *The will to meaning: Foundations and applications of logotherapy*. London: Souvenir Press.

Garland, D.R. (1999). *Family ministry: A comprehensive guide*. Grand Rapids: Intervarsity Press.

Garland, D.R. (2001). The faith dimension of family life. *Social Work & Christianity, 28*(1 (Spring)), 6-26.

Garland, D.R. (2002a). Faith narratives of congregants and their families. *Review of Religious Research, 44*(1), 68-91.

Garland, D.R. (2002b). Family ministry: Defining perspectives. *Family Ministry: Empowering Through Faith, 16*(2).

Garland, D.R. (2003). *Sacred stories of ordinary families: Living the faith everyday*. San Francisco: Jossey-Bass.

Glaser, B.G., & Strauss, A.L. (1967). *The discovery of grounded theory*. Chicago: Aldine de Gruyter.

Joanides, C. (1997). A qualitative investigation of the meaning of religion and spirituality to a group of orthodox Christians: Implications for marriage and family therapy. *Journal of Family Social Work, 2*(4), 59-75.

Lampe, P. (1992). "Family" in church and society of New Testament times. *Affirmation: Union Theological Seminary in Virginia, 5*(1 (Spring)), 1-19.

Lee, J. M. (Ed.). (1990). *Handbook of faith*. Birmingham: Religious Education Press.

Miles, M. B., & Huberman, A. M. (1994). *Qualitative data analysis* (2nd ed.). Thousand Oaks: Sage.

Nelson, C. E.. (1992). Does faith develop? An evaluation of Fowler's position. In J. Astley & L. Francis (Eds.), *Christian perspectives on faith development* (pp. 62-76). Grand Rapids: Eerdmans.

Nelson, R.A. (1990). Facilitating growth in faith through social ministry. In L. James (Ed.), *Handbook of faith*. Birmingham: Religious Education Press.

Osiek, C. (1996). The family in early Christianity: "Family values" revisited. *The Catholic Biblical Quarterly*, 58, 1-24.

Parks, S.D. (1992). Faith development in a changing world. In J. Astley & L. Francis (Eds.), *Christian perspectives on faith development* (pp. 92-106). Grand Rapids: Eerdmans.

Rubin, H. J., & Rubin, I. S. (1995). *Qualitative interviewing: The art of hearing data.* Thousand Oaks: Sage.

Straughan, H.H. (2002). Spiritual development. In *Christianity and Social Work: Readings on the Integration of Christian Faith and Social Work Practice.* (2nd ed.): Botsford, CT: National Association of Christians in Social Work.

Weiss, R.S. (1994). *Learning from strangers: The art and method of qualitative interview studies.* New York: Free Press.

Zinnbauer, B. J., et. al. (1997). Religion and spirituality: Unfuzzying the fuzzy. *Journal for the Scientific Study of Religion,* 36(4), 549-564.

CHAPTER 22

THE BLACK CHURCH AS A PRISM FOR EXPLORING CHRISTIAN SOCIAL WELFARE AND SOCIAL WORK

Timothy Johnson

The Black church's practice of Christian charity over the last 142 years and its current orientation to living out the Christian discipline of "holistic grace and hospitality" serve as a microcosmic case example of social welfare and systematic helping that undergirds the profession of social work. The Black church's commitment to 'holistic grace and hospitality' has a clearly documented history that has coexisted contemporaneously with legitimately sanctioned social welfare programs in our society.

The foundation of modern social welfare originated with the seventeenth century poor laws of England, which served as an ancestor and early influence on the formation of the social welfare system in the United States. The social welfare associated with the poor laws was a punitive and parsimonious response to need. Underlying this welfare system was the fear that the needy might become comfortable and lose the will to work. This example of social welfare stands as one of the two opposing poles of social welfare historically practiced in America. Jansson (2005) captures the issue here when he refers to United States as the "Reluctant Welfare State."

The second pole, standing in juxtaposition to the first, is the idea of Christian Charity. Lieby (1987) in his material on social welfare, in reference to reformers in the late 19th century asserts that:

> ...they believed the Biblical account of creation and human nature and destiny. They believed that a divine revelation defined right and wrong and pointed the way to Heaven or Hell. Charity, or love, was, in this view, the greatest commandment, and its practice manifested the spirit of God. To obey this command was a responsibility of individuals and of communities (p. 87).

Certainly the idea of "charity" within its Biblical definition was a precursor to the social welfare enterprise of our time. Charity as an obligatory Christian practice is given its fullest development in Paul's first letter to the Corinthian church. The text appears to depict charity or love as constant, tolerant, hopeful, and enduring (1 Corinthians 13). This stands in stark contrast to the reluctance and mistrust that may characterize prevalent forms of modern social welfare.

The modern social welfare system is a secondary system of resources, safety nets, and failsafe mechanisms designed to meet the needs of persons, and to maintain the stability of our society within a broadly acceptable range. In contrast to this secondary system, primary systems are those closest to client systems and are frequently comprised of their families, neighbors, friends, the church, and other organizations which anchor them to their communities. When persons cross over into secondary systems of social welfare, it is generally an indication that the client's primary systems have become compromised, inaccessible, overwhelmed, or inoperable. From a sociological perspective, secondary welfare system structures are 'artificial contrivances' of primary system entities. Yet in a mass society such as ours, where persons are often disconnected from primary systems, the secondary social welfare system is often related to as a primary system.

The Black church is a case example of social welfare within the primary relational context of African Americans. The Black church was forged as a surreptitious institution existing behind the bastions of chattel slavery. As human property, enslaved persons had little to no autonomy in matters of life, limb, and religion. After the Emancipation Proclamation and the end of the Civil War, Reconstruction found the Black church alive, religiously functional, and growing exponentially. The Black church at the threshold of freedom was the only institution that 4 million plus African Americans could claim as its own.

> The Black Church, then, is in some sense a "universal Church,"
> claiming and representing all Blacks out of a long tradition that
> looks back to the time when there was only the Black Church to
> bear witness to "who" or "what" a man was as he stood at the bar
> of his community (Frazier, 1974, p.116).

In the Reconstruction period, the community of post-enslavement Black Christians was suffering from what we now might call post-traumatic stress disorder. The truncated lives of the constituents of this institution and the existence of social constraints that prevented the needs of Blacks from being met bear a similarity to the communities of the early Christian church.

> All who believed were together and had all things in common; they
> would sell their possessions and goods and distribute the proceeds
> to all, as any had need. Day by day, as they spent much time together
> in the temple, they broke bread at home and ate their food with glad
> and generous hearts, praising God and having the goodwill of all
> the people (Acts 2:41-47).

Both churches demonstrated a concern for the members of the community and recognized the necessity of meeting the needs of the poor in their midst. For the post-Civil War Blacks, the Black church became the institution that anchored their lives.

Garland (1992) indicates that "the Church and its ministries provided the seed bed for the development of the social work profession" (p.1). In every sense the Black church was the seed bed for 'social uplift' and social welfare responses to needs of the Black community, for the reluctance that characterized social welfare in America proved to have ominous implications for African

Americans. Historically, second class citizenship, lack of political power, and the social invisibility of Black people have typically placed them outside the sphere of the social welfare system, or at best, has allowed African Americans to be mere marginal beneficiaries of the system of services and resources. Such has historically been the situation up to present time.

An Era of Buffering Social Welfare Reluctance: Profound Hospitality and Social Uplift

One of the critiques of the Black church within conservative religious circles regards its tendency to be a multipurpose social organization, in addition to being a locus for worship. It is true that the average Black church is a multi-focal institution. The explanation lies in an historical analysis of the social environment from the enslavement period to the present.

In its early years, the social environment of the Black church was characterized by "graciousness." Graciousness in this context means the grace of God underlying the practice of hospitality. Hospitality in this context comes closest to the shared root of the word "hospital" which is more than mere welcoming; rather, hospitality connotes "care," "cure" or "palliative ministrations." Over time, hospitality served to build communal cohesion and evolved into a sustained effort of "social uplift." To achieve the goals of social uplift, the Black church gave attention to the creation and mobilization of resources and empowerment of its members, thereby leading to social change and community building.

Profound Hospitality

The ending of slavery left over four million freed persons to their own devices. These former slaves comprised a wounded group of people, not without skills, but certainly with limited opportunity, and needing social, spiritual and psychological healing. It fell to the Black church as the Black community's single and pervasive institution to be a healing presence. The church embraced a form of profound hospitality that laid the foundation for all that was to follow.

The practical application of profound hospitality was demonstrated at the end of slavery when tens of thousands of freedmen wandered throughout the South looking for family members who had been lost to them by being sold away. The search to find family continued for decades after enslavement. The grace of profound hospitality that supported the nomadic searching of African Americans after the Civil War also had the impact of keeping very loose the boundaries around black families. Displaced persons and orphans were easily taken into black families and claimed as their own. This remarkable strategy of creating foster families was not so much a strategy of the mind, but of the heart and the psyche. It was understood that, for purposes of survival, persons needed connection and a communal location. Black family life was the gate through which fictive kin, once entering, were entitled to all the privileges of citizenship in the Black church and the Black community.

The institutionalization of foster families created an important alternative social welfare mechanism. Black families and the church became the network for providing accommodations when travel was necessary, given the largely "whites only" policy in accommodations throughout the United States. Frequently, Black persons who needed to travel cobbled together accommodations with other Black families through their churches. Friends of friends became very important if one needed to move around the country. This situation existed until well past the mid-20th century, when the civil rights movement achieved the legal standard for non-discrimination and parity in accommodations.

The Black church as a gracious institution stood as a protective buffer for the Black community. Through hospitality, the Black church involved itself in the everyday life needs of Black people. Frazier (1974) states that:

> The role of religion and the Negro church in more elementary forms of economic cooperation among Negroes may be seen more clearly in the rural mutual aid societies that sprang up among freedmen after Emancipation. They were formed among landless Negroes who were thrown upon their own resources. These societies were organized to meet the crises of life—sickness and death: consequently, they were known as "sickness and burial" societies.... [T]hese benevolent societies grew out of the Negro church and were inspired by the spirit of Christian Charity (p.42).

In the final analysis, profound hospitality meant that no one was a stranger in the Black community. Given the close identification of the Black church and the Black community, the function of the church as the primary social welfare mechanism remained largely hidden from public view.

Social Uplift

Because of the social and economic deprivation suffered by African Americans in enslavement, Black leaders were anxious for social uplift and economic parity for their people. The late 19th-century world was one of significant flux, fueled by the explosive social forces of the growth of technology, industrialization, and urbanization. The result was mass relocation of large sections of the Black population to urban centers of New York, Philadelphia, Chicago, Pittsburgh, and an array of smaller urban locations. The draw was the promise of better lives based on a money exchange economy. The late 19th-century was also the auspicious historical moment of the inception of the great progressive movements, marked by their goals for elevating the common life of the masses in terms of health, welfare, education, and refinement.

"Social Uplift" is the term used at the turn of the twentieth century to convey the need to raise the quality of life for the American public to higher standards. The object of social uplift was to prepare the masses for the new institutions coming into existence and the more sophisticated perspectives needed for viability in the social environment. The progressive movement was an equation of social, spiritual, and environmental forces. These were comprised of higher educational opportunity for women, scientific advances, industrialization, and the moral exigencies Christians believed were incumbent upon them. The result of this movement's progression toward modernity was the establishment of a benchmark to which citizens should be lifted. Inherent in the benchmark was the assumption that persons become 'humanized' by the refining aspects of education, that they embrace social interactions that bespeak of quality of character, and that they live out the moral dimensions of Christian principles. African Americans during this time were faced with extraordinary need because of the failure of resource systems in the social environment that normally would have served them. In this fomenting social context the Black community and the Black church felt all the more the urgency of social uplift.

With this sense of urgency regarding social uplift, the Black church prioritized its goals for meeting needs. They immediately gave particular attention to legitimizing slave marriages, which were based on the casual practice of "jumping the broom." One of the first tasks of organized churches in the South was to see that all couples joined in marriage by this practice, be remarried according to the tenets of the church and local law. The following quote from the January 3, 1871 minutes of the Green Street Baptist Church of Louisville Kentucky is insightful:

> On the motion and second the church voted to take up the subject respecting those members of the church not married by license, carried in the affirmative. Then the clerk read the resolution passed by the church on the third of October which resolution proclaims that all members of the church that was[sic] not married in 30 days from date shall be excluded from the church (Jones, circa 1979, p. 56).

The church also addressed breaches of public decorum which negatively reflected on the race, for example, vulgar language, gossiping and arguing. Such matters were brought up before the church (Jones, circa 1979, p. 75).

However, the Black church and the Black community were not only focused on the lives of their people, but they were also concerned about the social environment. Booker T. Washington, the president of Tuskegee Institute, was a dominant Black voice articulating the needs of African Americans. His strategy for social welfare was to push the Black community toward agricultural and industrial education, as well as property ownership. The other dominant voice during the same period was W.E.B. Dubois, whose vision and organizing efforts promoted classical educational opportunity for the intelligentsia of African American communities. The Black church served as the institution that not only provided an audience for these men, but disseminated their ideas.

Similar to the white women of this reform period who newly found their voices, Black women used the church as their base of operation for developing leadership skills, as attested to by the following quote:

> The Baptist women's preoccupation with respectability reflected a bourgeois vision that vacillated between an attack on the failure of

America to live up to its liberal ideals of equality and justice and an attack on the values and lifestyle of those blacks who transgressed white middle-class propriety (Higginbotham, 1993, p.215).

It is significant that Baptist women understood the necessity of paying attention both to the social environment and to the people for whom they wished to achieve social uplift. This view is consistent with today's social work emphasis on the person in the environment.

While education was a generally perceived route to social uplift, for African Americans education represented much more. It was the premier credential of personhood in a society within which males had been designated legally as three-fifths of a person. Not only was the ability to read an ontological issue for African Americans, (given that the penalty for learning to read while in slavery was death), but it was a spiritual issue. Freed persons coming out of slavery had a voracious desire to read, so that they could read the Bible for themselves. Often independently, or in collaboration with northern white missionaries, the Black churches created strategies for educating their people. The Sunday school was the principal setting in which this took place. Public education eventually became available for African Americans during this period, but the educational process was compromised as it was controlled by white power structures. Educational resources were constrained, and inferior, even though mandated by law. Whatever public education was available was usually provided in a church that served as both schoolhouse and worship center.

The Black church as a Christian social welfare institution made education one of its priorities. The fertility of the educational efforts of the Black church is demonstrated in the 1928 "Survey of Negro Colleges and Universities" (Klein, 1929). This survey lists over 50 schools listed in the survey that were operated by various African American religious denominations. Notably, the history of these schools demonstrates an evolving process from primary and secondary schools, to the establishment of college departments. The report documents the educational uplift of African Americans that can be attributed to the efforts of the Black church.

In response to the reluctance of social welfare during the late 19th century, the Black church gave its attention to the wellbeing of the African American community by focusing on the intersection of its social and religious life. Although there were outstanding efforts during this period to make resource systems in the social environment more appropriate to the needs of African Americans, the Black Church was primarily a church turned inward. The social welfare focus of the Black church in this period was to exercise care in welcoming strangers, not knowing when those entertained might be the angels of God (Hebrews 13:3). This inward concern was a combination of healing, nurture, and care because of the social and sometime physical wounds dealt to the African American community on a daily basis. Wimberly (1992) speaks to the development of the Black Church during this period:

> [African Americans] were systematically excluded from normal access
> to participation in the community that would lead to the fulfillment
> of his potential as a total person. The consequence of all of this is

the fact that many of the political, social, educational, recreational, economic, and social needs of the Black person had to be fulfilled within the Black church, his only institution. This was also true for the medical and mental health needs of the Black person. Often it was the Black Church that took care of the needs of the neglected sick and mentally ill....In fact it was through the efforts of the Black Church that hospitals were established in the Black Community (p. 412).

Elias C. Morris, in his 1899 presidential address to the National Baptist Convention, captures both the results and the dynamism of the profound graciousness of the period as an antithesis to the reluctance of social welfare.

Hence, I conclude that one of the marvels of the century will be that although it opened and looked for sixty-three years on a race of slaves, it closes with that same happy, free people, having built more churches and school houses, in proportion to their numbers, than any people dwelling beneath the sun....A little less than sixteen months from now that tireless steed, Time will come forth and announce the birth of the twentieth century....What is the duty of Negro Baptists: The answer comes back that as the nineteenth century opened upon us as slaves and closed upon us as freemen, so may the Gospel, borne on the tongues of the liberated, set at liberty during the twentieth century, the millions bound in heathen darkness (p.283).

The Church as a Primary Care Social Welfare Agency by Default

The period of the "great migrations" between the first and second World Wars and into the 1970's saw African Americans on the move from south to north. From 1870-1970, 7 million black people are reported to have moved from south to north (Lincoln & Mamiya, 1990, p. 121). The Great Depression and boll weevil infestation limited even further the subsistence resources of the Black community. If agricultural impoverishment was the push from the south, the pull from the north was the possibility of economic stability because of northern industries. As hundreds of thousands moved to northern urban sectors, particularly between the two World Wars, the problems already existing in these areas were further exacerbated. In northern cities, segregation, redlining,[1] and restrictive covenants[2] limited where African Americans could live. The populations of these areas increased rapidly, but the available housing remained static. While there were jobs available, employment opportunities were usually in the secondary job market which was characterized by instability, lack of benefits, and undesirable residual employment rejected by whites.[3] Access to skilled jobs was denied because of nepotism and union "whites only" hiring policies (Baron, 1969, pp. 146-147).

Given the compelling challenges of urban life for African Americans, the Black church willingly wrapped itself around the needs of its community. This culture of helping was part of the definitive fiber of the Black church. What was new in this era was the unparalleled growth of northern churches. As these northern churches grew exponentially, many in large urban areas became mega-churches before there was such a term. The northern church in its social welfare role became a figurative Ellis Island for the newly arrived southern immigrants. The social welfare activities of urban Black churches included residential location services, job referral services through word of mouth or the posting of opportunities, care for those who needed nursing services, after school activities, and childcare services for working parents.

Qualifying for the Black church's social service programs was on the basis of being a member of the Black community. Services were universal in nature and readily accessed. Distinctions were not made on the basis of longevity of membership or residence in the community. Need was the only criterion for receiving assistance.

Because the Black church itself was a primary system in terms of its functions and its potency in shaping spiritual and social perspectives, there was within it an ethos of family empathy because of shared deprivation. This family quality created within the church a pervasive awareness of the needs of brothers and sister in the church and a willingness to respond.

Fulop and Raboteau (1997), writing about Rev. J.C.Austin and Pilgrim Baptist Church of Chicago during this period, describe the church's social welfare programs.

> The church itself was organized into approximately one hundred auxiliary units, to assure that every member of the congregation had a "home" in Pilgrim's vast community. Austin was particularly effective in organizing groups of church women, who among their other roles, functioned as social workers, "missionary women whose job it was to go out…into these tenements and hovels these folks were living in and teach them hygiene and how to care for their babies and make sure they had food." With the aid of five assistant ministers and a deacon board of fifty-eight, Austin turned Pilgrim into a seven-day-a-week center for welfare, education, health care, job training and placement, youth activity, culture, and religion (p.318).

Abyssinia Baptist Church, in Harlem New York, also functioned as a social welfare institution and social service center:

> In each city there were a few leading churches and preachers who took a prophetic stance in attempting to meet the great needs of migrants by using their church's resources to provide help with food, shelter, clothing, and employment. In the 1920's Rev. Adam Clayton Powell, Sr., opened one of the first soup kitchens for the hungry migrants….In 1939 his son, Rev. Adam Clayton Powell, Jr., involved the church in welfare work, seeking employment, and supported black workers in their strikes and attempts to unionize (Lincoln & Mamiya,1990, p.121).

Pilgrim and Abyssinia Baptist churches serve as normative examples of the way in which the organizational and social welfare structures of large urban Black churches functioned during the years of the Depression.

The exigencies of life for many African Americans were great during this period. Brokenness and mental dysfunction were not uncommon. The Black church's tradition of profound hospitality meant that there was a great deal of tolerance for those who were dysfunctional and whose life-styles may have been out of sync with accepted Christian practices. Gilkes (1980) writes about the effectiveness of the Black church, whose members had limited access to established social welfare mechanisms, in mitigating the individual and collective mental dysfunctions of its members

The pastors of churches, north and south, on whose shoulders rested the spiritual, social, and physical wellbeing of their membership, served as the human linchpins for the various welfare roles in the church. Because ministers of this time were usually the most educated people in the congregation, they became paternal figures who protected their members' interests. Black ministers utilized a kind of shuttle diplomacy, in which it was their responsibility to collaborate with the white power structure, assist members with legal matters, and attempt to keep the stress of population increase from destabilizing the larger community. In this role Black ministers worked toward a goal of peaceful coexistence.

An undisputed and often autocratic leader of the local church, the pastor controlled the church's resources and often dispensed them himself, or controlled the organizational structure in the church designed to do so. The Black minister's power during this period, coupled with his expertise and the resources that he controlled, made him a figure of God-like proportions within the Black church. In my own childhood church during the 1950's and 1960's, some of the members of the church were able to become homeowners because the pastor of our church had an arrangement with a realtor that assured the availability of mortgages. In other instances, the pastor would co-sign for loans and other financial help for his members.

This period in the history of the Black church's social welfare and social services provision drew to a close with the coming of the civil rights era. The period just described was one in which the focus was on creating an organizational structure that would support the social service delivery system for the Black community. During the period of the great migrations, the Black church took seriously the biblical praxiological principle of the Apostle Paul, "being all things to all people that some might be won" (1 Corinthians 9:22). Rather than focusing on the reluctant nature of the established social welfare system, the Black church's own social welfare activities during the civil rights era included community organizing and empowerment of African Americans. The dynamism of the Black church vis-à-vis the reluctant social welfare system directed a sustained focus on the very foundations of social welfare in America.

Forcing Open the Gates to Social Welfare Equity

Following World War II, the homeostasis of white privilege supported by Black oppression began to unravel. The war itself had exposed African Americans to the possibilities of racial parity in other countries. President Truman had integrated the Armed Forces in 1948. The G.I. bill offered educational and housing opportunities along with increased aspirations. The war became a watershed of change in social relationships. These changes and opportunities served as social antecedents that began to bring African American citizens into direct conflict with existing social structures, ultimately leading to the civil rights movement of the 1950s and 1960s.

By this time, the Black church had achieved not only organizational complexity and solidity, but its relationship with the Black community was such that one could not be defined without the other. Also important was the evolution of a second Black institution of great influence, the Black ministers' conferences and episcopal districts which served to draw Black clergy together into well organized, prestigious, and powerful fellowship groupings. These supra-organizations served as a kind of social dynamo to concentrate and magnify the power of the Black church. In this context the fertile soil of unified protest was cultivated, and Black leaders began to focus outwardly on the inequities of the American social welfare system.

An excerpted statement by the National Committee of Negro Churchmen, July 31, 1966, captures the changing focus of the Black church from its own organizational concerns to the problems of the social environment:

> ...we must build upon that which we already have. "Black power" is already present to some extent in the Negro Church, in Negro fraternities and sororities, in our professional associations, and in the opportunities afforded to Negroes who make decisions in some of the integrated organizations in our society....The future of America will belong to neither white nor black unless all Americans work together at the task of rebuilding our cities. We must organize not only among ourselves but with other groups in order that we can, together, gain power sufficient to change this nation's sense of what is important and what must be done now...To accomplish this task we cannot expend our energies in spastic or ill-tempered explosions without meaningful goals. We must move from the politics of philanthropy to the politics of metropolitan development for equal opportunity (Sernett, 1985, p. 471).

The Black Church during this time became the catalyst both for raising social consciousness and fueling social protest. The major goals were the acquisition of power in the electorate through voters' rights and the integration of accommodations. In short, this was a campaign for equality of opportunity. At stake for the Black church was the social welfare of Black Americans in its broadest dimensions.

One of the most notable institutions created within the vortex of civil rights deprivation was the Southern Christian Leadership Conference (SCLC), begun in Montgomery, Alabama. The precipitating event was the arrest of Rosa Parks for refusing to give her seat up on the bus to a white man. The SCLC's first president was Rev. Dr. Martin Luther King, Jr.

In the northern cities, exclusion from the primary job market was part of the economic context of African Americans from the time of emancipation. A creative strategy called "selective patronage" came out of the ministers' conference in Philadelphia in the 1950's. The clergy recognized that the buying power of the Black community was a powerful force for leverage. Selective patronage targeted particular companies such as Tasty Baking Company, Pepsi Cola, and some of the oil companies. The ministers agreed to encourage their church members not to buy from these target companies. Unity of the Black ministers in the conferences and their influence in the Black community helped the strategy succeed. Because of the economic impact of lost retail sales, company after company came to the bargaining table. The goal was simple: employment opportunities for the Black community. This highly successful community organizing tactic eventually led to the organization of the Opportunities Industrialization Centers (OIC), which became international in scope. OIC's purpose was to provide the skill sets that the Black community needed in order to be qualified for the newly opening job opportunities (Lincoln & Mamiya, 1990, p. 263).

The Black churches' organizing efforts led to success in many of its social welfare aspirations for a more open society for African Americans, especially in the areas of economic and educational opportunity and residential mobility. But left in the wake of this successful social welfare agenda were those people on the economic and social bottom rungs. As the neighborhoods surrounding urban Black churches became depopulated, these isolated inner city areas became plagued with deteriorating housing, family disintegration, escalation of drug use and related crimes, unemployment related to a faltering economy, and continuing political invisibility. The problems of inner cities became the new community organizing targets for the Black church. In the late 20th century, the Black churches brought their expertise to bear in providing profound hospitality, mobilizing and multiplying scarce resources, and political and community organizing. What was newly added to this mix was a professionally trained clergy.

Social Change as Professional Practice

The training of African American clergy up to the civil rights movement was largely an apprenticeship model where learning took place primarily within the church, with some supportive ancillary educational experiences. With the opening of new educational opportunities and with college or seminary educated clergy becoming normative, the skill sets of clergy were vastly expanded. Their educational backgrounds gave this new cadre of men and women perspectives on the Black church in tandem with the social environment and skills in social service strategies for ameliorating some of the pressing social problems confronting the Black community.

Along with a transformed clergy, the congregations of large urban churches were changing. The 21st-century Black church is now amply populated with at least two to three generations of college-educated professionals. These professionals have shifted the social welfare dynamics of the Church away from a residual-based, crisis-oriented social welfare institution, where those in need often served others in need. Black churches in varying degrees have become fully functioning social service agencies in which professionals and volunteers in the congregation create non-profit corporations and social service programs to meet the needs of the Black community.

Billingsley (1999) in his documentation of Black churches and social reform, gives an extensive inventory of the social service ministries of an array of large urban Black churches across the country. The economic and social services programs are folded into the church structure so as to deal with the social and economic needs of the communities. The list of targets for change includes: housing development, rehabilitation of abandoned and deteriorating housing, housing corporations, programs for providing small business loans, nursing homes, medical clinics, conferences on social problems of African Americans, computer literacy, social services, shopping centers, mini markets, neighborhood revitalization programs, education and training programs, and credit unions.

Conclusion

The exploration of the social welfare role of the Black church points to five important conclusions that are of critical importance in the American social and economic landscape. 1) The Black church's role as social fiduciary over a huge area of social capital still remains untapped and mostly invisible to the larger society, but if tapped, validated and energized, can only enhance the common good. 2) The role of the Black church as a social welfare institution, if calculated in terms of its economic value and savings to the established social welfare system, would amount to an extraordinary sum of money. This kind of accounting ought to be acknowledged as an explicit and necessary economic value of the Black church as a social welfare institution. 3) The Black church's social welfare efforts have evolved over its history from ad hoc social welfare by default to sophisticated social welfare strategies and social services that bring together public and private resources focused on need. The experience of the Black church as a social welfare institution means that it is has all the attributes for being an effective force in Faith Based Initiatives. 4) The Black church itself is fulfilling the role (as identified by Warren (2001)) of renewing American politics by furthering the rebuilding of its foundation in the values and institutions that sustain community. Warren laments the "missing" middle in American political life. 5) The Black church in its welfare role with over a century of cultivating volunteerism, and now professionalism in service-giving, is actively involved in rebuilding community and filling in the missing middle. It now remains for those in power, and for those who control resources and shape social reality, to pull back the curtains of invisibility and showcase the Black Church as an effective model for social welfare and social services in the 21st century.

Notes

[1] "redlining" was a practice used by banks to exclude Black communities from securing mortgages. Black neighborhoods would be circled in red markings as areas for which mortgages would not be provided.

[2] "restrictive covenants" were secret agreements struck on the parts of white neighborhood associations that real estate would not be rented or sold to African Americans

[3] The distinction between secondary and primary job markets is a concept coming out of the book edited by LL. Knowles, *Institutional Racism in America*, New York, Prentice Hall, 1969. In an addendum, Jonathan Baron makes the distinction between these two job markets. The primary job market, an exclusionary one, was overwhelmingly white. It provided stable employment, with benefits and upward mobility. The secondary job market was overwhelmingly "minority" and was characterized by low wages, instability, seasonal work, and dead end jobs.

References

Baron, H. (1969). The web of urban racism. In L.L. Knowles & K. Prewitt, (Eds.), *Institutional Racism in America* (pp. 134-176). Upper Saddle River, NJ: Prentice Hall.

Billingsley, A. (1999). *Mighty like a river: The Black church and social reform*. New York, NY: Oxford University Press.

Frazier, E. F. (1974). *The negro church in America*. New York, NY: Schocken Books.

Fulop, T. E. & Raboteau, A. J. (1990). The Baptist church in years of crisis: J.C. Austin and Pilgrim Baptist Church, 1926-1950. In E. C. Lincoln & L. H. Mamiya, *The Black Church in the African American Experience* (pp. 309-339). Durham, NC: Duke University Press.

Garland, D. S. R. (1992). *Church social work: Helping the whole person in the context of the church*. St. Davids, PA: North American Association of Christians in Social Work.

Gilkes, C. T. (1980). The Black church as a therapeutic community: Suggested areas for research into Black religious practice. *The Journal of the Interdenominational Theological Center, 8*(1), 29-44.

Higginbotham, E. B. (1993). *Righteous discontent: The women's movement in the Black Baptist church, 1880-1920*. Boston, MA: Harvard University Press.

Jansson B. (2005). *The reluctant welfare state: American social welfare policies – Past, present, and future*. Monterey, CA: Thomson.

Jones, H. W. (circa 1979). *First hundred years plus 35. Unpublished history of Greene Street Baptist Church*. Louisville, KY.

Lieby, J. (1987). History of social welfare. In *Encyclopedia of Social Work Vol. 1*, (p. 755). Silver Springs, MD: National Association of Social Workers.

Lincoln, E. C. & Mamiya, L. H. (1990). *The Black church in the African American experience*. Durham, NC: Duke University Press.

Klein, A. (1929). Survey of Negro Colleges and Universities. *Department of the Interior Bureau of Education. Bulletin*, 1929, (7).

Sernett, M. C. (1985). *Afro-American religious history: A documentary witness*. Durham, NC: Duke University Press.

Warren, M. R. (2001). *Dry bones rattling: Community building to revitalize American democracy*. Princeton, NJ: Princeton University Press.

Wimberly, E. P. (1989). Pastoral counseling and the Black perspective. In S. Gayraud, (Ed.), *African American religious studies: An interdisciplinary anthology* (pp. 420-28). Durham, NC: Duke University Press.

CHAPTER 23

SOCIAL WORK AND INTERNATIONAL, INTER-CONGREGATIONAL RELATIONSHIPS: MULTI-DIMENSIONAL, TRANSFORMATIVE POWER

John Cosgrove

This chapter examines supportive relationships between religious congregations. The particular focus will be on the contemporary and growing phenomenon of formal relationships between individual congregations, particularly a major subset of these relationships, those between congregations in the developed and developing worlds. The semantic and substantive variations that make it difficult to discern commonalities in those relationships will be discussed and common themes will be identified. Stages and tasks leading to the establishment of these international, inter-congregational relationships or IICRs will be culled from the experiences of existing IICRs, following which there will be a description of opportunities of how social workers can make important contributions to the initiation, development and conduct of these relationships.

"Inter-National" Social Work

Social work has been prophetic in its view of the interrelatedness of the societies and peoples of the world. For nearly a century, social workers from around the globe have met, exchanged ideas, and created international[1] organizations (Healy, 2001). Social workers from the Global North[2] or so called developed nations have helped form the profession in the developing nations of the Global South. Initially, the approach was sometimes unintentionally patronizing and not always culturally relevant (Midgley, 1981). Over time, through experience and reflective scholarship, north-south relationships have become more empowering as well as reciprocal. Methods pioneered in developing countries are now considered for adaptation in the north (Hokenstad & Midgley, 2004). Overseas opportunities for social workers also have increased (Cosgrove, 2005). The lessons learned have been incorporated into social work curricula. In fact, content related to global issues and international social work is now mandatory (Council on Social Work Education, 2004).

The Impact of Globalization

These practice, scholarly, and educational trends have been accelerated by globalization. This amoral, amorphous, and largely unaccountable process is usually put in economic terms whereby the world has become one large market place. At the same time, globalization has accelerated the internationalizing of social problems including diseases, illegal drugs, terrorism and migration, to name a few. Ironically, we are more cognizant and knowledgeable about the world thanks to the truly remarkable advances in technology that have accompanied globalization. It is now difficult not to know that the vast majority of the peoples of the world have been living in conditions that North Americans[3] would find totally unacceptable and, too often, conditions that are getting worse. Many of us look on with feelings of helplessness at what is in happening to our brothers and sisters in the developing world. For any number of reasons such as family, finances, or career, we may not be ready or able to live and work in a developing country. There is much that we can do to advocate for reforms and support positive change from afar. Yet, for many, the longing to do more remains. Social workers who wish to have some direct "hands on" involvement in the developing world may need look no further than the local church for an option that is promising and powerful, as well as professionally, and spiritually rewarding.

International, Inter-Congregational Relationships

Background

The existing literature about international inter-congregational relationships is found mostly in popular and religious publications. These writings recount stories of participants in various associations between two or more organizations that identify themselves as churches, congregations, communities of faith, parishes or analogous terms. One of the first detailed and still quite useful works is Richard Fenske's *In the Good Struggle: The Sister Parish Movement* (1996). Additional comprehensive treatments of inter-congregational relationships can be found on Web pages of deanery, diocese, presbyteries, synods or denominational organizations. Overviews of the many different approaches are lacking. The literatures of social work and cognate disciplines fail to address the subject. Yet over the last several decades the exponential growth of this phenomenon has transformed the formation of inter-congregational relationships into a major social movement.

In preparing this chapter I drew on the limited extant literature and Web-based sources in addition to my own work with these partnerships. Furthermore, I spoke with a cross section of those participating in or promoting international, inter-congregational relationships. These informants and the print and Web sources were from diverse Christian denominations and ecumenical organizations; a representative list of these can be found at the end of the chapter.

There is no consistency in usage or meaningful categorization of these collaborations, which refer to themselves by a combination of the following words: "congregation" or "parish" and some version of "twinning", "partner" or "sister", i.e. twin, partnership, partnering or sistering. "IICR", an abbreviation for the inclusive "international, inter-congregational relationship," will be employed here as a short-hand, generic term.

History

In the latter part of the twentieth century, formal partnerships began to be established between congregations that were chronically or suddenly lacking in resources and those congregations that were relatively better off. The Haitian Parish Twinning Program (now the Parish Twinning Program of the Americas or PTPA) was originally formed in 1980 to match congregations in the US to ones in Haiti. Sister Parish Inc., founded in 1988, links churches and Christian communities in the US and in Central America. The most recent illustration of these relationships has been the outpouring of assistance to congregations and, through them, to victims of Hurricane Katrina on the Gulf Coast of the US.

Although relationships exist between congregations in the same country, partners are more likely to be in other countries. As part of a National Parish inventory, 80% of 5,831 US Catholic parishes responded to the question: Does this parish help fund or otherwise support another parish? Eighteen percent supported a parish outside the US, 10% in the US and 1% in both (Center for Applied Research in the Apostolate, 2003). These and congregational partnerships under other northern auspices are most frequently with congregations in the developing world. There are some linkages in nations in Central and Eastern Europe that are in transition to more democratic political institutions and decentralized economies. These states are occasionally equated with developing nations.[4]

Virtually every Christian denomination is involved in this movement. IICRs may be initiated by denominational hierarchies or by local congregations, with or without any third party involvement. There are ecumenical associations that promote partnering as well. In any of these arrangements, IICRs may be the sole mission or part of a larger strategy usually intended to have an impact on a geographic region, country or locality.

The Power of International, Inter-Congregational Relationships

What is so powerful about IICRs? The potency of IICRs begins with the characteristics of their constituent parts: the congregations. Local religious congregations are unique among community organizations in a number of ways. Connections among members are strong, arising from shared ceremonial observations of the fundamental milestones in life; among these are birth, coming of age, marriage and death. Lasting connections among congregations and their members are further strengthened by frequent opportunities for worship and social activities. It is not surprising then that researchers repeatedly found that people most often go to the clergy and to churches for help with difficulties when they cannot cope (American Red Cross, 2002: Cross; Chalfant et al., 1990; Gurin et al., 1960). In developing countries, if anything, bonds with and among congregations appear closer and are often quite visible in public ceremonies and celebrations.

Local religious congregations are among the most respected and viable of community organizations. This is especially true in poor communities. Congregations in impoverished communities in the US became trusted recipients of considerable government funding for community development during the 1960's "War on Poverty" (Schaller, 1967). Churches can be key mediating structures between ordinary citizens and their governments (Cosgrove, 2001). About the same time as the War on Poverty, congregations in Latin America and other developing regions fostered the establishment of civil societies[5] often in opposition to repressive governments (Berryman, 1994; Foley, 1996; Maclean, 2006). Thus there is a historical record of congregational activity to address concrete and spiritual human needs in the developed and the developing worlds. IICRs represent congregations bonded across borders and cultures by a shared faith and by institutional and interpersonal relationships. It is not difficult, then, to see the dynamic potential when such congregations combine as agents of change.

Common Themes

Mutuality, solidarity and personal contact are common themes in IICRs. Mutuality is the most consistent of these themes. To the uninitiated, the idea of IICRs may connote a benefactor-to-recipient relationship instead of a relationship of equals. Mutuality affirms a relationship with roots in human rights and social justice, not charity. An IICR educates and raises the consciousness of the northern congregation about the reality of the southern partner while enabling the empowerment of the marginalized[6] congregation. An empowered congregation then takes the lead in addressing not only immediate needs but the societal structures that perpetuate marginalization.

Besides a better sense of the realities of life and faith in the developing world, there exists in IICRs a less apparent but real possibility of personal and spiritual growth, refreshment, and renewal. This occurs through experiencing what has been called a spirituality of solidarity (Swedish & Dennis, 2004). This solidarity comes through northerners sharing the lives of people whose indomitable spirit makes it possible for them to persist in the face of deprivation and powerlessness. They, in turn, give hope to their southern partners. IICRs can thus become agents of transformation for their congregations and their individual members.

Visits between the partners, discussed at length below, are another common theme. Visitation facilitates consideration of whether and how to form an IICR. It does so through the medium of direct, personal contact. Once an IICR relationship is established, personal relationships that are developing can be extended to near-personal or virtual ones with the rest of the congregation through the returning visitors and the dissemination of information from and about the partner congregation. Where congregations partner without visitation there can be some benefits to both northern and southern counterparts. However, these relationships are not as potentially fulfilling and beneficial, absent the intimacy and understanding possible in face-to-face contact.

To assure the northern partner the closeness necessary for deeper experiences of mutuality and solidarity during visitation, the partner in the developing world should be a single, identifiable, community of faith composed of marginalized people (Fenske, 1996). Without this distinction, potential for closeness may be diffused in a number of ways, among them: trying to relate to congregations that are too large or too widely dispersed; involving multiple northern congregations with the same southern partner without coordination; or developing relationships with educational, social and medical services apart from an IICR. Mutuality, solidarity, and personal contact, three themes inherent in IICRs, are not sufficient to launch a partnership but do provide the foundation for doing so.

Developing an International, Inter-Congregational Relationship

Start-Up

Introducing IICRs and their value to congregations and communities is simple. To start, someone has to bring up the idea of congregation partnering. Once that happens, the exploration and creation of an IICR will, and should, take time to process. Protocols guiding this process may differ within the same denomination and region, and even how they are promulgated and practiced. For example, upper levels of denominational leadership may assert a range of direction and control over IICRs. Indeed, there are relationships between local and foreign denominational organizations of which congregations are a part. If there are any restrictions on congregational activities in the international arena, these are articulated or clearly implied by those higher organizational units based on views of mission, past ventures, or concern with maximizing impact. Limitations may be imposed involving the choice of countries and congregations where partnering can take place. The choice of partners may be restricted to those of the same denomination. Less often, the intent is to establish new congregations where other churches already exist.

Nonetheless, should the path to an IICR be through a denominational unit above the congregation, there can be several advantages to the congregation. These may include existing guidelines for these efforts, assistance throughout the exploration, development and continuation of the IICR and, at times, in the partnering country.

Organizing for Partnering

When the idea of a IICR has passed through the necessary systems far enough and agreement has been given to explore partnering, that responsibility is assigned to either an existing congregational unit, such as a social justice or social ministry committee, or, a separate group may be formed for the task. The unit with the ongoing responsibility for the IICR will be referred to here as the IICR Committee or Committee. A good deal of effort will be required from this point. When it comes to an actual commitment of the two congregations, the near universal minimum is three years. Continuity is important in the planning; therefore, potential IICR Committee members should consider not only their interest in the IICR but also their ability to devote themselves to the IICR for three years. Making information available on the responsibilities and tasks of the group, as described below, can help people assess their readiness to take part.

Sizes of IICR Committees have been reported from as few as three members at the beginning to as many as fifteen. Small dedicated groups seem to work best. As is good practice with any group, orientations should be given to any new members so they can move right into the life of the group and begin to make contributions rather than being left to catch up as best they can or using valuable group time to be brought up to date.

Pastors are generally not members of the IICR Committee although it is crucial for the success of the IICR that pastors and other congregational decision-makers are kept informed of progress. Their continued approval and support of the IICR are essential. Pastors have numerous and time consuming responsibilities in the home congregations, and IICRs take time and energy. However, the most frequently mentioned reason for lack of active, direct involvement of pastors is that the IICR belongs to the congregation and an IICR committee can offer greater stability and continuity over time. Both the northern and southern congregations need to take ownership of the IICR.

Engaging the Larger Congregations

Emphasis has already been placed on the importance of engaging parish leaders through communication about the development of the IICR. At the same time, every opportunity should be taken to inform and involve the rest of the congregation. The essence of the IICR is the relationship between two congregations, not just a select few congregants on the Committee. Proportionately few of the congregation may ever be directly involved in the operation of the IICR; nonetheless all may potentially be touched by it. There are a number of mechanisms to aid in the engagement of the congregation. These include: regular church or IICR bulletins and bulletin board postings, newsletters, websites, chat rooms, listservs, special and routine meetings, (parish council, social ministry, youth groups), and, announcements, sermons, homilies or updates at worship services. Feedback that is generated as a result of any of these activities can improve communication with the congregation, identify resources for the partnership and shape its design and operation.

The content of communications and discussions should initially speak to the questions: What is an IICR and why would our congregation want to establish one? The congregation should continue to be kept informed, if and when the partnering moves forward.

Choosing and Being Chosen

Matching developed with developing world congregations may be accomplished in several ways: by an organization which does matching, such as the aforementioned Sister Parish Inc. and the Parish Twinning Partnership of the

Americas; by a unit higher up in the denominational organization; through fortuitous contacts; or, by direct outreach by congregations. If there is a match-maker, modest fees may be involved to locate a partner and to provide some form of on-going support. Support occasionally extends to the country of the partner and comes from matching organization staff and/or through linkages to missionaries or other IICRs. Assistance in finding a partner congregation can be extremely useful particularly when the membership of the northern congrega-tion is not familiar with the developing world.

There are many examples of fortuitous or providential contacts made by travelers that have turned into vibrant IICRs. Those that originate in this manner also should take advantage of any expertise that is available. Potential partner-ships are limited only by the requirements of church bodies of which they are members. According to the director of the PTPA, a matching organization with several hundred members, if there is any difficulty locating congregations with which to twin, it is for the many southern congregations looking for partners in the north (Theresa Patterson, personal communication, August 6, 2006).

Whether the initial exploration of potential, promising partners was done at the congregation level or above or by one of the denominational or independent groups that make matches, sufficient vetting should have occurred so that there is a good likelihood that the match will work. Relationships that fail for lack of preparation are awkward and unnecessarily disappointing to both parties. Partner candidates should be explored one at a time. Simultaneous exploration of several partner candidates is not recommended. The IICR Committee could be pulled in different directions, stretching resources and resulting in a less than thorough exploration of a single possibility.

Once a possible partner is identified, formal communication between the congregations follows. The possible means of communicating are many including both traditional and electronic modes. Poor communities in the developing world may find postal mail, or "snail mail" to be the most practical form of contact and perhaps the most comfortable initial method of communication. Mailings can provide some necessary "space" early on for the southern partner in whose culture relationship-building can be more complex than for northerners who "get down to business" relatively quickly.

Whether or not there has been a prior visit from a member of the congre-gation or other representative, the formal, mutual exploration usually begins with both congregations describing their hopes and expectations for the IICR. These communications provide information about the congregations, the local community and people. They are often accompanied by photos or descriptive documents and materials. This is good place to cite an oft repeated caution. Frustrating slowness is often the norm for communications, of any form, from the southern partner. This may be the result of inefficient, unreliable and hard to access delivery systems, the pressures of daily life, all of which affect perspec-tives of time, priorities and urgency.

Early exchanges between congregations will give an idea of what the com-munication "turn around" might be like. Additionally, these exchanges are a window into the community and congregation-specific manifestations of culture. The culturally-sensitive, northern eye, for example, might see, in the formality of language and style or social pleasantries of a southern partner a preview of the gradual approach to relationships referred to above. In addition, the incoming messages can contain intimations of etiquette, protocol, status, and perceived relative position in the IICR, for example, from passive and dependent to active and self directed. Some not as yet culturally comprehensible information might be transmitted as well. Identifying that content and interpreting it will become easier for each partner as the relationship develops.

Few North Americans "buy into" anything they have not seen. The same holds true with IICRs. It is common for a delegation from the northern congregation to visit the would-be southern partner. It is rare that the reverse occurs in this exploratory stage. The reasons for this and the place of visits from the southern partner will be described further in the chapter.

Preparations for Visits

Visitation requires extensive preparation. The initial delegation must go through a pre-departure orientation to the country and culture of their partner that prepares them for their encounter with that culture. The basis of preparation includes material sent from the other congregation. Additional background material is available through libraries, bookstores, and the internet where extensive information on every nation can be found. This information includes detailed data on the population, government, economy, ecology, culture and religion, travel and tourism. Web versions of regional and national newspapers are often available, as are other sources of news and opinion.

Speakers, missionaries and others who have been immersed in other cultures long enough to have gone through of the struggles and rewards of acculturation, can make valuable contributions to the orientation. They can offer guidance about what it is like to be a foreigner in another culture. They can contribute to a framework and vocabulary for discussing the effects of geopolitical and economic forces on the partner congregation as well as offering theological and scriptural perspectives on partnering.

First time visitors, particularly North Americans, should be cognizant of how their countries are viewed by people in poorer nations. In the past, for example, I found that local citizens took pains to distinguish between the government of the United States and its citizens when expressing their views about US policies and actions affecting their nations. In recent years, a visitor is just as apt to be asked why we and our compatriots do not do more to alter what the questioners believe to be US policies that are harmful to the well being of their countries. While as people of faith we have confidence that our ideals of human rights, social justice and human dignity will ultimately prevail, visitors need to know and consider the reality and the perceptions that they will confront when they arrive.

It may be beneficial to arrange for delegates to meet with individuals or groups of people from the country or region. However, it is important to remember that information from your informants may be affected by their reasons for immigration, age at the time of departure and by issues of class, politics and experiences since their arrival.

Native film or literature can also be an excellent introduction to a culture. Despite translations or subtitles, popular media gives a beginning sense of the context and prevailing world view in the destination country. They convey communication styles, preoccupations, attitudes and behaviors and allow us to compare them with our own. All of these inputs provide the basis for discussions that not only benefit individual members but promote the development of a delegation as an informed, well functioning group.

The Special Case of Language

Language is the royal road to cultural understanding; it has an imbedded cultural code. Translations are helpful but what people tell us becomes fully alive when it is expressed and understood in the original language. People in other lands are more familiar with our culture and language than we are familiar with theirs. This comes as a result of our political and economic power and the hegemony of our popular culture such as music, TV and movies. Even in poor and isolated areas one can find persons who know some English, perhaps not well enough to translate, but generally better than our abilities to speak and comprehend their native tongue. Since early exchanges are encouraged between congregations, what can be done? While the congregation is developing its linguistic capabilities, hiring an interpreter or translator through the southern partner is much less expensive than doing so in the north and provides a source of income for someone in the impoverished community.

Gaining fluency is probably not practical in the short term. A realistic goal is to learn some common phrases and their responses. This will make delegates a bit more comfortable and serve as a foundation for further learning. The host congregation will appreciate and value that the visitors tried to learn some of the language. It is easy to obtain excellent learning materials for language training, particularly in electronic forms, like CD and DVD courses for every level of student. Some are independent of written text. Using native speakers, these aids take learners through a sequence of lessons that incorporate repetition of increasingly sophisticated phrases and sentences which progressively improve vocabulary, grammar, syntax, the command of verbs and other elements of the language.

Being immersed in the language during a visit or extended stay will considerably accelerate learning. Delegates may be surprised that they begin to get the gist of some conversations fairly quickly as some topics will be discussed over and over again using similar words and phrases. On a number of occasions I have sensed that an inaccurate interpretation was being made despite my knowing only a few words in a language. The intuition often proved to be correct when what the interpreter said was translated back into English. Frequently, this was because the subject was new to that interpreter. Sometimes a savvy interpreter will "edit", what is said without the speaker's knowledge. This is done for reasons of propriety or for "political" reasons; for example, the interpreter perceives that the other party may not likely be open to what was being asked or conveyed. Needless to say, finding and getting to know good interpreters and translators should be a high priority for the IICR Committee.

Selecting a congregational partner from an English-speaking country does not remove the difficulties of language. Culture so influences what and how things are said or not said, that it is difficult to be certain that words mean the same things to everyone. The almost unavoidable use of colloquial expressions from either culture compounds the difficulties in comprehension. Then there may be a *Creole*, *patois* or local dialect that comes from a mixture of a predominant language with vocabulary and grammar with different linguistic origins. This speech, even if English-based, can be as unfathomable to outsiders as any foreign language and, what is more, dictionaries, phrase books, and other learning tools may not be readily available. There are also completely different languages among some indigenous peoples. When faced with a dialect or indigenous tongues, turning to the official language of the country can be a feasible option since the locals are likely to have some fluency in it.

During visits, it is essential to have at least one person who speaks well both the language of the visitors and that of the locals. The burden of constant interpretation is best borne by having more than one bi-lingual person. Arrangements for these services are a critical part of preparations for the visit. Fortunately, as was previously indicated, the cost of translation and interpretation in southern nations is quite reasonable by northern standards.

The Visit(s)

Delegates should arrive prepared to work on an agenda jointly planned between partners during the preparation stage. The size of the delegation tends to be small, especially on the initial visit and includes members of the IICR Committee. On later trips, other members of the congregation augment this core group, preferably bringing new people each year so that congregational ownership will be broadened and strengthened. There is no set standard about how and when pastors and other clergy or church officials should participate in trips, but it seems advisable that they participate earlier in the process, rather than later. The capacity of the host congregation and local community to accommodate visitors will determine maximum group size. Limitations in terms of housing, transportation and availability of congregation leaders and members all need to be considered. Despite strong traditions of hospitality in the developing world, the demands of daily life cannot be put on hold when well meaning foreigners arrive.

Individual delegates customarily pay their own expenses for trips. This investment can reinforce the dedication of the delegates and the seriousness of their mission. Some person(s) may be deemed key participants whose expenses are subsidized. Donations of frequent flyer miles have been an easy way to reduce costs, but tighter regulations on their transfer make that resource less accessible. Other expenditures that the delegation should be prepared to cover include local transportation, accommodation, and meals. Delegates should understand that accommodations may be lacking some of the luxuries of North American hotels, though accommodations may be inexpensive and can be surprisingly comfortable.

When the people are relatively at ease with one another, home stays become a fairly regular component of IICRs, though this may not happen on the initial trip. Living together if only for a few days enhances relationships, joint prayer and worship (Fenske, 1996). However, visitors who have never spent time among the poor in the developing world may be hesitant to stay in homes lacking the amenities they have back home. Local families also may be embarrassed about their humble dwellings. If home stays with families are to be part of any visit, those arrangements should be worked out in advance, including mutual expectations and any costs involved.

The lengths of visits vary, customarily about a week, although longer stays are desirable and do occur. In the first few days, the delegation gets its bearings and becomes familiar with the region where their partner is located. There are official welcomes by the local pastor and other officials and tours of the area. As the days pass and social and cultural distances narrow, substantive meetings with the pastor, congregational committees, ministries, and the congregation as a whole can take place. The discoveries of particular areas of common interest, for example, music, social events, and youth ministries, may facilitate conversations and become the bases on which an IICR is built. Sharing spiritual beliefs and religious practices is customary on all visits and involves delegates in worship with their hosts, for the fundamental bond in an IICR is faith.

Northern visitors will see the need for material and other resources all around them; resources for the church, the congregation and for the larger community. The locals will have their own views of their needs and priorities that may vary, at least somewhat, from those of the visiting delegates. Both parties, but especially the visiting, "foreign" congregation, must exercise care in reconciling any differences in views.

Specific commitments are not made during the initial visit as a matter of course. The delegates and hosts need some distance from the excitement and stress of the visit to contribute thoughtfully to the decision-making process, which occurs at the individual congregational levels. Questions that are raised during or after the visit will need to be addressed. It would be of tremendous benefit to the IICR if, during the visit, arrangements could be made to use email, fax, or another form of electronic communication for future contacts.

Establishing and Maintaining an International, Inter-Congregational Relationship

As we have seen, sending the initial delegation takes a good bit of groundwork at home and with the destination congregation. In the event that an IICR is not the outcome, good preparation will make it easier to identify why the collaboration is not feasible and will help both parties accept that fact. A solid investment in thorough planning is more likely to lead to a delegation confirming the potential viability of a relationship. When both congregations agree the relationship has promise, the developing of a covenant describing the unique nature of this IICR will keep mutual expectations clear. The covenant will also be a living document that will change as the relationship evolves. It should be periodically reviewed, reaffirmed or, if indicated, revised.

Various types of support are provided by northern congregations to IICRs. The most frequent form of support, according to a follow up questionnaire in the report previously cited, was in the form of prayer, with 45% of the 245 responding parishes doing so at least monthly.. The next most frequent form of support from the parishes, all with partner congregations in the developing world, was "letter writing" with 21% corresponding at least several times a year. In terms of material support 45% gave less than $5,000 and 67% gave less than $10,000 annually. Many northern congregations provided non-financial resources at some time during a given year in the form of school supplies, food and clothing and religious supplies, in that order (Center for Applied Research in the Apostolate, 2003). Over-the-counter medicine and hygiene products were not mentioned in the survey but are typical of IICR "in-kind" contributions. Collecting these materials is a good way to involve members of the congregation who may not be traveling to the partner congregation or, are not able to donate financially.

Several caveats need to be observed in this regard. The expense of shipping and duties can make sending materials rather costly. These costs can be reduced if other IICRs or programs with partners in the same country join forces to cut the expense of shipping; for example, they might share a shipping container. It is also surprising how much a delegation of visitors can pack into suitcases or other containers and still stay under the allowable weight limit for airline passengers. Check the web sites of the destination country, their embassies or consulates if you have any question about what, if any, duties you will have to pay on different items. The host pastor will likely have experience in dealing with such issues as well. Second, when collecting personal items such as clothes for donation it is important that culture, climate, style, and sensibilities of the partner be considered. Third, there are issues of local availability. IICRs' actions should reinforce, rather that compete against the local economy. For example, providing fabric for the ubiquitous, required, school uniforms or aiding the development of a cooperative or micro enterprise that would make better uniforms is preferable to sending the uniforms themselves.

Members of the northern congregation may have talents to contribute as well. They can share relevant knowledge and skills through training or mentoring to enable their southern brothers and sisters to use what they learn in ways that will benefit their communities. Here again one must be careful to follow the lead of local colleagues regarding what is to be done and how to do it. When one is in a place where everything is strange and new, there is a universal tendency to fall back on what is familiar and has worked before. The emphasis should be on selecting the *best* means to accomplish local priorities.

To maintain an established IICR, annual visits are considered essential. That yearly norm is seldom violated in terms of the north-south visitation.

Representatives of the youth of the congregation are typically included. Besides the energy they bring to the IICR, the experience can have a profound effect on young people and their formation. They have yet to make life choices that may be influenced by their participation in an IICR. Minimally, by taking part, they will be able to better comprehend global issues.

Visits from the partner congregation in the developing country to the northern community are less frequent. Matters of cost, difficulty getting visas, and the day-to-day demands of living are all obstacles to "reverse" visits. Where they can occur, southern pastors are most likely to visit and usually stay with their counterparts. More accustomed to public speaking, and more apt to speak English, they can be extremely effective in engaging the larger northern congregation.

As for ongoing communication with the partner, email is an excellent and increasingly accessible option. Inexpensive personal computers specially designed for use in the developing world are currently on the market or in the technology pipeline (Markoff, 2006). Access to fax services in the south is probably better, at the moment, though often expensive. For emergency and routine contacts, phones service to just about anywhere can be had inexpensively through enrollment in special plans or by phone cards, either of which the northern congregation might underwrite for their southern partner. This same voice communication capability is still easier to attain through Voice Over Internet Protocol or VoIP, if conventional personal computers and internet connections can be procured. The same computers can further enhance relationship-building with Instant Messaging (IM) and audio and video teleconferencing capabilities built into the popular operating systems that come with computers or obtainable at little or no cost (although the video teleconferencing functions require high speed internet connections). With the addition of a digital projector, which is often available in northern congregations, a number of people can observe and take part in real-time video conferences with the partner congregation.

The kinds of projects in which partners can collaborate are as varied as each IICR. Projects most frequently address the needs of the southern congregation, its community or causes external to the community that affect it. Although distance is an obstacle, the chances for success are improved if both partners are involved in the planning and operation to the greatest extent possible. Micro credit and micro enterprise are among the most popular and successful projects for long distance collaboration. In these projects, people are organized into groups and receive small start-up loans that fluctuate according to the exchange rate but are roughly the equivalent of less than $100 US in local money. The whole group is then responsible for the repayment of each loan. The power of group and social sanctions reinforced by moral authority of the church are amazingly successful, particularly in small communities, in keeping default rates so low that they would be the envy of North American banks. The loans are used to start or upgrade small businesses or micro enterprises and interest charges increase the amount of money available for loans. Time and patience are required to set up these arrangements. Micro loan projects are often bolstered by training in basic literacy and "numeracy" (basic math geared to the practical needs of borrowers, such as budgeting, book keeping and the making of business plans). The loans are a powerful incentive to learn. Once arrangements are in place, regular reports to and periodic visits from the northern congregation, a usual source or conduit for funds, are normally sufficient to track progress and monitor accountability.

With sufficient advanced planning, there is no reason that projects cannot be done together on site. Sometimes special delegations have been formed of people with talents relevant to a certain project. A home or school construction project may benefit from the talents of skilled workers from the northern congregation. The skilled workers can be supplemented by less skilled locals and visitors to perform tasks like cleaning up, providing food and drink to the workers, or preparing for the liturgical and social celebrations that reinforce this shared experience. Of course, there are projects in which everyone can take part. It may just take a purchase, by the visitors, of some paints and brushes and a team of delegates and locals to make a church, school or health center brighter and more welcoming. With limited budgets and personnel resources, the congregation might not otherwise be able to do this refurbishing, or, with assistance, they may be able to save their limited resources for more pressing needs.

The Role of Social Workers in International, Inter-Congregational Relationships

Practice with IICRs

Now, we turn to our main question: What can social workers contribute to IICRs? Readers have undoubtedly seen connections between IICRs and opportunities for the application of social work expertise. Social workers are ideally suited for working at multiple societal levels at which IICRs are engaged. They may apply the broad knowledge base of the profession, including ecological and other comprehensive, interactive perspectives and relevant skill-sets such as methods of direct service, case and cause advocacy, training, community organization and development, administration, policy analysis, and research. Furthermore, social workers, with their well established strength in interdisciplinary collaboration, can facilitate the integration of these methods into a comprehensive plan in concert with people from various personal and working backgrounds.

Social workers need to consider what roles they wish to and can assume in an IICR. Will they be catalysts, consultants, co-equal participants with other congregation members, leaders, or some combination of these? Different roles require varying degrees of commitment, diverse investment of time and energy, and specific capacities. In any case, social workers will need a heightened "professional sense of self" to clarify for the IICR Committee and the congregation what they have to offer and how using their expertise will advance the attainment of the tasks ahead.

Social Work and the Northern Congregation

There are many tasks to be accomplished before and after visits to a partner parish. Who better to introduce the idea of an IICR than a social worker? Social workers have a professionally-formed awareness of the causes and effects of poverty and powerlessness and of their interaction with variables like culture, race, ethnicity and gender. Moreover, social workers have learned to view these issues through a global lens. Social workers may "see," conceptualize, and articulate what others might not, regarding events in other parts of the world making then ideal catalysts for IICRs.

Social work group skills are of especial importance. An IICR Committee is a task group. In the language of groups, social workers can help in the norming and forming stages of the IICR Committee and then assist in the performing stage, as the committee establishes and accomplishes its goals, objectives, tasks, assignments and timelines, with the social worker facilitating group process and team building.

Group skills are also essential in preparing the visiting delegation(s) prior to their visit and in debriefing them upon their return. These tasks involve a mix of educationally and developmentally oriented activities in which delegates learn, reflect on, and integrate new inputs that affect beliefs, attitudes, and behaviors. When preparing for the visits, inputs are mostly informational; in debriefing, the emphasis is on the experiential outputs.

During the preparation phase, trainees need to talk about their expectations, including their preconceived notions. Preconceptions are inevitable and necessary to fill gaps about the unknown with whatever existing knowledge one has that is then filtered through personal backgrounds, values and experiences. Social workers know how to sensitively reach for these perceptions and to make people comfortable with surfacing their preconceptions and associated feelings. They can then facilitate a discussion that will enhance individual self-awareness and understanding among group members.

Group members' views of immigrants and refugees from the target culture who have come to the US may be quite disparate and often firmly held. They can disproportionately influence or confuse prospective delegates who are exposed to these views during their preparation. Social workers can put these inputs into perspective by helping delegates find and consider alternative narratives intended to explain the situation in the destination country, particularly narratives that have currency in that country.

When preparing delegates for what they may face as North Americans in the developing world, there will be those prospective participants who are not as well versed as social workers in the policies that affect the developing world. These policies are formulated by northern countries and international agencies that deal with economic assistance, trade and other issues. Culturally sensitive social workers will notice attitudinal differences between visitors, members of the host congregation and the wider community that will need to be worked through. The southern partners can be ambivalent with ingrained senses of dependence and inferiority mixed with gratitude and resentment. These complex attitudes can be manifested in socially reticent, subservient or manipulative behaviors. Their northern partners may still find it difficult to admit to and to shed an unconscious paternalism. At the same time, northerners may harbor feelings of guilt or a need to be accepted that can be confusing or invite manipulation.

Debriefing is usually associated with the prevention, reduction or resolution of trauma and dysfunction among persons affected by a disaster. Social workers have been increasingly involved in responding to disasters (Cosgrove, 2000). Immersion in another culture can have analogous effects, though seldom as debilitating. Attention must be given to the effects of culture shock felt by visiting delegates. This may be one of the most helpful roles of social workers, particularly those with experience in other cultures. Social workers can facilitate the return of delegates as they articulate their thoughts and feelings. Returning delegates will need a supportive environment in which they may begin to integrate their experiences into their lives upon their return. They need to talk about their visits, to know what to expect and to have common reactions normalized. much as is done with persons affected by disasters.

Short visits will find people at different places in terms of what they need to work through. Some returning delegates may still be struggling with ambiguity or ambivalence about their time in the other culture. Many will be shaken by what they saw and felt. A surprising number will identify with the words "life changing experience." Some will be euphoric and anxious to tell everyone about their wonderful trip. Returnees need to be readied for the reactions their accounts will surface in others, from disbelief to disinterest, to the inability or unwillingness of family, friends and colleagues to absorb all that the returnees want to share. In some cases, visits may potentially create or reawaken troubling personal and interpersonal issues that require further attention. Social workers can assess the circumstances and, from their knowledge of community and congregational resources, identify appropriate services for those who are still troubled. It should go without saying that social work participants cannot exempt themselves from debriefing.

Social workers can also apply themselves to administrative tasks in an IICR, whether or not they actually make visits to the partner congregation. Among these tasks are program management, proposal writing, grant-seeking and other approaches to fundraising.

Social Work in the Developing World

In the developing countries, the mezzo-macro end of the social work skill spectrum, rather than the micro end, will be called on most. This is dictated by the often emergent and fundamental nature of the needs represented in the marginalized congregations. Primary targets for change are external to the congregation and the community. However, the immediate need may be to develop the human and social capital necessary to bring about change. Culturally adapted, community and program development techniques can address the more obvious human capital needs, such as. food security and nutrition, sanitation, and other public health issues, health care, education, literacy and numeracy. Social capital can be increased internally by explicating and strengthening natural support networks and by identifying and enabling natural helpers. Attempting to create or impose new structures without knowledge of or regard for existing ones would be extremely problematic. Providing experiences in leadership development and working in groups can enable the southern congregation to be more competent and more comfortable in effectively accessing larger social networks, non governmental organizations, and government agencies..

The evaluation of program and practice is another critical social work skill. Describing and measuring outcomes with often elusive social phenomena can be difficult. Furthermore, IICRs have not yet been subject to systematic research which could lead to improved performance and the sharing of best practices.

On the clinical end of the practice spectrum, the challenges of negotiating therapeutic relationships are complex enough in our native societies; in another society and culture direct clinical work is all the more problematic for a visitor. To the extent that the micro level issues emerge from the mutual assessment, social workers can aid in devising appropriate, cost effective interventions while enabling and empowering locals to implement them. This can be done by assisting local colleagues, health and community workers, in "indigenizing" or adapting and integrating northern practices into local formal and informal helping systems. At the same time, visiting social workers can assist in the conceptualization, validation and general application of interventions arising organically from the local culture, a process sometimes referred to as "authenticization." Focusing on preventive and therapeutic interventions that require minimal resources, such as community education, psycho education and other techniques, may ameliorate problems or slow or stabilize dysfunction until more individualized treatment options become available.

Inherent Limitations and Related Challenges of Practice with IICRs

There are also obstacles to be negotiated that represent inherent limitations of IICRs. Distance is one that has already been identified. These limitations will call on and test social workers' capacities. IICR delegations face a major challenge as uninformed newcomers entering the cultural reality of their new partners. Becoming part of a new culture to the point of seeing its reality through the eyes of its members requires an extensive investment of time. It also requires passing through a frequently disquieting transitional period during which neither one's native worldview nor what one can take from the new setting seems to make sense. Short-term or annual visitors cannot aspire to the level of biculturality that follows a lengthy and arduous period of acculturation. The emphasis in the profession on cultural diversity, although primarily in minority contexts in our society, will make it easier for social workers to accept and enable others to accept this hard but real truth. Long-time missionaries will attest to the struggle of being a minority in a society in which not only history, language, norms and customs are different but where these differences affect thought processes and the very shape of social institutions. Indeed, acceptance of this truth encourages a continual open mindedness, diminishes frustration, and leads to maximizing cultural competence.

Another challenge arises when the northern congregation provides financial support or when it obtains third party funding (grants), for a project in the developing country. In providing or overseeing that support, the congregation may understandably expect and require accountability based on northern practices. The southern partner, for whom mutual trust and community sanction may be the primary mechanisms for accountability, will need assistance in understanding the necessity for things like measurable outcomes and financial records. When trust and social sanction were the principle measures of accountability, communities were able to respond immediately to changes on the ground, as best they could, without the necessity of outside consultation. However, unfamiliar constraints come with resources of the northern partners and, all the more so, with those of third party grantors. Helping the southern partners understand expectations in this regard requires sensitivity and creativity, particularly with partners that may not be fully literate. Interventions could include explaining the grant making process in some detail using simulations, role playing, theatrical techniques, or other culturally accepted vehicles to communicate the less subjective and less flexible northern practices and the reasons for them.

Because of these gaps in cultural comprehension, northern partners end up influencing outcomes as much as they enable the empowerment of the partners. Social workers can reduce this possibility by encouraging the southern partners to formulate and express their thoughts about their own spiritual and material well being and encourage visitors to hear them with an open mind. Fortunately, shared commitment, trust, prayer and faith, which become stronger over time, can smooth over differences and misunderstandings.

Yet another limitation of IICRs in the developing world is that external forces can overwhelm and undo accomplishments of an isolated congregation. Agribusiness, cheaper imports, or decrease in demand can drive down prices of farm and other products and undermine a local economy despite the best efforts of an IICR to enhance productivity and well being. As social workers know, any community assessment must include an inventory of available and accessible resources which might be activated to accomplish objectives. Carefully nurtured contacts with other congregations and communities, as well as government agencies and non-governmental organizations, can lead to the formation of coalitions to address issues of human rights and social justice as well as other mutual or community specific needs. These coalitions can help ease necessary adjustments through such efforts as promoting more competitive farming cooperatives or creating or locating niche or fair trade markets for products, such as exotic coffees.

Summary

Contemporary inter-congregational relationships (IICRs) assume many forms for a variety of reasons. Of these relationships, a substantial and growing number are between congregations of marginalized people in the Global South and congregations in the economically developed and relatively democratic North. Collectively these relationships constitute a social movement fueled by an increasing awareness of, and response to, the interrelatedness of human kind, the uneven distribution of wealth and power, and the denial of fundamental human rights. Other attempts to respond to these problems by international institutions, governmental and non governmental agencies, are frequently much more ambitious in scale but without the kind of mutual personal commitment that is the essence of an IICR. Nor do they speak to or tap into spirituality, one of the few resources of the oppressed and the font of inspiration and direction for people of faith everywhere. Moreover, these larger projects seldom engage local religious congregations, which are apt to be among the few, viable institutions in marginalized communities, perhaps the only ones. IICRs combine the innate strengths of two otherwise disparate congregations in a synergistic collaboration that addresses inequities where they originate and at the points they are directly felt.

There are many reasons, personal and professional, that draw or call people of faith from the developed north to the suffering in the south. Often the intent is to give of themselves, but they find rather that they are the recipients of far greater riches. The would-be evangelizers are evangelized. An IICR is the perfect setting for persons who heretofore have seen few possibilities for sharing in the vibrant faith of the distant and downtrodden but who believe in a transcendent reality and universal kinship. In an IICR they can both achieve and occasion spiritual growth for themselves and others.

The work of the IICRs would not be possible without participants from various backgrounds who possess a wide range of talents. While some of these talents are essential, none alone is sufficient for the success of an IICR. The professional domain that best fits the complex nature and multiple functions of an IICR is that of social work. Where better than IICRs for northern-based, religiously-affiliated, social workers to express who they are and what they have chosen to be?

Notes

[1] Usually, *global* and *international* and words derived from them are used interchangeably. Strictly speaking, *global* is the more universal of the two. *International* may refer to multilateral relationships or actions that are less inclusive.

[2] *Developing* and *developed* are probably the most common terms used to denote, respectively, poor and well -resourced nations. The roughly geo-graphically-based *Global North* and *Global South* or simply *North* and *South* are

used frequently in this chapter. However, they are becoming less meaningful as more nations in the Southern Hemisphere are numbered among the developed. *Developing* also better reflects current reality than *Third World* originally a term originally used by a group of newly-independent, poor nations, it later morphed into short-hand for communist nations, losing much of its meaning with the end of the "Cold War" and, with it, the beginning democratization of countries of former the Soviet Union. The annual *Human Development Report* published by the United Nations Development Fund utilizes statistics on a number of social indicators to operationalize a more precise categorization of high, medium and low human development which are more indicative of quality of life. Nevertheless, *any* descriptors based on levels of development, especially *developing* and *underdeveloped* can be controversial to the extent that they are perceived as making negative inferences about the societies and peoples so described.

[3] The terms "North America (n)" are employed here not only because they describe the location and primary readership of this book, but to recognize that every country and every person in the Western Hemisphere is, in fact, "American". Most developing world peoples are accustomed to US citizens applying that appellation to ourselves and may even refer to us that way. However, some in this hemisphere will resent, silently, or openly, our exclusive appropriation of the title for ourselves. You have nothing to loose and everything to gain by internalizing the more inclusive American reality and referring to yourself as "North American", the most common form, or "US" American".

[4] Based on his experience in this Central and Eastern Europe, the author has come to see these countries as being different from those in developing world. Among the characteristics that distinguish the former are often considerable, functioning, physical infrastructure, albeit often neglected and in need of modernization; that includes roads, communications, and industrial facilities. These nations also have the human capital in the form of populations that possess education, training and skills for a modern economy, although there may not be jobs for that population. Then too, in many of these states, there is a recoverable memory of a more democratic way of life. These assets are negligible in the nations in Africa, Latin America and other locations in the developing world.

[5] "Civil society" refers to non-profit, non-governmental, voluntary organizations - e.g. fraternal, social, religious groups, unions - in which citizens have often multiple, cross memberships. Civil society acts as a mediator between citizens and the state and an active civil society is a hallmark of democracy.

[6] In this context, "marginalization" is generally considered in economic *and* political terms, the latter in the sense of the lack control people have over what happens to them.

References

American Red Cross (2002), *The lifecycle of a disaster: Ritual and practice: Understanding the impact of the 9/11 terrorist attacks on faith communities and their leaders.* New York: American Red Cross.

Berryman, P. (1994). *Stubborn hope: Religion, politics, and revolution in Central America.* New York: Orbis Books.

Center for Applied Research in the Apostolate (CARA). (Fall 2003). *Special report: Partnerships of solidarity with the church in Latin America and the Caribbean.* Georgetown University, Washington, D.C.

Cosgrove, J. (2000). Social workers in disaster mental health services: The American Red Cross. *Tulane Studies in Social Welfare, XXI-XXII,* 117-128.

Cosgrove, J. (2001). Religious congregations as mediators of devolution: A study of parish-based services. In B. Rock & R. Perez-Koenig (Eds.), *Social and Economic Justice: Devolution and Social Work Practice* (pp. 332-350). New York: Fordham University Press.

Cosgrove, J. (2005). International involvements for social workers. November 28, 2005 North American Association of Christians Social Workers (NACSW) Audio Conference Workshop.

Council on Social Work Education (CSWE). (2004). Educational Policy and Accreditation Standards. Alexandria, VA: Author.

Fenske, R. (1996). *In the good struggle: The sister parish movement.* Shippensburg, Pa: Ragged Edge Press.

Foley, M. W. (1996). Laying the groundwork: The struggle for civil society in El Salvador. *Journal of Interamerican Studies and World Affairs, 38*(1), 67 105.

Healy, L. M. (2001). *International social work: Professional action in an interdependent world.* New York: Oxford University Press.

Hockenstad, M. C., & Midgley, J. (Eds.). (2004). *Lessons from abroad: Adapting international social welfare innovations.* Washington, DC: National Association of Social Workers Press.

Markoff, J. (2006, November 30). For $150, third-world laptop stirs a big debate. *New York Times, p.A1.*

Midgley, J. (1981). *Professional imperialism, Social work in the Third World.* London: Heinemann.

Schaller, L. E. (1967). *The churches' war on poverty.* Nashville, TN: Abington Books.

Swedish, M., & Dennis, M. (2004). *Like grains of wheat: A spirituality of solidarity.* New York: Orbis books.

United Nations Development Programme. (2006). *Human development report: Beyond scarcity: Power, poverty, and the global water crisis.* New York: Oxford University Press.

Selected Web Resources for International, Inter-Congregational Relationships

Ecumenical and Mission Partnerships Presbyterian Church USA
http://www.pcusa.org/partnerships/protocols.htm

Global Ministries: United Methodist Church
http://new.gbgm-umc.org/work/evangelism/inmissiontogether/resources/

Parish Twinning Program of the Americas (PTPA)
http://www.parishprogram.org/

Parish Twinning of the Archdiocese of St. Paul-Minneapolis
http://www.catholicmissionmn.org/center_for_mission/global_solidarity.htm#current_status_parish_twin

Partnership for World Mission (PWM) Church Of England
http://www.pwm-web.org.uk/index.shtml

Sister Parish, Inc.
http://www.sisterparish.org/

Unitarian Universalist Partner Church Council (UUPCC)
http://www.uua.org/uupcc/docs/4-StepstoBecoming.pdf

CHAPTER 24

ETHICAL INTEGRATION OF FAITH AND SOCIAL WORK PRACTICE: EVANGELISM

David A. Sherwood

As I sat down to write this, I couldn't help but think of the old adage, "Fools rush in where angels fear to tread." Probably right. However, it seemed like it might be useful, at least as a conversation starter, to take a stab at trying to apply Christian and social work values, ethics, and practice principles to some of the controversial issues that seem to raise questions for most of us. I want to focus on the relationship between professional social work practice and evangelism.

I need to warn you from the beginning, on the other hand (my naturally cautious side coming out), that I do not propose to state the definitive Christian position on anything. What I do propose to do is to try to think through the application of Christian and social work values and practice principles to working with clients regarding evangelism in ways that maintain integrity for both our clients and ourselves.

Not Just an Issue for Christians

The first point I want to make is that this matter of trying to figure out how to have integrity and competence in the handling of our own beliefs and values as we work respectfully and ethically with clients is not just an issue for Christians. Every single one of us comes to our work profoundly influenced by assumptions, beliefs, values, and commitments that we hold in part on faith. That is part of what it means to be a human being. Our reason and our science can only take us so far, but they can never take us to the bottom line of values and meaning. "Facts," to the degree that we can ever really discern them, never answer the "so what" question. Values are never derivable from facts alone.

The first level of self-disclosure and informed consent that every social worker owes is critical personal self-awareness. This can be spiritual, religious, ideological, or theoretical—any "meta-narrative" that we use to make sense out of our experience of life. "Hello, my name is David and I'm a Christian." Or, "I'm a Buddhist," "I'm an agnostic," "I'm an atheist," "I'm a logical positivist," "I'm a behaviorist," "I'm a post-modernist." Or a Punk or a Goth or a Democrat or a Republican, for that matter. I'm not saying that we should greet our clients this way, but I am saying that we need to be aware of our beliefs and be self-critical in regard to how they affect our work.

What are my fundamental assumptions, beliefs, and values? How do they affect my practice? The way I interact with my clients? My selection of theories and interpretation of facts? It is not simply a matter of *what* I believe (important as that is), but *how* I believe it, how I handle my beliefs, which in itself comes back around to the nature of my value commitments.

Lawrence Ressler frequently tells the story of his MSW class at Temple University with Jeffrey Galper, who announced at the beginning of the semester, "I am a Marxist, and I teach from a Marxist perspective." I hope this meant that he had achieved this critical personal self-awareness that I am talking about and that his self-disclosure was in the service of facilitating informed consent on the part of his students. The proof of the social work practice pudding, of course, would be in his conscientiousness in not imposing this view on his students, his willingness to permit or even facilitate disagreement. Of course, the more deeply held the beliefs and the greater the disagreement, the more difficult it is to support self-determination. This is true even when self-determination is one of the core values believed in.

So—integrating faith and practice is not just a Christian thing. It is a human thing. Those who don't understand this basic truth are the ones who may pose the greatest risk of all of "imposing their beliefs on others," precisely because they may think that they are not susceptible to the problem (Sherwood, 2000). However, the rest of my comments are going to be addressed primarily to Christians in social work, even though I think the basic principles will apply to those who are not Christians. Many of us may feel tempted to "evangelize" in more way than one.

Addressing Spiritual and Religious Issues with Clients is Not (Necessarily or Normally) Evangelism

"Talking about God" with clients is not necessarily or normally evangelism. This is an important distinction. For too long social workers (secular and otherwise) have tended to "solve" the problem of evangelism by avoiding spirituality and religion and offering a blanket condemnation—"Thou shalt not discuss spiritual and religious issues with clients." If you do, it is automatically presumed that you are "imposing your own values on clients." This happens in spite of overwhelming evidence that issues of meaning and purpose are central in the lives of clients, that spirituality and religion have great importance to many people, and that religiously-based groups, congregations, and organizations are vital sources of support for people (as well as barriers, at times).

Well, sometimes social workers do impose their values (religious, political, or otherwise) on clients and it is an ethical violation when they do. I would stress that when this happens it is a violation of Christian ethics as well as social work ethics. But deliberately avoiding spiritual and religious issues is professional incompetence. The presumption has often been that spiritual and religious issues should simply be referred to chaplains or other clergy. In what other important area of life would social workers condone such a policy of withdrawal and referral? How can we say we deal with the whole person-in-environment while ignoring one of the most important dimensions of people's lives (for good or ill)?

Or how can we claim competence in dealing with diversity while ignoring or misunderstanding such a fundamental kind of diversity (Sherwood, 1998)?

The short answer is that we can't and shouldn't ignore spiritual and religious issues. The key is that we must do it from a client-focused and client-led perspective. This normally means that we may not ethically engage in evangelism with our clients. Exceptions would typically be when we are practicing in a faith-based context with a clearly identified Christian identity and with clients who clearly express informed consent. Even then, it is not transparently obvious that evangelism would be appropriate. I hope I can make it clear why I say this.

Proclamation versus Demonstration of the Gospel

"Twyla"

A perhaps simplistic but none-the-less useful distinction is this: It is always ethical and appropriate to demonstrate the gospel to our clients, but it is seldom ethical to proclaim the gospel to them in our professional role as social workers.

The Bible describes evangelism in the sense of demonstrating or living out the gospel as the calling of every Christian. "Therefore be imitators of God, as beloved children, and live in love, as Christ loved us and gave himself up for us" (Ephesians 5:1-2). "We know love by this, that he laid down his life for us—and we ought to lay down our lives for one another. How does God's love abide in anyone who has the world's goods and sees a brother or sister in need and yet refuses help" (I John 3:16 17).

The profession of social work provides us all with unique opportunities to demonstrate the gospel of Christ—to give to our clients the grace-filled gift of knowing what it feels like to be treated with love and justice, what it feels like to experience caring, grace, forgiveness, trustworthiness, honesty, and fairness, what it feels like to be treated with respect and dignity as a person with God-given value. Often our clients have few opportunities in their lives to be in a respectful, non-exploitive relationship. The power of this experience can be transforming. It can even be a form of "pre-evangelism," preparing the soil for the good seed of the gospel proclaimed.

We do not all have the same part to play in God's work in a person's life. The New Testament frequently talks about varieties of gifts among the various parts of the body, and evangelism is one of them (Romans 12:3-8, I Corinthians 12:4-31, Ephesians 4:11-16). "What then is Apollos? What is Paul? Servants through whom you came to believe, as the Lord assigned to each. I planted, Apollos watered, but God gave the growth" (I Corinthians 3:5-6). As Alan Keith-Lucas has said (1985, p. 28):

> Paul said that faith was the gift of the Spirit, which is true, but what we can do as social workers—and we do have a wonderful opportunity to do so—is to show such love and forgivingness that a confused and desperate person can understand the Spirit's message when it comes.

Compare to
Alan-Keith Lucas

A consideration of the Parable of the Sower may be helpful here. The seed only grows to maturity when there is good ground to receive it. But stony or even shallow ground can be converted to good ground by the addition of nutrients (love) or ploughing (facing reality) or breaking up of clots (getting rid of blocks) and perhaps what social workers can do for the most part is to be tillers of the ground, rather than the Sower, who must in the long run be God Himself. It is true that certain men and women, powerful preachers or prophets, may act, as it were, for God as sowers, but even they have for the most part audiences that have some readiness to listen.

On the other hand, explicit evangelism of clients (proclamation) in professional social work is almost always unethical. Why? What are the values and ethical principles involved?

Values and Practice: The Principle/Practice Pyramid

Christian and social work values largely agree at the level of principles. However, we may disagree on both the foundational assumptions/worldviews which support the principles, the rules/strategies for prioritizing the values principles when they conflict, and the practice implications of the value principles.

It helps me to conceptualize these relationships in the form of a "Principle/Practice Pyramid." The base of the pyramid is formed by our fundamental worldview and faith-based assumptions (religious or not) about the nature of the world, what it means to be a person, the nature of values, and the nature of knowledge.

On top of and growing out of this foundation sits our core values or principles. As a Christian I understand these to be the "exceptionless absolutes" of love and justice. The social work Code of Ethics might say (and Christians would agree) that this includes service, social justice, dignity and worth of the person, importance of human relationships, integrity, and competence.

On top of and growing out of this "principle" layer are the moral rules that guide the application of the principles to various domains of life. These are "deontological" parameters that suggest what we ought to do. Biblical examples would be the Ten Commandments, the Sermon on the Mount, and other Biblical teachings that help us to understand what love and justice require in various spheres of life. In the social work Code of Ethics, these would be the specific standards relating to responsibilities to clients, colleagues, practice settings, as professionals, the profession, and the broader society. These rules can guide us, but they can never provide us with absolute prescriptions for what we should do on the case level.

At the top of the pyramid sit the specific cases in which we are required to use the principles and rules to make professional judgments in the messiness of real life and practice. It is here that we will find ourselves in the most likelihood of conscientious disagreement with each other, even when we start with the same values, principles, and rules. The short answer for why this is true is that we are fallen (subject to the distortions of our selfishness, fear, and pride) and finite (limited in what we can know and predict). And even more challenging, our principles and rules start coming into conflict with each other on this level. It is here that we have to resolve ethical dilemmas in which any actual action we can take is going to advance some of our values (and the rules that go with them) at the expense of some of our other values (and the rules that go with them).

The Use and Limits of the Code of Ethics (and the Bible): Ethical Judgments Are Required Because Legitimate Values Come into Conflict

Ethical analysis and decision making is required when we encounter an ethical problem and at the case level we cannot maximize all values simultaneously. In my paradigm, the definition of an ethical problem or dilemma is that we have more than one legitimate moral obligation that have come into some degree of tension in the case that we find ourselves dealing with.

For example, I believe in client self-determination (one legitimate moral obligation) and I believe in the protection of human life (another legitimate moral obligation). Most of the time these values do not come into conflict. However, now I have a client who is threatening to kill his wife. I now have an ethical problem in which any action I take will compromise one or more of my moral obligations. Values and ethical principles can and do come into conflict on the case level.

It is important to realize from the beginning what the Bible and Code of Ethics can do for us and what they cannot. They can give us critical guidance and direction, but they can never give us prescriptive formulas that will tell us exactly what to do in every case, precisely because in the particular instance not all of the values can be fully achieved and not all of the rules can be completely followed. The Code of Ethics (1999, pp. 1, 2-3) says it very well:

> Core values, and the principles that flow from them, must be balanced within the context and complexity of the human experience. . . . The Code offers a set of values, principles, and standards to guide decision making and conduct when ethical issues arise. It does not provide a set of rules that prescribe how social workers should act in all situations. Specific applications of the Code must take into account the context in which it is being considered and the possibility of conflicts among the Code's values, principles, and standards.

Sometimes one of these biblical rules or Code of Ethics standards may have to give way to another in order for us to come as close to love and justice as the situation allows. At the case level, we are always going to have to take responsibility for making judgments that prioritize our values and approximate the good we seek as closely as we can.

Ethics and Evangelism

So, what are some of the core values and ethical principles from the Bible and the Code of Ethics that relate to evangelism with clients? I'll try to list a few and give some comments, although several of them overlap and interact with each other. And I would say that they all fall under the Biblical absolutes of love and justice.

1. The Great Commission:
Well, what Christians call the "Great Commission" is certainly one of these core values, the reason we are exploring this issue in the first place. While the imperative "Go therefore and make disciples of all nations" (Matthew 28:19) was given to Jesus' original disciples, the New Testament makes it quite clear that bearing testimony to the good news about Jesus' healing and saving work on behalf of humankind is in some sense the responsibility of all of us who are disciples of Jesus Christ. And if the gospel of Christ is true, what could be more important for people to hear? This value is real for us and explains why we struggle with the question of evangelism in our professional roles.

2. My Calling and Role:
Remember our discussion above about demonstration and proclamation? While it is true that not only evangelists bear witness to the gospel, it is also true that our particular calling and role in a given situation has a great impact on what it is appropriate for us to do. If you are convinced that your calling from God is evangelism in the sense of direct proclamation, then you should be an evangelist and not a social worker (or a nurse, or a car salesman, or a loan officer). Under what auspice are you working? What are the functions associated with your role? My father-in-law for many years demonstrated the grace and love of Christ in his role as a bank teller at the Potter's Bank and Trust in East Liverpool, Ohio, including taking money out of his own pocket to make sure that certain poor customers were able to get at least a little cash at the end of the month. But he could not, and did not, use his position to hand them tracts with the cash. As a social worker you may at times find it appropriate to share your faith directly, but most of the time you won't.

3. Self-Determination:
From the first chapter of Genesis on, the Bible presents a picture of human beings endowed with the gift and responsibility of choice with consequences. We are presented with the paradox and mystery (on our level of understanding) of God's sovereignty and our freedom. God is depicted as calling us, but not coercing us, warning us, but not protecting us. Conscience and commitment cannot be compelled, even though external behavior might be. Self-determination is also a standard of the Code of Ethics (1999, p. 7), growing out of the principle of the inherent

dignity and worth of the person. If ever a social work value stood on a theological foundation it is belief in the inherent dignity and worth of every person. While I may have my perceptions of what might be best for my clients, I have no right to compel or manipulate them to that end. I do have a responsibility to help facilitate their ability to exercise their self-determination, including the exploration of available alternatives and their possible consequences, so that their choices are as informed as possible. God grants us the fearful dignity of self-determination; we can hardly try to deny it to our clients, explicitly or implicitly.

4. Informed Consent:

A fundamental component of informed choice is informed consent, another standard of the Code of Ethics (1999, pp. 7-8). Informed consent essentially means that people should know what they are getting into and agree to it. This principle interacts intimately with the next one—integrity. Informed consent is one of the key determinants of whether or not evangelism with clients is ethical. Related concepts are agency auspice and client expectations. Why are clients coming to your agency or to you? What expectations do they have? Is there anything upfront that would lead them to understand that the sharing of your religious beliefs or evangelism would be a likely part of their experience with your agency or you? I have found that even in explicitly faith-based agencies there surprisingly few times when direct evangelism is the appropriate focus or outcome of interaction with clients. Christian clients struggle with the same kinds of issues as other clients. Sometimes we can help them sort through how their beliefs are resources or barriers for them. But sometimes religious clients want to use "religious talk" to avoid coming to grips with their issues. There would be almost no cases in a public or secular private agency when direct evangelism an appropriate focus or outcome of interaction with clients.

5. Integrity:

Honesty and integrity are core Biblical and social work values. A number of "rules" derive from this value, such as truth-telling, trustworthiness, and keeping agreements. Some of the standards in the Code of Ethics deriving from this principle come under the general heading of "Conflicts of Interest' (1999, pp. 9-10). These rules are particularly relevant to the question of engaging in evangelism with clients. These rules say, "Social workers should be alert to and avoid conflicts of interest that interfere with the exercise of professional discretion and impartial judgment" (1999, p. 9). They speak to the importance of setting clear, appropriate, and culturally sensitive boundaries and being careful of dual or multiple relationships with clients. Of particular relevance to the issue of evangelism is the standard that says, "Social workers should not take unfair advantage of any professional relationship or exploit others to further their personal, religious, political, or business interests" (1999, p. 9).

So, What about Evangelism?

The main reason that evangelism in the context of a professional social work relationship is normally unethical is that it almost always involves the risk of exploitation of a vulnerable relationship. It usually involves taking advantage of our professional role and relationship with our clients. It lacks the integrity of informed consent. And even when there seems to be a certain consent or even request from the client to go through the evangelistic door, it is the social worker's responsibility to be the boundary keeper. I am not saying that there can never be a legitimate open door under any circumstance, but I am saying that the social worker, acting in the professional capacity, bears a heavy weight of responsibility to avoid taking advantage of the client's vulnerability.

I think most Christians have little difficulty understanding the analogous rule in the Code of Ethics which says, "Social workers should under no circumstances engage in sexual activities or sexual contact with current clients, whether such contact is consensual or forced" (1999, p. 13). We also understand that it is the social worker's responsibility, not the client's, to maintain these boundaries. I hope no one is offended by my comparison of sexual exploitation to evangelism. Clearly there are significant differences. I believe in evangelism and I do not believe in sexual exploitation. However, we also need to understand the way in which evangelism in the context of a professional relationship does have some significant likeness to sexual exploitation, or any other taking advantage of the professional role.

For example, evangelizing a client coming to a public Rape Crisis Center would be unethical and, I would say, un-Christian. She is in a physically and emotionally vulnerable situation, there is nothing about the sign on the door that would lead you to believe that her coming is even giving implied consent to evangelism, and she is trusting you for specific kinds of help. The nature of your role and relationship means that you have a special responsibility not to exploit that role. What you can most certainly do with her is to give her the opportunity to experience what it is like to receive "grace," love and justice; what it is like to experience respect, caring, support, trustworthiness, honesty; what it is like to not be taken advantage of.

It would also probably be going much to far to ask her, "Are you a Christian?" Even if she said no, and you quietly moved on, the question would hang in the air, coming from a representative of the Rape Crisis Center to a person in a state of vulnerability who had a very particular reason for coming to this agency. How would she read that? How would it affect her response?

However, it might be quite competent and ethical professional practice to use a more appropriate probe that could be stated in "non-religious" terms—"This must be hard. Is there anything in your life that helps you get through things like this?" Then if she mentions something about her spiritual or religious beliefs, you are in a position to make a better judgment about how you might help her, even perhaps including engaging spiritual and religious resources. That could be good "spiritually-sensitive" social work practice (Sherwood, 1998).

Even then, you would be faced with the necessity of using good assessment skills, discernment, and judgment. For example, you would think that praying with clients in Christian agencies would be obviously the right thing to do. However, some clients are "religious" manipulators, and consciously or unconsciously use the appearance of spirituality to avoid dealing with hard issues. When a client says, "Let's just pray about that," or "I think we just have to trust the Lord," you have to try to discern whether doing that is helpful or their way of avoiding dealing with their anger, fear, abusive behavior, or whatever else they may need to face.

No Prescriptions, but Guidance

You will have probably noticed that I have avoided words such as "never" or "always" in what I have said. This is quite deliberate, and goes back to my earlier comments about what ethical principles and rules can do for us and what they can't. They can give us meaningful guidance but they can't give us simple formulas to prescribe our response to every situation. Although I might have come close to it, I have not argued that evangelism is never compatible with our professional role as social workers. I have tried to suggest ethical considerations as we try to make our best judgments about how we relate to our clients.

Morally and practically, a sense of certainty is highly attractive. Who doesn't want to be sure that they are "right" and that they are doing the right thing? But that level of certainty is often not available to us as human beings. And yet we do have to decide and act. These judgments always require prioritizing our values based on the best understanding we can achieve at the time regarding the relevant values involved and the potential consequences of the choices available to us.

Ultimately, how we respond in these hard cases has more to do with the moral virtue or character that we have developed, by God's grace and through God's Spirit, than it does with the specific facts and theories we have learned. Lord, help us to be people who hunger and thirst for your "more excellent way" (I Corinthians 12:31).

Note

This chapter is a revised version of an article first published in 2002 in *Social Work & Christianity, 29(1)*, 1-12.

References

Keith-Lucas, Alan. (1985). *So you want to be a social worker: A primer for the Christian student*. Botsford, CT: North American Association of Christians in Social Work.

NACSW. (1999). *Code of ethics*. Washington, DC: National Association of Social Workers.

Sherwood, David A. (2000). Pluralism, tolerance, and respect for diversity: Engaging our deepest differences within the bond of civility. *Social Work & Christianity, 26(2)*, 101-111.

Sherwood, David A. (1998). Spiritual assessment as a normal part of social work practice: Power to help and power to harm. *Social Work & Christianity, 24(2)*, 80-89.

ABOUT THE EDITORS

Beryl Hugen received a BA from Calvin College, a MSW from Western Michigan University, and a PhD from the University of Kansas. He is Professor of Social Work and Director of the Social Work Program at Calvin College in Grand Rapids, Michigan. He has served as a board member and publications editor for the North American Association of Christians in Social Work. He has published papers on mental health, the integration of Christian faith and social work practice, and social work history. He is co-editor of *Spirituality Within Religious Traditions in Social Work Practice* (Brooks Cole, 2001) and *Spirituality and Religion in Social Work Practice: Decision Cases with Teaching Notes* (Council on Social Work Education, 2002). He currently works part-time in the Social Work Program at the Russian American Christian University in Moscow, Russia.

T. Laine Scales earned her BA at University of North Carolina, MSW at Carver School of Church Social Work, and PhD at University of Kentucky. She is Professor of Social Work and Associate Dean of Graduate Studies and Professional Development at Baylor University, Waco, Texas. Dr. Scales has published in the areas of social welfare history, spirituality and religion in social work, and rural social work. She has authored, edited or co-edited seven books including *All That Fits a Woman: Training Southern Baptist Women for Charity and Mission, 1907-1926* (Mercer University Press, 2000). *Spirituality and Religion in Social Work Practice: Decision Cases with Teaching Notes* (Council on Social Work Education, 2002, *and Rural Social Work: Asset-Building to Sustain Rural Communities* (Wadsworth, 2004). Dr. Scales has been a leader in the North American Association of Christians in Social Work and served as Associate Editor of *Social Work and Christianity* from 2003-2006. She currently is Associate Editor of the journal *Family and Community Ministries: Empowering Through Faith*.

ABOUT THE CONTRIBUTORS

Gary R. Anderson received a BRE from Cornerstone University (Grand Rapids, Michigan), a MSW from the University of Michigan, and PhD from the School of Social Service Administration at the University of Chicago. Presently, he is a Professor and the Director of the School of Social Work at Michigan State University. He has social work practice experience as a child protective service worker. He has published extensively in the areas of child welfare, ethics, and health care. He is the Editor of the journal *Child Welfare*.

Cheryl K. Brandsen earned a BA from Calvin College, a MSW from the University of Michigan, and PhD from Michigan State University. Presently she is a Professor of Sociology and Social Work at Calvin College and department chair. Her research and practice interests are in gerontology, and specifically, end-of-life care, as well as in the integration of faith with social work teaching and scholarship. She has served as co-chair of the Social Work Research Group of the Michigan Partnership for the Advancement of End-of-Life care, a Robert Wood Johnson-funded initiative. She has served as project director for the Hartford Geriatric Enrichment in Social Work Education at Calvin College, and more recently, as a national faculty mentor for the CSWE Gero-Ed Center.

Mary Ann Brenden earned her BS at Cornell University and her MSW at the University of Minnesota. She has practiced social work in the areas of foster care, school social work and child welfare. She is an award-winning faculty member of the School of Social Work at the College of St. Catherine/University of St. Thomas in St. Paul, Minnesota. Mary Ann's teaching and research interests focus primarily on social policy, history and philosophy of social work, social change and social justice. She provides faculty development opportunities focused on 'teaching to mission' and the integration of social justice into curriculum. Mary Ann is the project director of *Social Work for Social Justice: Strengthening Social Work Practice through the Integration of Catholic Social Teaching* at the CSC/UST School of Social Work.

Rick Chamiec-Case earned a BA in Philosophy from Wheaton College, a MAR in Religion from Yale Divinity School, a MSW from the School of Social Work at the University of Connecticut, and PhD in Social Work from Fordham University. He worked for a number of years as Senior Vice President at ARI of Connecticut, whose mission it is to provide homes, jobs, and opportunities for people with disabilities and their families. He has several previous practice experiences in administering clinical, case management, quality assurance, family support, staff training, and management information services for people with disabilities like mental retardation. He has written and presented at conferences on various topics addressing the integration of faith with various management and disability issues, and has research and scholarship interests in the areas of spirituality in the workplace and faith-based social services. He has been the Executive Director of the North American Association of Christians in Social Work since 1997, and is also an Assistant Professor of Social Work at Calvin College in Grand Rapids, Michigan. He has been the managing editor of *Social Work and Christianity* since 1997.

John Cosgrove earned his MSW and PhD from Fordham University where he was Associate Dean for Research, receiving their alumni award in 2003. He is now Professor Emeritus, Board member of Fordham's Beck Institute on Religion and Poverty and is a consultant. He has been a member of the International Commission of CSWE and IFSW's Representative Team at the UN. He was both a Fulbright Senior Scholar and Senior Specialist. He is Chair of the International Interest Group of the NJ Chapter of NASW; he received their Trailblazer Award in 2002 for his international work. Before coming to academia, he spent seventeen years as a clinician, supervisor, field instructor, and administrator in domestic and overseas programs. His long standing interests in international issues and practice have resulted in articles in *Social Work and Christianity,* the *Journal of Global Awareness* (he is now a member of both their editorial boards), *International Social Work,* the *Journal of Progressive Human Services, Social Development Issues* and other publications. He has presented at a number of NACSW Conferences and other professional forums.

Diana R. Garland received her BA, MSSW, and PhD degrees from the University of Louisville. She is Professor of Social Work and inaugural Dean of the School of Social Work, Baylor University, Waco, Texas, where she has served on the faculty since 1997. She previously served as Gheens Professor of Christian Family Ministry at The Southern

Baptist Theological Seminary in Kentucky, where she was on the faculty for seventeen years and was Dean of the Carver School of Church Social Work and Director of the Center for Family Ministries. Dr. Garland is author, co-author, or editor of seventeen books. The most recent are *Flawed Families of the Bible: How God Works through Imperfect Relationships* (co-authored with David Garland, Brazos Books, 2007) and *Sacred Stories of Ordinary Families: Living the Faith Everyday* (Jossey-Bass, Inc., 2003). Her book *Family Ministry: A Comprehensive Guide* (InterVarsity Press) was winner of the 2000 Book of the Year Award of the Academy of Parish Clergy at Princeton Seminary. She has published more than 80 professional articles and book chapters. She has received more than $6 million in research and program grants since coming to Baylor in 1997, from organizations such as Lilly Endowment, Inc, Pew Charitable Trusts, Inc., the Annie E. Casey Foundation, the Henry Luce Foundation, the Council on Social Work Education, Baptist General Convention of Texas, and the Texas State Legislature. In 1996, Dr. Garland received the Jack Otis Whistleblower Award from the National Association of Social Workers to honor her public stance against unethical practices of the administration of The Southern Baptist Theological Seminary.

Helen Wilson Harris earned a BA from the University of Mary Hardin-Baylor, and a MSW from Our Lady of the Lake University in San Antonio, Texas. Presently she is a Senior Lecturer at the Baylor University School of Social Work where she teaches in both the BSW and MSW programs. Previously Helen served as Director of Graduate Field Education and Director of Field Education at the Baylor School of Social Work for ten years. Prior to coming to Baylor, Helen was the foundation director of the Hillcrest Hospice in Waco, Texas and served for eight years as foster care and independent living director at The South Texas Children's Home. Helen's research and practice interests are physical and mental health, end of life care, and faith-based child care and adoptions. She has written in the area of spiritual formation and grief and bereavement.

David R. Hodge received his PhD from the George Warren Brown (GWB) School of Social Work at Washington University in St. Louis. Currently, he is a senior nonresident fellow at the University of Pennsylvania's Program for Research on Religion and Urban Civil Society. He is also Assistant Professor in the Social Work Department at Arizona State University, where he teaches graduate courses on spirituality and spiritual assessment. Dr. Hodge is an internationally recognized scholar on the topic of spirituality and religion. His scholarship has been featured in over 100 peer-reviewed journal articles, encyclopedia entries, book chapters, and conference presentations, as well as in newspapers and other popular media around the world. Forthcoming, is a second edition of his book, *Spiritual Assessment: A Handbook for Helping Professionals* (NACSW, 2003).

Crystal R. Holtrop earned her BSW from Dordt College and her MSW from the University of Iowa. She has 14 years of experience as a Clinical Supervisor and Marriage and Family Therapist at Catholic Charities. A clinical member of the American Association of Marriage and Family Therapy, she has conducted in-service trainings, facilitated workshops, and participated in the redesign of a two-county social service delivery system. Currently, she is enjoying being a fulltime, stay-at-home mother with her two preschool children, Rachel and Esther.

Timothy James Johnson received a BS in Bible Social Work from Philadelphia Biblical University, a MSW from the University of Pennsylvania, and a PhD in African American

Studies from Temple University. His dissertation research was a study of the Black Church in America. In addition he completed extensive course work toward the PhD in social work and social research at Bryn Mawr College. With close to 30 years of teaching in higher education, he currently serves as Senior Professor of Social Work at Roberts Wesleyan College. He also served as associate professor of social work at Eastern University, and associate professor of Church Social Work at the Carver School of Church Social Work at The Southern Baptist Theological Seminary in Louisville, KY. A former NACSW board member, Timothy is the author of a number of articles, including NACSW'S 2002 Alan Keith Lucas lecture—"Reconciliation: a Paradoxical Idea and Ideal for Christian Social Work in the 21st Century," also published in the journal *Christianity and Social Work.* His current areas of teaching in social work education are social justice and ethics, macro social work, social work practice theory, human behavior in the social environment, and congregational and community practice theory. One of his primary commitments is to mentor African American men and women through the PhD process.

Sarah S. Kreutziger earned a BA from Columbia College (South Carolina), a MSSW from the University of Tennessee, and a PhD from Tulane University. Presently, she is Associate Professor Emeritus at the Tulane School of Social Work. Previously she served as Director of Communications for the Louisiana Conference of the United Methodist Church and as a clinical social worker in several mental health and health care organizations. Her research and practice interests are women's spirituality and religious beliefs; community planning and organization; policy development; and social work administration. She was recognized as social worker of the year in Florida, received the Continuing Education Award for Social Work Education, and was honored with several community service awards. Currently, she serves on the General Board of Higher Education and Ministry as well as the Foundation for Evangelism for the United Methodist Church (UMC). In the past, she was a member of the Board of Directors of the Council on Social Work Education and the Board of Visitors of Duke University's School of Divinity. She has been a delegate to three General and Jurisdictional Conferences (UMC) and to three World Methodist Conferences.

Jill Mikula received a BSW from Calvin College and a MSW from Michigan State University. She is presently employed as a program supervisor for the Families First of Michigan program at Catholic Charities of West Michigan, Lakeshore. Her professional experience includes direct and supervisory practice in family preservation and crisis intervention services, as well as solution-focused social work interviewing skills instruction at Calvin College. Her professional interests include child welfare, organizational and community practice, international social work, and the integration of social work and Christian faith.

Dennis R. Myers received a BA from Baylor University and a MSSW and PhD from the University of Texas at Austin. He is Professor of Social Work and Associate Dean for Graduate Studies, Baylor School of Social Work. He serves on the editorial board of *Social Work and Christianity.* He was recognized as a Distinguished Teacher by the Association for Gerontology in Higher Education and as an expert Gero-Ed Center Expert Trainer by the Council on Social Work Education. Recent publications include; Myers, D. R., Wolfer, T. A., & Garland, D. R. (forthcoming, 2008). Congregational service-learning characteristics and volunteer faith development. *Religious Education;* Garland, D.R., Myers, D.R., & Wolfer, T.A. (forthcoming, 2008). Social work with religious volunteers: Activating and sustaining community involvement. *Social Work*; and Singletary, J., Harris, H., Myers, D.R., & Scales, L. (2006). Student narratives on social work as a calling. *Arête*, 30 (1). He is published in the areas of educational gerontology, adult caregiving, productive aging, and faith-based community services. His current research and writing interests include the integration of faith and ethical social work practice, older congregational volunteers, personal and spiritual wellness in later life, and adult child and parent relations.

Mary Anne Poe earned a BA from Vanderbilt University, a MDiv from The Southern Baptist Theological Seminary in Louisville, Kentucky, and a MSSW from the University of Louisville. Presently she is Professor and Chair of the Social Work Department at Union University in Jackson, Tennessee and the Project Director for a grant from the Tennessee Center for Child Welfare. She has served previously as a social worker on church staffs in Minnesota and Kentucky. Her research and practice interests are how to engage congregations in effective and culturally sensitive ministry in the community, social and economic justice, and relationships among faith-based organizations, congregations, and other social service providers.

Jason Pittman earned a BA and MSW from Baylor University in Waco, Texas, as well as a MDiv from George W. Truett Seminary. He is presently working with the Cooperative Baptist Fellowship as the Executive Director of an inner-city ministry, Touching Miami with Love, www.touchingmiamiwithlove.org. He has social work experience in a variety of areas related to urban ministry and community development and was instrumental in establishing an alcohol and drug treatment center in Waco, Texas. Jason is the author of the book, *Substance Abuse and Spirituality* (2003) and his practice and research interests include faith-based substance abuse treatment programs, urban Christian ministries, community development, and congregational social work. Jason currently serves on the board of the North American Association of Christians in Social Work.

David A. Sherwood received his BA from Lipscomb University (Nashville, Tennessee), an MSW from Bryn Mawr, and a PhD in Social Work from the University of Texas at Austin. He is currently Professor of Social Work at George Fox University. His professional interests include the integration of Christian faith and social work practice, ethics, spirituality and religion, practice with individuals and families, and social work in health care and with the elderly. He has written numerous articles on ethics and topics related to the integration of Christian faith and social work practice. Dr. Sherwood is a co-editor of *Spirituality and Religion in Social Work Practice: Decision Cases with Teaching Notes*. He has served as a member of the Commission on Accreditation of the Council on Social Work Education, continues to chair accreditation site visit teams, and consults with social work programs in Christian colleges and universities. Dr. Sherwood has served on the Board and as President of the North American Association of Christians in Social Work and is Editor of the journal *Social Work & Christianity*.

Jon Singletary received his MDiv from the Baptist Theological Seminary at Richmond VA, and his MSW and PhD in Social Work from Virginia Commonwealth University. He is the Director of the Center for Family and Community Ministries and Assistant Professor in the School of Social Work at Baylor University. Jon is Co-Director of the Strengthening Congregational Community Ministries project and the Baylor Shepherd Poverty Initiative, two projects that look at the integration of faith and practice in working for social justice.

Hope Haslam Straughan earned a BA from Samford University (Alabama), a MSW and Certificate in Theology from the Carver School of Church Social Work at The Southern Baptist Theological Seminary (Kentucky), and a PhD in social work from Barry University (Florida). Presently she is Assistant Professor of Social Work at Wheelock College (Massachusetts). Previous social work experience has been as consultant to APERFOSA (Spain) around the establishment of an AIDS hospice, serving as a Volunteer Foster Care Case Reviewer for the Department of Social Services, and co-leading a dynamic collaborative within the community of Codman Square (Boston) in order to improve the lives of children and families in a diverse, impoverished, and complex neighborhood. Her research interests include spirituality within social work practice with children and families, spiritual development across the lifespan, transracial adoption narratives, and community and organizational collaboration. She is currently serving as an Associate Editor for the North American Association of Christians in Social Work journal, *Social Work and Christianity*, as well as the President of the Massachusetts chapter of the Association for the Advancement of Social Work with Groups.

S. Wade Taylor holds a BS from Indiana State University, a MSW from Baylor University, as well as a MDiv from George W. Truett Theological Seminary. Upon graduating from Baylor, he served as Lecturer in Research Methods in Social Work for three years at both the baccalaureate and graduate level. His professional interests include gender studies within the GLBT community, with special interests in the integration of faith and social work practice, social justice, and gender theory development. He is currently a doctoral student in the Boston College Graduate School of Social Work.

James R. Vanderwoerd received a BA from Calvin College, a MSW from Wilfrid Laurier University, and a PhD from Case Western Reserve University. He is currently Associate Professor of Social Work at Redeemer University College, and was formerly the Social Work Program Director at Dordt College. He worked for seven years as a community researcher with the Ontario government's innovative prevention project Better Beginnings, Better Futures. He is the co-author of Protecting Children and Supporting Families (Aldine de Gruyter, 1997), and has published articles in *Christian Scholar's Review*, *Social Work and Christianity*, *Journal of Baccalaureate Social Work*, *Critical Social Work*, and *Nonprofit Management & Leadership*. His research and teaching interests are in prevention of violence against women on college campuses, religion and non-profit organizations in social welfare, and social welfare policy and history.

Paul Vliem earned his BSW from Calvin College in 2006. He is presently employed as a group social worker through Plymouth Christian Youth Center, working with inner city youth in the Minneapolis public school system on social skill development necessary for academic success. He also works as the family case manager for a small non-profit that connects low income families with area churches in long-term mentoring relationships. His professional interests are in international social work and community development, with particular interest on how civil society can best influence peace, reconciliation, and sustainable growth in conflict and poverty stricken areas of Africa.